An Expanded Collection
of
Classics

Jan Bertoglio   JoLe Hudson

Cover Design & Illustrations by Pat Potucek

Additional copies of "A Cooking Affaire II"
and
The collectors' favorite "A Cooking Affaire"
may be obtained by addressing:
Butcher Block Press, Inc.
P.O. Box 6
Medicine Lodge, KS 67104
For your convenience, order blanks are located in the back of the book.
Copyright © 1991
Jan Bertoglio & JoLe Hudson
First Edition
First Printing 1991
Second Printing 1992
ISBN: 0-9614367-1-9

Printed in the United States of America

Wichita Press & Lithography, Inc.

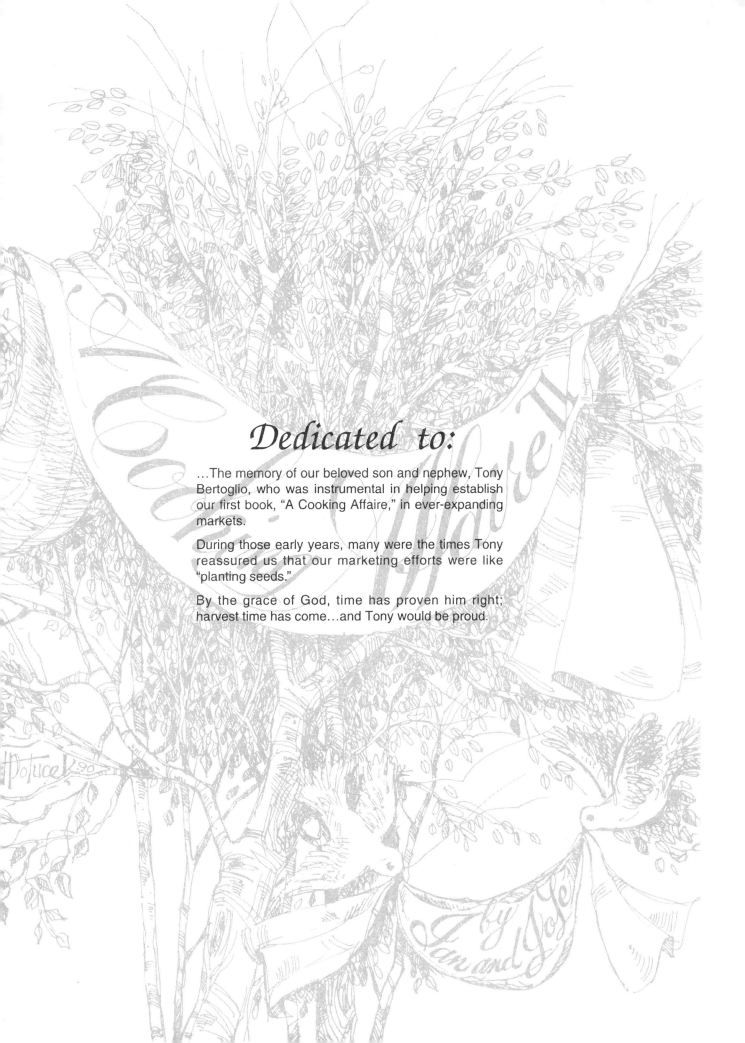

Dedicated to:

…The memory of our beloved son and nephew, Tony Bertoglio, who was instrumental in helping establish our first book, "A Cooking Affaire," in ever-expanding markets.

During those early years, many were the times Tony reassured us that our marketing efforts were like "planting seeds."

By the grace of God, time has proven him right; harvest time has come…and Tony would be proud.

Acknowledgements

Our families and friends have been so supportive of our endeavors. We gratefully acknowledge and thank them for sharing time, ideas and more of their wonderful favorite recipes for this second book.

We also thank the scores of new friends we've met through "A COOKING AFFAIRE." These friends have been so kind to share favorites; their contributions have helped fill "A COOKING AFFAIRE II."

About the Illustrator

In terms of talent, Kansas artist Pat Potucek would have to be considered one of the most feeling and versatile personalities in today's art world.

Whether she is creating portraits or landscapes in pen and ink, oils, acrylics, or watercolors, her readily recognizable style is her signature. But her abilities transcend what some might consider the usual gamut for an artist.

For example, she is considered by many to be one of the midwest's most talented muralist and some of her commissioned murals have been as large as 650 square feet; she is interested in a wide array of crafts; and she enjoys painting houses.

The latter, however, doesn't require a ladder and a bucket of paint. Instead, she works from photographs and reproduces homes in pen and ink, oils, or watercolors.

She has completed over 200 such paintings of city dwellings, ranches, farm homes, and businesses throughout the midwest. A number of such paintings have been done as gifts from children whose parents are moving into retirement centers.

A native Kansan, Potucek was born and reared on a farm in Cowley County. Her love of the rural life and Kansas, in particular, is readily mirrored in her lifelong interest in Americana art.

As Potucek explains, she has a tendency to create what she loves most.

A resident of Hutchinson, Kansas, where she works from a studio in her home, she has six children and is the grandmother of thirteen.

In addition to the delightful pen and ink illustrations she created for this book, she also illustrated the authors' very successful "A Cooking Affaire" which is expected to go into its seventh printing in 1991.

About the Authors

When I was a newspaper reporter years ago, our editors made a practice of posting kudos on the bulletin board recognizing reporters or photographers for assignments that were done especially well.

Such recognition by our peers seemed to go a long way in offsetting our somewhat pitiful salaries. And while most of us tried our cynical best to display a very cavalier attitude when we passed that board and found ourselves the subject of the moment, most of us would have had to admit that inside we were actually very pleased by the simple expression of professional respect.

Sadly, the kudo board seems to have gone the way of so many things that made for generally fond memories of that newsroom.

But there will always be a need of compliments for a job well done, regardless of what it is.

Therefore, with the reader's indulgence, I'd like to use the following space as something of a bulletin board and post the following kudos to a couple of very deserving women:

TO: JoLe Hudson and Jan Bertoglio, authors and publishers of "A Cooking Affaire II."

Congratulations on another job well done. Who would have thought that you could come anywhere close to matching the excellence of "A Cooking Affaire" in design, contents, or attention to detail?

Most of us, no doubt, felt that the uniqueness of your first delightful work would make it virtually impossible to ever match it. And some of us wondered why you'd ever want to try.

However, with "A Cooking Affaire II," you've displayed an unrivaled talent in design, culinary understanding, recipe selection, and overall good taste (intended), the result being another fantastic cookbook of cookbooks.

They do, indeed, compliment one another very nicely and the time and dedication that went into both books is most apparent.

Kudos to two of Kansas' (and the nation's) most outstanding cookbook authors and self-publishers.

About the only thing more enjoyable than handing out such plaudits to these deserving ladies is sampling the fare that they present to us through the pages of these outstanding cookbooks. They each stand above the crowd in that regard, as well, as Jan's husband, Jim, also will readily attest.

So, ladies, if you're ready for more kudos, how 'bout me sampling some of that Steak Diane again?

— *Jim Hudson*

JoLe Hudson and Jan Bertoglio   Photo by Jim Bertoglio

Contents

❖❖

Cheer Delights • Beverages & Appetizers

Here is a delectable array of appetizers and tantalizing drinks which will give your event a happy start.

Perhaps you picture yourself on a sundrenced island sipping a Bahama Mama, Pina Colada or a Mai Tai; or to bring you back to reality, you might plan to serve your guests from our selection of punches through cordials; an Irish Coffee, a Cafe' Calypso, or the Kansas-born Tumbleweed.

Whether your gathering is large or intimate we also offer a selection of appetizers such as Apple Dip, Spinach Stuffed Mushrooms, Beef Tenderloin Appetizers or Hot Dipping Sauce for tidbits.

❖❖

Cheer Delights

❖❖

Beverages

MAI-TAI

2 ounces pineapple juice
2 ounces lime juice
1 ounce orange juice
2 ounces orgeat syrup
1/2 ounce grenadine
4 ounces curacao
4 ounces light rum
4 ounces dark rum

Mix all ingredients and pour into 4 old fashion glasses filled with finely crushed ice. Garnish with a pineapple strip. Serves 4.

BAHAMA MAMA

1/2 cup coconut rum
1/2 cup light rum
1/4 cup orange juice
1/4 cup triple sec
1/4 cup pineapple juice
2 tablespoons grenadine syrup
4 orange slices
4 marachino cherries

Mix all ingredients except orange slices and cherries in blender and pour over crushed ice in chilled glasses. Garnish with slices and cherries. Serves 4.

PINA COLADA

3 cups cubed fresh pineapple
3 cups pineapple juice
1 can (15-ounce) cream of coconut syrup
1/4 cup half-and-half
7 cups crushed ice
2 cups rum
Shredded coconut (glass rims)
Pineapple juice (glass rims)
3 to 4 ounces rum

In batches, combine first 5 ingredients in blender. Mix thoroughly for about 3 minutes; add rum and blend 1 minute more. Repeat process with other half of mixture. Dip rims of glasses in pineapple juice, then in shredded coconut. Pour colada in glasses and top each with 1/2 ounce rum. Serves 6-8.

Jo and Jan say, "We think it's nice to have really chilled glasses, so dip the rims and place them in the refrigerator until ready to serve. We also like to use a spear of pineapple for a "swizzle." Stick a toothpick into a marachino cherry and top the spear. Fresh mint also adds that perfect touch."

FROZEN DAIQUIRIS

1 can (6-ounce) frozen limeade
1 limeade can light rum
1 large banana or equal amounts of strawberries or peaches
6 teaspoons confectioners' sugar
Ice

Place all ingredients in blender. Add ice to top of container. Blend quickly and serve. Can be made ahead and frozen. Serves 6-8.

STRAWBERRY DAIQUIRI

4 large strawberries
1 1/2 ounces dark rum
1 ounce sugar water (See index)
Heavy cream
Ice cubes
Fresh lime

Blend strawberries with rum, sugar water, a dash of cream and a scoop of small ice cubes until mixture is thick and there are no ice cubes left; about 30 seconds. Pour into a large stem glass and garnish with a fresh lime wheel. Serves 1.

SANGRIA

1 can (6-ounce) frozen lemonade, undiluted
1 fifth burgundy wine
1/4 cup light corn syrup
Orange and lemon slices
Fresh strawberries, bananas, peaches, cut up
8 ice cubes
1 bottle (28-ounce) club soda

Combine lemonade, corn syrup, wine and fruit. Let chill several hours. At serving time, add ice and club soda. Serve over ice in tall glasses. Makes 2 quarts.

WHITE SANGRIA

1/2 gallon white wine (we use Chablis)
1/4 cup lemon juice
1/2 cup orange juice
2/3 cup sugar
Orange slices
Lemon slices
Fresh peach slices

Combine ingredients and chill. Float slices of fruit in the bowl. Serves 6.

Jo and Jan say, " This is best when made a day before serving. You can adjust sugar amount to your taste. This is a very refreshing, light drink."

PEACH JULEP

1/2 cup sugar
1 tablespoon light brown sugar
2 tablespoons honey
1 cup water
2 whole cloves
1 stick (3-inch) cinnamon
1 cup fresh peaches, pureed
1/2 cup lemon juice
2 cups orange juice

Combine sugars, honey, water, cloves and cinnamon stick in a saucepan; heat, stirring constantly until sugar is completely dissolved. Cool; remove cloves and cinnamon.

Blend peach puree, lemon and orange juices into cooled syrup. Chill and serve in stemmed glasses. Garnish with fresh mint. Serves 12.

TEQUILA SUNRISE

2 ounces tequila
4 ounces orange juice
3/4 ounce grenadine

Stir tequila and orange juice with ice and strain into a glass. Add ice cubes. Pour in grenadine slowly and allow to settle. Stir. Serves 1.

BLUSHING COLADA

2 cups crushed ice
1 cup pineapple juice
3/4 cup rum
1/2 cup cream of coconut
2 tablespoons brandy
2 tablespoons grenadine syrup
Marachino cherries
Pineapple slices
Lime slices

Mix ice, juice, rum, cream of coconut, brandy, and grenadine in blender until a smooth and frothy. Pour into tall glasses. Garnish with cherries, pineapple and lime. Serve immediately. Serves 2.

STRAWBERRY SCHNAPPS

1 ounce strawberry schnapps
Club soda to fill the glass
Fresh mint for garnish

Pour schnapps and club soda into collins glass; add ice and sprig of mint. Serves 1.

GREEN LIZARD

1 can (6-ounce) frozen limeade concentrate, undiluted
1 can vodka
Ice
Fresh mint

Fill blender with ice, limeade, vodka and a handful of fresh mint. Blend until slushy; pour. Serves 2-4.

SALTY DOG

1 jigger vodka or gin
5 ounces grapefruit juice
Salt to taste

Fill a 12-ounce glass with ice cubes; add gin or vodka, grapefruit juice and several shakes of salt. Serves 1.

Jo and Jan say, "These are really delicious and so refreshing if you can take the time to use fresh grapefruit for your juice. Also, dip your glass rims in the juice, then into salt for extra pizazz. A Salty Dog without salt is called a Greyhound."

CRANBERRY VODKA SLUSH

1/4 cup sugar
1/2 cup water
1 cup frozen lemon juice
1 cup frozen orange juice
1 pint cranberry juice
1 pint vodka
1 quart ginger ale

Boil sugar and water for 5 minutes. Let cool and add juices; mix well. Add vodka and freeze overnight. Remove 1 hour before serving and add gingerale; mix until slushy. Makes 2 quarts.

RUM SLUSH

4 tea bags
2 cups boiling water
1 can (12-ounce) frozen orange juice, undiluted
1 can (12-ounce) frozen lemonade, undiluted
2 cups sugar
1 1/2 cups rum
7 cups water

Steep tea bags in boiling water for 10 minutes. In blender, combine orange juice, lemonade, tea, and sugar. Mix well and pour into a container that may be put in the freezer. Add rum and water; stir to blend well. Freeze at least 8 hours. Serves 16.

JOAN'S TROPICAL MANGO SLUSH

1 large ripe mango, peeled and sliced
Juice of 1 lime
5 tablespoons nonfat dry milk
5 to 6 tablespoons sugar (depends on sweetness of fruit)
1 1/2 tablespoons rum
Crushed ice
Vanilla ice cream (optional)

Mix all ingredients in blender until mixture thickens to a slushy consistency. Pour into tall, chilled glasses. Serve with a spoon and a straw. Serves 2.

BRANDY SLUSH

2 cups sugar
9 cups water
1 can (12-ounce) frozen lemonade concentrate
1 can (12-ounce) frozen orange juice concentrate
2 cups peach brandy
Lemon-lime soda

Combine water and sugar in a saucepan and bring to a boil. Let cool, then mix lemonade, orange juice and brandy; add to sugar-water and freeze. To serve, fill glasses 3/4 full then add the lemon-lime soda. Serves 8-10.

DRAGON WHISKERS

2 cups light rum
2 cups coconut cream
1 cup white creme de cacao
1 cup brandy
1 cup half-and-half
Crushed ice
8 tablespoons blue curacao
2 fresh pineapple slices, cored and quartered (garnish)
Fresh mint (garnish)

Combine rum, coconut cream, creme de cacao, brandy and cream in blender (in batches, if necessary) and mix until smooth. Divide mixture into 10-ounce glasses filled with crushed ice. Top each drink with 1/2 tablespoon Curacao (do not stir). Garnish with pineapple slices and mint. Serve immediately. Serves 16.

Jo and Jan say, "If you have the tall hurricane glasses (they hold about 20 ounces) the drink is even more impressive—be careful, though, they're bigger too!"

❖❖❖

WHITE RUSSIAN

1 ounce coffee liqueur
2 ounces vodka
Milk or cream
Ice

Pour coffee liqueur and vodka over ice. Add milk or cream. You can substitute ice cream for the milk or cream and blend the mixture. Serves 1.

OLD-FASHIONED EGGNOG

12 eggs, separated (6 egg whites in one
   bowl, 6 in another)
3 cups superfine sugar
1 quart brandy
1 pint rum
3 quarts heavy cream
1 quart milk
1 cup confectioners' sugar
Nutmeg, freshly grated

Beat egg yolks well in a large bowl. Add sugar and continue to beat until thick and lemon colored. With a whisk, beat in milk and 2 quarts heavy cream. Add brandy and rum very slowly and alternately, stirring constantly.

Beat 6 egg whites until stiff, but not dry peaks are formed, and fold into the yolk mixture. Beat remaining egg whites stiff and beat in confectioners' sugar. Lightly stir into egg whites the remaining cream and fold this mixture into the other. Cover and refrigerate overnight.

When ready to serve, pour into a large punch bowl, stir gently; ladle into punch cups and top each with freshly grated nutmeg. Serves 16-20.

Jo and Jan say, "If taste prefers, omit the brandy and rum in the above and gently stir in 1 pint bourbon, 1/2 pint rum and 1/2 pint brandy. You can also add eggnog ice cream after the initial servings to keep the mixture cool."

NON-ALCOHOLIC EGGNOG

6 egg yolks
1/4 cup sugar
3 tablespoons rum extract
1 teaspoon vanilla extract
1 1/2 cups heavy-cream, chilled
6 egg whites
5 tablespoons sugar
Nutmeg

Beat egg yolks, sugar, extracts until very thick and lemon colored. Add chilled cream gradually and continue to beat until blended; set aside.

Beat egg whites until frothy; add sugar slowly, beating well after each addition. Beat until stiff peaks are formed. Gently fold white into yolk mixture until blended. Chill.

To serve, pour into punch bowl and gently mix. Pour into cups and sprinkle with nutmeg. Serves 16.

PRALINE COOLER

1 1/2 ounces praline liqueur
1/4 ounce brandy
1 scoop vanilla ice cream

Blend all ingredients in blender with crushed ice. Serves 1.

COLD BUTTERED RUM

Butter Pecan ice cream
1 cup white rum

Fill blender with ice cream; add rum and blend for 20 to 30 seconds. Serve in frosted mugs. Serves 4.

Cheer Delights

❖❖

HOT SPICED CIDER

2 quarts apple cider
1 teaspoon whole cloves
1 teaspoon whole allspice
2 pieces (3-inch size) stick cinnamon
1/2 cup light brown sugar, firmly packed
Dash of salt
2 red apples, unpared and sliced (garnish)

Bring all ingredients except apple slices to a boil in a large saucepan; simmer, covered for 30 minutes. Remove spices and serve hot, garnished with apple slices. Makes 2 quarts.

CAFE´ CALYPSO

1 ounce brandy
4 ounces Kahlua
2 cups hot coffee
4 tablespoons whipped cream

Using 6-ounce heat-proof mugs or goblets, divide the brandy, add 1 ounce Kahlua and 1/2 cup hot coffee. Top each with a tablespoon of whipped cream. Serves 4.

CAFE´ AU LAIT

1 cup heavy cream
4 tablespoons sugar
2 teaspoons vanilla
2 bars (l-ounce size) German sweet
   chocolate, grated
4 cups hot coffee
Chocolate sprinkles or curls (garnish)

In a small mixer bowl whip cream, sugar and vanilla on low speed until soft peaks form. Fold in the grated chocolate. Pour hot coffee into 6-8 cups. Divide cream mixture over coffee in each cup. Top with chocolate sprinkles or curls and dash of cinnamon. Serve immediately. Serves 6-8.

CAFE´ ORANGE

2 oranges, sliced
Whole cloves
8 cups hot coffee
Heavy cream, whipped and sweetened with
   sugar
Brown sugar
Allspice
Cinnamon

Stud each orange slice with 4 cloves; pour hot coffee over slices and allow to steep for 30 minutes. Pour coffee through strainer and reheat. Pour into serving container. Accompany with bowls of the whipped cream, brown sugar and shakers or cinnamon and allspice. Guests may flavor coffee as desired. Serves 8.

CAFE´ A LA RUSSE

3/4 cup boiling water
1 ounce semisweet chocolate
1 1/2 tablespoons sugar
1 3/4 cups hot coffee
1/2 cup heavy cream, scalded
1/2 cup milk, scalded
2 ounces (1/4 cup) Cognac
2 ounces (1/4 cup) creme de cacao
Cinnamon & nutmeg

Combine water, chocolate and sugar in top of double boiler. Place over hot, not boiling water and simmer, stirring, 2 or 3 minutes, until chocolate is melted and sugar dissolved. Stir in coffee, cream, milk, Cognac and creme de cacao. Pour into 4 large preheated mugs and sprinkle with cinnamon and nutmeg to taste. Serves 4.

❖❖

IRISH COFFEE

6-ounce heatproof, stemmed glass
3 cocktail sugar cubes
Hot, black coffee
1 ounce Irish whiskey
Heavy cream

Preheat the glass with boiling water, put in the sugar cubes, fill glass 3/4 full with coffee; add whiskey and top with half an inch of fresh cream.

Jo and Jan say, "Our favorite bartender taught us that if you pour the cream slowly over the back of a spoon into the glass you will be assured it will float." Serves 1.

COFFEE SYRUP

1 cup sugar
3/4 cup water
1 teaspoon instant coffee
1/8 teaspoon almond extract
1/4 cup boiling water

Combine sugar and 3/4 cup water in a saucepan. Stir over low heat until sugar dissolves. Cover, bring to a boil and cook for 5 minutes; remove from heat.

Dissolve instant coffee in boiling water. Stir into syrup with almond extract. Cool and cover; store in refrigerator. Makes 1 cup.

PEACH RUM

3 pounds fresh peaches, halved, pitted, peeled and sliced
4 cups brown sugar, packed
Grated peel of 1 lime
Dark rum (about 6 cups)

Combine ingredients in a l-gallon container; using enough rum to fill. Seal and set container in a sunny place for 3 months; occasionally turning it. After 3 months, pour off the liquor and serve as a cordial. Makes 3 quarts.

VANILLA COGNAC

6 whole vanilla beans
1 bottle (25.4-ounce) Cognac

Rinse six 4-ounce glass bottles with corks in hot water. Soak corks in hot water for 30 minutes. Cut vanilla beans in half crosswise. Cut each half lengthwise 3/4 of the way, leaving 1 inch attached at each tip. Place 2 halves in each bottle. Fill each

with Cognac. Cork bottles tightly; Cognac should touch bottom of corks. Keep in a cool dry place at least 2 weeks.

Jo and Jan say, "The perfect gift for the friend who loves to make desserts! It is wonderful added to pastry creams, souffles, custards and tarts."

AMARETTO LIQUEUR

3 cups sugar
2 cups water
Zest of 1 lemon, cut in strips
6 tablespoons almond extract
2 tablespoons vanilla extract
1 tablespoon chocolate extract
3 cups vodka
1/2 cup bourbon

Combine sugar, water and lemon zest in large, heavy saucepan. Bring to a boil and simmer 20 minutes. Remove from heat; add remaining ingredients. Remove lemon zest and pour into decanter. Makes 6 cups.

❖❖❖

TIA MARIA

2 cups water
4 cups sugar
5 tablespoons instant coffee
1 tablespoon vanilla extract
1 bottle (4/5 quart) vodka or grain alcohol

Combine water and sugar in saucepan; bring to a boil, reduce heat and simmer about 20 minutes.

Remove from heat; stir in coffee and vanilla extract, then alcohol. Pour into a bottle with a screw top and store 1 month before serving. Makes about 5 cups.

SUE'S BLACKBERRY CORDIAL

8 cups ripe blackberries, picked over, rinsed
   and drained
1 cup water
Sugar
1/8 teaspoon ground mace
1 small cinnamon stick, broken in half; using
   only half
1/2 teaspoon whole allspice
1 whole clove
Freshly grated nutmeg
2 tablespoons fresh lemon juice
Vodka or brandy

Place berries in a noncorrosive saucepan; crush lightly. Stir in water and bring to a boil over medium heat. Reduce heat to low; simmer gently 10 minutes, stirring occasionally.

Place a sieve with dampened cheesecloth over a large bowl. Pour juice and blackberries into the lined sieve, allowing juice to drip through slowly. Press berries with the back of a large spoon. Discard pulp in sieve, leaving about 4 cups of juice.

Measure juice into original saucepan. For each cup of juice, add 1/2 cup sugar. Stir in spices. Bring to a slow simmer, stirring until sugar is dissolved. Increase heat slightly; boil gently 3 minutes. Remove from heat; cool to lukewarm. Stir in lemon juice. Strain spiced juice through a fine sieve into large bowl; discard spices.

Fill dry bottles or jars half full with juice. Fill jars to top with vodka or brandy. Cap tightly and store at room temperature. Makes about 2 quarts.

Appetizers

TIP
• Cut colorful squash in half, clean out and fill with your favorite dip to serve with chips or fresh vegetable relishes. Perfect for Fall entertaining!

APPLE DIP

2 packages (8-ounce size) cream cheese,
   softened
2 teaspoons vanilla
1/2 cup pecans, chopped
1/2 cup raisins, chopped
1/2 cup coconut
3/4 cup sugar, scant
1/2 cup maraschino cherries, diced and
   drained
1/2 cup crushed pineapple, well drained
1/4 teaspoon lemon juice
1/8 teaspoon nutmeg
1/8 teaspoon ground allspice
1/8 teaspoon mace (optional)

Mix all ingredients together until spreadable. Cool slightly in refrigerator then roll into a ball. Makes about 4 cups.

Jan says, "A very delicious dip or ball that may be served with apples for a wonderful appetizer. Especially good for those health-conscious souls."

Cheer Delights

AVOCADO DIP

1 small ripe avocado, peeled, seeded and cut
  in chunks
1 tomato, cup in chunks
1/4 cup sour cream
2 tablespoons canned green chili peppers,
  chopped
2 tablespoons milk
2 teaspoons lime juice
1 teaspoon onion salt
1/2 cup Cheddar cheese, shredded

Combine avocado, tomato, sour cream, chili peppers, milk, lime juice and onion salt in a blender or processor. Cover and process until smooth. Pour into serving bowl; stir in cheese. Cover and chill several hours to blend flavors. Makes 2 cups.

Jan and Jo say, "This is interesting used as a dip with French fries. Use the frozen and prepare according to package directions."

HOT BROCCOLI DIP

1/2 pound fresh broccoli, washed, trimmed
1/4 cup onion, chopped
1 garlic clove, finely minced
1 tablespoon butter or margarine
1 package (3-ounce) cream cheese
1/3 cup milk
1 tablespoon Dijon mustard
1 cup Swiss cheese, shredded
1/2 teaspoon salt
3 dashes cayenne pepper

Cut broccoli in 1/2-inch pieces. Cook in boiling water until crisp-tender. Drain and finely chop using food processor or sharp knife. Cook onion and garlic in butter until soft. Stir in broccoli and remaining ingredients. Cook over low heat, stirring frequently until cheeses melt and mixture is hot. Serve with vegetable relishes or chips. Makes about 1 3/4 cups.

HOT MUSHROOM DIP

4 slices bacon, fried crisp and crumbled
1/2 pound fresh mushrooms, sliced
1 medium onion, finely chopped
1 clove garlic, minced
2 tablespoons flour
1/4 teaspoon salt
1/8 teaspoon pepper, freshly ground
1/4 teaspoon thyme
1 package (8-ounce) cream cheese, softened
  and cut into pieces
2 teaspoons Worcestershire sauce
2 teaspoons soy sauce
1/2 cup sour cream
1/2 cup snipped fresh parsley

Drain bacon drippings from skillet, reserving 2 tablespoons. Add mushrooms, onion and garlic to reserved drippings and cook over medium heat until tender and most of liquid has evaporated from mushrooms; about 6 to 8 minutes. Mix in flour, salt, pepper and thyme. Add cream cheese, Worcestershire and soy sauce. Reduce heat to low and stir until cheese is melted. Remove from heat; stir in sour cream, parsley and crumbled bacon. Serve warm with crackers of your choice. Makes about 3 cups.

❖❖❖

"GOOD LUCK" BLACK-EYED PEA DIP

2 cans (15-ounce size) black-eyed peas,
   drained
1 can Rotel tomatoes, drained but
   reserve liquid
1/2 medium onion, chopped
1 can (4-ounce) chopped green chilies
1 clove garlic, minced
8 ounces sharp Cheddar cheese, shredded

Using blender, mix peas, tomatoes, onion, chilies and garlic. Mix well then heat over boiling water in top of double boiler. Add cheese and stir until well blended. Add some of the reserved liquid from tomatoes if desired for consistency. Serve hot. Makes 4 cups.

Jo says, "This is fun to serve on New Years' Day as part of the Good Luck tradition, observed in many regions of the U.S., which is, 'Eat black-eyed peas on New Years' Day and you will have good luck during the ensuing year.' If you want it even more spicy, add some hot pepper sauce. Serve with tortilla chips.

P.S. Our friend, John, has an addition to the tradition. He tells us that, when eating Black-eyed peas, you must leave three on the plate or the luck is shot. Wonder what would happen if we left 6 or 9 or 12?"

HUMMUS
(Chick-Pea-Sesame Dip)

1 can (17-ounce) Chick-peas (garbanzos)
1 large garlic clove
3 tablespoons tahini (sesame paste,
   available in Middle Eastern or
   health food stores)
2 tablespoons lemon juice
1/2 teaspoon salt
1/4 teaspoon ground cumin
Olive oil
Fresh parsley, chopped
Paprika

Drain chick-peas, reserving liquid; set aside. Finely chop garlic and tahini in blender or processor. Add 3 tablespoons of reserved liquid, lemon juice, salt and cumin. Puree until smooth. Add chick peas; blend until smooth adding more of reserved liquid if necessary for smoothness. Turn into a shallow bowl and sprinkle top lightly with olive oil and chopped parsley. Garnish with paprika. Cover and refrigerate until ready to serve. Makes 2 cups.

Jo says, "This is delicious served as a spread with warm cracker bread (lavash) or warm Pita triangles."

ISABEL'S GREEN PEA GUACAMOLE

2 cups frozen peas, cooked and chilled
2 tablespoons onion, chopped
2 tablespoons lemon juice
1 can (4-ounce) green chilies, chopped
2 garlic cloves, chopped
1/4 teaspoon pepper
1/2 to 1 teaspoon cumin
Dash hot pepper sauce, to taste
1 tomato, Roma preferred, diced small

Combine all ingredients except tomato in a blender or food processor. After thoroughly mixed, add the tomato and blend by hand. Makes about 3 1/2 cups.

Jan and Jo say, "We met Isabel at one of our signings and she wanted to share this recipe with us. It tastes like real guacamole. Thanks, Isabel."

CRANBERRY-CHEESE SPREAD

1 package (8-ounce) cream cheese, softened
1/2 cup cranberry relish
1/4 teaspoon nutmeg

Combine ingredients and beat with electric mixer until smooth and fluffy. Makes 1 1/2 cups.

Jo and Jan say, "This is wonderful served with smoked turkey sandwiches!"

WE-C'S CAVIAR SPREAD

1 stick butter, softened
6 hard-boiled eggs, chopped
1 package (8-ounce) cream cheese, softened
1 tablespoon mayonnaise
6 green onions, chopped
1 small jar caviar, drained and rinsed

Combine all ingredients except caviar and spread in a 9-inch pie plate. Spread caviar over mixture and chill until serving time.

HOT CRAB SPREAD

1 package (8-ounce) cream cheese, softened
2 tablespoons sherry
2 teaspoons Worcestershire sauce
1 can (7 1/2-ounce) Alaska King crab, drained and flaked
2 tablespoons chopped green onion
2 tablespoons toasted slivered almonds

Combine cream cheese, sherry, Worcestershire sauce, crab and green onion. Place in small baking dish and sprinkle with almonds. Bake, uncovered at 350 degrees for 15 minutes. Serve with crackers. Makes 2 cups.

Jo and Jan say, "You can substitute 1 tablespoon milk for the sherry, if you desire."

CAROL'S BOURSIN CHEESE

1 package (3-ounce) cream cheese, softened
4 tablespoons butter, softened
1/4 teaspoon garlic powder
2 tablespoons freshly grated Parmesan cheese
1 tablespoon dry white wine
1 tablespoon minced fresh parsley or 1 teaspoon dried
1 teaspoon thyme
1 teaspoon marjoram

Combine all ingredients and chill at least 4 hours before serving, better if overnight.

Jo and Jan say, "For a truly elegant presentation, use this recipe to stuff snow peas, miniature beets, or brussels sprouts. Instructions for preparation are under Shrimp Stuffed Snow Peas (See index)."

RUTHIE'S PIMENTO CHEESE

2 pounds Velvetta cheese
2 jars pimento, drained and chopped
1 medium onion, chopped
1 quart Miracle Whip

Melt cheese in top of double boiler. Blend in pimento and onion. Pour Miracle Whip into a mixing bowl; add melted cheese mixture and beat well. Makes about 2 quarts.

Jan says, "This may be served with crackers, chips or on hot veggies such as broccoli or cauliflower, as a sauce. It's yummy!"

FRIED CHEESE

1 pound kasseri cheese
2 hard-boiled egg yolks
2 tablespoons water
Flour
Olive oil
2 lemons, quartered

Mince egg yolks and mix with water. Slice cheese lengthwise in 1/4-inch-thick pieces. Dip cheese slices into egg-yolk mixture, then in flour, coating all sides. Shake off excess flour.

Heat about 1/4-inch layer of olive oil in a large skillet. Add cheese when oil is hot. Fry first on one side, then turn. Remove from oil and squeeze lemon juice on each slice. Serve immediately. Allow 2 slices per person. Serves 4.

SPINACH-STUFFED MUSHROOMS

1 pound fresh mushrooms
1 package frozen spinach souffle
Garlic salt to taste
Dash of hot pepper sauce
1/4 cup Parmesan cheese, grated
   (more, if desired)

Wash, dry and remove stems from mushrooms. Defrost spinach in microwave 4 1/2 to 5 minutes. Add garlic salt and pepper sauce to spinach and fill caps with mixture. Sprinkle tops with grated cheese. Microwave uncovered for 8 minutes on roast setting. This setting is important, as a higher setting may toughen the cheese. You can also finish these by placing them under the broiler for a few minutes, watching closely. Makes 20-30.

SWEDISH MEATBALLS

2 1/2 pounds lean ground meat
1/2 pound liver
1 onion
2 eggs
2 teaspoons salt, or as desired
1 teaspoon pepper
3/4 teaspoon nutmeg
3 slices bread, wet with water and pressed
   dry; torn into pieces
Oil for frying

SAUCE:

1/3 cup beef bouillon
2 tablespoons wine vinegar
1 cup heavy cream
2 tablespoons dry mustard, blended with 1
   tablespoon water
Salt. pepper and nutmeg, to taste
2 tablespoons minced parsley

Grind meats and onion 3 times. Mix thoroughly with rest of ingredients and let stand 1 hour. Dip hands into flour and form mixture into small balls. Brown balls in hot oil and drain on paper towels. Reheat in oven as appetizers and serve with dip. Makes about 75.

Jo says, "These can be reheated in sweet or sour cream for a dinner entree. Serve with boiled potatoes sprinkled with caraway seeds."

Pour oil out of skillet in which meatballs were cooked. Add bouillon and vinegar and boil down rapidly, scraping up coagulated meat juices until liquid has reduced to 2 tablespoons.

Stir in cream and mustard and boil slowly several minutes until lightly thickened. Season to taste with salt, pepper and dash of nutmeg. Strain in saucepan and reheat just before serving and stir in parsley. Serve hot in bowl beside meatballs. Makes about 1 cup.

✦✦

SWEET AND SOUR FRANKS

1 bottle (12-ounce) chile sauce
1 jar (10-ounce) grape jelly
2 pounds frankfurters, cut into
    1/2-inch pieces

Combine chile sauce and jelly. Heat, stirring constantly, until well blended. Add franks and heat thoroughly. Serve warm.

WE-C'S SAUERKRAUT BALLS

8 ounces sausage, seasoned as your taste
    dictates
1/4 cup onion, finely chopped
1 can (14-ounce) sauerkraut, drained and finely
    chopped
2 tablespoons bread crumbs
1 package (3-ounce) cream cheese, softened
2 tablespoons dried parsley
1 teaspoon dry mustard
1/4 teaspoon garlic salt
1/8 teaspoon pepper
1/4 cup flour
2 eggs, beaten
1/4 cup milk
3/4 cup bread crumbs

Saute sausage and onion; add sauerkraut, bread crumbs, cream cheese, parsley and seasonings. Mix well and refrigerate until chilled. Form mixture into small balls; dip first into flour, then into beaten eggs combined with milk, then into bread crumbs. Deep fry until golden-brown. Makes 24 .

We-C says, "These can be make, frozen, thawed and warmed when ready to serve. Great for drop-in company."

BEEF TENDERLOIN APPETIZER

Beef tenderloin, fat and skin removed (allow 3
    ounces per person)
2 lemons, halved and thinly sliced (garnish)
Watercress sprigs (garnish)
1 recipe Watercress Dressing (See index)
Parmesan cheese

Flash freeze tenderloin until slightly firm or about 45 minutes. Slice meat paper thin. A butcher will do this for you and it can be done one day before serving. If doing this, place slices on waxed paper and refreeze until ready to serve.

Prepare Watercress Dressing and chill. To serve, lightly coat a platter with dressing and arrange meat slices on top, overlapping slightly. Garnish with lemon slices and sprigs of watercress. Pass extra Dressing and Parmesan cheese separately.

SWEET-SOUR PARTY DRUMMETTES

1 cup pineapple juice
1 cup beer
1/2 cup soy sauce
1/4 cup brown sugar, packed
2 teaspoons minced onion
1 clove garlic minced
1 teaspoon ginger
40 chicken wing drummettes
1/4 cup butter or oil

Combine pineapple juice, beer, soy sauce, sugar, onion, garlic and ginger. Stir until sugar is dissolved. Marinate chicken in mixture several hours or overnight. Drain, reserving marinade.

Heat oil in large skillet and brown chicken on all sides. Add 1/4 cup marinade to skillet, cover, reduce heat and simmer 20 minutes or until chicken is done. Stir occasionally during cooking, adding more marinade as necessary to keep chicken moist. Serve hot. Makes 40 pieces.

❖❖

ORIENTAL CHICKEN WINGS

12 medium-size chicken wings
1/4 cup dark brown sugar, packed
1/4 cup soy sauce
1/4 cup water
1 tablespoon Worcestershire sauce
1 tablespoon dry sherry
1 teaspoon lemon juice
1 teaspoon ground ginger
1 1/2 teaspoons cornstarch

Remove and discard chicken wing tips; cut wings in half at the joint. Mix remaining ingredients except cornstarch in medium bowl; add chicken pieces; stir to coat well. Refrigerate, covered, stirring once, for 6 hours or overnight.

Drain chicken, reserving marinade. Arrange chicken in baking dish in single layer. Pour sauce over wings and bake uncovered in 325-degree oven until wings are done.

Mix cornstarch with reserved marinade in small saucepan and bring to a boil; cook until slightly thickened. Serve as a dipping sauce with wings. Makes 24 pieces.

ISLAND BEEF STRIPS

3 cups sesame oil
1 1/2 cups light soy sauce
1 1/2 cups sherry
1 1/2 cups firmly packed brown sugar
4 garlic cloves, finely minced
3/4 teaspoon ground ginger
3 pounds sirloin tip, flash frozen and cut across the grain into paper-thin strips
Bamboo skewers soaked in water

Combine first 6 ingredients in large shallow dish and blend well. Add beef strips, turning to coat. Cover and marinate in refrigerator at least 2 hours, preferably overnight.

Preheat broiler. Thread beef onto soaked skewers Dip into marinade, coating heavily. Place on rack and broil 6 inches from heat for 1 1/2 minutes. Remove, dip in marinade again and broil on second side to desired doneness. Serve hot or at room temperature. Makes 24 servings.

COCKTAIL PUFFS

1 cup beer
1/4 pound butter
1 cup sifted flour
1/2 teaspoon salt
4 eggs

Bring beer and butter to a boil; when butter melts, add flour and salt all at once. Cook over low heat, mixing steadily, until mixture leaves the sides of the pan.

Remove from heat; beat in eggs, one at a time until the dough is shiny.

Drop mixture onto a buttered baking sheet by the teaspoon, leaving 1 inch between each puff.

Bake in a preheated 450-degree oven for 10 minutes. Reduce heat to 350 degrees and bake 10 minutes longer, or until browned and free from moisture. Cool, split and fill with crab meat, cheese mixture, liver pate or other fillings of your choice. Makes 36 small puffs.

JAN'S HORS D'OEUVRE TART SHELLS

1 cup plus 2 tablespoons flour
1/4 pound butter, not margarine, softened
1/4 teaspoon salt
2 tablespoons grated Parmesan cheese
1 small egg, slightly beaten

While butter softens, measure flour and salt into sifter and sift into a medium bowl; add rest of ingredients mixing well, turn dough onto lightly floured board and gently work dough for a few seconds until formed; transfer to bowl; cover and chill several hours.

To form, pinch off pieces of dough about the size of a hazelnut and place in shell; press dough on bottom and sides of form with your thumb. Do not let dough extend above edge of form; edges might break off. To eliminate that problem, we press finished form against the palm of our hand.

Place forms on a baking sheet and bake in preheated 425-degree oven for 8 to 10 minutes. Gently remove shells from forms immediately upon removal from oven; when they can be handled. Makes 15-18 shells.

PARTY TURNOVERS

1 package (8-ounce) cream cheese, softened
1/2 cup butter, softened
1 1/2 cups flour
1 egg, beaten
 Filling (Crab, Herb-Mushroom,
  Artichoke-Cheese; See index)

Blend softened cream cheese and butter; mix with flour until smooth. Shape into a ball, wrap and refrigerate at least 1 hour. Divide in half and roll out 1/2 on a floured board to 1/8-inch thick. Cut into 3-inch rounds. Repeat until all dough is used.

Place about 1 teaspoon of filling on half of each circle, brush edges of circle with egg. Fold in half, crimp edges with a fork and prick tops. Bake on ungreased cookie sheet for about 12 minutes or until golden brown in a preheated 450-degree oven. Makes 50.

ARTICHOKE-CHEESE FILLING FOR TART SHELLS

1 cup mayonnaise
3/4 cup grated Parmesan cheese
8 to 10 canned marinated artichoke hearts,
  drained and chopped

Combine ingredients; fill baked pastry shells and broil until hot and bubbly.

CRAB FILLING FOR TARTS AND TURNOVERS

6 ounces fresh or frozen crab meat
1/2 cup mayonnaise
1/2 cup grated sharp Cheddar cheese
1 tablespoon green onion, minced
1 teaspoon Worcestershire sauce
1 tablespoon capers, drained (optional)

Combine ingredients; fill pastry rounds or shells as directed.

❖❖❖

SEAFOOD FILLER FOR TART SHELLS

4 1/2 cups shrimp or crab, drained and mashed
  with a fork
1 cup mayonnaise
1/2 cup grated onion
1 cup shredded Cheddar cheese
1 tablespoon lemon juice
1 teaspoon Worcestershire sauce
1/2 teaspoon garlic salt
Dash of cayenne

Combine ingredients; fill baked pastry shells and broil until bubbly or bake in a preheated 450-degree oven for 5 to 10 minutes.

HERB - MUSHROOM FILLING FOR TARTS AND TURNOVERS

1/2 pound fresh mushrooms, finely chopped
2 tablespoons scallions, minced
1/4 cup butter
1/4 cup flour
1/2 teaspoon salt
1 cup heavy cream
3 to 4 tablespoons dry sherry
1 teaspoon Worcestershire sauce
Juice of 1/2 lemon
1/4 teaspoon thyme
Freshly ground white pepper

Saute mushrooms and onions in butter. Stir in flour and salt. Stir in cream, sherry, Worcestershire sauce, lemon juice, thyme and pepper. Cook, stirring constantly, until thick and smooth. Taste and adjust seasoning, adding additional sherry, lemon juice, thyme or pepper, if necessary. Fill pastry rounds.

Jo and Jan say, "You may bake these tarts for about 8 minutes in a preheated 400-degree oven, then cool and freeze. When ready to serve, defrost for 1 hour, then bake at 400 degrees for 4 to 5 minutes or until golden and bubbly. Fills 48 tartlets."

CRESCENT CAPERS

1 package (10-ounce) frozen spinach,
  thawed, drained and chopped
1 package (8-ounce) cream cheese, softened
1 can (8-ounce) Crescent rolls
1/2 cup Parmesan cheese
1/4 cup green pepper, minced

Unroll can of roll dough. Combine drained spinach, cream cheese, Parmesan cheese and minced green pepper. Separate rolls and divide spinach mixture among rolls and spread to edges. Starting at short end, roll then cut into 2 slices. Place cut side down on ungreased cookie sheet. Bake in preheated 375-degree oven for 10 to 12 minutes. Serve warm or cold. Makes 16.

OR..... 1 can (8-ounce) Crescent rolls, 1 teaspoon parsley, or herbs to your liking, 1/4 cup Cheddar cheese, grated

Combine parsley and cheese; roll as for crescents and bake on ungreased cookie sheet according to package directions. Cut into bitesize appetizers.

OR..... Roll Crescent triangles around Vienna sausages and bake according to directions on package.

OR..... 1 package (8-ounce) Crescent rolls, 1/2 of a 5-ounce package Boursin, or Rondele cheese or Carol's Boursin (See index).

Place sheet of roll dough on flat surface. Spread with cheese. Roll and bake according to package directions. Makes 8.

RUSTEE'S TEA EGGS

12 eggs
2 star anise
1/4 cup black tea
2 teaspoons salt
2 tablespoons dark soy sauce

Cover eggs with cold water; boil 20 minutes over low heat. Cool in cold water; drain and tap shells with the back of a spoon until shell is completely crackled but do not remove shells.

Return eggs to pan, cover with cold water, salt, soy, anise and tea. Bring to a boil, reduce heat and simmer on low for 2 to 3 hours (yes, that's correct!). Turn off heat and leave eggs in liquid for 8 hours.

Drain and leave in shells until ready to use. Keep well wrapped in refrigerator, up to 1 week. Carefully peel and cut into halves or quarters. Makes 12.

SPICY HONEY-ROASTED NUTS

2 tablespoons butter, melted
2 tablespoons honey
2 teaspoons minced garlic
1 teaspoon ground red pepper
1 teaspoon ginger
1 teaspoon salt
1 pound nuts: peanuts, raw and skinned or pecans, walnuts, or your choice

Combine all ingredients except nuts in a medium bowl. Add nuts and stir until well coated. Spread in a shallow baking pan and roast in a preheated 325-degree oven for 25 minutes, stirring once or twice. Cool and store in an airtight container for up to 1 week. Makes 3 cups.

HOT DIPPING SAUCE

1/3 cup orange marmalade
1 clove garlic, minced
1/4 cup soy sauce
2 tablespoons lemon juice
1/3 cup water

Combine all ingredients in small saucepan. Cook to a boil and serve hot. Makes about 1 cup.

Jo says, "Try this with chicken or meat bites, shrimp or various meat balls."

JELLY AND BARBECUE SAUCE

1 cup currant jelly
1 cup barbecue sauce
1/4 cup honey
1 tablespoon soy sauce

Combine ingredients; heat and serve as a delicious dip for chicken or shrimp bites. Makes 2 cups.

❖❖❖

Super Bowls • Soups & Salads

A wonderful assortment is tucked in this section; whether you are looking for an enhancement to your meal - or perhaps for just a solo "Soup and Salad."

Our selections range from Annie's Clam Chowder, Santa Fe Soup, Pumpkin Soup baked in a shell to a cold Blackberry Soup. Salad choices are endless from tossed to molded. Included are Smoked Turkey, Cobb, Grand Hotel Spinach, Pepper Steak and from our illustrator, Pat's Raspberry Fluff Salad.

❖❖❖

◆◆

Soups

Beautiful Soup, so rich and green,
Waiting in a hot tureen!
Who for such dainties would not stoop?
Soup of the evening, beautiful Soup.
                    — *Alice in Wonderland*

CHEESE CROUTONS

2 loaves white bread
1 stick margarine
4 tablespoons Parmesan cheese
4 tablespoons parsley leaves, lightly packed
1 garlic clove
Dash dried red pepper, ground
3 tablespoons sesame seeds

Cut rounds from bread slices with a small biscuit cutter; place on baking sheet. Combine margarine, cheese, parsley, garlic and pepper; process on blender or food processor until smooth. Spread a teaspoon on each bread round and sprinkle with sesame seeds. Bake in preheated 225-degree oven for about 2 hours or until lightly brown.

Jan and Jo say, "If you would rather have the little squares, cut bread in strips one way, then across 5 times to make cubes. Place in a bowl; melt the margarine mixture instead of processing it and drizzle over bread, tossing to coat; sprinkle with seeds, spread out on baking sheet and bake as instructed above. They are delicious with salads, soup or cocktails."

PARMESAN ROUNDS

2 loaves sliced white bread
Butter
2 packages (8-ounce size) cream cheese, softened
1/2 cup butter, melted
1/4 cup plus 2 tablespoons mayonnaise
2 teaspoons Worcestershire sauce
6 green onions, chopped
Parmesan cheese, preferably freshly grated

Using 1-inch round cutter, cut 3 to 4 circles from each bread slice. Butter one side of each round. Arrange in single layer on baking sheet. Place under preheated broiler until lightly toasted. Turn and broil unbuttered side until lightly toasted. Transfer to rack and cool.

Combine cream cheese, butter, mayonnaise, Worcestershire sauce and green onion in large bowl. Spread about 1 teaspoon mixture over buttered side of bread. Dip into Parmesan cheese. (Rounds may be prepared in advance to this point and frozen.) Preheat broiler. Arrange rounds on baking sheet and broil until buttery and golden, about 5 minutes. Serve immediately. Makes 10 dozen.

PARMESAN TOASTS

8 slices (1/2-inch thick) white bread, crust removed and slices quartered lengthwise
1 1/2 sticks (12 tablespoons) unsalted butter, melted
2 1/2 cups grated Parmesan cheese, preferably fresh

Work with 1 strip at a time and using a fork, roll the strip quickly in butter, coating all sides. Remove and let the excess drip off, then press the Parmesan onto strip to help it adhere. Place the strip on a lightly buttered jelly-roll pan. Repeat with all strips. Bake in the top third of a preheated 375-degree oven for 10 minutes, turn and bake for 5 to 10 minutes more, or until strips are golden and crisp. Remove to paper towels to drain. The toasts may be made up to 1 day in advance and kept, covered loosely, at room temperature. If reheating, place toasts on a jelly-roll pan in preheated 325 degree oven for 5 to 10 minutes, or until they are heated through. Serve warm. Makes 32 toast strips.

TASTY ONION STICKS

1/2 cup butter or margarine
1 envelope dry onion soup mix
12 slices bread

Soften butter and add the dry soup, mixing well. Trim crusts from bread and spread onion butter on slices. Cut each slice into 4 strips. Place on ungreased baking sheet. Bake at 375 degrees for 10 minutes. Makes 48 sticks.

Jan says, "This onion butter is also very good on baked potatoes."

SOUP, STEW, POULTRY SEASONING BLEND

1 tablespoon thyme leaves
1 teaspoon rubbed sage
2 teaspoons rosemary leaves
1 tablespoon marjoram leaves

Blend all ingredients in a blender. Store in airtight container in a cool, dry place. Use as taste dictates.

BOUQUET GARNI

3 sprigs chervil
3 sprigs parsley
1 bay leaf
2 sprigs fresh thyme

Tie in a bunch and use for flavoring in stocks, soups.

WHITE FISH STOCK

1 pound bones and trimmings of any white fish
1 cup sliced onion
10 to 12 parsley stems
2 tablespoons fresh lemon juice
1/2 teaspoon salt
3 1/2 cups cold water
1/2 cup dry white wine

Combine bones and trimmings in a heavy, well greased saucepan. Add onion, parsley, lemon juice and salt. Cover and steam the mixture over moderately high heat for 5 minutes. Add water and wine; bring the liquid to a boil, skimming the top and cook over moderate heat for 25 minutes. Strain the stock through a fine sieve, pressing on the solids; let cool. Stock may be frozen. Makes about 3 cups.

BROWN STOCK

3 pounds cracked veal knuckles or veal bone
2 pounds beef bones, cut into 2-inch pieces
1 quart water
2 cups onion, chopped
2 cups carrot, chopped
1 cup celery, chopped
1 tablespoon crushed peppercorns
2 bay leaves, crumbled
2 garlic cloves
1 teaspoon dried rosemary
1 cup fresh parsley leaves
2 tomatoes, chopped
2 cups burgundy wine

Wash bones under cold water and drain. Place in a roasting pan and set in a preheated 500-degree oven until well browned, about 40 minutes. Turn after 20 minutes. Transfer bones to a large stockpot; pour 1 quart of water into the roaster, scraping all particles and add to the stockpot with the remaining ingredients. Bring to a boil over high heat; skim the top and lower heat to a simmer for 12 hours, skimming as necessary. Strain and remove fat. Refrigerate until cold; remove and discard fat from the surface. Refrigerate, covered tightly, up to 3 days or freeze up to 2 months. Reheat to a boil when ready to use. Makes 2 quarts.

Jo and Jan say, "We pour stock into ice cube trays, freeze it and transfer cubes to plastic bags. With small amounts like this you can take out just enough to meet any recipe requirement."

CHICKEN STOCK

3 quarts water
3 pounds chicken necks, backs and wings
1 large carrot, pared and and halved
2 ribs celery, including leaves, cut in
 1-inch pieces
2 medium onions, sliced
1 sprig parsley
1 bay leaf
1/2 teaspoon dried thyme
6 peppercorns

Combine all ingredients in a large stockpot and bring to a boil. Reduce heat; simmer, partially covered, 3 to 4 hours, skimming occasionally. Add water if necessary. Strain stock through a sieve lined with a double layer of cheesecloth, pressing solids with a spoon to extract all liquids. Discard solids and cool stock to room temperature; refrigerate, covered until cold. Remove and discard fat from surface of stock and refrigerate, covered, up to 3 days or can be frozen up to 2 months. To use, reheat to a boil. Makes 3 quarts.

TOMATO BOUILLON

2 cans (12-ounce size) tomato juice
2 cans water
3 beef bouillon cubes
6 whole cloves
1/4 teaspoon cinnamon
Sour cream (garnish)
Cinnamon (garnish)
Fresh parsley (garnish)

Pour tomato juice into saucepan; add 2 cans water, bouillon cubes, cloves and cinnamon. Heat, stirring occasionally until mixture just comes to a boil; do not let it boil. Lower heat and simmer on low for at least 30 minutes; strain.

To serve, heat just to a boil; pour into cups and add a dollop of sour cream and a sprinkling of cinnamon if desired. The soup can be frozen. Serves 6.

COLD TOMATO SOUP

2 tablespoons butter or margarine
1 large onion, minced
2 large cloves garlic, minced
1/4 teaspoon sugar
1 tablespoon fresh dill, finely chopped
1/2 teaspoon ground allspice
1 teaspoon salt, or to taste
Freshly ground black pepper, to taste
2 pounds ripe Italian plum tomatoes, peeled,
　seeded and chopped
3 cups chicken broth
2 1/2 tablespoons tomato paste
2 tablespoons cornstarch dissolved in 1/4
　cup cold broth
Sour cream
Chopped fresh parsley, chives or sprigs of
　dill (garnish)

Melt butter in large saucepan. Add onion and cook over low heat until soft. Add garlic; cook 5 minutes then add sugar, dill, allspice, salt and pepper. Cook for 2 more minutes; add tomatoes and 1 cup broth. Simmer, covered for 20 minutes. Add remaining broth, tomato paste, cornstarch and simmer 10 more minutes. Remove from heat and cool for a few minutes.

Puree mixture in blender or food processor. Chill thoroughly; taste and correct seasonings if desired. To serve, ladle into bowls and garnish each with a dollop of sour cream and a sprinkling of parsley, chives or a sprig of fresh dill. Serves 6-8.

If soup seems too thick for you, add a little more chicken broth.

RED BORDEAUX BEEF BROTH

6 cans (10 1/2-ounce size) condensed beef
　bouillon, undiluted
2 cups red Bordeaux
Lemon slices
Fresh parsley or watercress

Combine soup and wine in large saucepan; bring just to a boil. If served hot, pour into a warm tureen or soup cups. Float lemon slices on top; garnish each cup with a sprig of fresh parsley or watercress.

If served cold and jellied, combine soup and wine in large bowl. Refrigerate until slightly jellied, about 8 hours, or overnight. Spoon into soup cups. Serves 8.

FRENCH VEGETABLE SOUP

5 cans (14 1/2-ounce size) beef broth
1/4 teaspoon oregano, dried
1 teaspoon basil, dried
1 teaspoon parsley
1 teaspoon salt
1/4 teaspoon pepper
1/2 head cabbage, medium head
2 potatoes, large
1 carrot, large
1 leek, large
2 tomatoes, medium
1 cup green beans, fresh or frozen
1 cup peas, fresh or frozen
1/2 cup macaroni, Roni or Elbow
Parmesan cheese

Combine broth, oregano, basil, parsley, salt and pepper in a large kettle bringing it to a boil and letting it simmer, Meanwhile, clean and core cabbage and shred. Peel and chop potatoes, carrot, leek and tomatoes, Prepare the beans and peas. Add vegetables to broth and bring to a boil; simmer 30 minutes. Return to boil and add macaroni. Lower heat and simmer 1 hour. Serve hot, sprinkled with Parmesan cheese. Serves 8.

Jan says, "We simmer our soups and stews for several hours so the flavor of the ingredients have a chance to blend."

ITALIANA BEEF SOUP

4 pounds stew meat
2 tablespoons oil
1 can (28-ounces) tomatoes
6 cups water
1 large onion, chopped
1 clove garlic, minced
2 tablespoons brown sugar
1 tablespoon tapioca
2 tablespoons cider vinegar
2 teaspoons Italian seasonings
1 tablespoon chili powder
1 tablespoon salt
1/2 teaspoon dry mustard
1/2 teaspoon black pepper
1 package (4-ounce) pasta
1 green pepper, cut in chunks

Brown stew meat in oil. Drain off excess oil. Add rest of ingredients except pasta and green pepper to meat. Cover and simmer 3 hours. Add pasta and green pepper and continue to cook 15 to 20 minutes. Serves 8.

MINESTRONE

3 tablespoons olive oil
5 to 6 ounces salt pork
1 medium onion, sliced thin
1 leek, sliced thin
2 carrots, pared and cut into 2-inch match-
   like strips
2 potatoes, pared and cut into 2-inch match-
   like strips
6 ribs of celery, cut in bite-size pieces
1/3 head cabbage, shredded (1/2-inch)
1/2 cup frozen green beans or peas
2 quarts chicken stock (See index) or
   commercial chicken stock
1 can (16-ounce) tomatoes, drained,
   reserving juice
2 tablespoons tomato paste
2 cloves garlic, mashed
1 cup broken thin spaghetti
1 1/2 teaspoons basil
Black pepper, freshly ground
1/4 cup chopped fresh parsley
Parmesan cheese, freshly grated, if
   possible; to taste

Cut salt pork into 2-inch strips and saute in hot olive oil; but do not brown. Set aside the carrots, potatoes, shredded cabbage, and beans or peas.

After pork has sauteed, add tomato paste and season with pepper. Add pressed garlic, sliced onion, leek and the vegetables you set aside. Pour in the chicken stock and boil the mixture for 10 minutes, uncovered.

Add spaghetti and season with basil, oregano and parsley. Add salt only if needed. Cook until spaghetti is al dente. If desired, add the liquid from tomatoes. Sprinkle with Parmesan cheese before serving. Serves 12.

MARIE'S "CHOP SUEY"
(Vegetable Soup With A Different Flavor)

1 large cup onions, chopped
1 1/2 cups celery
1 green pepper
2 cups carrots
1 small jar pimentos, drained
1 can mushrooms, drained
1 can (303) tomatoes
1 can tomato puree
1 can bean sprouts, drained
2 to 3 pounds hamburger
2 tablespoons sugar
1 tablespoon chili powder
1 tablespoon Worcestershire sauce
1/3 to 1/2 cup soy sauce, to taste

In a large kettle fry hamburger and onions; drain off grease. Chop all vegetables, add to meat mixture; add all other ingredients and cook slowly until vegetables are tender.

Marie says, "This is very good served with biscuits or rolls and honey."

RUTHIE'S STEAK SOUP

1 stick margarine
1 cup flour
1/2 gallon water
2 cups ground beef or round steak, cut into
  bite-size pieces
2 tablespoons cooking oil
1 cup onions, diced
1 cup carrots, cubed
1 cup celery, chopped
2 cups frozen mixed vegetables
1 can tomatoes
2 cubes beef bouillon
2 tablespoons beef concentrate
1 teaspoon Accent
1 teaspoon seasoned salt
1/2 teaspoon coarsely ground black pepper

Melt margarine and stir in flour to make a smooth paste; add water. Saute beef in cooking oil; drain off grease, if any, and add beef to the kettle.

In saucepan, add onions, carrots and celery with water to cover. Bring to a boil; lower heat and cook 5 minutes longer. Drain and add vegetables to kettle.

Stir in mixed vegetables, tomatoes, bouillon, beef concentrate, Accent, seasoned salt and pepper. Bring to a boil, reduce heat and simmer gently until vegetables are done. Serves 16-20.

JOYCE'S WILD RICE - CHEESE SOUP

1 1/2 cups cooked wild rice
1/2 pound bacon, cooked and crumbled
1/4 cup chopped onion
3 cans potato soup
4 cups half-and-half
2 1/2 cups Velvetta cheese, grated

Cook wild rice following package instructions. Fry bacon and drain well. Saute onion in bacon fat and drain.

In large kettle, combine soup and onion; heat slowly and add cream. Cook on medium but do not allow to boil; add rice, bacon and onion; drop in cheese and stir until melted and soup is hot. Serves 4 - 6.

OLD-TIME BEEF STEW

1/2 cup flour
1 teaspoon salt
1/2 teaspoon pepper
2 pounds beef stew meat, cubed
1/4 cup vegetable oil
1 can beef bouillon
1 cup water
1/2 cup dry red wine
1 can (16-ounce) tomatoes, drained and
  chopped, reserving juice
1/2 teaspoon marjoram
1 bay leaf
4 carrots, sliced
1 pound pearl onions, peeled
1 1/2 pounds potatoes, cubed
1 package (10-ounce) frozen cut green beans
1 package (10-ounce) frozen mixed vegetables

Combine flour, salt and pepper; dredge meat until well-coated. Heat oil in Dutch oven over medium-high heat; add meat and brown in several batches. After browning meat, remove from kettle and set aside. Stir bouillon into drippings, scraping up brown bits from the bottom. Return meat to pot; add water, wine, tomato liquid, marjoram, bay leaf and remaining flour mixture. Bring to a boil and stir. Reduce heat; cover and simmer 1 1/2 hours. Add carrots, onions, potatoes and tomatoes. Cook uncovered 30 minutes, stirring occasionally. Add frozen vegetables and cook 15 minutes longer, stirring to break up vegetables. Serves 8.

WILD RICE SOUP

1/4 cup butter
1 medium onion, chopped
1/2 pound fresh mushrooms, thinly sliced
3 celery ribs, cut into l-inch matchsticks
4 small carrots, cut into l-inch matchsticks
6 tablespoons flour
6 cups chicken broth:
3 cups cooked wild rice
1 tablespoon Worcestershire sauce
1/2 teaspoon salt
1/4 teaspoon pepper
2 cups half-and-half
2/3 cup dry sherry
1 cup grated Cheddar cheese
Fresh parsley

Melt butter over medium heat in a 4 to 6-quart kettle. Saute onion until tender but not brown. Add mushrooms, celery and carrots; cook 2 minutes. Blend in flour then gradually add chicken broth. Cook, stirring constantly for 5 to 8 minutes until thickened. Stir in cooked wild rice, Worcestershire sauce, salt and pepper. Reduce heat to low, blend in cream and sherry. Add cheese and cook on low for 15 minutes ; do not boil. Garnish with parsley. serves 8.

ROMAN EGG DROP SOUP

1 1/2 quarts chicken broth
3 eggs, well beaten
4 tablespoons freshly grated Parmesan cheese
1/8 teaspoon salt
1/8 teaspoon pepper
1 tablespoon minced parsley
1 clove garlic, pressed
Fresh chives, chopped for garnish

Bring chicken broth to a boil. Combine beaten eggs, cheese, salt, pepper, parsley and garlic. Gradually add egg mixture to boiling broth, stirring constantly. Pour slowly to prevent lumping. Continue stirring and simmer for 3 to 5 minutes, only until egg strands are set. Top with chopped chives and serve hot. Serves 4.

PUMPKIN SOUP BAKED IN PUMPKIN SHELL

1 8 to 10-pound unblemished pumpkin
   with a 2-inch stem
1 tablespoon soft butter
2 1/2 cups fresh white bread crumbs,
   pressed down in cup to measure
6 tablespoons butter or margarine
2 cups onion, minced
1/2 teaspoon sage
1/2 teaspoon salt
Pinch of pepper
1/4 teaspoon nutmeg
11/2 cups Swiss cheese, finely diced
2 quarts chicken stock
1 bay leaf
1 cup heavy cream
1/4 cup fresh parsley, chopped

Spread bread crumbs in a shallow pan and allow them to dry out in a 300-degree oven, stirring occasionally; for 15 minutes.

Cut a lid out of the top of pumpkin, about 4 inches in diameter. Scrape and remove all stringy material and seeds from lid and inside of pumpkin. Rub inside of pumpkin and lid with 1 tablespoon soft butter.

In a large skillet, saute the onions in 6 tablespoons butter for 8 to 10 minutes over low heat until tender and translucent. Stir crumbs into the onion mixture, cook 2 to 3 minutes to absorb the butter. Stir in the sage, salt, pepper and nutmeg.

Remove from heat, stir in the cheese; spoon mixture into the pumpkin. Place pumpkin in a large, shallow, lightly buttered baking dish. Add chicken stock, adding enough so mixture comes to within 1 inch of pumpkin rim. Lay bay leaf on top and replace lid. Pumpkin may be prepared in advance to this point.

Carefully place baking dish in preheated 400-degree oven and bake for about 1 1/2 hours or until pumpkin begins to soften on the outside and the inside is beginning to bubble. Reduce temperature to 325 degrees and bake another 30 minutes or until pumpkin is tender but still holds its' shape solidly. Do not overcook or pumpkin will collapse. If pumpkin is browning too much, cover loosely with foil.

Keep warm in a 175-degree oven until ready to serve. Just before serving, remove bay leaf, heat cream in a saucepan to a simmer and stir into soup mixture and add parsley. Mix contents carefully, but well.

To serve, dip into pumpkin with a long-handled server, scraping bits of pumpkin from sides and bottom with each serving as soup is ladled into heated bowls. Serves 8 - 10.

PORK AND BEAN SOUP

3 cups chicken broth, fresh or canned
3 medium potatoes, cut into 1/2-inch cubes
1 small onion, finely chopped
1/2 cup celery, thinly sliced
1 garlic clove, crushed
1 small bay leaf
2 cans (1-pound size) beans in tomato sauce
2 cups ham, cooked and diced
Salt and pepper to taste

In saucepan, bring broth to a boil. Add potatoes, onion, celery, garlic and bay leaf. Cover and simmer until potatoes are tender. Add beans and diced ham. Stir and simmer; season with salt and pepper. Makes 2 quarts.

Jan says, "I do not peel my potatoes for this soup. The skins give it added flavor and vitamins."

FRENCH ONION SOUP

2 cans (14 1/2-ounce size) beef broth
2 red onions, sliced thin
2 tablespoons vegetable oil
2 tablespoons butter
1 garlic clove, finely minced
2 tablespoons flour
1 bay leaf
1/2 teaspoon parsley, minced
1/2 teaspoon thyme, crumbled
Freshly ground black pepper
Freshly grated nutmeg
4 slices French bread, sliced diagonally 3/4-inch thick
4 slices Gruyere or Swiss cheese
2 teaspoons Parmesan cheese, grated

Heat oil and butter in large kettle. Add onions and stir to coat. Reduce heat to low and cover; cook until onions are limp and golden in color. Stir in garlic and cook until garlic is soft. Sprinkle onions and garlic with flour; stir until well mixed. Stir in 1 can of broth, scraping the browned bits from the bottom of the pan, making a roux. Add bay leaf, parsley, thyme and the remaining can of broth. Simmer for 30 minutes while you toast the bread until golden brown. Place cheese on each slice; sprinkle with Parmesan cheese and return to oven until cheese is melted. Remove bay leaf and ladle soup into bowls; grind pepper and nutmeg on soup. Place bread on top of soup, using a spatula to lift slices. Serves 4.

Jan and Jo say, "Make this soup, toss a salad and dinner is done. The soup is rich, so you don't really need a lot more with it. Just a wonderful dessert."

SANTA FE CORN SOUP

4 cups fresh corn
1 cup chicken stock
1/4 cup butter
2 cups milk
1 garlic clove, minced
1 teaspoon oregano
Salt
Freshly ground pepper
2 tablespoons canned green chilies, rinsed and diced
1 chicken breast, boned and diced
1 cup tomatoes, diced
1 cup Monterey Jack cheese, cubed
2 tablespoons minced parsley (garnish)
Corn chips (garnish)

Combine corn and chicken stock in blender or food processor and puree. Combine butter and corn mixture in large heavy saucepan and simmer for 5 minutes, stirring constantly. Do not let corn stick. Add milk, garlic, oregano, salt and pepper; bring to a boil. Reduce heat, add chilies and simmer 5 minutes. Add chicken and tomatoes. (May be frozen or stored in refrigerator at this point).

At serving time, reheat soup slowly if refrigerated. Remove from heat, add cheese and stir until melted. Ladle into bowls and sprinkle with parsley and corn chips. Serves 6.

Jo and Jan say, "You can substitute Ro-Tel tomatoes for the 1 cup tomatoes in the recipe. It will make it more spicy."

QUICKIE CLAM CHOWDER

2 cans (6 1/2-ounce size) minced clams
2 cans (15-ounce) clam chowder
1 can (14 1/2-ounce) chicken broth
1 teaspoon minced, dried chives
1 teaspoon parsley flakes
1/2 teaspoon ground black pepper
1/4 teaspoon Tabasco sauce
2/3 cup heavy cream
Sherry (optional)

Drain clams and pour liquid into soup pan. Combine all ingredients except clams and bring to a boil. Reduce heat and simmer 5 minutes, stirring constantly. Add clams, stirring well and heat through. Serves 4.

Jan says, "When you do not have the time to fix Annie's Clam Chowder, take 10 minutes out of your day and make this version. I always add a half jigger of sherry. Hmmmmm, good!"

◆◆

ANNIE'S CLAM CHOWDER

1 pound bacon, fried and crumbled
7 tablespoons margarine
1 jar (6-ounce) mushrooms, diced
1 onion, diced
1/3 cup flour
1 teaspoon salt
1/4 teaspoon pepper
4 cups half-and-half
1 cup milk, or more
8 potatoes, cooked and diced
3 cans (6 1/2-ounce size) clams with juice
1 jar (16-ounce) Cheez Whiz
Paprika
Parsley

In 6-quart saucepan, fry bacon until crisp; remove and drain well on paper towels, crumble when cool. Drain bacon grease from pan and melt 3 tablespoons of margarine over medium heat. Saute onions and mushrooms and remove when tender to drain on paper towels.

Melt 4 more tablespoons margarine in pan. Stir in flour, salt and pepper until blended; cook for 1 minute. Gradually stir in half-and-half and milk. Add bacon, mushrooms, onion, potatoes and clams with juice. Fill to the level you want with milk (leave enough room to add cheese).

Simmer for 1 hour and add jar of Cheez Whiz. Simmer a while longer, to your liking. Garnish with paprika and parsley. Serves 10.

TURKEY SOUP

1 quart poultry stock
2 cups turkey, diced
1 package Knorr Vegetable mix
1 cup tomato juice
1 1/2 cups cooked rice
1/4 teaspoon basil
1/4 teaspoon parsley
1/4 teaspoon pepper
1/4 teaspoon sage
Pinch of nutmeg
1/4 teaspoon Kitchen Bouquet

Combine all ingredients in a large pan. Simmer for at least 1 hour. Serves 4-6.

This may be prepared in the microwave. Put the ingredients in a 2-quart glass bowl and microwave on high for 10 minutes.

BAKED POTATO SOUP

6 slices bacon, fried crisp, crumbled and set aside
4 medium-size baked potatoes; skins can be left on
2 tablespoons margarine
1/3 cup chopped green onion
1 can cream of chicken soup, undiluted
1 cup chicken broth
1 cup half-and-half
Salt and freshly ground black pepper
1/2 cup grated Cheddar cheese
Sour cream
Fresh chives or parsley, chopped

Prepare bacon and set aside. Bake potatoes, cool and cut in small chunks.

In medium-size saucepan, melt margarine and saute onions until clear. Add potatoes, chicken soup, broth, cream, salt and pepper to taste, and simmer until hot but do not boil.

Ladle into 4 individual soup bowls. Top each with grated cheese, crumbled bacon, a dollop of sour cream and fresh chives or parsley. Serves 4.

Jan and Jo say, "This makes such a marvelous meal! Toss a crisp, green salad and serve with hard rolls. The soup is rich and filling, so you do not need anything else."

JOYCE'S CHEESY CHOWDER

1 1/2 cups water
1 chicken bouillon cube
2 cups potatoes, cubed
1/2 cup onion, chopped
1 package (10-ounce) frozen mixed vegetables
1 jar (8-ounce) Cheez Whiz
1 can (16-ounce) creamed corn
1/2 cup milk
Fresh parsley or chives (garnish)

Boil potatoes in water with chicken bouillon, onion and mixed vegetables until potatoes are tender. Add Cheez Whiz, corn and milk. Stir until cheese is melted. Serve hot, topped with a few snips of fresh parsley or chives. Serves 4.

CHEDDAR CHEESE SOUP

1/2 cup butter or margarine, melted
1 cup onion, finely chopped
1 cup celery, finely chopped
1/2 cup grated carrot
1/3 cup flour
2 teaspoons dry mustard
1 1/2 cups chicken stock
2 cups half-and-half
2 cups milk
2 cups sharp Cheddar cheese, shredded
Salt and pepper to taste
2 tablespoons chopped fresh parsley
2 tablespoons chopped chives
4 slices bacon, cooked crisp and crumbled

Saute onion, celery and carrot in melted butter over low heat for 10 minutes. Add flour, dry mustard and paprika. Stir to blend and cook for 5 minutes. Combine chicken stock, cream and milk; add to vegetable mixture and stir until well blended. Cook for 15 minutes at a simmer. Add cheese and stir until melted. Salt and pepper to taste. Serve with chopped parsley, chives and crumbled bacon on top. Serves 8 -10.

JOYCE'S CHICKEN SOUP

2 chicken breasts
1/2 teaspoon salt
1/2 cup onion, chopped
1/2 cup carrots, sliced
1/2 cup celery, diced
1 can cream of chicken soup
1/2 cup milk
Pepper to taste
1/2 cup sharp Cheddar cheese, shredded

Simmer chicken breasts in 2 cups of water with salt. When done, remove chicken from bone and cut into pieces. Boil stock down to 1 cup. Place onion, carrots and celery in broth; simmer 10 to 15 minutes. Stir in chicken, soup, milk, pepper and cheese; heat slowly on low heat. Serves 2.

Joyce says, "This is excellent for a dinner with a salad and hot French bread. It can be frozen; when reheated, do not boil, just warm it slowly."

CHICKEN- VEGETABLE CHOWDER

1 3-pound broiler-fryer chicken, cut up
4 quarts water
1 teaspoon salt
4 bay leaves
6 black peppercorns
1 teaspoon dried parsley
1 teaspoon dried basil
1 teaspoon dried oregano
1 teaspoon dried thyme
1 onion stuck with 4 cloves
3 tablespoons flour
5 tablespoons water
1 can (16-ounce) tomatoes, undrained and cut up
4 medium potatoes, peeled and diced
1 package (10-ounce) frozen corn
2 packages (10-ounce size) frozen baby Lima beans
1 teaspoon Worcestershire sauce
1/4 teaspoon cayenne pepper
1 cup heavy cream
Salt and pepper to taste
4 sprigs fresh parsley, minced (garnish)

Place chicken in water with salt. peppercorns, herbs and onion. Bring to a boil; cover and simmer 45 minutes or until chicken is tender. Remove chicken, cool then bone and chop meat into 1-inch pieces; set aside. Strain broth and return to pot; bring to a boil.

Combine flour and 5 tablespoons water to form a roux. Add to boiling soup, stirring constantly until thickened. Add tomatoes and potatoes; simmer cover for 20 minutes. Add corn, lima beans, Worcestershire and cayenne. Simmer another 15 minutes. Add chicken and cream. Season to taste. Cook 1 minute longer; do not boil. Garnish with parsley. Serves 6-8

CREAM OF TURKEY SOUP

1/2 cup butter
6 tablespoons flour
1/2 teaspoon salt
1/4 teaspoon pepper
2 cups half-and-half
3 cups turkey or chicken broth
1 cup chopped cooked turkey
1 can corn, drained
Chopped green onion (garnish)

Heat butter in saucepan. Blend in flour, salt and pepper. Heat until bubbly. Gradually add half-and-half and 1 cup of broth, stirring constantly. Bring to a boil; cook, stirring constantly for 1 to 2 minutes. Blend in remaining broth, turkey and corn. Heat; do not boil.

To serve, ladle into bowls and garnish with chopped green onion. Serves 4-6.

BLACK FOREST POTATO SOUP

4 medium potatoes, pared and cubed
3 medium tomatoes, peeled and chopped
2 medium carrots, pared and chopped
1 cup celery, chopped
1 teaspoon parsley
1 small bay leaf
3 cans 10 1/2-ounce size) condensed beef broth
1 1/2 cups pumpernickel, wheat or whole-wheat bread, cubed
1 cup sour cream

In large pan combine potatoes, tomatoes, carrots, celery, parsley, bay leaf and beef broth. Bring to a boil and reduce heat and simmer, covered for 30 minutes or until vegetables are tender. In the meantime, place bread cubes on baking sheet and toast in 350-degree oven for 10 minutes; set aside. Remove bay leaf from soup before serving. Top each bowl of soup with toast cubes and a large dollop of sour cream. Serves 8.

TIP
• Garnish cream soups with herb flowers if they are available.

VICHYSSOISE

2 sticks butter or margarine
2 onions, sliced
4 leeks, chopped
5 small potatoes, sliced
2 quarts chicken broth
Prosciutto bone or piece of ham
Dash Worcestershire sauce
Dash hot pepper sauce
Salt and white pepper, to taste
Pinch of nutmeg
1 quart half-and-half
Chopped chives (garnish)

Melt butter in heavy saucepan. Add chopped vegetables and simmer 15 to 20 minutes. Add broth and bone or meat and simmer 2 hours until thick. Remove bone and strain; add seasonings. Cool and add cream until of desired consistency. Adjust seasonings and chill. To serve, ladle into serving dishes; top with chopped chives if desired. Serves 10-12.

ARTICHOKE SOUP

3 tablespoons butter
1 1/2 tablespoons green onions, minced
1 1/2 tablespoons flour
3 1/2 cups chicken broth
3 cans (1-pound size) artichoke bottoms, drained
1 cup half-and-half
Garlic croutons (garnish)

Melt butter and allow to brown slightly over medium heat. Add green onions and lightly saute; stir in flour and cook for 3 minutes.

Heat chicken broth in 2-quart saucepan; stir in flour mixture and cook over medium heat until slightly thickened, about 3 to 5 minutes.

Puree artichoke bottoms in blender or food processor; add chicken stock and half-and-half. Blend thoroughly for 30 seconds then season to taste with salt and pepper. Serve hot or cold. Serves 4-6.

Jan and Jo say, "We like recipes like this because they can be made ahead and refrigerated. Helps make for less kitchen time when you have guests."

BROCCOLI SOUP

3 packages (10-ounce size) frozen, chopped broccoli
5 cups chicken stock
1/4 cup onion, chopped
4 tablespoons butter
2 egg yolks
1 cup heavy cream
3 tablespoons flour
1 teaspoon salt
1 teaspoon pepper
1/4 teaspoon mace

In large saucepan, cook broccoli according to package directions, substituting chicken stock for water. While broccoli is cooking, saute onion in butter until tender.

Puree broccoli and onion in blender or food processor using as little of the cooking stock as possible. Add stock to pureed vegetables to bring it to desired consistency.

In separate bowl, blend yolks and cream. Gradually add flour and seasonings. Mix with a few drops of the hot mixture then stir back into the pot. Bring to a boil and cook for 30 seconds, stirring constantly. Correct seasonings if necessary. This soup is delicious hot or cold. Serves 8-10.

❖◆❖

BRUSSELS SPROUT SOUP

4 packages (10-ounce size) frozen Brussels
 sprouts, partially thawed
7 chicken bouillon cubes
5 cups boiling water
8 slices bacon
2 garlic cloves, minced
6 cups milk
3/4 cups uncooked rice
1 teaspoon oregano leaves, crushed
2 teaspoons salt
1/2 teaspoon pepper
1 package (10-ounce) frozen peas and carrots
1 teaspoon salt
2 cups water
3/4 cup shredded Parmesan cheese

Dissolve bouillon cubes in boiling water; set aside. Fry bacon in heavy pan; add garlic and saute. Add 3 cups of chicken broth to pot with milk, uncooked rice, oregano leaves, salt and pepper. Bring to a boil, reduce heat, cover and simmer 15 minutes.

Add frozen peas and carrots. Bring to a boil, reduce heat and simmer 10 minutes or until vegetables are tender.

Coarsely chop thawed Brussels sprouts. Combine the remaining 2 cups of broth, salt and 2 cups water, bring to a boil; add chopped sprouts. Return to a boil and simmer uncovered 10 minutes or until tender.

Add sprouts and liquid to rice mixture. Stir in Parmesan cheese. Serves 16-18.

BORSCH IN A JIFFY

1 can (16-ounce) sliced beets, chilled and
 undrained
1 can (10 1/2-ounce) beef consomme
8 ounces sour cream or unflavored yogurt
Juice of 1 lemon
Salt to taste
Chopped dill (optional)
Sliced green onions (optional)
Croutons (optional)
Grated hard-boiled eggs, (optional)

Puree beets, consomme, yogurt or sour cream and lemon juice until well-blended. Chill until ready to serve and garnish as desired. Serves 4.

CREAM OF MUSHROOM SOUP

1 medium onion, chopped
4 tablespoons margarine
1 pound fresh mushrooms, chopped
4 tablespoons flour
6 cups chicken broth
2 egg yolks
3/4 cup heavy cream or Creme Fraiche (See
 index)
Salt and pepper to taste

Chop onion and saute in margarine until golden. Add the chopped mushrooms and flour to onion mixture. Cook for a few minutes and add the stock. Cover and simmer for 1 hour; strain, working the onion and mushrooms through a sieve. Add a bit of the hot soup to the egg yolks and stir. Add a little more soup then add the yolk mixture back into the soup. Heat gently; add the cream or Cream Fraiche, salt and pepper to taste. Serves 8.

MINTED FRESH PEA SOUP

2 pounds fresh, shelled peas
1 green onion, chopped fine
1 tablespoon chopped fresh mint
1 1/2 cups heavy cream
Salt
Fresh chives, chopped

In saucepan, cover peas with water and bring to a boil. Add green onion and mint. Cover and simmer for 10 minutes or until tender. Puree in blender or food processor until smooth. Add cream and blend again; salt to taste. Reheat or serve chilled. Garnish with chives. Serves 6.

CURRIED CELERY SOUP

1 3/4 cups celery with leaves, sliced
1/2 cup onion, chopped
1/2 cup carrot, sliced
1 cup potato, diced
1/2 teaspoon garlic, minced
1/2 teaspoon parsley
1/2 teaspoon salt
1/2 teaspoon coarse black pepper
1/2 teaspoon curry powder
2 cups chicken broth, divided
1 cup half-and-half

In saucepan, combine celery, onion, carrot, potato, garlic, parsley, salt, pepper, curry powder and 1 cup of chicken broth. Bring to a boil; reduce heat and simmer, covered, until vegetables are tender. Pour half the mixture into a blender and blend at high speed until smooth. Remove and repeat with the remaining vegetable mixture. Return all pureed vegetable mixture to the saucepan. Add cream and the remaining 1 cup chicken broth. Mix well and simmer slowly until the flavor has a distinct taste. Serves 4.

Jan says, "We like this soup on a cold blustery day. I serve it for lunch with a sandwich and for dinner with a tossed salad and French bread."

CARROT CREAM SOUP

1/4 cup butter
1/2 cup onion, chopped
4 cups carrots, grated
1 cup flour
8 1/2 cups chicken stock
1/2 cup heavy cream
Salt and pepper

Melt butter in large heavy saucepan over medium heat. Add onion and cook until soft. Add carrots and stir in flour; mix well and cook about 2 minutes, stirring constantly using a wire whisk. Add chicken stock and bring mixture to a boil. Lower heat, cover and simmer 30 minutes, stirring occasionally. Blend in cream, salt and pepper to taste; serve immediately. Serves 12.

CREAM OF WATERCRESS SOUP

1/3 cup green onions, minced
3 tablespoons butter
4 cups (packed) fresh watercress leaves and
  tender stems, washed and dried
1/2 teaspoon salt
3 tablespoons flour
5 1/2 cups chicken broth
2 egg yolks
1/2 cup heavy cream
2 tablespoons butter, softened
1 cup watercress leaves - plunged in boiling
  water for 30 seconds then into ice water
  and drained

Melt butter in saucepan and cook onions, covered, until tender but not brown (5 to 10 minutes). Stir in watercress and salt; cover and cook slowly about 5 minutes until leaves are tender and wilted. Sprinkle in the flour and stir for 3 more minutes. In separate pan bring chicken stock to a boil. Remove watercress mixture from heat and beat in the boiling stock. Simmer for 5 minutes; remove from heat and puree. Return to saucepan. (If you are not serving immediately, set mixture aside, uncovered. Reheat before proceeding).

Blend yolks and cream in mixing bowl. Beat a small amount of hot mixture into yolks and stir well. Gradually beat in the rest of the soup in a thin stream. Return soup to saucepan and stir over medium heat for a minute; do not allow to simmer. Remove from heat; stir in butter a tablespoon at a time. Garnish with watercress leaves. Serves 6.

Super Bowls

CREAM OF SQUASH SOUP

1 butternut squash (2 to 2 1/2 pounds),pared, seeded and cut in 1-inch cubes
1 cup milk
1 cup heavy cream
1/2 to 1 cup chicken broth
1 tablespoon honey
1 tablespoon brandy or Cognac
1/2 teaspoon grated orange zest
1/2 teaspoon salt
1/8 teaspoon white pepper
1/4 teaspoon ground ginger
1/4 teaspoon ground nutmeg
1/4 teaspoon ground mace

Cook squash, covered, in boiling salted water until tender, 30 to 40 minutes. Rinse with cold water; drain.

Puree squash in blender or food processor and transfer to a large saucepan. Stir in milk, cream, 1/2 of the broth and rest of ingredients. If mixture is too thick add the rest of the chicken broth. Cook over low heat, stirring occasionally, until hot, about 10 minutes. Do not allow to boil. Adjust seasonings as to taste. Makes 6 cups.

CREAM OF CAULIFLOWER SOUP

2 packages (10-ounce size) frozen cauliflower
2 cups chicken broth
3 tablespoons butter or margarine
3 tablespoons flour
1/3 cup celery, chopped
1/2 teaspoon curry powder
1/2 teaspoon salt
2 1/2 cups milk
Chopped chives

In large saucepan, cook cauliflower according to package directions substituting chicken broth for water. When done, set some flowerettes aside if desired, to add as whole pieces and puree the rest in blender or food processor, using as little of the broth as possible in blending. Add the broth to the pureed cauliflower.

In a separate pan melt butter, gradually add flour and seasonings, stirring constantly with a wire whisk. Cook 1 minute to blend flavors. Slowly blend in milk and whisk until it just comes to a boil. Stir in pureed cauliflower and bring back just to a boil. Garnish with chopped chives. Makes 6 cups.

COLD BLACKBERRY SOUP

4 cups ripe blackberries
1 cup water
1 cup dry white wine
3/4 cup sugar
3 large strips lemon zest (cut strips 3x 1-inch)
1 stick cinnamon (2-inch size)
3 whole cloves
1 cup sour cream, chilled
1 cup plain yogurt, chilled

Pick over, rinse and drain blackberries; reserve a few for garnish. Combine rest of berries in noncorrosive saucepan with water, wine, sugar, lemon zest, cinnamon and cloves. Cook, covered, over low heat, stirring occasionally until berries have reddened and softened, about 10 to 15 minutes. Remove from heat; cool, uncovered about 10 minutes.

Remove lemon zest strips and cinnamon stick from mixture and press blackberry mixture through sieve; discard seeds. Refrigerate puree, covered, until cold.

Before serving, whisk puree together with sour cream and yogurt until smooth. Serve in chilled bowls; garnish with reserved blackberries. Serves 4.

Salads

SALAD TIPS

- Wash and pat dry salad greens. Wrap in towels and refrigerate to help retain crispness. Also, always break or tear leaves, never cut them; that will make the edges turn brown.
- Always try to have chilled bowls or plates ready to fill.
- As you pour dressing over a salad, follow a Z-line. It will give an even distribution. If pouring oil and vinegar or lemon juice, always add oil first; it will coat the leaves, allowing the salad to remain crisp.
- Practice the roll-toss method to mix your salads. Start with a salad spoon in your right hand, fork in the left. Go down to the bottom of the bowl with one, while going up and over with the other. Roll salad until all leaves are coated with dressing.
- Marinate green onions in lemon juice before adding to a salad.

HOW TO FORM TORTILLA CUPS

Press a Tortilla into a large ladle or a commercial potato basket holder. If using the ladle, hold the tortilla in place with a slightly smaller spoon and fry in deep fat (375 degrees) until tortilla is crisp. These can be held overnight in a turned-off oven. Tortilla cups are pretty containers for guacamole or other dips and sauces, but are used primarily for salads.

CROUTONS

1 cup bread cubes
Grated Parmesan Cheese
Garlic-flavored Olive Oil (See index)

Cut bread in strips one direction, then across, to make cubes. Spread on cookie sheet; drizzle a small amount of flavored oil over cubes. Heat in a preheated 225-degree oven for 2 hours. Sprinkle with Parmesan cheese. Store in a jar and refrigerate.

Jo and Jan say, "To ensure that croutons will stay crunchy, be sure to slow toast them. They should be very dry."

CHICKEN AND SPINACH SALAD

1/2 cup olive or salad oil
3 tablespoons Dijon mustard
2 tablespoons wine vinegar
2 whole small boneless cooked chicken
  breasts
2 large tomatoes
1 package (16-ounce) Mozzarella cheese
1/2 bag (10-ounce) spinach, washed and
  cleaned

In a small bowl, whisk oil, mustard and vinegar; set aside. Slice chicken breasts, tomatoes and cheese. Line platter with spinach leaves. Arrange chicken, tomatoes and cheese slices on spinach and pour dressing over the salad. Don't soak it; we usually drizzle some over the top then pass the rest for guests to use as they prefer. Serves 8.

❖❖

CHICKEN SALAD

1 large onion, sliced
4 stalks celery with leaves, sliced
Salt and pepper
4 whole chicken breasts
2 teaspoons minced onion
8 hard-boiled eggs, chopped
1 can (6-ounce) water chestnuts, sliced
3-4 stalks celery, chopped
1/2 cup seedless grapes
1/2 cup chopped nuts (pecan, cashew,
  macadamia)
3/4 cup mayonnaise

Place onion, celery, salt and pepper in large kettle of water. Bring to a boil and add chicken breasts. Simmer 1 hour, or until tender. Remove breasts and chill. Skin and bone chicken and cut into cubes. Add eggs, minced onion, water chestnuts, celery, grapes and nuts. Add only enough mayonnaise to mix thoroughly.

GRAND HOTEL'S SPINACH SALAD

1 package (3-ounce) lemon Jell-O
3/4 cup hot water
1 tablespoon lemon juice
3/4 cup mayonnaise
1/2 cup green onions, chopped
1/2 cup celery, chopped
1 small carton cottage cheese (small curd)
1 package (10-ounce) frozen chopped
  spinach, cooked, drained and cooled.

Mix together lemon Jell-O, water, lemon juice and mayonnaise. Cool slightly and add onions, celery, cottage cheese and spinach. Pour into an 8x8-inch pan and chill until firm. Serves 8-10.

MARY'S BEEF AND AVOCADO SALAD

2 avocados, peeled and sliced
1 pound rare roast beef, thinly sliced
1 red onion, thinly sliced
3/4 cup oil, half of it olive oil, the rest
  vegetable oil
1/2 cup red wine vinegar
2 teaspoons Dijon mustard
1 teaspoon salt
1/4 teaspoon freshly ground pepper
Lettuce
Parsley

In a casserole, layer 1/2 of the avocado, 1/2 of beef and 1/2 of onion. Repeat layers, set aside. Mix the oil, vinegar, mustard, salt and pepper together and pour over the layers. Cover and marinate 2 hours at room temperature. Drain well, refrigerate.

Return to room temperature before serving. Serve the salad on lettuce leaves, sprinkled with fresh parsley. A wonderful summer supper. Serve with hot bread or muffins. Serves 4.

Jo and Jan say, "Try this using David's 'Poor Man's Filet (See index). We think it's delicious."

TONIA'S CUCUMBER - DILL SALAD

1 medium onion
4 large cucumbers
1 small carton sour cream and chive dip
1 cup mayonnaise
3 tablespoons dill weed
2 tablespoons lemon juice
1 tablespoon vinegar
1 teaspoon salt
1 teaspoon pepper

Peel cucumbers and onion; slice thin into a bowl. Combine rest of ingredients; stir into cucumbers and onion and refrigerate until cold. Serves 8-10.

MILLIE'S SAUERKRAUT SALAD

2 1/2 cups sauerkraut (No. 2 can) drained
1 cup sugar
1 large onion, finely chopped
1 large green pepper, finely chopped
1 cup celery, finely chopped
1/4 cup pimento, chopped
1/2 cup salad oil
1/4 cup wine vinegar

Combine drained kraut and sugar. Let stand 10 minutes. Drain off liquid. Combine onion, green pepper, celery and pimento in medium bowl. Thoroughly mix vinegar and oil. Pour over vegetables; add kraut and chill several hours or overnight. Serves 6-8.

SMOKED TURKEY SALAD

2 pounds smoked turkey
1/2 pound Jarlsberg cheese
2 cups seedless green grapes, halved
2 cups seedless red grapes, halved
1 cup celery, thinly sliced
1 cup salted cashews or pecans
1 1/2 cups mayonnaise
1/4 cup medium-dry sherry
2 tablespoons Dijon-style mustard

Cut turkey in l-inch cubes; cut cheese in 1 1/2 x 1/4-inch strips. In bowl, combine turkey, cheese, grapes, celery and nuts.

In small bowl, blend mayonnaise, sherry and mustard until smooth. Pour over salad and toss to blend. Cover and chill until ready to serve. Serves 12.

SHRIMP – SCALLOP – SNOW PEA SALAD

2 dozen large shrimp, shelled and deveined
1 1/2 pounds scallops
2 cucumbers, peeled, seeded and sliced
1 can water chestnuts, sliced
4 celery ribs, chopped
1 bunch scallions, finely chopped
24 snow peas

DRESSING:
1/3 cup water
1/3 cup white vinegar
1/4 cup vegetable oil
1 garlic clove, minced
2-3 tablespoons dry mustard, or to taste
2 tablespoons sesame oil
2 tablespoons dry sherry
1 tablespoon sugar
Salt
1/4 cup salted shelled peanuts

Cook shrimp in boiling water until just pink. Drain well and place in bowl. Cook scallops in boiling water until translucent; drain well and add to shrimp, allow to cool.

Remove stem end and string snow peas. Place in a colander and pour boiling water over; drain well and transfer to another bowl and let cool. Add cucumbers, water chestnuts, celery and scallions; toss lightly.

Combine dressing ingredients except peanuts. Add half of dressing to seafood mixture and toss to coat. Add rest to snow pea mixture; toss well. Mound seafood on serving tray, surround with snow pea mixture. Sprinkle peanuts over snow pea mixture; Chill before serving. Serves 8-10.

Super Bowls

CITRUS AND ONION SALAD

2 tablespoons salad oil
3/4 cup chicken broth
1 clove garlic, minced
Dash of Italian seasoning
2 tablespoons vinegar
2 tablespoons lemon juice, freshly squeezed
Freshly ground pepper
2 grapefruit, peeled and sliced in rounds
2 oranges, peeled and sliced
1/2 red onion, thinly sliced

Combine salad oil, chicken broth, garlic, Italian seasoning, vinegar, lemon juice and pepper; chill well. One hour before serving, mix grapefruit, oranges and onions in a salad bowl. Pour dressing over fruit and onions; marinate in the refrigerator. To serve, drain with slotted spoon and arrange on a chilled platter lined with lettuce. Serves 4.

COBB SALAD

1 medium-size head iceberg lettuce,
  shredded
6 tablespoons white wine vinegar
1 teaspoon Dijon mustard
1/2 teaspoon salt
1/4 teaspoon garlic powder
1/4 teaspoon pepper
3 tablespoons chopped chives
1/2 cup vegetable oil
1 large tomato, chopped
1 1/2 cups cooked chicken, diced
1 large avocado, peeled, diced and sprinkled
  with lemon juice
1/2 pound bacon, sliced, cooked crisp,
  drained and crumbled
2 hard-boiled eggs, chopped
4 ounces Blue cheese, crumbled

Place shredded lettuce in a large bowl. Combine vinegar, mustard, salt, garlic powder, pepper, chives and the oil in a jar and shake vigorously. Pour dressing over lettuce and toss. Arrange the tomato, chicken, avocado, bacon and chopped eggs on top of the lettuce. Place crumbled cheese in center of the salad. Toss at the table. Serves 4.

SHRIMP SALAD IN PINEAPPLE BOATS

1 ripe pineapple
1 pound fresh cooked shrimp
1 cup celery, thinly sliced
1/2 cup onion, chopped
2 teaspoons grated fresh ginger root
1 cup water chestnuts, drained and chopped
1/3 cup mint leaves, minced
1/4 teaspoon salt
Tabasco sauce
Cashew nuts, chopped (garnish)

Cut pineapple in half lengthwise, including through the top of the leaves. Remove pineapple by cutting and scooping, being careful you do not cut through the "boat." Cut pineapple into bite-size pieces and chill. Combine rest of ingredients except Tabasco and nuts. Add a couple dashes of Tabasco, or to taste. When ready to serve, combine ingredients with chilled pineapple and fill the boats. Garnish with nuts. Serves 2.

COLESLAW WITH COOKED DRESSING

7 cups shredded cabbage
3/4 cup onion, minced
1/2 cup pimiento, chopped
1/2 cup sour cream
1/4 cup celery, minced
1/4 cup green pepper, minced
3 tablespoons minced fresh parsley
Salt
Freshly ground pepper
Paprika

DRESSING:
3 eggs
3/4 cup cider vinegar
1 1/2 tablespoons dry mustard
2 teaspoons sugar
1 teaspoon salt
1/2 teaspoon celery seed
1/8 teaspoon pepper, freshly ground
3 tablespoons bacon fat or butter
2 tablespoons flour
1 cup milk

Combine cabbage, onion , pimiento, sour cream, celery, pepper and parsley in a large mixing bowl; toss lightly. Cover and refrigerate while preparing Dressing.

Combine eggs, vinegar, mustard, sugar, salt, celery seed and pepper in mixing bowl and beat well and set aside. Melt butter in a heavy saucepan (nonaluminum, please) . Stir in flour and cook over medium-low heat, stirring constantly for about 3 minutes. Pour in milk and continue stirring until sauce begins to simmer. Cook, stirring constantly for about 5 minutes. Reduce heat to low, stir in egg mixture and cook until sauce thickens. Do not let the mixture boil; the eggs will curdle. Remove from heat; cool and refrigerate.

To serve, add cold dressing to cabbage mixture. Toss well and season with salt and pepper to taste. When serving, sprinkle top with paprika. Serves 12.

Jo and Jan say, "The Dressing can be made ahead up to 5 days. We like to toss the salad and Dressing one day ahead of serving to blend all the flavors. Just toss, cover and refrigerate until serving time."

MOM'S HOT SLAW

2 egg yolks
1 tablespoon butter
1/4 cup cider vinegar
1/4 cup water
4 cups shredded cabbage
1/4 teaspoon celery seed

In heavy saucepan mix yolks, butter, vinegar and water. Stir over low heat until thickened. Add cabbage and stir until well coated. Sprinkle with celery seed and stir again. Serves 4.

VEGETABLE SALAD

4 medium zucchini, sliced 1/4-inch thick
1 small red onion, sliced thin
1/4 teaspoon dill weed, dried or fresh
1/4 teaspoon parsley, dried or fresh
2 tomatoes, cut into wedges
1/2 cup Vinaigrette Salad Dressing (See index)
Ground black pepper

Combine zucchini, onion, dill, parsley and salad dressing in a glass microwave bowl. Cover bowl with plastic and cook on High 4 minutes or until zucchini is bright green. Cool. Add tomato wedges and toss gently. Cover and refrigerate overnight or several hours. Serves 6.

Super Bowls

GINA'S REFRIGERATOR FRUIT - PASTA SALAD

1 cup sugar
2 tablespoons flour
2 1/2 teaspoons salt
1 3/4 cup pineapple juice, from drained
    pineapple
2 eggs, beaten
1 tablespoon lemon juice
3 quarts water
1 tablespoon cooking oil
1 package (16-ounce) Acini de Pepe pasta
3 cans (11-ounce size) mandarin oranges,
    drained
2 cans (20-ounce size) pineapple chunks,
    drained; reserve juice
1 can (20-ounce) crushed pineapple, drained
1 carton (9-ounce) non-dairy whipped topping
1 cup miniature marshmallows
1 cup coconut, shredded

Combine sugar, flour, 1/2 teaspoon salt. Gradually stir in pineapple juice and eggs. Cook over moderate heat, stir until thick. Add lemon juice and cool to room temperature.

Boil water with rest (2 teaspoons) of salt and oil. Add pasta and cook at a boil until done. Drain thoroughly and rinse with cold water. Cool to room temperature. Combine egg mixture with pasta. Mix lightly but thoroughly. Refrigerate overnight in an airtight container. Add remaining ingredients lightly and refrigerate again until well chilled. This salad can be refrigerated for up to a week. Serves 18-20.

Jo and Jan say, "We like to use the large marshmallows, cut into fourths; we feel they absorb the flavors of the fruits better." This is a perfect salad to take to that covered-dish dinner. It makes a lot; so there is enough for second helpings."

BROCCOLI SALAD

1 cup mayonnaise
1/2 cup sugar
2 tablespoons vinegar
2 small bunches broccoli
3/4 cup white raisins
1/3 red onion, sliced
6 to 8 slices bacon, fried crisp and drained;
    crumbled

Mix mayonnaise, sugar and vinegar together in a small bowl; chill and let sit for a day. Combine broccoli, raisins, onion and bacon; add dressing.

Jan says, "When you mix the dressing a day ahead you can mix up the salad and set it aside in your refrigerator. At the last minute before serving, blend the dressing into the broccoli. This is a wonderful tasting salad which has a mystery flavor to it. It may be the raisins." Serves 8.

HONEY OF AN AMBROSIA

1/4 cup honey (or sugar)
2 pints plain yogurt
2 teaspoons vanilla
8 cups assorted fruits (melons, berries,
    grapes, kiwi)
1/4 cup orange liqueur
1/4 cup shredded coconut
1/2 cup walnut halves
1/2 cup white raisins
1/4 cup thinly sliced lemon and lime zest

Stir honey and vanilla into yogurt; cover and refrigerate. Toss fruit with liqueur; cover and refrigerate, basting occasionally for at least 2 hours. Drain fruit and reserve liquid. Stir liquid into yogurt and spoon into a chilled dish. Top with fruit and garnish with remaining ingredients. Serves 8.

ISLAND SHRIMP SALAD

2 pounds cooked large shrimp, shelled and
  deveined
2 papayas, peeled, seeded and sliced
2 mangoes, peeled, seeded and sliced
  (optional)
1/2 fresh pineapple, cut into spears
2 avocados, peeled, seeded and sliced
1 or 2 kiwi fruit, sliced
Butter lettuce

DRESSING:
1/2 cup heavy cream
2 tablespoons grated sweetened coconut
2 tablespoons lime juice
1 tablespoon grated lime or lemon rind
2 teaspoons honey
1 teaspoon grated fresh ginger
1/4 cup mayonnaise
Toasted coconut, chopped macadamia nuts,
  grapes and mint (garnish)

Arrange shrimp and fruit attractively on lettuce on a large platter or individual salad plates.

Combine all dressing ingredients except mayonnaise in blender and whirl until fluffy. Fold mixture into mayonnaise. Place a dollop of dressing on each salad and accompany with toasted coconut, macadamia nuts, grapes and mint. Serves 4-6.

Jo and Jan say, "Slices of cooked chicken breast may be substituted for the shrimp."

CRANBERRY - ORANGE COMPOTE

2 packages (12-ounce size) fresh cranberries
1 seedless orange, peeled and quartered
1 lemon, peeled, seeded and quartered
1 cup sugar or to taste
2/3 cup pecans, chopped
1/4 cup brandy
Thin slivers of orange peel (garnish)

Chop 1/2 of cranberries and 2 quarters of orange and 2 quarters of lemon in a blender or food processor. Remove to a bowl and repeat process with remaining berries and fruit. Stir sugar, nuts and brandy into berry mixture. Taste and adjust sugar. Refrigerate overnight. To serve, garnish with slivers of orange peel, if desired. Makes 3 1/2 cups.

ASPARAGUS SALAD

Fresh, frozen or canned asparagus
Hard-boiled eggs sliced
Strips of pimento for garnish
1 can (8-ounce) seasoned tomato sauce
2 tablespoons tarragon vinegar
1 teaspoon onion juice
1 teaspoon Worcestershire sauce
1/2 teaspoon salt
1/2 teaspoon dill seed
1/4 teaspoon basil

Prepare asparagus if frozen or fresh. Use proportions as to your liking; the same with the eggs. Combine dressing ingredients and mix well. Place asparagus spears on lettuce leaf, top with egg slices and strips of pimento. Drizzle dressing over top of salad. Serves 4.

Super Bowls

❖◆❖

CURRIED ASPARAGUS - MUSHROOM SALAD

2/3 cup mayonnaise
3 tablespoons sour cream
1 1/2 teaspoons curry powder
1 teaspoon grated onion
1/2 teaspoon sugar
3/4 teaspoon lemon juice
1/4 pound mushrooms, stems removed, caps
    sliced
2 cups chilled, cooked asparagus (1-1 1/2
    pounds) cut in 1 1/2-inch pieces
Salt and pepper

Combine first 6 ingredients and mix well. Add mushrooms and asparagus, salt and pepper to taste. Toss gently until well-coated. Serves 4.

Jo says, "This salad is wonderful with lamb. Asparagus and lamb, both gifts of Spring, give a blend of flavors that are truly a part of Mother nature's inspiration."

TABOULI

2 cups bulgur wheat
8 cups boiling water
1/2 bunch fresh parsley, finely chopped
1/2 cup fresh mint, finely chopped
1 bunch green onions with 2 inches of tops,
    finely chopped
4 medium tomatoes, finely chopped
2 cucumbers, finely chopped
1/2 cup lemon juice
1/2 cup olive oil
2 teaspoons salt
Freshly ground pepper

Put the wheat into a large container and pour the boiling water over it. Cover and let stand for 2 to 3 hours, or until the wheat is light and fluffy. Drain off excess water and shake the wheat in a strainer until it is very dry. Add the rest of the ingredients to the wheat and stir until thoroughly mixed. Chill for several hours before serving. Serves 8.

PEPPER STEAK SALAD

1 pound rare roast beef, cut into thin strips
2 medium tomatoes, cut into wedges
1 large green pepper, cut into strips
1 medium red onion, cut into thin slices
1 cup celery, sliced
1/2 cup fresh mushrooms, sliced
1/2 cup teriyaki sauce
1/3 cup olive oil
3 tablespoons wine vinegar
1/4 teaspoon ground pepper
1 cup fresh bean sprouts
4 cups Chinese cabbage, shredded

In a shallow dish, combine beef, tomatoes, green pepper, onion, celery and mushrooms. Set aside. In a jar combine teriyaki sauce, oil, vinegar and ginger. Shake well and pour over beef mixture and stir to mix well. Cover and marinate for 2 hours in the refrigerator, stirring occasionally. Just before serving lightly toss in the bean sprouts and cabbage. Serves 4-6.

SAUSAGE AND POTATO SALAD

1 1/2 pounds kielbasa sausage
2 pounds new potatoes
2 cans green beans, drained, reserving liquid

DRESSING:
1 cup sour cream
1 tablespoon wine vinegar
1 tablespoon horseradish
1/3 cup chopped red onion
1 tablespoon dill seed (optional)
Salt and pepper
Watercress
4 to 6 hard-cooked eggs
Sliced green pepper rings

Place sausages in skillet with just enough water to cover bottom of pan. Prick casings. Cook covered over medium heat about 10 minutes, turning frequently, until well-browned on all sides. Uncover and continue cooking until done; pricking casings occasionally to prevent bursting. Drain well, cool and cut into l-inch diagonal slices.

Cook potatoes in liquid from green beans, salted lightly, about 20 minutes. Slice into rounds. (We do not peel our potatoes).

Dressing: Combine sour cream, vinegar, horseradish, onion, dill, salt and pepper to taste in a large bowl. Add warm potatoes and toss lightly to coat.

Mound potatoes and sausage on watercress; garnish with egg wedges and pepper rings. Serve immediately. Serves 4-6.

Note: Potatoes may be cooked, dressed and chilled ahead and served cold with warm sausages.

CHILLED TURKEY SALAD

3 cups cold roast turkey, cut into bite-size
    pieces
3 green onions, chopped
1/2 green pepper, chopped
1/2 pound mushrooms, sliced
1/4 cup sliced stuffed green olives
3 tablespoons red wine vinegar
6 tablespoons olive oil
1 clove garlic, mashed
1/4 teaspoon dry mustard
Salt and pepper

Combine turkey, onions, green pepper, mushrooms and olives in large bowl.

Combine remaining ingredients in small bowl and whisk until slightly thickened. Pour dressing over salad mixture and toss to coat lightly. Mound salad on individual lettuce cups to serve. This is also excellent using roast duck. Serves 4.

EVELYN AND ALMA'S KIDNEY BEAN SALAD

1 can red kidney beans
2 cups chopped celery
1 tablespoon minced onion
1/2 cup chopped black walnuts
4 small pickles, chopped
1/4 cup salad oil
3 tablespoons wine vinegar
1/2 teaspoon salt
1/2 teaspoon pepper

Drain beans thoroughly, combine with celery, onion, nuts and pickles. Mix oil, vinegar, salt and pepper; pour over bean, celery mixture; toss. Serves 8.

Jo says, "Evelyn and Alma used a combination of wine and wine vinegar to give it a better flavor, and also say they use more pickles."

Super Bowls

NEW POTATO SALAD

3/4 pound whole tiny new potatoes
3/4 cup water
1 pound fresh green beans or 2 (10-ounce size) packages frozen
1/4 cup mayonnaise
1/4 cup sour cream
1/4 cup buttermilk
1/4 teaspoon salt
1/4 teaspoon pepper
1/4 teaspoon onion salt
1/4 teaspoon Italian seasoning
1/4 cup ripe olives, sliced
Tomato wedges

Wash and quarter the potatoes and cook in water until tender; drain. Remove ends and strings from green beans if you are using fresh and cook in 3/4 cup water, covered. Drain and set aside. In a large bowl, combine mayonnaise, sour cream, buttermilk, salt, pepper, onion salt and Italian seasoning. Stir in potatoes, beans and sliced olives. Cover and chill 4 hours. Garnish with tomato wedges. Serves 4.

SUMMERTIME PEACH SALAD

2 quarts fresh ripe peaches, peeled and sliced into 1/2-inch segments
8 to 10 kiwi fruit, peeled and sliced into rounds
Juice of 7 oranges
Juice of 2 lemons
3 tablespoons sugar, or to taste
4 to 6 fresh mint leaves

Place sliced fruit in a large bowl. Add sugar and the juices. Stir gently, just to blend. Place mint leaves on top, cover and refrigerate several hours. Serves 14-16.

Jo and Jan say, "Doesn't just reading this recipe bring summer into your home? Even on a cold, winter day we can begin to dream of summer entertaining."

NORMA'S FROZEN SALAD

1 can cherry pie filling
1 large can crushed pineapple, undrained
1 can sweetened condensed milk
2 cups small marshmallows
2-3 bananas, sliced
1 cup nuts, chopped
1 large container whipped topping

Mix all together and put into 2 9 x 13-inch baking dishes. Freeze until serving time. Makes 24 large squares.

CHILLED ITALIAN TOMATOES

4 medium tomatoes, sliced
4 green onions, sliced
3 tablespoons olive oil
1 tablespoon Vegetable Seasoning Blend (See index)
2/3 tablespoons lemon juice

Sprinkle green onions over tomato slices. Combine rest of ingredients and pour mixture over tomato slices. Cover and chill for 2 hours, stirring mixture over tomatoes after 1 hour. Serves 6-8.

RATATOUILLE SALAD

2 cups green pepper, cut in 1/2-inch squares
2 cups zucchini, cut in 1/2-inch cubes
2 cups eggplant, peeled and cut in 1/2-inch cubes
2 large tomatoes, cut in 1/2-inch cubes

DRESSING:
1/3 cup olive oil
3 tablespoons red wine vinegar
1 1/2 teaspoons basil leaves, crushed
1 1/2 teaspoon salt
1 teaspoon onion powder
1/2 teaspoon garlic powder
1/8 teaspoon black pepper

In large skillet, bring 1 inch of water to a boil. Add green pepper, zucchini and eggplant. Simmer, covered until just tender. Drain and toss with dressing. Refrigerate, covered overnight. Add tomatoes just before serving.

Combine ingredients well and set aside until ready to toss with vegetables. Serves 6-8.

COLD VEGETABLE SALAD

1 package (10-ounce) frozen broccoli
1 package (10-ounce) frozen French green beans
1 package (10-ounce) frozen asparagus
2 packages (10-ounce) frozen artichokes
1 green pepper, sliced fine
1 cucumber, sliced thin

DRESSING:
1/2 cup light cream
3 tablespoons lemon juice
2 tablespoons wine vinegar
1 clove garlic, minced
1/4 cup onion, chopped
1 cup mayonnaise
3 teaspoons anchovy paste
Salt and pepper to taste

Combine frozen vegetables in pan and cook half the time. Drain and add the green pepper, cucumber and chill.

Mix dressing ingredients together and add to the vegetables. Refrigerate overnight. Serves 6-8.

FOUR BEAN SALAD

1 can cut green beans, drained
1 can garbanzo beans, drained
1 can kidney beans, drained
1 can wax beans, drained
1 red onion, sliced into rings
1 green pepper, chopped
1 can water chestnuts, sliced
3/4 cup sugar
2/3 cup vinegar
1/3 cup oil

Combine beans, onion, green pepper and water chestnuts in large bowl. Mix sugar, vinegar and oil in saucepan. Bring to a boil and pour over bean mixture. Mix well; cover and chill overnight, or at least 12 hours. Serves 12.

Super Bowls

WILMA'S LEMON SALAD

1 package (3-ounce) lemon Jell-O
1 cup hot water
1 cup mayonnaise
1 cup celery, chopped
1/2 cup green pepper, chopped
1/2 cup cabbage, shredded
1 tablespoon onion, minced
1 cup cottage cheese
1/2 teaspoon salt

Mix Jell-O, water and mayonnaise in a bowl and beat together. Let this mixture set up and stir in the remaining 6 ingredients. Pour into an 8 x 8-inch pyrex dish and chill until firm. Serves 8-10.

RENE'S TOMATO - CHEESE SALAD

1 can (10 3/4-ounce) tomato soup
1 package (8-ounce) cream cheese
2 small packages lemon Jell-O
2 cups boiling water
1 cucumber, peeled and chopped
1 green pepper, chopped
1 1/2 cups celery, chopped
1 cup mayonnaise

Heat soup and set aside. Combine Jell-O, hot water and cream cheese. Stir until well-mixed. Cool.

In a small mixer bowl blend soup, Jell-O mixture, cucumber, green pepper, celery and mayonnaise. Pour mixture into a glass 8 x 8-inch dish. Serves 8.

PAT'S RASPBERRY FLUFF SALAD

1 package (3-ounce) raspberry Jell-O
1 can (8-ounce) crushed pineapple,
   undrained
1/2 cup sugar
1 carton (12-ounce) small curd cottage
   cheese
1/2 cup nuts, chopped
1 carton (8-ounce) Cool Whip
1 package frozen raspberries, thawed and
   drained

Combine package of Jell-O, pineapple and sugar in a small saucepan. Bring to a boil; remove from heat and cool. Transfer to a bowl, add cottage cheese and mix completely. Fold in nuts, Cool Whip and drained raspberries. Cover and refrigerate.

NANCY'S PRETZEL SALAD

2 cups crushed pretzels
1/4 cup sugar
1 1/2 sticks margarine, melted
1 package (8-ounce) cream cheese
1 cup sugar
1 1/2 cups Cool Whip
1 package (6-ounce) strawberry Jell-O
2 cups pineapple juice, heated
2 boxes (l0-ounce size) frozen strawberries,
   do not thaw

Mix crushed pretzels, sugar, margarine and press into a 9 x 13-inch or larger pan. Bake for 10 minutes at 350 degrees; cool. Mix cream cheese, 1 cup sugar and Cool Whip. Spread over cooled crumb mixture. Be sure cream cheese is sealing crust on all sides.

Dissolve Jell-O in hot pineapple juice. Add strawberries and stir until partially set. Spread over cheese mixture and chill.

Jo says, "This is really yummy' I served it over the Holidays and it is so pretty and festive. It's called a salad, but is really rich and could well be a dessert." Serves 12 big slices.

MOLDED CRANBERRY SALAD

2 cups cranberries
1 cup water
1 cup sugar
15 large marshmallows
1 package (3-ounce) raspberry Jell-O
1 cup hot water
1 cup celery, finely chopped
1 cup nuts, finely chopped
1 cup raw apple, finely chopped

Boil cranberries, sugar and water for 10 minutes. Stir often to mash berries. Remove from heat and add marshmallows, stir to melt. Dissolve Jell-O in 1 cup hot water and add to cranberry mixture. When cool, add celery, nuts and apples. Pour in 9 x 13-inch pan. Refrigerate until it sets. Serves 12.

CHRISTMAS TREE SALAD

1 envelope unflavored gelatin
1 cup cabbage, finely shredded
1/2 cup chopped walnuts
1/4 cup cold water
1 pound can jellied cranberry sauce, crushed
  with fork
1/4 cup celery, diced

Pour gelatin in a pyrex cup, add cold water. Let stand 2 minutes, then place cup in a pan of boiling water and heat until gelatin is dissolved. Add to crushed cranberry sauce. Fold in cabbage, celery and nuts. When mixture begins to thicken, pour into cone shaped paper cups. Support filled cups in small glasses and chill until firm. Place on lettuce and peel off paper cups. Trim with bands of softened cream cheese. Serves 6-8.

DOROTHY'S APPLESAUCE SALAD

2 packages (3-ounce size) red raspberry or
  cherry-flavored gelatin
2 cups hot water
2 cups applesauce
1 package (8-ounce) cream cheese, softened
1 cup chopped celery
1/2 cup walnuts or pecans
2 large tablespoons Miracle Whip

Dissolve gelatin in water, add applesauce. Pour into a 9 x 13-inch dish and refrigerate until set. Combine remaining ingredients and spread on top of set mixture. To serve, cut into desired-size pieces and set on a bed of lettuce. Serves 12-16.

CHILLED TOMATO SALAD

3 cups canned tomatoes
3 tablespoons sugar
2 teaspoons onion juice
1 teaspoon salt
Dash of pepper
2 tablespoons unflavored gelatin
1/3 cup cold water
1 medium cucumber, chopped
1/2 cup green pepper, chopped
1/2 cup celery, chopped
1 tablespoon grated horseradish
1/2 cup heavy cream, whipped
1 cup mayonnaise

Cook tomatoes with sugar, onion juice, salt and pepper for 10 minutes. Soak gelatin in cold water and dissolve in hot tomato mixture. Cool; add chopped cucumber, green pepper, celery and horseradish. Blend whipped cream and mayonnaise; add to gelatin and vegetable mixture and mix well. Pour into oiled mold or individual molds. Serves 12.

Super Bowls

❖✧❖

LYNN'S APRICOT JELL-O

1 package (6-ounce) apricot Jell-O
1 1/2 cups boiling water
1 package (8-ounce) cream cheese
1 small carton (9-ounce) non-dairy whipped topping
1 can (11-ounce) mandarin oranges
1 can (15 1/2-ounce) crushed pineapple with juice
3 large bananas, sliced

Place Jell-O and cheese in a large bowl; pour water over and beat with rotary beater. Add whipped topping and beat until very smooth. Add fruit and refrigerate until set. Serves 6.

CUCUMBER RING MOLD

1 tablespoon unflavored gelatin
1/4 cup cold water
1 cut garlic clove
3 packages (3-ounce size) cream cheese
2 cups drained, grated, pared cucumber
1 cup mayonnaise
1/4 cup minced fresh parsley
1/4 cup minced onion
1/2 teaspoon salt

Soften gelatin in cold water. Dissolve over hot water. Rub mixing bowl with garlic. Stir cheese to soften; add cucumber, mayonnaise, parsley, onion and salt; mix well. Stir gelatin into cheese mixture and pour into an oiled 5-cup ring mold. Chill until firm. Serves 8.

TIP

• Hollow out fruits, tomatoes or different colored peppers to hold individual salads or dressings.

SALAD SEASONING BLEND

2 teaspoons thyme leaves
2 teaspoons ground savory
1 teaspoon rubbed sage
2 teaspoons basil leaves
1 tablespoon marjoram leaves

Blend all ingredients in a blender. Store in airtight container in a cool, dry place. Use 1 to 2 teaspoons of Seasoning, or as taste desired, with salads.

ITALIAN DRY SEASONING MIX

1 tablespoon dried oregano
1 tablespoon dried marjoram
1 tablespoon dried basil
2 teaspoons dried savory
1 teaspoon dried rosemary
1 teaspoon dried sage

Combine herbs and store in an airtight container. Makes 1/4 cup.

GARLIC - FLAVORED OLIVE OIL

1 cup olive oil or salad oil (or 1/2 cup of each)
6 garlic cloves

Peel garlic cloves and slice lengthwise into quarters. Let stand in olive oil for several days.

VINAIGRETTE

2 tablespoons white wine vinegar
1 teaspoon Dijon mustard
1/2 teaspoon salt
1/4 teaspoon white pepper
1/4 teaspoon lemon pepper
1/2 cup olive oil
1/2 cup parsley, finely chopped

In small bowl combine vinegar, mustard, salt and peppers; add oil very slowly in a thin stream, whisking constantly with a wire whisk. After ingredients are well blended, stir in parsley. Cover and refrigerate. Makes 3/4 cup.

CREAMY RASPBERRY VINAIGRETTE

1 package (10-ounce) frozen raspberries in syrup, drained completely
6 tablespoons olive oil
1/4 cup heavy cream
2 tablespoons sherry vinegar
Salt
Freshly ground pepper

Puree raspberries in blender or processor. Strain into small bowl, discarding seeds. Combine remaining ingredients in blender and mix well. Add to raspberry puree. Taste and adjust flavoring as desired. Makes about 1 1/2 cups.

Jo and Jan say, "This is a perfect dressing for vegetable salads. Try it on fresh asparagus spears or heart of palm."

HERBED SALAD DRESSING

1/3 cup white wine vinegar
1/4 cup vegetable oil
1/4 cup olive oil
2 tablespoons water
1 tablespoon Vegetable Seasoning Blend (See index)

Combine all ingredients and shake vigorously. Makes 3/4 cup.

MUSHROOM SALAD DRESSING

1 tablespoon red wine vinegar
1 teaspoon Dijon-style mustard
1 egg yolk
7 tablespoons vegetable oil
1 clove garlic, crushed
1 teaspoon chopped fresh parsley
Salt and freshly ground pepper

Combine vinegar, mustard, and egg yolk in medium bowl. Beat with fork until blended. Gradually whisk in oil until thoroughly incorporated. Stir in garlic, parsley, and salt and pepper to taste. Toss with salad before serving. Makes 2/3 cup.

Jo and Jan say, "This is the perfect dressing for mushroom salads. Just leaf lettuce and sliced mushrooms; although we sometimes add a sprinkling of nuts."

BANANA DRESSING FOR FRUIT SALAD

2 ripe bananas
1 tablespoons fresh lemon juice
1/4 cup brown sugar
1/4 cup honey
1 cup heavy cream, whipped
1/2 cup chopped nuts (optional)

Combine bananas, lemon juice, sugar and honey in blender or processor until smooth. Gently fold into whipped cream; add nuts if desired. Serve with assorted fresh fruits.

Jo and Jan say, "We like to serve our fruits in a pineapple boat or in a lettuce cup on a clear plate. It seems to give an especially 'natural' look."

LEMON DRESSING

1/4 cup sugar
3 scant tablespoons lemon juice
1 egg yolk
6 tablespoons vegetable oil

In a medium mixing bowl combine sugar and lemon juice; whisk until sugar is almost dissolved. Add yolk and whisk until sugar is completely dissolved. Add oil, 1 tablespoon at a time, whisking constantly until dressing is thick and creamy. Cover and refrigerate.

To serve, rewhisk if necessary. Pour over salad and toss gently. This is delicious on spinach and fruit salad. Try oranges and strawberries with the spinach, and a few sunflower seeds sprinkled over the top. Makes about 3/4 cup.

LIME MINT DRESSING

1 1/4 cups lowfat yogurt
1/4 cup low calorie mayonnaise
2 tablespoons lime juice
Grated rind of 1 lime
1 tablespoon honey
3 tablespoons finely minced fresh mint.

Combine all ingredients and serve as a dressing for a chicken and fruit salad. It's wonderful!

ORIENTAL DRESSING

3/4 cup soy sauce
3 tablespoons fresh lemon juice
1 teaspoon sugar
1 teaspoon toasted sesame seeds
1 teaspoon chopped onion
1 1/4 cups peanut oil

Combine all ingredients except oil in blender. Blend on low speed until onion is minced. With blender running, add oil in thin stream and blend until oil is completely incorporated. Makes about 1 pint.

SOY - GINGER DRESSING

1/3 cup light soy sauce
1/4 cup cider vinegar
3 tablespoons sesame oil
1/2 teaspoon minced fresh ginger-root
2 green onions, minced
1 teaspoon sugar
Freshly ground white pepper

Combine all ingredients and whisk until completely mixed. A delicious dressing for Oriental salads. Also, try it on beef, asparagus and broccoli salad.

CRANBERRY SALAD DRESSING

2/3 cup sugar
1 teaspoon salt
1 teaspoon dry mustard
1/2 cup vinegar
1 teaspoon onion juice
1 cup oil
1 orange, peeled, cut and seeded
1 cup cranberries
1/2 cup sugar

Combine 2/3 cup sugar, salt, mustard and vinegar. Stir well and combine onion juice and oil. Beat until well-blended; set aside. Grind orange with cranberries. Stir 1/2 cup sugar into orange-cranberry mixture and blend with oil mixture. Makes 1 1/4 pints.

Jan says, "This recipe was given to me by my friend Ruthie. It keeps well in the refrigerator for 4 weeks or so. But, it won't be there that long because it is so delicious, especially on the grapefruit and orange slices; you will find it disappears quickly."

❖❖

DILL MUSTARD DRESSING

2 tablespoons Dijon mustard
1/2 cup tarragon vinegar
1/2 teaspoon coarse black pepper
Dash of salt
Pinch of sugar
1 cup olive oil
2 tablespoons chopped fresh dill

In a small bowl, whisk together the mustard, vinegar, sugar, salt and pepper. While whisking, slowly drizzle in olive oil until dressing thickens. Stir in fresh dill. Makes 2 cups

RUTHIE'S BLUE CHEESE DRESSING

7 tablespoons salad oil
2 tablespoons vinegar
1 teaspoon salt
1/4 teaspoon coarse black pepper
4 tablespoons blue cheese
4 tablespoons sour cream or cream

Combine oil, vinegar, salt and pepper in blender and blend until smooth. Add blue cheese and cream and blend until mixture is smooth.

Jan says, "If you have the chance to get the fresh Blue cheese from Wisconsin use it in this dressing and when you taste it, you'll think you have died and gone to Heaven."

CAROLYN'S MEXICAN SALAD DRESSING

1 cup vinegar
3 teaspoons salt
3 teaspoons sugar
1 teaspoon oregano
2 teaspoons black pepper
1 tablespoon basil
2 garlic cloves, slivered
3/4 cup salad oil

Combine all ingredients, except oil in a glass container and refrigerate for at least 24 hours before adding to the oil. Shake mixture well and pour over salad of greens, tomatoes and avocados.

MILLIE'S SPINACH DRESSING

1 cup Wesson oil
1/4 cup cider vinegar
3/4 cup sugar
1/3 cup tomato catsup
2 tablespoons Worcestershire sauce
1/2 cup onion, chopped

Combine all ingredients in sauce pan. Simmer 10 to 15 minutes. Cool and refrigerate. Makes 2 cups.

EPICUREAN DRESSING

1 can tomato soup
3/4 cup cider vinegar
3/4 cup sugar
2 tablespoons grated onion
2 teaspoons salt
1 teaspoon dry mustard
2 tablespoons Worcestershire sauce
1 1/4 cups salad oil

Combine all ingredients; you might want to mix a bit of the liquid with the dry mustard to dissolve it before adding to mixture. Beat and refrigerate unused portion. Makes 1 quart.

Jo and Jan say, "Ruthie told us this was a W. W. II recipe. It was served on Spam, veggies, etc. The first time we made it we used it for a dressing on Taco Salad in a tortilla shell—it was absolutely delicious!"

Super Bowls

HONEY YOGURT DRESSING

1 cup yogurt
1 tablespoon honey
1 teaspoon grated lemon or lime peel
1 to 2 teaspoons fresh lemon or lime juice
1 tablespoon toasted sesame seeds

Gently blend all ingredients. Chill and serve with fresh fruit, sprinkling with additional toasted sesame seeds, if desired. Makes 1 1/4 cups.

Jo says, "This is perfect with fresh fruit salads. Sometimes I will leave out the sesame seeds, add 1/2 of a mashed banana and some chopped nuts. It is wonderful on assorted fruits, perhaps served in a pineapple boat."

BEV'S POPPY SEED DRESSING

1 1/2 cups sugar
2 teaspoons dry mustard
2 teaspoons salt
2/3 cup vinegar
3 tablespoons fresh onion
2 cups Wesson oil
3 tablespoons poppy seeds

In blender or food processor mix sugar, mustard, salt and vinegar. Add onion and mix thoroughly. Add oil very slowly until mixture is thick. Add poppy seeds and pour into I-quart jar. Store in refrigerator. A wonderful dressing for fruit salads of all kinds. Makes 1 quart.

WATERCRESS DRESSING

1 large bunch watercress, stems included; but omit stems if you want a less peppery flavor
1 egg yolk
1 teaspoon Dijon mustard
1 garlic clove, minced
Juice of 1 small lemon
Pinch of salt
3/4 cup plus 1 tablespoon olive oil
1/2 cup heavy cream
1 tablespoon Cognac
Salt
Dash of cayenne pepper
Cracked black pepper

Puree watercress in blender or food processor; set aside. Combine egg yolk, mustard, garlic, half of lemon juice and salt in a medium bowl and blend well. Set aside for 5 minutes; add oil, 1 tablespoon at a time, mixing constantly after each addition until well blended. Add remaining lemon juice to taste and blend well. Mixture should be thin.

Beat cream in a small bowl until thick. Add Cognac and whisk this into the watercress puree. Add salt and cayenne pepper to taste. Refrigerate until ready to serve. Grind black pepper just before serving. Makes about 2 1/2 cups.

HUMMUS DRESSING

1/2 recipe Hummus Dip (See index)
1 cup yogurt (or sour cream and yogurt combined)
3 tablespoons olive oil
Juice of 1/2 lemon or to taste
Salt and freshly ground pepper

Prepare recipe for Hummus Dip as directed only to point where ingredients are pureed. Divide mixture and add Dressing ingredients to 1/2. Combine and blend well; chill thoroughly. Makes 2 1/2 cups.

Jo and Jan say, "This is excellent with green salads made with meats, avocados, tomatoes, onion, cheeses and black olives."

❖❖❖

MOM'S FRESH ORANGE FRUIT SALAD DRESSING

1/2 cup fresh orange juice
1 tablespoon fresh lemon juice
Dash of salt
2 eggs, separated
6 tablespoons sugar
1/4 cup heavy cream, whipped
Grated orange rind for garnish

Heat orange juice over low heat. Beat lemon juice, salt and egg yolks together in top of double boiler. Gradually beat in 4 tablespoons of sugar, slowly stir in hot orange juice. Cook over hot water until thickened, stirring constantly. Beat egg whites until they form soft peaks. Gradually beat in remaining 2 tablespoons of sugar. Fold into the cooked mixture. Chill. Fold in whipped cream just before serving. Garnish with grated orange rind. Makes 2 1/2 cups.

CITRUS SAUCE

1/2 teaspoon grated lemon, orange or lime
   peel
1 1/2 tablespoons lemon or lime juice or 3
   tablespoons orange juice
1/4 to 1/2 cup sugar
1 tablespoon cornstarch
1 cup water
Dash of salt
3 tablespoons butter

Grate rind of desired fruit, then extract juice. In top of double boiler combine sugar, cornstarch and water. Cook, whisking constantly until mixture thickens and is bubbly. Remove from heat and stir in grated rind and juice. Stir in salt and butter. Makes about 1 cup.

Jan and Jo say, "This sauce can be served warm or chilled. However, do refrigerate it in a covered container if not serving right away."

AVOCADO CREAM

2 small avocados
1/2 cup sour cream
1 tablespoon tarragon vinegar
1 teaspoon salt
1/2 teaspoon hot pepper sauce
1 cup milk

Remove peel from avocados and cut into chunks. Place avocado chunks in blender or food processor. Add sour cream cream, vinegar, salt, hot sauce and milk. Blend until smooth. Chill until serving time. Serve with Cold Poached Salmon (See index) or seafood salads.

GREEN MAYONNAISE

1 1/2 cups mayonnaise
1 cup torn raw spinach
1/4 cup parsley sprigs, omiting stems
1/4 cup watercress, omiting stems
1 tablespoon chives
2 tablespoons dry white wine

Prepare the day before serving. Place half of all ingredients in electric blender. Cover and blend at high speed until smooth. Add remaining ingredients and blend well. Refrigerate, covered, overnight. Excellent with cold poached salmon. Makes 1 1/3 cups.

Super Bowls

MANGO CURRY MAYONNAISE

1 jar (8 1/2-ounce) mango chutney
1 1/2 cups mayonnaise
1 1/2 tablespoons curry powder, or to taste

Chop chutney and place in small bowl. Add mayonnaise and curry, adding a small amount of curry at a time, to your taste; blend well. Cover and chill. This is a delicious mayonnaise to serve with chicken or duck salad.

JAN'S SALSA MAIONESE

1 large egg
3 teaspoons Dijon mustard
4 tablespoons lemon juice, fresh preferred
1 teaspoon salt
1 cup Bertolli olive oil

Measure out all the ingredients in blender except the olive oil. Add 1/3 cup oil, cover and blend at high speed for about 5 seconds. Add the remaining oil in a slow steady stream. Blend until thick and smooth. Makes 1 cup plus.

Jan says, "This is a wonderful dressing for a lettuce wedge or for sandwiches."

MOM'S HOMEMADE MAYONNAISE

1 teaspoon salt
1/2 teaspoon dry mustard
1/4 teaspoon paprika
Dash cayenne
2 egg yolks
2 tablespoons vinegar
2 cups salad oil
2 tablespoons lemon juice

In small mixer bowl combine dry ingredients; blend in egg yolks. Add vinegar and mix well. Add salad oil, 1 teaspoon at a time, beating at medium speed with electric mixer, till 1/4 cup oil has been added. Add remaining oil in increasing amounts, alternating last 1/2 cup with the lemon juice. Store in tightly-covered container in refrigerator up to 4 weeks. Makes 2 1/3 cups.

FRESH MUSTARD

2 large eggs
1/2 cup water
1/4 cup dry white wine
1/4 cup salad oil
2 teaspoons mustard seed
2 tablespoons white vinegar
2 tablespoons flour
2 tablespoons dry mustard
1 1/2 teaspoons salt

Place mustard seeds in a small plastic bag and crush them, using a rolling pin. Beat eggs, water, wine, oil and vinegar in a small bowl until blended. In a heavy saucepan combine crushed seeds and dry ingredients. Slowly add liquid to this and blend until smooth. Cook over low heat, stirring constantly, until mixture thickens and becomes the consistency of mayonnaise. Be very careful to keep your heat low. Pour into containers and cool at room temperature before storing in refrigerator. Makes 1 1/2 cups.

❖❖❖

Raising The Dough • Breads

Our illustration for this chapter might bring back many happy memories of Mother, Grandmother, or perhaps a favorite Auntie who taught you the fine art of bread making.

We offer delicious quick recipes which include Mom's Buttermilk Biscuits, Mexican Corn Bread, SuEllen's Dilly Cheese Bread and an assortment of muffins. Yeast breads which are a "must try" are Kathy's Cream Cheese Braid, Mary's Rolls and Rosalee's Cinnamon Rolls.

❖❖❖

❖❖

Bread

Be gentle
  When you touch bread
Let it not lie
  Uncared for-unwanted
So often bread
  Is taken for granted,
There is so much beauty
  in bread-
Beauty of sun and soil,
  Beauty of patient toil.
Winds and rains have caressed it,
  Christ often blessed it.
Be gentle
  When you touch bread.
        – Author Unknown

MOM'S BUTTERMILK BISCUITS

2 cups flour
1/2 teaspoon salt
4 teaspoons baking powder
1/2 teaspoon soda
5 tablespoons shortening
1 cup buttermilk

Combine dry ingredients. Blend in shortening using a pastry blender. Slowly add buttermilk, stirring in with a fork. Turn out onto a floured surface and knead several times with floured hands. Roll out 1/2-inch thick and cut with a floured biscuit cutter. Place on baking sheet and bake in preheated 450-degree oven for 12 to 15 minutes. Makes 16 biscuits.

SWEET CREAM BISCUITS

2 cups flour
2 tablespoons sugar
4 teaspoons baking powder
1/2 teaspoon cream of tartar
1/2 cup butter, cut into pieces
2/3 cup heavy cream

Sift dry ingredients; cut in butter until mixture resembles coarse meal. Add cream and stir just until incorporated. Turn out on a lightly floured board; knead about 15 seconds. Pat dough out 1/2-inch thick using heel of hand. Cut with 1 1/2-inch cutter. Arrange on 2 baking sheets, spacing 1 inch apart. Prick surface of biscuits with tines of a fork and bake in a preheated 425-degree oven for about 15 minutes or until tops are golden. Transfer to cooling racks. Serve hot or at room temperature. Makes 2 dozen.

Jo and Jan say, "These are nice party biscuits; wonderful with smoked turkey or shaved ham. Preslice them but do not butter or spead with a dressing ahead of time; they will get crumbly."

CHEESE BISCUITS

4 cups flour
6 teaspoons baking powder
2 teaspoons salt
1/4 cup shortening
1 1/2 cups grated Cheddar cheese
1 cup milk (approx.)

Sift flour, baking powder and salt. Cut in shortening; stir in cheese and add just enough milk to hold ingredients together to make a soft dough. Roll out on a lightly floured board to 1/2-inch thick. Cut into rounds with a small biscuit cutter and arrange on a well greased baking sheet. Bake in preheated 450-degree oven for 12 to 15 minutes. Makes 15 - 20.

HERBED BISCUITS

1/4 cup onion, finely chopped
1 teaspoon Italian Dry Seasoning Mix (See index) or use commercial brand
2 tablespoons butter or margarine
1 1/2 cups flour
2 teaspoons baking powder
1/2 teaspoon salt
1/4 cup shortening
1 egg, beaten
1/3 cup milk
2 tablespoons grated Parmesan cheese

Melt 1 tablespoon butter in small skillet; cook onion and dry seasoning until onion is tender. In a bowl stir the flour, baking powder and salt together. Cut in the shortening until the mixture resembles coarse crumbs. Combine onion mixture, egg and milk; add to flour mixture all at once. Stir until dough clings together; transfer to a lightly floured surface and knead 10 to 12 strokes. Roll or pat out dough to 1/2-inch thickness. Cut with a floured 2 1/2-inch biscuit cutter. Place close together in a greased 8-inch round baking pan. Melt remaining butter, brush over dough and sprinkle with cheese. Bake in preheated 450-degree oven for 12 to 15 minutes. Serve while hot. Makes 6.

GOLDEN YOGURT COFFEE CAKE

1 tablespoon margarine, melted
1 tablespoon brown sugar, packed
1/4 teaspoon ground cinnamon
2 Golden Delicious apples, cored and sliced
2 cups flour
1 teaspoon baking powder
1 teaspoon soda
1/2 teaspoon salt
1/2 cup margarine
1/2 cup sugar
2 eggs
1 carton (8-ounce) plain yogurt

STREUSEL FILLING:
1/4 cup sugar
1 tablespoon margarine, melted
1 tablespoon flour
1 teaspoon cinnamon
1/4 cup walnuts or pecans, chopped

Combine margarine, brown sugar, cinnamon in a 9 x 9 x 2-inch square pan. Smooth mixture evenly over bottom. Arrange apple slices over mixture. Combine flour, baking powder, soda and salt. Cream butter and sugar. Add eggs, one at a time; beat well after each addition. Add dry ingredients alternately with yogurt. Spread half of batter over apple slices. Sprinkle streusel filling over batter in pan. Spread remaining batter over filling. Bake in preheated 350-degree oven for 30 to 35 minutes or until cake tests done when pick is inserted in center. Invert onto serving plate. Serves 8.

Jan says, "I usually double the streusel filling. If you'd like, try different flavors of yogurt."

JEANNE'S GERMAN SOUR CREAM TWISTS

1 package dry yeast
1/4 cup warm water
1 cup margarine melted
1 cup sour cream
2 eggs, beaten
1 teaspoon salt
1 teaspoon vanilla
4 cups flour
1 cup sugar
1/4 teaspoon cinnamon

Dissolve yeast in warm water. Mix margarine, sour cream, eggs; add yeast, salt and vanilla. Beat in flour until smooth. Cover and refrigerate for 2 hours or up to 2 days. Combine sugar and cinnamon; working with 1/2 of dough, sprinkle some of cinnamon - sugar on board. Roll dough into a rectangle. Turn so both sides are coated to prevent sticking. Roll into a large thin rectangle. Fold 3 times; roll into another rectangle 1/2-inch thick. Cut into 1 x 4-inch strips; twist and place on a greased baking sheet. Bake immediately in a preheated 350-degree oven for 15 minutes.

KATHY'S CREAM CHEESE BRAID

2 packages dry yeast
1/2 cup warm water
1 cup sour cream
1/2 cup sugar
1 teaspoon salt
1/2 cup melted butter
2 eggs, beaten
4 cups flour

FILLING:
2 packages (8-ounce size) cream cheese
3/4 cup sugar
1 egg
1/8 teaspoon salt
2 teaspoons vanilla

GLAZE:
2 cups confectioners' sugar
4 tablespoons milk
2 teaspoons vanilla

Mix yeast and warm water; set aside. Slowly heat sour cream; stir in sugar, salt and melted butter. Cool to lukewarm and mix with yeast. Add eggs and flour. Cover and refrigerate overnight. Prepare filling; combine all ingredients. Divide dough into 4 parts; roll each into 12 x 18-inch rectangles. Spread cream cheese mixture on dough and roll up like a jelly roll. Place seam down on a baking sheet. Slit each roll at 2-inch intervals about 2/3 of the way through to resemble a braid. Cover lightly and let rise until double. Bake in preheated 375-degree oven. Prepare glaze and spread on baked braid.

ROSALEE'S CINNAMON ROLLS

3 cups milk
1 stick margarine or 1/2 cup solid shortening
3/4 cup granulated sugar
1 tablespoon salt
3 packages dry yeast
3/4 cup lukewarm water
3 eggs, lightly beaten
12 cups flour
2 sticks margarine, melted
3 cups light brown sugar
Cinnamon
Nuts, chopped (optional)
1 can (13-ounce) evaporated milk

Combine milk, margarine, sugar and salt in saucepan and heat until lukewarm and margarine is melted; sugar and salt dissolved. In a large bowl dissolve yeast in lukewarm water. Pour milk mixture and eggs into yeast. Add 4 cups flour and beat vigorously until blended. Continue to add flour and mix thoroughly until dough feels soft and slightly sticky. (Too much flour makes dough heavy).Turn out on lightly floured board and knead until smooth and elastic. Place in greased bowl, cover and let rise in warm place about an hour or until double in size. Punch down and let rise again. Prepare pans by generously covering sides and bottom with melted margarine and sprinkle lightly with brown sugar. (We use either 8-inch round or 9 x 13-inch pans). Turn bread out onto unfloured board and knead lightly. Divide into 2 parts. Roll one half into a rectangle 1/4-inch thick. Spread with melted margarine and 1 1/2 cups brown sugar until all is covered. Sprinkle lightly with cinnamon. You may add chopped nuts if desired. Roll up like jelly roll and cut into 1-inch rolls. Place in pan with each just touching. Repeat procedure with other half of dough or make plain rolls. Cover and let rise for 1 hour or until double. Pour evaporated milk over each pan until corners and cracks are covered. Bake in preheated 375-degree oven for 30 minutes or until lightly browned. Turn out to cool or may leave in pan to cool. You may glaze the tops with a confectioners' sugar frosting if you like. These have a yummy caramel bottom. Makes 40-45 rolls. May be frozen.

◆◇◆

ORANGE CINNAMON ROLL ICING

2 cups confectioners' sugar
1/2 stick butter, softened
1/2 teaspoon vanilla extract
1/2 teaspoon almond extract (optional)
1/4 to 1/3 cup fresh orange juice (only
  enough to make spreadable)

Combine sugar, butter and extracts in small mixer bowl. Beating at low speed slowly add orange juice, using only enough to make spreadable. Frost cinnamon rolls while they are hot. Frosts 1 pan of rolls.

Jo and Jan say, "You must try this icing on your next batch of rolls! Stand back and wait for the raves."

HERBED DINNER ROLLS

1 package clover leaf rolls
1/4 cup olive oil
1/4 cup margarine, melted
2 cloves garlic, minced
1 teaspoon thyme
Salt and Pepper
1/4 cup chopped parsley

Pull rolls apart and bake, following package directions, until browned (about 15 minutes).Combine oil and butter, garlic, salt and pepper. Place baked rolls in a large bowl. Drizzle oil mixture over them; toss rolls and sprinkle with thyme and parsley; toss again.

Jo and Jan say, "The oil-butter mixture may be prepared ahead and kept in a glass jar. The garlic flavor will be more blended."

PEPPERED CHEDDAR CHEESE LOAF

1 1/2 cups lukewarm water
1 package dry yeast
1/4 teaspoon sugar
3 1/4 cups flour
1 cup grated sharp Cheddar cheese
2 teaspoons coarsely ground pepper
1 teaspoon salt
1/4 cup grated sharp Cheddar cheese
Coarsely ground pepper

Dissolve yeast in water. Add sugar to yeast mixture and set aside. Combine flour, 1 cup cheese, pepper and salt in large bowl. Add yeast mixture and stir well with a wooden spoon. Knead dough until smooth. Place in greased bowl, turning so top is greased too. Cover with tea towel and place in warm draft-free area. Let rise until double, about 1 1/2 to 2 hours. Punch down and knead into a ball. Put bread ball on greased baking sheet. Cut diagonally every 2 inches with 1/4-inch deep cross in center of dough. Let bread ball rise again to about double in size. Just before baking, sprinkle 1/4 cup cheese on top and sprinkle pepper over cheese. Bake 20 minutes in preheated 400-degree oven, reducing temperature to 350 degrees for 25 minutes. Cool on rack. Loaf should sound hollow inside.

JUNE'S HOT ROLLS

4 1/2 cups water
1 1/2 cups sugar
1 cup Crisco
4 eggs
1 package yeast
3 teaspoons salt
12 cups flour

At 1:00 p.m., boil 4 cups water and sugar for 5 minutes. Add Crisco and cool. At 2:00 p.m. dissolve yeast in 1/2 cup warm water. Beat eggs well and add salt. Pour in sugar-water mixture.

Add flour 1 cup at a time and mix well. Let rise until 6:00 p.m. Punch down and let the mixture rise until 9:00 p.m. Form rolls on greased cookie sheets and let rise over night on the counter. Next morning, bake in preheated 350-degree oven for 15 minutes or until golden brown. Makes 10 dozen. These rolls freeze very well.

June says, "You may vary your time according to your schedule. I have found this is convenient for me."

❖❖

DILLY ROLLS

1 package dry yeast, softened in 1/4 cup
   warm water
1 cup cottage cheese, heated to lukewarm
2 tablespoons sugar
1 tablespoon minced dry onion
1 tablespoon butter
2 teaspoons dill seed
1 big teaspoon salt
1/2 teaspoon soda
1 unbeaten egg
2 1/4 cups flour
Melted butter - salt

Add heated cottage cheese to softened yeast. Add egg, butter and dry ingredients except flour. Add flour, 1/4 cup at a time, beating well after each addition. Dough will be stiff. Cover and let rise in a warm place until light and double in size (50 to 60 minutes). Punch dough down and pinch off desired amount; form into desired shape. Place in greased pan. Let rise until light, 30 to 40 minutes; bake in preheated 350-degree oven until golden brown. Cover tops with foil the last few minutes if you feel the rolls are getting too brown on the tops. After removing from oven, brush tops with melted butter and sprinkle with salt.

Jo and Jan say, "You can make the rolls as cloverleaf; place three to each greased muffin cup, or you can make a pan of rolls, form shapes and place them in a round cake pan. Any shape is delicious!"

MARY'S ROLLS

6 eggs
1 cup sugar
2 teaspoons salt
2 packages dry yeast
2 teaspoons sugar
1/2 cup warm water
2 cups milk, scalded
1 cup margarine, melted
8 cups flour, heaping
1 to 1 1/2 sticks margarine, melted
Sugar and cinnamon as desired

Beat eggs, sugar and salt. Mix yeast, sugar, water and let it bubble up good. Add it to eggs, then add milk, margarine and half the flour. Beat well; add rest of flour and beat again. Turn out onto floured surface and let it rest 10 minutes.

Do not knead. Using spatula, pick dough up and put it into a 2-gallon greased bowl; cover with plastic and let stand until bowl is heaping full. Turn out onto floured surface. Cut into 5 equal parts. Do not knead. Roll each part into a circle 1/2-inch thick. Spread with melted margarine and sprinkle with sugar and cinnamon. Cut into 12 pie-shaped pieces with a pizza cutter or serrated knife. Roll up and place on greased sheet. Allow a couple of inches between each roll. Let rise until very light and fluffy. Bake in preheated 350-degree oven for 10 minutes. Frost with powdered sugar glaze.

Jan says, "These rolls are the lightest I have ever tasted. I make them plain more than I do with cinnamon and sugar." Makes 6 to 7 dozen rolls.

ORANGE PUMPKIN BREAD

2/3 cup shortening
2 2/3 cups sugar
4 eggs
1 can (16-ounce) pumpkin
2/3 cup water
3 1/3 cup flour
2 teaspoons baking soda
1 1/2 teaspoons salt
1 teaspoon cinnamon
1 teaspoon pumpkin pie spice
1/2 teaspoon baking powder
1 medium orange
2/3 cup walnuts, chopped

Cream shortening and sugar thoroughly. Add eggs, pumpkin and water. Sift dry ingredients together and add to pumpkin mixture. Remove seeds from orange and grind orange, including peel. Add to pumpkin mixture; stir in nuts. Pour into 2 greased 9 x 5 x 3-inch loaf pans. Bake in preheated 350-degree oven for 1 hour.

Raising the Dough

LOIS' ICE BOX SWEET DOUGH

2 packages yeast
1 cup sugar
8 cups water (tepid - make sure it isn't too
  warm)
1 cup milk (scald and skim top after cooled)
1 cup shortening (may use half margarine)
1 1/2 tablespoons salt
4 eggs
10 pounds flour (approx.)

Put first three ingredients in large crock or bowl and let set for a few minutes to make sure your yeast is going to work; add milk, eggs, shortening and some of the flour. Mix well; the recipe takes most of the 10 pounds. Don't ever put salt directly on top of yeast as it may prevent it from raising correctly. Add salt and more of the flour; knead in flour until dough isn't sticky. Kneading is the secret to good bread dough. If you are going to use dough today, place it in a bowl that has been greased and cover it with a damp cloth. Let rise until double and make into rolls, loaf bread, doughnuts, or cinnamon rolls.

Let rise until double again and bake in preheated 375-degree oven about 30 to 40 minutes

Lois says, "If you don't want to use the dough today just put it in a bowl that will seal. Grease well and cover with a damp cloth; place in refrigerator and keep dough poked down. When you are ready, make into rolls of your choice and let raise until double and bake. This dough will keep 7 days in refrigerator if you keep it poked down. After the first day I punch the dough down once a day."

EDNA'S OATMEAL BREAD

2 packages yeast
1/2 cup lukewarm water
1 1/2 cups boiling water
1 cup quick oats
1/4 cup molasses
1/4 cup sugar
1 stick margarine
1 tablespoon salt
2 eggs, beaten
5 to 6 cups flour

Soften yeast in 1/2 cup water. Pour boiling water over oats. When oats are lukewarm, stir in 1 1/2 to 2 cups flour. Add eggs and beat, then stir in softened yeast mixture and add remaining flour. Dough will be sticky so refrigerate overnight and it will be easy to handle. Place in 2 bread loaf pans and let rise until doubled. Bake in preheated 350-degree oven for 40 minutes. Makes 2 large loaves.

Edna says, "This bread freezes beautifully so when you are in the bread-making mood make up a batch to have on hand when company comes, or a neighbor is in need."

BLUEBERRY BREAD

2 eggs
1 cup milk
1/2 cup blueberry juice
3/4 cup molasses
2 tablespoons melted shortening
4 cups flour
1 cup blueberries, well drained
5 teaspoons baking powder
1 teaspoon salt
2 teaspoons cinnamon
1/4 teaspoon nutmeg
1/2 cup sugar
1 cup chopped nuts

Beat eggs well and add 1 cup milk, juice, molasses and melted shortening. Mix and sift dry ingredients; add to liquid mixture. Stir in nuts and blueberries. Pour into 2 greased bread pans and bake in preheated 350-degree oven for 1 hour. Makes 2 loaves.

ALLECE'S SPOON BREAD

1/2 cup cornmeal
1/4 cup flour
1 tablespoon sugar
3/4 teaspoon salt
1 teaspoon baking powder
1 egg, beaten
1 1/2 cups milk
2 tablespoons margarine

Combine cornmeal, flour, sugar, salt and baking powder. Add egg and 1 cup milk. Blend until batter is mixed. Melt margarine in baking dish, pour in batter and pour 1/2 cup milk over the top. Bake in preheated 375-degree oven for 45 minutes.

Allece says, "This bread will have a soft center and a crusty top. It is very good to serve with chili, soups and casseroles."

PINEAPPLE - ZUCCHINI BREAD

3 eggs
3 tablespoons vanilla
2 cups sugar
1 cup oil
2 cups peeled, grated, well drained zucchini
3 cups flour
1 teaspoon baking powder
1 teaspoon baking soda
1 teaspoon salt
1 can (8-ounce) crushed pineapple, undrained
1 cup chopped walnuts or pecans

Grease and flour 2 loaf pans. Beat eggs until fluffy; add vanilla, sugar, oil and blend well. Add zucchini then dry ingredients and blend well. Stir in pineapple and nuts. Pour into pans and bake in preheated 350-degree oven for 1 hour or until pick inserted in center comes out clean. Makes 2 loaves.

MEXICAN CORN BREAD

1 can (8 1/2-ounce) cream-style corn
2 cups Cheddar cheese, shredded
1 cup cornmeal
1/2 cup sour cream
1/4 cup corn oil
4 green chilies (about 1/2 cup), rinsed and chopped
2 eggs
2 teaspoons baking powder
1/2 teaspoon salt

Combine all ingredients, reserving 1/2 cup cheese for sprinkling on top. Grease an 8 or 9-inch square baking pan; spoon in mixture and bake in preheated 350-degree oven for 1 hour or until set in center. Cut into squares and serve while hot. Serves 6.

BROCCOLI CORNBREAD

2 sticks margarine, melted
2 packages Jiffy cornbread mix
1 cup cottage cheese
4 eggs, well beaten
1 package (10-ounce) frozen chopped broccoli, well drained

Combine ingredients and pour into a greased 9 x 12-inch pan. Bake in preheated 350-degree oven for 45 minutes or until done. 12-16 squares.

Raising the Dough

RUBY'S CORNBREAD

2/3 cup flour
2/3 cup cornmeal
Pinch of salt
3 teaspoons baking powder
2 tablespoons sugar
1 cup milk
2 eggs, slightly beaten
2 tablespoons shortening, melted

Combine dry ingredients; mix milk and eggs and blend into dry ingredients. Stir in melted shortening and mix well. Pour into greased 8-inch pan and bake in preheated 425-degree oven for 10 minutes. Serves 4-6.

BROILED PITA BREAD

2 large pita pockets
3 tablespoons butter or margarine
2 tablespoons olive oil
2 teaspoons minced garlic
1 teaspoon Fines Herbs
Freshly grated Parmesan cheese

Split pita pockets into 4 rounds; cut each round in half. Arrange cut sides up on cookie sheet. In a small skillet melt butter with olive oil; add minced garlic and herbs. Brush butter mixture evenly over bread and sprinkle with cheese. Broil until topping is lightly golden, watching carefully to prevent burning. Serves 4.

SUELLEN'S DILLY CHEESE BREAD

3 cups Bisquick
1 1/2 cups sharp Cheddar cheese, shredded
1 tablespoon sugar
1/2 teaspoon dry mustard
1/2 teaspoon dill weed
1 egg, beaten
1 1/4 cups milk
1 tablespoon oil

Mix together Bisquick, sugar, mustard and dill. Add egg, milk and oil to the dry mixture and mix well. Pour into a greased bread pan and bake in preheated 350-degree oven for 50 minutes. Makes 1 large loaf.

FOCACCIA

1/2 cup hot water
2 tablespoons active dry yeast
1 teaspoon sugar
3 cups flour
1 teaspoon Italian herbs
2 teaspoons salt
1 cup warm water
1/3 cup olive oil
Olive oil for top
Parmesan cheese

Combine hot water, yeast and sugar in a small bowl; set aside until bubbles form, about 10 minutes. Combine flour and salt in a large bowl. Make a well in the center and pour in 1 cup water and olive oil; add yeast mixture. With mixer or by hand, blend until dough forms a ball. Turn out onto a floured surface and knead about 5 minutes, until smooth and elastic, but soft.

Place dough in a greased bowl, turning so all sides are greased. Cover and let rise until double, about 1 to 1 1/2 hours. Punch down and divide into portions you desire. At this point dough can be refrigerated to be used at a later time. Flatten dough by pulling and stretching to your desired thickness. Place on a baking sheet. Brush with olive oil and sprinkle with Parmesan cheese. Position rack in lowest position in preheated 450-degree oven and bake for 15 minutes or until bottom is well-browned. Makes 3 8-inch rounds.

Jo and Jan say, "This is the popular Italian flat bread which really is centuries old. You can put any topping on it you desire. (See index for Tony's Italian Bread). If you form the bread in small rounds, it can be sliced like hamburger buns and is great for sandwiches."

SALT RISING BREAD

3 medium sized potatoes
1 teaspoon sugar
3 tablespoons corn-meal
1 teaspoon salt
4 cups boiling water
2 cups lukewarm milk
1 cup water
1/8 teaspoon baking soda
1/8 teaspoon salt
2 tablespoons vegetable oil
Flour

Pare and slice potatoes. Add corn-meal, sugar, salt and boiling water. Wrap bowl in a heavy cloth. Cover and allow to stand in a warm area overnight. Next morning remove potatoes; add milk, water, soda, salt and oil. Add enough flour to make a dough just stiff enough to knead. Knead until smooth and elastic. Form into 3 loaves and place in well-greased pans. Cover and let rise until double. Bake in a preheated 400-degree oven for about 45 minutes. Makes 3 loaves.

APPLE PUFFS

2 cups flour, sifted
1 package yeast
2 tablespoons sugar
1/2 teaspoon salt
3/4 cup warm water
1/4 cup oil
1 egg, beaten
1 cup apples, chopped very fine
3 tablespoons margarine, melted
1/4 cup sugar
1 teaspoon cinnamon
1/2 cup pecans, finely chopped

In a large bowl, combine 1 cup flour, yeast, sugar and salt. Mix well; add very warm water and oil to flour mixture. Add egg and blend until well moistened. Beat for 2 minutes then gradually stir in apples and remaining flour by hand until you have a soft batter. Spoon into greased pans. Cover and let rise until double, about 35 minutes. Bake in preheated 375-degree oven 15 to 18 minutes. Combine 1/4 cup sugar, cinnamon and pecans. Dip tops of rolls into melted margarine and then into the sugar-cinnamon mixture. Serve warm if possible. Makes 12 puffs.

PINEAPPLE GEMS

2 cups flour
1 1/2 teaspoons baking powder
1/8 teaspoon salt
1/4 cup butter
2 tablespoons sugar
1 large egg
1 can (8 1/4-ounce) crushed pineapple in heavy syrup, undrained

Stir together the flour, baking powder and salt. Cream butter and sugar; beat in the egg, blend well. Add flour mixture and pineapple; stir only until flour mixture is moistened. Turn into greased muffin tin, filling each cup 3/4 full. Bake in preheated 350-degree oven for 30 to 40 minutes or until a tester, inserted in center comes out clean and muffins are golden. Serve warm. Makes 8-10.

CRANBERRY MUFFINS

2 cups unbleached all-purpose flour
1 cup whole wheat flour
4 teaspoons baking powder
1 teaspoon salt
1/2 teaspoon baking soda
2 cups cranberries
2/3 cup butter, softened
1 cup sugar
2 eggs
1 cup milk
4-6 tablespoons sugar
Grated peel of 2 lemons

Sift flours, baking powder, salt and soda; stir in cranberries and set aside. Cream butter in large bowl; gradually add sugar, beating until smooth, then beat in eggs. Blend milk into batter alternately with dry ingredients and berries. Spoon into 24 greased muffin pans. Combine sugar and lemon peel in small bowl, pressing with back of spoon or fingertips until sugar is moistened. Sprinkle evenly over batter. Bake in preheated 375-degree oven for 25 minutes or until muffins are light golden and tester comes out clean. Serve warm or at room temperature. Bakes 24.

Raising the Dough

NUTTY CORN MUFFINS

1 1/4 cups yellow cornmeal
1 cup sugar
3/4 cup flour
2 teaspoons baking powder
1/4 teaspoon salt
1 cup pecans, chopped
1 cup milk
1/2 cup margarine, melted
2 eggs

In bowl mix cornmeal, sugar, flour, baking powder, salt and pecans. In small bowl beat milk, butter and eggs with a fork and add to dry ingredients. Stir lightly until barely mixed. Pour into muffin cups. Bake in preheated 400-degree oven for 15 minutes. Makes 18.

RAISIN BRAN MUFFINS

1 cup oat bran
1 cup quick-cooking oats
2 cups raisin bran
1/2 cup honey
1/2 cup flour
1 teaspoon soda
1 teaspoon baking powder
1 teaspoon cinnamon
3 egg whites
1/2 cup Puritan oil
1/2 cup buttermilk
1/2 cup sunflower seeds, toasted
3/4 cup raisins

Combine oat bran, oatmeal, cereal, honey, flour, soda, baking powder and cinnamon. In large bowl combine egg whites, oil, buttermilk, sunflower seeds and raisins. Mix well and fold in dry ingredients . Fill greased muffin tins 3/4 full. Bake in preheated 375 degree oven for 20 minutes. Makes 16 muffins.

SIX-WEEK APPLE BRAN MUFFINS

2 large Jonathan, Delicious or Rome apples;
   pared, cored and chopped
1/2 cup butter or margarine
8 to 10-ounce box Bran Buds
2 cups boiling water
5 cups flour
3 cups sugar
5 teaspoons baking soda
1 teaspoon cinnamon
1 cup chopped walnuts or pecans
1 regular-size box seeded raisins
4 eggs
1 cup cooking oil
1 quart buttermilk

Saute apples in butter 10 minutes or until tender; set aside. Pour boiling water over 2 cups Bran Buds; set aside. Combine dry ingredients, remaining Bran Buds, sauteed apples, nuts and raisins. Mix together eggs, oil, buttermilk into Bran Buds with water. Add liquid mixture into dry ingredients; blend. Store in 4 l-quart covered containers or in a l-gallon jar. Let sit in refrigerator overnight. Spoon in to small muffin tins, lightly greased, or in paper muffin cups. Bake in preheated 350 degree oven about 25 minutes. Batter keeps 6 weeks in refrigerator. Makes 8-10 dozen.

PEANUT BUTTER MUFFINS

1/3 cup peanut butter
1/4 cup sugar
1 egg
1 1/2 cups flour
1/2 teaspoon salt
4 teaspoons baking powder
3/4 cup milk

Cream peanut butter and sugar. Add beaten egg, then sift dry ingredients and add alternately with milk. Bake in greased muffin tins 25-30 minutes at 350 degrees. Makes 12.

SHAWN'S HUCKLEBERRY MUFFINS

2 1/2 cups sifted flour
2 1/2 teaspoons baking powder
1/3 cup sugar
1/2 teaspoon salt
1 cup huckleberries
1 egg, well-beaten
1 cup milk
4 tablespoons melted butter

To sifted flour, add baking powder, sugar and salt; then resift twice. Use 1/3 of flour mixture with huckleberries. Combine egg, milk and shortening. Add to flour, beating only enough to dampen flour. Fold in huckleberries. Bake in greased muffin tins for 25 minutes in preheated 425-degree oven. Makes 18 muffins.

POPOVERS

3 teaspoons shortening
2 eggs
1 cup milk
1 cup flour
1/2 teaspoon salt
1 tablespoon cooking oil

Allowing 1/2 teaspoon shortening per cup, grease sides and bottoms of 6 (6-ounce) custard cups. Combine eggs and milk in mixing bowl; add flour and salt. Beat with rotary beater or electric mixer until smooth, about 2 minutes. Add oil and beat just 30 seconds more. Place greased cups on a baking sheet; fill half full and place sheet on lower rack of preheated 450-degree oven. Bake for 15 minutes, reduce heat to 350 degrees and bake for 20 to 25 minutes more or until popovers are golden brown and firm. Do not open oven door during baking, as the popovers may collapse. If the popovers brown too quickly, turn off the oven and finish baking in the oven until they are very firm. For extra-crisp popovers, turn off the oven and leave them inside for 30 more minutes, leaving the oven door slightly open. A few minutes before removing popovers from oven, prick each one with a fork to allow steam to escape. This will help the center to dry slightly. Serve hot with butter and jam. Makes 6.

YORKSHIRE PUDDING POPOVERS

1/2 cup drippings from rib eye roast
6 large eggs
2 cups milk
2 cups flour
1/2 teaspoon salt
1/4 teaspoon garlic powder
Black pepper, freshly ground

Using 2 tablespoons drippings, generously grease 8 to 10 5-ounce custard cups; set aside. Beat eggs in large bowl on medium speed until light. Add milk and remaining beef drippings. Reduce speed to low and beat in rest of ingredients. Fill prepared cups halfway with batter; place on a baking sheet and bake in preheated 375-degree oven for about 50 minutes. Remove cups from oven and make a slit in top of each popover to release steam. Return to oven and bake 10 minutes longer. Serve immediately. Makes 8 - 10.

RUTHIE'S DUMPLINGS

1 egg
1/3 cup milk
2 tablespoons oil
1 cup flour, sifted
1 1/2 teaspoons baking powder
1/2 teaspoon salt

In a medium-size bowl beat the egg, milk and oil together until well blended. Add sifted flour, baking powder and salt. Drop by heaping tablespoons into hot broth. They will take 15 minutes to cook. Always cover your pan when cooking dumplings.

Side Effects

❖❖

Side Effects • Vegetables & Accompaniments

Side Effects include rice dishes, vegetables, accompaniments, sauces, Pastabilities Part1 and an assortment of flavored butters to enhance your dishes, all of which will compliment your menu.

Some of our favorites are Black Beans and Rice, Shrimp-Stuffed Artichokes, Sweet Potato Balls and Tomatoes Florentine.

Special Pasta suggestions include Carol's Pasta Primivera, Fettucini and Spinach, and Pasta with Pesto Sauce.

Be sure to try the various flavored butters on vegetable and meat dishes.

❖❖

❖❖❖

Vegetables

FLUFFY RICE

1 cup long grain rice
1 teaspoon salt

Bring 2 quarts of water to a boil. Add salt and rice and cook, covered about 20 minutes. Pour rice into a strainer and run cold water through it until well rinsed. (Rice may be held at this point. Don't put it into the oven until you are ready to serve it.)

Put rice in a pyrex dish and place it in the upper part of a preheated 400-degree oven for about 10 minutes. No more gummy rice! Serves 6 - 8.

PARSLIED RICE

2 tablespoons butter
1 small onion, finely minced
1 1/2 cups converted rice
1/8 teaspoon white pepper
3 cups chicken broth
1 cup fresh parsley, minced
1 to 2 cloves garlic, pressed or finely minced
   (optional)
2 to 4 tablespoons butter (optional)

Heat butter in heavy saucepan; add onion and cook over low heat, stirring frequently until soft but not brown, about 5 minutes. Add rice, stirring to completely coat with butter. Add pepper and broth; heat to boiling; reduce heat and simmer, covered, until rice is tender, 20 to 25 minutes. Gently fold in parsley and, if desired, garlic and remaining butter. Serves 6.

LEMON RICE

4 cups chicken stock
2 teaspoons salt
1 tablespoon butter
Juice of 2 lemons
Peel of 2 lemons, cut into quarters
   (do not use white, spongy part)
2 cups raw rice
Lemon zest (garnish)

Combine stock, salt, butter, lemon juice and quartered rinds in a large pot; bring to a boil. Add rice and stir once. Cover; reduce heat and do not uncover for 20 minutes, liquid should be absorbed. If you are not ready to serve, place rice in a colander and put over boiling water until ready for it. Garnish rice with strips of lemon. Serves 8.

Jo and Jan say, "This is wonderful with fish! It is served a lot in the South with gumbo."

RICE SKILLET DISH

1 1/2 cups uncooked rice
2 tablespoons butter
1 onion, diced
1 can cream of mushroom soup
1 can cream of chicken soup
1 soup can water
Dash Worcestershire sauce
Dash Tabasco sauce
Salt and pepper to taste

Melt butter in large skillet; combine all ingredients and simmer, covered on low until done. Serves 6-8.

Jo and Jan say, "This is so easy and delicious served with barbecued chicken, chops, etc. You can use half wild rice for a variation or brown rice is delicious and so good for you!"

BLACK BEANS AND RICE

1 1/3 cups black beans
4 cups water (more if needed)
3 tablespoons vegetable oil
1/2 cup onion, chopped
1/2 cup ham, minced
4 tablespoons green pepper, chopped
2 garlic cloves, minced
1 bay leaf
1/2 teaspoon dried oregano, crumbled
1/4 teaspoon ground cumin
Tabasco to taste
Salt and freshly ground pepper
1 1/3 cups rice
2 cups water

Rinse beans well in cold water. Soak covered in cold water overnight.

Drain beans and place in heavy saucepan. Add 4 cups water and bring to a boil. Reduce heat, cover and simmer until beans are just tender, about 2 1/2 hours. Add more water if necessary.

Drain beans; heat oil in large, heavy kettle over medium heat. Add onion, ham, pepper, garlic, bay leaf, oregano, cumin, Tabasco, salt and pepper; cook until vegetables are soft, about 8 minutes. Add beans and rice. Stir in 2 cups water and bring to a simmer. Cover and cook until rice is tender and water is absorbed, about 20 minutes. Serve hot accompanied with Tabasco sauce. Serves 4.

RUTHIE'S WILD RICE WITH MUSHROOMS

1 cup uncooked wild rice, well washed
Boiling water
1 teaspoon salt
1/2 pound fresh mushrooms, sliced
2 tablespoons butter
4 strips bacon, finely chopped
2 cups celery, finely sliced
2 medium-sized onions, chopped
1 large green pepper, chopped
5 tablespoons olive oil
1/2 cup tomato juice

Cook rice until tender (about 30 minutes) in boiling salted water to cover. Drain thoroughly and turn into a greased 2-quart casserole.

Meanwhile, saute mushrooms in butter; in another pan, fry chopped bacon until crisp; add celery, onions, green pepper and saute until vegetables are limp. Stir mushrooms, the bacon-vegetable mixture, olive oil and tomato juice into cooked rice. Bake in preheated 350-degree oven until liquid is absorbed, about 30 minutes. Serves 8-10.

TIP

• Use red or green peppers, small acorn squash or miniature pumpkins as serving pieces for vegetables or condiments. They make a lovely and inexpensive alternative to dishes.

VEGETABLE SEASONING BLEND

1 teaspoon celery seed
1 tablespoon marjoram leaves
1 tablespoon thyme leaves
1 tablespoon basil leaves
1 tablespoon parsley leaves

Blend all ingredients in a blender. Store in airtight container in a cool, dry place. Use as taste dictates with vegetables.

SAVORY VEGETABLE SEASONING BLEND

3 tablespoons dried parsley flakes
2 tablespoons dried basil
2 tablespoons dried oregano
1 teaspoon ground savory

Combine all ingredients and process in blender. Store in airtight container in a cool, dry place. Use 1 to 2 teaspoons of Seasoning with vegetables, or as taste desires.

VEGETABLE MARINADE

1/2 cup vegetable oil
1/3 cup white or red wine vinegar
1/4 cup minced fresh parsley
2 garlic cloves, crushed
1 tablespoon Dijon mustard
1 teaspoon honey
1/2 teaspoon oregano
1/2 teaspoon basil
1/2 teaspoon tarragon
Salt and freshly ground pepper

Combine ingredients and blend well. Pour over raw or lightly steamed vegetables which have been chilled and refrigerate in marinade at least 2 hours. Makes 1 cup.

GREEN BEAN CASSEROLE

2 cups green beans, drained
1/2 cup onion, chopped
2 tablespoons margarine
1 cup sour cream
2 tablespoons white wine or wine vinegar
1/4 cup mushroom pieces
1 small jar pimentos, chopped
1/2 cup cashew nuts, chopped
Buttered bread crumbs or crushed
    potato chips

Saute onions in margarine. Add wine and blend in sour cream. Mix with remaining ingredients; top with buttered crumbs. Bake at 350 degrees for 20 minutes. Serves 4 - 6.

RENE'S GREEN BEAN CASSEROLE

3 cans (16-ounce-size) French-style green
    beans
1 can (10 3/4-ounce) mushroom soup
1 can (4-ounce) mushrooms
1 medium green pepper, diced
1 can (3 1/4-ounce) pimento
1/2 cup milk
1/2 pound Cheddar cheese, diced
1 tablespoon butter
1/2 cup bread crumbs

Take out and set aside 1/2 cup cheese and a few strips of pimento for the topping. Saute mushrooms, green pepper and pimento in butter. Add milk and cheese. Drain green beans and combine with sauce, mushroom soup and cheese. Pour into a greased 2-quart baking dish. Sprinkle with buttered crumbs and reserved cheese. Dot with reserved strips of pimento. Bake in preheated 350-degree oven for 30 minutes. Serves 8.

BRANDIED HEART OF PALM

1 can (1 pound 14-ounce) heart of palm
1/4 pound butter
2 tablespoons brandy

Cut heart of palm into 1/2-inch slices. Melt butter and baste heart of palm until glazed but not brown. Add brandy, baste and serve. Serves 6-8.

FRIED PARSLEY

Rinse and thoroughly dry very fresh parsley. Tear off any long stems and break into individual sprigs. Heat about 3/4 cup of equal amounts of light olive and vegetable oil in a deep-fat fryer to 375 degrees. Quickly stir in a handful of parsley, until the oil stops sizzling and spattering. Remove with a slotted spoon and drain on paper towels. Repeat with remaining parsley, adding handfuls, one at a time, keeping the temperature constant for each batch. Add more oil, if necessary, allowing the original to cool before adding more. Serve drained parsley warm and lightly salted.

CELERY REGAL

8 cups celery, sliced on the diagonal
1 can cream of chicken soup
1 can water chestnuts, sliced
1/2 cup slivered almonds, sauteed in butter
2 tablespoons butter
1/2 cup bread crumbs

Cook celery in slightly salted water until crunchy tender. Drain well; combine soup, water chestnuts and celery. Put into buttered casserole. Saute almonds in butter; remove with slotted spoon and set aside. Mix butter and bread crumbs; sprinkle over casserole, then the almonds. Bake in preheated 350-degree oven for 35 to 40 minutes. Serves 4 - 6.

Jo says, "I love to make this dish using cashews, but then, I really love cashews!"

DUTCH CHEESE FONDUE

2 cups dry white wine or beer
1 large clove garlic, crushed
1 pound Gouda cheese, coarsely grated
  (about 4 cups)
1 tablespoon cornstarch
2 tablespoons Kirsch liqueur
1/2 teaspoon nutmeg
1/2 teaspoon salt
Freshly ground pepper
1 large loaf French or Italian bread, cut
  into l-inch squares

Pour the wine or beer into a 2-quart fondue dish (or any 2-quart flame-proof enameled casserole), drop in the garlic and bring to a boil over high heat. Let the liquid boil briskly for 1 to 2 minutes, lower the heat so that the liquid barely simmers. Stir constantly with a table fork, add the cheese, a handful at a time, letting each handful melt before adding another.

In a separate dish, mix cornstarch with Kirsch. Add this to the cheese mixture and stir until fondue is creamy and smooth; add seasonings.

To serve, place the fondue pot over an alcohol or gas burner in the center of the dining table, regulating the heat so the fondue barely simmers. Place a basket of bread cubes alongside the fondue. Traditionally, each diner spears a cube of bread on a fork (preferably a long handled fondue fork) swirls the bread in the mixture until it is thoroughly coated, eat immediately. Makes about 6 cups.

❖❖❖

ALL ABOUT ARTICHOKES

• Artichokes really aren't so scary! We hope this "walk-through" will help you decide to experiment a bit.

Most American artichokes come from California, near Monterey. The best supplies and lowest prices are in April and May. Size has nothing to do with quality but is definitely something to consider for preparation. Large artichokes are best for stuffing and if you come across a recipe which calls for baby artichokes, don't substitute large ones.

When buying, allow 1 artichoke per serving. Our instructions are for 4. Select those which are firm, heavy, compact, with leaves just slightly open. They should be green in color, free of blemishes, and should yield a bit when pressed. Raw artichokes do not keep well. If storing for a day or two, keep in refrigerator crisper.

To prepare, lay artichoke on side; cut off 1-inch from the top and cut stem close to base to leave a smooth bottom. Remove outer, lower, tough leaves and cut thorny tip of each leaf with scissors. Rub artichoke all over with lemon juice to prevent discoloration.

If you are serving the artichoke hot and immediately after cooking; remove the "choke" now. To do this, open center of each artichoke with fingers and push leaves apart. With melon scoop or teaspoon (we use a grapefruit spoon) remove and discard the fuzzy "choke," scraping well.

Fill a large bowl with enough water to cover artichokes. Add more lemon juice to the water and after each artichoke is cleaned, drop it into the lemon water until ready to cook.

To cook artichokes, tie each with string to keep leaves in place. Stand upright in an enamel or stainless steel pan with boiling water l-inch deep on sides of artichokes. Season water with:

1 garlic clove, crushed
1 tablespoon olive oil
1 bay leaf
6 peppercorns
1 slice lemon for each artichoke

Bring water back to a boil, reduce heat and simmer, covered for 30 to 45 minutes, depending on size, until stem end is easily pierced with a fork and a leaf pulls away easily. Carefully remove from liquid and drain upside down. If you have not removed the "choke" before cooking, wait until cool enough to handle, then gently spread leaves apart and remove it at this time. Serve standing upright on a plate, accompanied with a sauce.

Artichokes may be prepared in advance and reheated by placing into a simmering bath for 5 minutes or until heated through. They will also keep covered and refrigerated for several days.

There really is no great mystery to eating artichokes. They are delicious hot or cold, as preference dictates, (try both ways) and they are a finger food. Pull off a leaf, dip the wide end into the sauce; and holding the tip, pull the leaf through your closed teeth to scrape the soft pulp from the base. Discard the rest of the leaf to the side of your plate and continue with each leaf.

Sometimes you may find that artichokes have been prepared without removing the "choke." Remove it with a knife and fork and proceed to cut and dip the delicious "heart" that remains into the sauce.

Sauces for artichokes include melted butter mixed with lemon juice; or Hollandaise Sauce (See index). Try mayonnaise mixed with mustard, lemon juice and herbs or make a dressing of mayonnaise, mustard and horseradish; as taste dictates. When ready to serve, fill center of artichoke with the mayonnaise dressing but serve melted butter sauces in a side dish.

Jo and Jan say, "We had such fun preparing artichokes in a cooking class. Although we had served them many times, we picked up some pointers which we have now passed on to you. Enjoy!"

Side Effects

- Artichokes make lovely, distinctive centerpieces. Try making a pyramid with them, filling spaces with fresh rosemary or dill.

TIP
- You can also stick candles in the center of artichokes for candle holders. This is very effective in the pyramid arrangement.

TIP
- A medium artichoke has only about 60 calories! What a wonderful, delicious diet food!

SHRIMP - STUFFED ARTICHOKES

1/2 stick butter
8 green onions, chopped
2 garlic cloves, minced
1 pound mushrooms, sliced
2 pounds shrimp, chopped
1/2 to 3/4 cup bread crumbs
1 teaspoon dried tarragon
1 tablespoon fresh parsley, minced
1 teaspoon dill
1/2 teaspoon celery seed
1/2 teaspoon paprika
1/4 cup dry sherry, optional
Salt and pepper to taste
1 1/2 cups Jan's Maionese (See index) or commercial mayonnaise
8 large artichokes, trimmed and cooked (See index for cooking instructions)

Melt butter in a large skillet. Quickly saute onions, garlic and mushrooms over medium heat. Add shrimp, bread crumbs, tarragon, parsley, dill, celery seed and paprika. Stir constantly until mixture is cooked. Add sherry if desired and simmer 2 minutes; season with salt and pepper; stir in 1/2 cup Salsa Maionese. Spread artichoke leaves apart and fill cavities with shrimp mixture. Top artichokes with remaining sauce. Place on greased baking sheet and lightly tent with foil. Bake in preheated 350-degree oven for 10 to 15 minutes. Remove foil and place under broiler until tops are lightly browned. Serves 8.

Jo and Jan say, "These may be filled ahead and refrigerated. Bring to room temperature before popping in the oven to bake."

BUTTER SAUCE FOR ARTICHOKES

2 sticks butter, melted
1/4 cup fresh lemon juice
1/4 cup fresh parsley, chopped
1 teaspoon salt
1/2 teaspoon dry mustard

Combine ingredients and simmer 5 minutes. Serve warm as a dipping sauce with hot, cooked artichokes. Makes 1 1/2 cups.

LEMON - BUTTER SAUCE FOR COOKED ARTICHOKES

1 cup butter, melted
1/4 cup lemon juice
1/4 cup chopped parsley
1 teaspoon salt
1/2 teaspoon dry mustard

Combine ingredients and simmer 5 minutes. Serve warm as dipping sauce. Serves 4.

BUTTERS FOR CORN ON THE COB

1/2 cup butter
1 teaspoon dried thyme

Melt butter and add thyme. Pour into a serving dish large enough to roll the ears to coat well. Coats 4 ears.

Jo and Jan say, "You can substitute 1 teaspoon dill or crushed dried red pepper for the thyme; or perhaps 1 tablespoon minced fresh chives?"

PERFECT CORN ON THE COB

The fresher the corn, the better it will taste; so it is best when eaten as soon after picking as possible. Keep corn refrigerated and unshucked until just before cooking.

Remove husks, silk and cut away any imperfect ends from ears. Rinse in cold water and drop into rapidly boiling unsalted water. (Salt toughens corn, so add later). You may line the bottom of pot with some of inner husks and place corn on top, or alternate layers. If the corn is more mature, add a little sugar; it helps the flavor.

After adding corn to pot, make sure water completely covers the corn. Allow water to return to a boil; immediately cover the pot and turn off heat. Let corn stand in water 5 to 10 minutes (5 for very young ears). Drain and serve immediately.

To get around the corn-buttering bother, put several lumps of butter, plus a tablespoon or so of minced fresh parsley or dill on a platter or large shallow dish. Just before serving, roll the ears until they're well coated. Have napkins handy!

CORN PUDDING

2 cups milk
1/4 cup sugar
6 eggs, well beaten
2 tablespoons flour
2 cans (16-ounce size) creamed corn
8 tablespoons butter

Combine milk, sugar, eggs and flour in mixing bowl. Beat well for 2 minutes. Stir in creamed corn and mix well. Pour into a buttered 9 x 13-inch baking dish; dot with butter and bake in preheated 350-degree oven for 45 minutes. Allow to set a few minutes before serving. Serves 6-8.

FRESH CORN CASSEROLE

2 cups fresh corn kernels
1/2 cup butter, melted
2 eggs
1 cup sour cream
1 cup Monterey Jack cheese, diced
1/2 cup cornmeal
1 can (4-ounce) diced green chilies
1 1/2 teaspoon salt

Puree 1 cup corn with butter and eggs in blender or food processor. Mix remaining ingredients in medium bowl. Add pureed mixture and blend well. Pour into a well-greased 2-quart rectangular casserole and bake, uncovered in a preheated 350-degree oven for 50 to 60 minutes.

Jo and Jan say, "If fresh corn is not available, substitute 2 packages of frozen corn. This may be prepared in advance and reheated before serving. It freezes beautifully; defrost before reheating." Serves 6.

MARSHA'S CORN CASSEROLE

1 can creamed corn
1 can whole corn
1 cup uncooked macaroni
1/2 stick margarine, melted
1 cup diced Velvetta cheese
1/3 cup buttered breadcrumbs

Combine corns, macaroni, margarine and cheese in casserole. Bake in preheated 350-degree oven for 30 minutes. Top with buttered breadcrumbs and bake for 15 minutes longer. Serves 4-6.

CORN STUFFING BALLS

1/2 cup chopped onion
1/2 cup chopped celery
4 tablespoons butter or margarine
1 can (17-ounce) cream-style corn
1/2 cup water
1/4 teaspoon pepper
1 teaspoon poultry seasoning
1 package (8-ounce) or 3 cups herb-
　seasoned stuffing mix
3 eggs, slightly beaten
1/2 cup butter or margarine, melted for
　topping. Note: If doubling recipe, do not
　double this ingredient; 1/2 cup is plenty.

Saute onion and celery in butter until tender but not brown. Add corn, water, pepper and poultry seasoning. Bring to a boil and pour over stuffing mix; toss together lightly and stir in the beaten eggs. Shape into 7 or 8 balls (mixture will be very moist but will set up when baking). Place balls in a baking pan. Pour melted butter over top. Refrigerate until ready to bake or bake for 25 minutes in a preheated 375-degree oven. Makes 7 or 8 balls.

Jo and Jan say, "We always double this recipe, because they are such a hit and if any happen to be left, they are just as delicious with that left-over turkey."

FRESH ASPARAGUS

2 to 2 1/2 pounds fresh asparagus
Boiling water
1 1/2 teaspoons salt
1/4 cup butter or margarine, melted
Lemon wedges (optional)

Break or cut off tough ends of asparagus stalks as far down as they snap easily. Wash asparagus tips well with cold water; if necessary use a brush to remove grit. Using a vegetable parer, scrape skin and scales from the lower part of stalk only. Stand the stalks upright in bottom of a double boiler or narrow, deep pan; form into a bunch, securing with string. Cook, covered, in 1-inch boiling, salted water, for 15 to 20 minutes, or just until tender. If just cooking tips, only boil for 5 to 10 minutes. Do not over-cook. Drain asparagus well. Drizzle with melted butter and serve hot with lemon wedges or a sauce, such as Hollandaise (See index).

Asparagus is delicious served cold; in a salad or by itself, with a cold entree. It's a wonderful diet food!

FRIED ASPARAGUS ITALIAN

3 pounds fresh asparagus
1 tablespoon Parmesan cheese
1/2 cup flour
1 egg
2 tablespoons white wine
1 cup bread crumbs
1/4 teaspoon garlic powder
1/2 cup olive oil
1 teaspoon salt

Clean asparagus, wash and thoroughly dry. Dip stalks in flour, then in egg beaten with wine, then into crumbs combined with cheese, garlic powder, salt and pepper. Saute in olive oil for 10 minutes or until tender. Serves 8-10.

SQUASH CASSEROLE

1 pound zucchini, crook neck or small white
  summer squash, sliced
1 large onion, diced
1/2 green pepper, diced
3 tablespoons butter
1 can cream mushroom soup
1 can mushrooms and juice
3 eggs, beaten
12 crushed soda crackers
1 cup cheese, grated

Parboil squash 5 minutes; drain and set aside. Saute onion, green pepper in butter until soft. Add squash to this mixture. Combine soup, mushrooms and juice, eggs, crackers and the grated cheese. Blend into squash mixture and pour into a greased 2-quart casserole. Bake in preheated 375-degree oven for 45 minutes to 1 hour. Serves 6.

SPAGHETTI SQUASH

1 spaghetti squash (2 to 3 pounds)
4 ounces butter or margarine
1 1/2 teaspoons garlic powder
1 teaspoon lemon pepper
1/2 teaspoon Italian herbs
1/2 teaspoon dill
1/2 teaspoon seasoning salt
4 tablespoons Parmesan cheese

Wash outside of squash and pat dry. Pierce in several places with fork. Place in microwave and cook on High 6 to 7 minutes per pound, turning once. It will feel soft to the touch. Let stand 10 minutes. When cool enough to handle, halve lengthwise and scoop out seeds. To release spaghetti-like strands, gently scrape squash lengthwise with two forks. Lift out pulp as it becomes free; place on paper towels to drain off liquid. Discard squash skin.

Melt butter, add other ingredients except Parmesan cheese. Place squash in casserole dish and pour butter mixture over all, mixing in well. Sprinkle with Parmesan cheese. Heat in microwave or oven; adding more butter, if necessary, depending on size of squash. Serves 6.

Jo and Jan say, "This is the way our families like it the best. Sometimes we add some cherry tomatoes before the last pop into the microwave. The added color is nice and the flavor is tremendous."

KATHY'S BUFFET SQUASH

2 pounds yellow squash, sliced
1/2 cup chopped onion
1/2 cup water
1 carton (8-ounce) sour cream
1/2 teaspoon salt
1/4 teaspoon pepper
1/4 teaspoon dried basil
1 cup soft breadcrumbs
1/4 cup shredded medium Cheddar cheese
1/3 cup butter or margarine, melted
1/2 teaspoon paprika
8 slices bacon, cooked crisp and crumbled

Cook squash and onion in boiling water until tender; drain and mash. Combine squash, sour cream, salt, pepper and basil. Pour into greased 2-quart casserole. Combine breadcrumbs, cheese, butter and paprika. Sprinkle over squash mixture. Top with crumbled bacon. Bake for 20 minutes in preheated 300-degree oven. Serves 6.

Side Effects

MAPLE WHIPPED BUTTERNUT SQUASH

2 pounds butternut squash, peeled,
quartered and seeded
1/2 cup butter or margarine, softened
1/4 cup maple syrup
1 tablespoon light brown sugar, firmly
packed
3/4 teaspoon freshly grated nutmeg
Salt and freshly ground white pepper, to taste

Bring 1 1/2 inches water to a boil in a 5-quart saucepan or Dutch oven. Add squash and steam, covered, until tender, about 20 minutes. Drain, then return to pot and mash and stir over low heat about 5 minutes to evaporate some of moisture. Transfer to large bowl and add butter, maple syrup, brown sugar, 1/2 teaspoon nutmeg, salt and pepper. Beat with electric mixer at medium speed, or with potato masher, until smooth. Sprinkle with remaining 1/4 teaspoon nutmeg to serve. Serves 6-8.

SAUTEED SPINACH WITH MUSHROOMS

1 1/2 pounds fresh spinach
2 tablespoons olive oil
1 tablespoon butter
1/2 pound fresh mushrooms, sliced
2 tablespoons shallots, finely chopped
1/4 teaspoon nutmeg
Salt
Pepper

Clean spinach well, discarding stems. Rinse, drain and pat dry on paper towels. Put spinach in skillet and cook over medium heat, stirring constantly. When spinach is wilted, transfer to colander and drain. Heat olive oil and butter in skillet and add mushrooms. Stir lightly over medium heat until slightly brown. Add spinach, shallots, nutmeg, salt and pepper. Toss until well blended. Serves 4-6.

Jan says, "This is a wonderful side dish, but is one that needs to be served right away."

SCALLOPED SPINACH

2 packages (10-ounce size) frozen chopped
spinach; cooked and drained
2 tablespoons onion, chopped
2 eggs, beaten
1 1/2 cups milk
1 1/4 cups Cheddar cheese, grated
Salt and pepper
1/2 cup buttered bread crumbs

Combine drained spinach with all other ingredients, except bread crumbs. Pour mixture into greased baking dish. Top with bread crumbs. Bake in preheated 350-degree oven for 20 minutes. Serves 4-6.

SPINACH - MUSHROOM BAKE

5 packages (10-ounce size) frozen chopped
spinach
2 cups chopped mushrooms
1/4 cup butter
1 cup Parmesan cheese
3/4 cup sour cream
3/4 cup heavy cream
1 tablespoon dried minced onion
1 teaspoon horseradish
1 teaspoon nutmeg
1/2 teaspoon salt
1/4 teaspoon pepper
1/3 cup Parmesan cheese

Cook spinach according to package directions; drain. Saute mushrooms in butter over medium heat until soft, 5 to 7 minutes. Combine spinach and rest of ingredients except the 1/3 cup Parmesan cheese in large bowl until well mixed. Spread mixture in buttered 9x13x1 1/2-inch baking dish; sprinkle with 1/3 cup cheese. Bake 25 minutes in preheated 350-degree oven. Sprinkle with additional cheese. Serves 8.

Jo says, "Try baking the mixture for 15 minutes, remove from oven and garnish with cherry tomatoes; return to oven and bake an additional 10 minutes." Serves 8.

RUTHIE'S BARBECUED LIMA BEANS
(Butter Beans)

2 cups lima beans, uncooked
1/4 pound salt pork (bacon may be used)
1/4 cup oil
1 medium onion, sliced
1 can tomato soup
1 tablespoon prepared mustard
1/4 cup vinegar
1/4 cup water
1 teaspoon chili powder
2 teaspoons Worcestershire sauce
1/2 teaspoon garlic salt, if needed
1 cup bean stock
1/2 cup brown sugar

Soak beans in water overnight. Pour off water and cover with fresh water. Cook beans with salt pork until tender. Brown onion in oil until well done. Mix the remaining ingredients together in a Dutch oven. Bake in 350-degree oven for 1 hour. Serves 6-8.

ONIONS ALMONDINE

1 1/2 tablespoons butter or margarine
1 1/2 tablespoons flour
1 can cream or mushroom or cream or celery soup
1/2 cup grated cheese
1/4 teaspoon salt
1/4 cup sherry
3 cans white onions, well drained
1/4 cup slivered almonds, toasted

Melt butter in saucepan; stir in flour and add soup. Add grated cheese and heat until cheese melts; add salt and sherry. Put onions in greased baking dish, top with sauce and then the almonds. Bake in preheated 350-degree oven for 30 to 40 minutes. Serves 10-12.

GLAZED ONIONS

2 tablespoons butter or margarine
1 tablespoon oil
Pinch of salt
Pinch of sugar
24 small onions
1/2 cup chicken broth
Fresh parsley, chopped (garnish)

Melt butter or margarine; add oil and season with salt and sugar in a large skillet. Add onions, making just one layer; stir to coat all onions and cook, covered, on low heat for 30 to 40 minutes or until tender. Remove cover and shake to glaze the onions. Garnish with fresh parsley. Serves 4-6.

BAKED ONIONS AU GRATIN

12 medium onions, peeled
Boiling salted water
1 cup Cheddar cheese, grated
1/2 teaspoon salt
1/4 teaspoon pepper
1/8 teaspoon nutmeg
2 tablespoons heavy cream

Cook onions in boiling salted water to cover for about 8 minutes or until slightly tender. Drain; carefully remove centers. Chop centers and mix with remaining ingredients. Fill onion cavities with mixture and place in a shallow baking pan with 1/2-inch water. Cover and bake in a preheated 375-degree oven for 30 to 35 minutes. Remove cover 5 minutes before onions are done. Serves 6, allowing 2 per person.

❖❖

ITALIAN SWEET - SOUR ONIONS

5 tablespoons vegetable oil
2 pounds tiny white onions, peeled
6 tablespoons dark brown sugar, firmly
  packed
1/2 teaspoon cinnamon
1/2 cup white wine vinegar
1/2 cup dry white wine
Salt
Freshly ground pepper

Heat oil in medium-size saucepan. Add onions and cook over medium-high heat, stirring frequently, until they begin to color. Add remaining ingredients; blend well and reduce heat to medium. Cover and cook until onions are tender, about 15 minutes. Shake pan occasionally to prevent sticking.

Remove lid, increase heat and shake pan constantly while reducing liquid to a glaze. Transfer to bowl and serve at room temperature. Serves 8-10.

Jo and Jan say, "These can be prepared up to 3 days ahead; cover and refrigerate."

PAT'S RED CABBAGE

4 pounds red cabbage
Boiling water
1/4 cup vinegar
1/2 cup shortening or 1/4 cup butter, 1/4 cup
  olive oil
2 teaspoons powdered caraway
2 apples, diced
1 onion, chopped
2 cloves
1 cup water
1/4 cup sugar, scant
2 teaspoons soy sauce

Cut or shred cabbage; pour boiling water over it and drain well. Mix cabbage with vinegar. Melt shortening; add caraway, apples, onion, cloves and 1 cup water. Simmer with cabbage for 90 minutes. Add sugar and soy sauce. Salt to taste. Serves 6-8.

FRENCH PEAS

2 tablespoons butter or margarine
1/2 cup sliced green onions
1 package (10-ounce) frozen peas
1/2 teaspoon sugar
1/4 teaspoon dried savory
1/4 teaspoon dried marjoram
1 tablespoon fresh parsley
1/2 cup water
1 teaspoon salt
1/8 teaspoon pepper

Saute green onions in butter until tender, but not brown. Add peas and remaining ingredients to saucepan and cook, covered, over low heat for 10 minutes or until peas are tender. Drain and serve. Serves 4.

GREEN PEAS IN CREAM SAUCE

3 slices bacon
5 tablespoons flour
1/4 cup chopped onion
1 cup half-and-half
2 cups sliced mushrooms
1/4 cup chopped pimento
1 1/2 pounds (about 3 cups) fresh tiny green
  peas or 2 packages (10-ounce size) frozen;
  cooked just until tender
Salt
Freshly ground pepper

Fry the bacon until crisp; drain on paper towels and reserve fat in skillet. Add flour to fat and mix well to make a roux. Cook over medium heat, stirring constantly until carmel colored. Add onion and cook 3 minutes. Whisk in the half-and-half until smooth. Gently fold in the mushrooms, pimento and peas; add salt and freshly ground pepper to taste. Heat thoroughly and pour into a serving dish. Crumble the bacon on top and serve immediately. Serves 8-10.

CAROL'S BROCCOLI

4 cups cooked broccoli stems and buds cut
    into 1-inch pieces or frozen/chopped
    broccoli
1 cup canned boiled onions
1/2 can cream of mushroom soup
2 ounces pimento
1 carton (8-ounce) sour cream
1 cup chopped celery
1 tablespoon Worcestershire sauce
Fresh ground pepper
1 tablespoon dry onion flakes
1 teaspoon salt
1/2 cup grated sharp Cheddar cheese

Combine all ingredients except cheese. Stir to blend well. Top with cheese and bake in preheated 350-degree oven for 1 hour. Serves 6-8.

BROCCOLI PUFF

2 packages (10-ounce size) frozen broccoli
1 can cream of mushroom soup
1/4 cup milk
1/4 cup mayonnaise
1 egg, beaten
2 ounces (1/2 cup) sharp American cheese,
    shredded
1/4 cup bread crumbs, finely ground
2 tablespoons butter, melted

Cook broccoli according to package instructions, omiting salt. Drain well and cut into 2-inch pieces if using spears. Combine soup, milk, mayonnaise, egg and cheese. Pour over broccoli in a 6x10-inch dish. Combine bread crumbs and melted butter. Sprinkle over casserole and bake for 45 minutes in a preheated 350-degree oven. To double recipe, place in a 9x13-inch dish. Serves 4-6.

BROCCOLI AND CAULIFLOWER STIR-FRY

1 large head broccoli
1 large head cauliflower
6 tablespoons olive oil
4 garlic cloves, chopped
1/2 cup chicken broth
Salt
Freshly ground pepper
Juice of 1 lemon
1/2 teaspoon finely grated lemon peel

Slice small stems of broccoli into thin rounds; discard large tough stems. Break flowerets into small pieces. Separate cauliflower into flowerets. Thoroughly rinse and drain vegetables.

Heat oil in large skillet or wok over medium-high heat. Add garlic and cook just until golden; remove immediately with slotted spoon and set aside. Increase heat to high; add broccoli and cauliflower and stir-fry for 2 minutes, stirring carefully so flowerets do not break apart.

Add broth and mix well. Cover and cook until vegetables are crisp but tender, 2 to 3 minutes. Add a little more liquid if needed to prevent scorching. Add salt, pepper, garlic and lemon juice; stir to mix. Sprinkle with lemon peel after you have transfered vegetables to a heated serving dish. Serves 8-10.

Jo and Jan say, "The degree of doneness of the vegetables is the secret to perfection of this recipe. They should not be overcooked, just tender-crisp."

79

Side Effects

MARLENE'S GLAZED BROCCOLI STEMS

6 or 7 broccoli stems (1 1/2 inches in
  diameter)
1 cup chicken broth
1 tablespoon fresh lemon juice
2 tablespoons butter, softened
1 tablespoon fresh parsley, chopped
Freshly ground pepper

Trim and peel broccoli stems and cut crosswise into 3/4-inch rounds. Combine broccoli and broth in a saucepan; bring to a boil and simmer, covered for 10 to 12 minutes or until tender. Transfer broccoli to a bowl with a slotted spoon, add lemon juice to broth and boil until liquid is reduced to about 1/4 cup. Whisk in the butter, parsley and pepper to taste. Add broccoli and stir until it is coated with glaze. Serves 4.

Jo and Jan say, "At last! Something to do with the broccoli stems that we think is so different. We combine the broccoli with baby carrots; make more glaze to coat well. It makes a very colorful accompaniment and is a beautiful buffet dish."

TIP
• For absolutely white cauliflower flowerets, blanch cauliflower with a little bit of lemon juice or milk in the water.

CAULIFLOWER CASSEROLE

1 medium cauliflower
2 tablespoons butter
2 tablespoons flour
1/2 teaspoon salt
1/8 teaspoon pepper
1 1/2 cups milk
2 hard-cooked eggs, chopped
2 tablespoons dried pimento
1/2 cup green onions and tops, finely
  chopped
2 tablespoons butter
3/4 cup bread crumbs
2 tablespoons grated Parmesan cheese

Wash cauliflower and separate into flowerets. Cook in boiling, salted water about 10 minutes or just until tender. Remove from heat, drain and place in a greased 1 1/2-quart casserole.

Make a white sauce with butter, flour, seasonings and milk in a saucepan. Add eggs, pimento and onion. Mix well and pour over cauliflower.

Melt butter; mix with crumbs and Parmesan cheese. Sprinkle over top of casserole. Bake in preheated 375-degree oven for 30 minutes. Serves 4-6.

SWISS VEGETABLE MEDLEY

1 bag (16-ounce) frozen broccoli, carrots,
  cauliflower; thawed and drained
1 can mushroom soup
1 cup Swiss cheese, shredded
1/3 cup sour cream
1/4 teaspoon pepper
1 jar (4-ounce) pimentos, chopped and
  drained
1 can (2.8-ounce) French Fried Onions

Mix all the above together except 1/2 cup cheese and 1/2 can of onions. Place in 1-quart casserole. Bake, uncovered at 350 degrees for 30 minutes. Remove dish from oven and top with remaining cheese and onions. Return to oven until brown. Serves 6.

❖❖❖

VEGETABLE MEDLEY STIR-FRY

1 medium bunch broccoli
2 medium carrots
2 celery stalks
1 medium zucchini
1 medium onion
1/2 pound mushrooms
1/4 cup salad oil
1/4 cup water
1 teaspoon chicken flavor base
1 teaspoon salt
1/4 teaspoon pepper
1/2 teaspoon sugar

Cut each carrot crosswise in half, then lengthwise into matchstick strips. Cut celery the same way. Thinly slice zucchini and onion. Cut broccoli into 1x1/2-inch pieces for the stalks and small flowerets. Cut mushrooms into quarters.

Heat salad oil in 12-inch skillet on medium-high. Add carrots, celery, zucchini, onions and broccoli; stir frequently. After 5 minutes, add mushrooms, water, chicken flavor base, salt, pepper and sugar; cover and cook 5 to 7 minutes longer until veggies are tender-crisp. Serves 6-8.

ORANGE - GLAZED CARROTS

1 pound fresh carrots, peeled and cut into
    2-inch pieces
1 1/2 cups orange juice
1 1/2 cups light brown sugar
1 1/2 tablespoons margarine
1 tablespoon cornstarch dissolved in 1/4 cup
    cold water
Pinch of ground ginger
Mint leaves (garnish)

Steam carrots until tender then transfer to serving bowl and keep warm. Heat orange juice, sugar and margarine in saucepan and bring to boil; reduce heat, stir in dissolved cornstarch and cook until clear and thickened. Add ginger and pour over warm carrots. Toss to coat with glaze and garnish with fresh mint leaves. Serves 4-6.

POTATO BALLS

16 medium baking potatoes
1/4 cup butter or margarine
Salt
Freshly ground pepper
Paprika (optional)
Chopped fresh parsley or dill for garnish
    (optional)

Peel potatoes and place in cold water. Using small end of melon baller, press down and twist to form a ball. Start at pointed end of potato and work down and around. To form perfect balls, there will be a lot of left-over potato which can be used for soup, mashed potatoes, etc. Drop balls back in cold water as they are formed and

drain on paper towels just before cooking.

Heat butter in a large skillet. Bring to medium heat and add potato balls and cook about 20 to 30 minutes. To brown evenly, shake pan occasionally. Salt and pepper to taste. When golden brown, remove from pan and sprinkle with paprika, parsley or dill, if desired.

Jo and Jan say, "Serve these sometime in Potato Baskets (See index). Remove them directly from the skillet into the baskets, using about 1 cup balls for each basket. Sprinkle with paprika and parsley or dill, as suggested. They are pretty mixed with other veggies too." Makes about 12 cups.

Side Effects

ITALIAN POTATOES

4 large baking potatoes
1 tablespoon olive oil
1/4 cup Parmesan cheese, grated
1 cup provolone cheese, shredded
1/2 cup mozzarella cheese, shredded
1/2 teaspoon oregano
1/2 teaspoon basil
1 1/2 teaspoons salt
1/8 teaspoon pepper
3 medium tomatoes, sliced
1 large onion, peeled and thinly sliced
2 tablespoons butter
Paprika

Peel and slice potatoes 1/4-inch thick. Grease a 9x13-inch casserole with olive oil. Combine the cheeses with oregano, basil, salt and pepper. Arrange potatoes, tomatoes and slices of onion in layers, sprinkling each layer with cheeses and seasonings, ending with a layer of cheeses and seasonings. Dot with butter and sprinkle with paprika. Bake, uncovered in preheated 400-degree oven for 50 minutes or until vegetables are done and the top is browned. Serves 6-8.

PARSLIED NEW POTATOES

2 tablespoons margarine
2 pounds small new potatoes, washed and
   halved
1/4 cup fresh parsley, chopped
1 tablespoon fresh chives, chopped
1/4 teaspoon paprika

Wash and slice the potatoes. Place in sauce pan with enough water to cover and cook over medium heat until just tender. Drain; add margarine, parsley and chives. Toss to coat and sprinkle with paprika. Serves 4.

VARIATION:

Cook potatoes according to the above directions. Drain and add potatoes to a small skillet with 2 tablespoons melted margarine. Heat until brown, sprinkle in 2 tablespoons Parmesan cheese with the herbs. Toss and serve.

POTATOES O'BRIEN

4 medium-size potatoes, boiled and diced
1 medium-size onion, chopped
2 tablespoons butter
2 tablespoons flour
1 1/2 cups milk
1/4 teaspoon salt
1/8 teaspoon pepper
1 can (3 1/4-ounce) pimento, chopped
1/2 green pepper, chopped
1 cup cheese, grated

Melt butter over low heat in heavy saucepan. Blend in flour, seasonings to taste. Cook over low heat and stir until smooth. Slowly add milk and stir until mixture is well blended and beginning to thicken. Boil 1 minute stirring constantly. Remove from heat; add cheese, pepper and pimento. Butter an 8x8-inch baking dish, place a layer of potatoes and onions, half the sauce; another layer of potatoes and onions and ending with sauce on the top. Bake in preheated 350-degree oven for 20 minutes until hot and bubbly. Serves 4-6.

FRIED POTATO BASKETS

Potato baskets can be made in two sieves, one slightly smaller than the other, but the special basket form that is available in cookware shops makes the job easier. The form should be 4 to 5 inches across, and the inside sieve or basket should be slightly smaller.

To make 12 baskets you will need at least 6 large-size baking potatoes. Grate the peeled potatoes, place them in a sieve under cold water. Making one basket at a time, leave rest of potatoes in water to prevent darkening. Squeeze moisture out with your hands and place potatoes on a paper towel.

In a kettle or deep-fat fryer, heat oil to a temperature of 375 degrees. Make sure oil is deep enough to completely cover form. Quickly dip the form in oil and place about a 1/2-inch layer of potatoes completely around the inside, overlapping slightly to form a tulip effect. Clamp on the insert or press down with the smaller sieve.

Dip the potato basket in hot oil until the bubbling subsides, then submerge it completely and fry for 3 minutes or until golden brown. Drain off as much oil as possible and allow to cool for 3 minutes. Carefully remove inside form and unmold basket by turning upside down and gently releasing it with the tip of a knife. Salt basket lightly and drain on paper towels. Repeat until all baskets have been made.

Baskets may be made ahead and frozen in cardboard or metal container. Place tissue paper between each one for protection. To serve, preheat oven to 375 degrees, then turn oven off. Place baskets on baking sheet and warm, about 5 to 10 minutes. If baskets are made the day they are served, they may be left out and rewarmed just before serving, as above.

These are delicious and so colorful filled with sauteed cherry tomatoes, baby carrots, green peas, brussel sprouts and/or potato balls (See index). Makes 12 baskets.

POTATOES WITH CAPERS

1 1/2 pounds small red potatoes, cut in
   bite size chunks
2 tablespoons olive oil
1 tablespoon lemon juice
1 tablespoon fresh dill, minced
1 tablespoon capers, minced
1 teaspoon salt
1/8 teaspoon pepper
1/4 cup olive oil

Heat oil in a 12-inch skillet over medium heat and add potatoes; cook until browned and fork-tender, stirring occasionally. Combine lemon juice, dill, capers, salt and pepper with 1/4 cup olive oil in a large bowl. Add potatoes to dressing; toss to coat well. Serve warm or chilled. Serves 12.

HASH BROWN POTATO CASSEROLE

2 pounds frozen hash brown potatoes
1/2 cup melted butter
1 teaspoon salt
1/4 teaspoon pepper
1/4 cup onion, chopped fine
1 can cream of chicken soup
2 cups sour cream
2 cups grated Cheddar cheese
1 cup buttered bread crumbs

Defrost potatoes, combine all ingredients except cheese and bread crumbs. Pour into a buttered 3-quart casserole and top with grated cheese and then buttered bread crumbs. Bake covered in preheated 350-degree oven for 1 hour. Serves 8-10.

Side Effects

DEE'S FRENCH FRY BAKE

3/4 cup green pepper, chopped
3/4 cup celery, chopped
1/3 cup margarine
1/3 cup flour
1/2 teaspoon salt
1/8 teaspoon pepper
3 cups milk
3/4 cup American cheese, shredded
3/4 cup carrot, coarsely shredded
1/3 cup pimento, chopped
1 package (32-ounce) frozen French fries

Saute green pepper, celery in margarine until tender. Stir in flour, salt and pepper. Add milk all at once. Cook until bubbly. Stir 1 minute more; add carrots, pimento and 1/2 of cheese. Stir until cheese is melted. Combine all ingredients except rest of cheese and place in a greased 9x13x1x-inch baking dish. Bake in preheated 375-degree oven for 45 minutes. Sprinkle remaining cheese on top and bake 5 minutes more. Serves 10-12.

POTATOES MARGARET

5 cups potatoes, cooked and sliced
1 cup sour cream
1/2 cup milk
1 tablespoon instant onion
Salt and pepper
2 tablespoons butter, melted
2 tablespoons fine, dry bread crumbs

Combine sour cream, milk and onion. Place half the potatoes in a greased 10x6x1 1/2-inch baking dish. Sprinkle with salt and pepper. Add half the sour cream mixture. Repeat layers. Sprinkle buttered bread crumbs over top. Bake in preheated 350-degree oven for 20 to 25 minutes. Serves 8.

SWEET POTATO PUFF

6 large sweet potatoes
4 eggs, separated
4 tablespoons butter or margarine
1 cup cream
1/2 teaspoon vanilla
3 tablespoons sugar
1 tablespoon grated orange rind
1/2 teaspoon cinnamon
1/4 teaspoon nutmeg

Cook potatoes; while they are cooling beat egg whites until they form stiff peaks. Drain potatoes and cut in chunks into large mixer bowl. Beat in egg yolks, butter or margarine and rest of ingredients. Continue beating until light and fluffy. Fold in beaten egg whites and spoon into a greased 2-quart baking dish. Bake in a preheated 325-degree oven 1 hour and 10 minutes or until slightly puffed and firm. Serves 8.

Jan and Jo say, "If you desire, top with marshmallows and return to oven for the last 15 minutes."

CRANBERRY APPLE SWEET POTATOES

5-6 sweet potatoes, cooked, peeled and cut into bite-size pieces
or
2 cans (18-ounce size) sweet potatoes, drained
1 can (21-ounce) apple pie filling
1 can (8-ounce) whole cranberry sauce
2 tablespoons apricot preserves
2 tablespoons orange marmalade

Lightly grease an 8x8-inch pan and spread the pie filling on the bottom. Arrange the potato pieces on top. Combine the cranberry sauce, preserves and marmalade in a small bowl and stir until well-mixed. Spoon over the potato mixture. Bake uncovered in a preheated 350-degree oven for 20 to 25 minutes or until bubbly. Serves 6-8.

SWEET POTATO BALLS

4 medium sweet potatoes
1 tablespoon butter
1 egg
1/4 cup sugar
1/3 cup flour
1/2 teaspoon nutmeg
1/2 teaspoon cinnamon
Marshmallows
Corn flake meal
Vegetable oil for frying

Pare and boil potatoes until well done; drain well. Cream butter, egg, sugar and flour. Add nutmeg and cinnamon, mix with potatoes. If potatoes are too soft, add a little more flour and cream well. Place in refrigerator several hours until well-chilled. Form into balls, using 1/2 marshmallow for the center. Roll in corn flake meal. Fry in deep fat until brown, about 3 to 5 minutes. Drain on paper toweling. Makes 15-16 balls.

Jo says, "When forming the balls, the mixture will be sticky, but holds form nicely when rolled in the crumbs. These can be made a day ahead except for frying or can be completed, frozen and heated, uncovered for 12-15 minutes in a 375-degree oven. Do not thaw before reheating. If reheating in a microwave oven, set them for only a minute or so, as the crust will get tough and chewy."

SAUSAGE - STUFFED PUMPKIN

1 pumpkin (6 to 8-pound)
1 teaspoon salt
1/2 teaspoon dry mustard
1 pound sausage
1 cup chopped onion
1 cup chopped celery
10 cups herb-seasoned stuffing mix
1 1/2 teaspoons poultry seasoning
1/4 teaspoon pepper
2 cups chopped raw apple
2 eggs, beaten
3/4 cup chicken broth

Wash pumpkin, cut off top and set aside. Scoop seed from pumpkin and prick cavity all over with a fork. Rub cavity with salt and dry mustard.

Saute sausage, onion and celery in a large skillet, stirring frequently, until meat is browned and vegetables are tender. Pour off drippings, reserving 1/4 cup. Add melted margarine if you do not have 1/4 cup drippings.

Combine in a large bowl the sausage mixture, drippings, stuffing, poultry seasoning, pepper and the chopped apple. In a smaller bowl, beat eggs and chicken broth; pour over sausage mixture and stir gently to mix. Spoon stuffing mixture into pumpkin; replace top.

Place pumpkin in shallow roasting pan; add 1 cup water to pan. Bake at 350 degrees for 1 1/2 hours or until pumpkin is fork-tender. Add more water during baking if necessary. Cut into wedges to serve or scoop out of pumpkin. Serves 6-8.

Jo and Jan say, "This will really add that touch of tradition to your Holiday table. It is truly an incredible edible."

HERBED CHERRY TOMATOES

6 tablespoons butter or margarine
2 pints cherry tomatoes, cleaned and stems removed
1 tablespoon chopped fresh chives
1 tablespoon chopped fresh parsley
Salt and freshly ground pepper

Melt butter in large skillet over medium heat. Add tomatoes and saute about 3 minutes. Add herbs and blend well. Season with salt and pepper. Serves 8.

SCALLOPED TOMATOES

4 large tomatoes, cut into chunks
1 3/4 cups croutons
1 tablespoon onion, minced
1/4 cup margarine, melted
1/2 cup mozzarella cheese, cubed
1/2 cup Cheddar cheese, cubed
1/4 teaspoon salt
1/4 teaspoon pepper
1/4 teaspoon parsley

Combine all ingredients in a 2-quart baking dish. Bake, uncovered in preheated 375-degree oven for 20 minutes. Serves 4.

TOMATO CASSEROLE

6 tomatoes, sliced 1/2-inch thick
6 shallots, chopped
1/4 cup olive oil
1/2 cup olives, chopped
1 teaspoon parsley
1 teaspoon tarragon, crumbled
1 teaspoon chervil, crumbled
1/2 cup butter, melted
1/4 cup Parmesan cheese
1/2 cup bread crumbs, coarse

Heat olive oil in small skillet and saute shallots until golden brown. Place shallots, drippings, tomatoes, olives and herbs into a greased 2-quart casserole. Season with salt and pepper; mix gently. Sprinkle combined bread crumbs and Parmesan cheese with melted butter over tomatoes. Bake in preheated 325-degree oven for 20-25 minutes. Serves 2-4.

TOMATOES FLORENTINE

2 packages (10-ounce size) chopped spinach
2 cups seasoned bread crumbs
6 chopped green onions
6 eggs, slightly beaten
3/4 cup butter, melted
1/4 cup Parmesan cheese
1/4 teaspoon Worcestershire sauce
1/2 teaspoon garlic salt
1 teaspoon salt
1/2 teaspoon black pepper
1 teaspoon thyme
1/4 teaspoon Tabasco sauce
12 thick slices tomato

Cook spinach according to package directions; drain. Add rest of ingredients except sliced tomatoes; mix well. Place sliced tomatoes in buttered baking dish and mound spinach mixture on top. Bake in preheated 350-degree oven for 15 minutes or until warm throughout. Freeze what is left in muffin cups so you can use only as many as needed. Serves 12.

CHEESE - TOPPED ZUCCHINI - TOMATO CASSEROLE

4 zucchini, sliced
1 small onion, chopped
2 tablespoons olive oil
1 can (16-ounce) stewed tomatoes
1 can (8-ounce) tomato sauce
1 tablespoon dried Italian herbs, crushed
4 ounces Cheddar cheese, grated
4 ounces Monterey Jack cheese, grated

Cook zucchini and onion just until tender crisp in hot oil. Add undrained tomatoes, tomato sauce and herbs. Bring to a boil, reduce heat and simmer, uncovered for 5 minutes. Reserve 1/4 of each of the cheeses and set aside. Stir the remaining cheese into hot mixture and transfer to a 1 1/2-quart casserole. Bake in preheated 350-degree oven for 10 minutes or until heated through. Sprinkle reserved cheese on top. Let stand until cheese melts. Serves 8.

STUFFED TOMATOES

6 medium tomatoes
1 1/2 cups fresh mushrooms, chopped
2 tablespoons butter
1/2 cup sour cream
2 egg yolks, beaten
1/4 cup bread crumbs
1 teaspoon salt
Dash of pepper
1/4 teaspoon dried basil
1 tablespoon butter
3 tablespoons bread crumbs

Cut stem ends of tomatoes. Scoop out pulp and drain shells. Chop pulp; you will have about 1 cup. Melt butter and saute mushrooms. Combine sour cream and egg yolks and add to pulp; add mushrooms. Stir in crumbs and seasonings and cook until thickened. Place tomatoes in baking dish and spoon in mixture.

Combine butter and bread crumbs and sprinkle as topping on tomatoes. Bake in preheated 375-degree oven for 25 minutes. Serves 6.

Jo and Jan say, "This is a dish that can be made ahead and chilled. A seasoned, cooked rice can be substituted for the crumb mixture."

TOMATOES A LA PROVENCAL

6 small tomatoes (1 1/2-2 inches in diameter)
   or 3 large tomatoes (3-4 inches in diameter -
   large preferred)
1 cup coarse dry white bread crumbs
2 tablespoons dried basil
1/2 cup chopped fresh parsley
2 tablespoons green onion tops, chopped
1/2 teaspoon salt
1/4 teaspoon pepper
1/3 cup olive oil

Cut tomatoes in half if using large ones. If using small, cut slice off top. Cut a small slice off bottoms so they will sit flat in pan. Arrange tomatoes cut-side-up in a lightly oiled baking dish.

Sprinkle each half with a few drops of oil; salt and pepper.

In mixing bowl, stir together the crumbs, parsley, onion tops, basil, salt, pepper and enough oil to moisten but still leave it crumbly. Top each tomato half with about 2 tablespoons of crumb mixture (for large tomatoes), patting it in and letting it mound up a little in the middle. Sprinkle a few drops of oil over each half. Bake in preheated 350-degree oven for 20 to 30 minutes or until they are hot but not limp. Serves 6.

TIP

• Make serving cups from zucchini. Trim ends from zucchini, peel strips lengthwise to make stripes then cut into 1 1/2-inch lengths. Hollow out one end, using a melon baller, leaving sides about 1/4-inch thick and bottom about 1/2-inch.

Bring salted water to a boil and cook cups about 4 minutes, until tender-crisp. Remove from water immediately, rinse with cold water and drain. Brush inside and out with melted butter and sprinkle with salt.

Jo and Jan say, "These are so colorful and unique. We fill them with tiny peas, miniature carrot rounds, the balls of zucchini removed when preparing the cups, or tiny broccoli or cauliflower florets. They are pretty with pimentoed corn too."

❖❖

Pastabilities

FETTUCINI AND SPINACH

1 package (8-ounce) fettucini noodles,
  cooked according to package
1 package (10-ounce) chopped spinach,
  thawed and drained
1 clove garlic, finely chopped or pressed
1/4 cup vegetable oil
1 teaspoon instant chicken-flavor bouillon
1/2 cup water
1/2 teaspoon basil
1 cup cottage cheese
1/4 teaspoon salt
1/4 cup Parmesan cheese, grated
1 tablespoon parsley, chopped

In large skillet, cook spinach and garlic in oil for 5 minutes, stirring often. Dissolve bouillon in the water. Add bouillon mixture, basil, cottage cheese and salt to spinach. Stir over low heat until blended. Toss spinach mixture, grated cheese and noodles. Serve immediately. Serves 4-6.

CAROL'S PASTA PRIMIVERA

2 cups broccoli flowerettes
2 cups snow peas, stem and string
1 1/2 cups zucchini, sliced
1 cup baby peas
12 asparagus spears, sliced
10 large mushrooms, sliced
4 large tomatoes
1/4 cup chopped parsley
1/3 cup fresh basil
1 tablespoon minced garlic
1/3 cup pine nuts or walnuts
1 pound spaghetti, cooked al dente and
  drained; keeping warm
1 cup heavy cream or sour cream
1/2 cup Parmesan cheese
1/2 cup butter, melted
Olive oil
Salt and pepper

Blanch first 5 ingredients in boiling water 3-4 minutes. (We cook snow peas first, then the rest separately in this order: zucchini, baby peas, broccoli and lastly asparagus. If blanched alone, each will retain it's distinctive flavor). Immediately after removing from boiling water, plunge the veggies into cold water and set aside.

Brown pine nuts in small amount of olive oil and reserve.

Heat about 2 tablespoons olive oil, add garlic and tomatoes. Cook until tomatoes are as "saucy" as you like. Add parsley, basil, salt and pepper; set aside.

In about 1/4 cup of olive oil, saute mushrooms. Add reserved vegetables and simmer until hot.

Add butter, cream, cheese, salt and pepper to pasta; toss gently. Arrange on platter, top with veggies, then tomato mixture. Sprinkle with pine nuts. Toss and serve. Serves 6-8.

Carol says, "I've found I really like using a can of crushed tomatoes in heavy puree sauce mixed with a small carton of fresh pesto in place of the cooked tomato sauce. It is fast and delicious."

SPAGHETTI PASTERE

1 pound spaghetti, cooked al dente and
  drained
12 eggs, beaten
1/4 cup coarsely ground black pepper
1 pound grated Italian cheese (Parmesan and
  Romano mixed)
1/2 pound butter or margarine

Add pepper and cheese to the beaten eggs, add butter and mix well. Add to drained spaghetti, toss to cover completely. Pour into lightly greased baking dish, bake at 325 degrees until brown and crisp. Serves 4-6.

❖❖

PASTA WITH PESTO SAUCE

2 cups firmly packed fresh basil leaves
3/4 cup freshly grated Parmesan cheese
1/4 cup pine nuts
4 garlic cloves
1/2 cup olive oil
1 pound pasta, freshly cooked and drained

Combine basil, cheese, pine nuts and garlic in processor or blender and puree. Keeping machine running, gradually add oil in a slow steady stream until mixture is consistency of a thick mayonnaise. Combine sauce with pasta and toss well. Serve immediately. Serves 4.

VEGETABLE PASTA

2 teaspoons Bertolli olive oil
2 garlic cloves, minced
3 medium zucchini, coarsely shredded
3 medium carrots, coarsely shredded
1 green pepper, cut into strips
1/4 cup chicken broth
1 package (8-ounce) spaghetti, cooked al dente and drained
1 tablespoon parsley
1/2 tablespoon basil
3 tablespoons Parmesan cheese

Heat oil in a saute pan; add garlic cloves and stir fry for 2 minutes. Add vegetables and stir constantly until veggies are done to a crisp look. Add drained hot pasta to vegetables and gently toss. Place pasta mixture on a platter or 4 individual plates, sprinkle Parmesan cheese over the top. Serves 4.

Hooray the Souffle - 1

SPINACH SOUFFLE

2 tablespoons Parmesan cheese (for dish)
2 tablespoons butter or margarine
2-3 shallots, minced
3 tablespoons flour
1 1/4 cups chicken broth
4 egg yolks, beaten
1 package (10-ounce) frozen chopped spinach
2 tablespoons grated Parmesan cheese
1/8 teaspoon nutmeg
6 egg whites
1/4 teaspoon salt
1/8 teaspoon cream of tartar

Prepare a 1 1/2-quart souffle dish (See index How To Prepare A Souffle Dish); sprinkle buttered dish with 2 tablespoons Parmesan cheese. Tap out excess.

Melt butter, add shallots and cook about 3 minutes; add flour and cook for 1 minute over low heat. Whisk in chicken broth to form a smooth sauce. Remove from heat and stir in the egg yolks.

Cook spinach according to package directions. Press all water from spinach and puree it in blender or food processor, adding 1/2 cup of sauce mixture. Combine the spinach, Parmesan cheese and nutmeg with the sauce.

Combine egg white, salt and cream of tartar in a bowl and beat to soft peaks. Fold egg whites into spinach mixture. Transfer to the prepared souffle dish and bake in a preheated 375-degree oven for 25-30 minutes. Serves 4.

❖❖❖

FRENCH CHEESE SOUFFLE

**3/4 cup coarsely grated Swiss cheese or a
mixture of Swiss and Parmesan**
3 tablespoons butter
3 tablespoons flour
1 cup heated milk
1/2 teaspoon salt
Freshly ground black pepper
Pinch of Cayenne pepper
1 teaspoon Dijon style mustard
1/8 teaspoon mace
4 egg yolks, room temperature
5-6 egg whites, room temperature
Pinch of salt
1/8 teaspoon cream of tartar

Prepare a 1-quart souffle dish (See index How To Prepare A Souffle Dish); coating dish with Parmesan cheese instead of flour. Chill dish in refrigerator.

Melt butter in saucepan; add flour and stir until mixture foams but do not let it brown. Remove from heat, stir in hot milk and beat well with a whisk. Beat in seasonings; return to heat and cook 1 minute, stirring constantly until thick. Remove from heat; add egg yolks, one at a time, beating vigorously after each addition. Beat egg whites until light and foamy; add salt and cream of tartar. Beat until stiff; fold in 1/3 of whites into egg yolk mixture; Stir in all but 1 tablespoon cheese, then fold in remaining whites. Pour into chilled mold, smooth the top, sprinkle with remaining cheese. Place in preheated 400-degree oven; turn back heat to 375 degrees and bake 25-35 minutes depending on your desire for creamy or firm texture. The souffle should rise 2-3 inches above the dish and be brown on top and should jiggle slightly when you move the dish. Serves 4.

Jo and Jan say, "If you desire, you can add 1/2 cup of chopped fresh herbs to the souffle mixture."

ANN'S MUSHROOM SOUFFLE

2 pounds mushroom caps
1 stick butter or margarine, melted
4 tablespoons flour
1 cup half-and-half
3 eggs, separated
White pepper

Chop mushrooms and saute in 4 tablespoons melted butter for 5 minutes. Drain and reserve the juice. You should have about 1 cup juice and 2 1/4 to 2 1/2 cups sauteed mushrooms.

Combine 4 tablespoons butter and flour, 1 cup of cream and 1 cup mushroom juice. Cook until thick. You will have two cups of sauce, but only need 1 cup for the recipe. Use the remaining to make a delicious mushroom soup.

Cool sauce and add 1 cup to sauteed mushrooms. Beat egg yolks and add to mushroom mixture. Salt and pepper to taste. Beat egg whites until stiff and fold into mushroom mixture. Taste again for seasoning. Spoon mixture into a buttered souffle dish and set in a pan of water in a preheated 350-degree oven. Bake for 40 minutes or until set. Serves 4-6.

Jo and Jan say, "This deserves a party."

BROCCOLI - CHEDDAR SOUFFLE

6 tablespoons butter or margarine
**3 packages (10-ounce size) frozen chopped
broccoli**
1/2 cup onion, finely chopped
6 large eggs
1 cup grated Cheddar cheese
1 cup heavy cream
1 teaspoon salt
1/2 teaspoon black pepper, freshly ground

Melt butter in a large skillet over medium heat. Add broccoli and onion and saute until onion is clear, about 5 minutes; remove from heat. Beat eggs well in a large bowl. Beat in cheese and cream; blend well. Stir in broccoli, onion, salt and pepper. Pour mixture into a greased 2-quart baking dish and set dish in a larger pan filled with 1 inch of hot water. Bake in preheated 350-degree oven for 45 minutes or until a wooden pick inserted in center comes out clean. Let stand 30 minutes before serving. Serves 6-8.

❖❖❖

SWEET POTATO SOUFFLE

2 cups mashed sweet potatoes
1 cup hot milk
1/2 teaspoon salt
2 teaspoons sugar
3 tablespoons butter
2 eggs, separated
1/2 cup raisins
1 teaspoon nutmeg
1/2 cup chopped pecans
Marshmallows

Mash potatoes; scald the milk and dissolve sugar and salt in it; add butter, and stir until melted. Add milk mixture to potatoes and beat until light and fluffy. Beat egg yolks and add to the potatoes; then add nutmeg, raisins and nuts. Beat egg whites until stiff, fold slightly into the potatoes and pour into a buttered casserole. Arrange marshmallows 1/2-inch apart on top. Bake in preheated 350-degree oven until the souffle is set and marshmallows are lightly toasted. Serve while hot. Serves 6-8.

SQUASH SOUFFLE

3 cooked and mashed winter squash
4 tablespoons butter or margarine
2 tablespoons brown sugar, well packed
1/2 teaspoon salt
1/2 teaspoon grated orange peel
1/8 teaspoon ground nutmeg
Dash pepper
4 egg yolks
4 egg whites

Prepare a 1 1/2-quart souffle dish (See index How To Prepare A Souffle Dish). In a large mixer bowl combine squash, butter, brown sugar, salt, orange peel, nutmeg and pepper. Beat until fluffy; add egg yolks, beat well. Beat egg whites until stiff peaks form; carefully fold into squash mixture. Turn into prepared souffle dish. Bake in preheated 350-degree oven for 55-60 minutes. Serves 8-10.

CREAMY PARSLEY CUSTARD

6 cups fresh parsley
2 eggs, beaten
1 cup milk
1/8 teaspoon nutmeg
1/2 cup Monterey Jack cheese, shredded

Microwave parsley and 2 tablespoons water, covered, at 80% for 8 minutes or until tender; drain well. Combine all ingredients and pour into 4 individual cups. Set cups in l-inch hot water bath in baking dish and bake in preheated 350-degree oven for 35 to 40 minutes. Serves 4.

YORKSHIRE PUDDING

1/4 cup beef rib roast pan drippings
4 eggs
2 cups milk
2 cups flour
1 teaspoon salt

Have milk and eggs at room temperature. Beat eggs until fluffy; add milk and beat in flour and salt until light and smooth, about 2 minutes. Cover batter and place in refrigerator until ready to use. Pour drippings from pan into a 9 x 13-inch baking dish and place in a preheated 400-degree oven. Quickly beat pudding again until large bubbles appear and pour immediately over hot drippings. Bake for 20 minutes in preheated 400-degree oven; reduce heat to 350 and bake another 20 minutes or until pudding is golden. Cut into squares and serve immediately with rib roast. Serves 12.

Side Effects

CLARIFIED BUTTER

Clarified butter is melted butter with the sediment removed. Cut unsalted butter into 1-inch pieces and melt in a saucepan over low heat. Remove from heat and let stand for 3 minutes allowing the milk solids to settle to the bottom. Skim the butterfat from the top and strain the clear yellow liquid into a container, leaving the milky solids in the bottom of the pan. Cover the container and refrigerate for 2 to 3 weeks or it may be frozen.

The milky residue left in the pan may be used as an enrichment to soups or sauces.

When clarified, butter loses about one fourth of its original volume.

BROWN BUTTER

1 stick butter
1 tablespoon fresh lemon juice
1/4 teaspoon freshly ground white pepper

Melt butter in small saucepan. Stir over very low heat until it becomes quite dark but not burned. It will take about 5 minutes. Add lemon juice and pepper; mix well and chill until ready to use. Serve with fish or eggs.

DILL BUTTER

2 sticks unsalted butter, softened
1/4 cup minced fresh dill
1 teaspoon minced dill seed
3 tablespoons fresh lemon juice
1/2 teaspoon white pepper

Combine all ingredients and process in blender or food processor until completely mixed. Shape into a roll and wrap in plastic. Refrigerate or freeze until firm. Excellent with chicken, seafood, veal or vegetables. The next time you roast chicken breast, place a pat under the skin before roasting; gives a wonderful flavor!

FINES HERBES BUTTER

2 sticks butter, softened
2 tablespoons minced fresh tarragon
2 tablespoons minced fresh chives
2 tablespoons minced fresh parsley
1/2 teaspoon white pepper

Combine all ingredients until well mixed. Transfer to plastic wrap and form into a cylinder. Wrap tightly and store in refrigerator or freeze. This is excellent with vegetables, meats and fish.

LEMON - PARSLEY BUTTER

1 stick butter
1 tablespoon fresh lemon juice
3 tablespoons fresh minced parsley
Salt
Freshly ground black pepper
Sprig of parsley (garnish)

Cream butter with electric mixer. Beat in lemon juice drop by drop until well blended. Mix in parsley, salt and pepper to taste. Pack into container and seal well or roll in cylinder shape; wrap in plastic wrap and refrigerate. Serve hot or cold over asparagus, broccoli, Brussels sprouts, fish, steak or chops. Makes about 3/4 cup.

❖❖

ONION - GARLIC BUTTER

2 medium garlic cloves
1/4 medium onion
1 teaspoon lemon juice
1 stick softened butter
1/4 teaspoon ground black pepper

Mince garlic and onion in blender or food processor. Add rest of ingredients and process until thoroughly mixed. Pack into a crock or transfer to plastic wrap; roll in a cylinder and wrap tightly. Store in refrigerator or freeze until ready to use. May be served chilled or at room temperature. This butter is excellent mixed with pan juices from sauteed meats or roasts. We also like to use it as a pasta sauce. Makes 1/2 cup.

LEMON - CHIVE BUTTER

2 sticks butter, softened
1/2 cup fresh chives, chopped
2 tablespoons lemon juice
Freshly ground pepper

Combine ingredients and mix thoroughly. Transfer to a sheet of plastic wrap and form into a cylinder shape. Seal well and refrigerate or freeze until ready to serve. Add a slice or two to a little wine and season sauteed dishes for a perfect flavor. Delicious on vegetables, poultry or fish. Makes 1 cup.

LEMON - MINT BUTTER

2 sticks butter or margarine, softened
1 teaspoon grated lemon peel
2 tablespoons fresh mint leaves, chopped

Combine all ingredients and beat until smooth. Transfer to plastic wrap and form into a cylinder. Wrap tightly and store in refrigerator or freeze. Makes about 1 1/4 cups.

SHALLOT BUTTER

6 shallots, minced
1 garlic clove, minced
1/4 cup dry white wine
2 sticks butter, softened
2 tablespoons minced fresh parsley
1/2 teaspoon freshly ground white pepper

Combine shallots, garlic and white wine in a small saucepan. Boil over high heat until liquid is reduced to 1 tablespoon. Remove from heat and allow to cool. Add cooled liquid to rest of ingredients and mix well. Turn mixture onto plastic wrap; smooth into a cylinder about 1 1/2 inches in diameter. Roll up in the plastic and seal. Store in refrigerator or freezer. At serving time combine butter with pan juices and a little wine. Excellent with fish, meats, vegetables and shellfish. Can be frozen up to 2 months.

PIMENTO - CHIVE BUTTER

2 sticks butter, softened
2 tablespoons finely chopped pimiento
1 tablespoon chopped fresh chives
1 teaspoon Worcestershire sauce
1 teaspoon minced garlic

Beat butter until creamy; gently stir in remaining ingredients. This butter can be refrigerated up to 5 days. Remove 1 hour before serving. This is delicious as a spread for bread. Makes 1 cup.

Side Effects

MAITRE D' HOTEL BUTTER

1 stick butter
1 tablespoon chopped parsley
1 teaspoon Worcestershire sauce or fresh
  lemon juice
Salt and freshly ground white pepper, to taste

Beat all ingredients together; shape into a log and wrap in plastic wrap. Chill until ready to use.

TARRAGON BUTTER

2 green onions
2 tablespoons chopped fresh parsley
4 teaspoons tarragon vinegar
1/2 teaspoon dried tarragon, crumbled
1/2 teaspoon freshly ground pepper
1 stick butter

Combine shallots, parsley, vinegar, tarragon and pepper in blender or food processor. Add butter and blend until thoroughly mixed. Transfer to plastic wrap and form into a cylinder. Refrigerate or freeze until firm. Slice butter into rounds and place on top of food. This butter is excellent on grilled steaks.

FRESH ROSEMARY BUTTER

1/4 medium onion
2 tablespoons minced fresh rosemary leaves
1/4 teaspoon ground black pepper
1 teaspoon lemon juice
Tabasco sauce, to taste
1 stick softened butter

Mince onion in food processor or blender. Add rest of ingredients and blend until thoroughly mixed, scraping sides of container. Butter may be used right away or form into a log l-inch thick and wrap in plastic. Refrigerate up to three days or freeze up to three months. This butter is delicious with lamb or veal; vegetables, pasta sauces and soups. Makes 1/2 cup.

CAROL'S BOURSIN ROLL

1 package (8-ounce) cream cheese, softened
1 clove garlic, minced
1 tablespoon fresh parsley, minced
1/2 teaspoon salt
1/4 teaspoon freshly ground black pepper

Mix all ingredients and form into roll or mold and chill or freeze. Makes 1 cup.

CHUTNEY BUTTER

1 medium shallot, peeled
1 1/2 tablespoon mango chutney
1 stick softened butter
1/4 teaspoon black pepper

Mince shallot; add chutney, butter, pepper and process in food processor or blender until thoroughly mixed, scraping sides of container so all ingredients are incorporated. Form into a roll wrap in plastic. Refrigerate up to 3 days or freeze up to 3 months. This is wonderful with pork, chicken; as a spread for sandwiches, such as turkey. Try it with squash for a unique flavor. Makes 1/2 cup.

◆◆

ZIPPY BUTTER

1/4 teaspoon Tabasco sauce
1 tablespoon Worcestershire sauce
1 stick butter

Combine ingredients and form into roll; wrap in plastic and chill or freeze.

ROQUEFORT BUTTER

2 ounces Roquefort cheese
1 stick butter

Combine cheese and butter and form into roll; wrap in plastic and chill or freeze.

WHITE SAUCE FORMULAS

White Sauce	Liquid	Thickening Material	Butter
No. 1 - Thin	1 cup milk	1 tablespoon flour	1 tablespoon
No. 2 - Medium	1 cup milk	2 tablespoons flour	1 1/2 tablespoons
No. 3 - Medium-Thick	1 cup milk	3 tablespoons flour	2 tablespoons
No. 4 - Thick	1 cup milk	4 tablespoons flour	2 1/2 tablespoons

Melt butter, add flour and stir to blend. Continue stirring over heat for 2 minutes to blend flavors. Add salt, pepper and any other seasonings you desire. Some prefer adding 1/2 teaspoon of paprika or dry mustard. Remove from heat and stir in the milk. When completely blended, return to heat and cook until the desired consistency. Makes 1 cup plus.

SAUCE FOR VEGETABLE LASAGNA

3/4 cup butter or margarine
8 tablespoons flour
2 tablespoons grated onion
6 cups milk, scalded
1/2 teaspoon salt
Freshly ground pepper
1/2 pound Gorgonzola cheese, crumbled

Melt butter in heavy saucepan. Add flour and stir until bubbly. Add onion and cook for about 5 minutes. Gradually whisk in hot milk; increase heat to medium and boil for 2 minutes stirring constantly. Add salt and pepper. Remove from heat and cool 15 minutes. Stir in cheese; cover surface with plastic wrap and cool to room temperature. Refrigerate if made ahead of serving day. Makes about 6 cups.

❖❖

LEMON BUTTER SAUCE

1/3 cup dry vermouth
2 tablespoons fresh lemon juice
1 stick unsalted butter, chilled and cup into
   1/2-inch pieces
1/8 teaspoon freshly grated nutmeg
Salt and freshly ground white pepper

Combine vermouth and lemon juice in a small sauce pan and cook over medium heat until reduced to 2 tablespoons. Add 2 tablespoons butter and whisk until blended. Place over low heat and whisk in remaining butter, a piece at a time. If sauce begins to separate, remove from heat and quickly whisk in 2 pieces of butter. When all butter has been added, stir in nutmeg and season with salt and pepper to taste. Makes about 2/3 cup.

Jo and Jan say, "This sauce can be prepared up to 2 hours ahead of serving time. Keep it warm on a rack or hot water, whisking frequently or in a thermos. It is a delicious sauce for vegetables such as broccoli, cauliflower, green peas or lima beans."

MORNAY SAUCE

1/4 cup butter, softened
1 teaspoon salt
4 tablespoons flour
1/4 teaspoon white pepper
1/4 teaspoon dry mustard
2 cups hot milk
4 tablespoons diced Swiss cheese
4 tablespoons Parmesan cheese

Place all ingredients into a blender, cover and blend at low speed until ingredients are thoroughly mixed. Turn to high speed for 30 seconds. Pour into top of double boiler and cook over simmering water for 15 minutes, stirring occasionally. Makes 2 1/2 cups.

MILLIE'S MUSTARD SAUCE

1 cup butter
2 cups plus 4 tablespoons sugar
4 eggs, well beaten
1 can tomato soup
1 cup apple cider vinegar
1 cup prepared mustard

Combine all ingredients in top of a double boiler and cook until thick. Cool and store in jars. Makes 1 quart.

Jan says, "This is one of the best mustard sauces I have ever eaten. It is a great gift giver."

JEANNE'S AVGOLEMONO SAUCE

2 tablespoons butter or margarine
3 tablespoons flour
3/4 teaspoon salt
1 can (13 1/4-ounce) chicken broth
3 tablespoons lemon juice
4 egg yolks
1 tablespoon chopped parsley

Melt butter in top of double boiler; remove from heat and stir in flour and salt, whisking until smooth. Gradually stir in broth and lemon juice.

Stirring constantly, cook over low heat until mixture comes to a boil. Remove from heat and place over hot but not boiling water. In a small bowl, beat egg yolks slightly and add a small amount of the hot mixture, slowly add back to rest of hot mixture, stirring constantly. Cook over hot water, stirring constantly, until thickened. Remove from heat and stir in parsley. Makes about 2 cups.

◆◆

Prime Thyme • Entrees

Prime Thyme is *THE* time to dazzle family and friends with our abundance of delicious selections of meat, poultry and seafood.

Some special delights include Fran's Sticky Chicken, Lemon Cream Chicken Breasts, Cajun Shrimp, Catfish Parmesan, Baked Stripped Sea Bass, Beef - Asparagus Stir-Fry and Herbed Lemon Veal.

This section also includes accompanying sauces for various dishes which will be a welcome addition to your meal preparation *AND* presentation.

◆◆

WALNUT CHICKEN

5 tablespoons Puritan oil
5 teaspoons soy sauce
3 teaspoons cornstarch
2 whole boneless chicken breasts, skinned
   and cut into 1-inch pieces
3/4 cup chicken broth
1/2 teaspoon ground ginger
1/2 teaspoon dried red pepper
1 medium onion, cut into 1-inch pieces
1/2 cup celery, cut into 1-inch pieces
1 garlic clove, minced
1/2 pound broccoli, cut into 1-inch pieces
1 green pepper, cut into 1-inch pieces
3/4 cup chopped walnuts
Hot cooked rice

Mix 1 tablespoon oil, 2 teaspoons soy sauce, and 1 teaspoon cornstarch in a small bowl. Stir in chicken to coat. Cover and refrigerate 30 minutes. Mix chicken broth, ginger, remaining soy sauce and cornstarch; set aside.

Heat remaining oil in a large skillet. Stir-fry refrigerated chicken mixture and dried red pepper over medium heat until chicken is no longer pink. Remove chicken from skillet; stir-fry onion, celery, garlic and pepper in skillet until onion is tender. Add broccoli, stir-fry until tender. Add chicken and broth. Cook, stirring until thickened; stir in walnuts. Serves 4.

Jan says, "You may serve this over the rice or on the side. It's delish."

GAILE'S GOURMET CHICKEN

1/2 cup butter
1/2 cup vegetable oil
6 whole chicken breasts, skinned and boned
1 1/2 cups carrot, chopped
2 medium onions, quartered
2 cups cooking sauterne
2 teaspoons garlic salt
1 teaspoon celery salt
1/2 teaspoon thyme
1/2 teaspoon cayenne
2 cups milk
1/4 cup butter, softened
1/4 cup flour
Cooked rice (6 servings)
1/2 cup slivered almonds (garnish)
Fresh parsley (garnish)

Heat half the butter and half the oil in a skillet. Dry chicken to prevent spattering, then fry until golden brown. Add more butter and oil if necessary while frying. When all the chicken is browned, put carrots, onion, wine and seasonings in a blender; cover and process on Chop only until vegetables are finely chopped.

Return all chicken to skillet and pour blended mixture over. Cover and simmer about 30 minutes. Remove chicken and keep hot in oven while preparing sauce. Pour vegetables and skillet juices, milk, butter and flour into blender. Cover and process on Whip until blended. Pour into skillet and cook over medium heat until thickened, stirring constantly. Serve chicken on a bed of rice. Spoon some sauce on chicken and garnish with almonds and parsley. Serve remaining sauce in a side dish. Serves 6.

FRAN'S STICKY CHICKEN

1/2 cup vinegar
1/2 cup sugar
1/2 cup soy sauce
4 1/4 pounds chicken pieces
3 garlic cloves, minced
1 tablespoon minced fresh ginger or 1/2 to
   1 teaspoon powdered, as taste dictates.

Combine vinegar, sugar and soy sauce in a shallow baking dish. Arrange chicken in a casserole in a single layer and turn to coat with the mixture. Cover and refrigerate overnight.

Transfer chicken and marinade to a heavy skillet. Add garlic and ginger; bring to a boil over

medium-high heat; cover and simmer for 15 minutes, turning occasionally. Uncover and continue simmering until chicken is tender; about 15 minutes. To test for doneness, prick with a fork; juices should run clear.

Transfer chicken to a heated platter, cover with foil and keep warm in a low oven. Turn up heat on sauce and cook until it is reduced and has carmelized; about 25 minutes. Note: Watch carefully so it does not burn. Return warmed chicken to sauce and coat well. Serves 4-6.

Jo and Jan say, "This is delicious! We serve it garnished with watercress or fresh parsley and cherry tomatoes. It is a beautiful presentation."

FORTY CLOVES OF GARLIC CHICKEN

2 1/2 to 3 pounds chicken pieces
40 UNPEELED garlic cloves
1/2 cup dry white wine
1 teaspoon mixed herbs

Arrange UNPEELED garlic cloves around pieces of chicken in roasting pan. Sprinkle with salt and pepper. Bake for 20 minutes in a preheated 350-degree oven then pour wine over chicken pieces and continue baking; basting every 15 minutes with pan juices for another 40 minutes or until chicken is tender.

Remove chicken to a heated platter, reserving pan juices. Surround with peeled garlic cloves or use the cloves in the sauce. The garlic mellows with cooking and may be eaten with ease. The centers pop right out of the peelings enabling you to enjoy.

SAUCE:
1/2 cup chicken stock
1/2 cup whipping cream
Reserved cloves of garlic, popped from peelings
Salt and freshly ground pepper

Skim fat from pan juices, place pan over high heat; add cream and stock. Boil for 2 to 3 minutes, stirring occasionally. Puree peeled garlic cloves in blender and stir into sauce; cook 1 more minute. Season with salt and pepper. Serves 4.

KING RANCH CHICKEN CASSEROLE

3-4 pounds chicken pieces
1 large onion, chopped
2 ribs celery, chopped
2 carrots, cut in pieces
1 bay leaf
Handful of parsley sprigs
2 teaspoons dried thyme
Salt and pepper
12 black peppercorns
1 package (12-ounce) Doritos
1 cup chicken stock
1 large onion, chopped
1 large green pepper, chopped
8 ounces Cheddar cheese, grated
1 can (10 3/4-ounce) cream of mushroom soup
1 can (10 3/4-ounce) cream of chicken soup
1 can (10-ounce) Rotel tomatoes with green chiles
1 teaspoon chili powder
1/2 teaspoon garlic powder
1/2 teaspoon salt
1/2 teaspoon pepper

Boil chicken with first 8 ingredients until tender. Water should cover solids by 2 inches. Cool the stock then strain it over a bowl, pressing on vegetables and chicken parts with a spoon to extract flavors. Cover and refrigerate stock overnight, if possible, and skim any fat before using.

Remove chicken from the bone and cut into bite-size pieces. Heat the stock and soak the chips until well wilted. Layer chips, cubed chicken, onion, green pepper and half of cheese in a 9 x 13-inch casserole. Heat the soups, tomatoes and seasonings. Pour sauce over layered ingredients in casserole and top with rest of cheese. Bake, uncovered, in preheated 350-degree oven for 30 minutes. If mixture seems a little dry, add a little more of the chicken stock. Serves 8-10.

Jo and Jan say, "This casserole freezes well. It may be made ahead and refrigerated until baking time. We feel the secret is a well-seasoned stock."

SESAME FRIED CHICKEN

2 chickens (3-pounds each) quartered
4 tablespoons sesame seeds
1 1/4 cups flour
1 teaspoon poultry seasoning
2/3 cup evaporated milk
1/2 teaspoon paprika
1 1/2 teaspoons salt
Ground black pepper
1/2 cup butter
1/2 cup oil

Combine sesame seeds, flour, poultry seasoning, paprika, salt and pepper. Dip chicken quarters into milk, then roll them in the sesame seed mixture. Saute chicken in combined butter and oil for 30 minutes or until golden brown and tender, turning frequently. Serves 6-8.

LEMON CREAM CHICKEN BREASTS

1 cup heavy cream
3 tablespoons fresh lemon juice
5 tablespoons butter
1/2 pound mushrooms, stemmed and sliced
3 whole chicken breasts, skinned, boned
   and halved
Salt
Freshly ground white pepper
Flour
1 tablespoon vegetable oil
1 medium onion, halved
1 cup chicken broth
2 to 3 tablespoons minced fresh parsley

Combine cream and lemon juice; reserve. Heat 3 tablespoons butter in a large skillet over medium-high heat. Saute mushrooms in butter, until nicely browned. Remove from skillet and reserve.

Sprinkle chicken breasts with salt and pepper; lightly dredge in flour and shake off excess. Add remaining 2 tablespoons butter and the oil to the skillet and heat until hot. Add halves of onion turned cut side down. Brown chicken over medium heat, for about 5 minutes per side. Remove chicken from skillet; remove and discard all but 1 tablespoon of the fat.

Add broth to skillet; heat to a boil and cook over high heat until reduced to 1/3 cup. Remove and discard onion; reduce heat to medium and add reserved lemon-cream mixture. Cook, stirring frequently until sauce is reduced to 1 1/4 cups. Return mushrooms and chicken to skillet; simmer, spooning sauce over chicken until chicken is heated through and no longer pink in center, 4 to 5 minutes. Garnish with fresh parsley. Serves 6.

SWEET - SOUR CHICKEN

1 large green pepper, cut into 1-inch squares
2 cups fresh carrots, sliced
1 1/2 cups cooked chicken, cut up
1 egg slightly beaten
1/4 cup cornstarch
1/2 teaspoon garlic powder
2 tablespoons cooking oil
1 can (13 1/2-ounce) pineapple chunks, drained,
   reserving syrup
1/3 cup cider vinegar
1/2 cup sugar
1/4 cup water
2 tablespoons cornstarch
2 teaspoons soy sauce
1/4 teaspoon ginger
1 can water chestnuts, sliced
4 cups cooked rice

Steam green pepper and carrots until just barely crunchy and set aside. Toss chicken pieces in egg until well coated. Combine cornstarch and garlic powder; sprinkle over chicken and toss until coated. Pour shortening into a medium skillet; add chicken and cook over medium heat until brown. Remove chicken and set aside. Add water to reserved syrup to measure 1 cup. Stir liquid, vinegar and sugar into skillet. Heat to a boil, stirring constantly. Reduce heat and simmer for about 2 minutes. Blend water and cornstarch; stir into skillet. Cook, stirring constantly until mixture thickens and boils. Cook and stir 1 minute. Stir in pineapple chunks, soy sauce, ginger, carrots, green pepper, water chestnuts and chicken. Heat thoroughly. Serve over hot rice. Serves 4-6.

CORNISH HENS IN COGNAC SAUCE

2 Cornish hens, split in half
Salt
Freshly ground pepper
1/2 stick butter (1/4 cup)
1 tablespoon oil
1/2 pound fresh mushrooms, sliced
1/2 teaspoon dried rosemary
Cooked wild or herb rice to serve 4
2 tablespoons Cognac
1/2 cup heavy cream

Season hens with salt and pepper. Melt butter with oil in a large heavy skillet until hot but not smoking.

Add hens and brown well on all sides. Add mushrooms and rosemary. Reduce heat to low, cover and cook until hens are tender, about 20 minutes. Spread rice onto heated platter. Warm Cognac in a small pan over low heat; sprinkle over hens and ignite, shaking pan gently until flame subsides. Set hens over rice. Add cream to skillet; cook gently about 5 minutes, whisking often. Spoon sauce over hens and rice. Serves 4.

COQ AU VIN

1 frying chicken cut in serving pieces
Flour seasoned with salt and pepper
6 bacon slices, diced
4 tablespoons butter
1/4 cup chopped onion
1 clove garlic, crushed
1/3 cup celery, chopped
1 can (3-ounce) sliced mushrooms
1/2 cup burgundy wine
1/2 cup chicken broth
1 bay leaf
1/4 teaspoon dried thyme
1/4 teaspoon salt
1 tablespoon tomato paste
1 can small onions, drained and rinsed
8 small new potatoes

Saute bacon until crisp and drain on paper towel. Roll chicken in seasoned flour. Add 2 tablespoons butter to bacon fat in skillet and brown floured chicken on all sides. Transfer chicken to casserole or Dutch oven. In another pan, melt 2 tablespoons butter. Add onion, garlic and celery; saute for a few minutes until onion is transparent. Add mushrooms and their liquid, wine, broth, bay leaf, thyme, salt, fried bacon and tomato paste. Mix well, bring to a boil and simmer 5 minutes. Pour sauce over chicken and arrange onions and potatoes between chicken. Bake, covered, in preheated 375-degree oven for 30-45 minutes or until chicken and potatoes are tender. Serve chicken with sauce poured over it. Serves 4.

CHICKEN OR TURKEY MORNAY ON BROCCOLI

1 package (10-ounce) frozen broccoli
1/4 cup butter or margarine
1/4 cup flour
1 cup poultry broth
1/2 cup heavy cream
1/2 cup dry white wine
Salt and pepper
1/8 teaspoon Worcestershire sauce
2 cups cooked poultry
1/3 cup grated Parmesan cheese

Cook broccoli until barely tender. Drain; arrange in buttered 1 1/2-quart size casserole or individual casseroles if preferred.

In separate saucepan, melt butter and stir in flour. Add broth and cream. Cook until smooth, stirring constantly. Stir in wine, salt and pepper to taste and Worcestershire sauce.

Top broccoli with poultry. Cover with sauce and sprinkle with cheese.

Bake, uncovered, in pre-heated 425-degree oven for 15 minutes. Serves 4.

Jo and Jan say, "You will need to bake this longer if you have prepared it in advance and refrigerated it."

LET'S TALK TURKEY

• Refrigerate turkey leftovers as soon as possible after your meal. Remove all stuffing that may remain and store it in separate container in refrigerator or freezer. Remove all meat from the bird; wrap and refrigerate or freeze. We separate it as to white meat, dark meat, slices or pieces.

• Make stock from the carcass; strain it well and refrigerate or freeze.

• To carve your turkey sever the joint joining the leg and back; remove the leg then sever the joint on the leg which separates the thigh and drumstick. Slice this meat then cut into the white meat parallel to the wing. Slice the breast meat down to the cut you just made.

• Arrange turkey slices on platter, and garnish the entire edge with fresh parsley.

TURKEY A LA KING

1/4 cup butter or margarine
1/4 cup flour
1 1/2 cups milk or part white wine if desired
1/2 cup chicken stock or turkey stock
1 tablespoon dry sherry
1 cup frozen green peas, thawed
1/2 cup artichoke hearts, chopped
4 ounces sauteed fresh mushrooms or well
    drained canned mushrooms
1/2 of 4-ounce jar, diced pimiento
1 1/2 cups cooked turkey, cut in chunks

Melt butter in medium saucepan; blend in flour until smooth. Slowly stir in milk and wine, then broth and sherry. Cook, stirring until thickened, then stir in peas, artichoke hearts, mushrooms, pimiento and turkey. Heat, stirring occasionally. Serves 4.

Jan and Jo say, "Serve this over toast points, biscuits or perhaps you might like to use puff pastry shells (found in the frozen food section of your grocery store.) Garnish with fresh parsley and cherry tomatoes."

BARBARA'S TURKEY CHILI

2 pounds ground turkey
1 large onion, chopped
1 package William's Chili Seasoning
2 cans Mexican-style beans
1 can (15-ounce) tomato sauce
2 tablespoons sugar
2 tablespoons flour
1 teaspoon salt
Pepper, to taste

Brown turkey and chopped onion; add remaining ingredients and simmer. Serves 8 - 10.

Jo says, "This is wonderful! No grease at all; freezes beautifully and you can't tell the difference from beef chili. My mother's art association served it at their Christmas bazaar and it was quite a hit."

CAJUN SHRIMP

6 sticks (3 cups) butter or margarine
1/4 cup fresh lemon juice
1/2 cup freshly ground pepper (Yes, this is
    correct, but if you prefer it not so hot,
    reduce the amount)
5 medium to large garlic cloves, minced
4 bay leaves
1 teaspoon dried rosemary
1 tablespoon Hungarian sweet paprika
1 teaspoon dried basil
1 teaspoon dried oregano
1 teaspoon dried thyme
1 teaspoon poultry seasoning
1 teaspoon freshly grated nutmeg
1 teaspoon salt
1 teaspoon cayenne pepper
6 pounds medium shrimp, unshelled, heads
    removed
1 1/2 cups dry vermouth

Divide and melt butter in 2 large skillets. Combine all remaining ingredients except shrimp and vermouth. Add 1/2 to each skillet and cook 20 minutes, stirring occasionally. Add 3 pounds shrimp to each skillet and cook just until pink. Add 3/4 cup vermouth to each skillet and cook 3 minutes. Remove bay leaves.

Ladle shrimp and sauce into serving bowls. Serve immediately. Serves 8.

Jo says, "Be sure to have some hot French bread to dip into the sauce. It's wonderful! You'll swear you are in Cajun country."

SHRIMP TETRAZZINI

1/2 pound spaghetti, cooked al dente and drained
1 pound cooked, coarsely chopped shrimp
1/2 cup butter
1/2 cup flour
2 cups hot chicken broth
1/2 teaspoon salt
1/4 teaspoon lemon pepper
1/4 teaspoon nutmeg
1/4 cup dry sherry
1/2 cup half-and-half
2 tablespoons butter
1/2 pound mushrooms, sliced
2 tablespoons chopped fresh parsley
1/2 cup Parmesan cheese
1/2 cup bread crumbs

Melt 1/2 cup butter; blend in flour and cook for a few minutes but do not let it brown. Gradually add broth and stir until smooth. Add salt, lemon pepper, nutmeg and sherry; simmer 5 minutes. Add cream and stir, barely simmering mixture. Set aside and keep warm.

Melt butter; saute mushrooms and chopped parsley, add to sauce. Stir half of sauce into cooked spaghetti and spoon into a baking dish. Stir cooked shrimp into remaining sauce and pour over spaghetti. Combine cheese and bread crumbs and sprinkle over top of mixture. Bake in preheated 350-degree oven for about 20 minutes or until mixture is bubbly. Serves 4-6.

Jo and Jan say, "You might prefer using a combination of crab and shrimp; or substitute lobster for the shrimp."

SHRIMP ETOUFFEE

6 tablespoons butter
2 cups chopped onion
2 cloves garlic, minced
1/2 cup green pepper, chopped
1 teaspoon tomato puree
1/2 cup green onions, chopped
1/2 cup fresh parsley, minced
2 cups celery, chopped
3 cups shrimp, cleaned
2 teaspoons Worcestershire sauce
Salt and pepper to taste
Tabasco sauce to taste
Cooked rice (for 8 servings)

Melt butter in large, heavy skillet. Saute onions, garlic and green pepper. Simmer until tender, about 10 to 15 minutes, stirring constantly. Add tomato puree and cook for 5 minutes. Add remaining ingredients, except rice and cook until shrimp turn to light pink color. Cook about 10 to 15 minutes more, stirring constantly so mixture will not stick. Turn off heat; let stand about 30 minutes so seasonings will blend. Serve with rice. Serves 6-8.

CATFISH PARMESAN

6 skinned catfish, pan-dressed
2 cups dry bread crumbs
3/4 cup Parmesan cheese
1/4 cup chopped parsley
1 teaspoon paprika
1/2 teaspoon oregano
1/2 teaspoon pepper
1 teaspoon salt
1/2 teaspoon basil
3/4 cup vegetable oil
Lemon

Clean, wash and dry fish and set aside. Combine bread crumbs, Parmesan cheese, parsley, paprika, oregano, basil, salt and pepper. Dip fish in oil and roll in crumb mixture. Arrange in a well-greased 9 x 13-inch baking dish and bake in a preheated 375-degree oven for 20 to 25 minutes or until fish flakes when tested with a fork. Serve with lemon wedges for garnish. Serves 6.

PAUL'S SALMON STEAKS

2 tablespoons butter or margarine
2 salmon steaks, cut 1-inch thick
4 green onions, chopped
2 tablespoons white wine vinegar
3 tablespoons green peppercorn mustard
1/2 cup heavy cream
Salt
Freshly ground black pepper

Melt butter in large skillet over low heat. Add onions and saute until soft; push to side of skillet. Add salmon and saute until lightly brown, about 5 minutes. Turn and cook about 5 more minutes. Transfer steaks to warm platter. Add vinegar to skillet with onions, scrape any browned bits and stir to reduce liquid slightly. Stir in mustard; add cream, salt, pepper and stir again. Reduce heat and cook until mixture is hot but do not boil. Return steaks to skillet, spoon sauce over tops. Cook until heated. Serves 2.

FRIED TROUT WITH CAPERS

4 medium trout
Juice of 1 lemon
1 teaspoon salt
1/4 cup flour
1/2 cup oil
1/4 cup butter
1/2 cup bread crumbs
2 tablespoons drained capers
Lemon slices
Parsley

Wash and pat the cleaned fish dry. Use half the lemon juice to sprinkle over the fish. Salt fish inside and out; dredge in flour. In a heavy skillet, heat oil and fry fish 5 to 10 minutes, turning several times; remove to heated platter when done.

In a small skillet, melt butter, add bread crumbs and brown; spoon over trout and sprinkle with remaining lemon juice and capers. Garnish with lemon slices and parsley. Serves 2-4.

POACHED FISH WITH HERBS

1 1/2 pounds fish fillets, perch, snapper, bass
3 tablespoons olive oil
1 garlic clove, crushed
2 tablespoons fresh parsley, minced
1/2 cup dry white wine
1/2 cup water
1 teaspoon salt
1/8 teaspoon pepper
1/4 teaspoon basil
1/4 teaspoon oregano

Rinse fillets in cold water and pat dry; cut into serving pieces. Saute garlic and parsley in hot oil in a deep pan or large skillet. Add wine and water; bring to a boil. Add fish, seasonings and herbs. Cover and bring to a boil; reduce heat to simmer and cook 5 to 10 minutes depending on thickness of fillets. Check at 5 minutes, test with a fork; if fish flakes, it is done. Fish may be served with a sauce, or chilled for salads. Serves 4.

BAKED STRIPED SEA BASS

1 stripped bass (4 to 5 pounds)
Salt and pepper
3 shallots, chopped
1 small onion, chopped
3 tablespoons parsley, chopped
6 mushroom caps, sliced
1/2 pound butter
1 pint white wine
1 garlic clove, finely chopped

Place bass in a large pan; salt and pepper all over. Add remaining ingredients and cook in a slow oven for about 45 minutes, basting the fish quite often. Before serving, add a tablespoon of butter to the sauce; stir well to incorporate. Serves 8.

Prime Thyme

❖◆❖

SOLE AU GRATIN

2 tablespoons butter
2 shallots, peeled and finely chopped
1 tablespoon parsley, chopped
1 teaspoon chives, chopped
1/2 pound fresh mushrooms, finely chopped
1 tablespoon flour
1/2 cup breadcrumbs
1 pound sole filets
1/2 teaspoon salt
1/4 teaspoon pepper
1/4 teaspoon dill weed
3/4 cup white wine
3 tablespoons grated Parmesan cheese
3 tablespoons butter

Melt butter in skillet and saute shallots, parsley, chives and mushrooms for 2 minutes. Spread 1/2 of this mixture in bottom of buttered shallow baking dish which has been dusted with flour. Sprinkle 1/4 cup of breadcrumbs over mushrooms. Place sole filets in dish and season with salt, pepper and dill. Cover with remaining mushroom mixture and pour in white wine. Sprinkle with remaining 1/4 cup breadcrumbs and Parmesan cheese. Dot with butter and bake in 350-degree oven for 15-20 minutes until top is slightly browned. Serves 4.

UNCLE JACK'S SOLE FILLETS WITH ORANGE GLAZE

2 pounds sole fillets
2 tablespoons butter, melted
2 tablespoons orange juice
1/2 teaspoon salt
Dash pepper
Orange Glaze (Recipe Below)

Rinse fillets with cold water; pat dry and if necessary, cut large fillets into serving portions.

Lightly grease broiler pan and lay fillets in a single layer. Combine butter and orange juice; brush over fillets. Sprinkle with salt and pepper. Broil about 4 inches from heat for 6 minutes. Baste with Orange Glaze. Continue cooking for 2 to 4 minutes, or until fillets flake easily when fork tested. Transfer to a warm serving platter and serve with remaining heated Orange Glaze. Serves 4 to 6.

ORANGE GLAZE:

2 tablespoons cornstarch
1 cup orange juice
1/4 cup butter
1/3 cup sliced almonds
1/4 cup dry white wine
1/4 cup apple jelly
1/4 cup lemon juice
1/4 teaspoon hot pepper sauce
1/8 teaspoon salt
1 teaspoon grated orange rind

Combine cornstarch with 1/4 cup orange juice; set aside. In saucepan, melt butter over medium heat. Add almonds and saute until slightly browned. Add remaining orange juice, wine, jelly and lemon juice; heat just to boiling. Stir in cornstarch mixture; continue cooking while stirring constantly. Add hot pepper sauce, salt, orange rind; mix well. Reduce heat to low and keep warm until serving. Makes 2 cups.

LEE ANN'S MEATLOAF

1 1/2 pounds ground beef
1 1/3 cups coarse cracker crumbs
2 eggs, beaten
1 cup milk
1/4 cup grated onion
1 teaspoon salt
1/2 teaspoon pepper
1/2 teaspoon sage

SAUCE:
6 tablespoons brown sugar
1/4 teaspoon nutmeg
1 teaspoon dry mustard
1/2 cup catsup

Combine all the ingredients except the sauce and place into a greased loaf pan. Spread the sauce over the meat before baking. Bake in a preheated 350-degree oven for 1 hour. Serves 6.

CHINESE PEPPER STEAK

1 1/2 pounds sirloin steak
2 tablespoons cooking oil
1 clove garlic, crushed
1 teaspoon ground ginger
1/2 teaspoon salt
1/2 teaspoon pepper
3 green peppers, cut in chunks
2 large onions, cut in chunks
1/4 cup soy sauce
1/2 teaspoon sugar
1/2 cup beef bouillon
1 can water chestnuts, sliced
1 tablespoon cornstarch
1/4 cup cold water
5 green onions, cut in 1-inch pieces
2 tomatoes, cut in chunks

Cut steak in very thin strips (it will slice easier if frozen for an hour). Heat oil in a skillet and brown steak; add garlic, ginger, salt, pepper. Saute about 2 minutes. Remove meat and saute green pepper and onion chunks for about 3 minutes. Add steak back to skillet and add soy sauce, sugar, bouillon, water chestnuts, cornstarch which has been dissolved in cold water, tomato chunks and green onion pieces. Simmer and stir until sauce is hot and thickened. Serve from a chafing dish over hot rice. Serves 6.

Jo and Jan say, "You might wish to cut back on the cooking time for the onion and green pepper chunks. We prefer them a bit crisp. We also will add snow peas and saute them to a light-crisp stage."

RIB EYE ROAST

1 rib eye roast
Salt
Cracked black pepper

Rub the roast with salt and pepper and place it in a shallow pan. Place the roast in a preheated 500-degree oven and close the door. For very rare meat, cook for 5 minutes per pound at 500 degrees. Keep the oven door closed while cooking. When meat has cooked the alloted time, turn off the oven. Leave meat in the oven for a total of 2 hours. Do not open the oven door during this time. For example, if the roast weighs 8 pounds, you will cook it for 40 minutes and turn off the oven, then leave it in the closed oven for 1 hour and 20 minutes.

For medium rare roast beef, add 5 minutes to the poundage cooking time before turning the oven off. For medium roast beef, add 10 minutes to the cooking time. From the time you start the roast until it is ready to slice, the time is 2 hours.

If you do not like your roast quite as pink, you may want to cook it for 6 minutes per pound. Beef prepared this way will wait for any latecomers. Serves 8-10.

AU JUS GRAVY

Beef drippings from rib roast
1/2 cup chopped onion
1/2 cup chopped carrot
1/2 cup chopped celery (with leaves)
3/4 cup port wine
3 cups beef broth
1 garlic clove, whole
1 garlic clove, crushed
1/2 teaspoon dried thyme

Pour off all but 1 tablespoon beef drippings from roasting pan; reserve poured-off drippings if you are making Yorkshire Pudding Popovers (See index).

Add vegetables to drippings left in roasting pan and cook over medium heat for 5 minutes, stirring occasionally.

Add wine, bring to simmer and cook until liquid is reduced by two-thirds; about 10 minutes, stirring occasionally. Add beef broth, garlic cloves and thyme. Bring to a simmer and cook 10 minutes. Remove whole garlic clove before serving. Makes 4 cups.

JEANNE'S MICRO STROGANOFF SUPREME

3 tablespoons margarine
1 pound round steak, cut into thin strips
1/2 cup chopped onion
1 can (4-ounce) sliced mushrooms, drained
1/4 teaspoon dry mustard
1/2 teaspoon salt
1/4 teaspoon pepper
1 package (8-ounce) cream cheese, diced or
  cubed
2/3 cup beer

Melt margarine in a 2-quart casserole on High for 30 seconds. Add steak strips to margarine and microwave uncovered on High for 10 minutes or until meat is browned. Add mushrooms, onion and seasonings to meat. Microwave, uncovered, on High for 4 minutes. Add cheese and beer to meat mixture; microwave on High for 6 minutes, uncovered. Stir occasionally. Serves 4.

Jeanne says, "This is a great tasty, quick meal. Serve over spaghetti or buttered egg noodles; and toss a salad. You may use sirloin instead of round and the fresh mushrooms are wonderful if you can get them."

CAROL'S MOUSSAKA

2 medium eggplant
1 pound ground beef
1 cup chopped onion
1/4 cup Burgundy wine
1/4 cup water
2 tablespoons snipped parsley
1 1/2 tablespoons tomato paste
1 teaspoon salt
Dash pepper
1 slice bread, torn into crumbs
2 eggs, beaten
2 ounces Mozzarella cheese, shredded
Dash ground cinnamon

SAUCE:
3 tablespoons butter or margarine
3 tablespoons flour
1 1/2 cups milk, room temperature
1/2 teaspoon salt
Dash pepper
Dash ground nutmeg
1 egg, beaten
2 ounces Mozzarella cheese, shredded

Cut eggplant into 1/2-inch slices. Sprinkle with a little salt, set on paper towels and set aside to draw moisture out. While this is happening, brown meat and onion in a skillet; drain off fat. Add wine, water, parsley and tomato paste; salt and pepper. Simmer until liquid is nearly absorbed; cool, then stir in half the bread crumbs, 2 beaten eggs, 2 ounces cheese and ground cinnamon to taste.

In saucepan, melt butter or margarine; stir in flour. Add milk; cook and stir until thickened and bubbly. Add 1/2 teaspoon salt, dash pepper and ground nutmeg to taste. Add a little of the hot sauce to the beaten egg; return to mixture. Cook over low heat for 2 minutes, stirring constantly.

Brown eggplant slices on both sides in hot butter or margarine until soft. Sprinkle bottom of a greased 9 x 13-inch baking dish with remaining bread crumbs. Cover with a layer of eggplant slices; spoon all of meat mixture on slices. Arrange remaining eggplant over meat mixture. Pour milk-egg sauce over all. Sprinkle with Mozzarella cheese. Bake at 350 about 45 minutes. Serves 10-12.

TONIA'S MEXICAN MEATLOAF

2 pounds ground beef
2 eggs
1 cup bread crumbs
1 can (4-ounce) taco sauce
3/4 cup chopped onion
1 garlic clove, minced
2 1/2 teaspoons chili powder
1/2 teaspoon salt
1/2 teaspoon cumin
1/8 teaspoon pepper
1 can (16-ounce) refried beans
2 tablespoons chopped green chilies
1 cup shredded Cheddar cheese
1/3 cup crushed corn chips
Lettuce, shredded, grated cheese, chopped
   onion, sliced black olives (garnish)

Combine first 10 ingredients; shape into a ball and place between 2 sheets of waxed paper. Roll into a rectangle (16 x 8 x 1/2-inch). Spread beans over meat; top with chili and cheese. Starting at the 8-inch side, roll up like a jelly roll, pulling off the waxed paper as you roll. Place roll in a 9 x 5-inch loaf pan, placing seam side down. Top with crushed chips and bake in preheated 375-degree oven for 1 hour. Drain grease and let stand 15 minutes. To serve, garnish with lettuce, grated cheese, chopped onion and sliced black olives. Serves 8-10.

BEEF - ASPARAGUS STIR-FRY

1 pound flank steak, partially frozen
3 tablespoons soy sauce
2 tablespoons dry sherry
2 tablespoons steak sauce
4 tablespoons oil, divided
1 medium garlic clove
1 pound fresh asparagus, trimmed and cut
   diagonally in 1/2-inch slices
1 can water chestnuts, drained and sliced
1/3 cup chicken broth
1 tablespoon cornstarch combined with 2
   tablespoons water

Cut steak in 2 1/2-inch lengthwise strips, then in 1/8-inch crosswise slices; set aside. Combine soy sauce, sherry and steak sauce; set aside. Heat 3 tablespoons oil in skillet or wok over high heat and brown garlic; discard. Add beef and stir-fry quickly until almost brown; remove to a warm dish with a slotted spoon. To pan drippings add remaining tablespoon oil and the soy sauce mixture. Add asparagus and water chestnuts and cook just until asparagus is crisp-tender, 3 to 5 minutes. Stir in beef and blended cornstarch; cook and stir until sauce thickens. Serves 4.

PAPRIKA GOULASH

1/4 cup peanut oil
2 1/2 pounds round of beef, cut into 1-inch
   cubes
1 1/2 teaspoons salt
1/4 teaspoon pepper
4 cups sliced onions
2 cloves garlic, minced
1 bay leaf
1 can (6-ounce) tomato paste
1 1/2 cups beer
1 tablespoon paprika
1 teaspoon lemon juice

Heat oil in heavy kettle and cook meat until well-browned on all sides. Sprinkle with salt and pepper. Add onions and garlic and cook, stirring occasionally, 10 minutes longer. Add bay leaf and tomato paste mixed with beer. Add paprika, cover and cook over low heat until meat is tender, 2 to 2 1/2 hours. Before serving, stir in lemon juice; correct seasonings with salt and pepper. Serves 6.

Jo and Jan say, "Serve this with buttered, parslied noodles and hard rolls."

HERBED LEMON VEAL

8 veal scallops
Salt and freshly ground pepper
1/2 cup flour
1/2 stick butter
1 tablespoon olive oil
2 garlic cloves, minced
1/2 pound fresh mushrooms, sliced
2 tablespoons dry white wine
1/2 cup chicken broth
2 tablespoons fresh lemon juice
1 tablespoon green onions, finely chopped
1 tablespoon fresh parsley, minced
1/2 teaspoon dried rosemary
2 tablespoons capers
1/2 lemon, thinly sliced

Sprinkle veal with salt and pepper on both sides and dredge meat in flour to coat lightly, shaking off excess. Heat butter and oil in a heavy skillet over medium-high heat until hot, but not smoking. Add veal and brown quickly on both sides, turning frequently. Transfer veal to a heated platter and set aside.

Add garlic and mushrooms to skillet and pour in wine. Saute until mushrooms are tender; remove and set aside. Blend in broth, lemon juice, onions, parsley and rosemary, stirring to scrap up any browned pieces. Reduce heat, cover and simmer gently, stirring frequently, for 3 to 5 minutes. Return veal to skillet; cover and simmer gently for about 5 minutes or until veal is tender. Add capers and sauteed mushrooms to just warm the last few minutes. Remove to a warm platter, sprinkle with parsley and garnish with lemon slices. Serve immediately. Serve 4.

MAPLE GLAZED HAM

1 10-pound precooked boneless ham
Whole cloves
3/4 cup light-brown sugar, firmly packed
1 cup dark corn syrup
2 tablespoons prepared mustard
1 tablespoon maple flavoring

Place ham, fat side up, on a rack in a shallow, open roasting pan. Insert meat thermometer in center and bake, uncovered, in a preheated 325-degree oven for 2 1/2 to 3 hours, or until internal temperature reaches 130. Remove from oven; turn oven to 450. Take out thermometer; carefully remove rind from ham and with tip of knife, cut fat into diamond patterns, being careful you do not cut into the ham. Insert a clove in each diamond. In bowl, mix rest of ingredients. Spread half of glaze over ham, and bake 10 minutes. Put on rest of glaze; bake 10 minutes. For easy slicing, let stand 20 minutes. Makes about 20 servings.

HAM LOAF

1/2 cup brown sugar
2 tablespoons pineapple juice
Pieces of pineapple; stud each with 1 whole
    clove
1 1/2 pounds ground ham
1 pound ground pork
2 eggs, beaten
1 teaspoon dry mustard
1 cup milk
3/4 cup crushed crackers

On bottom of a 9x5x3-inch loaf pan mix brown sugar and pineapple juice together. Add pieces of pineapple, placing clove side down.

Beat eggs in a large bowl and add ground ham, pork, mustard, milk and crackers. Mix well and shape into a loaf to fit pan. Place loaf on top of pineapple pieces; bake in a preheated 350-degree oven for 1 hour and 15 minutes. After baking, pour off excess juices and invert loaf onto a platter, pineapple side up. Serves 8-10.

RUTHIE'S SWEET - SOUR RIBS

5 pounds short ribs
Flour, salt and pepper
1 medium onion, sliced
2 tablespoons Worcestershire sauce
1/2 cup sugar, scant
4 tablespoons soy sauce
3/4 cup water
3/4 cup catsup
2 tablespoons vinegar

Dip meat in flour; salt and pepper. Do not brown the meat but place in a heavy Dutch oven or pan with a tight-fitting lid. Mix all ingredients together and pour over ribs. Bake at 300 degrees for 3 hours. Serves 6.

Jan says, "As Ruthie says, 'this dish is great for late starters.' It will not spoil if left longer in the oven. You may also use this sauce for chicken. It's great for a large group of people. The working gal or guy will love this for you may prepare it in advance and place in the oven to warm it up. So, let's have a party!"

CAROL'S CHINESE PORK TENDERLOIN

2 pound strip pork tenderloin
1 tablespoon sherry
2 tablespoons soy sauce
2 tablespoons brown sugar
Salt to taste
1/2 teaspoon ground cinnamon
1/4 teaspoon ground ginger
1/2 teaspoon ground clove

PLUM SAUCE:
1 cup plum preserves
1/2 cup chutney
1 tablespoon sugar
1 tablespoon vinegar

Mix sherry and remaining 6 ingredients; marinate tenderloin, turning often, for several hours. Line a broiler pan with foil and place a rack on the foil. Lay the pork on the rack. Brown in a preheated 450-degree oven for 10 minutes and baste. Turn oven to 325-degrees and bake for 1 to 1 1/2 hours, until tender, basting until all the marinade is used. Serve hot or cold with Hot Mustard Sauce (See index) and Plum Sauce. Serves 6-8.

To prepare Plum Sauce, blend ingredients and heat together until smooth.

Jo says, "Carol served this at a brunch and was rewarded with raves! I've prepared it for dinners ; but it's really delicious sliced and served cold. Great for picnics!"

PASTA AND AVOCADO WITH CREME FRAICHE / GORGONZOLA SAUCE

1/2 cup butter or margarine
1/4 pound gorgonzola cheese
1 cup Creme Fraiche (See index)
Pinch of nutmeg
1/2 cup walnuts, toasted and coarsely
  chopped (optional)
Salt and freshly ground pepper, to taste
1 pound pasta, cooked and drained
1 avocado, peeled and thinly sliced

Melt butter or margarine and cheese slowly over low heat, stirring until cheese melts. Add Creme Fraiche and nutmeg; heat thoroughly. Adjust seasoning, adding salt if desired, and some black pepper. Place drained pasta on a platter or shallow serving dish. Add walnuts to sauce just before serving and pour sauce over pasta. Add sliced avocado; grind some more black pepper over the top, toss gently and serve. Serves 4.

ANN'S FOUR CHEESE PASTA

2 tablespoons shelled natural pistachios
1 pound linguine pasta
Salt
1 tablespoon olive oil
1/4 cup butter
8 ounces (2 cups) Gruyere cheese, freshly
  grated
8 ounces Mozzarella cheese (2 cups) freshly
  grated
8 ounces Gorgonzola cheese (2 cups)
  crumbled Note: Use a mild unsalty
  Gorgonzola if you cannot find the sweet.
8 ounces (2 cups) Parmesan cheese, freshly
  grated
1 2/3 cups heavy cream
Salt and freshly ground black pepper
Fresh parsley (garnish)
Freshly grated Parmesan cheese (garnish)

Blanch pistachios in boiling water for 15 seconds; immediately rinse under cold running water; drain and slip off skins; and spread nuts on paper toweling to dry.

Add salt and olive oil to a large kettle of boiling water. Add pasta and cook just until tender; drain thoroughly.

While pasta is cooking, melt butter in a large saucepan over low heat. Add the four cheeses and stir until melted. Add cream slowly, stirring to thoroughly incorporate. Add nuts and heat through. Season to taste with salt and pepper. To serve, sprinkle with grated Parmesan cheese and fresh parsley.

CRAB CHEESE SOUFFLE

1/4 cup butter
1/4 cup flour
1 1/2 cups milk, scalded
1 cup sharp Cheddar cheese, grated
1 1/2 cups mild Cheddar cheese, grated
1 teaspoon salt
Pinch nutmeg
6 eggs, separated
1 can (7 1/2-ounce) crabmeat

Prepare 2-quart souffle dish (See index How To Prepare A Souffle Dish).

Melt butter in saucepan. Stir in flour; blend well and add hot milk, stirring constantly. Bring to a boil, add cheeses and stir until cheese is melted. Add salt and nutmeg; remove from heat. Add egg yolks, 1 at a time, stirring well after each addition. Add crabmeat and mix well. Beat egg whites until stiff and fold carefully into cheese mixture. Pour into prepared souffle dish. Bake in preheated 375-degree oven for 30 minutes. Serve immediately. Serves 6.

POULTRY SEASONING BLEND

1 1/2 tablespoons rubbed sage
1 1/2 tablespoons onion powder
1 1/2 tablespoons pepper
2 1/2 teaspoons paprika
1 1/2 tablespoons celery seeds
1 1/2 tablespoons dried thyme
1 1/2 tablespoons dried marjoram
2 1/4 teaspoons dried rosemary
2 1/4 teaspoons garlic powder

Combine all ingredients, mixing well. Store in airtight container in a cool, dry place. Use 2 teaspoons of Seasoning per pound of poultry. Makes 1/2 cup.

PASTIES

Jan and Jo say, "These peppery meat pies, pronounced 'pass-tees', were brought to this country by Cornish miners during the industrial boom that helped to open the American West.

To give pasties a tight seal with a ropelike edge, pleat the dough by pinching the pastry with the left hand and folding over with the right.

Baked pasties can by frozen up to 1 month. Cool completely on a wire rack; freeze in a single layer on baking sheets. Wrap each pastry in aluminum foil and return to freezer. When ready to serve, unwrap from foil and bake on ungreased sheets in preheated 325-degree oven about 30 to 40 minutes or until heated through."

PASTIES

1/2 to 3/4 cup shortening
3 cups flour
1 teaspoon salt
1/2 cup ice water

FILLING:
1 1/2 pounds round steak
1/2 pound pork steak
5 medium potatoes, peeled and chopped
  into small pieces
3 medium onions, minced
Salt and pepper to taste
2 tablespoons butter or margarine

Measure flour and salt into bowl; cut in shortening until coarse in texture. Mix in water lightly until dough sticks together; place in refrigerator.

Cut meat into small pieces; removing all gristle. Mix vegetables with meat, salt and pepper in a large bowl.

Divide pastry dough into 6 equal portions. Roll out 1 portion on a floured surface until the size of a medium pie plate. Place 1/6 of the filling on half the pastry; dot with small pieces of butter or margarine. Fold over other half of pastry over the filling; crimp edges to seal. Prick with a fork and place on a baking sheet.. Repeat with other portions of pastry and filling. Bake in a preheated 325-degree oven for 1 hour. Serves 6.

MEAT SEASONING BLEND

3 tablespoons dried thyme leaves
2 tablespoons onion powder
1 1/2 teaspoons ground cumin
1 tablespoon pepper
1 teaspoon ground paprika
1 teaspoon garlic powder
3 bay leaves, crumbled

Combine ingredients and store in an airtight container in a cool, dry place. Use 2 teaspoons of mixture per pound of meat. May also be added to soups and stews with meat. Makes 1/2 cup.

SEAFOOD SEASONING BLEND

1/4 cup plus 2 tablespoons dried parsley
3 tablespoons dillweed
3 tablespoons lemon-pepper
4 bay leaves, crumbled

Combine ingredients and store in an airtight container. Place in a cool, dry place. Use 2 teaspoons of seasoning mix per pound of seafood. Makes 1/2 cup.

CAJUN MIXTURE

1 tablespoon garlic powder
1 tablespoon onion powder
2 teaspoons black pepper
1 teaspoon lemon pepper
2 teaspoons white pepper
2 teaspoons cayenne pepper
4 teaspoons salt
2 teaspoons dried parsley
2 teaspoons dried thyme
2 teaspoons dried oregano
1 teaspoon paprika
1/2 cup oil

Combine all ingredients and blend well. Store in sealed container and refrigerate. The mixture is delicious on fish (try it on red snapper), and may be used on steaks. Makes about 3/4 cup.

BASIC BROWN SAUCE
(Espagnole)

6 tablespoons oil
1 onion, finely diced
1 carrot, finely diced
1 stick celery, finely diced
3 tablespoons flour
1 teaspoon tomato paste
1 mushroom, chopped
5 cups Brown Stock (See index)
Bouquet garni (See index)
Salt and pepper

Heat oil and add diced vegetables; no more than 6 tablespoons total of the vegetables. Cook over low heat until vegetables are clear and just about to start to brown. Stir in flour and brown slowly, whisking occasionally and scraping bottom of pan so mixture does not stick. When mixture is brown, but do not let it burn, remove from heat and allow to cool slightly.

Stir in tomato paste, chopped mushroom, 4 cups beef stock, herbs and seasoning. Bring to a boil, whisking constantly. Off set a lid on pan and gently cook mixture for about 40 minutes; check occasionally and skim off any scum that might rise to the top. Add half the remaining stock; bring to a boil and skim the top. Simmer 5 minutes; add remaining stock, bring to a boil again and skim once more. Cook 5 more minutes; strain, pressing vegetables to extract all juices.

Pour sauce in a clean pan; partially cover and simmer sauce until it is glossy and the consistency of heavy cream. Makes 2 cups.

Jo and Jan say, "The sauce can be used alone or as a base for others, such as Demi-glace (See index). A tablespoon of this added to a gravy, or pan juices of a steak is delicious."

SAUCE DEMI-GLACE

1/4 cup chopped mushrooms
2 teaspoons tomato paste
2 cups Basic Brown Sauce (Espagnole - See index)
1/4 cup Brown Stock (See index) or Canned beef consomme
1/4 cup sherry
1 tablespoon butter

Combine mushrooms and tomato paste; add to Espagnole sauce in a small saucepan. Simmer 5 minutes; add stock and simmer, uncovered, skimming often. When mixture is well reduced, add sherry and whisk in the butter. Remove from heat at this point. Keep warm over hot water or if reheat, do not allow to boil. Serve with dark meats. Makes 2 cups.

WHITE BUTTER SAUCE

1/4 cup dry white wine
3 tablespoons finely minced shallots
2 tablespoons white wine vinegar
Salt and freshly ground white pepper
2 sticks well chilled unsalted butter, cut into
   1/2-inch pieces

Combine wine, shallots, and vinegar in a heavy-bottomed, non-aluminum small saucepan over medium heat and cook until liquid is reduced to 2 tablespoons. Season with salt and pepper.

Remove from heat; add 2 pieces of butter and whisk quickly until just incorporated. Place over low heat and whisk in remaining butter 1 piece at a time without stopping, adding each only after the previous one is nearly combined;

sauce should be thick. If sauce becomes too hot and streaks or drops of melted butter appear, immediately remove from heat and whisk in 2 pieces of butter. Continue whisking in butter 1 piece at a time, off the heat, until sauce to thick and immediately emulsified. Return sauce to low heat and continue whisking in 1 piece at a time. Adjust seasoning and strain through a fine sieve if a smoother sauce is desired, pressing with the back of a spoon to extract all the liquid. Serve immediately. Makes about 1 cup.

Jo and Jan say, "This sauce can be kept warm for a short period on a rack set above water, whisking frequently to prevent any separation. It is a perfect sauce for lean, delicate foods; steamed, poached or broiled seafood, light meats such as chicken breasts or veal and for vegetables."

HORSERADISH CREAM

1 cup heavy cream, well chilled
2 teaspoons sugar
1/2 teaspoon salt
2 to 3 tablespoons prepared horseradish,
   drained

Combine cream, sugar and salt in chilled bowl. Beat with chilled beaters until cream holds stiff peaks. Fold in drained horseradish just before serving. Makes about 2 1/4 cups.

TARRAGON SAUCE FOR CHICKEN & SEAFOOD

2 egg yolks
1/4 teaspoon dried tarragon leaves
1 cup sour cream
1 bay leaf, crumbled
1/4 teaspoon garlic, crushed
1/2 teaspoon salt
1 tablespoons capers, washed and drained

Beat egg yolks and tarragon with rotary beater in small bowl until thick and lemon-colored.

In a small saucepan slowly heat sour cream, bay leaf and garlic just until bubbly around edges. Strain and discard bay leaf; pour a little of the hot sour cream into egg yolks, stirring constantly. Combine all egg yolks and sour cream back in saucepan. Bring just to a boil over low heat, stirring constantly; add salt and capers. Makes 1 cup.

MUSTARD DILL SAUCE

1 cup sour cream
3 green onion, finely chopped
1 to 2 tablespoons French-style mustard
1 teaspoon dill weed
1 tablespoon finely chopped fresh parsley
1/8 teaspoon ground white pepper

Combine ingredients and stir well. Heat, but do not boil. Excellent with fish; brush fish fillets prior to removing from oven, place under broiler for 2 minutes. Makes 1 1/4 cups.

MUSTARD SAUCE FOR COLD MEATS

1 cup sour cream
4 tablespoons Dijon mustard
2 tablespoons capers, well drained

Combine sour cream, mustard and capers until thoroughly mixed. Chill until ready to serve. Makes about 1 1/2 cups.

This sauce is excellent with sliced tenderloin and cold chicken, too.

FAR EAST MUSTARD SAUCE

3 tablespoons dry mustard
2 tablespoons hot water
1 tablespoon sesame seeds, toasted
1/4 cup soy sauce
1/4 garlic clove, crushed
3 tablespoons heavy cream, whipped

Combine mustard and water to form a paste. Place in blender with rest of ingredients except cream and blend at high speed for 1 minute. Remove and stir in whipped cream. Makes 1 1/4 cups.

CAROL'S HAM SAUCE

1/2 cup sugar
3 tablespoons dry mustard
4 egg yolks
1/2 cup vinegar
1 cup heavy cream

Combine sugar, mustard and egg yolks in top of double boiler. Add vinegar and cream; stir constantly until thickened. Cool and refrigerate. When sauce is cool and refrigerated, it will thicken more. Makes 2 cups.

Jo says, "Carol gave me this recipe many years ago. It is truly wonderful! Carol sometimes uses it as a dip for vegetables."

SYLVIA'S FLUFFY MUSTARD SAUCE FOR HAM

2 eggs
1/4 cup water
2 tablespoons prepared mustard
2 tablespoons vinegar
1/2 teaspoon salt
1 tablespoon sugar
1/2 cup heavy cream, whipped

Combine all ingredients except cream in small saucepan. Mix well and cook over very low heat, stirring constantly until thickened. Cool about 5 minutes and gradually fold into the whipped cream. Makes sauce for 6 to 8.

HONEY MUSTARD GLAZE FOR HAM

1/2 cup honey
2 tablespoons coarse-grained mustard
4 teaspoons Dijon mustard
Freshly ground pepper

Mix all ingredients in small bowl. Brush ham with glaze every 15 minutes after first hour of baking; use all of glaze. Makes 2/3 cup.

HOISIN SOY GLAZE FOR HAM

1/2 cup hoisin sauce
1 1/2 tablespoons fresh lemon juice
1 tablespoon soy sauce
1 teaspoon grated fresh ginger

Mix all ingredients in small bowl. Brush ham with glaze every 15 minutes <u>after</u> first hour of baking; use all of glaze. Makes 2/3 cup.

FLAVORED OIL FOR STIR - FRY

2 cups oil
2 tablespoons chopped fresh ginger
2 tablespoons dried-red-pepper flakes
3 large garlic cloves, chopped coarsely

Combine all ingredients and heat in a saucepan for several minutes; cool and transfer to a pint jar. Cover and refrigerate. To use, strain desired amount of oil for stir-frying. Makes 2 1/4 cups.

SOY GLAZE FOR STIR - FRY

2 tablespoons sugar
2 tablespoons cornstarch
1 cup cold water
1/2 cup soy sauce
3 ounces dry sherry

Combine ingredients in saucepan and stir until dissolved. Bring to a boil; cook until thick and shiny. Remove from heat and add to crisp stir-fried veggies. Toss until coated and reheat to serve. Makes 1 3/4 cups.

SOY - GINGER SAUCE

1 small onion
1/2 cup soy sauce
1/4 cup vinegar

1/8 teaspoon ground ginger or 1 small piece fresh ginger root. Combine all ingredients in blender and mix at high speed for 2 minutes or until onion and ginger are finely chopped. Makes 1 cup.

◆◆◆

Sweet Temptations • Desserts

Sweet temptations mean exactly that! Whatever your sweet tooth might be craving, we undoubtedly have just the perfect, delicious and satisfying answer.

We begin this section with Cookies and Brownies, continuing on with Pies and Cakes, not forgetting Frostings. Next we travel the sweet road to Cheesecake and Dessert Crepes; not forgetting such delectables as Creme Caramel, Creme Brulee, Puddings and Custards.

We could not forget all our wonderful sauces, Hooray The Souffle, Part II, Ice Creams and Toppings, our elegant offerings which we have titled Delectables, Candyland and Finishing Touches.

You may have noticed we have not given specific reference to particular recipes - we just happen to believe they are all wonderful!

◆◆◆

❖❖

Cookies & Bars

COOKIE HINTS

- Always keep your cookies in an air-tight container unless recipe specifically says to leave lightly-covered.
- Never put soft cookies in the cookie jar with crisp cookies. Keep them separate so they will retain their own texture.
- If soft cookies become hard, slice an apple and place it among the cookies.

- Freezing is the best way to preserve cookies.
- Cookies should be carefully wrapped. If freezing more than a week, double-wrap them so the air cannot penetrate the package and the cookies will remain fresh.
- Best to freeze cookies no longer than a month and two months at the most.

ANGEL COOKIES

1 cup flour
2 tablespoons cornstarch
1/2 cup confectioners' sugar
1 cup butter or margarine, softened
1 1/2 cups coconut

Mix flour, cornstarch and sugar in bowl. Blend in butter until forms a soft dough. If dough is too soft, cover and chill. Shape into 3/4-inch balls; roll in coconut and place 1 1/2 inches apart on ungreased baking sheets. Bake in preheated 300-degree oven for 20 to 25 minutes, or until lightly browned. Makes 3 dozen.

CASHEW COOKIES

2 cups sifted cake flour
1/2 teaspoon baking powder
1 cup butter or margarine, softened
1/2 cup confectioners' sugar
1 tablespoon vanilla
1 cup chopped, roasted and salted cashews
Confectioners' sugar (for sifting on top)

Sift flour with baking powder. Cream shortening and sugar until smooth; add vanilla and stir in flour mixture with nuts. Form into rolls about 1 1/2-inches in diameter. Wrap in clear plastic or foil and chill at least 1 hour. Slice with a sharp knife into 1/4-inch slices. Arrange on ungreased baking sheet. Bake in preheated 375-degree oven for 12 to 15 minutes or until golden brown.

Place a sheet of waxed paper on counter or tray, sprinkle paper with confectioners' sugar. Place cookies on sugar and sprinkle tops with more sugar. Cool completely and store in an airtight container. Makes 3 dozen.

COCONUT MACAROONS

3 egg whites, beaten until stiff
1 cup sugar
1 tablespoon cornstarch
1/4 teaspoon salt
2 cups shredded coconut
1/2 teaspoon almond extract

In top of double boiler combine egg whites, sugar and cornstarch. Cook over boiling water, stirring constantly for 20 minutes. Remove from heat; add salt, coconut and almond extract, stirring until well blended. Drop by teaspoon, 1/2-inch apart onto lightly greased cookie sheets; bake 18 to 20 minutes, or until lightly browned. Cool on wire rack. Makes about 2 dozen.

TONIA'S RICE KRISPIE SUGAR COOKIE

2 sticks margarine
1 cup sugar
1 teaspoon vanilla
1 1/2 cups flour
1/2 teaspoon baking powder
1/2 teaspoon baking soda
2 cups Rice Krispies cereal
1/2 cup chopped nuts

Cream margarine and sugar; add vanilla. Combine flour, baking powder and soda and add to first mixture. Fold in cereal and nuts. Roll in balls and place on cookie sheet; press with the bottom of a glass. Bake in preheated 325-degree oven for 7 to 8 minutes.

MAMIE'S GINGER COOKIES

1 cup sugar
1/2 cup plus 2 tablespoons oil
1 egg
1/4 cup dark molasses
2 cups flour
2 teaspoons soda
1/2 teaspoon salt
1 teaspoon cinnamon
1 teaspoon ginger
1/4 cup sugar, for dipping

Cream sugar and oil thoroughly. Add egg and beat well. Stir in molasses and add dry ingredients, mixing well. Drop balls of dough in sugar. Place on cookie sheet. Bake in preheated 350-degree oven for 10 to 12 minutes. Do not overbake. Makes 4 dozen.

DATE-NUT PINWHEELS

2 cups sifted flour
1 1/2 teaspoons baking powder
1/2 teaspoon salt
1 teaspoon cinnamon
1/2 teaspoon ginger
1/2 teaspoon nutmeg
2/3 cup butter or margarine, softened
1 cup sugar
1 egg
1 teaspoon vanilla

FILLING:
1 package (8-ounce) pitted dates, cut up
1/2 cup sugar
1/2 cup water
2 teaspoons grated lemon peel
1/2 cup walnuts, finely chopped

Sift flour with baking powder, salt, cinnamon, ginger and nutmeg; set aside. In a large bowl, beat butter until light and gradually beat in sugar. Add egg and vanilla; continue beating until very light and fluffy. Gradually add half of flour mixture. Mix in rest of the flour with your hands to form a stiff dough. Refrigerate 1 hour.

Make the filling in a small saucepan; combine dates and sugar with 1/2 cup water. Cook stirring over medium heat until mixture thickens, about 5 minutes. Remove from heat and stir in lemon peel and nuts. Cool completely.

Divide dough in half. On a lightly-floured surface, roll each half into an 8 x 10-inch rectangle. Spread each rectangle with half the date-nut mixture. From long side roll each in jelly roll fashion. Press edge to seal. Wrap separately, seam side down in plastic wrap or foil. Refrigerate until firm, about 6 hours or overnight.

Lightly grease cookie sheet. Using a sharp knife, cut as many 1/8-inch slices as desired for baking. Place slices 2 inches apart on cookie sheet. Bake in preheated 375-degree oven for 8 to 10 minutes or until brown to your desire. Remove to wire rack and cool. Makes about 9 dozen.

Jan says, "You may double or triple this recipe. It is a great one to make at Christmas as it is a favorite among many people. I always loved to come home from school to find these cookies waiting for me."

✧✦

A TRIBUTE TO THE CHOCOLATE CHIP COOKIE

The chocolate chip cookie—what would our lives be without it? It was first introduced to homemakers in 1939, but was created back in 1930.

That was the year a lady named Ruth Wakefield, proprietor of the New England Toll House in Whitman, Massachusetts cut up a bar of semisweet chocolate into small pieces and added them to her butter cookie dough. She had planned on them melting, but was astonished to discover the chocolate had merely softened into delicious creamy bits. Her cookie became so famous, called Toll House Cookies, that chocolate bars were made for cooks to break off squares as were needed; but the chocolate was still messy to cut.

Finally, in the late 30's, chocolate morsels appeared on grocers shelves and found their place in history. Many of us were little kids when they appeared and our mothers always had the cookie jar full.

The recipes using chocolate morsels are endless but the chocolate chip cookie is as American as baseball and apple pie—and you don't have to be a little kid to enjoy sitting down to a plate of these delicious goodies with a cold glass of milk!

CHOCOLATE CHIP COOKIES

2 cups flour
1 teaspoon baking powder
1/4 teaspoon salt
1 cup butter or margarine
1/2 cup granulated sugar
3/4 cup brown sugar
1/2 teaspoon vanilla
1 egg, beaten
1 package (6-ounce) chocolate chips
1 cup pecans, chopped

Combine flour, baking powder and salt in a medium bowl and set aside. In a large bowl combine butter, sugars and vanilla. Beat until creamy. Add beaten egg and blend well. Gradually add flour mixture. Stir in chips and nuts. Drop by teaspoon on greased cookie sheet. Bake in preheated 375-degree oven for 7 to 9 minutes.

Jan says, "I always double this recipe because they don't last long enough to fill the cookie jar."

REGINA'S TEA COOKIES

1 package (6-ounce) butterscotch chips
1/2 cup butter or margarine
3/4 cup flour, unsifted
1/4 cup granulated sugar
2 tablespoons 100% instant tea powder
1 teaspoon cinnamon
1 egg, slightly beaten
1/2 cup pecans, coarsely chopped

In large saucepan melt 2/3 cup butterscotch chips with butter over low heat, stirring until smooth. Remove from heat and stir in flour, sugar, tea powder, cinnamon and egg. Spread thinly in a greased 10 x 15 1/2 -inch jelly roll pan. Sprinkle with 1/2 cup pecans and remaining butterscotch chips. Bake in preheated 325-degree oven for 20 to 25 minutes. Cool and cut into bars. Makes 4 - 5 dozen.

R. E.'S SESAME COOKIES

2 cups butter, softened
1 1/2 cups sugar
3 cups flour
1 cup sesame seeds
2 cups shredded coconut
1/2 cup almonds, finely chopped

In large bowl cream butter; gradually add sugar and continue beating until light and fluffy. Add flour and mix until well blended. Stir in sesame seeds, coconut and almonds. Divide dough into thirds. Place 1/3 on a long sheet of waxed paper; shape into a long roll 2 inches in diameter. Repeat with remaining dough. Wrap and chill until firm.

Cut rolls into 1/4-inch slices. Bake on ungreased cookie sheets in preheated 300-degree oven for 30 minutes. Remove to wire racks to cool. Makes 4 dozen.

Sweet Temptations

ANNIE'S PEANUT BUTTER COOKIES

1 cup brown sugar
1 cup white sugar
1 cup crunchy peanut butter
1 cup shortening
1/2 teaspoon salt
2 eggs
2 1/2 cups flour
2 teaspoons soda
1 teaspoon vanilla

In a large bowl thoroughly mix sugars, shortening, peanut butter and eggs. Sift dry ingredients and stir into sugar mixture; mix in vanilla, and chill the dough.

Roll into large walnut-size balls. Place 3 inches apart on lightly greased baking sheet. Flatten with a fork dipped in flour, in a crisscross pattern. Bake in preheated 350-degree oven for 10 to 15 minutes. Makes 5 dozen.

GLAZED FRESH-APPLE COOKIES

2 cups sifted flour
1 teaspoon baking soda
1/2 cup soft shortening
1 1/3 cups brown sugar, packed
1/2 teaspoon salt
1 teaspoon cinnamon
1 teaspoon ground cloves
1/2 teaspoon nutmeg
1 egg, unbeaten
1 cup chopped nuts
1 cup finely chopped, unpared apple
1 cup raisins, chopped
1/4 cup apple juice

VANILLA GLAZE:
1 1/2 cups confectioners' sugar, sifted
1 tablespoon soft butter or margarine
1/4 teaspoon vanilla
1/8 teaspoon salt
1 1/2 tablespoons light cream

Sift flour and baking soda. Combine shortening, brown sugar, salt, spices and egg; mix until well blended. Stir in half the flour, then nuts, apple and raisins. Blend in apple juice, then rest of flour. Drop dough by rounded teaspoon, 2 inches apart on greased baking sheet. Bake in preheated 375-degree oven for 9 to 11 minutes or until done.

Prepare Vanilla Glaze by blending all ingredients and when cookies are done, and still hot, spread thinly with Glaze. Makes 3 1/2 dozen.

BANANA JUMBOS

1/2 cup butter
1 cup shortening
1 cup sugar
2 eggs
1 cup ripe bananas
1/2 cup buttermilk
1 teaspoon vanilla
3 cups flour
1 1/2 teaspoons baking soda
1/2 teaspoon salt
1 cup chopped nuts

Cream shortening and sugar until fluffy; add eggs and beat well. Add bananas then sift dry ingredients together and add alternately with buttermilk. Add nut chill dough for 1 hour. Drop by tablespoonful onto slightly greased cookie sheet and bake in preheated 375-degree oven 8 to 10 minutes. Makes 4 dozen cookies

Jo says, "This is one of my sisters' family favorites. They are delicious unfrosted but if you desire, you can frost them with Cream Cheese or Penuche Icing." (See index).

❖❖❖

NADINE'S SCOTTISH SHORTBREAD

2 cups butter
1 cup sugar
4 cups flour

Cream butter and sugar, add flour and blend well; divide dough. Place parchment paper on a cookie sheet and pat out the two rounds of dough on the paper. Flute the edges and prick the dough. Bake in preheated 300-degree oven for about an hour, less if you make dough into cookies.

Nadine says, "I have had this recipe for over 37 years. The mother of a friend came from Scotland to spend the winter with her daughter and this is her recipe. It is traditional to place the rounds of shortbread in front of guests and "break bread" with them. You can cut the dough with a diamond cutter and cut each in half, slightly prick each triangle and bake until slightly brown."

TONIA'S PFEFFERNUSSE

1 cup shortening
1 cup sugar (1/2 white 1/2 brown)
2 eggs, beaten
1 teaspoon cinnamon (more as desired)
1/2 teaspoon allspice
1/4 teaspoon cloves
1 teaspoon mace
1 teaspoon black pepper
1/4 teaspoon ginger (more as desired)
1/2 teaspoon nutmeg
1 teaspoon anise
1/2 cup light corn syrup
1 cup finely chopped nuts
1/2 cup molasses
1/3 cup water
1/2 teaspoon soda
6 2/3 cups flour

Cream shortening and sugars. Add beaten eggs and spices Combine syrup, water, molasses and soda, add to sugar mixture. Add flour, mix well and chill 4 hours. Form into rolls 1/2 inch in diameter, about dime-size or smaller. The smaller the rolls the crunchier the cookies will be. Cut into 1/3-inch pieces. Place on greased sheet and bake in preheated 400-degree oven for about 8 minutes. When cool, store in an airtight container,

Tonia says "You can adjust the spices to your own personal desires. I think theses cookies are great for the holidays. I stick a little baggy of them in Christmas stockings."

WILMA'S RAISIN CRUNCH BARS

FILLING:
2 1/2 cups raisins
1 1/2 cups water
1/2 cup sugar
2 tablespoons cornstarch
3 tablespoons lemon juice

CRUST:
1 1/2 cups quick oats uncooked
3/4 cup margarine
1 cup brown sugar
1 3/4 cups flour
1/2 teaspoon soda
1/2 teaspoon salt

FROSTING:
1 cup confectioners' sugar
1/2 teaspoon vanilla
Boiling water

Combine filling ingredients in saucepan. Cook over low heat until thick. Set aside to cool.

Combine crust ingredients and mix well. Press half of this mixture into a greased 9 x 13-inch baking pan. Pour cooled raisin mixture over crumb mixture. Bake in preheated 375-degree oven for 20 to 30 minutes. Frost while still warm.

Combine confectioners' sugar and vanilla. Add just enough boiling water to make it smooth and spreadable. Be very careful, it does not take much!

SUZANNE'S ONE-BOWL OATMEAL CARAMEL BARS

1 cup butter or margarine
2 1/2 cups all-purpose flour
2 cup brown sugar, packed
2 eggs
2 teaspoons vanilla
1 teaspoon baking soda
3 cups quick-cooking rolled oats
1 package (6-ounce) or 1 cup semisweet
   chocolate morsels
1/2 cup chopped nuts
1 package (7 ounce) or 24 vanilla caramels
2 tablespoons milk

Beat butter on high speed of electric mixer in the large bowl. Add 1 cup of the flour, sugar, eggs, vanilla and baking soda. Beat until well mixed. Add remaining flour; stir in the oats.

Press about 3 1/3 cups of the dough in an ungreased 10 x 15 x l-inch baking pan. Sprinkle with chocolate morsels and nuts.

Combine caramels and milk in a saucepan. Cook over low heat until caramels are melted. Drizzle mixture over chocolate and nuts. Drop remaining dough by teaspoons over the top. Bake in preheated 350-degree oven about 25 minutes or until top is light brown. Place pan on a wire rack and allow to cool. Cut into bars. Makes 60 bars.

SANDRA'S CHERRY MASH BARS

2 cups sugar
16 large marshmallows
2/3 cup evaporated milk
Dash salt
1/2 cup margarine
1 package (10-ounce) cherry chips
2 teaspoons vanilla
1 package (12-ounce) chocolate chips
3/4 cup peanut butter
1 cup chopped salted peanuts

Combine sugar, marshmallows, milk, salt and margarine in sauce pan over medium heat. Cook 5 minutes, stirring constantly. Remove from heat and add cherry chips and vanilla.Spread into a buttered 10 x 15 x l-inch jelly roll pan; Allow to cool. Melt chocolate chips in double boiler; add peanut butter and chopped nuts. Spread over cherry mixture and chill; cut into bars.

WILMA'S SOUR CREAM RAISIN BARS

CRUST:
1 cup brown sugar
1 cup margarine, softened
1 3/4 cups quick oats (uncooked)
1 3/4 cups flour
1 teaspoon soda

FILLING:
2 cups raisins
1 1/3 cups water
3 egg yolks
1 1/2 cups sour cream
1 cup sugar
2 1/2 tablespoons cornstarch
1 teaspoon vanilla

Prepare crust by creaming margarine and brown sugar. Add oats, flour and soda. Mix well and press half the mixture into a 9 x 13 inch pan, reserving the rest. Bake for 7 minutes in a preheated 350-degree oven.

Cook raisins in water for 10 minutes. Drain and cool set aside. Combine yolks, sour cream, sugar, cornstarch together and stir until mixture thickens. Add cooled raisins and vanilla. Pour mixture on baked crust and top with reserved mixture from crust. Bake at 350 degrees for 30 minutes. Cool before cutting into small bars.

Jan says, "We appreciate Wilma giving us this wonderful recipe. These bars freeze very well and she says they will keep forever, but when you make them you will find there won't be any left to put into the freezer."

❖❖❖

TURTLE BARS

1 3/4 cups flour
1 1/2 cups old-fashioned oats (uncooked)
3/4 cup firmly packed brown sugar
1/2 teaspoon salt
3/4 cup butter or margarine, melted
1 cup semi-sweet chocolate chips
1 cup pecans, coarsely chopped
1 jar (12 1/4 ounce) caramel ice cream
   topping

Combine 1 1/2 cups flour, oats, brown sugar and salt. Add butter and mix until crumbly; reserve 3/4 cup of mixture for topping. Press remaining mixture onto bottom of greased 9 x 13-inch baking pan. Bake in a preheated 375-degree oven for 10 minutes. Sprinkle chocolate chips and nuts over partially baked base. Combine caramel topping and remaining 1/4 cup flour and drizzle over chocolate and nuts. Sprinkle reserved crumb mixture over caramel mixture. Continue baking for 20 minutes. Cool thoroughly and chill to set chocolate. Cut into bars when set.

Brownies

EASY DELISH BROWNIES

1 1/3 cup shortening
4 eggs
2 cups sugar
1 1/2 cups flour
2 teaspoons baking powder
1 teaspoon salt
3/4 cup plus two tablespoons cocoa
1 teaspoon vanilla
1/2 cup pecans, chopped
Powdered sugar

Combine all ingredients in a mixing bowl and beat well. Spoon into 2 lightly greased 8 x 8-inch pans. Bake in preheated 350-degree oven for 25 minutes. Cool and sprinkle with powdered sugar.

Jan says, "This is a great quick brownie. Freeze one pan quickly before they are eaten so you'll have them when unexpected guests drop in. Each pan makes 25 squares."

CHOCOLATE BROWNIES

1 1/4 cups flour
3/4 teaspoon baking soda
1/4 teaspoon salt
3/4 cup margarine
1 1/2 cups brown sugar
3 eggs
2 teaspoons vanilla
3 squares (1-ounce size) unsweetened
   chocolate, melted and cooled
3/4 cup milk
3/4 cup walnuts, chopped
Chocolate Brownie and Bar Frosting
   (See index)

Stir flour, baking soda and salt into large bowl and set aside. In mixing bowl combine margarine, sugar, eggs, vanilla, cooled chocolate and milk. Beat until thoroughly mixed. Stir in dry ingredients and nuts. Pour into a greased 15 1/2 x 10 1/2-inch jelly roll pan. Bake in preheated 350-degree oven for 25 minutes.When cooled, frost with Chocolate Frosting and cut into bars. Makes 50.

Sweet Temptations

JEANNE'S MICRO BROWNIES

2 eggs
1 cup sugar
1/4 teaspoon salt
1 teaspoon vanilla
1/2 cup margarine, melted
3/4 cup unsifted flour
1/2 cup cocoa
1 cup chopped nuts

Beat eggs, sugar, salt and vanilla in a small bowl until the batter is light and fluffy. Add margarine and continue to beat until thoroughly blended. Stir in flour and cocoa at low speed on your mixer; stir in nuts. Spread evenly in a greased 8-inch dish. Microwave on High for 6 minutes. If you do not have a turntable unit, move the dish a 1/4 turn every 2 minutes. Sprinkle with powdered sugar.

Jo and Jan say, "Melt your margarine in the dish and when you have poured it into the batter your dish is already greased."

NORMA'S CHOCOLATE SYRUP BROWNIES

1 stick margarine
1 cup sugar
4 eggs
1 1/2 cups flour
1 can Hershey syrup

ICING:
6 tablespoons margarine
6 tablespoons milk
1 1/2 cups sugar
3/4 cup butterscotch chips
1/4 cup chocolate chip

Cream margarine and sugar well; combine rest of ingredients and pour into a greased 10 x 15-inch jelly roll pan, bake in a preheated 350-degree oven for 20 minutes.

Scald milk and add margarine and sugar. Bring to a full rolling boil and cook for 30 seconds. Add chips and beat well; pour onto brownies. Makes about 4 dozen.

CHOCOLATE MINT BROWNIES

2 ounces unsweetened baking chocolate
1/2 cup butter
2 large eggs
1 cup sugar
1 teaspoon vanilla
1/2 cup flour
1/8 teaspoon salt
1/2 cup pecans, chopped
1/2 cup After Eight mints, chopped

Melt chocolate and butter together in top of double boiler. Beat eggs well and gradually add the sugar to eggs, beating as you add the eggs so mixture will be well blended. Stir in chocolate and butter mixture, then vanilla. Sift flour and salt together and blend into batter. Fold in nuts and mints. Pour into an 8-inch square which has been greased and floured. Bake in a preheated 350-degree oven for 25 minutes. Makes 16 brownies.

KATHY'S BAKED FUDGE

2 cups sugar
1/2 cup plus 1 tablespoon flour
1/2 cup unsweetened cocoa
4 eggs, room temperature and well beaten
2 sticks margarine, melted and cooled
1 cup chopped pecans
2 teaspoons vanilla
Unsweetened whipped cream (garnish)
Ice Cream (garnish)

Combine sugar, flour and cocoa. Add well beaten eggs and blend melted margarine into dry ingredients. Add nuts and vanilla; stir well. Spread batter in an 8 x 10-inch baking pan. Set into larger pan of hot water. Bake in preheated 300-degree oven for 1 hour or until fudge is firm and knife inserted in center comes out moist but clean. Cool in refrigerator. Cut into squares and serve warm, topped with ice cream or whipped cream. Serves 8.

❖❖❖

CHOCOLATE BROWNIE AND BAR FROSTING

2 tablespoons butter or margarine
2 squares unsweetened chocolate
2 tablespoons warm strong coffee
1 tablespoon milk
2 teaspoons vanilla
2 cups confectioners' sugar, measured after
   sifting

Melt butter and chocolate in top of double boiler. Blend in coffee, milk and vanilla. Remove from heat and whisk in sugar until smooth. If too thick, add a bit more coffee or milk. Spread over cooled brownies.

CARAMEL BROWNIES

1 box (18 1/2-ounce) German chocolate cake
   mix
2/3 cup evaporated milk
3/4 cup melted margarine
1 package (14-ounce) caramels
1 package (12-ounce) chocolate morsels
1 cup chopped pecans

Blend cake mix, 1/3 cup of evaporated milk and melted margarine with a spoon. Press half of mixture in an ungreased 9 x 13-inch pan. Bake in preheated 350-degree oven for 7 minutes.

Melt caramels in remaining 1/3 cup evaporated milk over low heat. Spread over top of baked batter. Top with chocolate morsels and nuts. Spread with remaining batter; the batter will be very stiff so you will have to use your fingers.

Bake 18 minutes; cool before cutting into squares.

BROWNIE-RASPBERRY ELEGANCE

2 squares (1-ounce size) unsweetened
   chocolate
1/2 cup butter
2 eggs
1 cup sugar
1 1/2 teaspoons vanilla
1/2 cup flour

MOUSSE:
1 package (6-ounces) semisweet chocolate
   pieces
1 square (1 ounce) unsweetened chocolate
1/3 cup hot water
3 egg yolks, slightly beaten
1 1/2 teaspoons vanilla
6 tablespoons butter, softened
1 cup heavy cream, whipped
1 pint fresh raspberries, rinsed and well
   drained
1/3 cup sugar (optional, as taste dictates)
Heavy cream, whipped (garnish, optional)

Melt chocolate and butter over low heat; transfer to a mixing bowl. Beat in eggs, sugar and vanilla; blend well and mix in flour. Spread evenly over bottom of a well greased 8-inch springform pan. Bake in preheated 350-degree oven for 25 minutes. Brownie should be moist so do not overbake. Cool in baking pan while you make the mousse.

Combine chocolate pieces, unsweetened chocolate and water in top of double boiler; melt and stir until mixture is smooth. Remove from water and add a small amount to the egg yolks; add yolks back into the chocolate mixture; add vanilla and butter and whisk until well blended; cool slightly.

Fold cooled chocolate mixture into whipped cream and gently fold in raspberries and sugar, if desired. Spread mixture evenly over brownie layer in pan. Cover and refrigerate until firm, several hours or overnight. Serve sliced with additional whipped cream, if desired.

Jan and Jo say, "This is so delicious, and beautiful to behold' We like to garnish it with chocolate leaves and a few extra fresh berries." Serves 10 - 12.

Pies

**Dame, get up and bake your pies,
Bake your pies, bake your pies,
Dame, get up and bake your pies,
On Christmas day in the morning.**
—*Mother Goose*

TIPS ON PIES

- To make a lattice crust, divide dough in half. Press dough into bottom of pie pan, leaving a 1-inch overhang. Fill bottom crust with pie mixture. Roll out remaining pastry dough on floured board and cut into 1/2-inch strips. A pastry wheel will cut a more decorative crust. Lay half the strips horizontally 1 inch apart over filled pie. Starting at the center of the pie, weave the vertical strips, gently folding back corresponding portion of horizontal strips. Work over and under; do not press down hard. Repeat, working out from center to both sides, placing cross strips about 1 inch apart, until completed. Trim any overhanging strips to rim of pan. Fold the 1-inch overhang of lower crust and press firmly around edges to seal. Brush with an egg-water wash to glaze. Bake as directed.

- If you do not want to take the time to make a lattice crust, you can roll the pastry for the top into a 9 x 3-inch rectangle; cut into 4 strips and place on top of mixture forming 2 X's. Gently press at sides to seal. Bake according to recipe directions.

- To make leaf or flower shapes for top of pie, roll the pastry for the top crust about 1/8 to 1/4-inch thick. Use a leaf canape cutter and make leaves. You can use the dull side of a knife to etch veins. You can arrange several leaves to form flowers. Brush the edge of pie shell with an egg-water wash and place leaves around the edge; press lightly but firmly. Form a flower shape in center of filling, brush with additional glaze and bake as directed.

RUTHIE'S PIE CRUST

3 cups flour
1 1/3 cups shortening
1 teaspoon salt
1 egg, beaten
1 tablespoon white vinegar
5 tablespoons ice water

Mix flour, shortening and salt until crumbly. Add beaten egg, vinegar and ice water. Stir with a fork until mixture is moistened. Roll into a ball; wrap in plastic wrap and chill before rolling out. Makes 3 pie shells.

Jan says, "This is a wonderful pie crust given to us by Ruthie. I thought I had a good pie crust recipe, but this one is marvelous and a delight to work. It freezes well if you aren't ready to make a pie."

MOM'S PIE CRUST

FOR 2 CRUSTS
2 cups sifted flour
1 teaspoon salt
2/3 cup plus 2 tablespoons solid shortening
1/4 cup cold water

FOR 1 CRUST
1 cup sifted flour
1/2 teaspoon salt
1/3 cup plus 1 tablespoon shortening
2 tablespoons water

Measure flour and salt into a bowl. Add shortening and with a wire pastry cutter work the mixture until it looks like coarse meal. Add cold water all at once and mix until all the flour is moistened and dough comes away from the sides of the bowl. Quickly roll dough into circles and fit into the pie pan.

Jo says, "I think my Mother makes the best pie crust in the entire world! She tells me she thinks the secret is the pastry cutter, cool hands and above all, don't play with the dough. Work quickly and get it into that pie plate."

CREAM CHEESE PASTRY CRUST

1 1/2 teaspoons salt
1/2 cup butter
2 1/2 cups flour
1 package (8-ounce) cream cheese

Sift the flour and salt together. Cut in butter and cream cheese, using fingers to blend until crumbly; the dough will be moist. Form into a ball, wrap in waxed paper and refrigerate for 4 hours. Roll out to 1/8-inch thickness.

This is a wonderful crust for turnovers and tarts as well as your fruit pies. Makes 2 crusts.

TONIA'S NUTTY - COCONUT PIE CRUST

1 cup chopped nuts - we prefer cashews, macadamia, hazelnut or almonds
1 cup flaked coconut
2 tablespoons brown sugar
1/4 cup butter, melted

Combine ingredients and press into an 8 or 9-inch pie plate, slightly building up the sides. Bake in preheated 300-degree oven for about 15 minutes or until golden brown. Cool before filling.

Tonia says, "Tom and I use this crust with Mom and Jan's Banana - Cream Cheese Pie (See index). It's a real company pleaser."

NORMA'S STIR PIE CRUST

1 1/2 cups flour
2 tablespoons sugar
2 tablespoons milk
1/2 cup vegetable oil
Pinch of salt

Measure all ingredients into pie pan and mix with fork until well blended, then pat out with hands to form pie shell. Makes 1 pastry shell.

ALMOND SHORT CRUST

6 tablespoons butter, softened
2 tablespoons sugar
1 egg yolk
1 teaspoon grated lemon peel
1/2 teaspoon vanilla
3 drops almond extract
1/3 cup plus 2 tablespoons flour
1/3 cup blanched almonds, finely chopped

Cream butter, sugar, egg yolk, lemon peel, vanilla and almond extract in large bowl. Add flour and almonds; mix well until smooth. Gather into a ball and refrigerate about 30 minutes. Press chilled pastry into a 9-inch pie or tart pan, if necessary dust hands with flour to work the pastry. Chill at least 1 hour or freeze if not using for a few days

When ready to fill, bake in preheated 375-degree oven for 20 to 25 minutes; if air bubble forms during first 10 minutes, pierce pastry with tip of a knife. When pastry shell is golden, remove from oven and cool completely before filling. Makes 1 9-inch shell.

❖❖

COCOA PASTRY PIE CRUST

2 cups flour
1/2 cup sugar
1/2 cup cocoa,unsweetened
1/4 teaspoon salt
1/2 cup plus 6 tablespoons butter
1 teaspoon vanilla
4 to 5 tablespoons ice water

Combine flour, sugar, cocoa and salt in mixing bowl. Cut in butter with pastry blender until mixture resembles coarse crumbs. Sprinkle in vanilla and water. Mix with fork until ingredients are moistened. Shape into ball and chill until ready to use. Makes 2 9-inch crusts.

You may bake the crusts in a preheated 400-degree oven for 10 to 12 minutes. Just don't forget to prick the crust and rub a little shortening over the bottom to keep the crust from getting soggy.

Cool and fill with your favorite filling or ice cream.

SUGAR-WALNUT CRUST

1 cup flour
1/4 cup confectioners' sugar
1/4 cup walnuts, finely chopped
1/2 cup butter

Combine crust ingredients and mix with pastry blender until you can form a ball. Press into a 9-inch pie plate, using your hands to form a nice edge. Fill with pie filling and bake.

SUCCESSFUL MERINGUE

1 tablespoon cornstarch
2 tablespoons cold water
1/2 cup boiling water
3 egg whites
6 tablespoons sugar
Dash of salt
1 teaspoon vanilla extract

Add cold water to cornstarch in a small saucepan; add boiling water and cook stirring constantly until clear and thickened. Set aside until cold. Beat whites at high speed until foamy, add sugar gradually and beat until stiff but not dry. Reduce speed to low, add salt and vanilla. Gradually add cold cornstarch; turn speed to high and beat well. Spread meringue over pie filling making sure it completely covers filling around edges. Bake in preheated 350-degree oven about 10 minutes.

HAZELNUT PASTRY SHELL

1 1/2 cups flour
1 cup ground hazelnuts
1/3 cup sugar
1/2 teaspoon cinnamon
1/2 cup butter, cold and cut into pieces
1 egg

Combine flour, nuts, sugar and cinnamon in large bowl; cut in butter until mixture is like coarse crumbs. Add egg and stir until dough cleans side of bowl. Press into bottom of 9-inch pie plate; chill 1 hour. Line shell with foil or parchment and fill with uncooked beans. Bake in preheated 400-degree oven for 15 minutes. Cool pie shell completely before filling.

If making a baked pie, fill unbaked pie shell with pie mixture and follow recipe instructions. You can reserve 1/3 of the dough when forming the crust and cut dough strips or patterns for the top. Makes 1 9-inch shell.

SPICEY PECAN CRUST

2 cups all purpose flour
1 cup pecans, chopped fine
4 tablespoons sugar
1 teaspoon allspice
3/4 cup butter or margarine, cut into chunks
1 egg
2-3 tablespoons ice water

Combine first 5 ingredients and blend well. With pastry blender, cut in butter until mixture resembles coarse meal.

Beat egg with 2 tablespoons water. Add to flour mixture and mix with fork just until moistened, adding the additional tablespoon of water if needed. Be careful to not over beat. Gather into a ball and wrap; refrigerate overnight.

Divide dough and roll each half on floured board to 1/8-inch thickness. Lightly grease 2 8-inch pie pans and gently fit pastry into pans, trim off excess. Chill 1 hour. Line each shell with foil or parchment and fill with uncooked beans. Bake in preheated 400-degree oven for 15 minutes. Remove from oven and gently remove liners. Cool pie shell completely before filling. Makes 2 8-inch pies. Jo and Jan say, "Try this crust recipe with your next pumpkin pie."

Apple Pie without
Some cheese
It's like a kiss without
a squeeze -

FERN'S ENGLISH APPLE PIE

1/2 cup margarine
1/2 cup brown sugar
1 cup flour
2 teaspoons cinnamon
3 tablespoons water
1/2 cup pecans or walnuts
6 cups apples
1/2 cup granulated sugar
1 9-inch pie shell

In large bowl beat butter and sugar until fluffy. Stir in flour, 1 teaspoon cinnamon and water until smooth. Stir in nuts; set aside. Peel apples, quarter, core and slice them thin. Mound apples in prepared pie shell and sprinkle with sugar and 1 teaspoon cinnamon. Spoon nut topping over apples in dollops. Bake in preheated 375-degree oven for 35 to 50 minutes. Serves 8.

Jan says, "A great quickie dessert. You might want to serve ice cream or frozen yogurt over it to make it even more special."

RUTH'S DELICIOUS NO-SUGAR APPLE PIE

6 peeled, cored and sliced apples
1 can (6-ounces) frozen unsweetened apple juice concentrate (undiluted)
2 tablespoons cornstarch
Dash of salt
Cinnamon or apple pie spice (to taste)
1/4 cup margarine
1 double pie crust recipe (See index)

Dissolve cornstarch in apple concentrate. Combine with apples, salt and spice. Simmer together until thickened. Pour into unbaked pie shell. Dot with margarine; add top crust and bake in preheated 375-degree oven for 45 minutes.

RUTHIE'S HARVEST PIE

2-crust pie recipe (See index)
3 medium apples
3 medium pears
1 1/2 cups cranberries
1/2 cup raisins
1 cup mince meat (Home made, see index, or commercial brand, optional)
1 cup sugar
1 teaspoon cinnamon
1 1/2 cups whole walnuts
2 tablespoons flour
1 1/2 teaspoons butter

Peel apples and pears, quarter and core them; slice thin. Mix together in large bowl apples, pears, cranberries, mince meat, sugar, cinnamon, nuts and flour. Spoon mixture into bottom crust heaping up the mixture. Dot with butter and cover with top crust. Bake in preheated 425-degree oven for 50 to 60 minutes.

Jan says, "You will make many brownie points, as well as pie points when you bake this one! It is one of the very best. Do not substitute the walnuts; and you have an option of using the mince meat. A great pie for Fall."

MOM'S BLUEBERRY 'ALMOST PIE'

CRUST:
1 1/2 cups flour
Pinch of salt
3 tablespoons sugar
3/4 cup butter
1 1/2 tablespoons white vinegar

FILLING:
1/2 teaspoon cinnamon
1/2 cup sugar
3 tablespoons cornstarch
6 cups blueberries, rinsed and drained and divided to use
1 tablespoon butter

Combine flour, salt, and sugar in a small bowl. Work in butter with pastry blender or fingers; mix in vinegar. Pat crust in 8 or 9-inch springform pan, bring crusts up the sides about 1 1/2 inches.

In a large bowl, combine cinnamon, sugar and corn starch. Add 4 cups of blueberries. Pour into prepared crust and dot with butter. Bake in preheated 400-degree oven 1 hour. Remove from oven and place on cooling rack. Put remaining 2 cups uncooked berries on top. Cool, uncovered; to serve, remove rim of pan and cut in wedges. Serves 8

LAYERED FRESH PEACH CREAM PIE

1 9-inch baked pastry shell
1 envelope unflavored gelatin
1/4 cup water
1/2 cup sugar
1/4 teaspoon salt
3/4 cup milk
2 large eggs, separated
1 teaspoon vanilla
1/2 teaspoon grated lemon peel
1/4 cup sugar
1/2 cup heavy cream, whipped
3 cups fresh sliced peaches
2 tablespoons sugar
2 teaspoons lemon juice
Water
1 1/2 teaspoons cornstarch

Soften gelatin in water and set aside. Combine 1/2 cup sugar, salt, milk, egg yolks in saucepan; mix well. Stir over low heat until custard coats a spoon. Remove from heat, stir in gelatin, vanilla, lemon peel. Chill until partially set.

Beat egg whites until they stand in soft, stiff peaks, gradually beat in remaining 1/4 cup sugar. Fold egg whites and whipped cream into the gelatin mixture. Turn 1/2 of mixture into pie shell. Top with 2 cups sliced peaches. Spread on other 1/2 of mixture. Chill.

Combine remaining peaches, 2 tablespoons sugar and lemon juice. Cover and chill one hour or until juice has formed in the bowl. Drain juice into measuring cup and add water to make 1/2 cup. Blend in cornstarch; stir and cook 3 minutes or until juice is slightly thickened and transparent. Cool thoroughly.

Arrange sliced peaches over chilled pie. Spoon glaze over all. Chill until ready to serve.

What a wonderful summer pie! Garnish with fresh mint leaves.

FRESH CHERRY PIE

Pastry for a 9-inch 2-crust pie
4 cups fresh cherries
1 cup sugar
6 tablespoons flour
1/2 teaspoon cinnamon
Dash of nutmeg
1/8 teaspoon almond extract
1 1/2 tablespoons butter

Line pie plate with pastry. Mix cherries, sugar, flour, cinnamon, nutmeg and almond extract; pour into pie shell. Dot with butter over cherry mixture and cover with top crust. Prick the top with a fork and bake in a preheated 425-degree oven for 15 minutes. Reduce heat to 375 degrees and bake for 35 more minutes. Cool, but serve it warm if possible. Serves 8.

FRESH PEAR PIE

1 recipe Sugar-Walnut Crust (See index)
1/2 cup sugar
2 tablespoons flour
1/4 teaspoon salt
1 egg
1/2 teaspoon vanilla extract
1/8 teaspoon almond extract
1 cup sour cream
4 cups sliced fresh pears

CRUMBLE TOPPING:
1/4 cup butter
1/4 cup flour
2 tablespoons sugar
1/2 teaspoon cinnamon
3/4 cup walnut pieces and halves

Prepare crust; set aside. In medium bowl prepare filling by combining ingredients and pour into crust. Wrap a 2-inch strip of foil around crust edges and bake in preheated 400-degree oven for 30 minutes; remove foil strips. While pie is baking, prepare Crumble Topping.

In a small bowl combine butter, flour, sugar and cinnamon; mix with pastry blender until crumbly. Sprinkle topping over pie filling, scatter pieces and halves evenly over the top. Return to oven and bake an additional 25 to 30 minutes until topping is browned and walnuts are toasted. Cool completely before cutting. Serves 8.

INNES' RUM CREAM PIE

8 to 12 toffee candies
2 or 3 tablespoons cream
1/2 teaspoon rum flavoring
1 9-inch baked pastry shell
1 1/2 cups milk
1/2 cup cream
5 tablespoons sifted flour
1/4 teaspoon salt
2 eggs, well beaten
1 teaspoon rum flavoring
1/2 cup heavy cream,
  whipped
Whipped cream and shaved chocolate for
  garnish (optional)

In double boiler over hot water melt toffee candies and cream to a spreading consistency. Add rum flavoring. Spread candy mixture over bottom of baked shell.

In double boiler over hot water beat milk and cream. Mix together sugar, flour and salt; add to hot milk mixture. Cook and stir until thickened, about 15 minutes. Add a little of the hot mixture to the beaten eggs, then stir egg mixture into double boiler mixture and cook 2 or 3 minutes, stirring constantly. Cool; add rum flavoring and fold in whipped cream. Turn into pie shell; garnish with whipped cream and shaved chocolate, covering entire surface if desired. Serves 6 - 8.

Jan says, "This pie was one of my favorites when I went to the Innes Tea Room. I never make it that I don't have beautiful memories of times spent there."

FRESH RHUBARB PIE

1 10-inch baked pie shell
2 large eggs
1 1/2 cups sugar
1/4 cup flour
3/4 teaspoon salt
1 tablespoon cinnamon
3 cups fresh rhubarb (cut into 1/4-inch cubes)

Beat eggs until frothy in a large bowl; stir in rest of ingredients. Pour into baked crust; bake 30 to 40 minutes in preheated 350-degree oven until filling is set and golden brown. Let stand 30 minutes before serving. Serves 8 -10.

STRAWBERRY - RHUBARB PIE

1 double 9-inch pie crust (See index)
4 cups fresh strawberries, sliced
1 1/2 cups fresh rhubarb, cut into 1/2-inch
   pieces
1 3/4 cups sugar
2 tablespoons cornstarch
1/2 teaspoon ground cinnamon
1/4 teaspoon freshly ground nutmeg
1 egg, lightly beaten
1 egg beaten with 1 tablespoon water
Heavy cream, whipped and sweetened or
   Creme Fraiche (See index)

Combine strawberries and rhubarb in large mixing bowl. Mix sugar, cornstarch, cinnamon and nutmeg; sprinkle over fruit and toss to blend. Add egg and gently stir again. Spoon mixture into bottom crust.

Cover filled shell with top crust, brush with egg-water glaze and bake on lower third of preheated 400-degree oven for 40 to 45 minutes, or until crust is golden. Serve warm or at room temperature with sweetened whipped cream or Creme Fraiche. Serves 6 - 8.

WALNUT RUM PIE

1 partially baked sweet pastry pie shell (See
   index Cream Cheese Pastry)
3/4 cup sugar
1/2 cup butter, melted and cooled
1/2 cup flour
2 eggs, beaten
1 cup semisweet chocolate chips
1 cup walnuts, coarsely chopped
2 tablespoons dark rum
Unsweetened whipped cream (garnish)

Combine sugar, butter, flour and eggs; beat until smooth. Stir in chips, nuts and rum. Spoon mixture into shell and bake in preheated 350-degree oven for 30 to 35 minutes until filling is golden. Cool on a rack. At serving time, whip cream and spoon a dollop on each serving. Serves 8 - 10.

CHOCOLATE PECAN PIE

1 9-inch pie shell, unbaked
1 cup chocolate chips
2 tablespoons butter
2/3 cup evaporated milk
2 eggs, beaten
1 cup sugar
2 tablespoons flour
1/4 teaspoon salt
1 teaspoon vanilla
1 cup pecans, chopped

In medium-sized pan combine chips, butter and milk. Cook until smooth and set aside. Combine eggs, sugar, flour, salt, vanilla and nuts; stir into chocolate mixture. Pour in pie shell and bake in preheated 375-degree oven for 40 minutes or until firm. Serves 6 - 8.

PECAN PUMPKIN PIE

3 eggs
1 cup pumpkin
1/3 cup sugar
1 teaspoon pumpkin pie spice
1/2 cup sugar
2/3 cup corn syrup
3 tablespoons melted butter
1/2 teaspoon vanilla
1 cup pecan halves
1 unbaked 9-inch pastry shell

Stir together 1 slightly beaten egg, pumpkin, 1/3 cup sugar and pie spice. Spread over bottom of pie shell. Combine 2 beaten eggs, corn syrup, 1/2 cup sugar, butter and vanilla. Stir in nuts. Spoon over pumpkin mixture. Bake in preheated 350-degree oven for 60 minutes.

COCONUT CREAM PIE

1 cup sugar
1/2 cup cornstarch
1/4 teaspoon salt
3 cups hot milk
3 egg yolks, beaten
1 teaspoon vanilla extract
1/2 teaspoon almond extract
2 cans (3 1/2-ounce size) flaked coconut
1 9-inch baked pie shell (See index)
1 cup heavy cream, whipped

Combine sugar, cornstarch and salt; gradually add to milk in saucepan, stirring until smooth. Bring to a boil, stirring constantly, over medium heat and boil 2 minutes. Remove from heat, stir a little of hot mixture into beaten egg yolks; add back to saucepan. Cook, stirring over low heat until boiling and thick enough to mound from a spoon. Pour into bowl; add extracts and half of coconut. Place plastic wrap or waxed paper on filling and refrigerate for 1 hour. Spoon mixture into prepared pie shell; refrigerate 3 hours. At serving time, spread whipped cream over pie and top with remaining coconut. Serves 8.

LEMON VELVET PIE

1 8-inch pie shell, baked (See index, Ruthie's)
1 cup sugar
3 tablespoons cornstarch
1/4 cup butter or margarine
1 tablespoon grated lemon rind
1/4 cup lemon juice
3 egg yolks, slightly beaten
1 cup sour cream
1 cup heavy cream, whipped

Combine sugar and cornstarch in saucepan. Add butter, lemon rind, lemon juice and egg yolks. Cook and stir over medium heat until thickened and boiling. Remove from heat and cool slightly; fold in sour cream and cool thoroughly. Pour into pie shell and top with whipped cream. Refrigerate until serving time.

Jo and Jan say, "This is delicious and very pretty adorned with Glazed Lemon Slices (See index). It is also a wonderful filling for tarts. If you want to cut down a bit on the tartness, add 1 cup of milk to the custard ingredients before you cook it."

PEANUT BUTTER PIE

1 9-inch baked pie shell or Chocolate Cookie Crust (See index)
1 package (5 1/2-ounce) vanilla pudding mix (not instant)
1/3 cup creamy peanut butter
1/2 cup heavy cream, whipped
Sweetened whipped cream
1/4 cup peanuts, finely chopped

Prepare pudding mix according to package directions, adding peanut butter. Beat until thoroughly blended. Fold in whipped cream and spoon into prepared pie shell. Chill until firm; top with sweetened whipped cream and sprinkle with chopped nuts. Serves 8.

Jo says, "You might prefer using crunchy peanut butter instead of the smooth. We like to garnish this pie with milk chocolate curls."

SOUFFLE GRASSHOPPER PIE

1 chocolate cookie crust (See Frozen
   Grasshopper Pie, index)
1 envelope unflavored gelatin
1/2 cup sugar (divided)
1/8 teaspoon salt
1/2 cup cold water
3 eggs, separated
1/4 cup green creme de menthe
1/4 cup white creme de cacao
1 cup heavy cream, whipped

In top of double boiler combine 1/4 cup sugar, gelatin and salt. Slowly add water until gelatin is dissolved and mixture is slightly thickened, about 5 minutes. Remove from over water. Stir in liqueur and chill, stirring occasionally until the consistency of unbeaten egg whites. Into stiffly beaten, but not dry egg whites, gradually add other 1/4 cup sugar. Beat until stiff; fold into chilled mixture. Carefully fold in whipped cream; fill pie shell and chill before serving. Serves 8.

Jo says, "This recipe and the Frozen Grasshopper Pie can be make substituting Kahlua for the creme de menthe. We call it Tumbleweed Pie. We like to garnish the pie with fresh strawberries."

FROZEN GRASSHOPPER PIE

24 chocolate cookies with cream centers
1/4 cup butter or margarine, melted
24 large marshmallows
1/2 cup milk
4 tablespoons green creme de menthe
2 tablespoons white creme de cacao
1 cup heavy cream, whipped

Crush cookies with a rolling pin or in food processor. Add melted butter and mix well. Press mixture in pie plate, set aside.

Melt marshmallows in milk. Set aside to cool completely. Add liqueurs; fold in whipped cream. Spoon filling into cooled crust and freeze. Serves 8.

MILLIONAIRE PIE

1 cup crushed graham crackers (about 16)
10 tablespoons unsalted butter, melted
1 cup chopped pecans
1 cup sugar
1 quart vanilla ice cream, softened
1 quart raspberry sherbet, softened
5 egg whites
1 cup sugar

Combine graham crackers, melted butter, nuts and sugar and press into two 8-inch pie pans, forming a border crust at the top. Bake 15 minutes at 350 degrees or until golden brown. Set aside to cool then place in freezer for about 20 minutes. Fill bottom half of shells with vanilla ice cream, then top with sherbet. Freeze overnight.

Just before serving, make a meringue by beating egg whites to soft peaks then gradually beating in sugar until stiff. Cover entire top of pies with meringue, being careful to seal the edges. Place under broiler just until meringue browns slightly. Makes 2 pies.

RASPBERRY ANGEL PIE

1 recipe Meringue Shell (See index)
2/3 cup sugar
1 quart fresh raspberries
1 cup heavy cream
1 teaspoon almond extract

Prepare Meringue Shell recipe, spread meringue to make a 9-inch circle with a slightly raised edge. Bake as directed, cool and set aside.

Wash and drain berries; whip cream until stiff and fold in almond extract.

Fold 3 cups berries into whipped cream; turn into meringue shell and garnish with remaining berries. Serves 6 - 8.

RASPBERRY PIE

1 9-inch baked pie shell
1 quart fresh raspberries, washed
2/3 cup water
1/3 cup Framboise or raspberry liqueur
3 tablespoons cornstarch
1 cup sugar
1/2 stick butter
Red food coloring, if desired
Heavy cream, whipped

Cook 1/2 raspberries with water and liqueur for 5 minutes. Mix cornstarch and sugar together and add to boiling fruit. Add butter and a little red food coloring. Place other 1/2 of berries in the baked pie shell and spoon the glaze over all. Serve with sweetened whipped cream.

BANANA - CREAM CHEESE PIE

1 9-inch pie shell, either baked or cookie
  crumb
4 to 6 bananas
1 package (8-ounce) cream cheese
1 can (14-ounce) sweetened condensed milk
1/3 cup lemon juice
1 teaspoon vanilla

With mixer at high speed, beat cream cheese until smooth and creamy; add sweetened condensed milk and beat until thoroughly mixed. Add lemon juice and vanilla. Stir or fold with spoon until thickened. Slice 2 or 3 bananas onto crust to form a layer. Slice remaining bananas into cream mixture and fold gently to distribute. Pour filling into crust and refrigerate. Serves 8.

CHOCOLATE CHIP PIE

2 eggs
1/2 cup flour
1/2 cup sugar
1/2 cup brown sugar
1 cup butter, melted and cooled
1 package (6-ounce) chocolate chips
1 cup walnuts, chopped
1 8-inch unbaked pie shell (See index)

Beat eggs until foamy. Add flour, sugars and beat until well blended. Add butter; stir in chips and nuts. Pour into pie shell. Bake in preheated 325-degree oven for 1 hour. Remove and serve warm with whipped cream or ice cream.

Jan says, "You will want to make 2 of these pies. They freeze well and you'll be glad that you did. When company pops in, you will be ready."

FRENCH SILK PIE

CRUST:
1/2 cup butter
3/4 cup flour
1/3 cup pecans, chopped
2 tablespoons brown sugar

FILLING:
1 cup powdered sugar
1/2 cup butter, softened
2 squares (2 ounces) unsweetened
chocolate, melted
1 1/2 teaspoons vanilla
2 eggs
Heavy cream, whipped, for topping

Melt butter; add rest of ingredients and cook 3 to 4 minutes until brown and all the butter is absorbed. Press into an 8-inch pie dish from the center and on up the sides a little, Chill.

Combine all except eggs and blend well, then beat in 1 egg at a time, beating 5 minutes for each egg. Pour into chilled crust, and return to refrigerator to thoroughly chill the filling. Serve each slice with a dollop of whipped cream.

EVELYN'S CHOCOLATE PIE

1 9-inch baked pie shell (See index)
3 tablespoons cocoa
1 1/3 cups sugar
1/2 cup cornstarch
1/2 teaspoon salt
2 1/2 cups milk
3 egg yolks, beaten
1 teaspoon vanilla
2 tablespoons butter
Whipped cream, for topping

Mix dry ingredients together in a large heavy saucepan. Add milk, eggs and vanilla; stir constantly over medium-low heat until thickened. Remove from heat; add butter, cool and pour into baked pie shell. Chill and garnish with whipped cream if desired.

Cakes

BLITZ TORTE

1/2 cup butter
1 3/4 cups sugar
4 eggs, separated
1 teaspoon vanilla
1 1/2 cups sifted flour
1 1/2 teaspoons baking powder
1/2 teaspoon salt
1/2 cup milk
1/2 cup slivered almonds
1 recipe rum sauce (See index)

Cream butter and 3/4 cup sugar until light and fluffy. Add egg yolks and vanilla; beat well. Add sifted dry ingredients and milk alternately; beating until smooth after each addition. Spread in 2 greased and floured 8-inch round or square pans. Beat egg whites until stiff; add remaining sugar gradually and pile lightly on batter; sprinkle with nuts. Bake in preheated 350-degree oven for 30 minutes.Serve with Rum Cream Sauce. (See index). Serves 16.

PEGGY'S APPLE CAKE WITH HOT SOUR CREAM SAUCE

2 cups flour
2 teaspoons soda
Dash of salt
1/2 teaspoon nutmeg
1 teaspoon cinnamon
2 cups sugar
1/2 cup oil
2 eggs
6 Jonathan apples, chopped
1 cup nuts, chopped

SOUR CREAM SAUCE:
1 cup butter
1 cup brown sugar
1 cup granulated sugar
1 cup sour cream
1 teaspoon vanilla

Sift flour, soda, salt, nutmeg and cinnamon. Combine sugar, oil, eggs and mix well. Stir dry ingredients into liquid mixture; stir in apples and nuts. Pour into a greased and floured 9 x 13-inch baking pan or bundt pan and bake in preheated 325-degree oven for 35 to 40 minutes.

To make sauce, melt butter, add sugars and sour cream. Bring to a boil and cook until mixture thickens; stir in vanilla. Serve warm over cake slices.

Jo says, "Thank you, Peggy, for sharing this with us. Mother raved about it and she was right! It's truly yummy!"

Note - The sauce may be stored in a covered container and refrigerated until ready to use, or if there is any left...hardly possible!

Sweet Temptations

JUDI'S FABULOUS CARROT CAKE

1 1/2 cups Wesson oil
2 cups sugar
4 eggs
2 teaspoons baking soda
1 teaspoon lemon flavoring
1/3 cup buttermilk
1 teaspoon baking powder
1 1/2 teaspoons cinnamon
1/2 teaspoon nutmeg
1/2 teaspoon salt
3 cups all-purpose flour, sifted
3 cups grated carrots

TOPPING:
1/2 cup frozen orange juice concentrate
   (undiluted)
1/2 cup chopped walnuts
1/2 cup granulated sugar

Mix oil and sugar; add eggs, one at a time, beating until thick. Now, do the rest of mixing by hand! Add soda and lemon extract to buttermilk; add to first mixture. Add baking powder, cinnamon, nutmeg and salt to 1 cup of sifted flour; add to above mixture. Add remaining flour alternately with carrots. Bake in a greased tube pan in preheated 350-degree oven for 55 minutes to 1 hour or until cake springs up in middle when touched. While cake is baking, prepare Topping.

Mix all ingredients and spread on cake as soon as it comes from oven. Leave cake in pan until it is cool. Serves 12.

Jo says, "This my friends' colossal cake! It is so special I had to move out of town before she would share it with me. We really feel privileged to have it in A Cooking Affaire II. Thanks little friend!"

JULIE'S BANANA SPICE CAKE

2 3/4 cups sifted flour
2 teaspoons baking powder
1 teaspoon soda
1 teaspoon salt
1/4 teaspoon ground cloves
1 1/2 teaspoons cinnamon
3/4 teaspoon nutmeg
2/3 cup shortening
1 1/3 cups sugar
2 eggs, well-beaten
4 or 5 mashed bananas
2 teaspoons vanilla
1 recipe Cream Cheese Frosting (See index)

Sift flour, baking powder, soda, salt and spices together 3 times. Cream shortening and sugar until fluffy; add eggs, one at a time and beat well after each addition. Add sifted dry ingredients and bananas alternately in small amounts, beating well after each addition. Stir in vanilla and pour into greased and floured 9 x 13-inch baking pan and bake in preheated 350-degree oven for 35 minutes or until done. Remove from oven, cool and frost with Cream Cheese Frosting.

Jo and Jan say, "This makes a very nice layer cake too. It is great for those special times."

INDIVIDUAL PINEAPPLE UPSIDE DOWN CAKES

1 can (1 pound, 14-ounce) pineapple slices
1/2 cup butter, melted
1 cup brown sugar, packed
24 walnut halves
2 1/2 cups cake flour
1 1/2 cups sugar
4 teaspoons baking powder
1 1/2 teaspoons salt
2/3 cup soft shortening
1/2 cup milk
1 teaspoon grated lemon peel
2 teaspoons vanilla
2 eggs
Heavy cream, whipped (garnish)

Drain pineapple, reserve 1/2 cup syrup. Spoon 1 tablespoon melted butter into each of 8 (5-inch) individual foil pans; sprinkle with brown sugar and top with drained pineapple slice. Arrange 3 walnut halves around the edge. Place on baking sheet and bake in preheated 350-degree oven for 5 to 8 minutes.

Sift cake flour, then resift with sugar, baking powder and salt. Add shortening, 1/2 cup reserved pineapple syrup, milk, lemon peel, vanilla and eggs. Beat on mixer 2 minutes. Spoon batter on top of pineapple and return to oven to bake about 35 minutes or until cake tests done with a toothpick. Turn upside down on cake rack, remove pans and allow cake to cool. Top cooled cakes with whipped cream if desired. Serves 8.

FAVORITE SPICE CAKE

3/4 cup butter or margarine
1 1/2 cups sugar
3 eggs
2 cups flour
1/2 teaspoon baking powder
1/2 teaspoon soda
1/2 teaspoon salt
3/4 teaspoon nutmeg
1 teaspoon cinnamon
2 tablespoons cocoa
1 cup buttermilk
1 teaspoon vanilla
1 teaspoon lemon extract
1/2 cup nuts, toasted

FROSTING:
2 cups confectioners' sugar
1 tablespoon cocoa
1/2 teaspoon cinnamon
1/4 teaspoon nutmeg
4 tablespoons butter
Small amount hot coffee or milk.

Sift all dry ingredients except sugar together. Cream butter, sugar and eggs. Add buttermilk alternately with dry ingredients. Add vanilla and lemon extract, then nuts; mix well. Grease and flour 2 8-inch cake pans. Bake in preheated 350-degree oven for 25 to 30 minutes. Cool before spreading with Frosting.

Combine first 5 ingredients; add liquid to make spreadable. Serves 8 - 12.

PRUNE CAKE

2 cups sugar
2 cups flour
1 teaspoon baking soda
1 teaspoon salt
1 teaspoon cinnamon
1 teaspoon nutmeg
1 teaspoon ground cloves
1 cup vegetable oil
1 cup buttermilk
3 eggs
1 cup stewed pitted prunes, mashed
1 cup chopped pecans
1 teaspoon vanilla

SAUCE:
1 cup sugar
1/2 cup butter
1/2 cup buttermilk
1 teaspoon baking soda
1 teaspoon vanilla

Sift dry ingredients together in large mixing bowl. Add oil, buttermilk and eggs; mix well. Stir in prunes, nuts and vanilla. Pour into greased and floured 9 x 13-inch baking pan. Bake in preheated 350-degree oven for 35 to 40 minutes or until a toothpick inserted in center of cake comes out clean.

While cake is baking, combine sauce ingredients in pan and bring to a boil, stirring constantly. When cake is done and still hot, prick top several times with a fork and pour sauce over cake.

Jo says, "Sauce will be very thin and it will look like a lot, but keep pouring it over the cake and spreading it to cover. Use it all! This is. without a doubt. one of the best cakes you will ever make!"

TONIA'S TWINKIE CAKE

1 package butter cake mix
1 stick margarine, softened
3 eggs
2/3 cup water

FILLING:
1 cup milk
4 tablespoons flour
1 stick margarine,softened
1/2 cup solid shortening
1 cup confectioner' sugar
1 1/2 teaspoons vanilla

Mix cake as directed on box. Bake in greased and floured 9 x 13 inch pan and follow baking instructions on cake box. Prepare Filling.

Mix milk and flour together; cook until thickened; mix margarine, shortening, sugar and vanilla. Add to cooled flour-milk mixture and beat 4 minutes on electric mixer or until thick and fluffy. Split the cooled cake and fill.

RUTH'S PRETTY PLUM CAKE

2 cups sugar
3 eggs
1 cup oil
2 small jars plum baby food with tapioca
2 teaspoons red food coloring
2 cups unsifted flour
1/2 teaspoon salt
1/2 teaspoon soda
1 teaspoon cloves
1 teaspoon cinnamon
1 cup pecans, chopped

GLAZE:
1/3 cup butter
1 cup confectioners' sugar
3 tablespoons lemon juice
1 teaspoon red food coloring

In large bowl combine sugar, eggs and oil beating until well mixed. Add plums and red food coloring. Combine and add flour, salt, soda, cloves, cinnamon and nuts. Grease and flour bundt or angel food pan. Bake in preheated 325-degree oven for 1 hour. While cake is baking combine glaze ingredients in saucepan and bring to a boil. When cake is done, while still in the pan, brush some of hot glaze on the top. After turning cake out of pan brush remaining glaze over cake. Serves 16.

WHITE FRUITCAKE

1 cup butter
1 cup sugar
8 eggs
1/2 cup pineapple juice
3 1/2 cups flour
1 teaspoon vanilla
1/4 teaspoon almond extract
1 package (16-ounce) flaked coconut
1 box (15-ounce) golden raisins
1 package (16-ounce) pecans, whole
1 can (20-ounce) diced pineapple, drained
1 pound candied fruit
1 pound candied cherries

Cream butter and sugar together in a large mixing bowl. Add eggs one at a time and continue to beat. Add pineapple juice and vanilla. In larger bowl combine coconut, raisins, pecans, pineapple, candied fruit and cherries. Add 1 cup flour to fruit mixture and toss to coat ingredients. Beat remainder of flour into egg batter. Pour batter over fruits and mix until well blended.

Heavily spray or grease 6 small loaf pans. Divide batter among pans and fill to about 1/2 inch of rim. Bake in preheated 275-degree oven for 1 1/2 hours. Remove from oven and cool on rack about 30 minutes. When completely cool remove from pans and wrap in foil or freezer wrap. Makes 6 small loaves.

BLACKBERRY WINE CAKE

1 box white cake mix (2-layer size)
4 eggs
1/2 cup vegetable oil
1 small package blackberry Jell-O
1 cup blackberry wine

GLAZE:
1 1/2 tablespoons melted margarine
1 cup confectioners' sugar
1/2 cup blackberry wine

Combine all ingredients in mixer and beat well. Bake in greased bundt pan at 325-degrees for 1 hour. Glaze cake while warm.

Combine ingredients and bring to a boil. While cake is warm, spread with half of the glaze. Let cake set for 30 minutes; then turn out on a plate and add remaining glaze. Serves 14 - 18.

Jan says, "I like to make a little more glaze than the recipe calls for so it will spread all over the cake. You may use raspberry Jell-O and raspberry wine if you prefer, but the blackberry is so good!"

LOIS' ICEBOX GINGERBREAD

1 cup butter
1 cup sugar
3 eggs
1 cup sorghum
1 teaspoon soda
1 cup milk
1/4 teaspoon allspice
1/4 teaspoon cinnamon
2 teaspoons ginger
3 cups flour
1/2 cup nuts, chopped
1/2 cup raisins, chopped

Cream butter and sugar; add eggs one at a time and beat well. Add sorghum, soda and milk. Sift spices with the flour saving a small amount of flour to mix with nuts and raisins. Add flour, nuts and raisins to batter. Refrigerate at least 24 hours before proceeding. When ready to bake, grease muffin tins, spoon mixture in tins, filling 1/2 full. Bake in preheated 375-degree oven for 25 minutes or until done. Serve while warm. Makes 24.

Lois says, "These are excellent with a dollop of whipped topping."

LEMON CAKE

1 cup cake flour, sifted
1/4 teaspoon salt
1/2 teaspoon lemon rind, grated
1 1/2 tablespoons lemon juice
5 egg yolks, beaten until thick and lemon-colored
5 egg whites
1 cup sugar

Sift flour once, measure and add salt and sift 4 times. Add lemon rind and juice to beaten egg yolks and beat with rotary eggbeater until very light and thick. Beat egg whites until stiff enough to hold up in peaks, but not dry. Fold in sugar, a small amount at a time, then egg yolks. Fold in flour, a small amount at a time. Turn into an ungreased tube pan and bake in a preheated 335-degree oven for 1 hour. Test with a toothpick. Remove from oven and invert pan 1 hour or until cold.

Jan says, "This cake is a delight frosted with a Lemon Sauce." (See index)

Sweet Temptations

FLUFFY LEMON CAKE

9 egg whites
1 teaspoon cream of tartar
1/4 teaspoon salt
1 cup sugar
7 egg yolks
1 cup flour, sifted
1/3 cup lemon juice
2 teaspoons lemon zest

FILLING:
1 cup sugar
1/4 cup cornstarch
Dash salt
1 1/4 cups water
2 egg yolks
4 tablespoons lemon juice
1 tablespoon margarine
2 teaspoons lemon zest

TOPPING:
2 cups heavy cream
3 drops yellow food coloring

Beat egg whites until foamy in a large bowl. Add cream of tartar and salt; beat until peaks are formed. Gradually add 1/2 cup of sugar, beating until peaks are stiff and glossy; set aside.

Beat 7 egg yolks until lemon colored in a small bowl. Gradually add remaining 1/2 cup sugar, beating until thick and lemon colored. Lightly spoon flour into measuring cup. Add flour, lemon juice and zest to egg yolk mixture and beat at low speed. By hand, fold egg yolk mixture into egg whites. Pour into ungreased 10-inch angel food cake pan. Bake in preheated 325-degree oven for 45 minutes. Top should spring back when touched. Invert cake pan on cups and cool completely before removing from pan.

FILLING: Combine sugar, cornstarch and salt in a small saucepan. Gradually stir in water and cook over medium heat until mixture thickens and boils, stirring constantly. Remove from heat. Beat egg yolks in a small bowl and gradually blend small amount of hot mixture into egg yolks; return egg yolk mixture to saucepan and cook for 2 to 3 minutes, stirring constantly. Remove from heat and stir in lemon juice, margarine and lemon zest. Cool and reserve 1/2 cup filling for topping.

TOPPING: Whip cream until slightly thickened. Add 1/2 cup reserved filling mixture and food coloring. Beat until thickened and refrigerate until ready to use.

To assemble cake, slice it horizontally to make 3 layers. Place 1 layer on serving plate and spread with 1/2 cup filling. Place second layer on top and spread with remaining filling. Top with third layer and spread sides, center and top of cake with topping. Refrigerate until serving time. Serves 12 - 14.

Jo and Jan say, "This is a beautiful and delicious cake to serve at a springtime party. You might want to place Chocolate Leaves or Glazed Strawberries (See index) and garnish with fresh mint. Also, fresh flowers would make it extra special."

RUTHIE'S POPPY SEED CAKE

1/2 cup poppy seeds
1 cup milk
1 teaspoon vanilla
3/4 cup butter
1 1/2 cups sugar
2 cup flour
2 teaspoons baking powder
1/2 teaspoon salt
4 egg whites, stiffly beaten

Soak poppy seeds in milk and vanilla. Cream butter and sugar. Sift flour, baking powder and salt. Add to creamed mixture alternately with milk mixture. Fold in beaten egg whites and pour in 2 greased and floured 8-inch layer cake pans. Bake in preheated 350-degree oven for 30 minutes. Cool.

FILLING:
3/4 cup sugar
4 egg yolks, beaten
2 tablespoons cornstarch
1/2 cup milk
1/4 teaspoon salt
1/2 cup chopped nuts

Combine sugar, egg yolks, cornstarch, milk and salt in top of double boiler. Cook until thick; remove from over water, cool and add nuts. Chill and spread between layers of cooled cake. Serves 10-12.

❖❖❖

PAT'S FRUIT COCKTAIL CAKE

2 cups flour
1 1/2 cups sugar
2 teaspoons baking soda
1/4 teaspoon salt
2 eggs
2 cups fruit cocktail, undrained

Mix all ingredients by hand and pour into a greased and floured 9 x 13 inch baking pan. Top with:
1/2 cup brown sugar
1/2 cup pecans

Bake in preheated 350-degree oven for 35 to 40 minutes.

Topping:
1/4 cup granulated sugar
1/2 cup evaporated milk
1 stick butter or margarine
1 teaspoon vanilla
1 cup coconut

Boil sugar, milk and butter for 1 minute, add vanilla and coconut. Spread over cake while still warm.

Pat says, "I have made this cake for years. It is so easy, can be whipped up fast when company drops in. It is very moist and delicious served hot. Sometimes, I serve it with whipped cream."

JANE'S CHOCOLATE CAKE

2 squares unsweetened chocolate
1 teaspoon (scant) baking soda
1/2 cup warm water
1 1/2 cups sugar
1 stick butter or margarine
2 eggs, beaten
1 cup buttermilk
2 cups flour, sifted 3 times
1 teaspoon (scant) baking soda
Pinch of salt
1 teaspoon vanilla

FROSTING:
1 stick butter
2 squares unsweetened chocolate
1 1/2 cups confectioners' sugar
1 egg
1 teaspoon vanilla

To make cake, melt chocolate and dissolve soda in water. Cream sugar and butter; add beaten eggs then buttermilk. Add flour, second soda and salt. Lastly add chocolate, soda and water mixture and vanilla.

For a loaf pan, bake 35 minutes in a preheated 325-degree oven; for a layer cake, bake at 350 degrees for 25 minutes.

To make Frosting, melt chocolate and butter together. Beat sugar and egg, then add chocolate mixture and vanilla. Mix well. Serves 12 - 6.

ANNIE'S CHOCOLATE BUNDT CAKE

1 German chocolate cake mix
1 package (4-ounce) instant chocolate
   pudding mix
1/2 cup vegetable oil
4 eggs
1 package (8-ounce) sour cream
1 teaspoon vanilla
1/2 cup hot water
1 package (6-ounce) chocolate chips
1 cup chopped nuts

Combine cake mix, pudding mix, oil, eggs, sour cream and vanilla in large bowl of electric mixer. Blend well then add by hand the water, chocolate chips and nuts. Turn into a well greased bundt pan

and bake in preheated 325-degree oven about 1 hour; do not overbake.

Annie says, "If you want a dressy looking cake, put the chopped nuts on the bottom of the pan before spooning in the batter."

VARIATION:
1 package devils food mix in place of the German chocolate
6 ounces instant chocolate pudding in place of the 4 ounces
1 cup of vegetable oil in place of the 1/2 cup
12 ounces of chocolate chips in place of the 6 ounces
Rest of ingredients same as above. This cake is really a chocolate lovers' dream.

ALLECE'S SOUR CREAM POUND CAKE

1 cup butter, softened
2 cups sugar
1 cup sour cream
2 eggs
2 cups flour
1 1/2 teaspoons baking powder
1 teaspoon vanilla
2 tablespoons brown sugar
1 teaspoon cinnamon
1/2 cup chopped pecans or walnuts

Combine butter and sugar. Add sour cream and eggs and mix. Sift flour and baking powder in bowl. Beat into sour cream mixture and add vanilla. In a small bowl, combine brown sugar, cinnamon and nuts. Pour half of cake batter into a greased and floured bundt pan. Sprinkle cinnamon-sugar mixture over and top with rest of batter.

Bake in preheated 350-degree oven for 50 minutes. Remove cake from pan while warm and cool on wire rack. A powdered sugar icing may be drizzled over cake when cooled.

PATRICIA'S CHOCOLATE POUND CAKE

1/2 pound butter
1/2 cup shortening
3 cups sugar
5 eggs
3 cups flour
1/2 teaspoon baking powder
1/2 teaspoon salt
4 heaping teaspoons cocoa
1 cup milk
1 tablespoon vanilla

Cream butter, shortening and sugar. Add eggs, one at a time. Add sifted dry ingredients alternately with milk; add vanilla. Bake in a greased and floured tube pan in preheated 325-degree oven for 1 hour and 20 minutes. Ice the cake while it is hot. Prepare icing while cake is baking.

ICING:
2/3 stick butter, creamed
2/3 box confectioners' sugar, sifted
1 heaping tablespoon cocoa
1 teaspoon vanilla
3 tablespoons hot coffee

Mix all ingredients together and ice the hot cake.

ANNIE'S CHOCOLATE CHIP POUND CAKE

1 yellow butter cake mix
1 package (3-ounce) vanilla instant pudding
  mix
4 eggs
3/4 cup oil
1 cup sour cream
1 teaspoon vanilla
1 can (5-ounce) chocolate syrup
2/3 cup chocolate chips
1 cup nuts, optional

Combine cake mix and pudding mix in large mixer bowl. Add eggs and oil; beat well. Blend in sour cream, vanilla and chocolate syrup; lastly add chocolate chips and nuts. Stir well; mixture will be thick. Grease well but do not flour a bundt cake pan. Spoon mixture into pan and bake in preheated 325-degree oven for 45 to 50 minutes. Serves 12.

REBA'S STRAWBERRY ICE BOX CAKE

1 angel food cake
1 large box strawberry gelatin
2 cups boiling water
1 package (10-ounce) frozen strawberries
1 package (8-ounce) cream cheese, softened
1 cup sugar
1/2 pint heavy cream, whipped
1/2 cup chopped nuts

Dissolve strawberry gelatin in boiling water and add frozen strawberries. Stir well and let stand until mixture begins to gel. Combine cream cheese and sugar; blend with whipped cream and gelatin mixture, beating with electric mixer.

Crumble 1/2 of cake in rectangle or square pan. Add 1/2 of whipped mixture; crumble rest of cake and pour remainder of strawberry mixture on top. Sprinkle chopped nuts over top and chill several hours in refrigerator.

Jo and Jan say, "This is very pretty layered in a trifle bowl and served at a ladies' luncheon."

PUMPKIN DESSERT

1 can (29-ounce) pumpkin
4 eggs
1 can (13-ounce) evaporated milk
1 1/2 cups sugar
1 teaspoon cinnamon
1 teaspoon ginger
1/2 teaspoon nutmeg
1 yellow cake mix
2 sticks margarine, melted
1 cup nuts, chopped

Mix pumpkin, eggs, milk, sugar and spices well. Pour into a greased 9 x 13-inch pan. Sprinkle cake mix evenly over the mixture. Drizzle margarine over cake mix and sprinkle nuts over the top. Bake in preheated 350-degree oven for 1 hour. Serves 12 -15.

FROSTY SHERBET ANGEL CAKE

1 large package angel food cake mix or 1
    large bakery angel food cake, loaf size
3 pints orange sherbet, softened
2 cups heavy cream
Yellow food coloring
1 cup fresh lemon rind, finely grated (about 9
    lemons)

Prepare cake mix as directed. Pour batter into a 15 1/2 x 4 1/2 x 4 1/2-inch angel-cake loaf pan. Bake in preheated 375-degree oven for 35 to 45 minutes or until top springs back when lightly pressed with finger.

Cool completely by inverting pan with edges resting on raised surface to protect top of cake. Remove cooled cake from pan and split inverted cake lengthwise with sharp knife into three layers. Place top layer (of inverted cake) with bottom side down, in bottom of angel-cake loaf pan.

Carefully spoon 1 1/2 pints of orange sherbet on top of cake layer. Top with middle layer; spread with rest of sherbet, and top with last layer, crust side up. Cover with foil and freeze.

1 1/2 hours before you serve cake, dip loaf pan quickly in and out of water; dry and gently loosen edges with knife or spatula. Place oblong serving plate or tray on top of pan; invert, and shake gently until cake comes out. Refrigerate.

Whip cream until stiff; tint a pale yellow with food coloring and frost entire cake. Sprinkle top and sides with grated lemon rind. Refrigerate until served. Serves 12 -15.

Jo says, "If you are going to be any longer than an hour and a half before serving after removing cake from pan, refreeze it until you frost it. Make lemonade with the lemons you grated, serve it with the cake; so cool and refreshing."

CHOCOLATE CHARLOTTE

CAKE:
1 package (23-ounce) brownie mix
2 tablespoons water
3 eggs

Beat ingredients together at medium speed on electric mixer until batter is smooth. Grease an 11 x 15-inch jelly-roll pan and line it with waxed paper. Grease and lightly flour the paper, shaking off any excess; spread the batter evenly in the pan. Bake in a preheated 350-degree oven for 10 to 12 minutes or until cake is done. Turn cake onto a rack and peel off the paper. Lightly oil a 2-quart charlotte mold and line it with the cooled cake. Cut rounds of cake to fit both the top and bottom of the mold and a strip for the sides. Place the smaller round in the bottom of the pan. Wrap the strip around the inside of the mold; you will probably have to piece one section of the side to cover completely. Do not worry, any piecing will be covered.

Prepare Filling and Glaze; spoon the chilled Filling mixture into the mold. Fit the larger round of cake on top of the mold. Chill for 3 to 4 hours, or until firm. Unmold and cover with Glaze.

FILLING:
1 1/2 pounds semi-sweet chocolate squares
1/2 cup strong brewed coffee
3 eggs, separated

4 tablespoons sugar
1/2 cup Tia Maria liqueur
1/2 cup heavy cream

Melt the chocolate with the coffee in the top of a double boiler. When chocolate is completely melted. remove the pan from heat. Beat the egg yolks until pale yellow and stir into the chocolate. Gradually stir in Tia Maria and cool.

In a separate bowl, beat egg whites, gradually adding sugar until whites are stiff. Whip cream and gently fold cream into the cooled chocolate mixture and then fold in the egg whites.

GLAZE:
1/2 pound semi-sweet chocolate
1/2 cup water

Melt chocolate in water and stir until smooth. Spread over top of mousse-cake and drizzle down the sides. Chill again. Cut while chilled into slender slices.

Jo says, "Spoon some White Chocolate Sauce or Creme Anglaise on each dessert plate, place a slice of Chocolate Charlotte on top, and drizzle with Raspberry Sauce, sprinkled with a few fresh raspberries, if available. (See index for Sauce recipes). I first served this about 14 years ago at a dinner party and my friend Judie still talks about it!"

Icing

COFFEE ICING

1 stick butter or margarine
1/2 to 1 cup cocoa
1/2 cup cold coffee
1 tablespoon vanilla
1 box powdered sugar
Pinch of salt

Cream butter until very light. Alternate sugar, coffee and cocoa. Add vanilla and salt; blend thoroughly.

Jan and Jo say, "The amount of cocoa you use depends on your personal taste. Also, you can make a stronger coffee flavor by mixing 2 or 3 tablespoons instant coffee in a little water rather than using brewed coffee."

RUTH'S CREAM ICING

1 cup fine granulated sugar
1 cup heavy cream
1/2 teaspoon vanilla

In a medium-sized pan combine sugar and cream. Cover and cook on medium heat; remove cover when mixture comes to a boil.

Cook until a very soft ball stage. Pour into small mixer bowl with vanilla and beat at medium speed about 2 minutes. The icing will be runny.

Jan says, "Ruth ices her angel food cakes with this old family recipe and it is wonderful. This icing is a little tricky, but try it because it is worth the effort."

144

Sweet Temptations

CREAM CHEESE FROSTING

1/2 cup margarine, softened
1 package (8-ounce) cream cheese, softened
1 box (1-pound) confectioners' sugar
2 teaspoons vanilla
Dash salt
1/2 cup nuts, chopped

Blend ingredients on mixer until smooth and creamy.

PENUCHE ICING

1/3 cup butter or margarine
1 cup brown sugar, firmly packed
1/4 cup milk
1 3/4-2 cups confectioners' sugar

Melt butter or margarine; add sugar and milk; cook for 2 to 3 minutes and cool. Add sifted confectioners' sugar and beat until creamy and spreadable. If too thick, add a few drops of milk. Will frost 4 dozen cookies or 1 cake.

MRS. HALEY'S MOCHA FROSTING

2 tablespoons butter
1 square unsweetened chocolate, melted
1/4 to 1/3 cup strong coffee
1 package confectioners' sugar
1 teaspoon vanilla
Pinch of salt

Brown butter in a pan; add rest of ingredients and beat well. spread on cooled cake. Frosts a 2-layer cake.

Jo says, "Mrs. Haley was my Girl Scout leader and such a wonderful woman! She also was a marvelous cook and this frosting was one of my favorite delights. I remember really liking the cake, but always peeled away the frosting to 'save for last' You'll see why we were such good Scouts!"

ORANGE FROSTING

1/4 cup butter or margarine, softened
1 teaspoon grated orange rind
1 egg yolk
1 teaspoon aromatic bitters
1/8 teaspoon salt
1 package (1 pound) confectioners' sugar
2 tablespoons orange juice

Cream butter or margarine with orange rind. Stir in egg yolk, blending well. Stir in bitters and salt, then add sugar alternately with orange juice, beating until smooth. Fill and cover cooled cake layers. Frosts a 2-layer cake.

Cheese Cakes

GRAHAM CRACKER CHEESECAKE CRUST

1 1/2 cups graham cracker crumbs (about 20 crackers)
1/4 cup granulated sugar
1/2 cup melted butter

Lightly oil bottom and sides of a 9 or 10-inch springform pan. Combine crumbs, sugar and butter until thoroughly mixed and press into bottom of pan. Fill with your favorite cheesecake recipe and proceed with recipe instructions. (See index)

CHOCOLATE CRUMB CHEESECAKE CRUST

1 1/2 cups chocolate wafer crumbs
1/3 cup sugar
6 tablespoons butter, melted

Combine ingredients and press mixture in bottom and sides of a buttered springform pan.

Chill until ready to fill.

Jo and Jan say, "Sometimes, depending on the recipe, we'll add 1/4 teaspoon cinnamon and/or 1 cup chopped nuts, such as slivered almonds. It makes it special!"

BLACK AND WHITE CHEESECAKE

1 Chocolate Crumb Cheesecake Crust
(See index)

Blend all crust ingredients and press onto bottom of 10-inch springform pan. Refrigerate until firm, about 30 minutes.

FILLING:
4 packages (8-ounce size) cream cheese,softened
1 1/2 cups sugar
2 tablespoons flour
4 eggs, extra large
2 egg yolks, extra large
1/3 cup heavy cream
2 teaspoons vanilla
1 1/2 cups chocolate cream-filled cookies, coarsely ground
2 cups sour cream

TOPPING
1 cup heavy cream
8 ounces semisweet chocolate, chopped
1 teaspoon vanilla

Beat cream cheese with electric mixer until smooth. Beat in sugar and flour until well blended. Beat in eggs and yolks until mixture is smooth; stir in cream and 1 teaspoon vanilla. Pour half of batter into prepared crust and sprinkle with ground cookies. Pour remaining batter over, smoothing top. Bake in preheated 425-degree oven for 15 minutes. Reduce oven temperature to 325 degrees. Bake 50 minutes covering top loosely with foil to prevent browning too quickly. Increase oven temperature to 350 degrees; remove cake from oven. Blend sour cream, remaining vanilla in small bowl and spread over cake. Return to oven and bake 7 minutes. Refrigerate immediately. When cooled, cover with plastic wrap and chill overnight.

To make Topping, scald cream in heavy saucepan. Add chocolate and vanilla; stir 1 minute. Remove from heat and stir until chocolate is melted; refrigerate 10 minutes.

Set cake on serving platter and remove sides of pan. Pour glaze over top and smooth top and sides. Refrigerate until ready to serve. Serves 10-12.

CHOCOLATE CHEESECAKE

1 Chocolate Crumb Cheesecake Crust (See index)
1 package (8-ounces) semisweet chocolate
3 packages (8-ounce size) cream cheese, softened
1 cup sugar
3 eggs
2 teaspoons cocoa
1 teaspoon vanilla
2 cups sour cream

Prepare crust and chill. Melt chocolate in top of a double boiler, stirring occasionally. In large

bowl of electric mixer beat cream cheese until fluffy; add sugar. Add eggs, one at a time, beating after each addition. Add melted chocolate, cocoa and vanilla, blending thoroughly; beat in the sour cream. Pour mixture into prepared pan and bake in preheated 350-degree oven 1 hour and 10 minutes. The cake will become firm as it chills. Cool at room temperature; then chill for at least 6 hours before serving. Overnight is even better. Serves 12.

Jo and Jan say, "If cracks appear in the top of your cheesecake, you might try shaving chocolate over the top. It gives a pretty appearance and no one will ever know!"

Sweet Temptations

JEANNE'S LEMON CHEESECAKE SUPREME

CRUST:
1 1/2 cups graham cracker crumbs
1/4 cup granulated sugar
1 tablespoon grated lemon peel
1/2 cup butter, melted

LEMON CURD:
1/4 teaspoon unflavored gelatin
1 teaspoon water
1 tablespoon grated lemon peel
1/2 cup sugar
1/4 cup fresh lemon juice
3 large egg yolks
6 tablespoons butter

FILLING:
1 tablespoon plus
3/4 teaspoon unflavored gelatin
1/4 cup cold water
Peel from 2 lemons; use only yellow peel
3/4 cup plus 2 tablespoons sugar
3 large egg yolks
3/4 cup whole milk
12 ounces cream cheese, softened
1/3 cup fresh lemon juice
1 1/2 cups heavy cream whipped to soft
  peaks
Glazed Lemon Slices (garnish see index)
Mint leaves and fresh strawberries (garnish)

Combine ingredients and press onto bottom of lightly greased 9-inch springform pan. Bake in preheated 350-degree oven for 8 to 12 minutes or until golden brown. Cool thoroughly.

Sprinkle gelatin over water in a small dish; allow to soften. Combine lemon peel and sugar in blender or food processor until peel is sugar-fine. Transfer to a small, heavy saucepan. Mix in lemon juice and yolks, then butter. Stir over medium heat until very thick, about 5 minutes; do not let mixture boil. Pour into a bowl, add gelatin and stir to dissolve. Cool completely, stirring often.

Sprinkle gelatin over cold water in small dish. Let stand 10 minutes. Combine lemon peel and sugar in food processor or blender until peel is sugar-fine. Add yolks and blend until fluffy.

Scald milk in heavy saucepan; add slowly to lemon, sugar and egg mixture, stirring constantly; blend well. Return mixture to saucepan and stir over medium-low heat until it thickens, about 10 minutes; do not allow to boil. It should coat the back of a metal spoon.

Remove from heat, add gelatin to custard and stir until dissolved. Strain into bowl and refrigerate, stirring often until mixture thickens but is not set; about 20 minutes.

Blend cream cheese and lemon juice until smooth. Add cooled custard and blend well. Pour into large bowl and gently fold in whipped cream. Pour half of filling over cooled crust. Spoon half cooled lemon curd over filling. Swirl mixture with tip of knife. Repeat with remaining filling and curd. Swirl mixture on top and refrigerate overnight. At serving time, run knife around sides of cake. Release sides. Garnish with Glazed Lemon Slices or mint leaves and fruit. Serves 12.

Jo says, "I really love the combination of lemon and chocolate, so I do a variation on the above with the Chocolate Cookie Crust (See index) and garnish with Chocolate Leaves and fresh raspberries."

❖❖

PUMPKIN CHEESECAKE

**1 recipe Graham Cracker Cheesecake Crust
(See index)**
**2 packages (8-ounce size) cream cheese,
softened**
3/4 cup dark brown sugar, firmly packed
3 eggs
2 tablespoons flour
1/2 teaspoon cinnamon
1/2 teaspoon allspice
1/4 teaspoon nutmeg
1/8 teaspoon salt
1 cup canned pumpkin
**1 cup walnuts or pecans, toasted and
chopped**
1/2 cup maple syrup
Heavy cream, whipped (garnish)

Prepare Cheesecake Crust and set aside. Beat cream cheese until fluffy, gradually add brown sugar. Still beating, add eggs, one at a time, blending well after each addition. Sift flour, spices and salt, add to cream mixture and blend well. Mix in pumpkin and blend thoroughly. Turn into prepared crust and bake in preheated 325-degree oven about 1 hour and 20 minutes or until knife inserted in center comes out clean. Remove from oven and cool on rack 1 hour. Remove sides of springform pan and cool to room temperature. Chill thoroughly.

To serve, brush top with maple syrup and sprinkle with toasted, chopped nuts. Serve with whipped cream if desired.

Jo and Jan say, "We either serve the whipped cream unsweetened or will lightly sweeten it and add just a sprinkle of cinnamon or nutmeg on top. This is a delightful alternative to the traditional pumpkin pie." Serves 10-12.

CAPPUCCINO CHEESECAKE

**1 recipe Chocolate Cheesecake Crust; press
into 9-inch springform pan**
**2 cartons (15-ounce size) whole-milk ricotta
cheese**
1 cup sugar
3 tablespoons freeze-dried coffee granules
2 tablespoons flour
4 eggs, separated
3 tablespoons coffee-flavored liqueur
1 tablespoon vanilla
1 carton (16-ounce) sour cream
**1 square (1 ounce) semisweet chocolate,
melted**

Prepare Chocolate Crumb Cheesecake Crust and press into greased springform pan.

Combine ricotta, 3/4 cup sugar, coffee granules and flour in blender or food processor; blend until smooth. Add yolks, liqueur and vanilla. Blend until granules dissolve. Pour into bowl and whisk in sour cream.

Beat egg whites until foamy; beat in remaining sugar, a tablespoon at a time, until firm peaks form. Fold in cheese mixture and spoon into prepared pan. Spoon melted chocolate over batter and swirl with knife.

Bake in preheated 325-degree oven for 1 hour and 30 minutes. Center of cake will jiggle slightly when pan is moved. Turn off oven and let cake remain in oven with door closed for 30 more minutes.

Cool cake completely on wire rack and refrigerate overnight before cutting. Serves 16-20.

WHITE CHOCOLATE CHEESECAKE

Graham Cracker Cheesecake Crust
12 ounces white chocolate
**4 packages (8-ounce size) cream cheese,
softened**
1/2 cup sugar
1 cup heavy cream
4 eggs, room temperature and lightly beaten
3 tablespoons cornstarch, sifted
4 1/2 teaspoons vanilla extract

Prepare Graham Cracker Crust and press into bottom and sides of a buttered 9 x 5-inch springform pan.

Melt chocolate slowly; cool slightly. Combine in large bowl of electric mixer the melted chocolate, cream cheese, sugar, cream, eggs, cornstarch and vanilla. Beat until smooth and pour into prepared pan. Bake in preheated 325 degree oven for 65 minutes. Cool 1 hour on a rack. Remove sides and finish cooling. Serves 12.

Jo and Jan say, "You might want to make this with the Chocolate Cookie Crumb Crust (See index) and garnish the top with dark and white chocolate curls." (See index)

❖❖

Delectables

SWEET DESSERT CREPE BATTER

3 eggs
1 1/2 cup milk or half-and-half
3 tablespoons sugar
Pinch of salt
1 cup flour
2 tablespoons butter, melted and cooled
2 tablespoons brandy, cognac or other
  liqueur
1 teaspoon vanilla

Combine eggs, 3/4 cup milk, sugar and salt. Gradually add flour, beating with electric mixer or wire whisk until smooth. Add rest of milk and melted, cooled butter, beating steadily. The batter should have the consistency of fresh cream. Let batter stand at least an hour in the refrigerator before making crepes, then whisk in the brandy or other flavoring. Proceed with instructions as given with Basic Crepe batter (See index). Makes 30 - 36 5-inch crepes.

CHOCOLATE CREPES

1 cup milk
1/2 cup flour
1/4 cup sugar
2 eggs
2 tablespoons unsweetened cocoa
1 tablespoon butter, melted
1 teaspoon vanilla

Combine all ingredients in blender on low speed; just until combined. Cover and allow to stand for 1 hour before making crepes. Follow directions for making crepes (see index) and watch carefully because cocoa and sugar can cause crepes to burn easily. Let crepes cool; fill with a favorite filling. We like to fill them with flavored whipped cream or mousse and drizzle with warm chocolate sauce or Creme Anglaise. Makes 12 crepes.

CREPES SUZETTE SAUCE

3/4 cup butter
1/3 cup sugar
3/4 cup orange juice
1/3 cup orange liqueur
Finely grated rind of 1 orange
Sugar
3 tablespoons orange liqueur
6 tablespoons cognac

Melt butter in chafing dish. Add sugar, orange juice, liqueur and orange peel. Cook until mixture bubbles and reduces a little. Dip crepes in this hot mixture. Fold crepes in quarters. When all the crepes are folded, sprinkle with a little sugar, add remaining orange liqueur and cognac. To ignite, take a spoonful of sauce, light it, and pour into the dish. Spoon sauce over crepes. Will cover about 30 crepes, serving 10 people, 3 per person.

ALMOND CREME FILLING FOR CREPES

1 cup sugar
1/4 cup flour
1 cup milk
2 eggs
2 egg yolks
3 tablespoons butter
2 teaspoons vanilla
1/2 teaspoon almond extract
1/2 cup sliced almonds

TOPPING:
6 tablespoons butter, melted
1 1/2 squares bittersweet chocolate, shaved
1 1/2 pints sweetened whipped cream

Mix sugar and flour; add milk and cook, stirring until thickened then cook and stir 1 to 2 minutes longer. Beat eggs and yolks slightly; stir some of the hot mixture into eggs then pour this back into the remaining hot mixture. Cook and stir just to a boil and remove from heat. Beat smooth with an electric mixer; stir in butter, vanilla, almond extract and-almonds. Cool to room temperature; store in refrigerator.

To assemble crepes, spread 3 tablespoons of Filling on unbrowned side of a crepe; roll up and place folded side down in a 9xl3-inch baking dish. Continue with each crepe, brush crepes with melted butter and bake in preheated 350-degree oven until hot, about 5 to 10 minutes. Sprinkle tops of hot crepes with shaved chocolate and top each with a dollop of whipped cream and serve immediately. Makes 12 crepes.

❖❖

CREAMY STRAWBERRY CREPES FILLING

8 oz. cream cheese, room temperature
1 1/4 cups sifted powdered sugar
1 tbsp lemon juice, fresh
1 tsp. grated lemon rind
1/2 tsp vanilla
1 cup heavy cream, whipped
2 2/3 cups sliced strawberries
8 whole strawberries for garnish
8 6-inch crepes

Combine softened cream cheese, sugar, lemon juice, lemon rind and vanilla. Mix until well-blended. Fold in whipped cream. Fill crepe with about 1/4 cup cream cheese mixture, and 1/4 cup strawberries; roll up. Top with remaining cream cheese mixture and a whole berry. Serves 8

CHOCOLATE DESSERT CREPES FILLING

1 recipe Dessert Crepes (See index)
1 package (6 3/4-ounce) instant chocolate pudding mix
1 teaspoon instant coffee powder
8 cups heavy cream, divided in half
4 ounces bittersweet chocolate
1/2 cup unsalted butter
2 1/3 cups confectioners' sugar
1 1/4 cups evaporated milk
1 teaspoon vanilla
1 teaspoon rum extract (optional)

Combine pudding mix and coffee powder in a large bowl; blend well. Stir in 4 cups cream and mix until smooth. Whip remaining cream until stiff; gently fold into chocolate mixture and blend thoroughly.

Divide mixture among crepes and roll them up. Place seam side down on platters you will be serving them on. Cover and chill.

Melt chocolate with butter over low heat. Remove from heat and add sugar and milk; blend well. Place over medium heat and bring to a boil. Reduce heat and simmer about 8 minutes, stirring constantly. Remove from heat and stir in vanilla and rum (if desired). Serve warm, spoon over crepes.

Jo and Jan say, "This filling can be made 2 days ahead and refrigerated. The crepes can be filled 1 day ahead and the sauce can be made a far as a week ahead and chilled. Of course, the crepes can be made far in advance and frozen so we think this is an excellent party dessert; no last minute muss or fuss' To reheat the sauce, place over hot water and heat gently, stirring often. Fills 30 to 36 crepes.

BANANA CREPES FILLING

12 Dessert Crepes (See index)
1 package (8-ounce) cream cheese
3/4 cup sour cream
3 tablespoons sugar
1 tablespoon vanilla
1/2 cup slivered almonds, toasted and cooled
6 medium bananas
1/2 cup brown sugar
1 1/2 teaspoons cinnamon
1/4 teaspoon nutmeg
1/2 cup margarine
1/2 lemon

Combine cream cheese and sour cream; beat until smooth. Add sugar, vanilla, almonds; mix well. Spoon this mixture on crepes and roll up, leaving the ends open. Place on serving tray and refrigerate until ready to serve. Reheat in a preheated 350-degree oven for 5 minutes. Slice bananas in crosswise pieces 1/2-inch-thick into a baking dish. Combine brown sugar, cinnamon and nutmeg. Melt margarine and pour over bananas evenly. Squeeze juice of 1/2 lemon evenly over bananas and sprinkle the sugar-cinnamon mixture over all. Bake in 350-degree oven for 20 minutes. Remove from oven and spoon bananas and sauce over crepes. Serve while hot. Serves 6.

Jo and Jan say, "All you need to do is add a little vanilla ice cream to the crepes just before adding banana mixture, and you will have something very similar to Bananas Foster. The recipe can be doubled very easily."

Custards

TIPS ON BAKED CUSTARDS

• Whisk eggs only until smooth, not frothy. Gently whisk when adding hot milk. If foam appears, skim it off with a spoon before baking.

• Water in the water bath should be watched closely. If it comes close to a boil, cool it with ice cubes or very cold water to reduce the temperature to about 325 degrees. If water evaporates, add more to maintain starting level. Boiling water will result in a custard with holes.

• Watch your time closely and if baking individual custards, test each one. Remove from oven as soon as they are done.

• If your custard falls apart during unmolding, don't despair. Spoon it onto the dessert plates, top with fruit. The wonderful flavor and texture are still there.

• If there is still caramel in the bottom of the mold after you have turned out the custard, place the mold in a pan of hot water to dissolve any remaining caramel and pour over the custard.

CREME CARAMEL

1/2 cup sugar
1/8 teaspoon cream of tartar
3 tablespoons water
2 cups heavy cream
1/4 cup sugar
1 tablespoon vanilla
5 egg yolks
1 tablespoons light rum, Amaretto or liqueur
  of choice

Preheat oven to 325 degrees. Place a 1-quart mold or eight 4-ounce custard cups in oven so they will be hot for the caramel.

Combine sugar, cream of tartar and water in a small, heavy saucepan over low heat. Swirl pan occasionally until sugar dissolves. Increase heat to medium high and bring to a boil, without stirring, until mixture is a carmelized syrup and has turned a golden mahogany brown. Cool just until caramel stops bubbling then quickly pour into heated mold(s). Using pot holders, rotate and tilt dish to coat sides 3/4 of way up. Set aside to cool. The caramel will harden.

Combine cream, remaining sugar and vanilla in a heavy-bottomed saucepan. Cook over low heat until cream is scalded (between 180 and 185 degrees).

Combine egg yolks and rum in mixing bowl.

Whisking gently, slowly pour in the scalded cream. Gently strain mixture through a sieve into the carmelized mold(s). Let stand several seconds, then skim off any foam.

Set mold into larger pan and add enough very hot water to come halfway up sides of mold. Bake 50 to 60 minutes for large mold or about 25 minutes for small molds, or until a knife inserted halfway between center and edge of custard comes out clean. Custard will continue to cook when removed from oven. Do not pierce all the way to the bottom of mold.

Remove from oven and carefully lift dish from hot water bath. Place piece of plastic wrap directly on surface of custard to prevent a skim from forming. Place on a rack and cool at room temperature. Refrigerate at least 6 hours, preferably overnight, even a day or two ahead.

To unmold, loosen edges with a spatula. Carefully slip end of spatula down sides to let air in. Invert custard onto a serving platter; lift off mold. Spoon caramel mixture that remains in dish on top. Serves 6.

Jo and Jan say, "This is sinfully delicious and smooth as velvet! The secret is the egg yolks. We arrange sliced fruit around the edge. For an extra special taste treat, be sure to serve with sliced fresh nectarines!"

❖❖

TIP

- Another way to carmelize sugar for creme caramel is to spread 1/2 cup white sugar in a Pyrex casserole or souffle dish. Place in a preheated 350-degree oven and bake for 30 or more minutes. Pour this into your individual cups or pour the custard over this mixture and bake.

CREME BRULEE

8 egg yolks
1/4 teaspoon salt
1 quart heavy cream
1/3 cup sugar
2 teaspoons vanilla extract
1 cup brown sugar, sifted

Beat egg yolks and salt with a wire whisk. Heat cream in top of double boiler but do not scald; gently whisk in the eggs. Add sugar and stir until dissolved; add vanilla. Pour into a 6-cup mold or baking dish and place in a larger pan. Pour a hot water bath to about half the depth of the mold. Bake in a preheated 275-degree oven for 1 hour or until set.

Remove from oven and water bath; cool and chill overnight. Before serving, sprinkle brown sugar evenly over the surface; place mold in a baking pan, surround with ice cubes; place under broiler about 8 inches from heat. Do not take your eyes off. Broil until sugar melts. Watch carefully, as sugar has a tendency to burn. It should melt quickly so the cream remains cold. Remove at once and return to refrigerator until the crust hardens; however, refrigerating for more than 3 or 4 hours will cause the sugar to liquidify. Serves 8.

Jo and Jan say, "This is truly elegant served just as the recipe instructs, but we also love it sprinkled with fresh raspberries, blueberries, or 1/4 cup toasted slivered almonds or chopped hazelnuts. It will become one of your lifes' great pleasures!"

OLD-FASHIONED CUSTARD

1 3/4 cups milk
1/4 cup heavy cream
1/3 cup sugar
Pinch of salt
2 large eggs
1/2 teaspoon vanilla

Combine milk, cream, sugar and salt in top of double boiler over simmering water. Stir to dissolve sugar; when nearly scalding, remove from heat. Beat eggs with a wire whisk in a small bowl until foamy. Gradually stir a small amount of milk mixture into eggs, then gradually add warmed egg mixture into the hot milk, beating constantly. Continue to cook over simmering water, stirring constantly, until mixture coats back of spoon, about 10 to 15 minutes. Remove from heat and stir in vanilla

Cover surface of custard with plastic wrap or waxed paper; chill at least 2 hours. Makes 2 cups.

❖•❖

Pudding

GORDON'S STEAMED CHOCOLATE PUDDING

Our dear friend, Gordon, sent us on a search for this recipe, hoping to find one "like his Mother used to make." We knew we had a challenge when he told us his wife, Nadine, had never attempted to duplicate it.

The finished product was delivered to their home, and with great trepidation, Gordon was served the pudding topped with Creme Anglaise. To our delight, he cleaned the plate and we are proud to present Gordon's request!

• Check Tips On Steamed Puddings before your begin.

**Butter and granulated sugar for mold
   preparation
3 tablespoons butter
2/3 cup sugar
1 egg, well beaten
2 1/4 cups sifted flour
4 teaspoons baking powder
1/8 teaspoon salt
1 cup milk
2 1/2 ounces unsweetened chocolate,
   melted**

Butter a 1 1/2-quart mold and sprinkle with sugar. Cream butter and 2/3 cup sugar; add egg and beat well. Sift flour, measure, add baking powder and salt; sift again. Add alternately with milk to creamed mixture. Add melted chocolate and mix well.

Spoon batter into prepared mold, filling it 1/2 to 2/3 full. Cover the mold tightly with the lid or a double sheet of foil secured with kitchen string. Place mold on rack in center of kettle, cover kettle with a close fitting lid. Steam for 2 hours, checking occasionally to see if more boiling water needs to be added.

Remove mold from kettle, remove lid or foil and let pudding stand in mold on a rack for 10 minutes. Turn mold on its side; rap gently all the way around to loosen and slide pudding onto a serving tray. Serve with a desired sauce. Serves 8-10.

Jo and Jan say, "Steamed puddings are better served warm. If you prepare it ahead of time, reheat by steaming for 30 minutes. This is delicious with Creamy Sauce or Creme Anglaise (See index).

You can also flame puddings by pouring heated brandy over the top and then igniting it with a lighted match. Or, soak lumps of sugar in lemon or orange flavoring or liqueur, circle around the pudding; ignite one lump and the flame will travel around the pudding. When flames subside, cut the pudding."

TIPS ON STEAMED PUDDINGS

• To steam puddings, you can use a steamer with holes in the bottom and a tight cover; or a deep kettle that will hold water throughout the steaming time.

• You can use a tube center mold, which allows steam to quickly reach the center of pudding; or a round can or bowl, or lastly, individual molds or custard cups.

• Set a low rack in the bottom of a deep kettle large enough to hold a 1 1/2-quart steamed pudding mold and add enough water to reach 3 inches up the side of mold, allowing 4 inches between top of mold and kettle lid for steam to circulate.

• Bring water to a brisk, but not rolling boil; it should remain boiling when covered, the required length of steaming time.

Sweet Temptations

DORIE'S FAVORITE BREAD PUDDING

1 loaf (12 ounces) French bread, cut into 1 or 2-inch cubes
1/2 cup seeded raisins (or combination of raisins and currants)
2 teaspoons grated lemon rind
1/2 cup butter or margarine, melted
2 cups milk
2 cups heavy cream
4 eggs, beaten
2 egg yolks, beaten
1 cup granulated sugar
3/4 cup brown sugar
2 teaspoons vanilla
1 teaspoon nutmeg
2 teaspoons cinnamon
1/2 cup apricot preserves, heated and strained

Place cubed bread in a well-buttered 9 x 13 x 2-inch baking dish. Sprinkle raisins (and currants) and lemon rind over bread; drizzle melted butter over bread and mix carefully to coat bread.

Combine milk, cream, beaten eggs and yolks, sugars, vanilla, nutmeg and cinnamon; blend well. Pour over bread and allow to rest for 20 minutes.

Place baking dish in a larger pan filled with water halfway up the sides of the bread-filled pan. Bake, uncovered in a preheated 350-degree oven for 1 hour or until bread is lightly browned, custard has set and a knife inserted in the center comes out clean. Spread pudding with warm apricot preserves. Serve with warm Rum Sauce, Lemon Sauce, Whiskey Sauce or Pudding Sauce (See index). Serves 10 - 12.

VERA'S RICE PUDDING

6 cups milk
3/4 cup long-grain white rice, uncooked
1 cup heavy cream
3/4 cup sugar
3 egg yolks, beaten
2 teaspoons vanilla
1/4 teaspoon salt
1/2 cup seedless raisins
1/4 teaspoon nutmeg
1 whole blanched almond
1 teaspoon cinnamon

In heavy saucepan bring milk to a boil over medium heat. Stir in rice and return to a boil.

Reduce heat and simmer, uncovered, about 45 minutes or until rice is tender, stirring occasionally.

Combine cream, sugar, yolks, vanilla and salt. Stir into cooked rice and blend well. Heat to a boil; remove from heat and stir in raisins, nutmeg and the blanched almond. Spoon into a 2-quart casserole or individual sherbet dishes. Sprinkle with cinnamon. Serve warm or chill several hours. Serves 6.

Jo and Jan say, "The hidden almond brings good luck to the finder. You may substitute 1 8-ounce can of crushed pineapple, well drained,for the raisins. We like to serve it with Orange, Vanilla, Lemon or Thin Pudding Sauce (See index) or a pitcher of very cold cream."

DOWN SOUTH BANANA PUDDING

3 1/2 tablespoons flour
1 1/3 cups sugar
Dash of salt
4 eggs, separated, and room temperature
3 cups milk
1 teaspoon vanilla
1 package (12-ounce) vanilla wafers
6 medium bananas
1/4 cup plus 2 tablespoons sugar
1 teaspoon vanilla

In top of double boiler combine flour, sugar and salt. Beat egg yolks and combine with milk, mixing well. Stir into dry ingredients; cook over

boiling water, stirring constantly until smooth and thickened. Remove from heat and stir in vanilla.

Spread a small amount, about 1 tablespoon of custard on the bottom of a 3-quart baking dish. Cover with 1/3 of wafers. Slice 2 bananas and layer over wafers. Pour 1/3 of custard over bananas. Repeat layers twice, ending with custard.

Beat egg whites until stiff but not dry. Gradually add sugar, 1 teaspoon at a time, beating until sugar is well blended and meringue holds stiff peaks. Add vanilla and beat until blended. Spread meringue over custard, sealing to edge of dish. Bake in preheated 425-degree oven for 10 to 12 minutes or until golden brown. Serves 8 - 10.

COCONUT PUDDING

1 pint half-and-half
2 tablespoons unflavored gelatin
2 tablespoons cold water
1 cup sugar
1 teaspoon almond extract
2 cups flaked coconut
1 1/2 pints heavy cream, whipped

Bring cream just to a boil; dissolve gelatin in cold water and add to hot cream. Add sugar, flavoring and coconut; allow to set to cool; fold in whipped cream. Pour into an oiled mold and chill until firm. Remove from mold; garnish with coconut and serve with a sauce if desired. (See index)

AUNT JESSIE'S ICEBOX PUDDING

1 package lady fingers (or a light commercial sponge cake).
1 package (4-ounce) German Sweet Chocolate
3 eggs, separated
3 tablespoons sugar
Whipped cream

Line a round bowl with separated lady fingers, reserving half for second layer. Melt chocolate over boiling water.

Beat egg whites until fluffy. In another bowl, beat yolks with a fork adding sugar. Add yolk mixture to melted chocolate. If chocolate is stiff, add 1 to 2 tablespoons of water. Stir until thoroughly mixed. Fold chocolate mixture into egg whites.

Cover layer of lady fingers with half of the chocolate mixture. Add another layer of lady fingers then rest of chocolate mixture.

Place in refrigerator for 8 hours or overnight. To serve, top with whipped cream.

Jan says, "We thank you, Mary Ellen, for sharing Aunt Jessie's famous Icebox Pudding! It's a real 'Golden Era' recipe!"

APPLE CHART

Colors - Best Uses

- *Red Delicious* - red - fresh eating
- *Golden Delicious* - golden - fresh eating, cooking and baking
- *Jonathan* - red - cider, fresh eating, cooking and baking
- *Granny Smith* - green - fresh eating, cooking and baking (tart)
- *Rome Beauty* - red - cooking and baking
- *Winesap* - red - cider, fresh eating, cooking and baking

APPLE DUMPLINGS

2 cups sifted flour
1/2 cup shortening
2 1/2 teaspoons baking powder
1/2 teaspoon salt
3/4 cup milk
8 small apples, pared and cored
4 tablespoons butter
8 tablespoons sugar plus extra for topping
8 tablespoons cinnamon
Cinnamon-sugar to topping

Sift together the flour, baking powder and salt; cut in shortening. Add milk, stirring until soft dough is formed. Knead on lightly floured board and roll 1 1/2 to 2 inches thick. Divide into 8 pieces. Place an apple on each piece; fill each with 1 tablespoon sugar, 1 teaspoon butter, 1 teaspoon cinnamon. Fold dough up over apples, pressing edges together.

Place apples in baking dish, sprinkle with cinnamon-sugar then dot with another 1/2 teaspoon butter. Bake 30 to 40 minutes in preheated 375-degree oven. Serve with cream or Hard Sauce (See index). Serves 8.

GOLDEN APPLE SLICES

6 medium apples, preferably Granny Smith
1/4 cup sugar
1/4 teaspoon cinnamon
Pinch nutmeg
2 tablespoons lemon juice
1/2 stick margarine, melted

Peel, core and slice apples in 1/2-inch slices. In medium oven-proof bowl combine apples, sugar, cinnamon, nutmeg and lemon juice. Blend into apples and pour melted margarine over mixture.

Bake in preheated 400-degree oven for 35 to 45 minutes. Check after 20 minutes and baste apples. Serves 4.

APPLETS

1 1/2 cup grated apples
4 cups sugar
4 tablespoons unflavored gelatin
1 cup unsweetened applesauce
2 cups chopped walnuts
2 teaspoons vanilla

Combine grated apples and sugar in a heavy saucepan and bring to a boil. Soften gelatin in applesauce and add to sugar mixture. Boil hard for

15 minutes, stirring constantly. Watch carefully as mixture will burn easily. Remove from heat; add nuts and vanilla. Pour into 7 x 10-inch pan (or similar size) to depth of 1 inch. Depth is important. Let stand 24 hours at room temperature. Cut in squares; roll in powdered sugar. Makes 24 squares. May be kept in airtight container at room temperature, refrigerator or frozen.

These would be wonderful to send in a "care package" as they will not break or crumble.

JUDY'S ROSEY APPLE WHIRLS

3 cups apples, peeled and finely chopped
1 cup sugar
1 1/2 cups water
1/3 cup red hots
2 cups flour
2 teaspoons baking powder
1/2 teaspoon salt
1/4 cup sugar
1/3 cup shortening
1 egg
Milk
2 tablespoons butter, melted
1 cup heavy cream

Set chopped apples aside and combine sugar, water and red hots in a saucepan. Bring to a boil and simmer 5 minutes. Pour into 8 x 12 x 2-inch

pan, reserving 1/2 cup for topping.

Sift dry ingredients into a large bowl and cut in shortening until mixture resembles coarse meal. Break egg into measuring cup and add enough milk to measure 2/3 cup. Beat with fork to combine. Add to dry ingredients all at once. Stir until dough clings together in a ball.

Knead lightly on floured surface for 12 to 15 strokes. Roll out to a 12-inch square. Spread with melted butter and cover with chopped apples. Roll up jelly roll fashion and cut into 8 1 1/2-inch slices. Place on top of red cinnamon syrup in pan. Bake in preheated 400 degree oven 30 minutes. Spoon reserved syrup over whirls, 1 tablespoon on each one. Continue baking 10 to 15 minutes longer until golden brown.

Serve warm with plain or whipped cream. Serves 8.

POACHED APPLES

1 1/2 cups apple juice
1 tablespoon sugar
1 tablespoon lemon juice
6 apples, cored, cut into fourths
1/4 cup water
1 tablespoon cornstarch
1 container (8-ounce) whipped topping
1/2 cup walnuts, chopped
1/4 teaspoon nutmeg
1/4 teaspoon cinnamon

Combine apple juice, sugar and lemon juice in a saucepan. Add apples and simmer 15 minutes or until tender. Remove apples. Gradually add water to cornstarch and stir until blended. Add this mixture to hot liquid and stir constantly until mixture boils and thickens. Add apples and mix lightly. Combine whipped topping, nuts, cinnamon and nutmeg together and spoon over apples. Serves 6.

❖❖

APPLE CRUNCH

6 apples
7 tablespoons water
1 cup brown sugar
1/4 cup butter
3/4 cup flour
Cream, if desired

Slice apples into baking dish and cover with water. Mix brown sugar, butter and flour until crumbly. Spread over apples and bake for 45 minuted in preheated 375-degree oven. Serve with or without cream. Serves 6-8.

Jo says,"I always like to add a little cinnamon and nutmeg to the brown sugar mixture."

BLUEBERRY CRISP

1 cup flour
1 cup quick oats, uncooked
1/2 cup brown sugar
1/2 teaspoon cinnamon
1/4 teaspoon nutmeg
1/2 cup margarine
6 cups blueberries
1/2 cup sugar
2 tablespoons quick-cooking tapioca
1 1/2 tablespoons lemon juice

In medium bowl combine flour, oats, brown sugar, cinnamon and nutmeg. With pastry blender, cut in margarine until mixture resembles coarse crumbs; set aside.

In large bowl combine remaining ingredients. Press 1 cup crumb mixture onto bottom of a 2-quart baking dish. Spoon in berries. Sprinkle remaining crumb mixture on top. Bake in preheated 350-degree oven for 55 minutes. Toppings may be whipped cream or yogurt. Serves 8.

TIP

- For easy peeling of peaches, drop in boiling water for 30 seconds, plunge into cold water and remove peel with a sharp knife. Use the liquid for punch base, sangria or poaching other fruits.

PEACH COBBLER

2 cups fresh sliced peaches
1 cup sugar
3/4 cup flour
Dash of salt
2 teaspoons baking powder
1 cup sugar
3/4 cup milk
1/2 cup butter or margarine

In small bowl mix peaches and sugar together; set aside. In larger bowl combine flour, salt, baking powder and 1 cup of sugar. Stir in milk to make a batter. Melt butter in an 8 x 8-inch pan. Pour batter over melted butter. Do not stir. Carefully spoon peach mixture over batter. Bake in preheated 350-degree oven for 1 hour. Serves 6 - 8.

Jo and Jan say, "You might want to add a touch of cinnamon with the sugar. Serve with hot Lemon Sauce (See index)."

POACHED PEARS WITH RASPBERRY SAUCE

2 packages (10-ounce size) frozen raspberries, undrained
1/2 cup creme de cassis
8 firm ripe pears

Puree raspberries until smooth; strain through fine sieve to remove seeds. Add creme de cassis, blend.

Peel pears and core from the bottom, leaving stems on top. Cut a thin slice from the bottom so pears stand well. Arrange in a large saucepan; pour raspberry sauce over top. Bring to a simmer, cover and cook gently until fork tender. Remove pears, cool and chill.

Pour cooking liquid in a smaller pan; boil until reduced to a thick syrup, about 10 to 12 minutes. Cool.

To serve, spoon some syrup on individual plates; top with a pear and drizzle additional syrup over top. Serves 8.

❖❖

CAROL'S VARIATION ON POACHED PEARS

After poaching and chilling pears, spoon some chocolate sauce on plates. Dip bottom half of pear in a thick caramel sauce. Place the pear on top of the chocolate puddle; drizzle the thickened raspberry sauce over the top. Isn't it sinful?

Sauces

RUM CREAM SAUCE

8 egg yolks
1/2 cup sugar
2 cups heavy cream
3 tablespoons rum

Beat egg yolks and sugar until thick. Slowly add cream and cook in top of double boiler, stirring constantly until thick. Remove from heat, cool slightly and add rum. Makes 2 3/4 cups.

WHITE CHOCOLATE SAUCE

1 cup heavy cream
10 ounces white chocolate
1/2 cup Grand Marnier or Frangelico liqueur

Scald cream; remove from heat, break chocolate into pieces and add to hot cream. Process until smooth in blender or food processor. Add liqueur and chill until serving time. Makes 2 1/2 cups.

LILLIE'S CHOCOLATE SAUCE

1/2 cup butter or margarine
4 squares (1-ounce size) unsweetened chocolate
1/2 cup cocoa
Pinch of salt
1 box (pound) confectioners' sugar
2 cups half-and-half
1 1/2 teaspoons vanilla

Melt butter and chocolate in top of double boiler, stirring until smooth and creamy. Add cocoa, salt, sugar and cream. Stir while bringing just to the boiling point; remove from heat and add vanilla. Store in refrigerator and reheat if it thickens too much for you.

Jan and Jo say, "You have to try this! It is truly a chocolate lovers' delight. Drizzle it over our White Chocolate Mousse (See index) and you will be famous!"

FUDGE SAUCE

2 squared unsweetened chocolate
1 cup sugar
1/2 cup water
1 tablespoon butter
1 tablespoon light corn syrup
1 teaspoon vanilla
2 tablespoons heavy cream

Melt chocolate over hot water. Add sugar, water, butter and corn syrup. Cook without stirring until mixture thick and syrupy. Remove from heat; add vanilla and cream, mixing thoroughly.

CHOCOLATE CINNAMON SAUCE

1 pound semisweet chocolate
1/2 cup butter or margarine
1/2 cup milk
1/2 cup heavy cream
1 1/2 teaspoons cinnamon, more if desired
1/4 cup bourbon

Break chocolate into pieces and melt with butter in top of double boiler over simmering water. Scald milk and cream with cinnamon in small saucepan over medium heat; gradually stir into chocolate mixture. Blend in bourbon; add more cinnamon if desired. Serve hot. Makes 2 cups.

Jo and Jan say, "This is wonderful as a sauce for Profiteroles." (See index)

TIP

- Form a puddle of Chocolate Sauce on dessert plates; add a puddle on top of that of White Chocolate Sauce. With a toothpick, draw a design of swirls in the White Chocolate; the dark will come through the design. Place your dessert in the center. This can be done with other sauces, such as White Chocolate and Raspberry. (See index for sauce recipes).

CRANBERRY GLAZE

1/2 cup sugar
1 tablespoon cornstarch
3/4 cup fresh cranberries
2/3 cup water

In saucepan stir together sugar and cornstarch; stir in cranberries and water. Cook and stir till bubbly. Cook, stirring occasionally, just till cranberry skins pop. Cool to room temperature (do not chill). Makes 1 cup.

LIGHT RASPBERRY-ORANGE SAUCE

1 package (10-ounce) frozen raspberries in light syrup, thawed
1 tablespoon frozen orange juice concentrate, thawed and undiluted
2 teaspoons cornstarch
1/8 teaspoon grated orange rind

Process raspberries in blender or food processor until smooth; strain and discard seeds. Combine remaining ingredients in small saucepan; add raspberry puree and stir well. Cook over medium heat, stirring constantly until it comes to a boil. Cook 1 minute, stirring constantly; remove from heat, pour into a bowl, cover and chill. Makes 1 cup.

CHOCOLATE MARSHMALLOW SAUCE

6 ounces (6 squares) unsweetened chocolate
1 1/2 cups confectioners' sugar
1 cup hot water
8 large marshmallows or 1/2 cup miniatures
1 teaspoon vanilla

Place all ingredients in top of double boiler. Bring to a boil, stirring constantly. Remove from over water and continue stirring until chocolate is completely dissolved and mixture thickens. Serve hot or at room temperature. Makes 2 cups.

WHISKEY SAUCE

1/2 cup butter
1 cup sugar
2 eggs, beaten
1/4 teaspoon nutmeg
1/2 cup bourbon

Heat butter and sugar until sugar is clear. Remove from heat and cool. Add eggs and beat 1 minute. Add whiskey and nutmeg; continue to beat until well-blended.

❖❖❖

ORANGE SAUCE

3/4 cup sugar
3 tablespoons cornstarch
1 cup boiling water
1/2 cup orange juice
1 teaspoon grated orange rind
1 1/2 tablespoons butter

Combine sugar and cornstarch in a sauce pan. Add water to orange juice, pour into sugar mixture and stir constantly over medium heat until it boils and is clear. Remove from heat and stir in butter and orange rind.

Jo and Jan say, "We think this is delicious served hot over Rice Pudding and chilled, over fruit tarts."

HARD SAUCE

1 stick butter
1 cup white sugar
1 egg white
1/4 cup rum or bourbon
Grated nutmeg, for garnish

Cream butter and sugar until very light. Add beaten egg white. Continue beating and add flavoring, a little at a time until sauce is very fluffy. Sprinkle grated nutmeg on top of sauce.

VERA'S GRAND MARNIER HARD SAUCE

1 cup unsalted butter, softened
3 cups confectioners' sugar, sifted
1/4 cup Grand Marnier
1 egg yolk

Cream butter and sugar until light and fluffy. Add liqueur and egg; beat until smooth. Refrigerate until firm and bring to room temperature before serving. Makes 2 cups.

Jo says, "I really love this with my Mother's Plum Pudding, but it is wonderful with pound cake too."

LEMON BRANDY HARD SAUCE

1 1/2 cups powdered sugar
1/2 cup butter, softened
3 tablespoons brandy
1 teaspoon vanilla
1 teaspoon lemon zest

Combine all ingredients and beat with electric mixer until fluffy. Chill several hours or overnight

THIN PUDDING SAUCE

1/4 cup sugar
2 tablespoons flour
1 cup water
1 tablespoon butter
1/4 teaspoon nutmeg

Combine sugar and flour in small saucepan. Add water and butter; whisk together over medium heat. When slightly thickened, remove from heat and stir in nutmeg. This sauce is good with Rice Pudding and Bread Pudding (See index).

VANILLA SAUCE FOR RICE PUDDING

1 1/2 cups milk
1 cup heavy cream
1 teaspoon vanilla extract
7 egg yolks
1/2 cup sugar

In a medium saucepan, heat milk, 1/2 cup cream and vanilla. Do not boil. Beat yolks and sugar until stiff and white; slowly beat in the hot milk mixture. Pour back into the saucepan and heat, stirring constantly, until thick enough to coat a spoon. Place pan in cool water and stir 1 more minute. Makes 3 cups.

BLACKBERRY SAUCE

1 package (10-ounce) frozen unsweetened
  blackberries, thawed
3-4 tablespoons black currant jam
2 tablespoons sugar
2 1/2 teaspoons cornstarch
1 1/2 tablespoons creme de cassis liqueur

Puree berries and juices in blender or processor; strain into bowl. Mix jam, sugar and pureed berries in a saucepan. Combine cornstarch with creme de cassis and add to berry mixture. Mix well; simmer gently until sauce is thick enough to coat the back of spoon. Chill. Makes about 1 1/2 cups.

Jo and Jan say, "Try this sauce over poached fruits, such as pears and peaches. It's wonderful!"

MELBA SAUCE

2 teaspoons cornstarch
1 tablespoon water
1/2 cup light corn syrup
1/2 cup currant jelly
1 package (10-ounce) frozen strawberries or
  raspberries, thawed

Mix cornstarch and water in small saucepan. Stir in corn syrup, jelly and berries. Cook over medium heat, stirring constantly until mixture comes to a full boil and boil for 1 to 2 minutes. Remove from heat and strain. Cool slightly. Makes 1 1/4 cup

RASPBERRY SAUCE

1 pint fresh raspberries, pureed or 2
  packages (10-ounce size) frozen, thawed
1/2 cup sugar
1/4 cup kirsch, framboise, Grand Marnier, or
  brandy
Juice of 1/2 lemon

In small saucepan combine raspberry puree and sugar. Bring mixture to a boil, reduce heat and simmer 2 minutes. Carefully add liqueur and simmer 1 minute more. Strain mixture to remove seeds and add lemon juice. Cover and refrigerate. Makes about 1 1/3 cups.

BRANDIED RASPBERRY GLAZE

1 package (12-ounce) frozen dry-pack
  raspberries or 3 cups fresh
3/4 cup sugar
2 tablespoons cornstarch
1/4 cup brandy, Grand Marnier or other
  orange-flavored liqueur

Combine raspberries and sugar in saucepan. Dissolve cornstarch in liqueur in separate bowl then stir into raspberries and blend well.

Cook over medium heat, stirring occasionally, until sauce thickens and is bubbly, about 5 minutes; do not over cook. Cool to room temperature; store in covered container in refrigerator. Spoon over berries in pies and tarts. Makes 1 2/3 cups.

BANANAS FOSTER SAUCE

1/2 cup sugar
2 tablespoons butter
2 teaspoons cinnamon
1 teaspoon nutmeg
1 1/2 ounces (3 tablespoons) banana liqueur
1 1/2 ounces (3 tablespoons) white rum (100
  proof)

Combine sugar, butter, cinnamon and nutmeg. Heat in a small saucepan until butter

and sugar are melted, stirring constantly. Add banana liqueur and blend well. Heat the rum separately and add to flame the sauce.

Jo and Jan say, "This is an easy way to prepare Bananas Foster. We peel and slice firm bananas, lengthwise; place them in the heated sauce, coat them well and pour the rum over the top and flame them. Place a scoop of ice cream on a chilled plate, arrange banana slices on each side and spoon sauce over the top." Serves 4.

Sweet Temptations

TIP

- Our favorite bartender gave us this one. If you have doubts about your brandy igniting or don't want to take a chance, pour 1 or 2 drops of grain alcohol on the brandy. It works!

PECAN PRALINE SAUCE

1 cup heavy cream
1 cup brown sugar
1 teaspoon vanilla
1/2 cup chopped pecans

Stir cream and sugar together in saucepan. Bring to boil, reduce heat and simmer until syrupy, 6 to 8 minutes. Cool and stir in vanilla and nuts.

GRANDMOTHER MATTIE'S LEMON SAUCE

5 tablespoons flour
1 cup sugar
Dash of salt
2 egg yolks
3 tablespoons lemon juice
1/2 teaspoon grated lemon rind
3/4 cup boiling water
2 tablespoons butter

Mix flour, sugar and salt. Add beaten egg yolks, lemon juice, grated rind and boiling water; stir well. Cook in top of double boiler until thick. Add butter before removing from heat. Makes 1 1/2 cups.

CREAMY SAUCE FOR STEAMED PUDDINGS

1 egg
1/3 cup butter, melted
1 1/2 cups confectioners' sugar, sifted
1 teaspoon vanilla
1 cup heavy cream, beaten stiff

Beat egg until foamy. Blend in butter, sugar and vanilla. Fold in whipped cream.

CREME ANGLAISE

1 cup heavy cream
1 cup milk
4 egg yolks, room temperature
1/3 cup sugar
2 tablespoons cointreau, cognac or rum (optional)
1 teaspoon vanilla

Scald cream and milk in small heavy saucepan over medium heat; remove from heat. Whisk egg yolks and sugar in top of double boiler until thickened and pale yellow; gradually stir in hot cream mixture in thin, steady stream.

Cook custard mixture over simmering water, stirring constantly, about 10 minutes or until thick enough to coat the back of a spoon. Remove from heat; stir in liqueur and vanilla. Blend well; cool to room temperature, stirring occasionally. Cover and chill 4 to 6 hours before serving. Custard will thicken as it cools. Makes 2 cups.

Jo and Jan say, "You might like to try this without the liqueur, and add a cinnamon stick and 1/2 teaspoon of ground cinnamon to the mixture before cooking. Remove cinnamon stick when mixture is thickened. Try it over steamed pudding or rice pudding."

ENGLISH PASTRY CREAM

1/4 cup sugar
3 egg yolks
2 teaspoons cornstarch
1 cup scalded milk
1 cup light cream, heated
2 teaspoons vanilla extract

Beat sugar, egg yolks and cornstarch in saucepan until light and smooth. Pour the hot milk and cream into the egg mixture, beating constantly. Cook, stirring constantly over moderate heat until sauce coats the spoon, about 4 minutes. Do not let it boil or the eggs will curdle. Remove from heat and stir often until cool. Stir in vanilla, cover and refrigerate. Makes about 2 1/2 cups.

Jo and Jan say, "When making these kind of sauces, only add flavorings or liqueurs to cool mixtures, or flavors will evaporate."

BRANDIED ENGLISH CUSTARD CREAM

1/2 cup sugar
4 egg yolks
1 teaspoon cornstarch
1 3/4 cups scalded milk
1 tablespoon Cognac
1 teaspoon vanilla

Combine sugar, egg yolks and cornstarch in a medium-size saucepan; gradually stir in scalded milk. Heat over low heat, stirring constantly, until custard coats back of spoon, about 5 to 7 minutes.

Remove from heat and stir in Cognac and vanilla. Stir until cool and refrigerate, covered. Serve cold. Makes 2 1/3 cups.

FRANGELICO CREAM

4 egg yolks
1/4 cup sugar
Pinch of salt
1 cup milk
1/4 cup Frangelico liqueur

Set egg yolks out until room temperature. Combine yolks, sugar and salt in saucepan and whisk until creamy and light colored. Add milk while whisking; place over medium heat and cook while stirring constantly until mixture is thickened and coats the back of a spoon. Remove from heat; add liqueur and strain mixture. Makes about 1 1/2 cups.

Jo and Jan say, "This is delicious served warm over a chocolate brownie or cake."

CARAMEL WHIPPED CREAM

1/3 cup sugar
1 tablespoon water
1 cup heavy cream

Cook sugar and water in small, heavy saucepan over low heat, swirling pan until sugar dissolves. Increase heat and boil until mixture turns a mahogany color. Remove from heat and stir in cream; mixture will bubble. Return to heat and stir until caramel mixture dissolves. Cover and chill at least 6 hours.

With electric mixer, beat chilled mixture until soft peaks form. Cover and refrigerate until serving time. Makes 1 1/2 cups.

Jo and Jan say, "This is delicious spooned over pound cake, spice cake and brownies. It can be made a day or two ahead of serving time."

CREME FRAICHE

1 pint heavy cream
2 tablespoons buttermilk

Combine cream and buttermilk in glass jar and whisk until well blended. Cover with plastic wrap and let stand at room temperature in draft-free area, whisking several times, until mixture has thickened (about 24 hours).

Cover and refrigerate for at least 4 hours, it should be quite thick. It will keep for 10 days to 2 weeks if refrigerated in a tightly-sealed jar.

Seasoned with sugar and/or freshly grated nutmeg, it is "pure Heaven" with fresh fruits; and as it has a distinct tart, nut-like flavor, it can be used in soups and sauces.Creme Fraiche will quickly beat into soft peaks

IDEAS FOR CREME FRAICHE

To 1 1/4 cups Creme Fraiche add 1 teaspoon vanilla and 1/4 cup confectioners' sugar. Serve with pumpkin or apple pie. Add 1/8 teaspoon allspice and 1/4 teaspoon cinnamon for baked fruits.

To 1 1/4 cups Creme Fraiche add 1/4 cup confectioners' sugar and 1 oz. Cointreau.

Serve with fresh fruits and berries. To 1 1/4 cups Creme Fraiche whip 1/4 cup orange blossom honey and serve with biscuits, muffins, tea scones. Combine 1 1/4 cups Creme Fraiche with 1/2 cup Lemon Curd (See index, or available at specialty stores). Wonderful with spice cakes.

Hooray The Souffle - Part II

HOW TO PREPARE A SOUFFLE DISH

The average souffle dish will not be tall enough to accommodate a souffle after it has baked. It will need to have a 'collar' made to extend the sides. This can be done by making two thicknesses of foil folded to a width of 6 inches and tied around the dish so it will extend 4 inches above the top of the dish. Generously butter the bottom and sides of the souffle dish and the inside of the collar; sprinkle with flour or Parmesan cheese; or granulated sugar if the souffle is a dessert.

Spoon the souffle mixture into the dish, filling it 3/4 full. As the souffle bakes it will puff and rise up the sides of the collar. Remove the collar carefully after the souffle has baked.

WAXED PAPER COLLAR FOR COLD SOUFFLE DISHES

Fold a 26-inch long piece of waxed paper lengthwise into thirds. Lightly oil one side and sprinkle with sugar. The collar is oiled rather than buttered with a cold souffle, as butter hardens in the refrigerator and will stick to the souffle and pull away as the collar is removed. Wrap the collar around the souffle dish, sugared side against the dish to form a collar extending 2 inches above the top; tie with string.

TIP

- Refrigerate your souffle mixture for at least an hour before adding beaten egg whites, it will help prevent the souffle from falling.

❖❖❖

TIPS FOR SOUFFLES

- Be sure your souffle dish is thoroughly buttered. If you miss a spot, the souffle will stick to the dish and will not rise.

- Well-beaten egg whites at room temperature are the secret to a successful souffle. If you have forgotten to set them out, stand them in luke warm water for 15 minutes.

- Egg whites beaten in a copper bowl increase to 7 times their original volume; the bowl should be clean and shiny, free of any grease and not a speck of egg yolk in the whites.

- If you are using a copper bowl, do not add cream of tartar to the egg whites.

- Egg whites are beaten until they stand in soft peaks; when the beater is lifted, the peaks should bend slightly and be a bit moist. They should not be so stiff that you could cut them with a knife but should be firm enough to support the weight of a whole egg in its shell.

- The process of folding beaten egg whites into the custard should not take more than a minute. Be gentle and don't over fold. Add about 1/4 of the whites to the base and whisk thoroughly. Then add the lightened sauce to the remaining whites. Using a rubber spatula, with an up and over motion, turn the bowl as you fold.

- Form a circle with the spatula on the top of the unbaked souffle. Make it about 1 inch deep and 1 inch from the edge of the dish. This will create a top hat effect and allow the souffle to rise higher.

- A souffle is done if after 20 - 25 minutes it has a golden color and a light but firm consistency. If it is wobbly in the center, let it cook for 5 more minutes. A shorter baking time will create a creamier, more custard like center; the longer time a drier, firmer souffle.

- When serving a souffle, remove the collar in the kitchen, present the souffle dish at the table. With two serving spoons held back to back, spread the center of the souffle apart towards the sides. This allows steam to escape. Serve souffle onto warm plates.

- A 6-cup souffle recipe will fill 4 individual souffle dishes, but cooking time will need to be reduced to 15 minutes.

FROZEN STRAWBERRY SOUFFLE

6 large eggs, separated
2 cups pureed strawberries
1/2 cup Grand Marnier
2 cups sugar
1/4 cup orange juice
3 cups heavy cream
Chopped walnuts, pecans or pistachios
1/2 cup heavy cream
Whole strawberries
Raspberry Sauce (See index)

Oil and collar a 1 1/2-quart souffle dish (See index How to Prepare a Souffle Dish). Beat egg yolks in large bowl until thick and lemon colored. Add 1 cup sugar and beat until dissolved. Stir in 1/2 cup pureed strawberries. Place in top of double boiler and cook over hot water until thickened, about 15 to 20 minutes, stirring frequently. Allow to cool. Add Grand Marnier, a little at a time, until thoroughly blended.

Combine 1 cup sugar and orange juice in 1-quart saucepan. Cook, uncovered, over medium low heat, stirring until dissolved. Continue cooking without stirring until mixture reaches soft ball stage (245 degrees on a candy thermometer).

While orange juice and sugar are cooking, beat egg whites until soft peaks form. Very slowly pour in hot orange syrup, beating until stiff peaks form.

Whip cream and fold into yolk mixture. Fold in remaining strawberry puree. Gently but thoroughly fold in egg whites. Spoon into prepared souffle dish. Freeze about 1 1/2 to 2 hours. When firm, wrap in freezer wrap; secure edges with masking tape.

To serve, remove collar; press nuts around sides or top of souffle. Whip cream and garnish top. Decorate with strawberries and serve with Raspberry Sauce. Serves 12-16.

❖❖

CHOCOLATE ALMOND SOUFFLE

3 egg yolks
1/2 cup sugar
2 teaspoons almond extract
4 ounces unsweetened chocolate, melted
  over hot water
4 egg whites
Pinch of salt
1/8 teaspoon cream of tartar

Prepare a 1-quart souffle dish (See index How To Prepare A Souffle Dish) and dust with confectioners' sugar. Beat egg yolks; add sugar and beat until light in color. Stir in almond extract; fold in melted chocolate and cool slightly. In a separate bowl beat egg whites with salt and cream of tartar until stiff. Gently fold the chocolate mixture into the egg whites. Pour into prepared dish. Place in preheated 400-degree oven and reduce temperature to 375-degrees. Bake 15-20 minutes. Serves 4-6.

COLD HAZELNUT SOUFFLE

1 3/4 cups sugar
1 cup water
9 egg yolks
3 cups heavy cream, whipped
1 cup blanched hazelnuts, toasted and finely
  chopped
2 tablespoons Cognac
2 tablespoons Frangelico liqueur

    Prepare an 8-inch souffle dish. (See index How To Prepare A Souffle Dish).
    Refrigerate bowl until ready to fill.

Combine sugar and water in small saucepan until sugar is moistened then boil <u>without stirring</u> for about 5 minutes. While sugar water is cooking, place egg yolks in large mixer bowl and beat at medium speed until light and lemon colored. Increase speed to high and slowly pour in sugar syrup, beating until mixture is quite stiff and cool. Gently fold in all but 1/2 cup whipped cream until completely combined. Fold in nuts, Cognac and Frangelico. Spoon into souffle dish cover with remaining cream. Refrigerate overnight. Remove collar and serve immediately. Serves 10-12.

COLD RASPBERRY SOUFFLE

2 packages (10-ounce size) frozen
  raspberries
5 egg yolks
1 1/2 cups sugar
Juice of 1 orange, strained
2 tablespoons raspberry liqueur
2 packages unflavored gelatin
2 cups heavy cream
5 egg whites
1/8 teaspoon salt
1/8 teaspoon cream of tartar
Finely chopped nuts
1/2 cup heavy cream, whipped
Raspberry Sauce (See index)

Prepare a 1-quart souffle dish (See index How To Prepare A Souffle Dish).
    Thaw and drain raspberries; puree berries in blender or processor and strain to remove seeds. You should have a little more than 1 cup puree.
    Beat egg yolks and sugar together at high speed until very thick. Add all but 1/2 cup raspberry puree along with orange juice and liqueur. Place reserved 1/2 cup raspberry puree in a small saucepan and sprinkle with gelatin. Let sit for 5 minutes; heat gelatin until it has melted but do not let it boil.
    Whip cream until thick but not too stiff; beat egg whites with salt and cream of tartar until they stand in soft peaks. Fold melted gelatin into raspberry mixture. Fold in cream, then egg whites. Spoon into prepared dish and chill at least 6 hours before serving. To serve, remove collar and press nuts around sides of souffle. Garnish top with whipped cream and serve with Raspberry Sauce. Serves 8.

ORANGE SOUFFLE

3 egg yolks
1/2 cup sugar
2 tablespoons grated orange rind (from fresh
   oranges)
3/4 cup fresh orange juice
1 tablespoon unflavored gelatin
1/4 cup cold water
3 egg whites
2 cups heavy cream

Beat egg yolks and sugar for 5 minutes in a large bowl on medium speed of electric mixer. Stir in orange rind and juice. Soften gelatin in cold water and heat in a double boiler over hot water until thoroughly dissolved. Beat into egg mixture.

Beat egg whites until very stiff in another bowl. In yet another bowl, whip 1 1/3 cups of the heavy cream until stiff. Fold egg whites and whipped cream alternately into egg mixture. Transfer to a serving dish and chill until set.

Before serving, whip remaining 2/3 cup heavy cream and spread over top of souffle. Serves 6-8.

COLD MOCHA SOUFFLE

1 envelope unflavored gelatin
1/4 cup cold water
1 package (4 ounces) German sweet
   chocolate
1 tablespoon freeze-dried coffee
1/4 cup water
6 egg yolks
1/4 cup sugar
6 egg whites, stiffly beaten
2 cups dairy whipped topping

Prepare a 1-quart souffle dish (See index How To Prepare A Souffle Dish).

Soften gelatin in cold water; heat and stir chocolate with coffee and 1/4 cup water in saucepan over low heat. Add gelatin; stir to dissolve and remove from heat. Combine egg yolks and sugar in top of double boiler over hot water. Beat with electric mixer until thick and light, or about 4 minutes. Remove from heat, blend in chocolate mixture and pour into a bowl; fold in beaten egg whites. Cool about 10 minutes and fold in whipped topping. Pour into prepared souffle dish and chill about 3 hours. Gently remove collar and garnish if desired. Serves 10-12.

COLD PUMPKIN SOUFFLE

1 envelope unflavored gelatin
1/4 cup rum
4 eggs
2/3 cup sugar
1 cup canned pumpkin
1/2 teaspoon cinnamon
1/2 teaspoon ginger
1/4 teaspoon mace
1/4 teaspoon cloves
1 cup heavy cream, whipped
2 tablespoons finely chopped walnuts
Heavy cream, whipped for topping

Prepare a 1-quart souffle dish (See index for instructions).

Sprinkle gelatin over rum; heat over hot water until dissolved. Beat eggs thoroughly and gradually add sugar; beat until thick and smooth. Stir in pumpkin seasoned with spices. Add the gelatin and fold in the whipped cream. Fill prepared souffle dish with mixture, sprinkle with nuts and chill until set. Serve with whipped cream. Serves 6.

Jo and Jan say, "We prefer Creme Anglaise for a topping. You might want to try it sometime."

FROZEN RASPBERRY SOUFFLE

12 egg yolks
2 1/4 cups sugar
1 cup pureed and strained fresh or
  unsweetened frozen raspberries
2/3 cup framboise
2 cups heavy cream, whipped
8 egg whites, room temperature
Pinch of salt
1/8 teaspoon cream of tartar
Sweetened whipped cream and fresh berries
  (garnish)

Prepare a 3-quart souffle dish with oiled foil collar extending 4 inch above rim. See directions on How To Prepare A Souffle Dish (index).

Beat egg yolks in a large bowl until thick and lemon colored. Add 1 1/4 cups sugar and beat until dissolved; blend in raspberries. Transfer to a double boiler and cook over hot water until custard coats a metal spoon; do not let it boil. Strain mixture into a bowl set in ice and stir until cool. Gradually add framboise, blending thoroughly after each addition. Gently fold in whipped cream.

Beat egg whites until light and foamy. Add salt and cream of tartar and, gradually adding 2 tablespoons at a time, beat in the remaining sugar. Mix 1/3 of egg whites into the custard, then fold in the rest. Pour into prepared dish, smooth top and freeze overnight. When it is firm, cover with foil or plastic wrap.

To serve, remove collar and smooth sides. Garnish with whipped cream and berries. Serves 12.

Jo and Jan say, "This melts very quickly so serve directly from the freezer. It is also delicious served with Creme Fraiche (See index)."

ICED LEMON SOUFFLE

1 envelope unflavored gelatin
2 tablespoons water
Grated rind of 4 lemons
1/2 cup lemon juice, strained
1 cup superfine sugar
1 cup egg whites (7 or 8 eggs)
1 cup heavy cream, whipped
Whipped cream (garnish)
Lemon, sliced paper-thin (garnish)
Fresh mint leaves (garnish)

Soften gelatin in water in a small saucepan. Add grated lemon rind, juice and sugar. Stir over low heat until gelatin is thoroughly dissolved. Chill until consistency of syrup. Beat egg whites until very stiff and beat into the lemon-gelatin mixture. Fold in whipped cream, mixing well.

Pour into a prepared 1-quart souffle dish. See directions on How To Prepare a Souffle Dish (index). Chill the souffle.

To serve, remove collar; decorate top of souffle with additional whipped cream, slices of lemon and mint leaves. Serves 6.

Jo and Jan say, "This is a lovely summertime dessert."

HOT CHOCOLATE MOCHA SOUFFLE

1 stick butter
4 squares (ounces) unsweetened chocolate
1 cup sugar
4 egg yolks, room temperature
1 tablespoon instant coffee granules
  dissolved in 1 tablespoon rum
1 teaspoon vanilla
1/4 cup flour
5 egg whites, room temperature

Prepare a 1-quart souffle dish (See index How To Prepare A Souffle Dish).

Melt butter and chocolate in heavy large saucepan over very low heat, stirring until smooth. Blend in 1/2 cup sugar, egg yolks, coffee mixture and vanilla; stir in flour.

Beat whites in large bowl until soft peaks form. Gradually add rest of sugar, beating constantly until whites are stiff but not dry. Fold 1/4 of whites into chocolate, then fold chocolate back into remaining whites. Turn batter into prepared dish. Sprinkle lightly with sugar. Place on rack in center of oven and bake in preheated 450-degree oven for 5 minutes. Reduce heat to 400 degrees and continue baking about 20 minutes or until souffle is puffed. Serve immediately with Creme Anglaise (See index). Serves 6.

Jo and Jan say, "The center of this souffle will remain moist. It's truly delicious."

COLD LIME SOUFFLE

1 envelope gelatin
1/4 cup water
3/4 cup milk
4 egg yolks
1/2 cup sugar
1/2 cup fresh lime juice (6 to 7 limes)
1/4 teaspoon grated lime rind
1 cup heavy cream
3 drops green food coloring
7 egg whites
Fresh lime slices (garnish)

Prepare a 1-quart souffle mold, oiling the collar rather than butter. (See index How To Prepare A Souffle Mold).

Sprinkle gelatin over water to soften. Heat milk in top of a double boiler. Beat egg yolks with sugar until light and lemon-colored; pour hot milk into them. Return mixture to top of double boiler and add gelatin. Cook mixture over hot water, whisking constantly until thick and creamy; do not let it boil. Remove from heat and from over water; let it cool and add lime juice and rind. Refrigerate mixture until it begins to mound from a spoon.

Whip cream until thick but not stiff and fold into chilled lime mixture, add the food coloring. Refrigerate the mixture until it is just beginning to set. Beat egg whites until stiff but not dry and fold them gently into lime mixture . Spoon the souffle into prepared mold and chill at least 3 hours. Decorate with paper-thin slices of fresh lime. Make a slice halfway-through each slice and give it a twist. Set around edge of souffle. Serves 6-8.

BITTERSWEET CHOCOLATE SOUFFLE

3 egg yolks
2 tablespoons butter or margarine
2 tablespoons flour
1/4 teaspoon salt
3/4 cup milk
2 squares (1-ounce size) unsweetened
    chocolate, melted and cooled
1/2 cup sugar
2 tablespoons hot water
3 egg whites
1/2 teaspoon vanilla
Sweetened whipped cream

Prepare a 1 1/2-quart souffle dish (See index How To Prepare A Souffle Dish).

Beat egg yolks until thick and lemon-colored; set aside. In saucepan melt butter or margarine; stir in flour and salt. Add milk, all at once; cook, stirring constantly, until mixture is thickened and bubbly. Stir a small amount of hot mixture into beaten egg yolks; mix well. Return to remaining hot mixture in saucepan, cook and stir 2 minutes more; remove from heat. Stir together cooled chocolate 1/4 cup sugar, and hot water. Stir chocolate mixture into egg mixture.

Beat egg whites and vanilla until soft peaks form; gradually add remaining sugar, beating to stiff peaks. Fold the egg whites into chocolate mixture. Turn into prepared souffle dish. Bake in preheated 325-degree oven until a knife inserted just off-center comes out clean, about 55 to 60 minutes. Serve immediately with sweetened whipped cream. Serves 6.

BRANDIED CHERRY-CHOCOLATE SOUFFLE

1 jar (1 pound, 4 ounces) brandied dark bing
  cherries (pitted)
1 ounce dark sweet chocolate
3 ounces bitter chocolate
2 tablespoons butter
3 tablespoons flour
3/4 cup hot milk -do not boil
4 tablespoons sugar
3 tablespoons rum
5 eggs (separated)
1/8 teaspoon salt
1/8 teaspoon cream of tartar
Confectioners' sugar
1 cup heavy cream, whipped

Drain cherries, saving liqueur. Melt chocolate in 4 tablespoons cherry liqueur in top of double boiler.

Melt butter in a quart and a half saucepan. Blend in flour, add milk and stir constantly until mixture thickens and is smooth. Add sugar and rum; just stirring in. Remove from heat, add melted chocolate mixture; blend well. Cool to room temperature.

Prepare a 6-cup souffle dish. (See index on How To Prepare a Souffle Dish). Preheat oven to 375 degrees. Place in it a pan large enough to hold souffle dish in 2 inches of hot water.

Line bottom of souffle dish with drained cherries. Beat egg whites until stiff, adding salt and cream of tartar at half-way point. Beat egg yolks until lemon colored, and stir them into the chocolate mixture. Fold in the egg whites gently but thoroughly. Pour on top of cherries, and place in hot water bath in oven. Bake for 45 minutes. Remove from oven and dust top with confectioners' sugar. Serve with whipped cream. Serves 6-8.

GRAND MARNIER SOUFFLE

2 cups milk
3/4 cup sugar
1/2 stick butter, melted
1/3 cup flour
1/4 cup Grand Marnier
5 egg yolks, room temperature
7 egg whites, room temperature
1/8 teaspoon salt
1/8 teaspoon cream of tartar
1 recipe Creme Anglaise (See index)

Prepare a 1 1/2-quart souffle mold (See index, Directions on Preparing A Souffle Mold).

Heat milk, add sugar; stir and bring to a boil. In another saucepan mix the melted butter with flour and cook for 1 minute over low heat. Stir into hot milk, blend until thick and creamy. Remove from heat and add Grand Marnier.

Beat egg yolks until lemon colored and add to mixture, stirring constantly.

In a separate bowl, beat egg whites until frothy. Add salt and cream of tartar and beat until whites stand in soft peaks. Fold one third of whites into custard base with a rubber spatula. Gently fold in remaining whites until just a few small streaks of white remain.

Spoon into prepared souffle mold. Smooth top of mixture with spatula; run thumb around edge of dish to form a 1/2-inch border of souffle mixture flush with rim. Bake in preheated 375-degree oven, in center of oven until top is golden brown and center is set, about 20-25 minutes.

Remove souffle from oven; remove collar and serve immediately. Spoon souffle onto warmed serving plates, including a portion of crust and creamy center with each serving. Drizzle Creme Anglaise sauce over each. Serves 6.

KIM'S HOT RASPBERRY SOUFFLE

3 tablespoons butter
3 tablespoons flour
1/2 cup milk
2 tablespoons sugar
4 large egg yolks, well beaten
1/4 cup almond liqueur
2 packages (10-ounce size) sweetened
    frozen raspberries, thoroughly drained,
    reserving 1/4 cup syrup
3 tablespoons raspberry jam
6 large egg whites, room temperature
1/4 teaspoon cream of tartar
Pinch of salt
Confectioners' sugar Raspberry sauce
    (See index)

Prepare recipe of Raspberry Sauce. Prepare a 1 1/2-quart souffle dish (See index, How To Prepare A Souffle Dish).

Melt butter in a small saucepan. Stir in flour and blend until smooth over low heat. Remove from heat and slowly whisk in milk and sugar. Cook over medium heat, stirring constantly until mixture is thickened; remove from heat.

Combine beaten egg yolks, liqueur, reserved raspberry syrup and jam; beat well. Stir in 1/3 of hot mixture. Return mixture to pan, stirring constantly and cook 1 minute. Transfer to a large bowl and stir in raspberries; cool.

Beat egg whites until foamy. Add cream of tartar and salt; beat until stiff peaks form. Fold half of whites gently but thoroughly into raspberry mixture. Carefully fold in remaining whites. Lightly spoon into souffle dish.

Position rack in lower 1/3 of oven and preheat oven to 375 degrees. Bake souffle 35 to 45 minutes, or until a deep golden color. Sprinkle with confectioners' sugar and serve immediately with Raspberry Sauce. Serves 6.

FRESH PEACH MOUSSE

1 1/2 pounds fresh peaches
1/4 cup peach schnapps liqueur
1/4 teaspoon salt
3 tablespoons sugar
1 envelope unflavored gelatin
1/4 cup warm water
2 cups heavy cream
2 tablespoons sugar
2 tablespoons lemon juice

Peel fresh peaches and cut into chunks; puree in blender or food processor. Pour 2 cups puree into large bowl, stir in peach schnapps, salt and sugar.

In a small pan, dissolve gelatin in warm water. Cook over heat, stirring occasionally, until completely dissolved. Stir into peach mixture and refrigerate; stirring occasionally for about 45 minutes, until mixture mounds slightly.

Prepare collars for 8 6-ounce ramekins. Tear off 8 4-inch strips of foil. Fold each in half into a 2-inch strip. Wrap each tightly around outside of each ramekin to collar stands about 1/2 inch above rim. Secure with string or tape. Oil inside of ramekin and collar and sprinkle with sugar.

Beat heavy cream and 2 tablespoons sugar to stiff peaks. Fold 2 cups of whipped cream into the chilled peach mixture. Fold lemon juice into the remaining whipped cream. Alternately spoon cream mixture and peach mixture into prepared molds. Using a knife, cut through mixtures to make a swirled design. Refrigerate until firm, at least 3 hours. Remove collars before serving. Serves 8.

Jo and Jan say, "This mousse is lovely for a ladies' luncheon! You might serve it in a 1 1/2 quart souffle dish."

AMARETTO MOUSSE

6 egg yolks, room temperature
1/3 cup confectioners' sugar, sifted
1/2 cup Amaretto liqueur
1/4 cup fresh orange juice
1 cup heavy cream
1/2 cup slivered almonds, well-toasted

Beat egg yolks and sugar until thick and pale yellow; beat in liqueur and orange juice.

Transfer to top of double boiler and whisk over low heat until mixture is very thick (you can see bottom of pan between strokes). Remove from heat and beat until cool.

Beat cream until stiff and stir 1/4 into cooled yolk mixture; gently fold in the rest. Cover and refrigerate several hours or overnight.

To serve, spoon into 4 goblets; sprinkle toasted almonds on top. Serves 4.

CHOCOLATE MOUSSE

2 packages (12-ounce size) semi-sweet chocolate chips
1/4 cup water
10 egg yolks, lightly beaten
14 egg whites
Pinch of salt
Heavy cream, whipped

Melt chocolate with water in top of double boiler. Slowly whisk in egg yolks and cook about

3 minutes until mixture is smooth. Beat egg whites with salt until stiff peaks are formed.

Fold cooled chocolate mixture into egg whites until well mixed. Pour into dishes/bowl of choice and chill. To serve, top with whipped cream and garnish with a fresh or crystallized flower. Serves 20.

Jo and Jan say, "This mousse may be made in advance and refrigerated, so it is perfect for a dinner party. No last minute scurrying about in the kitchen. It is also so delicious as a filling for chocolate dinner crepes."

WHITE CHOCOLATE MOUSSE

10 ounces white chocolate (we use Belgian)
3 tablespoons milk
2 eggs, beaten
2 egg yolks, beaten
2 teaspoons vanilla or desired liqueur
2 cups heavy cream, stiffly beaten

Place a 2-quart serving dish in refrigerator to chill. Combine chocolate and milk in top of double boiler and melt over simmering water. Remove from over water and heat; slowly add beaten eggs, a spoon or so at a time to the hot mixture.

When eggs are all incorporated, return to over heat to just thicken the mixture. Once again, remove from heat, add vanilla or liqueur and transfer to a large bowl. Set bowl in ice water to quickly chill the mixture. When thoroughly cold, fold in whipped cream and spoon into the well chilled bowl. Cover and refrigerate several hours or overnight. This can be made a day or two ahead of serving. It keeps very well. Easily serves 12.

Jo and Jan say, "Make a puddle of Lillie's Chocolate Sauce or Raspberry Sauce (See index) on each plate; spoon a mound of the Mousse on top, garnish with fresh fruit or berries if you desire. It's fit for royalty!"

❖❖

MOCHA POT DE CREME

1 package (6-ounce) semi-sweet chocolate
   morsels
3 tablespoons sugar
1 1/3 cups half-and-half
1 1/2 tablespoons Kahlua
1/2 teaspoon instant coffee granules
3 egg yolks, beaten
1 teaspoon vanilla
Sweetened whipped cream

Melt chocolate morsels in top of double boiler. Stir in sugar until dissolved. Gradually whisk in half-and-half; cook until thickened. Combine Kahlua and coffee granules, stirring until coffee is dissolved. Add to chocolate mixture and stir well.

Beat egg yolks well, then gradually stir in about 1/4 hot chocolate mixture into yolks, quickly add back to chocolate, stirring constantly. Stir in vanilla and pour into 4 pot de creme cups or container of your choice. Chill 3 to 4 hours and garnish with sweetened whipped cream before serving. Serves 4.

RASPBERRIES SABAYON

4 egg yolks
2 tablespoons sugar
1/4 cup Grand Marnier
1/3 cup heavy cream, whipped
2 pints red raspberries, washed and drained

Beat egg yolks until thick in top of double boiler with electric mixer at medium speed. Gradually beat in sugar; beat until mixture is light and soft peaks form.

Place double boiler top over simmering water

being careful that water does not touch the bottom of the top pan. Slowly beat in the Grand Marnier, continuing to beat until mixture is fluffy and mounds; about 5 minutes.

Remove double boiler top from hot water and set in ice water. Beat the mixture until cool. Gently fold in the whipped cream; refrigerate, covered, until ready to serve.

Place berries in serving dishes and spoon sauce over fruit. Serves 6.

CRANBERRY TORTE

1 1/2 cups graham cracker crumbs
1/2 cup chopped pecans
1/4 cup sugar
6 tablespoons butter or margarine, melted
2 cups whole fresh cranberries, ground
   (makes 1 1/2 cups) * See Note
1 cup sugar
2 egg whites
1 tablespoon frozen orange juice
   concentrate, thawed
1 teaspoon vanilla
1/8 teaspoon salt
1 cup heavy cream
Fresh orange slices, thin and twisted for
   garnish
1 recipe Cranberry Glaze (See index)

Combine crumbs, pecans, 1/4 cup sugar and melted shortening. Press onto bottom and up sides of an 8-inch springform pan; chill.

In large mixer bowl combine cranberries and 1 cup sugar; let stand 5 minutes. Add unbeaten egg whites, juice, vanilla and salt. Beat on low speed until frothy; then beat on high for 6 to 8 minutes or until stiff peaks form; in small mixer bowl whip cream until soft peaks form. Fold into cranberry mixture. Spoon into crust, cover and freeze until firm. Prepare Cranberry Glaze.

To serve, remove torte from pan; place on serving plate. Spoon Cranberry Glaze over top and garnish with orange twists. Serves 8 - 10.

* Note - When buying cranberries, check amount needed for Glaze as well as Torte.

STRAWBERRY SQUARES

1 cup sifted flour
1/4 cup brown sugar
1/2 cup chopped walnuts
1/2 cup butter or margarine, melted
2 egg whites
1 scant cup granulated sugar
1 package (10-ounce) frozen strawberries,
  partially thawed
1 tablespoon lemon juice
1 cup heavy cream, whipped

Mix flour, brown sugar, nuts and butter. Spread in shallow baking pan. Bake in preheated 350-degree oven for 20 minutes, stirring occasionally. Sprinkle 2/3 of the crumbs in a 9x12-inch baking dish.

Combine egg whites, sugar, berries and lemon juice in large bowl; beat at high speed to stiff peaks, about 10 minutes. Fold in whipped cream and spoon over crumbs, then top with remaining crumbs. Freeze 6 hours or overnight. Trim with whole berries, if in season. Serves 12.

Jo says, "Our family loves raspberries, so I make this using chocolate wafers for the crust and frozen raspberries. Try it sometime."

STRAWBERRY MARLOW

1 pint ripe strawberries
24 large marshmallows
1/4 teaspoon salt
1 cup heavy cream, whipped

Crush washed, stemmed strawberries. Heat marshmallows and 2 tablespoons juice from

berries in top of double boiler, stirring constantly until marshmallows are almost melted. Remove from heat and continue folding until mixture is smooth; cool. When cooled, add strawberries and salt; chill. Fold whipped cream into chilled mixture and freeze. Garnish with a whole fresh berry and/or mint leaves. Serves 6-8.

STRAWBERRIES ROMANOFF

2 pints ripe strawberries
1/2 cup sugar
1/3 cup Grand Marnier or Cointreau
3/4 cup heavy cream, whipped
2 tablespoons sugar

Rinse and drain the strawberries; pat dry with paper towels. Remove stems and place strawberries in a bowl. Add sugar and liqueur. Cover bowl and refrigerate until ready to serve. Add remaining sugar to whipped cream and serve with the berries. Serves 8.

PATTI'S RASPBERRY FOOL, GALLIANO

1 pint fresh raspberries
1/4 cup sugar
1/4 cup Galliano liqueur
2 cups heavy cream

Puree raspberries with sugar and Galliano in blender or food processor. Strain through a fine

sieve to remove seeds. Chill at least 1 hour. Meanwhile, whip cream then swirl it in chilled puree. Refrigerate until serving time. Serves 6.

Jo and Jan say, "Raspberry Fool is beautiful served in a clear, stemmed dish. Garnish with mint or perhaps a fresh pansey."

MOLDED CHOCOLATE CREAM

2 packages (4-ounces each) German
  chocolate
2 tablespoons hot coffee
4 eggs, separated and at room temperature
2 teaspoons confectioners' sugar
1 teaspoon vanilla
2 cups heavy cream, whipped and
  sweetened
Shaved chocolate curls for garnish
  (optional)

Oil a 1 to 1 1/2-quart mold and set aside. Melt chocolate with hot coffee in double boiler. Using beater, add egg yolks one at a time; then add sugar and vanilla and mix well. Set aside to cool.

In another bowl, beat egg whites until stiff but not dry and gently fold into cooled chocolate mixture. Pour into oiled mold and refrigerate 24 hours.

To serve, remove from refrigerator and unmold onto serving dish. Frost mold with sweetened whipped cream or serve in a side bowl. Decorate with shaved chocolate curls if desired. Serves 6 - 8.

Jo and Jan say, "Once again we add that a dash of cinnamon in the whipped cream, or even in the chocolate mixture will give a wonderful touch of flavor."

CELEBRATION CREME

1 tablespoon unflavored gelatin
1/4 cup cold water
1 cup Asti Spumante champagne, room
  temperature
6 egg yolks, room temperature
1/2 cup sugar
1 cup heavy cream, whipped
16 fresh raspberries or strawberries

Sprinkle gelatin over cold water in a small bowl and set aside until softened, about 5 minutes. Combine wine, yolks and sugar in top of double boiler over simmering water. Whisk until mixture doubles in volume, becomes thick and heavy and pale yellow; about 20 minutes. Add gelatin and whisk until completely dissolved, about 2 more minutes. Remove from over water and set on a rack to cool; whisk occasionally.

Gently fold whipped cream into cooled mixture. Drop 1 berry into each of 8 dessert glasses. Divide mixture evenly among glasses and refrigerate for at least 2 1/2 hours or overnight. Top each with a berry and serve chilled. Serves 8.

PUMPKIN-BOURBON MOLD

2 tablespoons gelatin
1/2 cup water
1 cup bourbon
1/2 cup sugar
1 tablespoon lemon juice
1 1/2 cups canned pumpkin
1 cup sour cream
1 cup heavy cream, whipped
1 1/2 teaspoons cinnamon
1 teaspoon ginger
1/2 teaspoon mace
Whipped cream and chopped nuts for
  garnish

Dissolve gelatin in water in top of a double boiler. Add bourbon, sugar, lemon juice. Stir until blended and slightly thickened; remove from heat.

Combine pumpkin with sour cream and whipped cream; add spices. Blend this into thickened mixture, stirring well. Pour into a greased 6-cup mold. Chill until firm. To serve, garnish with whipped cream and nuts.

Sweet Temptations

❖❖

TONIA'S "DIRT" CAKE

1 package (16-ounce) Oreo cookies
1 stick margarine, melted
1 package (8-ounce) cream cheese
1 cup confectioners; sugar
1 carton (8-ounce) whipped topping
2 packages (3 1/2-ounce size) instant vanilla
  pudding mix
1 teaspoon vanilla
3 cups milk

Crush cookies and spread 1/2 in a 9 x 13-inch baking dish. Whip together the melted margarine and cream cheese. Add confectioners' sugar and whipped topping; set aside. Prepare instant pudding with vanilla and milk, Add pudding to topping mixture and mix well. Pour over crushed cookies. Sprinkle top with remaining crushed cookies. Chill at least 2 hours before serving. Serves 12 - 14.

Jo and Jan say, "The little ones think it's really fun to go home from Auntie's or Grandma's and report to Mom that they were fed "dirt!"

Ice Creams

ELEGANT PARTY BOMBES

A bombe is a combination of 2 or more flavors of ice cream or sherbet usually formed in a round mold or bowl, and can be prepared days in advance of serving.

To prepare the mold, oil lightly and line with plastic wrap, allowing a 1 to 2-inch overlap and carefully smooth out all wrinkles. Chill thoroughly.

Smooth a 3/4-inch layer of softened ice cream onto bottom and sides of prepared mold; freeze. Fill center with different ice cream or sherbet; freeze. Just before serving, remove from freezer and tug gently at plastic wrap to release bombe. Invert onto serving plate; gently peel off plastic wrap and decorate with any garnish desired.

SUGGESTIONS FOR COMBINATIONS:
Chocolate - Raspberry
Cherry - Vanilla
Chocolate almond - Banana
Strawberry - Pistachio
Lemon - Coconut

GARNISHES:
Whipped cream
Coarsely grated chocolate
Chopped cherries
Chopped nuts
Chopped fruit
Crystallized flowers

LEMON ICE CREAM

5 1/3 cups heavy cream
5 1/3 cups milk
1 1/4 cups fresh lemon juice
4 cups sugar
2 teaspoons lemon extract
1 tablespoon grated lemon peel

Thoroughly mix all ingredients and pour into ice cream freezer cannister. Freeze according to manufacturer's directions. Makes 3 1/2 quarts.

COCONUT ICE CREAM

1 1/2 quarts half-and-half
2 cups milk
1 1/2 cups sugar
1/8 teaspoon salt
5 eggs
5 egg yolks
2 tablespoons cornstarch
2 cups heavy cream, whipped
1 tablespoon vanilla
2 cups grated coconut

Heat the cream, milk, sugar and salt in a heavy 4-quart saucepan; stir until sugar dissolves. In a separate bowl beat the eggs, egg yolks and cornstarch. Beat in a little of the hot cream; add egg mixture to the saucepan, stirring constantly. Cook over low heat 10 minutes; cool. Add whipped heavy cream and vanilla to cooled custard and pour into ice cream freezer. Freeze according to manufacturer's directions. Churn until mixture thickens and machine slows down, add coconut and continue churning until firm. Makes 1 gallon.

COCONUT-ALMOND ICE CREAM

1 1/2 quarts ice cream (See Jo says:)
1 cup flaked coconut
3/4 cup finely chopped slivered almonds

Stir the ice cream to soften slightly and pack into a chilled 1 1/2 quart mold or small individual molds. Freeze until solid.

While freezing ice cream, preheat oven to 350 degrees. Spread coconut and almonds on a baking sheet and toast for 15 minutes, or until browned, stirring occasionally. Remove from oven and cool completely.

Unmold ice cream by dipping mold quickly in hot water, give it a shake, loosen around edges with a small spatula or knife. Turn mold upside down on a tray; remove mold. Working very quickly, pat a thick coating of the coconut-almond mixture on the ice cream, covering completely. Return ice cream to freezer until serving time. Makes 12 1/2-cup servings.

Jo says, "Use your favorite ice cream for this wildly delicious dessert. We love a mocha-chocolate, but vanilla is just as sinful. Also, for a variation, try setting the ice cream on a thin sliver of fudge cookie and drizzle caramel or fudge sauce over the top! Check the index for our array of toppings. Need more be said?"

MOM'S OLD-FASHIONED LEMON DROP ICE CREAM

3 quarts milk (approximate)
7 eggs, beaten
4 cups sugar
Juice of 4 or 5 lemons (about 10
    tablespoons)
Grated rind of lemons (about 8 teaspoons)
1 quart cream
1 tablespoon vanilla
2 cups crushed or ground old-fashioned
    lemon drops

Combine 1 quart milk, eggs and sugar. Stir well and add lemon juice. Heat in top of double boiler, stirring until thick and custard like. Remove from heat and flavor with vanilla; add lemon rind. When cool, add quart of cream. Pour into container and fill to within 1 1/2-inch of top with remaining 2 quarts of milk.

When about half frozen, add crushed lemon drops and complete freezing process. Use a 6-quart freezer.

VARIATION: VANILLA ICE CREAM

For one of the best vanilla ice cream bases you will ever find, just leave out the lemon juice, rind and candy from the above recipe. Make the recipe the same; if you are adding fruit to the mixture toward the end of the churning process, add more sugar to the custard base.

MARIE'S HOMEMADE ICE CREAM

4 eggs
2 cups sugar
1/2 teaspoon salt
1 cup heavy cream
1 tablespoon vanilla
1 teaspoon vanilla butternut flavoring
1 quart half-and-half
Milk

Combine eggs, sugar and salt. Beat until sugar is dissolved and mixture is very thick and creamy. Add heavy cream and beat in well; add vanilla flavorings. Add half-and-half and mix in thoroughly. Pour into 1 gallon freezer cannister and fill to the line with milk; mix thoroughly. Freeze with lots of salt and ice. Makes 1 gallon.

Marie says, "I have made ice cream for years but I think I have finally figured out the right combination and it is very good. The secret is beating and beating the eggs and sugar."

LEMON - SHERBET CUPS

Cut the top from one end of lemons about 1 inch from the end. Scoop out insides and slice the other end off so lemons stand upright. Fill lemon cups with sherbet, tuck fresh mint sprig in the top and set the 'lid' on at a jaunty angle. Freeze until serving time. A unique, refreshing and pretty dessert.

PEACH SORBET

4 cups frozen peaches, thawed
Juice of 1/3 lemon
1 1/4 cup sugar
1 bottle champagne
2 cups peach liqueur

Puree peaches in blender or food processor. Combine with remaining ingredients and mix well. Freeze until firm. Break up and mix with electric mixer or processor and refreeze until ready to serve. Makes about 2 quarts.

CRANBERRY ICE

1 can (1-pound) jellied cranberry sauce
1 cup lemon-lime soda
Mint leaves (garnish)

Beat cranberry sauce on electric mixer at high speed until smooth, about 5 minutes. Gently fold in lemon-lime soda. Divide mixture in 2 ice cube trays and freeze until firm. Place cubes in blender or food processor and mix until frothy. Transfer to a 1-quart container, cover and freeze until ready to use. Let stand at room temperature 30 minutes before serving. Garnish with fresh mint. Serves 4 - 6.

BELLINI ICE

2 pounds rips peaches
4 to 6 tablespoons sugar
2 tablespoons water
1 1/2 cups Asti Spumante

Peel peaches and cut in quarters. Puree in blender or food processor. You will have about 3 1/2 cups.

Mix water and 4 tablespoons sugar in small pan. Bring to a boil; remove from heat and stir in peach puree. Add champagne and place in freezer until firm. Break into chunks and puree, in batches, until smooth but not liquefied. Taste and add more sugar is desired. Refreeze immediately. Makes 5 cups.

Jo and Jan say, "Use a good spumante, you do not want a grapy-tasting champagne."

WATERMELON SORBET

1 cup sugar
1 cup water
3 cups watermelon, pureed

Bring sugar and water to a boil. Cook for 1 minute and cool. Add mixture to pureed watermelon and place into freezer. When frozen 1 inch from edge of bowl, remove from freezer and beat with electric mixer. Freeze and whip three times. After the third time, let the mixture freeze in the bowl. Serves 4 - 6.

RASPBERRY SHERBET

4 cups fresh raspberries, pureed to make 2
  cups
1/4 cup Framboise de Bourgogne or
  raspberry liqueur
1/3 cup lemon juice
2 cups water
1 cup granulated sugar
Whole raspberries (garnish)

Puree raspberries; set aside. Combine lemon juice, water and sugar in a saucepan and cook, over low heat, stirring for 10 minutes, until it becomes a very light syrup. Remove from heat and cool.
  Combine puree with syrup and the liqueur; blend well. Pour the mixture into a shallow freezer dish and freeze until crystals begin to form around the edge. Remove from freezer and beat until smooth. Return to freezer for several hours or until ready to serve. Makes 1 quart.

PINEAPPLE SHERBET

1 cup boiling water
3/4 cup sugar
1 package (3 ounces) lime Jell-O
Juice and rind of 2 large lemons
1 can (8 1/2 ounces) crushed pineapple
3 cups milk

Pour boiling water over sugar and Jell-O. Stir to dissolve; add lemon juice and grated rind. Stir well and add pineapple and milk. Turn into a 2-quart container and freeze. When frozen, remove from container, place in large mixer bowl and beat thoroughly until smooth with electric mixer. Return to freezer container and refreeze. Serves 12.

CHAMPAGNE SHERBET

4 pints lemon sherbet
1 bottle (4/5 quart) champagne (We like to
  use pink)
1/8 teaspoon red food color (if using pink
  champagne)

  Beat sherbet until smooth but not melted in a large bowl. Quickly stir in champagne and food color. Stir to blend well. Pour into a 12-cup mold or individual serving dishes. Garnish with fresh mint leaves or fruit.
  Jo and Jan say, "If you freeze the sherbet in a large mold, invert over your serving utensil, place a hot, damp cloth over the mold and shake it to release. Garnish and serve at once."

BLACKBERRY SORBET

6 cups blackberries, washed and drained
  (fresh or frozen)
1/2 cup sugar
3 tablespoons Kirsch

Puree ingredients in blender or processor. Strain to remove seeds. Place in individual dishes and freeze. Remove to refrigerator 1 hour before serving. Serves 8.
  Jo and Jan say, "This is so good added to a vanilla ice cream base about 3/4 of the way through churning process."

Sweet Temptations

❖❖❖

OUR TERRIFIC TOPPINGS

- Toast shredded coconut and slivered almonds on a baking sheet in preheated 300-degree oven until light brown. Roll preshaped and frozen ice cream balls in cooled mixture and place in freezer until ready to serve.
- Marinate 6 pitted dark cherries in 6 tablespoons Cognac for 2 hours. Place a scoop of chocolate ice cream in each of 6 frosted champagne glasses. Pour 1 jigger of cherry-chocolate liqueur over each serving and top with a marinated cherry.
- Roll preshaped and frozen banana ice cream balls in crushed peanut brittle until well coated.
- Roll preshaped and frozen espresso, vanilla or pumpkin ice cream balls in crushed English toffee candy until well coated.

Special Touches

MERINGUE SHELLS

3 egg whites
1/4 teaspoon cream of tartar
Dash of salt
1 teaspoon vanilla
1 cup superfine granulated sugar
1 cup chopped nuts (Optional)

Separate eggs while still cold; bring to room temperature so they'll beat to fullest volume. In small bowl, with electric mixer at high speed, beat whites until frothy. During beating, do not scrape sides of bowl, or meringue will break down. Continue beating at high speed until whites form soft peaks.

Still beating at high speed, begin adding sugar, 2 tablespoons at a time. Beat for about 2 minutes or until sugar is dissolved. continue beating until all sugar is dissolved. Test by rubbing meringue between fingers. If grainy, continue beating; it will take about 15 minutes. Continue beating at high speed until very stiff peaks form and meringue looks glossy and moist, not dry. Peaks should not curl when beaters are removed. Add nuts if desired.

Cover baking sheet with plain ungreased paper or foil. Draw 6 circles 4 inches in diameter. Spoon meringue evenly on circles, spreading with back of a spoon to shape inside of meringue shell, mounding around the edges to make a nest shape.

Bake in preheated 200-degree oven for 3 1/2 hours. Remove from oven and cool completely on cookie sheet. Loosely wrap each nest with waxed paper and store in an airtight container. Makes 6.

Jo and Jan say, "The long baking time at low temperature allows meringue to bake crisp without browning."

FORGOTTEN TORTE

5 egg whites
1/4 teaspoon salt
1/2 teaspoon cream of tartar
1 teaspoon vanilla
1 1/2 cups superfine sugar

Beat eggs until frothy; sprinkle salt and cream of tartar over top and beat until stiff. Gradually beat in sugar, 2 tablespoons at a time. Add vanilla and continue to beat on high speed until peaks are formed.

Pour into a well-buttered springform pan. Place pan in preheated 450-degree oven and turn off heat at once! Bake overnight in stored up heat; don't peek! Do not remove torte until the next morning.

Serve torte covered with ice cream and fresh berries.

GLACED STRAWBERRIES

1 pint fresh strawberries with leaves
1 cup sugar
1/2 cup water
1/2 teaspoon cream of tartar

Leaving stems and leaves on strawberries rinse berries; pat dry with paper towel and set aside on a dry paper towel until ready to glaze. In a heavy saucepan heat sugar, water and cream of tartar over medium heat until mixture reaches a boil and sugar is completely dissolved. Use a pastry brush on the sides of the pan to remove any crystals that may have started to form. Set a candy thermometer in pan and continue to cook without stirring until temperature reaches 300°F. or a hard crack stage. If you are without a thermometer, drop a small amount of mixture into a cup of cold water; mixture should form a hard ball.

Grease a cookie sheet while mixture is cooking and when mixture is done; remove thermometer and work quickly. Hold a strawberry by the stem and dip it into the hot syrup swirling it around to coat completely. Be sure there is no excess syrup on the bottom of the berry. Brush it against the side of the pan and place on the greased tray. Continue with rest of berries. Let stand on tray 1 hour.

Jan and Jo say, "These are really delicious and give just that special finished touch guests love. The strawberries need to be eaten soon after they are finished as they will soften."

CHOCOLATE SHELLS

8 shells (4 1/2-inch size)
8 squares semi-sweet chocolate
1 pint fresh strawberries
1 cup heavy cream, whipped
2 tablespoons almond liqueur
2 teaspoons sugar
8 foil strips (6 to 8 inches)

Melt chocolate over low heat in a small heavy pan; stirring occasionally. Keeping chocolate warm, and using a pastry brush, very carefully spread chocolate over foil covered shell. Place coated shells on a cookie sheet and refrigerate until good and firm. Hold shell lightly and quickly remove foil from shell and immediately put back into refrigerator. Be sure your hands are quick and cool.

Fill shells with strawberries; add liqueur to whipped cream and top strawberries. For an added attraction lightly swirl chocolate sauce over the cream. Serves 8. A dazzling dessert for your guests.

ALMOND SHELLS

8 baking shells (4 1/2-inch size)
1 1/2 cups flour
1 cup sugar
2 teaspoons baking powder
1/4 teaspoon salt
2 eggs
2/3 cup milk
2/3 tablespoons salad oil
1/2 teaspoon vanilla extract
1/2 teaspoon almond extract

Combine flour, sugar, baking powder and salt in a large bowl. In a smaller bowl combine eggs, milk, salad oil and extracts. Beat together lightly until well mixed. Pour mixture into flour and stir until flour is moistened. Lightly spray inverted with cooking spray. Spread batter over the shells leaving a 1/2-inch border. Place shells on top of upside down muffin tins and bake in preheated 350-degree oven for 25 minutes. Cool shells on racks; then carefully loosen with tip of a knife. Fill with ice cream or fresh fruit and garnish with fresh mint. If shells are not used the day of baking, store in an air-tight container.

Sweet Temptations

✦✦

BRANDY LACE CUPS

1 cup flour
1 cup nuts, finely chopped
1/2 cup corn syrup
1/2 cup butter or margarine
2/3 cup brown sugar, packed
1 teaspoon grated orange rind
1 teaspoon cinnamon
1/4 teaspoon nutmeg
2 tablespoons brandy

Combine flour and nuts; set aside. Blend corn syrup, butter, brown sugar, orange rind and spices in saucepan. Stir constantly over medium heat until it comes to a boil; remove from heat and gradually stir in flour-nut mixture, then the brandy and stir until smooth.

Set the pan over simmering water so mixture will stay spreadable. Preheat your oven to 300 degrees. Grease and flour large cookie sheets and have custard cups 4 1/2 inches in diameter and 2 inches deep close by.

You will be preparing 2 cups at a time. Drop 2 tablespoons of mixture onto one end of a cookie sheet; spread it into a 3-inch round. Prepare another on the other end of the sheet; this is to allow room for the cookies to spread.

Bake for 10 to 12 minutes or until cookies are golden and bubbling in the center. Remove from oven and let stand for 1 minute. Working very quickly, loosen cookies from the sheet, one at a time, using a spatula. If cookies begin to harden, return the sheet to the oven for several seconds. Now, quickly press each cookie into a custard cup; let cool before removing from cups. Repeat procedure with remaining mixture.

Arrange cups in an airtight container with paper towels between cups. Store in a cool, dry place. Makes about 16.

To serve, fill Lace Cups with a scoop of ice cream, spoon your favorite sauce or fresh fruits over the top. Serve immediately.

Jo and Jan say, "We particularly like to suggest a splash of brandy or a topping like Caramel Sauce." (See index)

BRANDY SNAP CORNUCOPIAS

1 1/2 sticks butter or margarine
1 cup brown sugar
1/2 cup dark molasses
2 tablespoons brandy
1 1/2 cups flour
1 1/2 teaspoon ginger
1 teaspoon nutmeg

Combine butter, sugar, molasses and brandy; stir in dry ingredients. Drop by teaspoon onto baking sheet, leaving 2 1/2 inches between each. Bake in preheated 300-degree oven for 10 to 15 minutes. Let cool only until they can be handled. While warm, roll around the handle of a wooden spoon, reheating if they harden too quickly. Place cones, seam side down on a wire rack to cool completely. Store in tightly covered tins placing paper towels between layers as they are very fragile. They will stay crisp several weeks. Do not fill until ready to serve. Makes 4 dozen.

FILLING:
1 pint heavy cream
4 tablespoons confectioners' sugar
1 to 2 tablespoons brandy

Just before serving, beat cream, sugar and brandy until stiff peaks form. Pipe or spoon filling into each cone.

LYNN'S PROFITEROLES WITH ESPRESSO SAUCE

1 recipe Basic Cream Puff Paste (See index)
1 quart vanilla, coffee or butter pecan ice cream
1 1/4 cups light brown sugar, firmly packed
1 tablespoon instant expresso coffee
1/4 cup light corn syrup
1/2 cup water
2 tablespoons butter or margarine
1 to 2 tablespoons brandy (optional)

Prepare Basic Cream Puff Paste according to directions, bake and cool completely. Cut a slice from top of each puff; remove any soft dough. Fill puffs with small scoops of ice cream of your choice; replace tops. Freeze until serving time.

(If keeping puffs frozen over 4 hours, wrap in plastic wrap of foil).

Combine sugar, coffee, corn syrup and water in saucepan. Bring to a boil, stirring constantly. Cook over low heat for 5 minutes, stirring frequently. Remove from heat; stir in butter until melted. Stir in brandy and cool, stirring several times.

When ready to serve, mound profiteroles on a deep serving plate or rounded compote. Spoon sauce over and serve. Makes 36, serves 12.

Jo and Jan say, "Our sweet tooth cannot let this go by. We love these with Lillie's Chocolate Sauce (See index) and will even go so far as to spoon a little Chocolate syrup with the espresso sauce."

CHOCOLATE CURLS

4-ounce piece of white or dark chocolate

Warm chocolate slightly in microwave on defrost for 20 seconds. Shave off strips along one side of chocolate using a vegetable peeler. If chocolate hardens and curls split, return chocolate to microwave for an additional 10 seconds. Transfer curls to your dessert with a toothpick.

ROASTED CHESTNUTS

2 pounds fresh chestnuts
3 tablespoons water

Cut a cross into the flat side of each chestnut. This allows steam to escape during roasting. Place nuts in a single layer on a generously greased shallow pan and sprinkle with water. Shake pan to lightly coat chestnuts. Roast in a preheated 400-degree oven for about 30 minutes until skins pop slightly. Serve warm.

Jo and Jan say, " 'Chestnuts roasting on an open fire'....those words always bring the Holidays to mind; but you don't have to wait for that magical time of the year to enjoy this treat.

For a truly festive touch, have them ready to roast when your guests arrive. You can make the slits a day ahead and refrigerate in a plastic bag. Pop them in the oven to roast during your meal and they will be ready to serve by the fire with dessert or a last glass of wine. Serve them on a bed of green boughs."

Sweet Temptations

❖❖❖

Candy

OUR FAVORITE OLD-FASHIONED FUDGE

4 cups granulated sugar
2/3 cup unsweetened cocoa
1/8 teaspoon salt
1 1/4 cups half-and-half
1 tablespoon light corn syrup
2 tablespoons butter
1 1/2 teaspoons vanilla
1 cup chopped nuts

Butter the inside of a 4-quart heavy-bottomed saucepan. Combine sugar, cocoa and salt in the pan; stir so cocoa is completely mixed. Add cream and corn syrup and stir to mix well.

Stirring constantly, bring mixture to a full rolling boil over medium low heat. After it reaches a boil, do not stir or scrape the sides of the pan. Cook until mixture reaches 234 degrees on a candy thermometer or a soft ball stage.

Remove from heat, add 2 tablespoons butter and vanilla. Do not stir! Cool at room temperature to 110 degrees on candy thermometer. Beat with a wooden spoon until fudge thickens and begins to lose some gloss. Quickly stir in nuts, if desired, and spread in buttered 8 or 9-inch square pan, smoothing it into an even layer. If it starts to set up too quickly, butter your hands and pat it into the pan. When fudge is completely cool, cut into squares. Store in a covered container.

TONIA'S PEOPLE CHOW

1 stick butter or margarine
1/2 cup peanut butter
1 package (12-ounce) chocolate chips
1 box Crispix cereal
3 cups confectioners' sugar

Melt butter, peanut butter and chocolate chips in top of a double boiler. Pour cereal into a large bowl and pour melted mixture over cereal, mixing carefully. Pour confectioners' sugar into a large paper bag and pour chocolate mixture, a little at a time, into the sugar. Shake the bag, and like magic, the chocolate-covered cereal pieces are all covered, individually, with sugar. Believe us, you will not be able to eat just one! These are great for those holiday gift boxes."

CHOCOLATE COVERED MARSHMALLOWS

1 package chocolate almond bark
30-50 marshmallows
Pecans, finely chopped

Melt almond bark in double boiler over low heat. Remove from stove and dip each marshmallow in bark using a toothpick. Roll in crushed nuts.

Jan says, "This is so easy, and delish! You will want to add it to your list of Holiday goodies."

KAREN'S PRALINES

3 cups sugar
1 cup buttermilk
1 teaspoon baking soda
8 tablespoons butter
Dash of salt
2 tablespoons light or dark corn syrup
1 teaspoon vanilla
2 to 3 cups chopped pecans

Measure sugar into a deep, heavy saucepan. Combine buttermilk and soda; add to sugar and stir until well mixed. Add butter, salt and corn syrup; stir to mix. Cook slowly over medium heat until mixture reaches soft ball stage (234 degrees on a candy thermometer).

Remove from heat; beat in vanilla and pecans until mixture begins to thicken. Working very quickly, drop by teaspoon onto waxed paper; cool. Makes about 3 dozen small pralines.

RUTHIE'S BUGLE CLUSTERS

1 large box Bugle crackers
1 package (1 1/2 pound) almond bark
2 tablespoons solid shortening
1 pound salted mixed nuts
1/2 pound pecans

Melt almond bark and shortening in top of double boiler. Add Bugles and nuts; mix lightly until well coated. Drop by teaspoon on waxed paper. When dried, store in an air-tight container.

Ruthie says, "For something that is so simple these are wonderful, especially at Christmas time for your goodie boxes."

TONIA'S CHERRY MASH CANDY

2 boxes cherry frosting mix
1 small jar maraschino cherries, drained and chopped
1 can sweetened condensed milk
1/2 cup butter or margarine, melted
1 package (24-ounce) chocolate chips
1 ounce (1/4 slab) paraffin
1 pound salted peanuts, chopped

Combine the first four ingredients and form into balls. Chill in refrigerator on cookie sheets lined with waxed paper. Melt chocolate in top of double boiler. Melt paraffin separately then add to melted chocolate along with chopped nuts. Dip chilled balls into chocolate mixture and chill or freeze.

Jo says, "Talk about nostalgia! Seems like only yesterday we would gather at the local drug store 'hang-out' and order up a cherry mash and lime-coke. We never would have survived our day-to-day teenage traumas without those staples!"

The Lady Has Taste

The Lady Has Taste • Tea Time

Once upon a time, when we were very small, Tea Time was the simplest of pleasures. We set our tea table under a shady tree in the back yard. Our favorite dolly and perhaps a bunny or teddy bear were our special guests. We dressed up in our Mother's long dresses, high heels, big hats and <u>always</u> wore white gloves. We poured for our guests then sipped a cup of tea and nibbled on dainty cookies while we visited.

The years have passed, bunnies, teddy bears and favorite dolls have been replaced with <u>real</u> best friends; but we still love to dress up, wear big hats and white gloves and present tea. Yes, tea time has endured, perhaps we serve a bit more than dainty cookies, but it is still the simplest of pleasures.

The Lady Has Taste

Tea Time

There are few customs more dear to the English than afternoon tea, a pleasant and restorative ritual that has been popular since Victorian times when the Duchess of Bedford began taking tea with sandwiches, cakes and breads to sustain herself until dinner. Now, as then, afternoon tea fare can range from simple to elaborate. It can also be prepared with the most natural and nutritious of ingredients.

Whatever your pleasure, take time for tea, be it a quick cup to begin your day or a proper English high tea with your friends. Always a gracious gesture of hospitality, tea time is gaining in popularity.

Generally, tea time is between three and five o'clock. If you are serving tea to a few friends, it should be a relaxed time for you to sit down and have an informal visit, perhaps serving from a small table in your living room.

You would bring in the tea service on a large tray or tea cart and then place teapot, sugar bowl, milk pitcher, plate of lemon slices, cups, saucers, teaspoons and napkins on the table. We also include a small vase of fresh flowers on the table.

If you have room on the table, you might wish to place the tea refreshments on it, using small plates. Or, you could place the refreshments on a table close by. If this is the case, food should be kept simple and easy to handle—perhaps slices of nut bread spread with a cream cheese; a plate of cookies or sliced cake; or cheese, crackers and some slices of fruit.

Women are like tea bags.... You don't know their strength until they are in hot water....

In true English tradition, afternoon tea includes savory sandwiches, such as the classic cucumber or watercress, filled puffs or shells, scones or biscuits and sweets. If you have a tiered server, present the food in the order it is to be eaten. The bottom tier holds sandwiches; the middle tier holds tea cakes and biscuits; and the top tier, dessert. If you are using trays, place them on the table in the order the food is to be eaten.

If gentlemen will be present you may wish to set up a tray or cart with some spirited beverages and add a couple of more substantial items to your food table.

A proper cup of tea is always brewed in a pot and must be freshly brewed and hot. To make a perfect pot of tea, always start with a clean teapot. Choose your teapot carefully; the best is glazed china or earthenware. Never use aluminum.

Fill the kettle with fresh cold water, place over high heat and bring to a boil. When the water is nearly boiling, warm the teapot by rinsing it with hot water then discard the water. It is important for proper brewing that the tea water remains boiling when it is poured on the tea.

Measure 1 teaspoon of loose tea for each cup, plus 1 more for the pot, or 1 tea bag per cup. When the water starts to boil, pour it over the tea and quickly cover the pot. The larger the tea leaves, the longer they steep; 5 minutes for large-leaf teas, 3 minutes for herbal and small leaf teas, and only 1 minute or 2 for tea bags.

If you are brewing loose tea, stir through once and pour it through a tea strainer into the cups.

The Lady Has Taste

❖❖

You, the hostess, pour the tea, offering each guest a choice of milk, lemon or sugar. Americans often take lemon and sugar with tea while the British generally prefer sugar and milk. If your guests desire "cream," pour cold milk into the cup first, then the hot tea.

If you are serving a fragrant, herbal, or spiced tea, you will only offer sugar. When all cups are served, the tea refreshments are passed or guests may serve themselves.

Tea also may be served in more formal settings. These are known as invitational teas and are more elegant occasions where guests are encouraged to mingle. Refreshments are served in the dining room or in the garden and you have the opportunity to use your finest china and silver, linens, candles and flowers.

In this case, you, as hostess, would not serve tea but would have two of your friends act as stewards and others to replenish the foods.

We have included in this chapter the recipes we think are wonderful for teas. We encourage you to also look in the Cheer Delights and Sweet Temptations sections for more ideas.

TEA TIPS

• Do not use a silver or metal pot to brew tea
• 1 teaspoon loose tea equals 1 tea bag
• Use loose tea in a tea ball or cheesecloth to brew.
• If tea becomes cloudy, stir in boiling water. Boiling water should be added to the tea, not the other way around.

• To store iced tea, cover and chill
• Always put a teaspoon into the cup before pouring a hot cup of tea. That will prevent cracking or breakage of the cup.

BREWED ICED TEA

OLD-FASHIONED:

Place 4 to 8 tea bags in a teapot. Add 4 cups boiling water, cover and steep 4 to 6 minutes. Remove bags and serve over ice cubes.

COLD AND HOT TEA:

Place 4 to 8 tea bags in a teapot. Add 2 cups boiling water, cover and steep for 4 to 6 minutes. Add 2 cups cold water and serve over ice.

SUN TEA:

Place 6 to 8 tea bags in a clean 2-quart clear glass jar. Add 1 3/4 quarts cold water and cover with lid. Let stand in full sun all day, at least 4 to 6 hours. Remove bags and serve over ice.

REFRIGERATOR TEA:

Place 3 teaspoons tea or 3 tea bags in 6 ounces cold water. Measure tea into quart glass container; add cold water to fill. Cover; set in refrigerator for 12 to 24 hours. Strain and pour over ice.

SIMPLE SYRUP

4 cups sugar
1 cup water

Combine sugar and water in saucepan. Stir over low heat until sugar is dissolved. Reduce heat and simmer about 3 minutes until liquid is clear. Cool and use as needed. To store, refrigerate in a glass container. Makes 3 1/4 cups.

FRESH LEMONADE SYRUP

1 1/2 cups sugar
1 cup water
1 1/2 cups freshly squeezed lemon juice

Bring sugar and water to a boil in saucepan. Cook and stir just until sugar dissolves. Remove from heat and allow to cool; then stir in lemon juice. Store covered, in refrigerator until ready to serve. Makes 2 2/3 cups.

Pitcher of lemonade: Combine full recipe with 5 cups cold water, add ice and stir. Garnish with lemon slices and fresh mint. Makes 1 3/4 quarts.

Glass of lemonade: Pour 1/3 to 1/2 cup of syrup in tall glass. Add 1/4 cup cold water. Add ice and stir. Garnish with lemon slices and fresh mint.

SHAKER LEMONADE

1 lemon, juiced
1 cup sugar
1 cup boiling water
6 cups cold water
Ice

Squeeze the juice from the lemons and add sugar; set aside. Pour boiling water over lemon

rinds and let stand until cool. Strain the lemon-rind water into the sweetened juice. Add cold water to mixture and serve over ice. Serves 4.

Jan says, "I remember my Mother making this lemonade on hot summer days. She would roll the lemons on the counter top with the palm of her hand to release the juices from the lemons. There is nothing like a real lemonade."

TIP

• ZEST - The colorful outer coating of lemons, oranges, limes and tangerines. Can be obtained with a hand grater or a small device found in food specialty shops called a "zester."

The rind of fruit is more intense in flavor than the juice because of the high concentration of oil, so a light touch is necessary when zesting the fruit. Use only the colored portion, as the white spongy part under it is bitter.

• Dip rim of glasses in a saucer of fresh lemon juice then in granulated sugar. Set in refrigerator to chill until ready to serve lemonade or iced

tea. Pour drink over ice cubes and garnish with a sprig of fresh mint. This is very attractive and something just a little special for your guests.

APRICOT TEA

4 tea bags
4 teaspoons sugar
1/4 cup dried apricots
Boiling water
Fresh mint

Warm a 5-cup tea pot with boiling water. Pour out the water and add apricots with enough boiling water to cover them. Set pot aside for 5 minutes; add tea bags, sugar and enough boiling water to fill the pot. Let steep for 5 minutes. Strain tea into glasses over ice cubes. Top with fresh mint leaves. This tea is also very soothing when served hot. Serves 4.

BEV'S SPICY ICED TEA

1 cup water
1 cup sugar
1/8 teaspoon ground nutmeg
6 whole cloves
4 whole allspice
4 pieces stick cinnamon, cut in 2-inch pieces
3 tablespoons tea or 4 tea bags
4 cups freshly drawn cold water

Combine all ingredients except tea in saucepan. Stir over low heat until sugar dissolves. Cover and simmer 20 minutes; strain, cool and chill.

Draw 2 cups fresh cold water and bring to a full boil in saucepan. Remove from heat and add tea; stir and let tea steep 5 minutes. Stir and drain into a pitcher of 2 cups cold water.

(If tea bags were used, remove and omit straining). Blend in spicy syrup and pour into ice-filled glasses. Serve with slices of lemon or lime and fresh mint. Makes 1 quart.

LAUREN'S DRESSY TEA

1 quart freshly drawn water
1/2 cup sugar
4 whole cloves
1 stick cinnamon
2 rounded teaspoons tea or 2 tea bags
1 cup orange juice

Combine water, sugar, cloves and cinnamon in a 2-quart saucepan. Set over medium heat and stir until sugar is dissolved. Bring mixture to a boil.

Put tea into preheated teapot. Pour in the spice mixture; cover and let steep 3 to 5 minutes.

Heat orange juice; strain tea and return to teapot. Mix in the hot orange juice. Serve with lemon slices. Serves 6.

MILLIE'S MINT TEA

6 lemons, juiced
1 3/4 cups sugar
2 cups boiling water
10 teaspoons mint, approximately 18 sprigs
4 cups boiling water

Pour the first 2 cups boiling water over the sugar and lemon juice. Pour the 4 cups boiling water over the mint. Steep this mixture at least an hour. Add more water to make a gallon.

Jan says, "Mint grows abundantly in the summer garden and it is so easy to start. This makes a wonderful glass of tea in the summer or a hot cup of tea to share with a friend when the snow flies."

ALMOND TEA

2/3 cup sugar
1 quart water
2 tablespoons lemon juice, bottled
1 1/2 teaspoons vanilla
1 1/2 teaspoons almond extract
2 cups very strong tea (5 to 6 bags)
1 1/2 pints water

Boil sugar and 1 quart water together in a large pan. Set aside and add lemon juice, vanilla, almond, tea and water. Simmer on low for 30 minutes. This tea is good hot or cold.

PEACHY TEA

Prepare a pitcher of your favorite iced tea and add several fresh peaches, peeled, seeded and halved. This was served to us as the standard order of iced tea while we were in Venice. We were so impressed we have been doing it this way at home ever since, when fresh peaches are available.

HOT CRANBERRY CIDER

2 quarts cranapple or cranberry juice
5 cups strong tea, unsweetened
4 sticks cinnamon
3-4 slices orange
1 cup sugar

Combine all ingredients; heat to a boil, strain and serve. Serve 12-14.

JO'S PUNCH

2 cups plus 4 tablespoons honey
12 cups hot strong tea
4 cups orange juice
2 cups lemon juice
6 cups cold water
3 cups pineapple juice
8 tablespoons lime juice
2 bottles ginger ale

Combine all ingredients except ginger ale. To 3 1/2 quarts of punch base, add 2 bottles ginger ale.

ANN'S PINEAPPLE PUNCH

2 cups strong tea
3/4 cup lemon juice
1 1/3 cups orange juice
2 tablespoons lime juice
1 cup sugar
Leaves from 12 sprigs of fresh mint
8 slices pineapple and juice
2 quarts ginger ale
2 quarts club soda
Crushed ice

To the tea, add fruit juices and sugar; stir well. Refrigerate at least 2 hours before serving. When ready to serve, add pineapple, ginger ale and club soda. Pour over crushed ice in punch bowl.

NORMA'S RUM SLUSH

4 tea bags
2 cups boiling water
1 large can frozen orange juice
1 large can frozen lemonade
2 cups sugar
1 1/2 cups rum
7 cups water

Steep tea bags in boiling water for 10 minutes. Add rest of ingredients and freeze in a sealed container. To serve, scoop slush into glasses.

TARTLET MERINGUE

1/2 cup egg whites, room temperature
Pinch of salt
1/2 cup granulated sugar
1/2 cup confectioners' sugar
Confectioners' sugar, for dusting

Add salt to egg whites in large bowl and beat until soft peaks form. Gradually add granulated sugar and beat until stiff but not dry. Sift confectioners' sugar over top and gently fold into beaten mixture.

Using a pastry bag fitted with large star tip, pipe meringue a high mound atop each tart, still in shell, making certain meringue touches shell. If you do not have a pastry bag, use a knife to mound the meringue. Bake on center rack of a 400-degree oven about 5 minutes or until meringue is light brown. Remove from oven and cool on a rack. Gently slip tartlets from pans. Tartlets can be prepared up to 8 hours before serving; dust with confectioners' sugar just before presentation. Tops 24 miniature tartlets.

TEA TARTLETS

2 cups all-purpose flour
1/2 teaspoon sugar
1/4 teaspoon salt
1 stick unsalted butter (if using salted butter, omit 1/4 teaspoon salt)
3 tablespoons margarine
1/4 cup ice water

Cut butter and margarine into dry ingredients until mixture resembles coarse meal. Add ice water gradually and gather dough into a ball. Wrap in plastic wrap and refrigerate at least 2 hours.

Preheat oven to 375 degrees. Roll dough to 1/8-inch thick. Cut slightly larger than 2 1/2-inch tartlet mold and press into mold. Trim edges and press pastry down into mold with another tartlet mold. Bake for 8 to 10 minutes until golden. Carefully remove from molds and cool before using. Makes 24 tartlets.

Jo and Jan say, "Fill these with any of tart fillings we have for you, or you might have a favorite of your own. At any rate, they will be a delight."

ALMOND PASTRY

1 cup sifted all purpose flour
6 tablespoons butter
3 tablespoons powdered sugar, sifted
1 egg yolk
1/4 cup almonds, finely ground and sifted
1/2 teaspoon vanilla
Almond extract, about 2 drops, or to taste

Cut butter into dry ingredients until mixture resembles coarse meal. Add yolks, almonds, vanilla and extract; mix well and form into a ball; flatten into a disc shape, wrap in plastic and refrigerate at least 2 hours.

For instructions on forming into shells, see recipe for Tea Tartlets (index); and bake as directed. Makes 24 2-1/2-inch tartlets.

CREAM CHEESE TARTLET SHELLS

1 package (3-ounce) cream cheese
1/2 cup butter, softened
1 cup flour

Combine ingredients, cream until smooth and shape into ball. Chill 1 hour then divide into 24 pieces. Press each on bottom and sides of miniature tart pans. Bake in preheated 350-degree oven for 5 to 6 minutes or until golden. Cool and gently remove from pans. If not using right away, store in tightly covered container until ready to fill with your choice of tart fillings (In this chapter).

The Lady Has Taste

JANE'S TART SHELLS

1 cup slivered almonds, finely ground
1/2 cup (1 stick) butter, softened
1/2 cup sugar
1/2 teaspoon salt
1 large egg white
1/2 teaspoon almond extract
1 1/4 cups all-purpose flour

Combine almonds, butter, sugar, salt, egg white and almond extract in medium bowl. Stir with fork until well blended. Gradually stir in flour, mixing until smooth.

Grease 12, 4 to 5-inch fluted tart pans. Divide dough into 12 equal portions and press into the greased pans. Be sure to press dough up to the top edges of pans. Prick bottoms of shells with fork and place on baking sheet. Place in freezer for 30 minutes.

Preheat oven to 350 degrees. Bake shells 15 to 18 minutes or until golden-brown. Place baked shells on wire rack to cool for 10 minutes in pans.

Using the tip of a sharp knife, loosed shells from edges of pans; gently remove shells and cool completely. Store in airtight containers until ready to fill. Makes 12.

PECAN TART PASTRY

1 cup all purpose flour
1/2 cup pecans, finely ground
2 tablespoons sugar
1/4 teaspoon salt
6 tablespoons unsalted butter, well chilled and cut into pieces
1 1/2 tablespoons (about) heavy cream, well-chilled

Combine flour, pecans, sugar and salt. Cut in butter using pastry blender or food processor until mixture resembles coarse meal. Slowly add enough cream to moisten, stir until dough forms a ball and leaves sides of bowl. Wrap in plastic and refrigerate at least 30 minutes.

Divide dough into 8 pieces. Work with 1 piece at a time, refrigerating the rest, flatten dough and roll between waxed paper to a 1/4-inch-thick round; peel off paper. Fit into 3 1/2-inch tartlet mold. Trim edges and repeat procedure with remaining dough. Refrigerate for 30 minutes.

Pierce dough with fork and place on center rack of preheated 375-degree oven. Bake about 10 minutes or until lightly browned. Cool in molds on rack about 10 minutes. Gently unmold and cool completely. Makes 8 3 1/2-inch tartlets.

Jo and Jan say, "These can be prepared a day or so ahead; wrap in plastic and store in an airtight container until ready to serve with your favorite fillings."

LARGE TART SHELL

1 1/4 cups unsifted flour
2 tablespoons sugar
1/8 teaspoon salt
1/3 cup butter or margarine
1 egg, lightly beaten

Mix flour, sugar and salt in bowl. With pastry blender, cut in butter until dough is like small peas. Stir in egg with a fork and blend well. Shape into a ball on a floured pastry cloth. Flatten slightly with your hands and roll out to a 12-inch circle. Line a 10-inch tart pan with a removable bottom with the pastry. Trim pastry edge even with the rim of pan. Bake in a preheated 375-degree oven for 25 minutes or until lightly browned. Fill with tart filling of your choice. Serves 10 - 12.

To serve, carefully remove side rim from pastry, keeping tart on the pan bottom. Transfer to a plate and decorate with whipped cream, meringue, glazed fruits or your desired topping.

BASIC VANILLA CREAM FOR TARTLETS WITH VARIATIONS

BASIC VANILLA:
4 egg yolks
7 tablespoons sugar
1/4 cup flour
1 2/3 cups scalded milk
1 1/2 teaspoons vanilla extract

Add to top of double boiler, yolks, sugar and flour. Stir to blend. Add scalded milk and vanilla extract. Cook slowly 20 minutes or until bubbles appear, stirring constantly. Remove from heat, cool and chill. Fill prepared tartlet shells. Makes about 2 cups.

CHOCOLATE:

Stir into hot cooked Basic cream, 4 ounces grated sweet cooking chocolate.

COFFEE:

Add to Basic cream: 3 teaspoons instant coffee powder to hot milk in recipe. Add 1 tablespoon rum, 2 tablespoons ground pecans to cooked cream.

LEMON:

Add to Basic cream: 1 1/2 teaspoons grated lemon rind 1 tablespoon lemon juice 1 teaspoon grated orange rind.

QUICK N' EASY FRUIT TARTS

1 package (3 ounces) cream cheese, softened
2 tablespoons sugar
3 tablespoons fruit-flavored brandy (your choice)
2 cups thawed commercial whipped cream topping
6 prepared tart shells
1 1/2 cups fresh sliced fruit of choice
1/4 cup apple jelly, melted

Beat cheese, sugar and brandy until smooth and creamy. Blend in whipped topping. Spoon mixture into tart shells. Chill for at least 2 hours. Just before serving, top with fruit and brush with melted jelly. Serves 6.

GRAND MARNIER TARTLET FILLING

1 package (8-ounce) cream cheese
1/4 cup confectioners' sugar
2 tablespoons Grand Marnier liqueur
2 teaspoons orange zest
1/3 cup frozen whipped topping, thawed
2 tablespoons sliced almonds, lightly toasted and cooled
1 recipe Grand Marnier Sauce (See index)
Maraschino cherries, halved (garnish)

Combine first 4 ingredients in small mixer bowl and beat until smooth. Blend in topping, then cooled nuts. Fill tart shells and refrigerate until ready to serve. Cover with Grand Marnier Sauce and garnish with cherry halves. Refrigerate again if not serving right away. Fills 24 tartlets.

❖❖❖

PECAN TARTS

1/4 cup sugar
2 tablespoons flour
1/2 teaspoon salt
3 eggs, beaten
2 cups dark corn syrup
2 tablespoons butter, melted and cooled
1 teaspoon vanilla (or 3 tablespoons
    bourbon or Grand Marnier)
1/4 teaspoon white vinegar
1 cup pecan halves

Mix dry ingredients together in a bowl. Stir in the eggs and mix well. Whisk in corn syrup, butter, vanilla and vinegar. Stir in pecans and pour mixture into unbaked tartlet shells. Bake in a preheated 350-degree oven for 15 minutes or until set. Serve topped with whipped cream. Makes about 4 dozen 1 1/2-inch tartlets.

PECAN TART FILLING

1/2 cup margarine
1/3 cup dark corn syrup
1 cup confectioners' sugar
1 cup chopped pecans
Pecan halves for tops
1 cup heavy cream, whipped
Vanilla and sugar to taste (for whipped
    cream)
24 miniature tartlet shells, baked and cooled

Bring margarine, syrup and sugar to a boil. Stir in chopped pecans and spoon into baked miniature tartlet shells. Top with pecan halves and bake in preheated 350-degree oven for 5 minutes. Cool and top with sweetened whipped cream. Makes 24.

CHOCOLATE PECAN TARTS

1 recipe for tart pastry, do not bake (see
    index)
2 tablespoons butter or margarine
2 squares (1-ounce size) semisweet
    chocolate
4 large eggs
1/2 cup granulated sugar
1/2 cup dark corn syrup
1 tablespoon white vinegar
1 cup chopped pecans
1 cup pecan halves

Melt butter and chocolate in small saucepan over very low heat, stirring occasionally; let cool slightly. Combine eggs, sugar, corn syrup and vinegar in medium bowl. Whisk until well blended. Stir in cooled chocolate mixture along with chopped nuts. Pour filling into pastry-lined tart pans. Arrange pecan halves on top. Place tarts on baking sheet and bake in preheated 350-degree oven. Allow about 25 minutes for 4-inch tarts and about 15 minutes for miniature tartlets. Watch closely to see that filling is set and crust is golden brown. Remove to rack to cool carefully remove tarts from pans. Makes approximately 2 dozen miniature tarts.

CREAM CHEESE TART FILLING

2 eggs, separated
1/2 cup sugar
2 packages (8-ounce-size) cream cheese,
    softened
1 tablespoon fresh lemon juice
1 teaspoon grated lemon peel
1/2 teaspoon vanilla
Pinch cream of tartar

Beat egg yolks and sugar with electric mixer until smooth and pale. Add cream cheese, lemon juice, lemon peel and vanilla. Beat until smooth. Beat egg whites with cream of tartar until stiff and fold a small amount into cheese mixture to lighten, then fold in remaining whites. Spoon into a baked tart crust and bake in preheated 350-degree oven until filling is firm to the touch, or about 20 minutes. Cool completely on a rack then refrigerate at least 1 hour. Serves 10-12.

LEMON CURD TART FILLING

1 cup sugar
6 egg yolks, lightly beaten
1/2 cup lemon juice, freshly squeezed and
  strained
1 tablespoon lemon peel, finely grated
1/2 cup butter, softened
12 miniature tartlets, (See index for choice)
  or 1 8-inch tart shell)

Combine sugar, egg yolks and lemon juice; cook over low heat but do not boil. Cook until mixture thickens to coat a spoon, or about 10 minutes. Remove from heat and gradually beat in butter and lemon peel. Cool at room temperature and refrigerate at least 2 hours. When mixture is cold, fill shells. Makes 12.

Jo and Jan say, "We love to garnish the tartlets with fresh raspberries and our large tart with Glazed Lemon Slices and Frosted Flowers (See index)."

ORANGE CURD

2 eggs
2 egg yolks
1/4 cup sugar
1/4 cup fresh orange juice, strained
2 tablespoons orange peel, finely grated
1 tablespoon fresh lemon juice, strained
3 tablespoons unsalted butter, well chilled
1 1/2 tablespoons Cointreau

Whisk eggs and yolks in small saucepan until foamy. Add sugar, juices and orange peel, whisking until smooth. Stir over low heat until mixture thickens and heavily coats a spoon, about 15 minutes. Remove from heat and whisk in butter, a little at a time. Blend in liqueur. Cool completely at room temperature; cover and refrigerate. Will fill 8 3 1/2-inch tart shells half full. Arrange fruit on top and brush with a glaze, if desired. (See index).

SOUR CREAM LIME TARTE

CRUST:
1 1/2 cups graham cracker crumbs
1/2 cup sugar
6 tablespoons butter or margarine, melted

FILLING:
1 cup sugar
3 tablespoons cornstarch
1 cup heavy cream
1/3 cup fresh lime juice
1/4 cup butter
1 tablespoon lime peel, finely grated
1 cup sour cream

TOPPING:
1 cup whipping cream
1/4 cup sugar
1 1/2 teaspoons vanilla
3/4 cup sour cream

To prepare crust, combine all ingredients in a medium bowl. Press on bottom and sides of a 9-inch pan. Freeze at least 15 minutes.

Preheat oven to 350 degrees. Bake crust until lightly browned, about 12-15 minutes. Place on rack to cool completely while preparing filling.

Mix sugar and cornstarch in heavy saucepan. Gradually stir in cream, lime juice, butter and lime peel. Bring to a boil over medium high heat, whisking constantly, then reduce heat to simmer and stir until thick and smooth, about 10 minutes. Cool mixture to room temperature, stirring occasionally. When cool, fold in sour cream and spread evenly into prepared crust.

To prepare topping, whip cream, sugar and vanilla until it holds soft peaks. Gently fold in remaining sour cream and spread over filling. Chill at least 4 hours before serving. Serves 10-12.

Jo and Jan say, "Fresh limes hold the secret to this delicious tarte. Please do not use the bottled juice or commercial rind. The flavor will not be the same."

TANGY LEMON TART

1 8-inch unbaked tart shell
Juice of 6 lemons (about 1 cup)
Zest of 6 lemons
1/2 cup butter, melted
6 eggs
1 cup sugar

Combine juice, zest and butter. Stir in eggs and sugar; mix well. Pour into prepared tart shell and bake in preheated 400-degree oven for 20 minutes or until golden brown. Serves 6 - 8.

PASTRY CREAM FOR TARTS
(Creme Patissiere)

2 cups half-and-half
1/2 cup sugar
2 eggs
2 egg yolks
5 tablespoons cornstarch
1/4 cup (1/2 stick) unsalted butter, room temperature
2 teaspoons vanilla

Dissolve 1/4 cup sugar in cream over low heat, stirring constantly. Increase heat and bring to a simmer. In a medium bowl, whisk other 1/4 cup sugar, eggs and yolks until lemon-colored. Add cornstarch and whisk until dissolved; then whisk in 1 cup milk mixture. Return this mixture to saucepan, increase heat and boil until custard thickens, stirring constantly, about 1 minute. Continue stirring until smooth. Strain into a bowl; stir in butter and vanilla. Cover with plastic wrap on surface and refrigerate until mixture is well-chilled. Makes 2 1/2 cups. Will fill 12 3-inch tarts or 24 miniature tartlets.

Jo and Jan say, "This cream can be made at least 2 days before filling tart shells. We spread it in the shells then arrange fresh fruit on top and glaze. They are beautiful and delicious!"

BLUEBERRY TARTS

1 recipe of Janes's Tart Shells (See index)
1 pint fresh blueberries
3/4 cup sugar
2 tablespoons cornstarch
1 teaspoon ground cinnamon
3 tablespoons lemon juice
1/4 cup water
2 tablespoons butter
1 teaspoon grated lemon peel
1 package (8-ounce) cream cheese, softened
1 tablespoon milk
Prepare tart shells are directed in recipe.

Wash berries; drain and reserve 1 cup. Place remaining berries in a saucepan. Combine sugar, cornstarch and cinnamon and add to the berries in saucepan. Crush berry-sugar mixture to make juice; add lemon juice and water. Let stand 10 minutes.

Bring crushed berry mixture to a boil over medium-high heat, stirring often. Boil 3 minutes, stirring constantly. Remove from heat; stir in butter and lemon peel. Cool to room temperature, then stir in reserved berries. Transfer to a bowl, cover with plastic wrap and refrigerate.

About 6 hours before serving, combine cream cheese and milk. Place half of mixture in a pastry bag fitted with a 1/4-inch star tip. Cover tip with plastic wrap and refrigerate. Spread remaining cream cheese over bottom of each tart shell. Pour 1/4 cup fruit filling into each tart shell. Using pastry bag, pipe 6 strips of cream cheese into a lattice design on top of each tart. Set tarts in a covered container, allowing 1 inch above tarts to avoid smearing. Refrigerate until ready to serve. Makes 12 4 to 5-inch tarts.

FRENCH CREAM TARTS

1 8-ounce package cream cheese
1 cup confectioners' sugar
1/2 pint heavy cream, whipped
1 teaspoon vanilla flavoring
6 pastry shells
Fruit
Additional whipped cream

Soften cream cheese; add sugar and whip. Fold in whipped cream and flavoring. Pour into baked pastry shells and place fruit on top. Suggested fruits; strawberries, blueberries, pineapple chunks, raspberries, cherries. Garnish with whipped cream. Serves 6.

FRUIT GLAZES FOR TARTS

Jo and Jan say, "Choose a jelly or preserve that compliments the fruit you are using. Strain the preserves and add cognac if desired. The proportion we use is 1 tablespoon cognac to 1 cup preserves or jelly. Individual preference and taste will dictate the addition of cognac.

If you desire the fruit glaze but do not want a liqueur, combine 1/2 cup of your desired jelly and 1 tablespoon of sugar in a small saucepan. Stir over low heat until sugar dissolves; increase heat and boil 3 minutes, stirring often. Cool to room temperature and glaze fruits. Will glaze 8 tarts (3 1/2- inch)."

GRAND MARNIER SAUCE

1 cup heavy cream
6 egg yolks
1/2 cup sugar
2/3 cup butter, melted
6 tablespoons fresh lemon juice
6 tablespoons Grand Marnier liqueur
2 teaspoons finely minced lemon zest

Pour cream into chilled bowl and beat until thick and glossy, but not stiff; refrigerate. Beat egg yolks until thick and lemon-colored; gradually add sugar. Slowly beat in butter, lemon juice and liqueur. Gently fold in the lemon zest and whipped cream. Chill thoroughly. Makes about 2 1/2 cups.

CHOCOLATE GRAND MARNIER SAUCE

2 squares (1-ounce size) semi-sweet
  chocolate
2 tablespoons water
1/4 cup sugar
2 tablespoons butter
3 tablespoons Grand Marnier liqueur

Combine chocolate and water in small saucepan. Place over low heat until chocolate melts. Add sugar, stirring constantly, then butter, and blend. Add liqueur and bring to quick boil. Turn off heat; cool and spoon over tarts.

PINEAPPLE CHEESE BALL

2 packages (8-ounce size) cream cheese,
  softened
1 can (8-1/2-ounce) crushed pineapple,
  drained
1/4 cup green pepper, finely chopped
2 tablespoons onion, minced
2 ounces Cheddar cheese, grated
1/2 teaspoon seasoned salt
1 dash Tabasco sauce
1 cup nuts, chopped

Combine all ingredients except nuts. Form into ball and roll in nuts. Chill. Serve with crackers. Makes 3 cups.

Jo and Jan say, "We prefer macadamia nuts with this, they give a hint of the tropics."

The Lady Has Taste

STUFFED CUCUMBER ROUNDS

1 package (8-ounce) cream cheese, softened
2 green onions, finely minced
1/4 teaspoon Worcestershire sauce
1/4 teaspoon garlic powder
1/4 teaspoon dill
1/8 teaspoon white pepper
1 medium cucumber, scored, cored and
  drained
24 bread rounds, cocktail-size
Capers, drained (optional)
Fresh watercress (optional)

Beat cream cheese, onions, Worcestershire sauce, garlic powder, dill, and pepper until smooth. Cut cucumber into thirds and fill hollowed core of each piece with cream cheese mixture. Wrap cucumber pieces in plastic wrap or foil and refrigerate overnight.

When ready to serve, slice cucumbers into thin rounds (a little over 1/8-inch thick) and place on bread rounds. Garnish with capers if desired or a single watercress leaf. Makes 2 dozen.

SKIDDY WATERCRESS SANDWICHES

7 bunches watercress
1/2 cucumber, peeled, seeded and chopped
  fine
1/2 teaspoon Accent
1 package (8-ounce) cream cheese, softened
1/4 teaspoon salt
3-4 drops Tabasco sauce (to taste)
1 3/4 loaves white bread, thin sliced

Wash and pick watercress. Pull off stems and chop fine. Add cucumber to softened cream cheese and mix into watercress. Add salt and hot pepper sauce; mix in Accent. Adjust seasonings to taste.

Cut crusts from bread and make sandwiches, spreading mixture on half the slices, topping with other half. It will make 100 square party-size sandwiches. If you desire round sandwiches, you will not have as many, but they are very pretty especially for a tea. We cut each large sandwich on the diagonal, both ways, which gives you 4 pretty triangles, and no waste.

Jo says, "When I'm invited to my friend Carol's ancestral home, we pick watercress in a fresh water stream. The commercial seems bland by comparison."

HOT ASPARAGUS BITES

20 slices white bread, thin-sliced. Cut off crusts and roll each slice flat.
3 ounces blue cheese
1/2 pound butter, melted
1 egg
20 asparagus spears, fresh or frozen
  (cooked)

Blend cheese and egg thoroughly. Spread cheese mixture over each bread slice. Roll an asparagus spear inside each slice and fasten with a toothpick. Dip each roll in melted butter and place on a baking sheet and freeze. When the roll-up is firm, slice each roll into 3 pieces. Place back on baking sheet and bake in preheated 400-degree oven for 25 minutes or until lightly browned. Makes 5 dozen bites.

Jan says, "Let us all remember our ovens vary in degrees so let's peek at 20 minutes."

POTTED SHRIMP BUTTER

1 package (7-ounce) frozen, shelled and deveined shrimp
1/2 cup butter
1 clove garlic, minced
2 tablespoons finely chopped parsley
1 tablespoon finely chopped onion
1 teaspoon grated lemon rind
1/2 teaspoon salt
1/8 teaspoon pepper
Cucumber slices

Cook shrimp, drain and cool; chop fine. Beat butter in small bowl with mixer. Stir in shrimp and remaining ingredients except cucumber slices. Spoon into a crock, cover and refrigerate several hours. Allow to soften slightly before serving.

To serve, center crock on a platter and surround with cucumber slices, accompanied with sesame seed crackers. Makes about 1 cup.

PEA POD BOATS

1/2 pound fresh snow peas

Blanch snow peas in boiling water for 10 to 20 seconds. Immediately plunge into ice water to stop the cooking process. Crisp in ice water, then drain well. With a sharp knife, pick off stem end and make a slit through the vein that runs along the top to form a boat. Remove peas from

inside and set aside. The peas can be used as part of the fillings or in a salad at a later time. Fill boats with the following filling or simply fill with Boursin Cheese or Peppered Jelly Cream Cheese (See index). Arrange filled boats on a bed of red leaf lettuce or the beautiful lettuce called Savoy.

AMANDA'S SMOKED SALMON MOUSSE

4 ounces smoked salmon, minced
1 teaspoon grated onion
1 1/3 cups heavy cream
2 tablespoons cognac
2 teaspoons dill weed
Ground white pepper
Endive spears (optional)
Brown bread (optional)

Combine minced salmon, grated onion and 2/3 cup cream in blender or processor and

blend about 1 minute. Add cognac, dill and white pepper; blend well. Refrigerate until chilled. Whip remaining cream until stiff peaks form and fold into the chilled mixture. Makes about 1 3/4 cups.

Amanda says, "This makes an elegant statement. I like to pipe a small amount in the tip of endive spears. I also cut triangles or rounds from brown bread or use slices of party pumpernickel and rye, spread the slices with the mousse, then lay a thinly slivered slice of smoked salmon on top, garnished with a thin twist of lemon and a sprig of dill."

NUTTY CHEESE WAFERS

1 pound cheddar cheese, grated
3 cups all-purpose flour
1 cup butter, room temperature
1 teaspoon salt
1/4 teaspoon cayenne pepper
1 cup chopped pecans

With electric mixer, beat all ingredients except nuts until well-blended. Add pecans and mix well. Divide dough in thirds and form into 1 1/2-inch logs. Wrap each in wax paper and refrigerate about 1 hour or until firm.

To bake, cut dough into 1/4-inch-thick slices. Arrange on baking sheet, spacing about 1 1/2 inches apart. Bake in preheated 325-degree oven 15 to 18 minutes or until golden brown. Transfer to paper towels and cool completely. Store in airtight container. Makes 10 dozen.

SHRIMP, CRAB AND WATER CHESTNUT FILLING

1 can cocktail shrimp, well drained
1 box (6-ounce) frozen Alaskan king crab. If you prefer just the shrimp, substitute equal amount of shrimp for crab. Drain, squeeze out excess liquid and chop fine.
1 can water chestnuts, chopped fine
1 teaspoon Dijon mustard
1 tablespoon scallions, chopped fine
1 teaspoon Worcestershire sauce
2 dashes Tabasco sauce
1 teaspoon dill weed
1/3 cup mayonnaise or just enough to make spreadable
2 teaspoons capers, drained (optional)
Peas from pods (optional)
Fresh parsley sprigs (garnish)

Combine all ingredients except parsley. Fill pea pod boats, tuck a sprig of parsley in one end of each; chill until ready to serve. Arrange on red leaf lettuce and wait for the raves!

BASIC CREAM PUFF PASTE
(Choux Paste)

1 cup water
1/2 cup butter or margarine
1 teaspoon sugar
1/4 teaspoon salt
1 cup sifted all-purpose flour
4 eggs

In large, heavy saucepan, heat water, butter, sugar and salt to a full rolling boil. Reduce heat to low, add flour all at once. Stir vigorously with a wooden spoon until mixture forms a thick smooth ball that leaves the sides of pan clean, about 1 minute.

Add eggs, one at a time, beating well after each addition with wooden spoon or electric hand mixer until paste is shiny, smooth and well blended. Cover lightly and let stand until cool.

Drop by slightly rounded teaspoonful into 36 even mounds, I-inch apart, on large greased baking sheet.

Bake in a preheated 425-degree oven for 20 minutes or until puffed and golden brown and crusty. If time allows, refrigerate puffs on baking sheet for 30 minutes or freeze for 15 minutes; place directly in preheated oven. This extra step will give a higher rise to the pastry. When done, remove from oven and turn off heat. Pierce side of each puff with sharp knife and return to oven. Leave door ajar and let set for 10 minutes to dry inside of puffs. Let cool on racks in a draft-free area. Makes 36 small puffs.

Jo and Jan say, "The baking time for puffs or eclairs depends on their size. Care must be taken to bake them until they are browned and completely done. If they are removed from the oven too soon, before they are completely done, they will fall exactly the way an undercooked souffle falls. If you are not certain whether they are done, take 1 from the oven, cut a slit in the side, let it cool for a couple of minutes and check the inside. It should be soft, but not doughy. If the puffs are removed too soon and fall, they will not rise again, even if put back in the oven immediately, so watch them closely. Unfilled puffs can be frozen. Place unthawed in 375-degree oven for 10 to 15 minutes."

❖❖

TEA TABLE HORS D'OEUVRE PUFFS

Place a tray of unfilled miniature or bite-size puffs on the table, with a selection of fillings (See index). When making hors d'oeuvre puffs, brush them with mayonnaise and sprinkle with Parmesan cheese and paprika just after they come out of the oven.

See Cheer Delights section for other fillings.

TEA TIME EGG SALAD
(filling for puffs)

6 hard-boiled eggs, finely minced
6 tablespoons bleu cheese salad dressing
1 tablespoon bleu cheese salad dressing
   mix
2 tablespoons undrained India relish
Mayonnaise (optional)
Minced parsley (optional)

Combine all ingredients except parsley. Chill. Just before serving, mound in bowl and sprinkle with parsley. Makes 1 1/2 cups.

FRENCH CUSTARD FOR TINY CREAM PUFFS

1/3 cup sugar
1 tablespoon flour
1 tablespoon cornstarch
1/4 teaspoon salt
1 1/2 cups milk
1 egg yolk, slightly beaten
1 teaspoon vanilla
1/2 cup heavy cream, whipped

Mix first 4 ingredients. Gradually stir in milk. Cook and stir until mixture thickens and slightly boils. Cook, stirring constantly, 2-3 minutes longer. Add some of the hot mixture to the egg yolk, then return egg mixture to custard. Return custard to heat, stirring constantly, until mixture comes just to a boil. Remove from heat, add vanilla and cool. Beat smooth.

Before serving, fold in whipped cream and fill puffs. Keep custard refrigerated if made ahead. Fills about 5 dozen puffs.

HOT CHEESE PUFFS

1 loaf unsliced white sandwich bread
1/2 cup butter
1 package (8-ounce) Monterey Jack cheese
   with Jalapeno peppers
1 package (8-ounce) cream cheese
2 egg whites, stiffly beaten

Remove crusts from bread and cut into l-inch cubes. In top of double boiler melt butter and cheeses, stirring well. Cool to room temperature; then fold in beaten egg whites. Dip bread cubes into cheese mixture; covering completely. Place on cookie sheets and freeze. After freezing, they can be stored in bags.

To serve, place frozen cubes on cookie sheets, bake in preheated 400-degree oven until slightly browned and puffy, (about 12-15 minutes). Serve hot. Makes 8 dozen.

TOASTED ROUNDS

1 loaf thin-sliced white bread
1 small can grated Parmesan cheese
1 large onion, grated
2 cups mayonnaise
2 teaspoons Worcestershire sauce
Paprika
Chopped parsley

Cut sandwich bread into rounds with biscuit cutter. Lightly toast bread, but not too crisp. Combine cheese, onion, mayonnaise and Worcestershire sauce until well-blended. Refrigerate at least 2 hours. Spread thickly on toasted rounds. Sprinkle lightly with paprika and chopped parsley. Place under broiler for about 3-4 minutes until lightly browned. Makes 50 rounds.

BRIE CRISPS

4 ounces Brie cheese, room temperature
1/2 cup butter, room temperature
2/3 cup all-purpose flour
2 dashes ground red pepper
1/2 teaspoon dried mixed herbs
1/8 teaspoon salt
Paprika

Combine cheese and butter and mix until creamy with electric mixer or food processor. Add rest of ingredients except paprika and mix well, until it forms a loose ball. Place ball in plastic wrap and refrigerate for at least 30 minutes.

Smooth dough and shape into a roll 1 1/2 inches in diameter and about 8 inches long. Rewrap tightly and refrigerate overnight.

To serve, slice into 1/4-inch rounds. Arrange on baking sheet about 2 inches apart. Bake in a preheated 400-degree oven about 10 to 12 minutes or until edges are slightly browned. Cool on a rack and sprinkle with paprika. Makes 3 dozen.

TEA SANDWICHES

1 large egg
2 tablespoons lemon juice
2 tablespoons Dijon mustard
2 tablespoons fresh chives, minced
2 tablespoons capers
1 small garlic clove, minced
1/4 teaspoon salt
1 cup olive oil
36 slices white or whole wheat bread, thin-sliced

Combine first 7 ingredients in a blender. While processing, very slowly add the olive oil in a thin steady stream until mixture is thickened. Pour into a bowl, cover and chill.

Cut the bread into desired shapes with cookie cutters. Use remaining bread and crusts for bread crumbs. Spread about 2 teaspoons of the mayonnaise mixture on each piece of cut-out bread. You may use different toppings such as shrimp, cherry tomatoes, sliced radishes, parsley, watercress, cucumbers, etc. Cover with a damp tea towel and refrigerate until ready to serve. You will be a hit at the tea'

Note: To make bread crumbs, place bread on a cookie sheet and leave in a low oven half a day until crisp. Roll out or grind on blender or food processor. Makes wonderful bread crumbs and much cheaper than the store brands.

❖❖

DOROTHY'S CREAM CHEESE SPREAD

2 packages (8-ounce size) cream cheese,
   softened
1 can (8-ounce) crushed pineapple, drained
1 cup chopped pecans
1/4 cup green pepper, finely chopped
1 tablespoon onion, finely chopped
1 tablespoon seasoned salt

Mix ingredients together and chill. Makes 1 1/2 cups.

Jan says, "This makes a delicious luncheon or tea sandwich. I have never made it that there weren't many raves."

MUSTARD BUTTER FOR PARTY BISCUITS

1 small garlic clove, crushed
1/2 cup (1 stick) unsalted butter, room
   temperature
1 tablespoon coarse-grained mustard
1 1/2 teaspoons Dijon mustard
1 teaspoon fresh lemon juice

Cream butter, add garlic, mustards and lemon juice; mix well. Serve with small biscuits served with thinly sliced or shaved ham. Makes about 1/2 cup.

WHIPPED BUTTER

1/2 pound butter
1/2 pound margarine
1/4 cup sour cream

Mix butter and margarine at medium speed on electric mixer until well blended. Beat in sour cream, a tablespoon at a time, until smooth and fluffy. Makes about 2 cups.

ORANGE PEEL CREAM CHEESE

2 packages (8-ounce size) cream cheese,
   softened
1/2 cup powdered sugar
2 tablespoons orange peel, grated
2 tablespoons Cointreau
2 tablespoons frozen orange juice
   concentrate

Combine all ingredients in bowl and blend thoroughly. Cover tightly and refrigerate overnight before using. Makes 2 1/2 cups.

Jo and Jan say, "Try this delicious spread on nut breads, or on party sandwiches with sliced breast of turkey or chicken."

CRANBERRY FRUIT DIPPING SAUCE

1 carton (8-ounces) vanilla yogurt
1/2 cup cranberry-orange relish
1/4 teaspoon ground nutmeg
1/4 teaspoon ground ginger
1/4 cup chopped pecans

Combine ingredients in small bowl; mix until blended. Cover and chill. Serve with assorted fruit. Makes 1 1/4 cups.

The Lady Has Taste

LIME FRUIT DIP

2 eggs
1/2 cup sugar
4 teaspoons cornstarch
1 can (6-ounce) frozen limeade, undiluted
1 cup heavy cream, whipped
Fresh lime slices (garnish)
Mint leaves (garnish)

Beat eggs and combine with sugar, cornstarch and limeade in top of double boiler. Cook until thickened, stirring frequently. Remove from heat and when completely cool, fold whipped cream into mixture. Refrigerate until ready to serve. Mound in bowl and surround with fresh fruits and berries. Garnish with a thin twisted slice of lime and mint leaves. Makes 2 cups.

BANANA DIPPING SAUCE

2 ripe bananas
2 tablespoons lemon juice
1/4 cup brown sugar
1/4 cup honey
1/4 cup chopped pecans
1 cup heavy cream, whipped

Combine bananas, lemon juice, sugar and honey until smooth in a blender. Add nuts and fold in whipped cream.

Jo says, "This is delicious served with fresh fruit; or mound assorted fruits in pineapple shells for a beautiful as well as tasty luncheon entree." Makes about 2 cups.

FRUIT AND BERRIES DIPPING SAUCE

1/2 cup sour cream
1/4 cup heavy cream, whipped
4 tablespoons brown sugar
2 tablespoons Grand Marnier liqueur
1/4 cup Cucacao liqueur
1 tablespoon dark rum

In a small bowl, combine sour cream, whipped cream and sugar. Stir in the liqueurs and rum. Mix well and chill until serving time. Serve with 3 pints of fruit or berries.

GINGERED FRUIT DIP

1 package (8-ounce) cream cheese, softened
1 jar (16-ounce) marshmallow cream
1/4 teaspoon powdered ginger
1/4 teaspoon grated fresh orange rind

Blend ingredients, chill and serve with fresh fruit. Makes about 2 1/2 cups.

LEMON CRESCENTS

1 can (8-ounce) Crescent rolls
1 package (3-ounce) cream cheese, softened
1 teaspoon lemon juice
1/2 teaspoon grated lemon rind

Unroll package of rolls. Mix cream cheese, lemon juice and rind until creamy. Separate rolls and spread mixture on rolls, spreading to edge. Starting at short end, roll and place on ungreased sheet. Bake in 375-degree oven for 12 minutes. Makes 8.

Jo and Jan say, "These are wonderful with hot tea!"

MINIATURE ORANGE PARTY MUFFINS

3/4 cup golden raisins
Zest and juice of 1 orange
1 cup sugar
1/2 cup butter
2 eggs
1 teaspoon baking soda
1 cup buttermilk
2 cups sifted all-purpose flour
1/2 cup sugar (for tops)

Grind raisins and orange zest in blender or food processor and set aside. Set aside the juice from the orange, about 1/2 cup. Cream sugar and butter on electric mixer until smooth; add eggs and beat until fluffy.

Combine soda and buttermilk; add sifted flour to butter mixture alternately with buttermilk. Stir until well-mixed; stir raisins and orange zest. Spoon batter into greased miniature muffin tins and bake for about 12 minutes in a preheated 400-degree oven until golden brown and firm. Remove from oven and set on a rack. While still warm, brush tops with reserved orange juice and sprinkle with sugar. After 5 minutes, turn out of pans. Cool completely and cut in half before placing on serving platter. Makes 36 miniature muffins.

Jo says, "Serve the muffins with slivers of smoked turkey or ham and place a bowl of Sour Cream Cranberry Sauce or Cranberry Cheese Spread (See index) at the side of the platter."

PEAR NUT BREAD

2 large ripe bartlett pears, (1 1/4 cups) peeled, cored and finely chopped
2 eggs, beaten
1 cup whole bran
1 1/2 cups sifted all-purpose flour
1/2 cup sugar
1 teaspoon baking powder
1/2 teaspoon salt
1/2 teaspoon baking soda
1/2 scant teaspoon cinnamon
1/2 stick (1/4 cup) margarine, softened
1/2 cup walnuts, chopped
1 1/2 tablespoons freshly grated orange zest (optional)

Combine pears, eggs and bran in medium bowl; stir to moisten. Set aside while preparing remaining ingredients. Sift flour, sugar, baking powder, salt, soda and cinnamon into mixing bowl. Cut in margarine until mixture resembles small peas. Stir in pear-bran mixture, then walnuts and orange peel, if desired. Turn into a greased loaf pan. Let stand 20 minutes.

Bake in preheated 350-degree oven for 60 minutes, or until tester inserted in center comes out clean. Cover with foil if top browns too quickly during last few minutes. Remove from oven and let stand 10 minutes, then invert loaf onto wire rack to cool. This freezes well.

Jo and Jan say, "This is a lovely bread for a tea or a picnic. You might want to spread it with Lemon-Mint Butter or Picnic Lemon Butter (See index) Also if you are on a low-sugar watch, substitute 1/4 cup firmly packed brown sugar for the 1/2 cup of white." Makes 1 loaf.

STRAWBERRY NUT BREAD

3 cups flour
1 teaspoon soda
1 teaspoon salt
1 teaspoon cinnamon
2 cups sugar
4 eggs, beaten
2 cups frozen sliced strawberries, thawed
1 1/4 cups salad oil
1 cup pecans, chopped

Sift dry ingredients; add beaten eggs, strawberries, oil and nuts. Stir until ingredients are well moistened and blended but do not beat. Spoon into two 9 x 5 x 3-inch loaf pans which have been greased on the bottom. Bake in a preheated 350-degree oven for 1 hour. Cool in pans for 10 minutes before removing.

Jo and Jan say, "This makes excellent tea sandwiches. Spread slices with Strawberry Spread (See index)."

RUBY'S SCONES

2 cups flour
1/4 teaspoon salt
1/4 teaspoon soda
4 tablespoons butter
1 tablespoon sugar
1 cup commercial sour cream
1 egg, beaten

Sift flour, salt and soda together in a large bowl. Cut in the butter and mix until crumbly like peas. Add sugar, egg and enough cream to make a soft dough. Turn out on a floured board, knead lightly, roll out and cut into round cakes with 2-inch cutter. Bake in preheated 400-degree oven for 15 minutes or until nicely browned.

Jan says, "Ruby used to serve these scones when she had her friends in for a chat and a cup of tea. She used to make with scones in diamond shapes or stars. I remember also that she used sour milk instead of the commercial sour cream because there wasn't such a thing back when..." Makes 12 scones

ELIZABETH'S SCONES

2 cups all-purpose flour
1 1/2 tablespoons sugar
1 tablespoon baking powder
1/4 teaspoon salt
1/4 cup butter, cut into pieces
1 large egg
1/2 cup milk

Sift flour, sugar, baking powder and salt into bowl. Add butter and blend until it resembles meal. In another small bowl, beat the egg and milk well. Reserve 1 tablespoon for brushing tops of scones. Stir remaining mixture into flour mixture only until it forms a dough.

Roll or pat dough 1/2-inch thick on a lightly floured surface. Cut into rounds with a 2-inch cutter and arrange on a lightly greased baking sheet. Repeat with scraps of dough. Brush tops of scones with reserved milk mixture and bake on middle rack of preheated 425-degree oven for 12 to 15 minutes or until tops are golden. Makes 16.

Jo and Jan say, "These are a "must" for your tea table. Place them on a serving plate accompanied by dishes of butter and jam."

IRISH SCONES

3 cups all-purpose flour
1 teaspoon baking powder
4 tablespoons unsalted butter, cut into
    pieces
1 cup milk
1 egg

Sift flour and baking powder in a large bowl. Work in butter with pastry blender or fingers until texture is fine crumbs. Make a well in the center; lightly beat milk and egg in a small bowl and pour into the well, reserving 1 tablespoon of the liquid. Gradually work dry ingredients into the liquid until dough is formed.

Turn dough out onto a lightly floured board. Knead gently until it holds its shape. Roll dough out to 10 x 8-inch rectangle; transfer to a baking sheet with a large spatula. Score dough with a sharp knife into 2-inch squares; being careful to not cut through the dough.

Brush dough with the reserved milk and egg mixture. Bake in a preheated 350-degree oven about 25 minutes until light brown. Break into squares and serve warm. Makes 20.

POPPY SEED TEA CAKE

1/3 cup poppy seeds
1 cup buttermilk
1 cup butter or margarine
1 1/2 cups sugar
4 eggs
2 1/2 cups flour
2 teaspoons baking powder
1 teaspoon baking soda
1/2 teaspoon salt
1 teaspoon orange extract
Cinnamon sugar (2 tablespoons sugar and
    1 teaspoons ground cinnamon)

Combine poppy seeds and buttermilk. Refrigerate overnight for full flavor.

Cream butter with sugar until light and fluffy. Add eggs, one at a time, beating after each addition. Sift flour, baking powder, soda and salt. Add orange extract to creamed mixture. Blend in flour mixture alternately with poppy seed mixture, beginning and ending with dry ingredients. Turn half the batter into greased and floured 10-inch bundt or tube pan. Sprinkle cinnamon sugar on top. Add remaining batter. Bake in a preheated 350-degree oven 1 hour or until cake tests done. Cool 10 minutes; remove from pan and finish cooling.

DORIE'S MINIATURE TEA CAKES

1/2 cup butter or margarine
1/2 cup sugar
1/4 teaspoon vanilla extract
1/8 teaspoon almond extract
1 tablespoon light rum
Grated zest of 1 orange
2/3 cup plus 2 tablespoons flour
3/4 cup almonds, finely ground
4 large egg whites, stiffly beaten
2-3 tablespoons confectioners' sugar, sifted

Cream butter and sugar; add extracts, rum, orange zest, salt, flour and almonds. Mix well. Fold in 1/3 of the egg whites to the mixture, then carefully fold in the rest.

Pour into greased 2-inch muffin tins and bake for about 45 minutes in preheated 375-degree oven. Remove from tins and place on a rack to cool. Sprinkle tops with confectioners' sugar. Makes 12.

LEMON TEA CAKES

1 1/2 teaspoons vinegar
1/2 cup milk
1/2 cup butter or margarine
3/4 cup sugar
1 egg
1 teaspoon finely shredded lemon peel
1 3/4 cups all-purpose flour
1 teaspoon baking powder
1/4 teaspoon baking soda
1/4 teaspoon salt

LEMON GLAZE:
3/4 cup sugar
1/4 cup lemon juice

Stir vinegar into milk. Cream butter and sugar until fluffy; add egg and lemon peel then beat well. Combine flour, baking powder, soda and salt; add to creamed mixture alternately with milk, beating smooth after each addition. Drop from teaspoon, 2 inches apart, onto ungreased baking sheet. Bake in 350-degree oven 12 to 14 minutes. Remove from sheet; immediately brush with Lemon Glaze.

Combine sugar and lemon juice and brush on warm tea cakes. Makes 4 dozen.

AUSTRIAN JAM COOKIES

1/2 cup butter, softened (do not use margarine)
1/2 cup sugar
1 teaspoon vanilla
1 egg, separated
1 1/4 cups sifted flour
2/3 cup finely chopped almonds
Raspberry, strawberry, blackberry jam

Cream butter and sugar; add vanilla and egg yolk. Blend well and add flour. Put egg white in a small dish and chopped almonds in another dish. Form small balls with the dough; roll balls in egg white, then in nuts. Place on lightly greased cookie sheet and press with thumb so you have an indentation on each cookie. Fill space with jam and bake in preheated 300-degree oven for about 20 minutes. Keep in airtight container. Makes 2 dozen.

COCONUT-ALMOND DROPS

3/4 cup sweetened condensed milk
2 cans (3 1/2-ounce size) flaked coconut
1 teaspoon vanilla extract
1/2 teaspoon almond extract
1 cup toasted slivered almonds

Combine condensed milk with remaining ingredients, stirring until well mixed. Drop by teaspoon 1-inch apart onto lightly greased cookie sheets; bake in preheated 300-degree oven for about 12 minutes, or until lightly-golden. Cool on wire rack. Makes about 4 dozen.

CHOCOLATE NUT SLICES

4 squares (1-ounce size) unsweetened baking chocolate
2 cups sugar
1 1/2 cups butter or margarine
2 eggs
2 teaspoons vanilla
3 1/2 cups flour
4 teaspoons baking powder
1 teaspoon salt
1 cup chopped nuts

Melt chocolate and cool. Mix remaining ingredients; add chocolate and nuts. Shape into rolls, wrap in plastic wrap and chill until firm. Slice; roll in powdered sugar, if desired. Bake in preheated 350-degree oven for 10 minutes. Makes 4 dozen.

VANILLA REFRIGERATOR COOKIES

1 1/2 cups sifted all-purpose flour
1/2 teaspoon baking soda
1/4 teaspoon salt
1/2 cup soft shortening
1 cup granulated sugar, or
1/2 cup each, granulated and brown sugar, packed
1 egg
2 to 3 teaspoons vanilla extract, or 1/2 teaspoon almond extract
1/2 cup chopped nuts (optional)

Sift first 3 ingredients. Cream shortening, sugar, egg and vanilla. Gradually add flour mixture, nuts; mix well. On sheet of waxed paper, shape dough into a roll about 2 inches in diameter. Chill or freeze until ready to use. Slice dough 1/8 to 1/4-inch thick and bake on ungreased cookie sheet at 375 about 10 minutes, or until golden brown. Makes 5 dozen.

REFRIGERATOR COOKIE VARIATIONS

CHOCOLATE:

Add 3 squares (3 ounces) unsweetned chocolate, melted, to egg mixture just before adding flour mixture. Decrease vanilla to 1 teaspoon.

SPICE-NUT:

Sift 1/2 teaspoon cinnamon and 1/4 teaspoon nutmeg with flour mixture. We like to add 1/2 cup chopped nuts to these cookies.

ORANGE:

Add 1 tablespoon grated orange rind to egg mixture; substitute orange juice for vanilla. Nuts are very good in these cookies, we like pecans.

COCONUT:

Increase shortening to 3/4 cup; use 1/2 cup brown sugar, packed, and 1/2 cup granulated sugar; add 2 cups shredded coconut.

BROWN-SUGAR REFRIGERATOR COOKIES

3 1/2 cups sifted flour
1 teaspoon baking soda
1/2 teaspoon salt
1 cup butter or margarine, softened 2 cups brown sugar, firmly packed
2 eggs
1 teaspoon vanilla
1 cup pecans or walnuts, finely chopped

Sift flour with baking soda and salt; set aside. In a large bowl beat margarine or butter until light. Gradually beat in sugar. Add eggs and vanilla, continuing beating until very light. Beat in the flour mixture until smooth. Add nuts, mixing to combine ingredients.

Divide dough in thirds. Shape each third into a roll 8-inches long. Wrap in plastic wrap or foil. Refrigerate until firm; about 6 hours or overnight.

Using a sharp knife, cut slices about 1/8-inch-thick and place 2 inches apart on ungreased cookie sheet. Bake in preheated 375-degree oven for 8 to 10 minutes or until browned to your liking. Remove to wire rack to cool. Makes 8 to 10 dozen.

Jan says, "This is a great cookie to make ahead to have on hand and ready to bake when you need a really yummy cookie in a hurry."

❖✦❖

LEMON REFRIGERATOR COOKIES

1 cup butter or margarine
1/2 cup light brown sugar
1/2 cup granulated sugar
1 beaten egg
2 tablespoons lemon juice
1/2 cup chopped nuts
1 tablespoon grated lemon rind
3 cups sifted flour
1/4 teaspoon soda
1/4 teaspoon salt

Cream butter; add sugar, egg, lemon juice and rind. Mix well, then add dry ingredients and nuts. Mix well. Form into a roll about 2 inches in diameter, wrap in waxed paper and chill in refrigerator until ready to use. Slice and bake on lightly greased cookie sheet for 12 to 15 minutes in a 350-degree oven. Makes 4 dozen.

CHOCOLATE CHEESE CUPS

1 1/2 cups flour
1 cup sugar
1/2 cup unsweetened cocoa
1 teaspoon baking soda
1/2 teaspoon salt
1 tablespoon vinegar
1 teaspoon vanilla
1 cup water
1/3 cup cooking oil

Sift dry ingredients together into mixing bowl. Add remaining ingredients; beat until well blended. Spoon into greased miniature muffin tins, filling 1/3 full.

FILLING:
1 package (8-ounce) cream cheese, softened
1 egg
1/3 cup sugar
1/8 teaspoon salt
1 cup chocolate chips
Additional sugar (optional)
4 ounces chopped almonds (optional)

Combine cream cheese, egg, sugar and salt. Beat until smooth then add chocolate chips. Place 1 tablespoon of this mixture in the center of each cup. Sprinkle with additional sugar and chopped nuts if desired. Bake in preheated 350-degree oven for 30 minutes. Refrigerate upon removal from pans. Makes 24.

MARGO'S CHOCOLATE DREAMS

24 ounces semisweet chocolate
1 stick butter
1 1/4 cups flour
2 cups ground almonds, lightly toasted
1 1/2 teaspoons baking powder
6 eggs
1 cup sugar
1/2 cup Kahlua
Powdered sugar
Granulated sugar

Melt chocolate and butter in top of double boiler over simmering water. Sift together flour, almonds and baking powder. Combine eggs with sugar and beat with electric mixer until light. Fold chocolate mixture into egg mixture. Add flour mixture alternately with Kahlua, ending with dry ingredients. Cover and chill several hours or overnight.

To bake, preheat oven to 350 degrees. Form dough into 1-inch balls; roll each first in granulated sugar then in powdered sugar. Place on lightly greased baking sheet and bake for 15 minutes or until firm in center. Cool completely before removing from baking sheet. Makes 6 dozen.

Margo says, "When melting butter and chocolate, do not overheat or the chocolate will become hard. If that happens, stir in a little vegetable shortening."

✦✦

ORANGE TEA PUFFS

1/2 cup plus 2 tablespoons butter or margarine, softened
1/2 cup sugar
1 1/2 cups flour
1 1/2 teaspoons baking powder
1/4 teaspoon grated nutmeg
Zest of 1 orange
1/4 cup orange juice
1/4 cup milk

Beat butter and sugar until light; stir in egg. Sift dry ingredients into another bowl. Stir into butter mixture alternately with orange juice and milk. Add grated zest. Grease 2 1/2-inch muffin cups and half-fill with the mixture. Bake in preheated 350-degree oven for 20 to 25 minutes or until lightly browned.

TEA TIME LEMON WAFERS

1/2 cup butter
1/2 cup sugar
1 egg
1 teaspoon fresh lemon juice
1 teaspoon grated lemon rind
1/8 teaspoon lemon extract
3/4 cup sifted cake flour

Cream butter and sugar until light; beat in egg, lemon juice, rind and extract. Continue to beat and add flour just until mixed.

Chill dough for a few hours, then drop dough, a 1/2 teaspoon for each cookie, at least 2 inches apart on a greased baking sheet. Bake for about 7 minutes in a preheated 375-degree oven, or until the paper-thin rims brown slightly. Cool completely and store in an airtight container.

Jo and Jan say, "These are the most delicious tea wafers! You will want to make extra batches of these because they will not stay around too long. They make wonderful vanilla wafers too. Just substitute vanilla for the lemon juice and delete the lemon extract from the recipe. Add just 1/4 teaspoon of lemon rind for a hint of flavor." Makes 3 dozen.

CASHEW TEA COOKIES

1 cup brown sugar, packed
1/2 cup butter or margarine
1 egg
1/2 teaspoon vanilla
2 cups all-purpose flour
3/4 teaspoon baking soda
3/4 teaspoon baking powder
1/4 teaspoon salt
1/2 teaspoon cinnamon
1/4 teaspoon nutmeg
1/3 cup sour cream
1 cup salted cashew nuts, broken into small pieces

BUTTER ICING:
3 tablespoons butter or margarine
2 cups powdered sugar, sifted
2 to 3 tablespoons milk
1 teaspoon vanilla

Cream brown sugar and butter. Beat in egg and add vanilla. Stir in dry ingredients; add to creamed mixture alternately with sour cream, then stir in nuts. Drop from teaspoon onto greased cookie sheet. Bake in 375-degree oven for 8 to 10 minutes. Frost with Butter Icing.

Heat butter and stir until browned. Slowly add powdered sugar, milk, and vanilla. Beat until mixture is smooth. Spread on cookies. Makes 4 dozen.

ALMOND MERINGUE COOKIES

8 ounces slivered blanched almonds (1 1/2 cups)
2 egg whites, room temperature
1/8 teaspoon salt
3/4 cup powdered sugar
1/4 cup granulated sugar
1/4 teaspoon almond extract
1 cup pine nuts, coarsely chopped

Toast almonds on baking sheet in preheated 350-degree oven until lightly browned around edges, about 10 minutes. Stir occasionally. Cool and grind to a dry meal.

Grease and flour a large baking sheet; shake off excess flour. Beat egg whites and salt until soft peaks form. Mix sugars in small bowl and add to egg whites, a tablespoon at a time, beating constantly until stiff. Blend in almond extract and gently fold in almonds. Drop meringue onto baking sheet by heaping tablespoons, about 1 inch apart. Sprinkle tops with pine nuts. Bake about 15 minutes, until lightly browned. Cool on racks and store in airtight container. Makes 2 dozen.

FRENCH LACE COOKIES

1 cup unsifted flour
1 cup pecans, finely chopped
1/2 cup butter
1/2 cup light or dark corn syrup
2/3 cup brown sugar, packed

In a large mixing bowl, combine flour and chopped nuts. Place the butter, syrup and sugar in a saucepan. Bring to a boil, remove from heat. Cool. Combine this with flour and nuts. Mix well. Drop by teaspoonful 4 inches apart, on a well-greased baking sheet (8 cookies to a sheet). Bake in preheated 325-degree oven for 8 to 10 minutes. Cookies will be very thin. Allow to cool 2 minutes before removing from pan. Makes 3 dozen.

Jo and Jan say, "You might try adding 4 teaspoons unsweetened cocoa and 1/2 teaspoon instant coffee powder to this recipe for a delicious mocha cookie."

CHOCOLATE LACE COOKIES

1 recipe of French Lace Cookies
3 1/2 ounces semisweet chocolate, melted

Prepare French Lace Cookies as directed. Using a thin spatula, spread a layer of chocolate on bottom side of half the cooled cookies. Cover with flat side of plain cookie to form a sandwich. Cool on rack until chocolate is set. Serve within 1 hour or wrap in foil and freeze.

MACADAMIA SNOWBALLS

1 stick butter, softened
1 cup flour
4 tablespoons dark rum
1 teaspoon vanilla
1 1/4 cups macadamia nuts, finely chopped
1 tablespoon vegetable shortening
1 cup confectioners' sugar

Cream butter in bowl of electric mixer; gradually add flour, rum vanilla and salt, beating well. Add chopped nuts and beat at low speed until thoroughly mixed.

Wrap dough in plastic and chill 1 hour. Form balls about 3/4 inch in diameter and place on a greased cookie sheet. Bake on middle rack in a preheated 300-degree oven for 35 minutes. Remove from oven, cool slightly and roll in confectioners' sugar. When completely cool, roll in sugar once again. Makes 30 balls.

ORANGE NUT TEA DROPS

1/2 cup butter or margarine
1 package (3-ounce) cream cheese
1/2 cup sugar
1 egg
1 teaspoon grated orange rind
1 teaspoon vanilla
1 cup sifted flour
1/2 teaspoon salt
1/2 cup pecans and walnuts, mixed

Cream butter, cream cheese and sugar. Add egg, orange rind and vanilla. Combine flour and salt and add to butter mixture. Stir in nuts. Drop by teaspoonfuls 1 inch apart on a greased baking sheet. Bake at 350 degrees for 15 minutes or until just lightly brown.

VARIATION: COFFEE LIQUEUR FILLING FOR LACE COOKIES

1 1/3 cup unsifted confectioners' sugar
6 tablespoons cocoa
4 teaspoons hot water
3 tablespoons coffee liqueur

Combine sugar, cocoa and water until smooth. Add coffee liqueur. Mixture should be thick. Spread on cookies as directed above.

BETTY'S HAZELNUT COOKIES

1 cup butter
1 1/2 cups hazelnuts, ground fine
2 teaspoons vanilla
1 teaspoon grated fresh lemon peel
2/3 cup sugar
2 1/2 cups sifted all-purpose flour
Confectioner's sugar

Cream butter in large bowl; stir in nuts, vanilla and lemon peel. Mix well then beat in sugar and gradually add flour. Roll on lightly floured surface to 1/4-inch thick. Cut out dough with a 2 1/2-inch cutter and place on ungreased baking sheet. Bake in preheated 325-degree oven for 12 to 15 minutes or until light brown. Remove from sheet; cool on racks and dust with confectioner's sugar. Makes 4 dozen.

The Lady Has Taste

CAROL'S POLISH COOKIES

1/2 pound (2 sticks) butter or margarine
1 package (8-ounce) cream cheese
2 cups flour
1 cup powdered sugar
2 teaspoons baking powder
Prepared fruit filling or lemon pudding

Combine butter and cheese. Sift together flour, sugar and baking powder; blend into cheese mixture.

Form dough into long rolls 2 inches in diameter. Wrap in wax paper or plastic wrap and chill until firm.

Cut dough in slices 1/4-inch thick. Place slices on greased baking sheet. Using thumb, make an indentation in center of each slice. Spoon on filling of choice. Bake in preheated 350-degree oven for 15 minutes or until lightly browned and spring to touch. Makes about 4 dozen.

Carol says, "Do not store these in a covered container; they will become soggy."

KEY LIME SQUARES

1 cup margarine
1/2 cup confectioners' sugar
2 cups flour
Pinch of salt
4 eggs
2 cups sugar
6 tablespoons lime juice
6 tablespoons flour
Rind of 1 lime, grated
Confectioners' sugar (garnish)

Combine margarine, confectioners' sugar, flour and salt; mix well. Press in bottom of a well-greased 9x13x2-inch pan. Bake in preheated 350-degree oven for 15 to 20 minutes.

Beat eggs, add rest of ingredients except confectioners' sugar. Pour on top of baked pastry and bake 25 minutes. Garnish with confectioners' sugar while warm. Cut into squares; refrigerate. Makes about 5 dozen squares.

DRESSY GRAPES

1 1/4 cups unroasted, shelled nuts
1 package (8-ounce) cream cheese
1/4 pound Roquefort or Bleu cheese
2 tablespoons heavy cream
1 pound red or green seedless grapes

Wash and dry grapes; set aside. Chop nuts coarsely and spread on a baking sheet. Toast lightly in oven and allow to cool.

Combine cream cheese, Roquefort or Bleu cheese, cream and beat until smooth. Coat dry grapes with cheese mixture and roll in toasted nuts and place on tray lined with waxed paper. Chill until ready to serve.

Jo and Jan say, "We prefer pistachio nuts or pecans. Also, if you do not care for the flavor of Roquefort and prefer a milder cheese, try one of the new fruit-flavored cheeses available in most cheese sections of grocery deli sections."

❖❖

CREAM CHEESE - STUFFED STRAWBERRIES

2 packages (3-ounce size) cream cheese,
  softened
1 teaspoon grated lemon peel
1 teaspoon fresh lemon juice
1 teaspoon sugar (or honey)
48 large fresh ripe strawberries
Fresh Mint

Mix cheese, lemon peel, lemon juice and sugar in blender or food processor until fluffy; refrigerate until chilled. Gently scoop centers from strawberries with melon-baller or fruit knife. Fill with cheese mixture. Arrange berries on serving plate and garnish with fresh mint. Makes 4 dozen

GLAZED APRICOTS

2 cups sugar
1 cup water
2 packages dried apricots

Bring sugar and water to a boil. Turn down heat and add apricots; boil gently for 5 minutes (watch for boiling over). Remove apricots with a fork and spread on waxed paper (not touching) for a least 20 minutes. Save syrup for next batch; it keeps in refrigerator. Press apricots into a plate of sugar, using your fingers. Place on a rack and let dry overnight.

Jo and Jan say, "This recipe was in our Under The Mistletoe section of A Cooking Affaire. It has been so popular and is so wonderful for teas and gift-giving, we decided to repeat it. We know you will enjoy them."

FROSTED CRANBERRIES

2 tablespoons light corn syrup
1/4 cup fresh cranberries
2 tablespoons sugar

In a small saucepan, heat corn syrup over low heat. When heated, remove pan and stir in cranberries until coated. Remove cranberries with slotted spoon to a bowl and toss with sugar to coat well. Spread out on waxed paper. These are lovely as a garnish on your holiday or party table.

GLAZED LEMON SLICES

4 lemons, unpeeled and sliced 1/4-inch thick
3 cups water
1 cup sugar
2/3 cup light corn syrup
1/2 cup water

Bring water to a boil and remove from heat. Add lemon slices; cover and let stand 5 minutes. Drain slices and in the same pan boil sugar, corn syrup and 1/2 cup water. Add lemons and simmer 10 minutes. Remove from heat and let stand overnight.

Drain lemon slices, reserving 1/2 cup syrup. Boil syrup over medium heat until reduced to 1/4 cup. Allow to cool. Arrange lemon slices, overlaping, on dish to be decorated and brush with syrup.

FROSTED GRAPES

2-3 pounds seedless grapes
2 egg whites
Granulated sugar

Whisk egg whites in bowl until foamy. Dip small clusters of grapes into egg whites, turning to coat; hold cluster over bowl to let excess drip back into bowl. Place clusters on a waxed paper-lined tray and sprinkle with granulated sugar. Place tray in refrigerator for several hours or overnight before using.

Jo and Jan say, "We also have dipped the grapes into white wine, let them sit for a few minutes, then sprinkle with the sugar. Tap the tray against the counter to remove excess sugar; it will keep it from forming clumps on the grapes."

CANDIED VIOLETS

Violets of any shade, heads only
2 egg whites
Confectioners sugar, sifted

Violets are better if they have been picked in the sun; they will be more fragrant and will taste better. Beat egg whites slightly. Dip each violet in the egg white, then the sifted sugar. Shake off excess sugar and place on a baking sheet, being careful that they do not touch. Place in oven to dry at the lowest temperature. These make lovely decorations for food, and are also good to eat.

FRESH - FLOWER ICE BUCKET

Fill an ice bucket or metal bowl to 2/3 level with water. Place a plastic container about 7 inches high and 5 inches in diameter in the water. Weigh the container with dried beans or a rock to submerge it about 6 inches. Center the plastic container and secure rims in position with tape.

Cut about 3 dozen flowers close to the bud and place in the water. Freeze. Remove the tape and weight; place a hot towel inside the plastic container for 1 minute. Remove the container and immerse the bowl briefly in a pan of hot water to unmold.

Jo and Jan say, "This is absolutely beautiful filled with an assortment of flowers and colors. Wrap a lovely lace-edged napkin around the neck of your favorite bottle of wine, place it in ice in the flower bucket and you have a unique and lovely wine cooler."

Light Hearted·

The reoccurring theme for the 90's seems to be an awareness of good health. It seems that even casual conversations eventually come around to the subject of cholesterol, stationary bikes, stairmasters, spas and a score of other health-related topics.

Since we sent you into sugar shock with our Sweet Temptations section, we thought it only fair to give equal attention to light hearted foods.

This section is one of our mini-books, with delicious and healthy recipes ranging from appetizers to desserts. Have a deLITEful time!

THE DIETERS' PRAYER

Lord, grant me the strength
That I may not fall
Into the clutches of cholesterol
The road to Hell is paved with butter,
Cake is cursed, cream is awful
And Satan is hiding in every waffle.
Beelzebub is a chocolate drop
Lucifer is a lollipop.
Teach me the evils of Hollandaise
of pasta and gobs of mayonnaise,
And crisp fried chicken from the South,
If you love me Lord, shut my mouth.
—*Author unknown*

SALT-FREE SEASONING

1/2 teaspoon garlic powder
1/2 teaspoon onion powder
1/2 teaspoon dry mustard
1/2 teaspoon white pepper
1/2 teaspoon paprika
1/4 teaspoon powdered thyme
1/4 teaspoon ground celery seed

Combine all ingredients; store in airtight container in a dry place. Makes 3 tablespoons.

MAGIC MIX

4 cups instant nonfat dry milk
1 cup flour or 1/2 cup cornstarch
2 sticks margarine

Combine dry milk, flour and margarine in a large bowl and mix until it looks like cornmeal. Keep mix tightly covered in the refrigerator. Makes 5 cups.

MAGIC CREAM SOUPS

4 cups water
3 cups Magic Mix
1 cube or 1 teaspoon bouillon granules

Combine water, Magic Mix and bouillon in a saucepan. Stir over medium heat until slightly thickened. Add one of the following:

3 cooked carrots, mashed
3 potatoes, cooked and chopped and
  1 tablespoon chopped onion
1 package (6-ounce) chopped spinach,
  cooked
1 can (8-ounce) cream-style corn and
  1 tablespoon minced onion
2 cups cooked broccoli, cauliflower or
  carrots

You can use Magic Mix for all milk base soup recipes or add to soup stock to make a cream soup.
Add 1 cup grated cheese to make vegetable cheese soup.

MAGIC SAUCE

2/3 cup Magic Mix
1 cup water

In saucepan, combine Magic Mix and water. Stir over medium heat until it starts to bubble. Add cooked meat, cheese or vegetables to the hot sauce. Makes 1 cup.

Use Magic Mix Sauce for all recipes calling for a white or cream sauce.

MAGIC PUDDING

1/2 cup sugar
2 cups Magic Mix
2 cups water
1 teaspoon vanilla

Combine sugar, Magic Mix and water in a saucepan. Stir over medium heat until pudding bubbles. Add vanilla and beat. Cover and cool.

Chocolate Pudding: Combine 3 tablespoons cocoa with the sugar and follow the above recipe and steps.

THE SPICE OF LIFE
• TO BRING OUT THE FLAVORS OF YOUR FOODS •

FRUITS:

Apples - cinnamon, allspice and nutmeg
Bananas - cinnamon, nutmeg, ginger and allspice
Peaches - cinnamon, nutmeg and cloves
Pears - cardamon, cinnamon and black pepper
Oranges - cinnamon and cloves
Cranberries - allspice, ginger and cinnamon
Strawberries - cinnamon

VEGETABLES:

Beans - marjoram, basil, rosemary, caraway seeds and mustard
Broccoli - ginger, sesame seed and garlic powder
Carrots - Cinnamon, nutmeg, mint, basil and dill
Corn - Chili powder, cumin, garlic and onion powders

Peas - Mint, onion powder, parsley, rosemary and marjoram
Spinach - Nutmeg, onion powder, sesame seed and garlic powder
Squash - Cinnamon, nutmeg, ginger, dill, onion powder and sesame seed.
Tomatoes - Basil, rosemary, parsley, cinnamon onion, garlic
Potatoes - dill, onion powder, parsley flakes, caraway seed and onion powder.
Rice - tumeric, coriander, curry powder, chili powder, cumin
Pasta - basil, garlic powder, parsley, garlic onion and red pepper

FISH:

Tarragon, onion powder, paprika, thyme, parsley, fennel seeds, black and red peppers, sesame seed, ginger and white pepper.

FRESH PEACH SHAKE

1 cup sliced peaches
1 cup buttermilk
1 tablespoon lemon juice
3 tablespoons honey

Combine all ingredients into blender and beat until smooth. Pour into glasses and serve immediately. Serves 2.

GRAPEFRUIT SPRITZER

1 can (6-ounce) frozen grapefruit juice, undiluted
2 1/2 to 3 cups club soda, chilled

Pour grapefruit juice into a pitcher and add chilled club soda slowly; mix well. Serves 4.

CHEATA-RITA

4 ounces frozen lemonade, undiluted
16 ounces lime-flavored mineral water
1 ounce lime juice

In blender, combine all ingredients. Blend at high speed for 10 seconds or until liquid becomes light and frothy. Salt rim of margarita glass (if desired) and serve. Serves 2.

PEACH CLOUD

1/2 cup frozen orange juice concentrate, thawed and undiluted
2 cups low-fat vanilla yogurt
3 cups peaches, sliced
2 cups low-fat milk, chilled

Combine juice concentrate and yogurt in blender. Add peach slices a few at a time until the peaches are pureed. Add milk and serve at once in chilled glasses. Serves 6.

NECTARINE SHAKE

1 large nectarine, peeled and diced
2 tablespoons frozen orange juice, thawed and undiluted
1 cup buttermilk

Combine ingredients into blender and blend until smooth. Pour into chilled glass. Serves 1.

Heart-T Snacks

SPINACH -YOGURT DIP

1 package (10-ounce) frozen spinach, thawed and chopped
1 carton (8-ounce) plain low-fat yogurt
1 teaspoon dried oregano, leaves crushed
1/2 teaspoon lemon juice
1/2 teaspoon onion powder

Thaw spinach and allow to drain. Squeeze out remaining liquid until dry. In medium-size bowl, combine all ingredients. Chill until ready to serve. Makes 1 1/2 cups.

Light Hearted

YOGURT - HERB DIP

1 cup low-fat yogurt
1/3 cup green onions, sliced
2 tablespoons parsley, chopped
2 tablespoons dill weed, diced
1/2 teaspoon basil leaves, dried
1/4 teaspoon garlic powder
1/8 teaspoon ground pepper
1 teaspoon salt, optional

Blend all ingredients in a blender until smooth. Chill until serving time. Makes 2 cups.

ITALIAN TOMATO DIP

1 can (8-ounce) stewed tomatoes
2 teaspoons Italian seasoning, dried
1/4 teaspoon garlic powder
1 green pepper, chopped
1/4 teaspoon salt
1/4 teaspoon pepper, ground

Process all ingredients in blender until smooth. Chill until ready to serve. Makes about 1 1/2 cups.

LOW-CAL SALSA

1 can (16-ounce) tomatoes, mashed
1/4 cup green pepper, chopped
3 tablespoons onion, minced
3 tablespoons water
1 tablespoon chili powder
1/4 teaspoon garlic powder
Dash cayenne

Combine all ingredients in blender. Place in medium-size bowl. Chill to serve. Makes about 2 cups.

CHEESE DIP

1 carton (16-ounce) part-skim Ricotta cheese
2 tablespoons skim milk
2 tablespoons water
2 teaspoons onion, minced
2 teaspoons capers, drained
1 teaspoon lemon juice
1 teaspoon caraway seeds
1 teaspoon dry mustard
1 teaspoon salt
1 teaspoon paprika
1/4 teaspoon pepper

Combine all ingredients in blender and process. Chill in covered container. Makes about 2 cups.

EGG DROP SOUP

1 egg
1/2 teaspoon water
3 cups chicken broth
1/4 teaspoon salt
1/8 teaspoon peanut oil
1 small onion, minced
2 teaspoons finely-chopped chives

In a small bowl, beat the egg with the water. Bring the broth to a simmer and add the sugar, salt and peanut oil. Stirring constantly, add the egg to the simmering broth. As you stir, the egg will form strings. Stir in onion and remove from heat. Sprinkle chives on top of individual bowls. Serves 4.

LOW-CAL CLAM CHOWDER

1 1/2 teaspoons Puritan oil
1/2 cup carrots, thinly-sliced
1/2 cup celery, thinly-sliced
1/2 cup green pepper, thinly-sliced
1/2 cup onion, finely-chopped
2 cups tomatoes, chopped
1 1/2 cup minced clam meat
2 cups water
3 tablespoons tomato paste
1 1/2 tablespoon parsley
1/2 teaspoon rosemary leaves
1/4 teaspoon salt
1/4 teaspoon lemon pepper

Heat oil in large heavy pan and saute carrots, celery, green pepper and onion. Add tomatoes, including the juice and all the remaining ingredients. Simmer 25 minutes; add the clams and heat thoroughly. Serves 6.

RUBY'S CHICKEN STOCK

1 baking hen
2 quarts cold water
1 medium onion, peeled, sliced
2 carrots
2 ribs celery with leaves
1 teaspoon whole black peppercorns
1/2 teaspoon dried thyme
1/2 teaspoon dried parsley
2 bay leaves

Combine all ingredients in a 4-quart soup pot or saucepan. Bring to a boil, then simmer for 3 hours. Strain broth and refrigerate over night; next morning skim off the fat. Pour broth into a 2 quart jars and store in refrigerator. You must freeze the broth after 5 days in the refrigerator. This is great for soups, sauces and stir-fry.

Jan says, "I remember my Mother fixing this for her soup broth. You may substitute a fryer. Don't forget to make chicken and noodles, sandwiches from chicken salad with the deboned chicken. This is that wonderful broth to cure all ills. Jo and I like to add some of the chicken and some rice to the broth."

TOMATO BOUILLON

2 teaspoons margarine
3/4 cup onion, chopped
6 cups tomato juice
1 bay leaf
1/2 cup celery with leaves, chopped
1/2 teaspoon dried oregano leaves
1/4 teaspoon salt
1/4 teaspoon lemon pepper

In medium sauce pan saute onion, stirring until golden. Add remaining ingredients and simmer 15 minutes, stirring occasionally. Strain. This may be served hot or cold. Serves 4.

CUCUMBER AND PORK SOUP

3/4 teaspoon cornstarch
1/4 teaspoon salt
1/4 teaspoon white pepper
1 teaspoon sherry
1/2 cup thinly sliced pork
3 cups beef broth
1/2 cucumber, peeled seeded and cut into thin strips
1 1/2 teaspoons light soy sauce

In a small bowl, combine cornstarch, salt, pepper and sherry. Add pork strips and toss to coat them thoroughly. Bring broth to a boil; add the pork. Reduce heat, cover and simmer 10 minutes. Add cucumber strips and simmer three more minutes. Stir in soy sauce. Serves 4.

LITE 'N LIVELY GAZPACHO

3 cans (10-ounce size) spicy Bloody Mary mix
1 can (46-ounce) tomato juice
1/2 cup fresh lemon juice
2 cucumbers, peeled and chopped
1 green pepper, chopped
1 medium onion, chopped
1 garlic clove, crushed
2 small tomatoes, peeled and chopped
2 teaspoons artificial sweetener
Salt and freshly ground pepper
Worcestershire sauce to taste
Tabasco sauce to taste

Blend vegetables and lemon juice in food processor or blender. Add juices and seasonings and blend again. Refrigerate until serving time. Garnish with cucumber sticks or celery spears. Serves 10-12.

Salad Slimmers

SALAD SLIMMER BASIC BLEND

1 tablespoon lemon juice
1 cup nonfat yogurt
1/4 teaspoon lemon pepper
1/4 teaspoon dill
1/2 cucumber, chopped

THOUSAND ISLAND DRESSING

1 recipe Basic Blend
2 tablespoons tomato paste
1/4 teaspoon garlic, minced
1 tablespoon pickle relish
1 tablespoon onion, minced
1/4 cup celery, chopped

Combine all ingredients and chill.

GREEN GODDESS DRESSING

1 recipe Basic Blend
1 teaspoon garlic, minced
1 teaspoon chives, dried or fresh
1 teaspoon parsley, fried or fresh
1/4 teaspoon tarragon

Combine all ingredients and chill.

RANCH DRESSING

1 recipe Basic Blend
1/2 cup buttermilk
1 tablespoon Dijon mustard
1 teaspoon garlic, minced
1 teaspoon parsley, chopped
1 teaspoon chives, chopped

Combine all ingredients and chill.

❖❖

WAIST-LINE DRESSING

1/2 cup red wine vinegar
1/2 cup safflower oil
1 1/2 tablespoons lemon juice
1 tablespoon Dijon mustard
2 teaspoons Worcestershire sauce
2 teaspoons honey
1 1/2 teaspoons dried tarragon
1 teaspoon dried basil
1 teaspoon minced garlic
3/4 teaspoon dried oregano
3/4 teaspoon salt
1/4 teaspoon pepper
1 cup water

Combine all ingredients except water in a jar with a tight-fitting lid. Shake well; add water and shake again until well blended. Refrigerate. Makes 2 cups.

Jo and Jan say, "We like to make this at least a day ahead of serving so the flavors will blend."

CUCUMBER DRESSING

1 cup cucumber, pared and finely chopped
1/2 cup green pepper, chopped
1 clove garlic, finely chopped
1/2 teaspoon salt
1/4 cup low-fat yogurt
1/4 cup light mayonnaise
1/4 cup chili sauce
1 tablespoon prepared horseradish

Combine all ingredients in blender. Mix well and refrigerate until well chilled. Makes 2 cups.

NO-FAT DRESSING

2 tablespoons powdered fruit pectin
1 1/2 teaspoons basil, dried
1 1/2 teaspoons thyme, dried
1 1/2 teaspoons parsley, dried
1 1/2 teaspoons oregano, dried
1 1/2 teaspoons tarragon, dried
1 1/2 teaspoons dillweed, dried
1 teaspoon sugar
1/4 teaspoon dry mustard
1/2 cup water
2 tablespoons vinegar
1 tablespoon lemon juice
1 small clove garlic, minced

In small bowl crush all the herbs together. In a medium-size bowl combine crushed herbs, pectin, sugar, and mustard. Stir in vinegar, water and garlic. Stir well and cover. Store in the refrigerator. Makes 1 cup.

LITE-HEARTED RASPBERRY VINAIGRETTE

1/2 teaspoon unflavored gelatin
2/3 cup plus 1 tablespoon water, divided
1/4 cup Raspberry Vinegar (See index)
2 tablespoons balsamic vinegar
1 teaspoon honey
1 tablespoon minced fresh cilantro
1/8 teaspoon salt

Dissolve gelatin in 1 tablespoon water; stir well and set aside. Combine remaining 2/3 cup water, vinegars, and honey in a small non-aluminum saucepan. Bring to a boil over medium-high heat. Remove from heat and gradually stir in gelatin mixture, cilantro and salt. Cover and chill 8 hours. Stir well before serving. Makes 1 cup.

❖❖

LIVING RIGHT - LITE DRESSING

1 bunch parsley
1 bunch watercress
1/2 cup safflower oil
1/2 cup olive oil
1/3 cup tarragon vinegar
2 egg yolks
8 shallots, sliced
2 teaspoons dry mustard
1 teaspoon horseradish
1 teaspoon MSG
1 teaspoon Worcestershire sauce
Vegge-Sal seasoned salt to taste

Blend ingredients in blender. If dressing is too thick, add a few drops of ice water until desired consistency. Makes 2 to 3 cups.

LIGHT-HEARTED HOLLANDAISE

1/3 cup nonfat yogurt
3 tablespoons thawed egg substitute
1 tablespoon lemon juice
1/4 teaspoon cayenne

Blend all ingredients together and chill. Makes 1/2 cup. Jan says, "This is a wonderful substitute for you in place of that rich version. This goes well on chicken salads, vegetables, etc."

LITE-HEARTED MAYO

1 cup tofu puree
2 teaspoons white vinegar
2 teaspoons lemon juice
1/4 teaspoon dry mustard
Dash of cayenne pepper

Blend all ingredients in a blender until smooth. Store tightly in refrigerator. Be adventurous and add herbs and garlic to the mayo. Makes 1 cup.

PARSLEY DRESSING

1 cup Bertoli olive oil
1/2 cup lemon juice
1 clove garlic, minced
1 small bunch green onions, minced
1 egg
2 cups fresh parsley, stems removed
1/8 teaspoon paprika

Blend all ingredients in a blender until smooth. Place in refrigerator until ready to use. This dressing is wonderful on top of veggies or over salad greens. Makes 1 1/2 cups.

MOCK SOUR CREAM

3/4 cup nonfat buttermilk
1 cup uncreamed cottage cheese
2 teaspoons lemon juice
1 teaspoon vinegar

Pour 1/2 cup buttermilk into blender and add cottage cheese, a little at a time, blending and stirring to mix well. Add the other 1/3 cup of buttermilk and blend until smooth. Makes 1 1/2 cups.

YOGURT SAUCE

1 tablespoon Puritan oil
1 onion, chopped
1/4 cup sesame seeds
1 tablespoon lemon juice
1 cup yogurt
1/8 teaspoon salt
1/8 teaspoon pepper

Saute onion in oil. Toast sesame seeds in another skillet, stirring often until seeds are brown. Combine onion, sesame seeds, lemon juice, salt, pepper and yogurt in blender. Blend until smooth. Serve cold or slightly warm. Great dressing for potato salad or a dip for raw vegetables. Makes 1 1/2 cups.

SPINACH-MUSHROOM SALAD

1/2 cup dry white wine
2 tablespoons lemon juice
1/2 cup dried apricots
1 1/2 pounds fresh spinach, washed, stemmed, torn into bite-size pieces
1/2 pound fresh mushrooms
6 tablespoons olive oil
1/2 teaspoon dill
Salt and pepper
Sliced almonds (optional)

Add wine, lemon juice, dried apricots and simmer over low heat about 20 minutes. Cover these ingredients tightly for 1/2 hour. In the meantime, slice mushrooms thin. Then, drain apricots (saving liquid) and cut into bite-size pieces. Add liquid, olive oil, salt and pepper, and beat until well blended. Toss with spinach; sprinkle apricots and almonds on top. Serves 4 - 6.

SMOKED SALMON AND FETTUCCINE SALAD

1 medium-size cucumber, peeled and thinly sliced
3 tablespoons Bertoli extra light olive oil
4 teaspoons lemon juice
1 tablespoon red wine vinegar
1/2 teaspoon Dijon mustard
1 teaspoon lemon pepper
2 cups cooked fettuccine
3 green onions, thinly sliced
1/4 cup fresh parsley, chopped
4 ounces smoked salmon, thinly sliced or
   1 can (7-ounce) salmon, drained and flaked
4 hard-boiled eggs, halved
Romaine lettuce leaves or watercress
Lemon wedges

Sprinkle 1/2 teaspoon lemon pepper on thinly sliced cucumber rounds; set aside. In large bowl, whisk oil, lemon juice, vinegar, mustard, and 1/2 teaspoon lemon pepper. Add pasta and toss to coat well. Add cucumber, onions and parsley. Toss until well mixed. Fold in salmon. To serve, arrange the lettuce or watercress leaves on salad plates and spoon salad mixture on leaves topped with egg slices and garnish with lemon wedges on the side. Serves 4.

SPRING VIDALIA SALAD

2 cups Vadalia onion, sliced
2 cups low-fat cottage cheese
2 tablespoons lemon juice
1/4 teaspoon lemon pepper
Spinach leaves or romaine lettuce

In blender, combine onion, cottage cheese, lemon juice and lemon pepper. Blend until smooth. Toss with spinach leaves or romaine. Makes 2 cups of dressing.

GARDEN FRESH PASTA SALAD

2 tablespoons extra light olive oil
2 tablespoons red wine vinegar
1 garlic clove, minced
1 tablespoon shallots, minced
1/4 teaspoon salt
1/4 teaspoon lemon pepper
2 cups cooked linguine or shells
1 cup matchstick-sliced Jarlsberg cheese
1 cup mushrooms, sliced
1/2 red onion, thinly sliced
1/4 cup fresh parsley, minced
1/4 cup fresh basil, minced
3 medium tomatoes, diced
Parsley sprigs

Combine oil, vinegar, garlic, shallots, salt, lemon pepper in small bowl and mix well. In large bowl, combine pasta, cheese, mushrooms, red onion, minced parsley and basil. Add dressing and toss well. Line a platter or shallow bowl with spinach leaves and arrange pasta on top. Sprinkle with diced tomatoes and garnish with sprigs of parsley.

SEAFOOD PASTA SALAD

2 tablespoons extra light Bertoli olive oil
2 tablespoons lemon juice
1 tablespoon fresh chives, chopped
2 tablespoons fresh parsley, chopped
Lemon pepper to taste
2 cups cooked pasta shells
1 cup cucumber, diced
1/2 cup green pepper, diced
1 can (6 1/2-ounce) salmon
1 can (6 1/2-ounce) tuna
Lemon wedges

In large bowl, whisk together oil, lemon juice, parsley, chives, and lemon pepper. Add pasta, cucumber and green pepper; toss to coat evenly. Drain salmon, removing any bones and skin; break salmon into chunks. Drain tuna and flake. Gently fold salmon and tuna into pasta. Chill 45 minutes. To serve, arrange lettuce leaves on platter or salad plates and spoon salad on top. Garnish with lemon wedges. Serves 4.

NEW POTATO AND BEEF SALAD

1/2 cup light mayonnaise
1/2 cup low-fat milk
3 tablespoons Dijon mustard
1/4 teaspoon salt
1/4 teaspoon lemon pepper
1 pound small new potatoes, cooked, cooled
  and quartered
3/4 pound flank steak, cooked and thinly
  sliced
1/2 pound green beans, blanched
1 small red onion, sliced
1 medium-size head romaine lettuce

Combine mayonnaise, milk, mustard, salt and lemon pepper in a small bowl. Stir until well blended. In medium-size bowl, combine potatoes and 1/3 cup of the dressing. Toss to coat well. To serve, line individual salad plates with lettuce leaves; arrange steak, beans, onion and potato mixture on top. Serve with remaining dressing. Serves 4.

CRUNCHY CHICKEN SALAD

3 cups cooked chicken cut into bite-size
  pieces
1 package (10-ounce) snow peas
1 cup water chestnuts, sliced
1/2 cup green onion, sliced
1/4 teaspoon lemon pepper
Salt to taste

DRESSING:
1 cup sour cream
1 teaspoon lemon juice
1 teaspoon curry powder

In large bowl combine chicken, water chestnuts, snow peas, green onion, and lemon pepper. In another bowl stir together sour cream, lemon juice and curry powder. Pour dressing over chicken mixture and toss to mix. Season with salt if you like. Refrigerate. Serves 4.

Jan says, "When I make this salad, I use fresh snow peas. I do not cook them, only blanch them with hot water and drain immediately, because I like them crunchy. If you would rather cook them, follow the directions on the package."

GARDEN YOGURT SALAD

2 medium zucchini, sliced 1/4-inch thick
1 cucumber, sliced 1/4-inch thick
1 ripe tomato, chopped
1/2 cup green onion, thinly chopped
1 teaspoon garlic, minced
1 cup plain yogurt
1 tablespoon parsley, fresh or dried
1 teaspoon dill weed
1/4 teaspoon lemon pepper
Salt to taste
1/4 cup sesame seeds, toasted
1/2 cup bean sprouts, fresh

Arrange zucchini in a 2-quart casserole. Cover and microwave on high 2 to 3 minutes. Drain and cool. Add cucumber, tomato, onion and garlic. Ross with yogurt, parsley, dill, salt and pepper. Refrigerate 2 hours. Top with sesame seeds and sprouts. Serves 4 to 6. Note: To toast sesame seeds, put in pan and place in a low oven for 1 hour.

PARSLEY POTATO SALAD

6 medium new potatoes
6 tablespoons Bertoli olive oil
2 tablespoons wine vinegar
2 tablespoons lemon juice
1 teaspoon Dijon mustard
1/4 teaspoon salt
1/2 teaspoon lemon pepper
2 tablespoons green onion, minced
2 tablespoons capers
2 tablespoons fresh parsley, minced

Boil potatoes in enough water to cover them until tender. Cool and slice into 1/2-inch slices; set aside in a medium size bowl. In a small bowl combine olive oil, vinegar, mustard, salt, pepper and green onion. Whisk until blended. Pour over cooked potatoes and toss gently. Sprinkle capers and parsley over the top. Serves 4.

Jan says, "This is one of my family's favorite potato recipes. I like to serve it cold in the summer. It is a great side dish with grilled chicken."

Light Hearted

❖❖❖

MARINATED ASPARAGUS

2 cans (14 1/2-ounce size) asparagus
1 green pepper, chopped
1 small bunch green onions, chopped
1/2 clove garlic, minced
1 celery stalk, finely chopped
1/2 cup wine vinegar
1/2 cup sugar
3/4 cup vegetable oil
1/4 teaspoon paprika

Drain asparagus. In a large bowl, combine remaining ingredients together and pour over the asparagus. Marinate 4 to 5 hours before serving. Serves 6-8.

NEW POTATO AND SNOW PEA SALAD

6 small new potatoes, quartered
1 head romaine lettuce
1 1/2 tablespoons wine vinegar
1 1/2 tablespoons Bertoli olive oil
1 tablespoon fresh chives, chopped
1 cup snow peas, fresh or frozen
Salt
1/4 teaspoon lemon pepper
Paprika

In a small saucepan cook potatoes in small amount of water. Wash pea pods and trim. In medium-size bowl combine wine vinegar, olive oil, chives, salt and lemon pepper. Arrange romaine leaves on salad plates. Toss potatoes and pea pods together in dressing. Arrange on top of leaves. Sprinkle with paprika.

Note: If using frozen snow peas let water run over them until thawed. You don't have to cook pea pods, particularly if you like them crunchy.

WATERCRESS SALAD

2 large bunches watercress
1 to 2 teaspoons minced garlic
2 tablespoons Dijon mustard
1 teaspoon salt
1/2 teaspoon freshly-ground black pepper
3 tablespoons red wine vinegar
1/2 cup olive oil
2 cups fresh mushrooms, sliced
1/2 cup toasted slivered almonds

Wash and dry watercress. Combine minced garlic, mustard, salt, pepper and vinegar in a bowl. Whisking continuously, add oil in a thin stream. Toss with watercress, adding nuts and mushrooms at the last moment.

ELAINE'S WAIST WATCHER'S SALAD

2 envelopes unflavored gelatine
3 1/4 cups tomato juice, divided
1/2 teaspoon salt
1 teaspoon sugar
1 teaspoon Worcestershire sauce
1/4 teaspoon Tabasco sauce
1/4 cup lemon or lime juice

Sprinkle gelatin over 1 cup tomato juice in a saucepan. Stir constantly over moderate heat until gelatin dissolves, about 3 minutes.

Remove from heat; stir in remaining 2 1/4 cups tomato juice and rest of ingredients. Pour into a greased I-quart ring mold and chill until firm. Unmold and fill center with coleslaw or chicken salad. Serves 6.

PEACH BRAN MUFFINS

1 1/2 cups all-bran cereal
3/4 cup orange juice
1 1/2 cups flour
3/4 cup sugar
3 1/4 teaspoons baking powder
1/2 teaspoon salt
1 egg, beaten
3/4 cup Puritan oil
2 large peaches, peeled and chopped

In a small bowl combine cereal and orange juice. Let stand until bran has absorbed juice. In a large bowl, combine flour, sugar, baking powder and salt. Stir egg and oil into bran until well-mixed. Add bran mixture, chopped peaches to dry ingredients. Stir lightly until mixture is blended. Spoon batter into muffin tin. Bake at 350 degrees for 25 minutes. Makes 24 muffins.

Jo and Jan say, "Remember that muffin batter should never be smooth. Leave those lumps in it after the ingredients have been blended well into the batter."

CURRANT OAT MUFFINS

1 cup oat bran
2/3 cup rollet oats
1/3 cup whole wheat flour
1/3 cup unbleached flour
1 tablespoon baking powder
1/4 cup egg substitute
3 tablespoons dried currants
1/2 cup pecans
1 1/4 cups buttermilk

In a large bowl combine bran, oats, whole wheat flour, unbleached flour, baking powder, currants and nuts. Stir in egg substitute and buttermilk. Blend until well moistened. Spoon batter into muffin tins. Bake at 350 degrees for 20 minutes. Makes 12 muffins.

APPLESAUCE OAT BRAN MUFFINS

1 cup oat bran
1/2 cup all-bran
1/3 cup whole-wheat flour
2 teaspoons baking powder
1/2 teaspoon cinnamon
1/4 teaspoon nutmeg
2 egg whites
1/3 cup applesauce
1 cup skim milk

Combine oat bran, all-bran, wheat flour, baking powder, cinnamon and nutmeg in a large bowl. Set aside. In a smaller bowl, combine egg whites and applesauce. Whisk in the skim milk, then pour liquid into flour mixture. Mix until moistened. Spoon batter into 12 muffin cups. Bake at 375 degrees for 20 minutes. Makes 12 muffins.

GARDEN GREEN BEANS

1 pound fresh whole green beans
1 small onion, thinly sliced
1 clove garlic, minced
1 tablespoon olive oil
1/4 teaspoon coriander
1/4 teaspoon lemon pepper
1/4 cup toasted slivered almonds

In a large saucepan cook fresh beans, covered, in a small amount of water 15 minutes or until tender. In another small saucepan saute onion and garlic in olive oil until tender. Stir in coriander and lemon pepper. Cook 1 more minute. Toss garlic mixture with green beans. Before serving, sprinkle slivered almonds on top. Serves 4-6.

VEGETABLE LASAGNA

2 cans (15-ounce) salt-reduced tomatoes,
  cut up
2 cans (8-ounce) salt-reduced tomato sauce
1 can (6-ounce) salt-reduced tomato paste
2 tablespoons olive oil
1 medium onion, chopped
2 cloves garlic, minced
1 medium green pepper, chopped
1 cup mushrooms, sliced
1 teaspoon oregano, dried
1 teaspoon rosemary, dried
1 teaspoon thyme, dried
1 teaspoon basil, dried
2 bay leaves
8 ounces lasagna noodles
2 cups loose-pack frozen mixed broccoli,
  cauliflower and carrots
1 egg, beaten
1 carton (15-ounce) ricotta cheese
1 cup part-skim Mozzarella cheese

In large skillet heat olive oil for 2 minutes. Add onion, garlic, mushrooms and green pepper and saute until tender. Add herbs, tomatoes, tomato sauce and tomato paste. Simmer slowly for 1 hour. Meanwhile, cook noodles according to package directions. Omit salt but add 1 teaspoon olive oil to water. Drain. Cook vegetables according to package directions and drain well. Cut up large pieces. Combine egg, ricotta and half of the Mozzarella cheese.

In a 9 x 13-inch baking dish layer one-third of the noodles, one third of the cheese mixture, one third of the vegetables and one-third of the tomato mixture. Repeat layers twice. Cover with foil and bake in preheated 375-degree oven for 40 minutes.

Remove foil; sprinkle with remaining Mozzarella cheese and bake 10 minutes more or until cheese is melted. Let stand 10 minutes before cutting. Serves 8-10.

VEGETABLE MARINADE

1 can (16-ounce) French cut green beans,
  drained
1 can (16-ounce) peas, drained
1 can (16-ounce) white shoe peg corn,
  drained
4 stalks celery, chopped
1/2 cup onion, chopped
1 small jar pimento, chopped
1 green pepper, chopped

MARINADE:
1 tablespoon salt
3/4 cup vinegar
1/4 cup Puritan oil
1 tablespoon water

Combine all marinade ingredients together and blend well. Pour over vegetables and let stand in refrigerator for 24 hours. This salad will keep for days. If you cannot find the shoe peg corn, buy the small yellow or white kernel corn.

ROASTED POTATOES

2 large baking potatoes, cut into l-inch chunks
1 1/2 teaspoons prepared mustard
1 1/2 teaspoons Dijon mustard
1 teaspoon olive oil
1 clove garlic, minced
1 teaspoon parsley, dried
1/2 teaspoon tarragon
1/4 teaspoon paprika
1/4 teaspoon lemon pepper

Mix prepared mustard, Dijon mustard, oil, garlic, parsley, tarragon, paprika and lemon pepper in a large bowl and blend into a smooth paste. Add the potatoes and toss until well-coated. Place on a lightly greased baking sheet in a single layer. Bake in a preheated 425-degree oven for 45 minutes. Serves 2-3.

❖❖❖

LITE LIFE MIXED VEGETABLES

1 large onion, chopped
1 teaspoon minced garlic
1/4 cup water
1/2 cup chopped fresh parsley
1 1/2 teaspoons dried basil
1/4 teaspoon salt
1/4 teaspoon pepper
1 cup carrots, freshly cooked and cut into
  thin slices
1 cup zucchini, freshly cooked and cut into
  slices
1 cup red or green bell pepper, parboiled and
  cut into 1/2-inch pieces

Cook onion, garlic and water in a covered skillet over medium heat for 12 to 15 minutes until onion is tender. Stir several times during cooking. Stir in parsley, basil, salt and pepper; then the vegetables. Heat thoroughly. Serves 8.

PEGGY'S WALNUT BROCCOLI STIR FRY

1 pound tofu
2 tablespoons oil
1 cup water
1/2 teaspoon salt
2 carrots, cut in thin slices
2 cups broccoli floweretes
2 or 3 bunches green onions, thinly slices
2 tablespoons oil
1 cup sliced mushrooms
1 cup walnut halves
1 tablespoon cornstarch
3 tablespoons soy sauce
1/2 teaspoon freshly ground black pepper
Rice, prepared to serve 6

Cut tofu into 1-inch cubes and brown lightly in oil. Bring water to a boil with salt in a small saucepan. Boil carrots and broccoli for 1 minute. Drain, reserving liquid. Sauce green onions in 2 tablespoons oil; add sliced mushrooms and walnut halves.

Increase heat to medium, add carrots and broccoli. Stir and add tofu. To reserved vegetable stock add cornstarch, soy sauce and pepper. Pour over vegetables and stir, cooking until bubbling. Serve over cooked rice. Serves 6.

BROWN-RICE PILAF

1 1/2 cups boiling water
1 chicken bouillon cube
1/2 cup brown rice, uncooked
1/2 cup onion, chopped
1 can (3-ounce) sliced mushrooms
1 teaspoon salt
1/4 teaspoon pepper
Dash dried thyme leaves
1/2 cup celery, thinly sliced

In a 1-quart casserole, add water to bouillon, stirring until dissolved. Add remaining ingredients, except celery. Bake, covered in preheated 350-degree oven for 1 hour. Stir in celery with a fork. Bake 15 minutes longer; fluff rice with fork. Serves 6.

GREEN PEPPER AND MUSHROOMS

1 tablespoon vegetable oil
1 cup onion, thinly sliced
3 green peppers, sliced in 1/4-inch rings
1/2 pound fresh mushrooms
1 teaspoon salt, optional
1/8 teaspoon crushed dried red pepper
1/8 teaspoon dried oregano leaves
1/4 teaspoon dried parsley leaves

Heat oil in skillet; saute onion, stirring until golden. Add remaining ingredients and cook over medium heat for 5 minutes, stirring occasionally. Serves 4.

Light Hearted

STIR-FRY VEGETABLES

1 1/2 pounds fresh broccoli
3 tablespoons Puritan oil
1 teaspoon sesame oil
1 clove garlic, minced
1 cup chicken broth
1 can (16-ounce) bean sprouts, drained
1 can (8-ounce) water chestnuts, drain and
 sliced
1/4 pound fresh mushrooms, sliced
1 package (6-ounce) frozen snow peas,
 thawed
2 teaspoons cornstarch
1 teaspoon sugar
1/8 teaspoon ground ginger
1 tablespoon light soy sauce
1 tablespoon toasted sesame seeds

Remove flowerets from broccoli and cut in half. Cut stalks in 2 x 1/4-inch strips. In a 12-inch skillet or wok, heat oil until hot. Add broccoli and stir-fry 1 minute. Add garlic and 1/2 cup of the chicken broth. Cover and cook 3 minutes. Uncover and stir-fry 2 more minutes. Add bean sprouts, water chestnuts, mushrooms and pea pods. Stir-fry 2 minutes. Combine cornstarch, sugar, ginger, soy sauce and remaining 1/2 cup of chicken broth and stir to blend. Stir cornstarch into skillet, cook until mixture comes to a boil. Boil 1 minute; spoon onto heated platter and sprinkle sesame seeds over the top. Serves 4.

STIR-FRY PEPPERS AND ZUCCHINI

4 tablespoons Bertoli olive oil
1 large red onion, cut into strips
1 large green pepper, cut into thin strips
2 small zucchini, cut into thin strips
1 cove garlic, minced
2 tablespoons basil, fresh or 2 teaspoons
 dried
1/4 tablespoon thyme, fresh or 1/4 teaspoon
 dried
2 teaspoons parsley, fresh or 1/2 teaspoon
 dried
1/2 teaspoon lemon pepper
Dash of salt

Heat olive oil in large skillet over high heat. Add onion, garlic and stir-fry until golden, about 2 minutes. Add zucchini, green pepper and herbs; stir-fry another 2 minutes. Sprinkle with lemon pepper and salt (optional).

Jo and Jan say, "We think this is delicious with steak and rice."

COOKIE SHEET POTATOES

5 baking potatoes, thinly sliced
1/2 cup margarine
Salt to taste
Pepper to taste
Sprinkles of parsley
Sprinkle of red pepper

Wash and thinly slice potatoes. Arrange slices on a jelly roll pan with slices overlapping. Pour melted margarine over potatoes and sprinkle with salt and pepper. Bake in preheated 400-degree oven for 45 minutes or until potatoes are crisp. Sprinkle with parsley and red pepper. Serves 3 - 4.

Note: If potatoes seem a little dry, add more margarine.

❖❖❖

DILL YOGURT SAUCE

1 tablespoon diet margarine
2 teaspoons flour
1 tablespoon onion, minced
1/2 teaspoon paprika
1/4 teaspoon parsley
1/4 teaspoon dill weed
1/2 cup skim milk
3 tablespoons Parmesan cheese
1 cup plain yogurt
1 egg, beaten

Saute onion in margarine. Blend in flour, paprika, dill weed and parsley. Slowly blend in the milk. Cook and stir until mixture is smooth and thickened. Stir in Parmesan cheese. Blend yogurt with the beaten egg and stir into sauce. Cook and stir over low heat until mixture is well-blended and hot. Makes 1 1/2 cups.

TIPS FOR MARINADES:

- Low-calorie oil and vinegar bottled dressing for steak and ribs
- Tomato marinara sauce for chicken and fish
- Orange juice for chops

LEMON-PEPPER MARINADE

1/4 cup lemon juice
1/4 cup water
1 tablespoon olive oil
1/2 teaspoon fresh dill weed
1/2 teaspoon cracked black pepper
Dash of salt, optional

Combine ingredients and blend well. Makes 1/2 cup.

FLAVOR BLEND FOR BROILING

1/4 cup Dijon mustard
1 garlic clove, minced
1 green onion, minced
1/2 teaspoon basil

Combine mustard, garlic, green onion and basil in small bowl and mix well. Spread on both sides of meat and broil.

MARINADE FOR STEAK

1/4 cup red wine vinegar
2 cloves garlic, minced
1 tablespoon Worcestershire sauce

Combine ingredients and pour over meat. Turn after 1 hour and let marinade season the other side of meat.

❖❖❖

PLUM SAUCE

1 cup fresh plums, finely chopped
1/4 cup dried apricots, soaked in warm water
  1 hour then finely
1/2 teaspoon cayenne pepper
1 teaspoon salt
2 tablespoons water
3/4 cup sugar
1/2 cup vinegar

Combine the plums, apricots, cayenne pepper, salt and one tablespoon water in a heavy saucepan. Bring to a simmer over low heat and cook 15 minutes. Add a little water if the mixture becomes dry. Stir in sugar to taste and vinegar. Simmer 30 minutes more until mixture becomes a chutney-like consistency. Store the sauce in a covered jar in the refrigerator. Wonderful with hot or cold meats.

LOW-CAL SPAGHETTI SAUCE

2 tablespoons Bertoli olive oil
1 large onion, finely chopped
2 large cloves garlic, crushed
2 cans (6-ounce) low-sodium tomato paste
1 can (16-ounce) low-sodium tomatoes with
  liquid, chopped
1 can (16-ounce) low-sodium tomato sauce
2 tablespoons parsley, finely chopped
1 teaspoon dried basil leaves
1/2 teaspoon dried oregano leaves
1/2 teaspoon dried rosemary
1 small bay leaf
1 tablespoon vinegar
1/4 teaspoon salt
1/4 teaspoon freshly-ground pepper

Heat oil over medium heat in a 4-quart saucepan. Saute onion, garlic, parsley, basil, oregano, rosemary and bay leaf for 10 minutes. Stir in vinegar, tomato paste, tomatoes, tomato sauce, salt and pepper. Simmer, partially covered on low heat for 2 hours. Remove from heat and remove bay leaf. Makes 5 cups.

SWEET AND SOUR SAUCE

1 cup sugar
1 cup vinegar
4 tablespoons soy sauce
4 tablespoons sherry
1/2 cup catsup
4 tablespoons cornstarch
1 cup pineapple juice

Combine sugar, vinegar, soy sauce, sherry and catsup in a heavy saucepan and bring to a boil. Add the cornstarch to pineapple juice and stir well. Add the cornstarch mixture to the catsup base, stirring constantly until the sauce thickens.

SOY DIPPING SAUCE

4 tablespoons oil
2 teaspoons green onion, minced
3/4 teaspoon fresh ginger root, minced
2/3 cup soy sauce

Heat oil in saucepan. Add onions and ginger root. Stir-fry 30 seconds and stir in soy sauce; remove from heat. Serve with cooked chicken.

STIR-FRY SEASONING SAUCE

1/2 cup soy sauce
1/2 cup beef bouillon or chicken broth
1/2 cup dry white wine
2 teaspoons sugar
Dash pepper

Combine all ingredients and blend well until sugar is dissolved. Store in refrigerator until ready to use in recipes. Use as taste dictates, usually about 1/2 cup is enough. Makes 1 1/2 cups.

STIR-FRY PEPPER STEAK

2 pounds flank steak, trimmed
2 tablespoons soy sauce
1 tablespoon dry sherry
2 teaspoons cornstarch
4 tablespoons Puritan oil
1 medium-size green pepper, cut into 1/2-inch chunks
1/4 teaspoon ground ginger
Rice

Cut meat lengthwise into thirds and then crosswise into 1/4 inch strips. Combine soy sauce, sherry, cornstarch in a bowl, turning meat to marinate for 30 minutes in the refrigerator. Heat skillet over medium-high heat and add 1 tablespoon oil and thoroughly coat bottom of skillet. Add pepper and stir-fry until crisp-tender, about 2 minutes. Transfer to dish. Pour remaining oil in skillet and heat over medium-high heat. Add ginger and steak with marinade and stir-fry until meat is lightly browned and marinade is reduced, about 2 minutes. Return pepper to skillet and stir-fry until heated through, about 1 minute. Serve over rice. Serves 4.

STIR-FRY SHRIMP WITH BROCCOLI

1 pound shrimp, shelled and de-veined
1/2 pound broccoli
2 teaspoons light soy sauce
3 teaspoons white wine
1 1/2 teaspoons cornstarch
1 tablespoon water
3 tablespoons peanut oil
1 clove garlic, minced
1/4 teaspoon ginger

Cut broccoli floweretes into bite-size pieces. Parboil for 3 minutes, drain and set aside. Mix soy sauce, wine, cornstarch and water and set aside. Heat 1 tablespoon oil in wok or skillet and stir-fry broccoli. Remove and set aside. Heat 2 tablespoons oil, add garlic and ginger. Add shrimp and stir-fry until pink in color. Add broccoli and pour soy sauce mixture over all. Serves 4.

SHRIMP AND CUCUMBERS

1 pound fresh shrimp
1 tablespoon sherry
2 teaspoons salt
2 teaspoons cornstarch
2 medium cucumbers
3 tablespoons oil
1/2 teaspoon sugar
2 slices ginger root
Dash soy sauce

Clean and shell shrimp. Slit lengthwise and rinse in cold water. Mix shrimp with sherry, 1 teaspoon of salt and cornstarch. Peel cucumbers, quarter lengthwise, and cut into1-inch chunks. Heat 1 tablespoon oil in skillet on high heat; add remaining salt and sugar. Add cucumbers and stir-fry until slightly transparent; do not overcook. Remove from heat and transfer to a bowl. Stir-fry shrimp in remaining oil with ginger root. When shrimp turns pink, return cucumber mixture to skillet and mix well. Serves 4.

CHICKEN-CASHEW STIR-FRY

1 pound boneless chicken breasts
2 tablespoons light soy sauce
1 tablespoon cornstarch
2 tablespoons oil
1/2 teaspoon salt
1 small onion, peeled and chopped
1/2 pound mushrooms
2 tablespoons oil
1 package (6-ounce) cashews
1 can (3-ounce) Chinese fried noodles

Cut chicken into strips. Place strips in bowl with soy sauce and cornstarch; blend well. Let stand at room temperature for 10 minutes. Heat oil in wok or skillet over high heat. Add chicken strips and stir-fry until white in color. Add onion and mushrooms. Continue to stir-fry until vegetables are crisp-tender. Add cashews just before transferring mixture to a heated bowl. Sprinkle with Chinese noodles just before serving, or have noodles in a side bowl. Serves 4.

Light Hearted

HOISIN CHICKEN

2 whole chicken breasts
2 teaspoons cornstarch
3 tablespoons oil
2 tablespoons sherry or white wine
6 water chestnuts, sliced
1/2 cup bamboo shoots, sliced
1 medium green pepper, diced
6 fresh mushrooms, sliced
2 tablespoons hoisin sauce

Skin and bone chicken breasts. Cut into large chunks. Mix chicken with sherry and cornstarch. Heat oil in wok or skillet over high heat; stir-fry chicken about 3 minutes until white in color. Do not brown the chicken. Add vegetables and stir-fry thoroughly. Be sure you keep them crispy. Add hoisin sauce and mix carefully through the mixture. Serves 4.

Jo and Jan say, "We like to sprinkle slivered almonds over the mixture before serving. Serve with a side dish of rice."

BEEF STIR-FRY

4 teaspoons cornstarch
1 tablespoon Worcestershire sauce
1 cup beef broth
1/4 cup light soy sauce
1 1/2 pounds beef strips, round, flank or sirloin
1 tablespoon vegetable oil
1 onion, chopped
1 green pepper, chopped
2 stalks celery, sliced diagonally
10 fresh mushrooms, sliced

Dissolve cornstarch in Worcestershire sauce. Mix together with beef broth, soy sauce and set aside. Heat wok or skillet to high heat and stir-fry beef strips until browned. Remove from wok and drain fat. Heat oil in wok and stir-fry onion, celery, green pepper and celery until crisp-tender, about 3 minutes. Add mushrooms, beef and beef broth mixture. Cook and stir until thickened. Delicious served over rice. Serves 4.

HEARTY CLUB SANDWICH

6 slices oat-bran bread, toasted
12 slices onion, thin slices
8 lettuce leaves
8 spinach leaves, stems removed
8 ounces smoked turkey breast, thinly sliced
4 teaspoons Dijon mustard

Layer half of the onions and lettuce on each of 2 slices of toasted bread. Add another slice of bread per sandwich, then the spinach and turkey. Spread remaining bread with mustard and complete sandwiches. Serves 2.

FLANK STEAK WITH BROCCOLI

1 bunch broccoli, stems cut
2 tablespoons oil
1 clove garlic, minced
1 medium onion, sliced
3/4 pound flank steak, cut into 2 x 1 1/2-inch strips
8 mushrooms (optional)
1 teaspoon light soy sauce
1 cup beef broth
1 teaspoon cornstarch
1/4 cup cold water
3 tablespoons hoisin sauce
1/4 teaspoon salt

Blanch broccoli in boiling water for 3 minutes; drain. Heat oil in wok or skillet for 1 minute on high heat, add garlic, onion and salt. Stir and add steak; stir-fry until redness is gone. Add broccoli; stir-fry thoroughly and add mushrooms if desired. Combine soy sauce and beef broth; add to mixture and mix gently. Cover and lower heat to medium and cook 3 minutes. Remover cover and return to high heat. Thicken sauce with cornstarch mixture. Season with hoisin sauce. Serves 4.

BEEF STROGANOFF

1 1/2 pounds beef tenderloin
1 tablespoon flour
1 1/2 tablespoons vegetable oil
1 pound mushrooms, sliced
1 cup green onion, finely chopped
1 clove garlic, minced
1 cup white wine
1/2 cup tomato soup, undiluted
1 cup nonfat yogurt
6 drops Tabasco Sauce
Salt and pepper
Pasta noodles

Cut meat into 1 x 1/4-inch pieces. Season with salt and pepper; toss with 1 tablespoon flour. Melt oil in skillet over medium heat. Add meat strips and saute, turning to brown on both sides. Remove to another container. Melt 1/2 tablespoon oil and add mushrooms, onion, garlic; saute until golden. Stir in tomato soup, Tabasco and wine; simmer a few minutes then add yogurt and meat to this mixture. Simmer slowly for 45 minutes. Serve over hot noodles. Serves 4.

BARBECUED SPARERIBS

2 pounds spareribs
3 tablespoons light soy sauce
1 tablespoon sherry
3 tablespoons hoisin sauce
2 cloves garlic, minced
1 tablespoon sugar
1 tablespoon honey
2 tablespoons chicken broth
1 tablespoon oil

Remove fat and trim ribs. Leave the ribs in one or two sheets, but cut halfway between each rib. Combine the sauce ingredients and pour over the ribs. Marinate 4 hours, turning the ribs every hour. Place the ribs on a foil covered rack and bake at 375 degrees 1 hour. Serve immediately.

Jo and Jan say, "If you can find the boneless 'country ribs,' they are wonderful. So much meat and no waste from bones." Serves 4.

SWEET AND SOUR CHICKEN

1 3-pound fryer
1 can (15 1/4 ounce) chunk pineapple
1 cup sugar
2 tablespoons cornstarch
3/4 cup cider vinegar
1 tablespoon soy sauce
1/4 teaspoon ground ginger
1 chicken bouillon cube
2 green peppers, cut into 1/2-inch chunks
1/2 cup celery strips

Flour and brown chicken. Meanwhile, drain pineapple juice and mix with water to measure 1 1/4 cups. Blend in sugar, cornstarch, vinegar, soy sauce, chicken cubes and ginger. Boil for 2 minutes.

Place chicken pieces in casserole; pour sauce over and top with pineapple, pepper and celery strips. Bake 30 to 40 minutes in a preheated 350-degree oven. Serves 4.

HERBED CHICKEN A LA ORANGE

4 chicken breasts, cleaned and deboned
6 tablespoons chopped scallions
1 teaspoon paprika
1/2 teaspoon dried crushed rosemary
1 teaspoon dried basil
1/2 teaspoon curry
1/2 teaspoon garlic salt
1/2 teaspoon white pepper
1 1/2 cups fresh orange juice
Fresh carrots, peeled and cut into strips

Prepare chicken breasts. Mix scallions, herbs, paprika, herbs, salt and pepper. Rub chicken pieces with mixture, covering well. Place in shallow casserole. Place carrot strips around chicken and bake in preheated 300-degree oven for 1 hour or until tender. Baste frequently with orange juice until chicken is brown. This is delicious with brown rice. Serves 4.

❖❖❖

SHRIMP-CHICKEN ORIENTAL

1 small boneless, skinless chicken breast
8 shrimp
1/2 green pepper, diced
1/2 cup broccoli buds
1 cup snow peas pods
1/2 onion, minced
1/4 teaspoon ginger
1 can (6-ounce) water chestnuts
1 tablespoon soy sauce
1/4 cup water
1 cup cooked rice

Clean and shell shrimp. Cut in half lengthwise. Cut chicken breast in cubes. Steam green pepper, broccoli buds, pea pods and onions until tender, but still crisp. Heat skillet with a little oil; saute shrimp and chicken, stirring constantly, until almost done. Add steamed vegetables, soy sauce, lemon pepper and water chestnuts. Dissolve cornstarch in water and add to mixture. Cook and stir until sauce thickens. Serve with cooked rice on the side. Makes 2 small servings.

Jo and Jan say, "We think this is a wonderful dish for two ladies. We prepared it often when we were working on the book."

CHICKEN GARDEN SKILLET

3 to 4 pound fryer or breasts, legs and thighs
1/4 cup oil
3/4 cup chicken broth
3/4 cup cooking sherry
1 package (10-ounce) frozen artichoke hearts
2 tomatoes, cut in wedges
1 onion, sliced
1/2 green pepper, sliced
Garlic salt and pepper to taste

Preheat wok or skillet. Brown chicken pieces, turning once. Reduce heat; pour in chicken broth and sherry. Cover and cook 45 minutes. Push chicken to side, add artichokes, tomatoes, onion and green pepper. Cover and cook just until artichokes are done. Serves 4.

Jo and Jan say, "We like to use just chicken breasts. Also, we have been known to throw everything in the crisper into it. We love veggies, and this presents a great opportunity to use bits and pieces."

ORANGE GLAZED CHICKEN BREASTS

3 medium chicken breasts, split and skinned
Salt, pepper and paprika to season
1/4 teaspoon finely shredded orange peel
1/2 cup orange juice
1 tablespoon sliced green onion
2 teaspoons instant chicken bouillon granules
1 tablespoon cornstarch
1/2 teaspoon paprika
1- tablespoon cold water
1/2 cup seedless green grapes, halved
Fresh parsley (garnish)

Place chicken in baking dish. Combine orange peel, juice, onion, and bouillon granules. Sprinkle chicken with a little salt, pepper and paprika; cover with orange juice mixture. Cover and bake for 1 hour in a preheated 350-degree oven or until chicken is done. Remove chicken and keep warm. Measure juices in pan, adding water if necessary, to measure 3/4 cup. Combine cornstarch, paprika and cold water in saucepan and stir in pan juices. Cook and stir until mixture thickens and bubbles. Stir in grapes; heat through. To serve, place chicken on serving plate, spoon sauce over chicken and garnish with orange slices and parsley. Serves 6.

LEMONY CHICKEN BREASTS

2 chicken breasts
1 tablespoon dill, dried
1 tablespoon parsley, dried
2 tablespoons green onion, minced
1 clove garlic, minced
1/4 teaspoon lemon pepper
4 tablespoons margarine, melted
Paprika
1 lemon, thinly sliced

Place breasts in small oven dish. Pour melted margarine over breasts and sprinkle with dill, parsley, onions and garlic. Cover with foil and bake in preheated 325-degree oven for 45 minutes. After removing from oven, place lemon slices and paprika on the breasts. VARIATION: You can substitute 2 tablespoons Parmesan cheese for the lemon slices. Serves 2.

SHRIMP ELEGANTE

3 pounds fresh or frozen shrimp in shells or 50 large shrimp
Boiling water
2 packages (6-ounce size) frozen pea pods or may use fresh
3 chicken bouillon cubes
2 1/2 cups boiling water
1/3 cup sliced green onion with tops
3 tablespoons soy sauce
1 teaspoon salt
1/4 cup cold water
1/4 cup cornstarch
4 medium tomatoes, cut into eighths

Thaw frozen shrimp. Peel and devein shrimp; set aside. Pour a little boiling water over pea pods and carefully break apart with fork; drain immediately and set aside. In large saucepan dissolve bouillon cubes in the 2 1/2 cups boiling water; add shrimp, green onions, soy sauce and salt. Return to boiling; cook for 3 minutes, stirring occasionally. Slowly blend cold water into cornstarch, stir into shrimp mixture. Cook, stirring constantly until mixture is thick and bubbly. Add tomatoes and pea pods. Cook until tomatoes are heated through, about 3 minutes. Serves 12.

LOW-CAL FISH SAUCE

1 carton (8-ounce) plain low-fat yogurt
1 small cucumber, finely chopped
1 tablespoon Dijon mustard
1 teaspoon horseradish sauce
1 1/2 teaspoons green onions, minced
3/4 teaspoon dried dillweed
1/2 teaspoon lemon juice
1/4 teaspoon lemon pepper
1/2 clove garlic, minced

Combine all ingredients. Chill in a covered bowl. Makes 2 1/4 cups.
Jan and Jo say, "This is a wonderful sauce for your fish. No longer will you be tempted to reach for the rich Hollandaise sauce."

SEAFOOD ROLLUPS

6 lasagna noodles
1 can (16-ounce) Italian-style tomato sauce
1 can (6-ounce) crab
1 cup ricotta cheese
1/4 cup Parmesan cheese, grated
1 egg, beaten
1 tablespoon dried parsley flakes
1/4 teaspoon onion powder

Cook noodles according to package directions. Rinse in cold water and drain well. Combine crab, cheese, Parmesan cheese, egg, parsley and onion powder. Spread 1/3 cup filling on each noodle. Roll tightly and place seam-side down in a 9-inch square baking pan. Pour sauce over rollups. Bake covered in a 375-degree oven for 30 minutes. Serves 6.
Jo and Jan say, "This is a wonderful filling to use with orange roughie. Use the same procedure with the fish fillet as with the lasagne noodle. You might have to use a toothpick to seal the rollup; it depends on the fish."

❖❖

GOOD NEWS FOR CHOCOHOLICS

Are you a chocoholic? You may still have your chocolate and eat it too. Use unsweetened cocoa. Yes, the American Heart Association recommends that people on low-fat diets cook with unsweetened cocoa. You can do this if...

The recipe calls for 1 ounce of chocolate, use 3 level tablespoons cocoa and 1 tablespoon shortening.

The recipe calls for 1 package (6-ounce) or 1 cup semi-sweet chocolate chips or 6 blocks (1 ounce each) semi-sweet chocolate, use 6 tablespoons cocoa, 7 tablespoons sugar and 1/4 cup shortening.

CHOCOLATE MERINGUES

3 egg whites, room temperature
1/4 teaspoon cream of tartar
3/4 cup sugar
1/4 cup unsweetened cocoa

In small bowl, beat egg whites with electric mixer on high speed until they start to peak. Gradually add sugar, beating after each addition of sugar. When mixture is thickened and forms peaks, stop beating. Sift half of cocoa over egg whites and blend carefully into whites. Gently fold in the remaining cocoa.

Preheat oven to 275 degrees. Grease 2 cookie sheets. With 2 heaping tablespoons of mixture, drop on sheet and build up sides about 1 inch. Be sure you have the bottom thick enough so that when you fill them there is enough base under the filling. Bake in preheated oven for 1 hour. Makes 6.

Jan and Jo say, "We like to make meringues in the evening. Put the cookie sheets of meringues in the preheated oven. Turn off your oven and let them sit in the oven all night and don't peek. A great way to let them sit where there is no moisture, which is so important to making meringues. Fill with fresh fruit of any kind. It is all delicious. Top the filling with a dab of whipped topping if you like."

CHOCOLATE MONK ICE

3/4 cup sugar
1/2 cup unsweetened cocoa
2 cups low-fat milk
2 tablespoons Frangelico liqueur
1 cup strawberries, sliced

Combine sugar and cocoa in a small saucepan. Gradually stir in milk and cook over low heat, stirring constantly until mixture is smooth; do not boil. Remove from heat and stir in liqueur. Pour mixture into a medium-size bowl; cover and freeze until firm. Stir several times while freezing. Stir in strawberries and freeze until firm. Spoon mixture into blender and blend until mixture is smooth; return to bowl and freeze again until firm. Set out until it softens and spoon into chilled dishes. Serves 2.

RUTH'S OIL PIE CRUST

1 cup plus 2 tablespoons flour
1/4 teaspoon salt
1/3 cup Mazola oil
3 tablespoons milk or cold water

Combine ingredients and mix well. Dampen table or counter top. Lay a strip of waxed paper on damp counter, then dough and top with a strip of waxed paper. Roll until thin. Peel off top paper; pick up paper with crust and place on pie pan. Peel off waxed paper and shape in pan. Roll out the top crust in the same manner. Makes 1 small pie. If making a 9-inch pie, you may want to double the recipe.

Ruth says, "This is a great pie crust for diabetics."

STRAWBERRY ANGEL TORTE

1 package angel food cake mix
1/3 cup unsweetened cocoa
1 package (2.8-ounce) whipped topping
1 cup cold skim milk
2 cups strawberries, mashed
1 teaspoon vanilla
Whole strawverries, for garnish

In medium-size bowl, combine cocoa and contents of cake flour packet. Mix ingredients as directed on package. Bake and cool as directed.

In large bowl, combine topping mix, milk and vanilla. Whip according to package directions. Blend in mashed strawberries.

Using a serrated knife, cut cake in two and place the bottom half on serving plate. Spread with 1/2 of the topping mixture. Place other half of cake on top and frost with the remaining topping. Garnish with whole strawberries. Serves 12.

SUMMER MEDLEY

1/2 cup frozen orange juice concentrate, thawed and undiluted
1 tablespoon candied ginger, chopped
2 tablespoons honey
1 medium-size peach, sliced
1 medium-size pear, sliced
1 medium-size nectarine, sliced
2 medium-size plums, sliced
1 medium-size orange, sliced
Few sprigs mint

Combine juice concentrate, honey and ginger in a small bowl. In a large glass bowl arrange fruit slices and pour ginger sauce over fruit. Cover and chill. Toss lightly before serving; top with mint sprigs. Serves 4.

PEACH CREME FRAICHE

4 medium-size peaches, peeled and sliced
2 cups plain low-fat yogurt
1 tablespoon honey
Few drops almond extract
2 envelopes unflavored gelatin
2 tablespoons water
Mint

Combine peaches, yogurt and almond extract in blender and blend until smooth; add honey. In small saucepan combine gelatin and water and stir until gelatin is dissolved. Remove from heat and add to peach mixture. Turn blender on medium and blend until smooth. Spoon into glasses and the creme fraiche will thicken as it chills. Garnish with sprigs of mint. Serves 3-4.

MINTED MELON BALLS

1 ripe, firm cantaloupe, halved and seeded
1 ripe, firm honeydew melon, halved and seeded
1/4 ripe watermelon, seeded
2/3 cup Cointreau (optional)
2/3 cup fresh mint leaves, chopped

Using a melon-ball scoop, cut balls from the melons and place in chilled glass bowl and cover with Cointreau. Stir well and chill. Just before serving, sprinkle mint over the top. Serves 8. This is a wonderful summer dessert or side dish. It is so pretty in the glass bowl, but you might like to serve it in the decorated and carved watermelon shell.

Light Hearted

LOW - CAL CHEESECAKE

1/2 cup fine graham crackers
4 tablespoons margarine, melted
1 cup low-fat cottage cheese
2 packages (8-ounce size) Neufchatel cheese
3/4 cup sugar
2 tablespoons flour
1 teaspoon vanilla
3 eggs
1/4 cup skim milk
1 cup fresh strawberries, peaches or blueberries
1/2 cup low-fat yogurt
2 teaspoons skim milk
1/4 teaspoon vanilla

Combine crumbs and margarine and press on bottom of an 8-inch springform pan. Process undrained cottage cheese in blender until smooth. Beat in Neufchatel, sugar, flour and 1 teaspoon vanilla. Add eggs and beat until mixture is smooth, but do not overbeat. Stir in 1/4 cup milk. Turn into prepared pan. Bake in preheated 375-degree oven for 45 minutes; cool. Remove springform and chill pan with mixture. Arrange fruit on top of cheesecake. Combine yogurt, milk and vanilla; drizzle over fruit and chill until ready to serve. Serves 12.

BRANDY ALEXANDER SOUFFLE

1 envelope unflavored gelatin
1 cup skim milk
4 eggs, separated
Non-nutritive sweetener equivalent to 1/3 cup sugar
1/8 teaspoon salt
2 tablespoons brandy
3 tablespoons creme de cacao
1/3 cup sugar

Prepare a 1-quart souffle dish (See index How To Prepare A Souffle Dish).

Soften gelatin in 1/2 cup cold milk in top of double boiler. In bowl, beat together egg yolks and remaining milk; add to gelatin mixture. Place over boiling water and cook, stirring, until gelatin dissolved and mixture thickens slightly, about 5 minutes. Remove from heat; stir in sweetener, salt, brandy and creme de cacao. Chill, stirring occasionally, until mixture mounds slightly when dropped from a spoon.

Beat egg whites until stiff but not dry; gradually add sugar and beat until very stiff. Fold into gelatin mixture. Spoon into prepared souffle dish. chill until set; several hours, or overnight. Remove collar and garnish with frosted grapes if desired. Serves 6-8.

POACHED PEAR FANS

2 medium-size firm, unpeeled pears
1 1/2 cups water
2 tablespoons frozen orange juice, thawed and undiluted
1 stick cinnamon (2-inch)
Raspberry Sauce (See index)

Cut pears in half lengthwise; core and place cut-side down in a large kettle or Dutch oven. Combine water and orange juice; stir well and pour over pears. Add cinnamon stick; bring to a boil over medium heat. Cover, reduce heat and simmer 10 minutes or until pears are tender but firm. Remove from heat; let cool in liquid. Make Raspberry Sauce.

Remove pears from liquid; place each half cut-side down and slice lengthwise into 1/4-inch strips, leaving stem end or pear unsliced.

Spoon prepared Raspberry Sauce onto each of 4 dessert plates; place a pear half on each plate, fanning out the slices. Serves 4.

Jo and Jan say, "This is a beautiful dessert and low in calories. We garnish it with fresh mint and fresh raspberries, if in season."

OATMEAL - RAISIN COOKIES

1/2 of 1 package (8-ounce) lite cream cheese
1/3 cup sugar
2 tablespoons honey
2 teaspoons vanilla
1 large egg
3/4 cup flour
1/8 teaspoon soda
1/4 teaspoon cinnamon
3/4 cup old-fashioned rolled oats
1/2 cup seeded raisins
1/2 cup pecans, chopped

In medium-size bowl beat cream cheese, sugar, honey, vanilla and egg until well blended. In small bowl combine flour, baking soda and cinnamon. With mixer on low combine flour mixture into cream cheese mixture until blended. Stir in oats, raisins and nuts. Drop onto greased cookie sheets and bake in a preheated 350-degree oven for 10 to 12 minutes. Makes about 3 dozen cookies.

FIG BARS

1 1/2 cup figs
2 cups boiling water
1/2 teaspoon cinnamon
1/4 teaspoon nutmeg
1/4 teaspoon salt
1 cup pecans, chopped
1 1/2 cups whole-wheat flour
1 1/2 cups oatmeal
1/2 teaspoon cinnamon
3/4 cup margarine
1/2 cup pecans, chopped

Cook figs in water until tender. Mash and continue to cook until slightly thick. Add cinnamon, nutmeg, salt and nuts.

For pastry, combine flour, oats and cinnamon. Add margarine and nuts. Mix until crumbly and pack half of mixture into a greased 9 x 9-inch pan. Spread filling over pastry; top with rest of pastry mixture. Pack firmly and bake in preheated 375-degree oven for 25 minutes. Cool and cut into bars. Makes 36.

Jan and Jo say, "Try this recipe with apricots instead of figs."

APPLESAUCE SPICE COOKIES

1 cup flour
1 1/4 teaspoons cinnamon
1 teaspoon soda
1/4 teaspoon salt
1/4 teaspoon nutmeg
1/4 teaspoon cloves
1 teaspoon allspice
3/4 cup chopped pecans
1 cup quick oats
1 cup seeded raisins, chopped
1 cup unsweetened applesauce
1/2 cup Puritan oil
2 egg
1 teaspoon vanilla

Combine flour, cinnamon, soda, salt, nutmeg, cloves, allspice and nuts. Stir in raisins, applesauce, oil, eggs and vanilla. Drop by teaspoons onto greased cookie sheet. Bake in preheated 375-degree oven for 12 to 15 minutes. Makes 2 dozen.

DIABETIC DATE NUT CAKE

1/2 cup margarine
1 egg
1 tablespoon diabetic liquid sweetener
1 teaspoon vanilla
1 1/2 cups unsweetened applesauce
2 cups flour
1/4 teaspoon cloves
1/2 teaspoon cinnamon
2 teaspoons soda
1 cup dates, chopped
1 cup pecans, chopped

Cream butter and egg until well blended. Add sweetener, vanilla and applesauce. Mix and beat with electric mixer until creamy. Sift together flour, cloves, cinnamon and soda; add to above mixture. Fold in dates and nuts. Pour into a greased and floured 8 x 8-inch baking dish and bake in a preheated 350-degree oven for 1 hour.

NO CHOLESTEROL DEVIL'S FOOD CAKE

3 cups sifted flour
2 cups sugar
2 teaspoons soda
1 teaspoon salt
6 tablespoons cocoa
3/4 cup Puritan oil
2 cups lukewarm water
2 tablespoons white vinegar
2 teaspoons vanilla

Sift dry ingredients into mixing bowl; add liquids to dry mixture; mixing well. Pour into a greased and floured 9 x 13-inch baking dish. Bake in preheated 375-degree oven for 30 minutes. This batter will be very thick and the cake will stay very moist.

FRESH FRUIT TRIFLE

1 3/4 cups Amaretti cookies, coarsely crushed
3 medium peaches, sliced
3 tablespoons lemon juice
1 quart strawberries, sliced
1 1/2 cups seedless red or green grapes
2 cartons (8-ounce size) vanilla yogurt
1 carton (8-ounce) sour cream

In a 2-quart trifle bowl or large glass bowl sprinkle 3/4 cup of the crushed cookies. Dip peach slices in lemon juice and arrange half of slices, strawberries and grapes over the cookie layer.

In a small bowl combine yogurt and sour cream; blend well. Spoon half of this mixture over the fruit layer. Repeat layers with remaining 1 cup of crumbs, fruit and yogurt mixture. Chill for 2 hours. Serves 14 to 16.

Jan says, "This is a lovely dish to serve to the ladies' groups. Women prefer it more than men. Serve it in view of your guests for added appeal. Also, vary your fruit. I have used blueberries, kiwi, pears and pineapple. A lot of variety in this dish."

YOGURT TOPPING

1 3/4 cup ricotta cheese
1 teaspoon vanilla extract
1/4 teaspoon almond extract
2 tablespoons sugar
1/2 cup low-fat vanilla yogurt

Combine all ingredients in a blender and blend until smooth; refrigerate until ready to use. This is a delicious topping for angel food cake. Top with a fresh strawberry.

–Jan and Jo's Lite Talk–

- Lemon pepper sprinkled over cucumbers is delish.

- Always top your homemade soups with parsley and a little green onion or chives.

- Give your omelettes a boost with chopped fresh tomatoes and parsley.

- Give your biscuits a different flavor by adding chopped parsley or fresh dill to your margarine.

- Use nonfat yogurt blended with parsley and chives for your baked or steamed new potatoes.

- Nonfat yogurt will thicken your soups.

- When a recipe calls for whole milk or cream, substitute the same amount of skim milk, evaporated milk or buttermilk.

- Instead of using rich cookie fillings, try fruit puree or allfruit preserves.

- To bread chicken, dredge it in flour, then in egg whites, then in crushed bran flakes.

- Brazil nuts are good for topping muffins and casseroles.

- Instead of butter sauce on broccoli, use 1 teaspoon corn oil, 2 tablespoons lemon juice, some tarragon, thyme or parsley to taste. Good hot or cold.

- Try apples and raisins tossed in your cabbage slaw. Top with an herb vinaigrette or dressing made with nonfat yogurt, celery seed and honey. Use your imagination.

- Butternut squash is so good topped with pineapple chunks instead of butter.

- Forget the cheese sauce on your cauliflower. Use tomato sauce seasoned with oregano and basil.

- Make a great salad with seafood, grapefruit sections, sliced red onion and drizzle dressing made with honey and citrus juices.

- A great fish idea is to wrap your fish fillets in steamed kale leaves and bake, basting frequently with chicken broth, laced with lemon juice.

- Mix nonfat yogurt or low fat cottage cheese with dill, chives and pepper for baked potato topping instead of sour cream.

- Use the seeded raisins sprinkled on salads to give it a high fiber lift.

- Marinate Tofu in a small amount of low-sodium soy sauce mixed with oil. Stir-fry with vegetables.

- Apricots steamed with chopped dried apricots are good. Put in baking dish and glaze with apricot nectar; bake 15 minutes.

- Dip fillets of white fish in egg white, dredge in mixture of wheat germ and Cajun spices before baking. Such a flavor!

- Cut potatoes into chunks, steam and toss with oil-free salsa and some chili powder.

- Make a paste of prepared mustard, hot pepper sauce, thyme and dill. Rub on fish fillets before baking, grilling or broiling.

- Cottage cheese with lemon juice, garlic, hot pepper sauce, paprika and parsley is great on salad greens or marinated veggies.

- Horseradish and honey is a great dipping sauce for shrimp or crab.

- Substitute olive oil or canola oil for other fats.

- Defat your dairy products by choosing skim and low-fat products over whole-milk products.

- Snack on popcorn, pretzels, ginger snaps, vanilla wafers, fig bars, raisins, dates and apples.

- Always drink 8 glasses of water each day.

- Eat oat-bran muffins of 1/3 cup of dry oat-bran or 1/2 cup cooked beans each day.

- Avoid Cheddar and cream cheese. Use ricotta mozzarella and lowfat cottage cheese.

- Try pungent garlic, onions or leeks to replace the salt in sauces.

- Brush 1/2-inch egg plant slices lightly with olive oil and broil 2 to 3 minutes till tender and flavorful. Yummy!

- Replace up to half the flour in your favorite muffin recipes with oat bran and bake as usual.

- Substitute oat bran for two-thirds of the flour in pancake, waffle and crepe batters.

- Toss a salad together with raw spinach, raw julienned beets, sliced apples and sunflower seeds. Then top the salad with orange juice.

- Make a quick fish sauce by combining mashed avocado, chopped tomato and a dash of hot pepper sauce.

- Fill taco shells with assorted fresh fruits.

-Jan and Jo's Lite Talk Cont.-

- Don't cook your potassium away. Always steam, microwave, stir-fry or eat vegetables raw. Boiling destroys at least 30 per cent of the potassium.

- Eat more sardines. Add to salads or even add them pureed in the salad dressings.

- Put soup stock into a jar and screw the lid on tightly. Invert the jar and place it in the refrigerator. When the soup is cold, the fat will have solidified in the bottom of the jar. Open and pour out the stock. This way the fat can be discarded and you have fat-free soup.

- You can store your bananas in the refrigerator if you place them in a white plastic bag and store them in the crisper. Also, bananas are delicious when put in the freezer. Have you ever tried a frozen banana? You will like!

- Prepare scrambled eggs or omelettes using fewer egg yolks and extra egg whites. Example: scrambled eggs for 4: Use only 4 whole eggs and 4 to 8 egg whites.

- To make gravy without fat, don't use the meat drippings. Combine 1 tablespoon of cornstarch with 2 tablespoons low-sodium fat-free broth. Simmer and stir until mixture has thickened.

- Fill pita pockets with sliced avocado and sprouts.

- Spread English muffins with low-fat cottage cheese and stack with thinly sliced turkey breast.

- Stuff crepes with sardines, onion slivers and sprinkle with low-fat cheese.

- Are you craving an egg? Try the egg substitutes which have about half the fat of whole eggs and none of the cholesterol. Use 1 yolk for every 2, 3 or 4 whites.

- Scramble whites and mix with fresh herbs and low-fat cottage cheese.

- Better believe it! Pasta is actually a slimming complex of carbohydrates. Pasta got the reputation of being fattening because it was dressed up with those rich and creamy sauces. Use olive oil rather then the oils which contain fat. If you do not think you care for olive oil, we suggest you try the extra virgin olive oil that Bertoli puts on the market. The following is a listing of various oils for your use.

- *Virgin:* Top grade of olive oil. Not mixed with refined oils.

- *Extra Virgin:* Has a perfect flavor. It must not have more than 1 percent free oleic acid.

- *Fine Virgin:* This oil meets the same standard, but it may have 1.5 percent free oleic acid.

- *Semi-Fine:* Labels say simply "Virgin." Must have good flavor and no more than 3 percent free oleic acid.

- *Refined:* Oil comes from the processing of oil that is too high in acidity or has an "off" flavor, refining the oil removes extra acid along with color, odor and flavor.

- *Pure:* A mixture of refined and virgin oils. Manufacturers add enough virgin oil to give the mixture the desired flavor and aroma.

- *Light:* The newest variety. Not for the caloric count but for the flavor. Light is pure olive oil made with very little virgin oil. If you want to use olive oil and only want a hint of the olive flavor this one is the best.

- The new heart-friendly factor is that monounsaturated fat should be part of our diet. Olive oil, avocados and nuts are abundant in the monounsaturated fat. A tablespoon of olive oil averages almost 10 grams of monounsaturated fat. So don't forget...a diet enriched with olive oil, served Italian style; salads, vegetables, bread and pasta will lower LDL even more than the low-fat diet without changing HDL.

- *Coconut oil:* High in saturated fat. The only oil from non-animal source that contains cholesterol.

- *Palm oil:* Almost as high in saturated fats as coconut oil.

- *Safflower oil:* High in polyunsaturated fats and highly refined. It has almost no flavor and is good for frying, sauteing, vinaigrettes and mayonnaise.

- *Sesame oil:* Made from toasted sesame seeds. Amounts dropped into Oriental cooking like stir-fry and fried rice at the end of the cooking time lends a distinct sesame flavor.

- *Sunflower seed oil* is high quality. It is nearly orderless, tasteless and pale gold. It is an all-purpose oil used for frying, stir-frying, salads, mayonnaise and salad dressings.

- *Soybean oil:* Most used in the United States. It is used commercially in margarine, vegetable shortening, salad dressing, mayonnaise and ordinary salad and cooking oil. It is high in polyunsaturated fats, but low in monounsaturated fats.

- *Peanut oil:* Adds a great taste to salad dressings. It is high in monounsaturated fats as olive oil.

✧✧

Petals To Parsley

The first blush of spring stirs thoughts to endless hours enjoying Mother Nature.

Sun-kissed days, spring soft rains and soft breezes will entice you to stroll through our garden in great anticipation of what will be.

Upon entering the gate you will discover the wonders of annuals, perennials, bulbs and roses. As you continue further down the path you come upon edible varieties and recipes to savor their bounty.

Perhaps you will find a shade tree where you can rest and muse upon Jan and Jo's Garden Talk and plan your own lifetime friendship with an enchanted garden.

✧✧

Petals to Parsley

❖❖❖

LOVE SEEDS

"Love is something to scatter
Love is something to sow
Where it lands doesn't matter
For love seeds always sow."

ANNUALS

Annual seeds are an ideal start in planting your garden for the beautiful bouquets you will have all summer. They cost very little and most varieties of annuals are very hardy.

Prepare your soil in early spring. Work bone meal into your soil. After planting seeds, lightly cover them with compost, peat moss or potting soil. Cover gently and sprinkle lightly. If you have a memory like us, label your seeds as to what you have planted. Gently sprinkle every day.

Annual flower seeds to plant are zinnias, marigolds, snapdragons, sweet peas, hollyhocks, nasturtiums. Heliotrope is an annual that will permeate a room with its fragrant scent. Sanvitalia is a great yellow bloom like a sunflower that doesn't fade after cutting. It is wise to have scented flowers in your flower bed.

Low growing annuals are verbena, dwarf phlox, sweet alyssum, varigated marigolds petunias and lobia.

Medium growing annuals are lemon-yellow marigolds, salvia and zinnias.

Tallest growing annuals are cosmos, hollyhocks, sunflowers and four o'clocks.

There are many more annual seeds, but these are hardy and look great with your nursery plants.

PERENNIALS

Before you plant perennials, always prepare your soil, Since perennials come up year after year, it is wise to keep the soil well fed and weed free. We use shredded bark among our flowers to keep the weeds out and the moisture in the ground. It gives the bed a finished look.

Low growing perennials are moss phlox, sedum, candytuft, pinks, ajuga.

Medium growing perennials are the poppy, daylily, columbine, and chrysanthemums.

Tall perennials are the iris, delphinium, yarrow, baby's breath, phlox, foxglove and many more.

Let us remember the time to plant and what to plant depends on the planting zone you live in. Consult your nursery.

"To think we used to plant our flowers all in a row like tin soldiers and kept the varieties together..nice..but with the color and variety of flowers, now our beds look like a busy spring hat."

HINT: When planting plants, take a table fork to loosen the ball around the plant so it may breathe when put into the ground. So many plants you buy, you will notice the soil and roots are tightly bound and cannot breathe, so this is important.

Petals to Parsley

CHRYSANTHEMUM

A wonderful pretty, hardy plant that will honor you with its presence summer and fall and come back to see you the followering season, if given TLC. Mums need to have a good soil that has been fed with peat moss, compost or well-rotted manure. Mums will thrive in full sun and should be planted in soil that is well drained. They really like their own plot of ground and will spread readily.

In planting cushion mums, plant them 18 inches apart. To grow taller mums plant them 12 inches apart. Don't crowd your mums and always give them enough room for air to circulate.

There are three rules of thumb to care for your mums in order to have them bloom.

Water mums well at the roots once a week or twice a week in the hot summer. Our nursery man told us to pour a bucket of water on our mums once a week during the winter, if we are having dry weather; they are thirsty plants. During the summer, they thrive on being fed once a month. Use a good food that your nursery man will recommend. When your mums are 6-8 inches tall, begin pinching off the light green growing tips so the plant's foliage will branch out. Pinch back until July 1st. If you want larger blooms, pinch off the growing tips. The third rule is to have a pest control program. If you see aphids, be sure to give the plants immediate attention.

Mums will last a long time as a cut flower if you slit the bottoms of the stems and give the foliage a good soaking before arranging. Our mothers used to soak the bottoms of the stems in freshly boiled water for three minutes so that the sap would come up into the slit stem.

Jan and Jo say, "Be sure to pick off the dead blooms and cut the plants back about 4 inches in the fall. Don't forget mulching with bark around your plants to help keep the moisture in and the weeds out. Happy planting!"

"The kiss of the sun for pardon
The song of the birds for mirth
One is nearer God's heart in a garden
Than anywhere else on earth."

Bulbs

DAHLIAS

Plant 4 inches deep; add 1 tablespoon bone meal to each bulb. Water thoroughly.

Feed in July with a good fertilizer. Continue to pinch off tips of stems to encourage bushier growth. Remove all but one bud from each flower cluster for a single big bloom.

Dig bulbs in fall and store in a dry, cool place. Replant in the spring.

CANNA LILY

Plant cannas after frost. Place bulb in 3-inch soil; sprinkle with 1 tablespoon bone meal, setting the bulbs 18-24 inches apart. Cover with soil and dampen ground well. Plant cannas in a sunny spot that is well-drained.

Canna bulbs come in talls; about 5 feet or dwarfs; about 3 feet high. Very vibrant orange, red, salmon, yellow and pink are the colors to choose. These make a wonderful background or to use for hiding an unsightly scene. The bulbs are very effective planted in clumps.

Dig bulbs in the fall and store in a dry, cool place.

CALLA LILY

Plant callas after danger of frost. Space the bulbs 12-15 inches apart in a rich-moisture soil, adding 1 tablespoon bone meal to each bulb. Callas like partial shade and they grow 15 to 24 inches tall.

The colors are pink, yellow and white. Calla lilies also make wonderful houseplants. Set them in a sunny window.

TUBEROUS BEGONIA

Start bulbs indoors in the early spring and move to the garden after danger of frost. In you cannot plant early, go to the nursery and buy your plants.

Begonias come in many varieties and colors. There are trailing plants for flower boxes or hanging baskets for patio or trees; and they are nice to plant among your other flowers in the garden. Be sure to plant the bulbs in a moist, rich soil in the shade. These bulbs are great to plant in pots so that dogs and children can look, but not touch.

Dig your bulbs in the fall before frost and store in a cool, dry place for the winter.

GLADIOLUS

There are two varieties of gladiolus that stand either 5-feet or 3-feet tall.

Plant the big bulbs 6-inches deep and the smaller bulbs 4-inches deep. Space the bulbs about 5 to 6 inches apart. Sprinkle 1 tablespoon bone meal in the hole and cover lightly. Always moisten the soil. Gladiolus are one bulb you may plant every 2 weeks between May and August. That way, you will have beautiful, colorful spikes all summer.

CALADIUM

You may start your Caladium bulbs indoors in the spring or buy the young plants at your nursery when you start the spring planting. We like to plant our caladiums in pots so we can move them around in our garden or on our patio whenever we like.

If you want the caladiums in your garden, sink the pot into the soil and then when fall comes, just lift the pot out and store it in a dry, cool place. Caladiums prefer partial shade to full sun.

TULIPS

Plant bulbs in a semi-rich soil in October or early part of November. Do not wait until the ground becomes frozen, or you get so involved with the coming Holidays. Dig a 4-inch hole and place the bulb in the hole with the eye up. Sprinkle 1 tablespoon bone meal in the hole and cover it well. Water lightly and patiently wait until spring. If you do not want to wait until spring; plant bulbs in clay pots. Place in a sunny window and keep the soil moist with light watering. You will have spring during the winter months. P.S. They make a wonderful gift for a shut-in or someone in the hospital.

Petals to Parsley

❖❖

DAFFODIL

THAT...TAKE THE WINDS OF MARCH WITH BEAUTY...

Springtime in the winter with the pretty yellow to white daffodils. You may plant these bulbs in clay pots giving them the same care as tulips.

You can make these bulbs bloom early by giving them artificial periods of cold and darkness, forcing the bulb to bloom. Ask your nursery about the precooled bulbs that bloom without forcing.

We personally like to plant the daffodil bulbs in the late fall with our tulips so the beauty may be shared with everyone who passes by.

CROCUS

Another colorful springtime debut! Plant your crocus bulbs in groups around your garden. The planting procedure is like tulip and daffodil bulbs.

Crocuses are so tiny, but vibrant. They are not a cutting flower, but are a wonderful breath of springtime when they are the first to make their appearance along with robin redbreast, saying "spring is just around the corner."

HYACINTH

The perfume-scent hyacinth bulb is another great one to have in your garden. Plant the bulb in a 4-inch deep hole, sprinkle 1 tablespoon bone meal and cover the hole lightly and moisten.

Hyacinths may be planted 3 to 4 inches apart like the other spring bulbs. Also, for a perfume scent in your home, plant the bulbs in clay pots and be sure the fragile hyacinth is not in direct sunlight and is away from heat ducts.

To force hyacinths, tulips and daffodils, move them to a cool, dark place for 13-16 weeks. Keep the bulbs moist, but not wet. The temperature should be between 35° and 50°, In about 10 weeks, check your bulb growth. If the stems are visible; about 1 inch to 2 inches, move them to a warm but not hot area and enjoy watching them grow.

After you realize spring is on the way, get out your seed catalogs and plan your flower and vegetable gardens!

HINTS ON BULB AND FLOWER FOLIAGE

Always pinch the dead flowers off to encourage more beautiful growth and flowers.

When the bulb flowers have withered down, never remove foliage to make room for your oncoming flowers. Braid the leaves and stake them down on the ground because the food from the foliage goes back to the growth of the bulb for the coming season. After this has been done and the foliage has withered away, you may dig the bulbs up and plant them in a spot you won't be using and dig them up next fall to plant. Personally, we haven't had that much luck and like leaving them where they are.

❖❖❖

ROSES

One of the most beautiful perennials of all is the rose. There are Hybrid Tea, Floribundas, Grandifloras and Miniatures. The following roses are ones to start with if you are a novice in the rose garden.

Hybrid Tea	Floribundas	Grandiflora	Miniatures
Peace	Ivory Fashion	Sonia	Beauty Secret
Mr. Lincoln	Little Darling	Love	Rise n' Shine
Chrysler Imperial	Cherish	Prominent	Judy Fisher
Tropicana	French Lace	Camelot	Party Girl
Tiffany	Angel Face	Montezuma	Cinderella
Granada	Iceberg	Pink Parfait	Dreamglo
Pristine	First Edition	Queen Elizabeth	Peaches n' Cream

PRUNING:

Late March or early April is the time to prune your roses.

How much to prune depends on the effect winter has had on your plants. If the canes are blackened down to live wood it is wise to cut that dead wood off and if you have to prune down to the bud union, it won't hurt the bush. It depends on your rose bush. Some will be cut back 12-16 inches others 6-8 inches. Personally, we like to prune back all the dead wood so the bush will be nice and full and not left to be a stringy, unattractive one. Start feeding your roses with a standard rose food or Epson salts. We have used the salts and the roses have done very well. It is cheaper than commercial rose food too. Put Epson salts around each bush about two weeks after pruning. Use about 1 tablespoon of salts per gallon of water and apply about a half-gallon per bush. Make another application in the middle of June. Use a regular schedule. Six weeks after the first application, and again in August. Epson salts make the foliage greener and it encourages basal shoots and makes them stronger.

Roses like to be watered by soaking rather than sprinkling. Start a spraying program after the first few weeks in Spring. Different sprays for different problems are available; consult with your nurseryman. HINT: Put your banana peelings under the leaves of your roses. You may use 7 banana peelings to a plant. Watch the leaves get greener and firmer. Potassium is even good for the roses.

CUTTING YOUR ROSES:

Roses should be cut early morning or in the evening. In France, the roses which are gathered for perfume are picked while they are still wet with dew, before the sun touches them. They are more fragrant at that time. Always cut your rose stem just above a five leaf stem.

Fill a tall vase with 100 degree water mixed with a packet of floral preservative. If you do not have a packet on hand use a mixture of half lemon-flavored soft drink and half water. Warm liquid is always best. Cut the stems diagonally with a sharp knife and put them in the water immediately. Always remove leaves below the water line.

Keep your roses in a cool location and out of direct sunlight. Never put a cut flower on top of the T.V. due to the heat of the set.

Remember, roses need plenty of water, so add fresh water every day.

Roses are red
Violets are blue
Glad to bring our secrets to you...

"Always count your garden by the flowers and not by the falling leaves."

Petals to Parsley

❖❖

AFRICAN VIOLETS

A beautiful flowering houseplant that seems to be the easiest, but hardest to grow with continuous flowers. We hope the following tips will help you to have your non-flowering violet grow into a flowering array of color.

First, you must have the right kind of violet. The Rhapsodie and Ballet violets are best to start in your home. These violets are very compact plants with a single stem and a flat circle of leaves, clear-colored flowers are borne continuously on sturdy stalks.

CARE:

If a violet is too crowded in the pot there are too many suckers growing around the base. Lift the plant from the pot and brush off the soil. With a sharp paring knife, cut away the suckers from the main plant being careful not to disturb roots. Repot all suckers in plastic pots with soilless mix of equal parts of spagnum, peat moss, vermiculite and perlite. Add a finely crushed egg shell to a quart of mix. When watering violets, do not soak. Water lightly until water comes through drainage hole or set pot in a dish of water. Always use tepid water.

To fertilize your violet, use a 15-30-15 to a quart of water once a week. Once every two weeks, use the following mixture. One gallon of rain water combined with a teaspoon of each: baking powder, epson salts, salt peter and household ammonia. Mix and dissolve. Wow! That would make anyone bloom! Amazing results.

Violets do well in a bright, indirect light. They seem to like a northern exposure or a sunny window shielded by a curtain that filters light.

TEMPERATURE:

Violets like temperatures about 65-85 degrees. They will go into shock lower or higher than those temperatures.

INSECTS:

The insects you need to look out for are mealybugs and mites.Mealybugs appear as a white goo under the leaves.Use a cotton swab dipped in alcohol and remove the bugs from the leaves. Repeat every day for a week. Mites are only visible with a magnifying glass. Wash the leaves thoroughly in lukewarm water with a little detergent. Repeat at least 4 times at intervals of 3 days.

A NEW START:

You may start a new violet by suspending the stalk of the leaf by poking a hole into cardboard laid over a glass of water. When roots form, dip the tip of the leaf into hormone powder and put it in to a small container of vermiculite. Cover the container with plastic and set in a warm place. Good luck!

"APRIL SHOWERS BRING MAY FLOWERS"
HINTS TO MAKE CUT FLOWERS LAST DAYS LONGER

a) Pick flowers from your garden early morning or late evening. Never during the hot afternoon.

b) Flowers do best when you cut the bud except for peonies or poppies. If you can't get the flowers in water immediately, put a damp newspaper in your basket with a plastic covering and place the basket under a tree.

c) Always recut the stem on a slant with a 2-inch vertical slit up the middle of the stem. This allows the stem to take more water into the flower.

Stems which are hard and woody should be crushed with a hammer to increase water intake. The stems of woody plants are lilac, peony, hydrangea, mock orange. Daffodils, iris, hyacinths and dahlias bleed a clear sap that causes blockage. To avoid this, squeeze the sap from the lower 2 inches of the trimmed stem and plunge it into boiling water. Or you may pass the stem quickly over a flame to seal the stem.

d) To revive drooping flowers, plunge into 2 inches of boiling water.

ARRANGING:

a) Have a clean container.

b) Use brass pin holders to hold stems, or metal or glass frogs, mesh bag of marbles, foam blocks, but need to check frequently to make sure there is ample water. Never use blocks for tulips, daffodils, etc.

c) When arranging long-stemmed flowers in a wide-mouthed vase, crisscross strips of cellophane tape just inside the top of the vase. This will hold the flowers upright.

TAKING CARE OF THE BOUQUET:

a) Change water daily and clean vase with soapy water.

b) Keep out of direct sunlight and drafts.

c) Rinse stems and recut stems 1/4 inch.

d) Add flower food to water.

FRIENDS AND FOES:

a) Avoid combining poppies, orchids or daffodils with other flowers.

b) Never use fruits and vegetables in the same flower arrangement. As fruit ripens it gives off gas that is harmful to flowers.

c) Tulips and roses are friends who like to be together.

d) A few sprigs of evergreen will keep nasturtiums alive longer.

LONG-LASTING FLOWERS:

Carnation, chrysanthemum, clematis, daisy, cosmos, geranium, marigold, zinnia, gladiolus and snapdragon.

Petals to Parsley

GARDENIA

This plant has to bring back more memories than any other one. And if the truth were known, it has been bought, nurtured and thrown out when one has tried to grow it.

TIPS ON THE GARDENIA

a) A range of temperature 60-70 degrees is ideal.

b) A half day or more in direct sun in winter, much less in summer. Ideal to have on a shady porch or patio.

c) Ideal humidity is 40 per cent during the winter months.

d) Frequent misting is a must.

e) Repot gardenias in the spring with one part each of all-purpose potting soil, sand, sphagnum and peat moss.

f) Gardenias like fish emulsion or a flowering houseplant fertilizer that contains acid. Don't forget your compost dirt. It would be wonderful when you repot.

g) Keep moist soil at all times.

h. If you see bugs rinse the plant good and use a cotton swab dipped in alcohol.

A joy of the garden is its abundance of flowers. The more you cut, the more blossoms you will pick. Share them with your family in the home or take a basket to your friend.

FLOWERS TO DRY

a) Statice
b) Cockscomb, celosia
c) Blue Salvia
d) Baby's breath
e) Starflower
f) Daisy
g) Bells of Ireland
h) Strawflowers
i) Helipterum

Sow the seeds, when plants are grown cut the flowers before they are fully open and hang them in any airy spot until dry. With tender, loving care, the flowers will maintain their color.

ALTERNATE WAY TO PRESERVE:

Your flowers will look garden fresh if you choose flowers that are fresh and free from morning dew. Choose containers with tight-fitting lids. There are many on the market now that would be great for drying flowers. Be sure they are deep enough to cover the whole flower head. Sift in a layer of silica gel and lay selected flowers with a half-inch of their stems in a row. Gently add more crystals until the whole head is covered. Place lid on the container and tape around the edges so that no air can get through. Flowers are ready when petals are dry, but not brittle. Attach wire to end of toothpick protecting and wrap with green florist tape.

Have fun experimenting and seeing the colors change. Flowers tend to darken like pink to red. You may buy the silica-gel at your hobby or garden shop.

COMPOST PIT

A compost pit is so simple and produces such wonderful dark, rich soil. First find a spot that is out of the way and dig a hole 5' x 5' in diameter and at least 3 feet deep. The measurements are to your liking but you need to start at least with this size and making it bigger if you find you can use more. Turn the soil, working it until it is free of chunks, clods or rocks. Start adding grass clippings, small twigs, dry leaves. If you have any fertilizer, dump that in the hole too. Moisten well and start adding your garbage out of the kitchen. We aren't saying table scraps, but peelings from potatoes, oranges, carrots, bananas, apples, tea leaves, coffee grounds and egg shells. Your wood chips are good, also wood ashes, but don't add a lot of ashes at a time. Continue to cover the vegetable matter with grass clippings and such, continuing to to turn it over. This will have no odor as long as you cover with leaves, clippings and such.

Work the soil every two weeks completely turning it over and over. You will find the soil gets darker, richer and begins to feel like your grandma's silk gown. The compost hole will provide you rich dirt as long as you feed it. Also, it is wise to put a wire around it to keep the animals out.

Come spring, you will be glad you have started a compost because the richness of the dirt makes for beautiful flowers and vegetables; you may decrease the amount of peatmoss and potting soil in your garden.

PRETTY AND EDIBLE

Chrysanthemums are the most edible flower. Leaves and flowers are great in stir-fry dishes.

Lavender is very good in savory and sweet Provencal dishes. The flavor is delicate and fragrant.

Impatients are great for garnish, but are not edible.

Rose petals look and smell pretty among desserts or salads. An added attraction is to paint the petals with egg whites and sprinkle with sugar. Set on racks to air dry. Rose hips are used in teas.

Nasturtiums are the blossoms used in salads to give it a spicy taste and that pretty touch.

"To see a world in a grain of sand
And a Heaven in a wild flower
Hold infinity in the palm of your hand
and Eternity in an hour."
—*William Blake*

WILDFLOWERS

Spring and fall are the best times to start wildflowers from seed. Before planting, spade the ground to a dept of 8-10 inches making the surface free of stones and very smooth. It is very important to have a rich, moist soil so use the dirt from your compost pit or vermiculite. After the soil is prepared, sow the seeds thinly in clumps and keep the area moist until the seeds have germinated. You may start your wildflower seeds in a flat to transplant to their bed when time.

If you are planting plants, pick a cloudy, cool day. This is best for the wildflowers. If this isn't possible and the day is warm and sunny, keep the roots covered by wet newspaper until you are ready to plant. This is a rule of thumb for all plantings.

Wildflowers thrive in partial shade. They flourish along the north side of the house and large shrubs like a lilac and forsythia bush. Of couse, if you have large spaces, you can have your own beautiful meadow of wildflowers!

Petals to Parsley

✦✦

Jan And Jo's Garden Talk

• Buttermilk is a cure for spider mites on outdoor ornamental plants. Mix 1/2 cup buttermilk, 4 cups wheat flour, 5 gallons water. Strain mixture through cheesecloth and spray on plants.

• Fruit cocktail is great for Japanese beetles. Open 1 can fruit cocktail and let it sit in the sun for a week to ferment. Stand it on bricks or wood blocks in a light-colored pail. Fill the pail with water to just below the top of the can and put it 25 feet from the plants you want to protect. Now the bad news. If it rains and dilutes the mixture, you will need to start over.

• Soapsuds make a good killer for soft-bodied pests such as aphids. Mix 1 teaspoon of liquid dishwashing detergent in a gallon of water and spray the underside of leaves every 5 days for 15 days and repeat once a week thereafter until the insect problem is gone.

• Bleach is good to protect ripening tomatoes from fungus diseases. Wash with a solution of 1 tablespoon of bleach to a quart of water and dry with a paper towel. Wrap each tomato in newspaper and store in a tray in a cool place, around 55 degrees.

• Talcum powder is great if you are plagued by rabbits. Try dusting your plants with ordinary talcum. It works like a charm in getting rid of flea beetles on tomatoes, potatoes, peppers and other plants.

• Garlic is a great way to keep cats and dogs away. Chop a large onion or a bulb of garlic, add a tablespoon of cayenne pepper and steep in a quart of water for an hour. Add 1 teaspoon of liquid dishwashing detergent to help the mixture stick to the plant. Strain what you need into a sprayer or watering can and sprinkle it on the plant leaves. The rest will keep for several weeks in the refrigerator so you may use it again.

• If your azaleas and gardenias need an acid soil you may use vinegar. Add 2 tablespoons vinegar to a quart of water and pour a cupful or so around the base of a plant every 2-3 weeks until the yellow leaf disappears.

• Vinegar is also useful in making a preservative for cut flowers. Mix 2 tablespoons of white vinegar and 2 teaspoons of cane sugar in a quart of water. Use in the vase instead of plain water.

• Epson salts is not only great for roses but your vegetable garden. Use a foliar spray, apply at the rate of 3 ounces per gallon of water. For a soil application, use 4 tablespoons per plant.

• Clay pots - never throw away your broken clay pots. Use large pieces to cover the drainage hole for plants you are potting up. If you don't have broken pots, use gravel. Plant your young plants in pots in the spring. Be sure you don't overcrowd.

• Pots are great fillers in a garden when you have an empty space or when you entertain. They may be placed in precarious places that are pleasing to the eye. If the plants get too big in the pots, transfer them to the garden. Great when you have lost a flower and have a sad, empty space.

• To prevent clay pots from cracking during the winter months, bury small pieces of an old garden hose crosswise in the potting soil. Allow for expansion when the pot freezes.

• Fish emulsion is a wonderful fertilizer for your summer plants. Use it once a month.

"If the day and night be such that you greet them with joy, and life emits a fragrance like flowers and sweet-scented herbs, is more elastic, more immortal, that is your success. All nature is your congratulation, and you have cause momentarily to bless yourself"

— Henry David Thoreau

HERBS

BASIL: Fragrant with a sweet taste. Several fragrances are offered. Buy seeds or plants. Pick fresh by picking leaves. Very good in tomato dishes, soups, salads, stew, meats, potatoes and egg dishes. Annual.

CHERVIL: Has an anise flavor. Buy plants or seeds and plant in partial shade. Use in salads, soup, egg dishes, spinach and fish. Annual.

CHIVES: A mild-flavored herb that is from the onion family. Snip leaves as needed for omelets, dips, salads, soups and sauces. A nice filler in bouquets because of the pretty purple flowers. Use it anywhere you would use a mild onion flavor. Perennial.

GARLIC CHIVES: A garlic-flavored chive that may be substitutes for garlic. It has a pretty white flower. Perennial.

DILL: Plant the seeds in your garden. The leaves can flavor salads and meats. Also good in fish, vegetables, sauces and used a lot in pickle preserving. Annual.

FENNEL: A pleasant sweet licorice-flavored herb. Good for fish, breads, pastry, salads, pickles. Annual.

MARJARAM: This herb likes a hot, dry location. It sprawls so give it some room. Seeds or plants do well. Use leaves in soup, tea, salad, meat, fish, egg dishes and vegetables. Perennial.

MINT: A very easy healthy herb to grow. Put it in a moist location and give it plenty of room to grow. Will take over most any flower around. Great to pick for ice-tea, hot tea, jelly, most summer drinks, peas, lamb sauce. Perennial.

OREGANO: A strong heavy flavor known as the pizza herb. Has bitter undertones so taste the leaf to be sure you are getting the plant you want. Use leaves in tomato sauces, stews, egg dishes, vegetables, salads and soups. Annual.

PARSLEY: Different leaf types. Buy plants or if you buy seeds soak overnight before planting. A wonderful garnish and a breath sweetener. A wonderful source of potassium. Also looks great in your garden as an edging plant or among the flowers. A "must" in salads, soup, sauces, stew, egg dishes, vegetables. We always keep some on hand for a touch of garnish on serving plates or platters. Biennial.

ROSEMARY: Sweet scent and a bold flavor. It is a small evergreen shrub and not hardy so take it indoors during the winter. The leaves are resinous and spicy. Use sparingly with pork, lamb, vegetables, fish, stew, egg dishes, sauces and save some to put in your potpourri and sachets.

SAGE: A wonderful dressing herb. Buy plants, they look like shrubs. Use it in cheese, meats, fish, stew and tea.

TARRAGON: A very aromatic, full-flavored herb. Use leaves in vinegars, sparingly in salads, sauces, fish and poultry. Perennial.

THYME: A strong and slightly sharp taste. Good in meats, soups, vegetables, dips, omelets, dressing and soups. Perennial.

Now that you have grown your herbs and had them at your fingertips, whether at your back door or windowsill, you will want to start picking them to have during the winter months.

DRYING HERBS

To preserve the harvest for year-round cooking, tie the fresh herbs in small bunches and hang them on an overhead pot rack to dry. Easy to get to when you need to reach for herbs for your soups, salads, etc. Also, hang them in a dry, warm place out of direct sunlight where the air will circulate around the plants. Let the herbs dry until the leaves are brittle which will take a few weeks. Then pick off the leaves and discard the stems. Store in a tightly-covered container.

Petals to Parsley

HARVESTING

Herbs are more flavorful when your plant starts to produce. The more oil in the leaf, the more flavor your herb will produce.

Remember, you will have two good cuttings with Summer Savory and Tarragon. Oregano has three cuttings and the great thing about Parsley, you can pick it all summer.

Rinse the herbs in cool water and discard any damaged leaves. We like to pick them early in the morning and put them in a glass of water covered by plastic and put them in the refrigerator. Parsley is a great herb to have for a long period of time. Rinse it good, put it in a plastic bag and stuff it in a jar with a lid. It will keep a good two weeks. It is great in the winter when you have to buy it at the store. By storing this way, you can always have parsley on hand. Also, if your parsley is limp, douse it in warm water then plunge it in ice cold water. It will perk up like a wilted daisy.

Pick herbs before blossoming. Gather herbs on a clear day as soon as the dew has dried and before the oils begin to evaporate in the heat of the sun. Wash gently in cold water, then spread on towels to dry. Put a handful of herbs in a clean sterilized bottle, pour in enough vinegar to cover the herbs completely and cap the bottle. Place the bottle in a sunny window for about 10 days. The heat of the sun draws the flavor from the herb and the wilting leaves.

FREEZING HERBS

Dill and chives freeze well. Basil, parsley and tarragon will freeze for about 2 months but will be limp when taken out of the freezer. The taste is still there, but put them in a dish that requires cooking. Always put your herbs in a moisture-free bag, seal, label and freeze.

Fresh herbs are not as strong as dried herbs, so you have to use more of them in a recipe. It takes three times as much fresh herb to give you the same flavor. Use about one-third as much of the dried herb in a recipe.

Herbs are a wonderful sodium-free replacement and always gives that recipe an extra boost. That's why they are excellent for those of us on diets.

HINT: Use the pungent herbs such as rosemary, thyme or marjoram in your barbecue grill. Wait to add branches just before the food is to be put on the grill; it will give a wonderful flavor to your fish, meat and chicken.

What gives more satisfaction then growing herbs for culinary purposes, vinegars, oils, potpourris or making wreaths. Such a small item to give such pleasure for you or your friends.

Jan and Jo say, "when our flowers are resting and there are no blossoms to pick, we use the herb foliage to make our bouquets. They are great for a picnic or patio get-together."

"He who plants trees loves others beside himself."

—*English Proverb*

"The earth yields us blessings every year, and friendship every moment."

— *Unknown*

TOMATOES:

Preparing the soil: If you are aware that your soil is not good for your new crop of tomatoes it is a good idea to broil (yes, broil) the soil. Kills off fungus and it will give your tomatoes a lift to be planted in soil that has been more or less purified. Cover your tomato bed with a sheet of plastic. When the sun hits the plastic the soil will heat up. It will take four days of hot sun to broil your dirt. The temperature must get up to 160 degrees. An old gardener told us this trick and it really works.

After frost, plant tomato plants in a well-drained soil and in a location that will be sunny and out of the wind. Never plant tomatoes in the same location as the year before. Mulch plants to keep soil moisture and temperature constant. Straw or grass clippings are a good mulch.

PROBLEMS

Tomatoes may have the following problems:

• Blossom-end rot: Caused by change in soil moisture.

• Blossom drip: Unseasonable cool or hot weather during the blooming stage. The remedy is to keep plants warm at night by covering them with cloths. Protect from the wind.

• Sun scald: Too much sun. Plants damaged by disease or insects have insufficient leaf cover. The remedy is to let plants sprawl on the ground so they'll shade themselves from full sun.

• Fruit cracks: Cracks often found on tomatoes are caused by sudden change of weather. Full exposure to sun due to lack of foliage can cause cracking. The remedy is to mulch plants to keep soil moisture constant.

ROSE POTPOURRI

6 cups dried rose petals
1/2 teaspoon ground cloves
1/2 teaspoon ground cinnamon
2 teaspoons orange peel strips, dried
1/2 teaspoon rosemary
1/2 teaspoon mint flakes
1 tablespoon orris root

Add spices to dried rose petals. Dry strips of orange peel in oven on low heat for 1/2 hour. Sift in orris root. Mix in wide bowl and pack in large glass jar. Cover tightly but open the container every few days to stir the mixture. Variation: Add summer daisies or marigolds for fresh color in glass jar with spices.

SPICE POTPOURRI

1 quart rose petals
1/2 pint lavender flowers
1/2 pint geranium flowers
1 teaspoon anise seed
1 tablespoon cloves
1 tablespoon nutmeg
1 tablespoon cinnamon
1 tablespoon crushed benzoin
Floral oil of choice

Mix rose petals with lavender and geranium flowers. Mix anise seed, cloves, nutmeg and cinnamon; crush. Add jasmine, patchouli, spring or rosemary oil to crushed benzoin. Blend all together.

GARDEN ITALIAN SEASONING

2 tablespoons dried oregano
2 tablespoons dried marjoram
2 tablespoons dried basil
4 teaspoons dried savory
2 teaspoons dried rosemary
2 teaspoons dried sage

Mix the herbs together. Store in airtight container. Makes 1/2 cup.

SALAD HERBS

1 tablespoon dried parsley
1 tablespoon dried basil
1 tablespoon dried tarragon
1 tablespoon dried thyme

Mix herbs thoroughly and store in an air-tight container. Add to salads, meats and vegetables in place of salt.

HERB DRESSING

1/2 cup Bertoli olive oil
1/3 cup red wine vinegar
2 tablespoons salad herbs
1 teaspoon sugar
1/4 teaspoon salt
1/4 teaspoon ground pepper

Combine above ingredients into a jar and shake vigorously. Spoon over mixed greens, tomatoes or cucumbers. Makes 1 cup.

HERB ZESTY

1 cup fresh basil leaves
1 cup fresh oregano leaves
1 cup fresh parsley leaves
1 cup fresh thyme leaves
2 1/2 tablespoons Dijon-style mustard
2 cloves garlic, minced
1/2 cup olive oil
1/4 cup Parmesan cheese, grated

Combine the leaves of the four herbs, garlic and 1/2 cup olive oil in a blender or food processor. Blend until mixture is smooth. If mixture seems to be thick, add more oil until the mixture is the consistency of mayonnaise. Stir in Parmesan cheese. Cover and chill. Makes 1 cup.

AUNT MARIE'S SPICED PEACHES - 1934

8 pounds peaches
8 1/2 cups sugar
4 cups vinegar
2 cups water
7 pieces stick cinnamon
2 tablespoons whole cloves
2 tablespoons allspice

Prepare syrup of sugar, vinegar, water and spices. Boil for 5 minutes. Add peeled peaches and cook until tender, about 5 minutes.

❖❖❖

AUNT MARIE'S PEACH PRESERVES - 1937

2 pounds sliced fresh peaches
3 cups sugar
1/2 cup water

Prepare peaches. Boil sugar and water 5 minutes. Add peaches and boil slowly until clear and thick.

SPICED PEACH PRESERVES

8 medium peaches
1 3/4 ounce package powdered fruit pectin
7 cups sugar
1 tablespoon lemon peel, grated
2 teaspoons lemon juice, fresh
1/4 teaspoon allspice

In a 4-quart kettle mash peaches with potato masher. Stir in pectin and cook over high heat for 5 minutes, stirring constantly until mixture comes to a boil. Stir in sugar, lemon peel, lemon juice and allspice. Cook, stirring constantly until mixture comes to another boil. Boil 1 minute. Remove from heat and skim foam off the top.

Ladle preserves into hot sterilized jars within 1/2-inch of top. Spoon hot paraffin over preserves at least 1/4 inch thick. When cool, cover jars with lids. Makes 4 10-ounce jars.

BLUE PLUM RASPBERRY PRESERVES

4 pounds blue plums
2 packages raspberries
1 cup sugar for each cup fruit

Grind plums, add 1 cup sugar for each cup fruit. Boil briskly for 20 minutes. Pour in jars. Makes about 9 cups.

THREE-FRUIT MARMALADE

1 cantaloupe
1 can (15 1/4-ounce) crushed pineapple
6 fresh peaches
2 tablespoons lemon juice
1 package powdered pectin
8 cups sugar

Peel cantaloupe and put in food processor with medium blade. Drain cantaloupe and pineapple. Grind peeled, pitted peaches and drain; add to other fruits to make 6 cups. Put in kettle with lemon juice and pectin and bring to a boil, stirring constantly. Add sugar and bring to a hard boil, stirring. Boil 8 minutes then pour into 8 sterilized medium-size jelly glasses and seal.

PEAR PRESERVES

12 cups peeled, sliced pears
3 cups sugar
Juice of 1 lemon
1 cup water

In large kettle, simmer all ingredients over medium heat about 45 minutes or until pears are tender and syrup is thick. Ladle in hot sterilized jars to 1/4 inch from top. Seal and process 5 minutes in a boiling water bath.

Petals to Parsley

CRANBERRY CHUTNEY

1 pound fresh cranberries
2 cups water
2 cups sugar
1/4 cup vinegar
1 cup seeded raisins
2 tablespoons light brown sugar, firmly
   packed
1/4 teaspoon powdered ginger
1/2 teaspoon salt

Wash and discard soft berries. Bring water and sugar to a boil; add berries and rest of ingredients. Simmer, stirring occasionally, until berries have popped. Cool and serve warm or chilled. Makes 1 quart.

MINT CHUTNEY

2 ounces fresh mint leaves
2 to 3 tablespoons chopped onion
1 tablespoon chopped green chilies
1 teaspoon chopped fresh ginger
1 teaspoon sugar
Salt
1 tablespoon cider vinegar

Combine mint, onion, chilies, ginger, sugar and salt in blender or food processor and blend into a paste. Keeping machine running, gradually add vinegar. Store in small container with tight-fitting lid. Will keep up to 2 days. Makes 1/2 cup.

BETTY'S MANGO CHUTNEY

1 1/2 cups cider vinegar
1 1/4 cups sugar
1 1/4 cups dark brown sugar, firmly packed
3 cups mangoes, papayas or peaches,
   peeled and coarsely chopped
1/2 cup golden raisins
1 tablespoon fresh lemon juice
1 teaspoon minced fresh ginger
1 teaspoon cinnamon
1 teaspoon salt
1 teaspoon mustard seed or dry mustard
1/2 teaspoon minced garlic
1/2 teaspoon ground red pepper

Bring vinegar and sugars to a boil in 5-quart saucepan over high heat. Reduce heat to medium-low and add remaining ingredients. Simmer until mixture thickens slightly, 20 to 25 minutes. Cool; chutney will continue to thicken. Store in sterilized jars in refrigerator.

PICKLED OKRA

2 pounds fresh okra
5 pods hot red pepper
5 cloves garlic, peeled
3 cups white vinegar
5 tablespoons pickling salt
1 tablespoon celery seed or mustard seed

After washing okra, pack in 5 sterilized pint jars. Put 1 pepper pod and 1 garlic clove in each jar. Bring remaining ingredients and 1 cup water to a boil. Pour over okra with 1/2 inch of top and seal. Process 5 minutes.

NECTARINE CHUTNEY

1 teaspoon whole peppercorns
1 teaspoon mustard seed
1 teaspoon celery seed
8 whole juniper berries
8 whole allspice
8 whole cloves
11/2 cups sugar
1 3/4 pounds nectarines, chopped (about 6)
3 tart apples, peeled and chopped
1 cup chopped onion
1 red pepper, julienned
1 cup cider vinegar
Peel of 1 lemon, julienned
1 tablespoon minced jalapeno pepper
1 tablespoon chopped ginger

Place first 6 ingredients in a piece of cheesecloth; tie into a bag. Place bag in a large kettle with remaining ingredients. Bring to a boil over medium-high heat, stirring to dissolve sugar. Reduce heat and simmer 35 to 40 minutes, until thickened. Cool and remove spice bag. Refrigerate in a glass container overnight before serving. Cover and refrigerate up to i week. Let stand at room temperature 1 hour before serving.

Makes 4 1/2 cups.

SPICED OR BRANDIED FRESH PLUMS

15 plums, medium-size
1 1/2 cups water
1 cup sugar
2 sticks cinnamon
6 whole cloves

In a kettle combine water, sugar, cinnamon and cloves. Bring to a boil and cook until sugar is dissolved. Prick plum skins with fork in several places. Add fruit to boiling syrup and cook 2 minutes. Remove kettle from heat, cover and let stand 20 minutes. Remove plums from syrup and leave out in a bowl until syrup thickens. Pour syrup over plums and refrigerate.

VARIATION: Omit the spices and add 1/2 cup brandy to the syrup before you pour the syrup over the plums. Refrigerate. A wonderful Side Effect.

PICKLED BABY CORN ON THE COB

1 1/2 cups sugar
1 cup vinegar
1/2 teaspoon ground turmeric
1/2 teaspoon celery seed
1/4 teaspoon dry mustard
1 clove garlic, finely minced
1 1/2 pounds fresh baby corn on the cob

Combine sugar, vinegar, turmeric, celery seed, mustard and garlic in a large saucepan. Add corn and bring to a boil. Cook gently for 2 minutes and remove from heat. Cool. Put corn in 2 l-quart jars and pour liquid to cover corn. Screw lids on tight and refrigerate. Keeps for a week. Serves 6 to 8.

Jan and Jo say, "If you do not have fresh corn in your garden, buy the 8-ounce packages of frozen baby corn on the cob."

OLD-FASHIONED CORN RELISH

1/2 cup vinegar
1/3 cup sugar
1/3 cup vegetable oil
1 teaspoon salt
1/2 teaspoon celery seed
1/4 teaspoon mustard seed
1/4 teaspoon hot pepper sauce
2 packages (10-ounce size) frozen corn, thawed
2 tablespoons chopped green pepper
1 tablespoon chopped pimento
1 tablespoon minced onion

Combine first 7 ingredients in medium saucepan and bring to a boil. Cook 2 minutes; remove from heat and cool.

Place remaining ingredients in medium bowl. Add cooled mixture and blend lightly. Chill.

Jo and Jan say, "This will keep indefinitely in the refrigerator; the flavor improves with standing. Makes 1 2/3 cups.

PEAR RELISH

4 quarts pears, firm, ripe, peeled, cored and quartered
1/4 teaspoon cayenne pepper
4 sweet green peppers, seeded and cored
1 pint dill pickles, drained
1 quart chopped onion
1 cup pickling salt
2 cups sugar
1 1/2 tablespoons flour
1 teaspoon turmeric
2 tablespoons dry mustard
1 quart white vinegar

Put first 5 ingredients through food chopper, using medium blade. Add salt and mix well. Let stand overnight in refrigerator. Drain off liquid, cover pulp with cold water and drain again. In a big kettle, mix remaining ingredients. Stir until smooth. Bring to a boil and cook 5 minutes. Add pear mixture, bring to boil and cook 5 minutes more, stirring constantly. Pack in 8 sterilized pint jars and seal. Process 20 minutes.

RED PEPPER PRESERVES

12 red peppers, large and sweet
1 tablespoon pickling salt
2 cups white vinegar
3 cups sugar

Wash and seed peppers and force through food chopper with medium blade. Add salt and let stand overnight. Drain well, pressing out all liquid. Put in kettle with vinegar and sugar. Cook, uncovered, stirring every few minutes, about 45 minutes or until marmalade is thick, but not gummy. Pour into 6 sterilized jars and pour within 1/2 inch from the top and seal. Process 5 minutes.

FREEZING GRAPEFRUIT AND ORANGES

Peel grapefruit and oranges; separate into sections. Spread on a flat pan, or put them in ice cube trays in their own juice; quickly freeze.

Remove frozen sections from pan or tray and package in airtight containers. Seal, label and date; store from 2 to 4 months.

Add frozen sections to fruit cups or serve alone. They are excellent partially thawed.

VIDALIAS

Vidalia onions are grown in southeastern Georgia from May through July. The onions are so sweet in taste you can eat them like an apple. They have the same sugar content that an apple does.

Vidalia onions have a flat and squatty shape with a creamy-white interior. They are low in calories and high in Vitamin C. But you must remember they will vary from onion to onion.

Use the Vidalia onion for special dishes for they tend to be expensive. Always check to see if the onion has a Vidalia sticker on it to ensure its authenticity.

Vidalia onions must be kept in a cool, dry place away from direct sunlight. The onions should not touch each other when stored. They either can be wrapped individually in plastic or use a pair of pantyhose with a knot between each onion. (Please check to see you have all the onions out of your hose before you put them on.)

Use the Vidalia onion in soups, stews and other dishes. They may be frozen, whole or chopped. It is wise to do this because the season is so short.

GRILLED VIDALIA ONIONS

2 onions, whole
2 tablespoons butter or margarine Herbs,
 fresh, chopped

Wrap onions in aluminum foil and butter and a sprinkling of herbs over the onions. Grill 4 inches from coals until fork tender, about 30 minutes. Serves 2.

BAKED VIDALIA ONIONS

Vidalia onions, peeled and cored
1 tablespoon margarine, each onion
1 tablespoon soy sauce, each onion

Place onions in baking dish and fill the core with the margarine and soy sauce. Cover and bake at 350 degrees for 45 minutes, continue baking uncovered for 15 minutes longer.

SKILLET VIDALIA

1/4 cup butter
2 cups onions, thinly-sliced
1/2 pound fresh mushrooms, sliced
1 teaspoon salt
1 cup sour cream
2 teaspoons paprika
2 tablespoons flour

In large skillet melt butter; add onions and mushrooms. Cook over low heat until crisp and tender, about 12-15 minutes. Mix sour cream, paprika, salt and flour. Add to onions and mushrooms. Stir over low heat until heated through. Serves 4-6

STUFFED VIDALIA ONION SALAD

4 to 6 large Vidalia onions
2 tablespoons deviled ham
1 tablespoon pimento, chopped
1 package (8-ounce) cream cheese
1 teaspoon dry mustard
1/4 teaspoon salt
Dash of pepper

Peel onions and remove core with apple corer. Beat cream cheese until soft and creamy. Blend in deviled ham and remaining ingredients. Fill centers of onions with mixture and chill several hours or until cheese centers are firm. To serve, slice onions and place on lettuce leaves. Serves 6-8.

VADALIA ONION MEAT PIE

FIRST LAYER:
1 can biscuits

SECOND LAYER:
1/2 pound ground beef
1 medium Vidalia onion, chopped
1/2 pound fresh mushrooms, sliced
1 teaspoon parsley
1/2 teaspoon salt
1/4 teaspoon oregano
1/2 teaspoon pepper
1 egg slightly beaten

THIRD LAYER:
1 cup Swiss cheese, grated
1 cup milk American cheese, grated
3 eggs
1/4 cup sour cream
1/2 cup half-and-half

First Layer: Make a pie shell out of the biscuits.

Second Layer: Mix next seven ingredients together and cook over low heat. Mix egg thoroughly with ingredients so it will help hold pie together. When done, layer on top of biscuit shell.

Third Layer: Mix next 5 ingredients together and layer on top of ground beef mixture. Bake in 350-degree oven for 30 to 40 minutes, until brown. Serve hot. Serves 3-4.

SCALLOPED VIDALIA ONIONS

3 cups onions, peeled, cut into cross-wise slices
5 tablespoons butter or margarine
1 teaspoon salt
1/8 teaspoon pepper
1 1/2 cups half-and-half
3 tablespoons flour
1 cup celery, diced, cooked and drained
1/2 cup pecan halves
1/4 cup Parmesan cheese, grated
Dash of paprika

Saute onions in 3 tablespoons of margarine. Remove from saucepan while golden. Add 2 more tablespoons butter and melt. Blend in flour, salt and pepper. Gradually add half-and-half and simmer over low heat until thickened and smooth, stirring constantly.

Place onions, cooked celery and pecans in alternate layers in a buttered 2-quart baking dish. Cover with the cream sauce and sprinkle with Parmesan cheese and paprika. Bake at 350 degrees for 20 to 30 minutes until bubbly and hot. Serves 6.

Jan and Jo say, "This delicious casserole may be made ahead and heated just before serving."

SHALLOTS

Shallots are becoming popular among cooks who are aware of the least known member of the onion family.

Cooks find that shallots have a delicate onion flavor sweeter and less bitter than a green onion and have a similarity to garlic so you have a combination of garlic-onion. Shallots are used to flavor sauces, soups, meat and fish dishes. They are best when cooked over moderate heat. Slow cooking the whole bulb produces a sweet and smooth paste inside the bulb. The paste is good on crisp toast. Also, adding the whole shallots around the edge of a beef or pork roast while cooking adds a distinct flavor.

When you go to market to buy shallots they should feel firm and solid and free from rot and mold. Shallots grow in multiple cloves similar to garlic. Skin ranges from a deep copper color to a light purple. Store shallots in a cool, dry place, but not in the refrigerator. They tend to mold and get limp.

BEAN SPROUTS FROM SCRATCH

Quart Jar
1/4 cup mung beans

Buy whole beans at a health store or Chinese market. Place the beans in a bowl, cover with lukewarm water, allowing enough room for the beans to swell. Let stand overnight. Drain, then rinse the beans thoroughly.

Place 1/4 cup of the soaked beans in a quart jar. You may have several jars going at one time. Depends on how many sprouts you need.

Cover the top of the jar with two layers of cheese-cloth and fasten with two rubber bands or a canning lid band. Place jars on their sides so the beans form a layer. Store in a warm, dark place. Once a day, rinse the sprouts by pouring lukewarm water into the jars, swirling to moisten all the beans, then pour off the water. Sprouts are ready to use in about three or four days.

These are a wonderful addition to your salads, Oriental dishes, sandwiches or a great substitute for lettuce.

FRIED ZUCCHINI

4 zucchini
2 tablespoons flour
1/2 teaspoon salt
1 egg, beaten
1 tablespoon lemon juice
3/4 cup cracker crumbs
4 tablespoons cooking oil

Wash zucchini, but do not peel. Slice and coat thoroughly with the salted flour. Add lemon juice to the beaten egg and dip pieces into mixture. Coat with crumbs and fry in cooking oil. Drain on paper toweling. Serves 2 to 3.

HERBAL RED WINE VINEGAR

1 quart red wine vinegar
1/4 cup fresh parsley
1/2 cup fresh basil or 1 1/2 tablespoons, dried
1 tablespoon fresh marjoram or 1 teaspoon, dried
1 bay leaf
1 1/2 teaspoons mustard seed
1/2 teaspoon black peppercorns, cracked

Snip the herbs so they will look pretty in the jar or bottle. Pour vinegar, mustard seed and peppercorns on the herbs. Cap the bottle or jar and store in a dark place for at least 6 days before using. turning the bottle down once or twice a day to blend flavors.

LEMON DILL VINEGAR

1 quart cider or white vinegar
4 sprigs dill
2 lemons, stripped peel to be used, not juice

Place the dill and lemon peel in the glass jar and fill with vinegar. Cap and store in a dark place for at least 5 days before using, turning the bottle upside down once or twice a day to blend.

Jan and Jo say, "You may use any herbs from your garden to make an herbal vinegar. Try basil, oregano, or chile rather than dill. Just cram the jar full of the herb and fill the jar with pickling vinegar, which is the 5 percent strength. It is better to warm the vinegar before you pour it over the herbs.

Petals to Parsley

RASPBERRY VINEGAR

2 cups white wine vinegar
2 cups fresh raspberries (about 2 half-pints)

Combine vinegar and raspberries in a sterilized glass jar; cover with lid. Let stand at room temperature 3 days. Place raspberry mixture in a non-aluminum saucepan over medium heat. Bring to a boil; remove from heat, and let cool.

Strain raspberry mixture through several layers of cheesecloth into decorative jars; discard raspberry pulp. Seal jars with a cork or other airtight lid.

Makes 2 1/2 cups.

DID YOU KNOW?

• Vinegar is a sodium-free seasoner.

• The acid in vinegar will tenderize meat, fish and poultry.

• A great ingredient for a marinade.

• Rice vinegars are milder than cider or wine vinegars.

• Vinegars have 4 to 6 percent acid content. Use vinegar content according to taste.

• Always use 5 percent vinegar when pickling or preserving.

MUSTARD VINAIGRETTE

1/2 cup tarragon vinegar
2 tablespoons Dijon-style mustard
1/2 teaspoon black pepper
1 cup olive oil
2 tablespoons fresh dill, chopped

Whisk mustard, vinegar and pepper in a small bowl. Slowly drizzle olive oil until vinaigrette thickens, whisking all the time. Stir in dill. Store in a pint jar and refrigerate. Makes 1 pint.

BEETS

Don't pass up beets. Raw beets are great in salads and side dishes. To retain the color of beets, cook before peeling. The garden beets may be put into storage, layered in sand in a cool, moist cellar.

To cook beets, wash thoroughly and leave 3 inches of stems attached to the beet. Cover with water and boil until tender. Drain and cover with cold water. Slip off skins and stems. Slice or leave whole.

SWEET PICKLED BEETS
(Respectfully snitched by Ruthie Smith)

Small, young beets, amount of your choice
Boiling water
Salt
5 cups sugar
3 cups distilled vinegar
Cinnamon, allspice and cloves (Optional)
Cinnamon sticks (Optional)

Wash beets, leaving about 3 inches of tops and the roots. Cook with water to cover beets in a covered pan until skins slip easily. Place in cold water. Remove skins, top and roots.

Ruthie says, "I like to do mine in pint jars, so I pack beets into jars within 1/2 inch of top. Add 1/2 teaspoon salt to each jar of beets and pour boiling syrup of sugar and vinegar over beets to within 1/2 inch of top. Process 30 minutes in boiling water bath.

If desired, you can add cinnamon, allspice and cloves. For 'years' I didn't process in water bath, and never lost a jar, but these days, a water bath seems the thing to do!"

Jan and Jo say, "Ruthie brought us a sample of these beets, (a jar for each of us) when she brought this recipe. Upon sampling, we decided we had to serve these at our Fourth of July picnic with 'pink eggs' (hard-boiled eggs marinated in the syrup)!"

❖❖

SIMPLE BUTTERED BEETS

6 cups beets, diced
2 tablespoons butter
Salt and pepper

After cooking beets, add butter, salt and pepper and toss lightly. Or, add cooked beets to 1/4 cup vinegar, salt and sugar to taste.

HARVARD BEETS

3 cups beets, cooked and diced
3 tablespoons cornstarch
1/4 cup water
6 tablespoons sugar
1/2 cup vinegar
2 tablespoons butter, melted

Combine sugar, cornstarch, butter, water and vinegar.
Cook over hot water until smooth and thick. Season to taste.
Add beets and heat thoroughly. Serves 6
Jan says, "This is an old recipe of my Mothers'. I used to hide the beets under my napkin at the table. Now I've learned to keep them on my plate."

MOM'S PICKLED BABY BEETS

Baby beets
2 quarts vinegar and 1 pint water
4 cups sugar
2 teaspoons salt
3/4 teaspoon pepper

Mix and let boil. Fill jars with cleaned and cooked baby beets. Fill jars to top with boiling mixture and seal.

FRIED GREEN TOMATOES

4 medium tomatoes
2 tablespoons flour
1/2 teaspoon salt
1 egg, beaten
3/4 cup bread, cracker crumbs or cornmeal
4 tablespoons cooking oil

Wash and slice tomatoes 1/2-inch thick. Coat thoroughly in flour which has been seasoned. Dip pieces into beaten egg. Coat with crumbs and fry in oil, turning slices until a golden brown. Serves 2-3.

SUN-DRIED TOMATOES

6 tomatoes, sliced
2 cloves garlic, slivered
3 sprigs basil

Spread sliced tomatoes in a 200-degree oven overnight and into the next day. Do not remove the tomatoes until they resemble a dried piece of fruit. Put in a clean jar, cover with olive oil, garlic and basil. Cap the jar and refrigerate.
Be sure to prepare quite a few jars if you would like to use them during the winter. We prefer the sun-dried tomatoes to the canned ones when making our Italian sauces.

Petals to Parsley

HOW TO PEEL AND SEED TOMATOES

Place whole fresh tomatoes into boiling water for 3 to 5 minutes. Using your fingers or a sharp knife, pull the skin off. Slice the stem end from the peeled tomato and squeeze to remove seeds and liquid. You may use a grapefruit spoon to scoop out the seeds.

GARDEN-FRESH TOMATO SAUCE

4 medium-size tomatoes
1/4 cup Bertoli olive oil
1 garlic clove, minced
1/2 cup fresh basil leaves
1/2 cup fresh parsley leaves

Cut tomatoes into 1/4-inch slices and dice. Heat olive oil in skillet over medium heat. Add garlic and heat until golden.

Add diced tomatoes and heat for 15 minutes. Reduce heat to low and add salt and pepper to taste. Simmer another 5 minutes, then add basil and parsley leaves. Remove from heat and set aside while you cook the pasta. Serve sauce warm over pasta. Makes 1 cup sauce.

A great quick meal for 1. Recipe may be doubled or tripled to your liking.

MICROWAVE GREEN TOMATO DISH

3 medium green tomatoes, each cut into 6
  wedges
1 clove garlic, minced
2/3 cup celery, sliced
4 green onions, sliced into 1/2-inch pieces
4 tablespoons olive oil
2 tablespoons parsley
Fresh black coarse pepper, to taste

In a small glass bowl combine garlic, olive oil, celery, and onion. Microwave on high for 1 1/4 minutes. Arrange tomato wedges in a glass pie dish and spoon the mixture over the tomatoes. Sprinkle parsley leaves over all. Cover lightly with waxed paper and cook on high for 2 minutes or until fork tender. This depends on the tomatoes. Season with pepper. Makes 4 side dishes.

CUCUMBER PICKLES

2 pounds cucumbers
2 cups cider vinegar
1/2 teaspoon mustard seed
1 cup sugar
1 teaspoon mixed pickling spice
1 cup water
4 teaspoons salt
2 medium onions, sliced

Soak cucumbers in cold water overnight; drain. Slice about 1/4-inch thick with serrated cutter. Bring the next 5 ingredients to a boil in a kettle. Add cucumbers and boil 3 minutes or until cucumbers lose their green color. Pack cucumbers into 4 hot sterilized pint jars. Add 1 teaspoon of salt and a few onion slices to each jar. Bring remaining syrup to a boil and pour over pickles and seal. Process 5 minutes. Makes 4 pints.

GRANDMA SNAZZY'S PICCALILLI

3 quarts green tomatoes
3 quarts ripe tomatoes
2 red peppers
3 onions
1/2 cup salt
2 quarts vinegar
1 quart sugar
1 teaspoon cinnamon
1/2 teaspoon cloves
4 tablespoons white mustard seed

Run vegetables through the food chopper, using coarse cutter, sprinkle with salt. Let stand overnight then drain and add other ingredients. Cook about 45 minutes. Pour into jars and seal. Process 5 minutes.

ZUCCHINI PICKLES

2 pounds zucchini
2 medium onions
1/4 cup pickling salt
1 pint white vinegar
1 cup sugar
1 teaspoon celery seed
1 teaspoon mustard seed
1 teaspoon turmeric
1/2 teaspoon dry mustard

Wash and cut unpeeled zucchini and peeled onions in very thin slices into a bowl. Cover with water and salt. Let stand 1 hour; drain. Mix remaining ingredients and bring to a boil. Pour over zucchini and onions. Let stand 1 hour. Bring to a boil and cook 3 minutes. Pack in 3 hot sterilized pint jars and seal. Process 5 minutes. Makes 3 pints.

SWEET PICKLE STICKS

6 medium, firm cucumbers
3 3/4 cups white vinegar
3 cups sugar
3 tablespoons pickling salt
2 1/2 teaspoons celery seed
2 teaspoons turmeric
3/4 teaspoon mustard seed

Wash cucumbers and cut in sticks. Cover with boiling water and let stand 4 to 6 hours. Then drain and pack solidly into 6 pint jars. Mix remaining ingredients in saucepan and bring to a boil. Boil 5 minutes and pour over cucumbers, filling jar within 1/2 inch of top. Put on lids and process 5 minutes.

PICKLED ONION RINGS

4 large sweet onions
2 cups white vinegar
1 cup sugar
1 teaspoon mustard seed
1 teaspoon celery seed
1 teaspoon ground turmeric
1/4 teaspoon powdered alum

Peel and slice onions 1/8-inch thick and fill pint jars. Bring remaining ingredients to a boil and pour over onions. Cool, then cover and refrigerate. Let stand several days before serving. Will last several months in refrigerator.

FRESH KOSHER-STYLE PICKLES

30 to 36 cucumbers, 3 to 4 inches long
3 cups white vinegar
3 cups water
6 tablespoons pickling salt
Fresh or dried dill
1 clove garlic, sliced
1 1/2 teaspoons mustard seed

Combine vinegar, 3 cups water and salt in saucepan and bring to a boil. Put a generous layer of dill, garlic, and mustard seed in the bottom of each quart jar. Pack cucumbers into jars. When jar is half filled, add another layer of dill, garlic, mustard seed and complete filling the jars. Fill within 1/2 inch from the top with boiling brine. Seal and process 15 minutes.

GREEN TOMATO PICKLES

4 quarts green tomatoes, thinly sliced
1 quart onions, thinly sliced
1/3 cup pickling salt
3 cups white vinegar
1 teaspoon whole allspice
1 tablespoon black peppercorns
1 teaspoon celery seed
1/8 teaspoon cayenne
1 lemon, thinly sliced
3 cups brown sugar

Place sliced tomatoes and onions in a large bowl and sprinkle with salt. Cover and let stand overnight; drain. Bring remaining ingredients to a boil and add tomatoes and onion. Bring to a boil and simmer stirring gently several times. Cook about 10 minutes then pour into 5 sterilized pint jars and seal. Process 5 minutes.

BREAD-N-BUTTER PICKLES

8 cups cucumbers, unpeeled and thinly-sliced
2 onions, thinly-sliced
1/2 cup salt
2 cups cider vinegar
2 teaspoons celery seed
2 teaspoons ground turmeric
1 cinnamon stick

Combine cucumbers, onions and salt in an enamel or stainless steel pan. Let stand overnight; drain and discard liquid. Add remaining ingredients and bring to a boil, then reduce heat. Simmer 20 minutes or until cucumbers are tender. Pack while hot in hot sterilized jars to 1/4-inch from the top. Seal and process 15 minutes in boiling water bath. Makes 4 pints.

AUNTIE K'S DIXIE WATERMELON PICKLES - 1937

4 pounds prepared watermelon rind
2 quarts water
3 tablespoons salt
2 teaspoons powdered alum
1/2 cup bark cinnamon
1/4 cup whole cloves
3 cups sugar
3 cups vinegar
1 1/2 cups water

Remove pink and green portions from melon rind. Weigh out 4 pounds and cut into 1 x 2-inch pieces or triangles. Add salt and water and soak overnight. In the morning, drain well and cover with ice water for 2 hours. Drain and cover by 2 inches with cold water and add alum. Boil gently until rind is tender when tested with a fork. Drain well and add to syrup.

To make syrup, loosely tie cinnamon and cloves in cheesecloth bag; add to rest of ingredients and boil 5 minutes. Add prepared melon rind and simmer until syrup is very thick and rind is well-glazed. Remove spice bag and pour into sterilized jars and seal.

AUNT TOTTIE'S DILL PICKLES - 1936

Cucumbers
Fresh dill
Grape leaves
Garlic
Red peppers
1 pint vinegar
1 1/2 pints water
3 tablespoons salt

Select large cucumbers and wash. Pack in jars with plenty of dill and grape leaves, 1 piece of garlic and 1 piece of red pepper.

Prepare syrup of vinegar, water and salt. Bring to a boil; pour over pickles and seal.

GREAT AUNT ADELAIDE'S 14 DAY SWEET PICKLES - 1936

75 small cucumbers (3-4 inch)
Water
2 cups salt
1 tablespoon alum
5 pints strong vinegar
6 cups sugar
1/2 ounce celery seed
1 ounce stick cinnamon
3 cups sugar

Thoroughly wash cucumbers and cut into 4 pieces (makes 2 gallons). Place in stone crock. Cover with 1 gallon boiling water mixed with salt. Let stand 7 days. Skim every day and stir slightly each day.

8th Day - Drain well and pour 1 gallon boiling water over cucumbers. Let stand 24 hours.

9th Day - Drain and pour 1 gallon boiling water mixed with alum over cucumbers. Let stand 24 hours.

10th Day - Drain and pour 1 gallon boiling water over cucumbers. Let stand 24 hours.

11th Day - Drain and put pickles in clear jar. Prepare syrup of vinegar, sugar, celery seed and cinnamon. Bring to a boil and pour while hot over pickles.

On days 12-13-14, drain off and reheat syrup and pour over pickles. Add 1 cup sugar each time you reheat syrup.

FRESH TOMATO SAUCE

6 medium fresh tomatoes
1/4 cup olive oil
1 clove garlic, minced
1/4 teaspoon salt
1/4 cup basil leaves, fresh and shredded
1/4 cup parsley, fresh and shredded
Ground black pepper

Peel tomatoes and cut into 1/4-inch slices. Heat olive oil in heavy skillet over medium heat. Add garlic and saute until golden. Stir in diced tomatoes and heat to boiling point. Cover and simmer until liquid has diminished to a moist point and not a dry one. Stir in parsley, basil and black pepper. Set aside and cook the pasta. Makes 2 cups.

MOM'S TOMATO SAUCE

3 tablespoons butter
1 stalk celery
1 medium onion, chopped
1 tablespoon chopped parsley
1 clove garlic, mashed
1 can (1 pound, 13-ounce) tomatoes
1 tablespoon tomato paste
1 teaspoon salt
Freshly ground pepper to taste
1 teaspoon dried basil
1 bayleaf

Heat butter and saute celery, onion, parsley and garlic. Add tomatoes and tomato paste, season with salt and pepper; simmer gently 45 minutes. Add basil and bay leaf; simmer 15 minutes longer. Remove bay leaf. Makes 3 cups.

AUNT LE'S CHILI SAUCE - 1937

18 tomatoes, peeled
2 large onions
3 red peppers
1 cup sugar
2 cups vinegar
2 teaspoons salt
1 teaspoon cinnamon
1 teaspoon cloves
1 teaspoon allspice

Grind tomatoes, onions and peppers. Combine remaining ingredients and add to first mixture. Bring to a boil and cook until thick. Makes 4 - 5 pints.

TOMATO CATSUP

Tomatoes - Cook tomatoes in their own juice until soft. Then strain. To 1 gallon of tomato pulp add these ingredients:
1 quart cider vinegar
1 pint sugar
1 teaspoon salt
1 teaspoon ground cinnamon
4 red peppers
5 large onions

Rub mixture through a sieve and then cook slowly until thickened which will take between 3 and 4 hours. Pour into hot sterilized bottles or jars and seal immediately.

MOM'S CHILI SAUCE

10 pounds tomatoes
1 pound onions
1 1/2 ounces red pepper
3 ounces salt
6 ounces stick cinnamon
2 ounces whole cloves
1 1/2 pounds sugar
1 1/2 quarts vinegar

Pour boiling water over tomatoes and let stand about 1 minute. Then peel them and cut into small pieces. Peel onion, cut open the peppers and discard stems and seeds, and put both vegetables through food chopper.

Cook the spices in a cheesecloth bag in vinegar for about 5 minutes. Then add vegetables, sugar and salt and cook down to about 3 1/2 quarts of sauce or until thick. Seal in hot jars.

SALLY'S SPICY CHILI SAUCE

4 quarts peeled, cored, chopped ripe tomatoes (about 24)
1 1/2 cups chopped green peppers (about 3)
2 cups chopped onions
1 1/2 cups vinegar
1 1/2 cups sugar
1 tablespoon salt
1 tablespoon celery seed
1 teaspoon ground ginger
1 teaspoon ground cinnamon
1 teaspoon ground allspice
1 teaspoon ground cloves

Combine all ingredients and simmer until thick as desired, stirring frequently to prevent sticking. It will take about 1 1/2 hours.

Pour boiling hot sauce into hot pint jars, leaving 1/4 inch at top. Process for 15 minutes. Makes 8 pints.

Sally says, "Because you are using ground spices, the sauce will not be a bright red."

BLENDER CHILI SAUCE

1 peck tomatoes
3 onions, cut in chunks
4 green peppers, cut in pieces
4 sweet red peppers, cut in pieces
1 1/2 cup white vinegar
1 tablespoon whole allspice
2 sticks cinnamon
1 tablespoon whole cloves
1 cup sugar
3 tablespoons salt

Tie allspice, cinnamon sticks and cloves in a bag. Blend tomatoes; then blend onions and peppers in vinegar. Drain and reserve vinegar. Add peppers and onions to tomatoes, then add spice bag. Cook until volume is reduced to 1/2.

Remove spice bag, add sugar, salt and vinegar and boil rapidly for 5 minutes. Pour into sterilized jars and seal.

MOCK MINCEMEAT

2 cups green tomatoes, chopped
3 cups apples, chopped
1 pound of either: raisins, currants or
   prunes, chopped
or 3/4 cup of each
3/4 cup sugar
2 teaspoons cinnamon
1 teaspoon salt
1 teaspoon allspice
1 teaspoon powdered cloves
1/4 cup vinegar

Combine all ingredients in large kettle; bring to a boil and simmer until thickened. Pour, while hot into jars. Makes 4 pints.

MOM'S WINTER CHILI SAUCE

1 can tomatoes
2 onions, finely chopped
1/3 cup brown sugar
1 1/2 teaspoons salt
1 teaspoon paprika
1/8 teaspoon cayenne
1/2 teaspoon cinnamon
1/4 teaspoon cloves
1/3 cup vinegar

Mix ingredients and simmer about half an hour or until thick.

MOM'S TABLE SAUCE
- catsup -

12 ripe tomatoes
1 onion, sliced
3 green peppers, sliced
2 tablespoons sugar
1 1/2 tablespoons salt
2 teaspoons mustard
1 teaspoon paprika
1/2 teaspoon pepper
1 cup vinegar
1 teaspoon ground cloves
1 teaspoon ground cinnamon

Wash tomatoes, cut in halves and put in kettle. Add onion and peppers and seasonings. Simmer 2 hours; press through a sieve and return to kettle. Simmer 1 more hour and seal in jars or bottles. When cool, pour melted paraffin on tops.

PICNIC BASKETS

If you with litter would disgrace
And spoil the beauty of this place...May
indigestion rack your chest...And ants invade your
pants and vests...!

✧✧✧

Picnics

Savor the idle hours of spring, summer and fall with one or all of our wonderful picnic ideas. Whether you are a short-order cook or lean toward the gourmet, you will find a variety of fun picnics to fit your style! Menus are presented on the following pages but you certainly do not have to follow them to the letter. For instance, perhaps the day of the big game is cold and blustery; a hearty bowl of chili might by just the ticket for your Tailgate Picnic rather than our suggestion. A good rule to follow: Be flexible, experiment, go with the flow!

P.S. Don't forget the bottle opener, a corkscrew and plenty of food for those outdoor appetites. Have fun!

✧✧✧

❖❖❖

Let's Go On A Picnic...

Picnics have been around for a long time, probably having their origin way back when cavemen sat around firepits roasting game. It was around the first part of the 19th century when these outdoor gatherings began taking on a different social significance. That's when the English started going to the countryside carrying their hampers (as they were known then) full of goodies ranging from sandwiches to cakes. The ladies and their gentlemen were elegantly dressed and usually attended by their servants who toted the wicker hampers. Games such as tag and charades were played.

As time went by, the basket became the symbol of picnicking and picnics evolved into social gatherings which the working man and his family could look forward to after a hard weeks' work.

Picnics today are more popular than ever and, fortunately, are one of the few family happenings that have survived social change. They may be very casual with simple sandwiches, fruit, cookies, disposable cups and plates, and thermals full of lemonade tucked down in the basket. But an elegant picnic, in contrast, is wonderful with the basket packed with crystal, china, flowers and lacy linens.

Picnics create a togetherness as everyone pitches in and helps, be it gathering wood for the fire or slicing the tomatoes. Young and old have a great time from the moment they arrive at the picnic spot until they toss the plates into the trash in order to leave the place the way they found it. It is important to clean up our outdoor kitchen!

TIPS

- Pin a whistle on children's shirt. If they get lost, all they have to do is whistle!

- Before storing your thermos, stuff it with paper toweling which will absorb any odors that may be inside.

- Make a novel serving piece or centerpiece for your next patio party or picnic. Using a container about 12 inches in diameter (we use large ice cream cartons) tape fresh asparagus spears close together, with tips toward top of container. Tie a ribbon around the center of container making a pretty bow. Fill your creation with fresh vegetables, and you have a conversation piece as well as a useful one. Keep asparagus fresh before your party by mixing it lightly, wrapping it in plastic wrap (use a cleaners' plastic bag) and chill it until ready to fill.

Lover's Picnic

Ramos Fizz
Cornucopias
Dorothy's Freezer Cold Slaw
Chicken Boursin
or
Alfalfa and Bean Sprout with Chicken Sandwiches
Poached Peaches
Edith's Chocolate Topknot Cookies
Tonia's "Gimme' a Little Kiss" Cookies
Wine - Iced Tea

❖❖❖

The King and Queen

There was a princess in a land far away, who wanted to be a queen, and in a land, the other way, a knight who wanted to be king. From one land to the other, they called out to each other, not knowing for sure if they were to be heard. With the other in mind, they seemed not to worry about time, because love, and destiny were meant for them. With love as their energy, they began a journey into time, really not knowing when, only to find the other within. With this discovery of wanting to be with each other, they knew they needed one another. Together they could explore the world with the spirit of their hearts and minds and the freedom of forever to be themselves, always searching for the truth. They were at peace then, to enter side by side the kingdom of heaven with God and destiny as their guide, and the love of one's, a feeling from within.

A King and Queen they became, and side by side they traveled on. Always free to be, to share a world from within, through each other's spirit as they felt it then. They knew by now, there was only a change in time, there will be no end for them. So divine they became one, with the truth right at hand. A King and Queen, within the kingdom, always together, one in Trinity - forever and ever -

— *Tony Bertoglio*

Make this a special time, a summer memory that will remain in your hearts forever....

It is said that it doesn't really matter where you are if you are with the one you love, but let us imagine you are planning a special picnic in the country, park, seashore or mountain top. For this time together pack your treasured wicker hamper or baskets with a feeling of pleasure and anticipation. This would be a good time to show your lover your creativity in making this a very memorable day.

First you need the essentials, such as wineglasses, winebucket, a wine opener, crystal wine glasses, china, silverware, and above all, cloth and napkins. In another bag pack hand wipes, sun-screen and repellent to prepare yourselves for the unexpected.

Begin your lovers' picnic with a dreamy mood. Pick out a spot with a big shade tree and lush green grass. If your picnic is on the beach, and no trees are in sight, we hope you have remembered that nifty beach umbrella stored in the hall closet. Spread out your cloth and napkins and add a bouquet of flowers to add to the decor of the great outdoors. If you are in a meadow, you can pick wildflowers right on the spot; what could be more beautiful?

Above all, have a sense of leisure when starting your summer picnic; there should be no sense of urgency in getting back to town, no deadlines to meet, put your watches in that picnic basket and forget about time. Your food will be cold and delectable and wine will have an endless flow. You will dazzle your lover with the food and don't forget to tuck a love note in with the dessert.

RAMOS FIZZ

1 can (6-ounce) frozen lemonade, undiluted
1 lemonade can gin
1/2 lemonade can heavy cream
Whites of 2 eggs
1/4 teaspoon vanilla
Dash of orange-flower water
1 cup crushed ice

Combine all ingredients except ice in blender. Add ice; cover and blend 10 seconds on high speed. Pour into chilled champagne flutes; garnish with an orange slice. Serves 4 to 6.

❖❖❖

CORNUCOPIAS

Salami or summer sausage, thinly sliced
Cream cheese
Horseradish
Midget sweet gherkin pickles
Fresh parsley

Soften cream cheese at room temperature and season with a small amount of horseradish, to taste. Spread on meat slices and shape into cornucopias. Tuck a tiny gherkin into cornucopia and fasten with a wooden pick. Tuck a tiny sprig of parsley on top of each cornucopia to garnish.

To serve, arrange on a tray with cubes of cheese and some fruit.

DOROTHY'S FREEZER COLD SLAW

1/2 cup water
2 cups sugar
1 cup white vinegar
1 head cabbage. shredded
1 green pepper, chopped
1/2 cup celery, chopped
2 carrots, finely chopped

Combine water, sugar and vinegar in saucepan and bring to a boil. Let cool. Combine cabbage, green pepper, celery and carrots. Let it refrigerate 2 hours. If there is any liquid, press out and pour the vinegar mixture over the mixture of cabbage. Let stand in refrigerator overnight. This may be packed in freezer containers so it will be ready for unexpected company or a picnic.

CHICKEN BOURSIN

8 chicken breast halves, boned
8 ounces cream cheese, softened
1 clove garlic, minced
1 tablespoon fresh or 1 teaspoon dried
  parsley, minced
1/2 teaspoon salt
1/4 teaspoon pepper
1/4 cup flour
1 egg mixed with 1 tablespoon water
1/2 cup dried bread crumbs
1/2 cup margarine
1/4 cup oil

Remove skin from chicken breasts and flatten. Combine cream cheese, garlic, parsley, salt and pepper. Shape this mixture into a roll about 11/2 inches in diameter. Cover with plastic wrap and refrigerate until firm, about 2 hours. Cut this roll into 8 equal portions and place each on a flattened chicken breast. Roll up, tucking in ends to make sure cheese is completely enclosed. Secure ends with toothpicks. Coat chicken with flour, then dip in egg-water wash. Roll each breast in bread crumbs and chill 1 hour.

Heat margarine and oil in a skillet. Saute chicken rolls for 5 minutes on each side or until done. Drain on paper towels.

Jo and Jan say, "These rolls can be served immediately after preparation or kept warm in a 200-degree oven for up to 1 hour. We think they are wonderful for warm weather meals or make delicious picnic fare chilled and sliced. They also freeze beautifully."

◆◇◆

ALFALFA & BEAN SPROUT - CHICKEN SANDWICH

1 cup chicken, cooked and finely chopped
1/2 cup celery, chopped
2 tablespoons fresh parsley, chopped
1/4 cup mayonnaise or salad dressing
Margarine, softened
8 slices whole wheat bread
1 cup fresh bean sprouts, washed and
  drained
1 cup fresh alfalfa sprouts, washed and
  drained

Combine chicken, celery and parsley. Add mayonnaise to chicken mixture and stir lightly. Spread margarine on bread slices and spread filling on buttered side of 4 slices. Top each with 1/4 cup each of bean and alfalfa sprouts and top with remaining bread. Makes 4 sandwiches.

Jo and Jan say, "This is a very nice filling for pita pockets. Just the ticket for that picnic you're planning."

POACHED PEACHES

1 cup water
1 cup sugar
2 cups dry white wine
6 large fresh peaches, peeled
1 recipe Raspberry Sauce (See index)

Bring water, sugar and wine to a boil and cook 20 minutes; reduce heat and add peaches. Cook, covered for 4 minutes. Remove from heat, let stand in poaching liquid until cool. Refrigerate and prepare Raspberry Sauce. To serve, drain peaches and top each with Raspberry Sauce. Serves 6.

Jo and Jan say, "This is lovely for a picnic dessert. You might want to slice the peaches in half, fill the cavities with a sweetened cream cheese mixture, surround with fresh raspberries and spoon the Sauce over all."

EDITH'S CHOCOLATE TOPKNOT COOKIES

3/4 cup butter or margarine
1/4 cup heavy cream
1 teaspoon vanilla
1 3/4 cup flour
6 tablespoons powdered sugar
1 cup pecans, chopped

Cream butter in large bowl, beating in cream and vanilla. Sift flour and sugar; add to mixture. Mix in pecans. Chill and prepare Frosting.

FROSTING:
2 cups confectioners' sugar
1 package (3-ounce) cream cheese
2 squares (I-ounce size) unsweetened
  chocolate, melted
1/2 teaspoon vanilla
1 to 2 tablespoons water

Form chilled dough into small balls. Place 2 inches apart on greased sheet. Make a depression in center of each cookie. Bake in preheated 325-degree oven for 20 minutes. Cool and swirl frosting in depression of each cookie. Makes 4 dozen.

TONIA'S "GIMME' A LITTLE KISS" COOKIES

1 1/2 cups margarine, softened
3/4 cup sugar
1 tablespoon lemon extract
2 3/4 cups flour
1 1/2 cups almonds, finely chopped
1 package (14-ounce) milk chocolate Kisses
Confectioners' sugar
1/2 cup semi-sweet chocolate chips
1 tablespoon shortening

Cream margarine and sugar until fluffy; add lemon extract then flour and almonds. Beat on low speed of mixer until blended. Cover and chill 1 hour.

Remove wrapper from kisses, shape 1 scant tablespoon of mixture around each kiss, forming a ball. Place on ungreased baking sheet and bake in preheated 375-degree oven for 8 to 12 minutes, or until lightly golden. Remove from oven and cool 1 minute; sprinkle with confectioners' sugar.

Melt chocolate chips in shortening and dip tops of cookies in melted mixture. Set on waxed paper until tops are solid and ready to store. Freeze nicely. Makes 4 dozen.

Fourth of July Picnic

Long Island Tea
Tonia's Spinach Dip Supreme
Jack's Chicken For A Mob (See index)
Or
Picnic Southern Fried Chicken
Roasted Spareribs With Hoisin - Honey Glaze
Capri Salad
Marinated Potato Salad
Baked Beans
Carol's Party Cheese Bread
Vanilla Ice Cream with Sauces
Double Fudge Brownies
Tonia's Hummingbird Cake
Lemonade - Iced Tea

Flags are flown proudly from the porch, patio and flag pole, and the bunting is hung on the porch railing. Let the children help decorate with rolls of patriotic crepe paper. It will always look like a ticker tape parade; but you will have lots of color! String twinkle lights among the trees so when darkness falls the lights will resemble hundreds of flickering fireflys.

Have your tables a blaze of color with red, white and blue cloths. Baskets of red and white geraniums with flags tucked among the flowers are centered on each table with small drums, bugles and toy soldiers surrounding the baskets. You might like to use commercial Uncle Sam hats inverted with flowers and flags set inside. Be sure to buy enough hats because experience has taught us that younger children want to wear them all day long and truly are Yankee Doodle Dandies!

As we go down memory lane we would like to share with you our ways of making a Fourth of July picnic a big bang!

To begin with, it isn't only our country's birthday but one of your authoress', JoLe. This has been a time when our families had their yearly get-together...and what times we have had!

Looking back into our diaries, we thought it would be fun to give your our ideas. First, it was always a prerequisite that everyone, young and old, wore red, white and blue. A parade presented by the children and young adults in honor of the "birthday girl" and good old USA was always the highlight of the day.

Between shooting firecrackers and churning ice cream various and sundry games were played. "Losers" took the last turns on the crank freezer handle while winners got the first "licks" from the dasher.

All of us anticipated the evening fireworks, always followed by ice cream and cake. The children loved to see us light the sparklers which had been placed on the birthday cake.

Even before the sparklers had burned down, another dandy Yankee Doodle Day was etched in our book of memories.

❖❖❖

LONG ISLAND TEA

1/2 ounce vodka
1/2 ounce gin
1/2 ounce rum
Tea
Coke
Lemon slice

Pour vodka, gin and rum in collins glass. Fill 2/3 with tea; add dash of iced Coke for color. Stir and garnish with lemon slice. Serves 1.

TONIA'S SPINACH DIP SUPREME

2 large green onions with tops, minced
1 pint sour cream
1 package (8-ounce) cream cheese, softened
1 cup cheddar cheese, shredded
1 cup chopped pecans
1/2 teaspoon lemon juice 1
1 teaspoon Worcestershire sauce
1 package Hidden Valley Original Salad
　 Dressing mix (dry)
1 package (10-ounce) frozen, chopped
　 spinach, thaw, drain well and squeeze dry
1 can water chestnuts, chopped fine

Mix all ingredients and chill thoroughly, several hours, preferably overnight. Serve in hollowed loaf of rye or pumpernickel bread, with cubes of bread in basket to the side.

Tonia says, "Sometimes I make this with 1 package of dry vegetable soup mix, but it is a little more salty. It is very pretty in a red cabbage shell."

Jo says, "Tonia brought this to our last Christmas gathering and it was the hit of the day! Nary a crumb was left, and she doubled the recipe!"

PICNIC SOUTHERN FRIED CHICKEN

3 frying chickens (2 1/2 to 3 pounds each),
　 cut into pieces
3 cups evaporated milk
2 tablespoons Worcestershire sauce
1 1/2 cups flour
1 1/2 cup cornmeal, finely ground
1 1/2 teaspoons salt
1/8 teaspoon freshly ground pepper
1/2 teaspoon ground red pepper
4 cups cooking oil
Fresh parsley (garnish)

Place chicken pieces in shallow dishes. Combine milk and Worcestershire and pour over chicken. Cover and refrigerate at least 8 hours. Drain chicken and pat dry. Combine and mix flour, cornmeal, salt, pepper and red pepper in a large plastic bag. Add chicken pieces in batches and shake bag to coat the pieces. Remove from bag and shake off excess flour mixture.

Heat oil in large skillet to 365 degrees. Add chicken legs and fry about 15 to 20 minutes, turning to brown evenly. Watch your heat and try to keep it between 365 to 375 degrees. When legs are done, remove from oil with a slotted spoon and drain on paper towels. Repeat frying process with thighs, frying for 15 minutes, and breasts, frying for 10 minutes or until browned. Cool at room temperature and transfer to a covered container and refrigerate. Garnish with fresh parsley sprigs. Serves 12.

Jo and Jan say, "We like to prepare this a day before our picnic; we think the flavor is better."

❖❖

ROASTED SPARERIBS WITH HOISIN - HONEY GLAZE

1 12-ounce bottle beer
3/4 cup hoisin sauce
3/4 cup honey
3/4 cup soy sauce
3/4 cup minced green onion
3 tablespoons minced fresh ginger or 1
  tablespoon ground
9 pounds lean spareribs

Combine all ingredients except ribs in medium saucepan over low heat and cook 5 minutes to blend flavors. (Glaze can be prepared ahead to this point, cooled, covered and refrigerated. Reheat before proceeding with recipe.

About 2 hour before serving time, position racks in upper and lower thirds of oven and preheat to 350. Brush ribs with glaze. Arrange on racks set in 2 large roasting pans. Roast until well browned, 1 1/2 to 1 3/4 hours, turning ribs every 30 minutes and basting with glaze. Transfer to work surface and cut between ribs. Arrange on heated platter and serve immediately.

CAPRI SALAD

1 package fresh Mozzarella cheese, sliced
  1/4-inch thick
6 tomatoes, cut in quarters or eighths
1 large red onion, cut in rings
Sprinkling of fresh basil - if using dried, add
  to dressing
DRESSING:
1/2 teaspoon salt
1/2 teaspoon pepper
1 tablespoon dried mustard
1 teaspoon basil - if using dried
1 tablespoon red wine vinegar
3 tablespoons olive oil

Blend salt, pepper and dried mustard with a fork. Blend in vinegar, then add olive oil. Arrange cheese, tomatoes, onion and fresh basil on platter. Drizzle dressing over salad, lightly toss to cover. Serves 4 to 6.

MARINATED POTATO SALAD

6 medium-sized potatoes, cooked and diced
1 cup Italian salad dressing 1
 onion, finely chopped
1 cup mayonnaise
2 teaspoons prepared mustard
4 hard-boiled eggs, chopped
1/2 teaspoon celery seed
1/2 cup celery, chopped
2 tablespoons sweet pickle relish
Seasoned salt to taste
Salt and pepper to taste

Marinate potatoes in Italian dressing in refrigerator for several hours. Combine with other ingredients and chill until serving time. May garnish with hard-boiled eggs, cherry tomatoes, or green pepper rings. Serves 6-8.

❖◆

BAKED BEANS

4 cans (l-pound size) pork and beans
2 small onions, chopped
4 teaspoons Worcestershire sauce
1 cup catsup
1/2 cup brown sugar
4 tablespoons molasses
4 teaspoons prepared mustard
1 cup bacon, chopped, fried crisp

Combine all ingredients; adjust seasonings. Bake uncovered in a preheated 250-degree oven for at least 2 hours, or until mixture thickens. Serves 12.

Jo says, "This past 4th, my sister Jeanne made up these beans and added a pound of spicey sausage, crumbled, fried and well-drained. It added a delicious flavor."

CAROL'S CHEESE BREAD

1 loaf French bread, cut horizontally
1 1/2 cups grated mild Cheddar cheese
1 1/2 cups grated sharp Cheddar cheese
1/2 to 2/3 cup mayonnaise (or enough to bind)
2 teaspoons Beau Monde seasoning
1 teaspoon mixed herb seasoning
1 large or 2 small bunches green onions, chopped

Combine cheeses and remaining ingredients. Spread on cut halves of bread. Place halves together and wrap in foil. Bake 25-30 minutes at 350 degrees. Remove from foil, open halves quickly and slice.

Jo and Jan say: "This is one you must try! It is the perfect answer to a patio dinner, or a tail-gate picnic. This is so delicious it has become a 'must-have' for special times and there are threats of pouting if we don't serve it."

DOUBLE FUDGE BROWNIES

1 1/2 cups sifted flour
3/4 cup plus 2 tablespoons unsweetened cocoa
1/2 teaspoon salt
1 teaspoon baking powder
1 1/3 cups butter or margarine
2 cups sugar
4 eggs
1/4 cup corn syrup
2 teaspoons vanilla
2 cups coarsely chopped and toasted nuts
Chocolate Brownie and Bar Frosting (See index)

Grease a 9 x 13-inch baking pan. Sift flour, cocoa, salt and baking powder. Cream butter and sugar in large mixing bowl. Add sifted dry ingredients and mix well. Beat in eggs, corn syrup and vanilla; mix well and stir in nuts. Spread in pan and bake in preheated 350-degree oven for 40 to 45 minutes or until soft in center but firm around edges. Watch closely and do not overbake. Cool completely before frosting. Cut into squares and store in airtight container. Makes 3 dozen squares.

Jo and Jan say, "If you don't love chocolate, you are really missing out on this one! It's tremendous and perfect for parties. We usually use chopped hazelnuts; (you can fine them at bulk or gourmet shops). They need to be toasted so we chop them first, spread out on sheets and then toast. They give a distinctive flavor to the brownies, but of course, you can use your favorite."

TONIA'S HUMMINGBIRD CAKE

3 cups flour, sifted
2 cups sugar
1 teaspoon salt
1 teaspoon soda
3 eggs, beaten
1 1/2 cups oil
1 1/2 teaspoons vanilla
1 1/2 cups crushed pineapple, drained
1 1/2 cups bananas, mashed
1 cup pecans, chopped

Combine flour, sugar, salt and soda in a large mixing bowl. Add eggs, then oil. Mix well then add remaining ingredients and mix again. Grease and flour 3 round 9-inch cake pans. Divide cake mixture among pans and bake in a preheated 350-degree oven for 30 minutes. Remove from oven and cool layers before frosting with Cream Cheese Frosting (See index).

Tonia says, "This really delicious cake is one of our family favorites. It is my hubby's choice for his birthday cake, and is requested at Mom's 4th of July birthday party, so you know it's great."

Pumpkin Patch Festival Picnic

Apple - Wine Bowl
Quick Snack Mix
Vegetable - Cheese Soup
Curly Pasta Salad
Ten Minute Sloppy Joes
Or
Submarine Sandwiches
Judy's Sunflower Seed Cookies
Or
Rick's Pumpkin Bars (See index)
Apple Cider

With fall in the air, now is the time to celebrate the last of the lingering days of autumn. You and your children are invited to the pumpkin patch for a fall festival. This is the finale to a family outing after selection of the largest pumpkin in the patch to be used for a Jack-O-Lantern.

Use autumn-colored tablecloths such as orange and brown felt or colored burlap; the look will be smashing. To make arrangements for your fall table, hollow out pumpkins and fill them with mums. Surround the pumpkin bases with mums and fall leaves. Another idea for an arrangement is to hollow out the pumpkin, puncture it at random with an ice pick and place small buttonmums in all the holes, pushing stems all the way in so only the flower heads show. Surround the base with additional mums and leaves.

Use a pumpkin as a server for your appetizers. Spear cheese cubes and relishes with toothpicks or bamboo sticks into the pumpkin; intertwine parsley on top for 'hair' so ole' Jack-O looks alive.

Miniature pumpkins can be hollowed out for condiments or place votives in them to light up your table.

A popular pastime is to create your own pumpkin faces with acrylic paint. If your picnic lingers into the twilight hours, have your Jack-O-Lantern carved so his glowing face will shine and keep away the goblins.

If at all possible; if fire codes allow it, or if you live in the country, add to the atmosphere by building a small bonfire in a secluded corner. Not only would it brighten the yard, but would show the happy glow of faces around the fire while toasting marshmallows. Apple bobbing is always fun for young and old; and perhaps someone who is good at weaving tales could tell some hair-raising ghost stories. Boo!

Picnics

APPLE - WINE BOWL

2 cups apple cider or apple juice
1/2 cup sugar
2 sticks cinnamon
2 dozen whole cloves
2 quarts dry white wine

Combine all ingredients except white wine in a large saucepan. Bring to a boil and simmer 5 minutes. Strain spices from mixture; add wine and cook only until mixture is thoroughly warm; but do not boil. Serves 16 to 20.

Jo and Jan say, "This is a very nice punch for your fall party activities. Cinnamon sticks may be used for stirrers, and you might want to float apple slices in the punch."

QUICK SNACK MIX

1 box plain Captain Crunch cereal
1 medium size package M & Ms with peanuts
1 medium size package M & Ms chocolate
1 large jar dry roasted peanuts
1 large can shoestring potatoes
1 large box raisins
1 medium size package Reeses Pieces

Mix all together and store in airtight container.

VEGETABLE - CHEESE SOUP

4 small carrots, cut into 1-inch matchsticks
3 celery stalks, cut into 1-inch matchsticks
1 1/2 cups chicken broth
2 tablespoons butter
2 tablespoons onion, finely chopped
1/4 cup flour
3 cups hot chicken broth
1 cup sharp Cheddar cheese, shredded
1 can (8 3/4-ounce) whole tomatoes, undrained, chopped
1/8 teaspoon Tabasco sauce
1/8 teaspoon nutmeg
Salt and freshly ground black pepper to taste
1/4 cup dry white wine
1 1/2 cups heavy cream, heated
Chopped parsley (garnish)
Croutons (garnish)

Combine carrots, celery and chicken broth in a 2-quart saucepan. Bring to a boil; reduce heat and simmer until vegetables are tender. Set aside and melt butter in a large saucepan over medium heat. Add onion and saute until transparent. Blend in flour and cook for 5 to 7 minutes, stirring constantly; don't let it brown. Slowly add other 3 cups chicken broth into flour mixture and cook over low heat, stirring constantly until thickened. Blend in cheese and stir until melted. Add tomatoes and undrained vegetables. Season with Tabasco, nutmeg, salt, pepper and wine. Just before serving, stir in heated cream. Garnish with parsley and croutons, if desired. Serves 6.

CURLY PASTA SALAD

1 package (8-ounce) Curly Roni-Rotini pasta
1 green pepper, chopped
1 red pepper, chopped
1 cucumber, chopped
3/4 cup ripe olives, slivered
1 red onion, sliced thin
16 mushrooms, sliced
1/2 bottle Italian salad dressing
1/2 cup mayonnaise
1 cup mild Cheddar cheese, grated

Cook pasta according to package directions. Drain and set aside to cool. In a large bowl, mix green and red peppers, cucumber, olives, onion and mushrooms with the dressing and mayonnaise. Gently fold in the cheese. Refrigerate until chilled. Serves 10-12.

Jan says, "This is a wonderful summer salad. It makes a nice light dinner with chicken breast and hot French bread. When mixing the dressing, add according to taste. We like our salads moist with flavor but not swimming in the dressing."

TEN MINUTE SLOPPY JOES

2 tablespoons butter
1 1/4 pounds ground beef
1 medium onion, chopped
3/4 cup catsup
2 tablespoons sugar
2 tablespoons mustard
1 tablespoon vinegar
1 teaspoon salt

Brown meat and onion in melted butter. While browning, mix remaining ingredients together and pour over browned mixture. Simmer 10 minutes; skim off any fat on surface. Serve on hamburger buns or fill pita pockets. Serves 4.

SUBMARINE SANDWICH

1 loaf Italian bread, about 16-inches long
1 package (8-ounce) sliced bologna
1 package (8-ounce) salami
1 package (8-ounce) Swiss cheese, sliced
1 cup shredded lettuce
1/4 cup hot cherry peppers, sliced
1/2 small cucumber, thinly sliced
1 small tomato, thinly sliced
1 small red onion, thinly sliced
6 pitted ripe olives, sliced

Slice bread horizontally in half. Arrange all ingredients on bottom half of bread. Top with Mayonnaise or Vinaigrette (See index). Makes 6 servings.

JUDY'S SUNFLOWER SEED COOKIES

1 cup margarine
1 cup brown sugar
1 cup granulated sugar
2 eggs, beaten
1 teaspoon vanilla
1 1/2 cups flour
1/2 teaspoon salt
1 teaspoon baking powder
3 cups quick oats , uncooked
1 cup sunflower seeds, shelled

Cream margarine and sugars. Add eggs, vanilla and blend well. Add flour, salt, baking powder and oats. Mix and blend in sunflower seeds. Form into rolls about 1 1/2-inch in diameter. Wrap in plastic wrap or foil and chill. Slice with a sharp knife into 1/4-inch slices. Place on ungreased cookie sheet. Bake in preheated 350-degree oven for 10 to 12 minutes. Cool and store in airtight container. Makes about 9 dozen.

Picnics

Tailgate Picnic

Brandy Milk Punch
Roca - Chive Cheese Ball
Crackers - Apples
Judie's Sausage Puffs
Tailgate Pea Soup
Betty's Crunchy Cabbage Salad
Janet's Make - ahead Sandwiches
Assorted Relishes
Mocha Bars
Coffee

An Indian Summer day is a great time to have an end-of-season picnic. Let Mother Nature set the scene for the football event and the opportunity to enjoy friends. The great outdoors is not only a casual way to entertain, but the appetites seem to soar in great anticipation of the ensuing activity. To be organized in your planning is a must. Make yourself a list of necessities ahead of time which are needed to make your picnic error-free. As our Mothers used to say, "keep your hot food hot and your cold food cold," so... that takes extra careful planning.

One of our favorite ways of packing plates, cups, silverware and napkins is to take a large bandana and place it flat on the table. Put utensils inside and gather up the ends and knot; it will look like a hobo sack. Hand these out before serving the food and you are on your way.

You might set a basket of shiny apples on the tailgate for a centerpiece or for those who wish to take a snack into the game. Also, the Roca-Chive Ball is delicious spread on apple wedges.

If you are having such a good time at the stadium and time gets away with you, tie a pennant with the team logo or school colors on the aerial of the car so you can find your way back easily after the game. When the final seconds have ticked off the scoreboard and you are waiting for traffic to clear, enjoy dessert and coffee while replaying the strategic points of the game with your friends.

We are sure as your Tailgate picnic ends and the sun is setting in the west you will find yourselves making plans for another soon.

BRANDY MILK PUNCH

1/2 gallon milk
8 tablespoons sugar
5 tablespoons vanilla
3 cups brandy
Nutmeg or cinnamon
Ice

Combine all ingredients except ice in blender. Blend on high speed for 10 seconds. Pour punch into thermos. To serve, pour over ice and sprinkle with cinnamon or nutmeg. Makes 16 1/2-cup servings.

Jo and Jan say, "This is written for a picnic, to be poured over ice. If you are serving at home, blend with ice."

ROCA - CHIVE CHEESE BALL

1 jar Kraft Roca-Blue cheese
1 package (8-ounce) cream cheese
1 package (8-ounce) chive cheese
1 cup celery, chopped fine
2/3 cup nuts, chopped (optional)

Combine all ingredients except nuts. Shape into ball or log; roll in chopped nuts if desired and chill before serving. Makes 1 ball.

JUDIE'S SAUSAGE PUFFS

1 roll (1-pound) seasoned sausage
1 cup whole pimento-stuffed olives; more if
  needed
1 package (8-ounce) Crescent rolls

Divide sausage and pastry in 2 parts. Keep other parts chilled while working on one.

Roll 1/2 of sausage between waxed paper to a 4 x 12-inch rectangle. Remove top waxed paper; line 1/2 the olives end to end just off-center of sausage strip. Fold sausage over olives and roll tightly like a jelly roll. Transfer to refrigerator and repeat with other 1/2 of sausage, using remaining olives.

Roll 1/2 of chilled pastry to a rectangle about 1 1/2 x 14 inches; pinching the dividing perforations together. Place a chilled sausage roll along one edge of pastry. Roll pastry around

sausage; wet pastry edges and press to seal. Return to refrigerator and repeat with remaining chilled pastry and sausage roll. Chill then slice into 1/2-inch slices. Place on parchment paper on baking sheet. Bake in preheated 350-degree oven for 15 minutes or until pastry is puffed and golden brown; watch closely. Serve warm or reheat just before serving. Makes 4 dozen.

Judie says, "If you want to freeze the puffs, slightly undercook and freeze them; finish baking at serving time. To reheat, please don't microwave them, they will become soggy. Also, when serving, do not cover with napkins."

Jo says, "Judie brought these to one of my family's outings; they were such a hit we thought the guys were going to arm wrestle for the last ones. This year she'll probably double the amount!"

TAILGATE PEA SOUP

1 tablespoon butter or margarine
2 tablespoons onion, chopped
1/4 cup celery, chopped
1/4 teaspoon ground thyme
1 can condensed green pea soup
1 soup can water
1 can (8-ounce) tomatoes, drained and
  chopped
Herbed croutons (garnish)

Melt butter in saucepan; add onions, celery and cook until tender and add thyme. Blend in soup; add water gradually, stirring constantly. Add tomatoes and heat, stirring occasionally. Serves 2-4.

BETTY'S CRUNCHY CABBAGE SALAD

1/2 head cabbage, chopped in 1/2-inch wide
  pieces
1 or 2 green onions, chopped
1 package Raman noodles "Oriental flavor"
  (crush pack with hands before opening).
1/2 cup salad oil
2 tablespoons sugar
3 tablespoons cider vinegar
1 teaspoon salt
1/2 teaspoon pepper
1/2 cup sunflower seeds
2 tablespoons sesame seeds
1 small package slivered almonds

Chop cabbage and onions, combine and chill until ready to toss. Make dressing by combining oil, sugar, vinegar, salt and pepper. Add seasoning packet from noodle package and blend well.

Just before serving, combine cabbage, onions, seeds almonds and package of noodles. Toss with dressing at last minute. Serves 6-8.

Jo and Jan say, "This is one salad we cannot stop eating! It is a delicious buffet dish. It is just as good the next day (if there is any left); but the noodles will not be crunchy."

❖❖

JANET'S MAKE AHEAD SANDWICHES

1 pound shaved ham
1 cup American cheese, grated
1 medium onion, finely chopped
1/2 cup stuffed green olives chopped
3 tablespoons barbecue sauce
1 cup mayonnaise
10 medium-size hamburger buns

Mix together cheese, onion, olives, barbecue sauce and mayonnaise. Spread mixture on top and bottom halves of buns. Put ham between and close buns. Wrap each sandwich individually in foil. Store in refrigerator if using soon, or they freeze beautifully. Bring to room temperature. Still wrapped in foil, heat in preheated 350-degree oven for 20 minutes.

Jan says, "'These are wonderful to make ahead and serve with soup or a salad. Thank you, Chapter EM, P.E.O. of Wichita, Kansas for sharing this wonderful recipe!"

MOCHA BARS

7 squares (1-ounce size) semi-sweet
   chocolate
1/2 cup butter
1 1/3 cups flour
2 teaspoons instant coffee granules
1/2 teaspoon salt
1 teaspoon baking powder
5 eggs
1 1/2 cups sugar
3 teaspoons vanilla extract
11/3 cups graham cracker crumbs
1 cup pecans, chopped

GLAZE:
2 tablespoons milk
1 tablespoon butter
3 teaspoons instant coffee granules
2 cups confectioners' sugar

Melt chocolate with butter in small saucepan over low heat; cool. Combine flour, coffee, salt and baking powder; set aside. Beat eggs and sugar in large bowl at medium speed until light. Beat in chocolate mixture; add vanilla. Stir in flour mixture, graham crackers crumbs and nuts. Pour into a greased 9 x 13-inch pan and bake in preheated 350-degree oven for 35 minutes.

While baking prepare glaze by heating milk, butter and coffee in saucepan. Add confectioners' sugar and blend until smooth. Glaze bars while warm. Cool and cut in squares. Makes 3 dozen.

Mothers Day Picnic

Pea Pod Boats (See index)
Mom's Cheese Spread For Celery
Soup St. Germain
Margaret's Mushroom Salad
Sugarless Blueberry Muffins
Picnic Lemon Butter
Cold Poached Salmon
Tomatoes Provencal (See index)
Trish's Chocolate Filled Lemon Roll
Picnic Iced Tea - Wine
Fresh Flower Ice Bucket (See index)

"God could not be everywhere so He made mothers."

A special day, a special token of love for Mother on Mother's Day begins with serving her breakfast in bed. We recommend Derelys' Lemon French Toast (see index).

Whether it will be a picnic in the backyard garden or on the patio, let us help make it a memorable occasion for Mother and all her family. To give the table an elegant touch, use your Battenberg lace or the cherished lace or crocheted cloth your grandmother gave you. Since roses are beginning to blossom, a bouquet in an heirloom vase or in individual bud vases could grace the table. Pictures of your mother in small frames among the vases are a beautiful way to elicit treasured memories.

Fan the napkins and tie with matching ribbon for each place. Let a rosebud peek out of each napkin; guests can pin them on dresses or lapels.

Have your table embellished with a mixture of your cherished heirloom dishes for serving the meal. Remember, you do not need to have a matching motif.

For a unique touch which says "I love you and you are so special," form the Fresh Flower Ice Bucket to chill your favorite wine with which you will propose a toast to a beautiful lady.

MOM'S CHEESE SPREAD FOR CELERY

1 package (8-ounce) cream cheese, softened
1 1/2 tablespoons mayonnaise
1 tablespoon cream
1/4 teaspoon salt
1 teaspoon grated onion
1 garlic clove, minced
1 teaspoon Worcestershire sauce
Paprika
Celery

Combine all ingredients except paprika and celery. Wash celery and cut ribs into desired lengths. Stuff celery with creamed mixture and sprinkle with paprika. Chill until ready to serve.

Jo says, "I remember that stuffed celery was always part of our Christmas Eve buffet, and there was never any left for next-day munching."

SOUP ST. GERMAIN

1 can (17-ounce) green peas, drained
1 cup chicken broth
1 cup heavy cream
Salt to taste
Pepper to taste
Sour cream, for garnish
Chopped chives, for garnish

Puree peas in blender. Combine with chicken broth and cream. Season with salt and pepper. Chill and serve in chilled cups garnished with spoonful of sour cream and chopped chives. Serves 6.

MARGARET'S MUSHROOM SALAD

2 heads Boston lettuce
1 head Romaine lettuce
1 bunch scallions
1 1/2 pounds fresh mushrooms
1/4 cup fresh parsley, chopped
Salt and pepper to taste
Juice of 1/2 lemon
1/4 cup red wine vinegar
1/2 cup olive oil (Margaret says, "use a good
    grade"
1/2 cup salad oil
2 tablespoons Dijon mustard
3 tablespoons chopped chives
Juice of 1/2 lemon

Wash, dry, remove spines and tear lettuce into bite-size pieces. Slice scallions thin, including most of green tops.

Brush clean the mushrooms, remove stems and slice tops. Squeeze juice from 1/2 lemon over mushrooms to prevent turning dark.

Place chilled greens in bowl. Add onions, parsley and sliced mushrooms. Add salt and pepper, then dressing. Toss and serve. Serves 12-14.

DRESSING:

Combine vinegar, olive oil, salad oil, Dijon mustard, chives and lemon juice. Mix together and shake well. Serves

Margaret says "I do my greens early in the day and seal them in plastic bags until ready to use. This keeps them cold and really crisp."

SUGARLESS BLUEBERRY MUFFINS

1 3/4 cups flour
2 teaspoons baking powder
1/2 teaspoon baking soda
1/2 teaspoon allspice
1/4 teaspoon cinnamon
1/4 teaspoon nutmeg
1/4 teaspoon salt
1 cup blueberries, washed and well drained
2 eggs, lightly beaten
1/4 cup vegetable oil
3/4 cup orange juice
Zest of 1 orange

Combine dry ingredients; toss blueberries with about 1/4 cup of dry mixture and reserve. Combine eggs, oil, orange juice, zest and beat well. Combine batter with dry ingredients, stirring only until ingredients are moistened. Fold in blueberries. Pour into 10 or 12 greased muffin cups, filing 2/3 full. Bake 20 to 25 minutes in preheated 400-degree oven. Makes 10 to 2.

PICNIC LEMON BUTTER

3 eggs
2 cups sugar
1 large lemon, juice and rind
2 teaspoons butter

Beat eggs well in top of double boiler white adding sugar. Place over water and cook over medium heat, stirring occasionally until thickened. Remove from heat, add lemon juice, rind and butter. Stir and allow to cool; then chill. Makes 2 cups.

PICNIC ICED TEA

2 family size teabags
3 quarts boiling water
1/2 cup sugar
1 can (12-ounce) frozen lemonade
    concentrate, undiluted
1 quart ginger ale

Steep teabags in water. Combine tea, sugar and lemonade. Just before serving, stir in ginger ale and pour over ice. Serves 10.

❖❖❖

COLD POACHED SALMON

4 cups fish stock or clam broth
2 cups white wine (preferably a Chenin
 Blanc or French Colombard)
6 peppercorns
1 small onion, coarsely chopped
1 carrot, coarsely chopped
1 bay leaf
3 coriander seeds
2 parsley sprigs
Pinch of dried thyme
6 salmon fillets (6 to 8-ounce size), skinned
 and boned
1/4 cup vegetable oil
2 tablespoons fresh lemon juice
Watercress
Chopped fresh chives, lemon wedges, fresh
 dill sprigs (garnish)

Combine stock, wine, peppercorns, carrot, onion, bay leaf, coriander, parsley and thyme in a large saucepan and bring to a boil over medium-high heat, skimming foam off the top as it forms. Partly cover, reduce heat and simmer about 30 minutes. Strain stock through a colander into a large skillet. Place over medium heat and bring to a gentle simmer. Reduce heat to low, add salmon and poach until almost cooked, about 6 minutes. Remove from heat and let fish cool in stock. Drain fillets well. Arrange in a single layer in a shallow baking dish. Sprinkle with oil and lemon juice. Cover and refrigerate overnight.

Drain salmon and pat dry with paper toweling. Arrange salmon on watercress; sprinkle lightly with salt and pepper. Cover and refrigerate. Serve with Avocado Cream (See index) and garnish with chives, lemon wedges and fresh dill. Serves 6.

TRISH'S CHOCOLATE - FILLED LEMON ROLL

1 cup cake flour, sifted
1 teaspoon baking powder
1/4 teaspoon salt
3 eggs
3/4 cup sugar
1/3 cup water
2 teaspoons grated lemon rind

Grease a 10 x 15 x l-inch jelly-roll pan; line the bottom with waxed paper. Grease the paper and sprinkle lightly with flour.

Sift cake flour, baking powder and salt and set aside. Beat eggs with electric mixer in a medium-

size bowl until light and fluffy. Still beating, gradually add sugar until mixture is very thick. Gently add water and lemon rind and mix well. Fold in the flour mixture; spread batter into prepared pan.

Bake in preheated 375-degree oven for 12 minutes or until cake is golden and center springs back when lightly touched.

Using a knife or small spatula, loosen cake around edges. Invert pan onto clean towel dusted with confectioners' sugar. Peel off waxed paper and trim 1/4-inch from sides of cake. Roll up cake, jelly-roll fashion, starting at a short end. Place seam-side down on a wire rack to cool completely. Prepare Filling.

FILLING:
1 package (3 1/2-ounce) chocolate pudding
1 2/3 cups milk
2 tablespoons butter

Combine pudding mix, milk and butter in small saucepan. Cook over medium heat, stirring constantly until mixture comes to a full rolling boil. Cool Completely.

Unroll cooled cake and towel. Spread cake evenly with Filling. Reroll cake and chill while making Frosting.

FROSTING:
1/4 cup butter or margarine
2 cups confectioners' sugar
1 tablespoon lemon juice
1 tablespoon (approximately) milk

Cream butter or margarine in small bowl. Beat in 1 cup of confectioners' sugar and lemon juice until blended; add other cup of sugar and enough milk to make frosting smooth and of spreading consistency.

Spread Frosting over chilled cake roll; refrigerate until ready to serve.

Jo and Jan say, "We happen to think the combination of lemon and chocolate is divine, so this recipe is right up our alley. It is a beautiful Springtime dessert, so pretty and delicious too."

❖❖❖

Father's Day Picnic

Fuzzy Navel Cocktails
Cheddar - Blue Cheese Spread
Crackers
Fix Ahead Ham Sandwiches
Or
Marinated Grilled Sirloin Steak
Tomato Salad
Roasted Potatoes
Tony's Italian Bread
Blueberry Slump
Or
Black Russian Cake With Glaze
Iced Tea - Coffee

Have this special Sunday-in-June picnic mark one of the best occasions in your man's life! Use a theme which compliments Dad's favorite sport. If he usually does the grilling, give him a day off, a comfortable lawn chair, a cold drink so he can relax, and let him just be "The Boss" that day.

If he insists on managing the grill, give him a new apron, hat and mitts, and let him choose the menu.

After you have enjoyed the food, it would be fun to have a game of softball, volleyball, badminton, or croquet. If tennis is his raquet, or golf his bag, a game of doubles or a hearty foursome might fit in the plans. Just remember, let Dad make the choice.

It might be that your man-of-the-day is a fisherman; if so, disregard all the above, pack your hamper for a picnic and head for the fishin' hole...and you bait the hook!

Whatever your Father's Day brings, make it an affair of the heart; a time for families to gather together to let Dad know how much he's loved and appreciated!

FUZZY NAVEL

2 parts orange juice
1 part peach schnapps
Fresh mint (garnish)

Pour juice and schnapps over ice in glass, stir well. Garnish with fresh mint, if desired.

Jo and Jan say, "As always, we prefer using the fresh-squeezed juice, but it is a matter of convenience and availability, so suite your own individual taste."

Jo and Jan also say, "You can make wonderful "shakes""with the peach schnapps. Combine vanilla ice cream, orange juice and peach schnapps for a milk shake and mix orange sherbet and peach schnapps for a really refreshing cooler."

CHEESE SPREAD

2 packages (8-ounce size) cream cheese, softened
1 medium onion, chopped fine
1 cup mild cheddar cheese, grated
1 cup sharp cheddar cheese, grated
2 ounces Blue cheese, crumbled
Several dashes of Worcestershire sauce
1 cup pecans, chopped

Combine all ingredients and blend thoroughly. Chill for several hours before serving. Can be made into 1 large or 2 small cheese balls. If you like, roll the balls in chopped fresh parsley.

FIX AHEAD HAM SANDWICHES

1 pound ham, shredded
2/3 cup margarine, softened
3 tablespoons green onion, finely chopped
3 tablespoons Dijon mustard
1 tablespoon poppy seed
8 sliced Swiss cheese
8 buns

Combine margarine, green onion, mustard and poppy seed. Cut buns in half and spread with 2 tablespoons of mixture on each. Top with a slice of cheese and ham as desired. Wrap in foil and bake in preheated 350-degree oven for 20 minutes. You may freeze these until you need them. Bring to room temperature and bake. Makes 8.

MARINATED GRILLED SIRLOIN STEAK

1 sirloin steak (about 2 1/2 pounds, cut 2
  inches thick)
3/4 cup catsup
3/4 cup chili sauce
1 1/2 tablespoons soy sauce
3 tablespoons honey
3 tablespoons green onions, chopped
3 cloves garlic, mashed
1/2 teaspoon salt
1/4 teaspoon pepper

Place steak in a plastic bag. Combine rest of ingredients in a bowl and mix well. Pour into bag with steak. Fasten bag with twistie and place in a shallow pan. Refrigerate for 24 hours, turning occasionally.

To prepare, remove steak from marinade and pat dry with paper towel. Grill 6 inches from grayed coals, brushing several times with marinade for about 8 minutes on each side for rare. Serves 6-8 hearty appetites.

TOMATO SALAD

6 large tomatoes, sliced 1/4-inch thick
1/2 cup olive oil
1/4 cup red wine vinegar
1 clove garlic, mashed
2 tablespoons grated onion
1 tablespoon Italian herbs

Slice tomatoes and place into shallow glass bowl. In a small bowl combine remaining ingredients and stir until blended. Pour over tomatoes and chill 1 hour. Serve cold on a bed of romaine or fresh spinach leaves. Serves 4.

ROASTED POTATOES

1 1/2 pounds small, red potatoes
2 tablespoons olive oil
2 cloves garlic, pressed
3 tablespoons butter or margarine
1 tablespoon dried rosemary leaves
Salt
Freshly ground pepper

Scrub potatoes; peel a strip around the middle of each. Add pressed garlic to olive oil. Melt butter and add to oil mixture; then add rosemary leaves. Toss the potatoes in this mixture to coat well. Roast in preheated 375-degree oven for 35 to 45 minutes, until potatoes are tender, turning gently every 10 minutes. Before serving, sprinkle with salt and pepper. Serves 6-8.

❖❖

TONY'S ITALIAN BREAD

1 16-ounce round shell bread (Focaccia, Italian bread, found in refrigerator section at markets or see index for recipe.
2 tablespoons olive oil
1 garlic clove, minced
Dash of pepper
1 tomato, peeled, seeded and chopped
1/4 cup Gorgonzola cheese or blue cheese, crumbled
1 teaspoon rosemary
1 teaspoon oregano
1 teaspoon basil

Place bread on lightly greased baking sheet. In a small bowl, stir together oil, garlic and pepper. Brush over bread very generously. Sprinkle tomato, cheese over bread and bake in preheated 400-degree oven for 10 to 15 minutes or until cheese melts. Cut into wedges. Serves 12.

VARIATION:

Instead of the cheeses, slice 1/2 red onion over the bread and sprinkle with Parmesan cheese.

Jan says, "I was served this bread at an Italian dinner and I asked the hostess for the recipe. I was delighted until I started looking for the flat bread, but finally found it. So keep looking."

BLUEBERRY SLUMP

1 quart blueberries
1/2 cup sugar
1/2 cup water
2 cups flour
2 teaspoons baking powder
1/2 teaspoon salt
I teaspoon sugar
1 teaspoon cinnamon
1/3 cup butter
1 tablespoon buttermilk

Sift together the flour, baking powder, salt and sugar. Cut in butter and add enough milk to make a soft dough.

Boil berries, sugar and water in saucepan until there is plenty of juice. Drop the dough mixture by tablespoons over berries, cover and cook 15 minutes.

This is a very old recipe, "Oldie and goodie!" It is equally delicious with raspberries or blackberries.

BLACK RUSSIAN CAKE WITH GLAZE

1 package (18 1/2 ounce) devil's food cake mix
1 package (3 1/2-ounce) instant chocolate pudding mix
4 eggs, beaten
3/4 cup brewed strong coffee, room temperature
3/4 cup coffee liqueur
3/4 cup creme de cacao
1/2 cup vegetable oil
GLAZE:
1 cup sifted confectioners' sugar
2 tablespoons brewed strong coffee, room temperature
2 tablespoons coffee liqueur
2 tablespoons creme de cacao
Confectioners' sugar for dusting

Combine cake ingredients in large mixing bowl. Blend at medium speed until a smooth batter. Pour into greased and floured 10-inch bundt pan. Bake in preheated 350-degree oven for about 45 minutes or until tester inserted in center comes out clean. Let cool 10 minutes in pan.

While cake is cooling, combine sugar, coffee and liqueurs. Invert cake and prick top several times with a fork. Spoon glaze over top and cool completely before storing in airtight container. Dust with additional confectioners' sugar before serving. Serves 10-12.

Jan and Jo say, "This is a variation of the very popular Black Russian Cake featured in A Cooking Affaire. It was the recipe Jan wouldn't give before the book was published. It has been so popular we thought you would enjoy this version."

❖❖❖

Mexican Fiesta Picnic Buffet

**Perfect Margaritas - Fruited Sangria
Kay's Guacamole With Chips
Ann's Chili Con Queso
Chili - Cheese Bean Dip
Chili - Cheese Squares
Mexican Layer Dip
T-N-T Drummettes
Quesadillas
Carol's Gazpacho
Allece's Enchiladas
Jolece's Chicken Fajitas
Virgil's Pozole & Carne Adovada
Chili - Cheese Cornsticks
Cheesecake Bars
Brandied Cafe Mexicano**

With summer in the air it is time to have a Mexican Fiesta in the back yard.

String twinkle lights and pinatas in the trees. Use lots of balloons and place luminaries among plants in the garden.

Dress tables with colored burlap or colored sheets, using bright accents of handcrafted tin pieces that are so popular in Mexico. This would be a great opportunity to use the tin foil pie plates for dishes. When your fiesta comes to an end you will be glad you can toss the plates in the trash.

Use a large tin kettle for your drinks. If you do not have the kettle, carve out a watermelon; it is great for holding drinks. Using an upright melon, cut a sliver from one end so that it stands evenly. Cut about 3 inches from the top for the opening. With a melon baller, scoop out melon balls, leaving a 1 1/2-inch shell.

Sombreros filled with flowers and vegetables would look smashing on the buffet table. Clay pots or hollowed out green, red and yellow peppers will hold votive candles. Have a lot sitting around so they will shine on all the tempting goodies you are serving. If you have used enough votives and have extra pots, fill them with relish sticks and the hollowed out peppers will hold the salsa and guacamole.

If you aren't too relaxed after your scrumptous meal, choose teams for charades. The winners get to take whacks at the pinatas!

P.S. A Mexican Fiesta isn't complete without music! If you know a guitarist, perfect. If not, play Mexican or guitar tapes as background music. It adds that extra touch to the party.

PERFECT MARGARITAS

**1 cup lemon juice
Coarse salt
2 1/3 cups tequila
2/3 cup Cointreau
1/2 cup superfine sugar
4 cups cracked ice
Fresh lime**

Squeeze lemons for juice in a flat dish; dip rims of 8 glasses (we use the popular margarita size) in juice, then dip in salt and refrigerate until ready to serve, at least an hour.

Combine lemon juice, tequila, cointreau, sugar and ice in blender in half portions; blend on high for 30 seconds. Pour into chilled glasses and garnish with a lime wheel. Serves 8.

✦✦

FRUITED SANGRIA

1 lemon, sliced
1 orange, sliced
1 apple, sliced
2 cups watermelon, cubed
1 pint strawberries, halved
1 small bunch seedless grapes
1 bottle dry red wine
1 bottle rose' wine
3 tablespoons sugar
1/2 cup brandy
1 bottle (28-ounces) club soda
Ice cubes
Fresh mint (garnish)

Place all fruit in a large container and gently stir in sugar, wine and brandy. Cover and marinate for at least 3 hours. To serve, add ice and club soda, garnish with fresh mint, if desired. Serves 12.

KAY'S GUACAMOLE DIP

3 large avocados
1 can (4-ounce) diced green chilies
2 packages green onion dip mix
1/2 cup sour cream
Taco sauce
Monterey Jack cheese, shredded
Sliced black olives

Peel and mash avocados; mix with green chilies, onion mix and sour cream. Spread on a large plate, about 1/2 to 3/4-inch thick.

Spread a small amount of Taco sauce over top and sprinkle with cheese and black olives. Refrigerate until serving time. Serve with tortilla chips.

Jo says, "If you prepare the avocados early and do not mix with the other ingredients, place an avocado seed in the middle of the mixture, cover and refrigerate until serving time. The seed will keep the avocado from turning dark."

ANN'S CHILI CON QUESO

16 ounces Velvetta cheese, chopped
1 can (15-ounces) chili without beans
1 bunch green onions, chopped
1 can (4-ounce) green chilies, drained and chopped
1/4 teaspoon hot pepper sauce

Remove seeds from chilies if milder flavor is desired. Mix all ingredients; pour into baking dish and bake for 45 minutes to 1 hour in a 275-degree oven. Serve hot in chafing dish with chips. Makes about 4 cups.

CHILI - CHEESE BEAN DIP

1 can (9-ounce) bean dip
1 package (3-ounce) cream cheese, softened
1 cup sour cream
1 can (7-ounce) chopped green chilies
1/2 cup chopped onions
11/2 teaspoons taco seasoning mix
1/2 pound Monterey Jack cheese, grated
1/2 pound Cheddar cheese, grated

Combine bean dip, cream cheese and sour cream; mix well and add chilies, onion and seasoning mix. Blend well and spread half of mixture in a 9 x 13 x 2-inch oven-proof baking dish. Layer cheeses on top and spread with remaining bean mixture. Bake in preheated 350-degree oven for 20 to 30 minutes or until bubbly. Serves 8-10.

CHILI - CHEESE SQUARES

1/2 cup butter, melted
10 eggs
1/2 cup flour
1 teaspoon baking powder
Dash of salt
1 can (8-ounce) chopped green chilies
1 pint cottage cheese
1 pound Monterey Jack cheese, grated

Lightly grease a 9 x 13 x 2-inch pan. Beat eggs lightly in large bowl. Blend in flour, baking powder and salt. Add melted butter, chilies, cottage and Jack cheeses; mix until just blended. Turn batter into prepared pan and bake in preheated 400-degree oven for 15 minutes; reduce heat to 350 degrees, bake 35 to 40 minutes. Cut into squares and serve hot. Makes approximately 100 squares.

MEXICAN LAYER DIP

1 can (15-ounce) refried beans
1 carton (16-ounce) sour cream
1 carton (16-ounce) guacamole
6 to 8 green onions, topped and chopped
1/2 to 1 cup cheddar cheese, grated
1/2 to 1 cup ripe olives, diced
Tortilla chips

Using a l-quart bowl, layer ingredients, starting with the beans. Layer twice. Serve with chips.

Jan says, "This dip may be layered twice, three times or more. Depends on how many you are serving. Make plenty for guests love it. I set out knives with it because you need to get to the bottom layer for the flavor blending."

T-N-T DRUMMETTES

3 dozen chicken wing drummettes
2 onions, chopped
6 garlic cloves, chopped
2 tablespoons chili powder
2 tablespoons dry mustard
1 teaspoon ground coriander
2 teaspoons ground cumin
1 teaspoon cayenne
2 teaspoons sugar
4 tablespoons Worcestershire sauce
3/4 cup bourbon
1 1/4 cup ketchup
1/2 cup cider vinegar
2 tablespoons lemon juice

Combine onions and garlic; set aside. Mix dry ingredients in a large bowl; add liquids, one at a time, stirring after each addition. Add onion-garlic mix. Pour marinade over chicken drummettes and marinate for 24 hours in the refrigerator; basting or turning if necessary.

Drain chicken wings, reserving marinade. Arrange chicken in baking dish in single layer. Pour sauce over wings and bake uncovered in 325-degree oven until wings are done and well coated. Baste as necessary. Makes 3 dozen.

Jan and Jo say, "You can also cook these on your outdoor grill; baste with sauce as needed. Also, sometime try this marinade with ribs. Excellent."

QUESADILLAS

Vegetable oil
12 flour tortillas
1 pound Monterey Jack cheese
3/4 cup Green Chile Relish (See index) or
  use commercial brand Sour cream
  (garnish)
Guacamole (garnish)
Picante Sauce (garnish)

Heat 1/2-inch shortening in a skillet over medium-high heat. Quickly dip each tortilla into shortening to soften. Drain on paper towels. Divide cheese into 12 slices; place a slice of cheese and 1 tablespoon of relish on half of each tortilla. Fold tortilla in center as a turnover. Place filled tortillas in an ungreased skillet and heat on medium, turning once, for 3 to 4 minutes or until cheese is melted and tortilla turns crisp. Serve accompanied by sour cream, Guacamole and picante sauce. Serves 12.

Jo and Jan say, "We're hooked on these! For a fun appetizer, use the larger tortillas. Do as above, except double the ingredients, spread cheese and relish on one tortilla and top with another to make a sandwich effect. After frying, cut into wedges and serve. You can get 4 to 6 triangles out of 1 'sandwich'.If you desire, you can use corn tortillas, we prefer the flour."

GREEN CHILE RELISH

1 large tomato, chopped
1 small onion, chopped
1/2 teaspoon garlic salt, or to taste
1 small can green chiles, drained and
  chopped

Combine all ingredients in mixing bowl and marinate at least 15 minutes. Makes about 2 cups.

Jan and Jo say, "This is what we use as the filling for our Quesadillas (See Index). Adjust amounts as your taste dictates."

CAROL'S GAZPACHO

1 can (10-ounce) tomato soup
1 can cold water
3 tablespoons olive oil
2 tablespoons wine vinegar
1 teaspoon garlic salt
1/2 teaspoon cayenne
1 medium tomato peeled and cut into small
  pieces
1 can chopped black olives
1/2 cup thinly sliced cucumber, cut into
  pieces
2 tablespoons sliced green onion
1 avocado, chopped

Combine all ingredients except avocado and chill well. Add chopped avocado to top of mixture just before serving. Serves 4.

❖◆◆❖

ALLECE'S ENCHILADAS

TORTILLAS:
2 cups flour
3 teaspoons shortening
1/2 teaspoon baking powder
14 tablespoons water (approx.)

CHILI WATER:
1/2 cup water
1 heaping tablespoon chili powder
MEAT MIXTURE:
1 pound ground beef
1/4 teaspoon garlic, crushed
1 teaspoon salt
3 tablespoons chili powder
1 tablespoon cumin
1 cup water
1 medium onion, chopped fine
1/4 pound Monterey Jack cheese, grated
Melted shortening

Mix and then roll mixture paper-thin or thin enough to handle. Be sure there are no holes. Roll out into circles of desired size. Fry on a very hot griddle, ungreased, on both sides until dried out, or until still pliable. Makes approximately 12-15.

Make chili water and set aside. Brown ground beef with garlic and salt. Add chili powder and cumin. Add 1 cup water and simmer until water is absorbed. Dip a tortilla in chili water; drain off excess water; place a tablespoon of meat mixture on tortilla. Sprinkle with cheese and chopped onion. Roll up and set aside. Continue until all tortillas are rolled. Fry quickly on both sides in hot melted shortening for 2 to 3 minutes on each side. Garnish with sour cream. Makes 12-15.

JOLECE'S CHICKEN FAJITAS

1/2 envelope Italian salad dressing mix
1/2 cup light rum
1/2 cup lime juice
1/4 cup vegetable oil
1 to 2 teaspoons hot pepper sauce
2 pounds boned, skinned chicken breasts
1 large onion, sliced in rings
1 red bell pepper
1 green bell pepper

Make a marinade by combining first 5 ingredients. Mix well and set aside. Combine chicken and vegetables in a large bowl; pour marinade over and refrigerate at least 4 hours or overnight.

Remove breasts from marinade, reserving 2 to 3 tablespoons of the liquid. Cook chicken stovetop or charcoal grill 10 to 15 minutes or until done. Do not overcook. Slice into strips.

In a large skillet, cook onion and peppers in the reserved marinade until crisp-tender. Set aside to serve with the chicken. Serves 4-6.

VIRGIL'S POZOLE

3 cups chicken stock
2 1/2 pounds boneless pork steak, trimmed
   and cut into 3/4-inch pieces
1 can (28-ounce) stewed tomatoes
1 medium onion, chopped
4 garlic cloves, pressed
1 can (15-ounce) white hominy, drained
1 1/4 cups chopped green or red chilies
1/2 teaspoon dried oregano, crumbled
1/2 teaspoon salt
1/2 teaspoon pepper

Combine all ingredients in Dutch oven or slow cooker. Cover and cook on low for 8 to 9 hours then serve hot. Serves 8 - 10.

Jo says, "Virgil is my brother-in-law. He and Carolyn live in Albuquerque and Virgil prides himself on being a connoisseur of Mexican cuisine (he makes the best margaritas ever). The first time I tasted Pozole they had come to Kansas and Virgil made a huge batch, keeping it warm in a crock-pot and served it with corn bread. You can serve side relishes such as chopped green onion, avocado, sliced mushrooms, shredded Monterey Jack cheese."

VIRGIL'S CARNE ADOVADA

1 quart unseasoned CHILE CARIBE (recipe
   follows)
3 cloves garlic, minced
2 teaspoons salt
2 tablespoons crushed oregano leaves
5 pounds lean pork loin strips

Add garlic, salt and oregano to the chili base and mix well in a blender; pour into bowl. Add pork strips to mixture, covering each strip well with chili. Cover and refrigerate at least 24 hours.

Into a 9 x 13-inch baking dish pour 1 cup of water and place meat strips in dish. Cover and place in a preheated 150-degree oven for 4 to 6 hours.

CHILE CARIBE (base for chile sauce)
10-12 red chile pods (seeded, stemmed)
1 teaspoon salt
1 clove garlic
1/4 teaspoon oregano leaves
2 1/2 cups cold water

Place all 5 ingredients in blender. Blend to a smooth paste and pour into a quart jar. Add 1/2 cup water to the blender and run at high speed. Pour remaining sauce in jar. This makes 1 quart of thin paste.

Jo says, "This is another of Virgil's favorites direct from Albuquerque. You can see why we look forward to their visits--Virgil cooks!"

TONIA'S MEXICAN CASSEROLE

1 pound hamburger
1 small onion, chopped
2 small cans chopped green chilies
1 can cream of chicken soup
1/2 can milk
1 cup sour cream
1 package small flour tortillas
Grated Mozzarella and Colby cheese
Black olives

Brown hamburger and onion; drain excess grease. Combine chilies, soup and milk and heat to a boil. Remove from heat and add sour cream. Place flour tortillas in a 9 x 13-inch pan. Spread hamburger mixture over tortillas, then cover with sour cream mixture; top with grated cheeses and black olives. Bake in preheated 350-degree oven for 30 minutes.

CHILI - CHEESE CORNSTICKS

1 1/4 cups yellow cornmeal
1/2 cup flour
2 tablespoons sugar
1 tablespoon baking powder
1/2 teaspoon salt
1 large egg
1 cup milk
1/4 cup salad oil
1/2 cup (2 ounces) Cheddar cheese,
   shredded
2 tablespoons chopped mild green chilies

In medium bowl combine cornmeal, flour, sugar, baking powder and salt; mix well. Add egg, milk and oil; beat just until smooth, about 1 minute with a whisk. Stir in cheese and chilies.

Grease 2 cornstick pans and spoon batter into them. Bake in preheated 425-degree oven for 12 to 15 minutes, or until golden. Loosen with tip of knife and turn out of pan. Makes 10 large or 14 small cornsticks.

CHEESECAKE BARS

5 tablespoons butter or margarine
1/3 cup brown sugar
1 cup flour, sifted
1/4 cup nuts, chopped
1/2 cup sugar
1 package (8-ounce) cream cheese, softened
1 egg
2 tablespoons milk
1 tablespoon lemon juice
1/2 teaspoon vanilla

Cream butter and brown sugar; add flour and nuts. Mix well and set aside 1 cup for topping. Press remainder in the bottom of an 8x8x2-inch baking pan. Bake in preheated 350-degree oven for 12-15 minutes.

Blend sugar and cream cheese until smooth. Add rest of ingredients and beat well. Spread over baked crust and sprinkle with the reserved topping. Bake for 25 minutes. Cool, then

chill. Cut into bars when ready to serve. Makes about 16 bars.

BRANDIED CAFE MEXICANO

1 1/2 squares (1 1/2-ounces) semisweet
  chocolate
1 cup milk
1 tablespoon sugar
1/4 teaspoon almond extract
1/4 teaspoon cinnamon
1 cup strong, hot coffee
1/4 cup brandy
2 cinnamon sticks (garnish)

Combine chocolate and milk in small pan over low heat and cook, stirring constantly until chocolate melts and milk is hot. Do not boil. Transfer to blender and add sugar, almond extract and cinnamon. Blend for 15 seconds.

Fill 2 mugs half full with chocolate, then pour hot coffee into each mug to almost fill. Add brandy to each and garnish with a cinnamon stick, if desired. Serves 2.

Jo says, "I usually add a dollop of whipped cream, with a sprinkling of cinnamon on top for a little pizazz."

MEXICAN CHOCOLATE SOUFFLE

1 cup milk
2 ounces unsweetened chocolate
1/2 cup sugar
1/2 teaspoon cinnamon
1/8 teaspoon salt
3 eggs
1/2 teaspoon vanilla
1 cup heavy cream, whipped
2 tablespoons confectioners' sugar

Heat milk, chocolate, sugar, cinnamon and salt in top of a double boiler, stirring to melt chocolate. Add eggs and vanilla; beat with rotary beater for 1 minute. Cover pan and cook for 20 minutes without disturbing. Whip cream with confectioners' sugar. Serve souffle warm or chilled topped with whipped cream. Serves 6.

For the Good Times

◆◆

For The Good Times

You are cordially invited…

For those special times of your life; when friends gather to celebrate meaningful events, here is an offering of some of our favorites. Included are some "Parties," Wedding suggestions, "Ladies Only" and Brunches. Also included are some very special ideas for your own Bed and Breakfast and "Something For A Mob."

Your own personality and unique touches will make your event very special and your guests will have such a good time they will leave your home hoping you will be entertaining again soon.

◆◆

Putting on the Ritz

**They came for the party
with a simplicity of
heart that was its
own ticket of admission."**
— *F. Scott Fitzgerald, "The Great Gatsby"*

**Martinis - Champagne - Wine
Jan's Hors D' Oeuvre Tart Shells with Assorted Fillings (See index)
Avocado Consomme With Bread Sticks
Caesar Salad
Grapefruit Sorbet
Roast Glazed Loin of Pork
Spinach Ramekins - Blue Cheese Stuffed Potatoes
Ruthie's Rolls
White Chocolate Mousse with Lillie's Chocolate Sauce and Raspberry Sauce (See index)
Coffee - Brandy**

One of our favorite dinner parties is a stylish sit-down dinner. The black-and-white theme of "Putting On The Ritz" will bring to mind images of the Art Deco period. Well thought-out plans are a "must" for the success of this party. Give special though to your guest list and send hand-written invitations bordered in black.

The mood of the evening will be set as your guests enter the front door. We suggest soft background music, dim lights, and candles galore. Be careful not to ruin appetites by serving cocktails too long or offering an over-abundance of hors d'oeuvres.

Your table can be covered with an always-elegant white damask cloth or it can be utterly dramatic covered with mirror place mats. Whichever, definitely use votive lights at each place and scatter them at random on the table. We suggest a mirror under your centerpiece for depth. Perhaps a tall crystal vase holding an arrangement of calla lillies will give you the dramatic look your guests will love. Of course, candle light reflecting off the mirrors creates a beautiful setting.

Tie narrow, black, satin ribbons on long-stemmed white carnations and lay one at each lady's place with the place card tucked close by. Each man's place card will have a white carnation boutonniere.

After you and your guests have enjoyed your wonderful dinner, return to the living room for demitasse and brandy...a fitting and beautiful finale for a memorable evening.

P.S. This is a wonderful party for the gentlemen to wear their tuxedos and the ladies their loveliest dresses; perfect for a New Year's Eve dinner. And, if your imagination runs rampant, try this for your favorite charity fund-raiser; complete with white gloves, top hats and tails!

TIP
• Where to sit? When hosting a party with 8 or 12 guests, you might wish to avoid having two men or two women seated together. In this case, you, the hostess should move 1 place to the left so the man on your right will be sitting opposite the host at the other end of the table. With 6 or 10 guests, the seating is evenly alternated, men and women, with the host and hostess sitting at opposite ends of the table.

For The Good Times

AVOCADO - CONSOMME APPETIZER

6 small avocados
Lemon juice
1 can (13-ounce) jellied chicken consomme, chilled
1 carton (8-ounce) sour cream
12 teaspoons red caviar
Cracked ice
12 lemon wedges (garnish)

Cut avocados lengthwise and remove pits. Brush cut surface with lemon juice. Spoon chilled jellied consomme into avocado centers; top each with a tablespoon of sour cream, then a teaspoon of caviar. Arrange avocados on cracked ice; serve with a wedge of lemon on the side to squeeze over the top. Serves 12.

Jo and Jan say, "This is a wonderful first course, elegant but easy, and so colorful!"

TONIA'S CAESAR SALAD

1 head romaine lettuce, washed, patted dry and crisped overnight in plastic bag
1 egg, coddled 1-2 minutes, cooled
2 large garlic cloves
6 oil-packed anchovy fillets (optional)
2 teaspoons lemon juice
1/2 teaspoon Dijon mustard
1 teaspoon Worcestershire sauce
1/3 cup olive oil
1/2 cup freshly grated Parmesan cheese
Fresh and coarsely grated black pepper
1 cup croutons (See index) or commercial onion-garlic croutons

Wash lettuce, coddle egg, set aside. Rub wooden salad bowl with garlic clove., then in a separate bowl, mash garlic and anchovies to make a paste. Add lemon juice, mustard, Worcestershire sauce and olive oil; mix well. Break chilled romaine into salad bowl; break egg over lettuce and toss lightly. Drizzle garlic dressing over lettuce and toss lightly until all traces of egg disappear and romaine is lightly coated with dressing. Sprinkle with cheese and add croutons; pepper generously and toss again. Divide on salad plates, sprinkle with more Parmesan cheese and pepper if desired. Serves 4.

Jo and Jan say, "Check index for our tips on croutons and dressing a salad."

PINK GRAPEFRUIT SORBET

5 large pink grapefruit
3/4 cup sugar
2 tablespoons grenadine syrup

Halve grapefruit; squeeze juice and strain. They should yield 4 cups. Combine sugar with 1 cup juice in saucepan and heat on low. Stir constantly until sugar is dissolved; but do not boil. Pour into a bowl, add remaining juice and grenadine. Refrigerate until chilled.

Transfer to container for ice-cream maker. Freeze according to manufacturer's directions until ice begins to stiffen. Remove container; remove dasher. Cover and freeze overnight. Makes 1 quart.

❖❖❖

ROAST GLAZED LOIN OF PORK

1 loin of pork (4 1/2 to 5-pound - 10 chops)
2 teaspoons salt
Freshly ground black pepper
2 teaspoons garlic powder
1 cup orange juice
1/2 cup light brown sugar
2 teaspoons ginger
1/4 teaspoon powdered cloves
1/4 teaspoon cinnamon

Rub salt, pepper and garlic powder over roast. Place in roasting pan, fat side up. Ribs will serve as a rack. Insert meat thermometer at a slant, bulb in center of meat, not touching bone.

Roast uncovered in preheated 325-degree oven for 35 minutes per pound or until thermometer registers 185 degrees.

Meanwhile, combine orange juice and rest of ingredients in a small saucepan. Simmer for 30 minutes. Brush this glaze generously over roast during the last 1 1/2 hours of roasting time; at least 4 times. Serves 8.

Jo and Jan say, "A nice variation of the glaze is to substitute 1 cup sweetened applesauce for the orange juice. It can be spread on an hour before roast is done and returned to the oven without any more glazing."

BLEU CHEESE STUFFED POTATOES

6 baking potatoes
4 tablespoons butter
3 tablespoons milk
1 cup sour cream
5 tablespoons bleu cheese, crumbled
3 tablespoons minced scallion
1 teaspoon salt
Freshly ground black pepper

Wash, grease and bake potatoes in a 450-degree oven for 45 minutes or until tender when tested with a fork. Remove from oven at once and cut a slice from the top of each potato.

Scoop out the inside of each, being careful you do not damage the skin. Mash the pulp, then beat in butter, milk and sour cream until mixture is light and fluffy. Stir in cheese, scallions and salt. Add grated black pepper to your liking.

Fill the shells with the mashed potato mixture, mounding them slightly. Return stuffed potatoes to oven for 8 to 10 minutes, making sure they are thoroughly heated. Serves 6.

Jo says, "We have always praised the potato, but these are absolutely the ultimate! Do try these for your next dinner party as they can be made ahead; perfect for relaxed entertaining!"

SPINACH RAMEKINS

Margarine (to prepare molds)
1/2 cup minced green onions, include tops
3 tablespoons margarine
3 packages (10-ounce size) frozen chopped
  spinach, cooked and drained
3 eggs, well beaten
3 egg yolks, well beaten
1 1/2 cups half-and-half
3/4 cup dry bread crumbs
1/3 cup grated Parmesan cheese
1/2 teaspoon salt
1/4 teaspoon white pepper
1/8 teaspoon nutmeg

Prepare 8 to 10 ramekins (6-ounce size) by buttering then lining the bottoms with waxed paper and buttering the paper.

Saute onions in margarine until soft. Combine with rest of ingredients in large bowl; mix well. Spoon mixture into prepared molds. Place molds in large baking pan and pour 1 inch of water around molds. Bake in preheated 350-degree oven for 20 to 25 minutes or until a knife inserted halfway between center and edge of mold comes out clean. Unmold onto serving plates, remove waxed paper and turn molds right side up. Serves 8 - 10.

Jo and Jan say, "These make wonderful picnic fare, serve cold, drizzled with olive oil and lemon juice or if you prefer to serve them hot, they are very nice garnished with sauteed mushrooms."

◆◆

RUTHIE'S REFRIGERATOR ROLLS

1 cup Crisco
1 cup boiling water
1/2 cup sugar, heaping
1 teaspoon salt
1/2 cup cold water
3 eggs, slightly beaten
2 packages dry yeast
1/2 cup water, very warm
6 cups flour

Combine and mix Crisco, water, sugar and salt in a large bowl. Add cold water and eggs. Mix yeast and warm water together and add to first mixture. Add flour all at once, mixing and kneading only slightly. Cover well and place in refrigerator 4 hours or overnight before using. Dough will keep a week.

Form into rolls and let stand 2 to 3 hours before baking in a preheated 375-degree oven for 10 to 15 minutes.

Black Tie Gourmet
For the Ladies

French '75's
Dazzling Caviar Mold
Allece's French Bread
Tomato - Herb Soup
Spinach Salad Flambe
Kiwi Sorbet
Veal Marsala
Rosemary - Garlic Roasted Potatoes
Elegant Circle of Cream
Wine - Coffee - Liqueurs

Jan and Jo say, "We would like to thank Jack Houlihan and his host group for sharing their Gourmet Dinner Presentation. We happen to think they have some very lucky ladies!

We are passing their idea on to you fellows. Get the creative juices flowing as to your invitations and menu, then dazzle your own true loves."

PLEASE COME FOR DINNER
Date:_____ Time:_____
Place:_____ Hosts:_____
Dress: Black Tie, String of Pearls!
R.S.V.P.

FRENCH '75'S

4 ounces brandy
4 ounces fresh lemon juice
4 ounces Simple Syrup (See Index)
Chilled champagne
Fresh strawberries

Pour 1 ounce of brandy, lemon juice and Simple Syrup in each of 4 champagne glasses. Stir and top with chilled champagne. Drop a fresh berry in each glass. Serves 4.

DAZZLING CAVIAR MOLD

GELATIN MIXTURE:
2 envelopes unflavored gelatin
1/2 cup water

EGG LAYER:
4 hard-boiled eggs, chopped
1/2 cup Homemade Mayonnaise (See index)
   or Hellmans
1 teaspoon lemon juice
2 scallions, minced
1/4 cup fresh parsley, minced
3/4 teaspoon salt
Dash Tabasco sauce
Freshly ground pepper

AVOCADO LAYER:
2 medium avocados, pureed just before
   using
2 medium avocados, diced just before using
2 large scallions, minced
2 tablespoons Homemade Mayonnaise or
   Hellmans
1 teaspoon lemon juice
1/2 teaspoon salt
Dash Tabasco sauce
Freshly ground pepper

SOUR CREAM AND ONION LAYER:
1 cup sour cream
1/4 cup minced onion

TOPPING:
1 jar (4-ounce) black caviar
Fresh lemon juice
Lemon slices
Freshly chopped parsley

In a small bowl, soften gelatin in water and set bowl in a pan of hot water; set aside. This gelatin mixture will be divided and used in all the layers. If making Homemade Mayonnaise, proceed with recipe as directed.

Oil an 8-inch spring-form pan with mayonnaise; set aside and prepare layers beginning with egg layer.

EGG LAYER: Combine all ingredients with 2 tablespoons of gelatin mixture. Taste and adjust seasonings. Neatly spread egg mixture into prepared pan with a spatula, smoothing the top. Wipe any egg mixture from foil with a paper towel; set aside and prepare avocado layer.

AVOCADO LAYER: Combine all ingredients with 3 tablespoons mixture. Taste and adjust seasonings. Gently spread over egg layer as described above. Set aside and prepare sour cream layer.

SOUR CREAM LAYER: Mix sour cream, onion and remaining gelatin. Spread carefully over avocado layer. Cover dish tightly with plastic wrap and refrigerate overnight.

Just before serving, place caviar in a fine sieve and rinse gently under cold water. Sprinkle with lemon juice and drain well. Open spring-form pan and transfer mold to serving plate with a wide spatula. Spread caviar over top and garnish with parsley and lemon slices around bottom of mold. Decorate top with a large lemon twist. Serve with thin slices of dark pumpernickel bread. Serves 18-20.

ALLECE'S FRENCH BREAD

1 tablespoon salt
1 tablespoon sugar
2 tablespoons shortening
1 cup boiling water
3/4 cup cold water
1 package yeast
1/4 cup warm water
5 to 5 1/2 cups flour
1 egg white, beaten

Mix salt, sugar, shortening and boiling water together. To this mixture, add cold water and the package of yeast which has been dissolved

in the warm water. Mix well, adding the flour slowly. Knead 5 minutes and put in a greased bowl. Cover and let rise 1 1/2 hours.

After rising, divide dough into 2 portions. Roll each portion in jelly-roll fashion. Pinch ends together and put seam side down on a cookie sheet. Brush with beaten egg white and make diagonal slashes across the top of each loaf.

Let rise for 1 hour. Bake bread in preheated 425-degree oven for 15 to 20 minutes. Reduce heat to 350 degrees and bake 30 more minutes. Let cool and slice bread through the slashes. Makes 2 loaves.

For The Good Times

TOMATO - HERB SOUP

1/4 cup olive oil
1/4 cup bacon
1 cup chopped onion
1/4 cup chopped leek (include white and
　　green part)
4 tablespoons chopped celery
1 cup tomato sauce
1 can (16-ounce) tomatoes, chopped
1/4 teaspoon oregano
1/4 teaspoon basil
1/4 teaspoon sage
1/8 to 1/4 teaspoon curry
1 quart chicken stock
2 tablespoons sugar
Salt and freshly ground white pepper
1/3 cup gin
1/2 cup sour cream
Sprigs of fresh dill

Heat oil over medium heat in heavy saucepan. Add bacon and cook until lightly browned. Add onion, leek and celery; cook until vegetables are tender, stirring occasionally. Stir in tomato sauce, tomatoes. Simmer 10 minutes then add herbs and simmer another 10 minutes or until mixture becomes like a puree. Add chicken stock and sugar, season to taste with salt and pepper, adjusting herb seasoning if your desire. Simmer 10 minutes, stirring occasionally then puree in blender.

Return to pan, bring to a boil, and stir in gin. Ladle into soup cups or bowls, top each with a dollop of sour cream and garnish with a sprig of fresh dill. Serves 6.

Jo and Jan say, "This can be prepared a day ahead up to the point of adjusting seasonings. It is wonderful for dinner parties!"

SPINACH SALAD FLAMBE

6 12-ounce bunches spinach, washed and
　　thoroughly dried
6 hard-boiled eggs, sliced
1 bunch green onions, sliced
1/2 pound fresh mushrooms, sliced
1/4 teaspoon salt
1/2 teaspoon ground pepper
1/2 teaspoon dried oregano, crumbled
1/4 teaspoon dried tarragon, crumbled
1/4 teaspoon dried rosemary, crumbled
12 bacon strips, chopped and fried crisp
Bacon drippings
1/2 cup red wine vinegar
1/4 cup lemon juice
4 teaspoons sugar
1 teaspoon Dijon mustard
1 teaspoon Worcestershire sauce
1 1/2 ounces brandy (100 proof)

Tear spinach into bite-size pieces and place in large bowl. Add egg slices, onions, mushrooms, salt, pepper, oregano, tarragon and rosemary.

Mix remaining ingredients except brandy in small saucepan and heat until very hot. Heat brandy briefly, add to saucepan and ignite. Pour flaming dressing over spinach mixture and toss gently but thoroughly. Serve on warm salad plates. Serves 8-10.

KIWI SORBET

1 cup water
1/2 cup sugar
1/2 cup light corn syrup
3 or 4 kiwifruit, pared and pureed to make
　　3/4 cup
5 teaspoons lemon juice
1/4 teaspoon grated lemon peel

Combine water, sugar and corn syrup in saucepan. Cook until sugar is dissolved, about 2 minutes. Add kiwi puree, lemon juice and lemon peel to sugar mixture. Pour into shallow pan and freeze until firm but not solid, about 1 hour. Remove from freezer and turn into a chilled bowl. Beat with mixer until smooth but not liquid. Return to freezer for about 2 hours or until firm. Serves 4.

VEAL MARSALA

2 pounds thin veal scallops
2/3 cup flour
2/3 cup butter
Salt and pepper
1/2 cup dry Marsala wine
1/2 pound fresh mushrooms, sliced
3 tablespoons butter
2 tablespoons chopped parsley

Pound meat very thin; dip into flour and saute for 2 to 3 minutes per side. Sprinkle with salt and pepper; remove from skillet and set aside, keeping them warm.

Add wine to skillet and stir to deglaze pan; simmering until thickened, about 2 to 3 minutes. Saute mushrooms in butter in a separate skillet; place veal on serving dish, cover with mushrooms and pour wine sauce over all. Sprinkle with parsley. Serves 8.

ROSEMARY - GARLIC ROASTED POTATOES

2 1/2 pounds small red new potatoes
1/4 cup fresh rosemary leaves, finely
  chopped
or 1 tablespoon dried
2 cloves garlic, finely chopped
3 tablespoons butter or margarine, melted
2 tablespoons olive oil
Salt and freshly ground pepper

Scrub potatoes and peel away a strip of skin around the center of each one. Combine melted butter and olive oil with rosemary and garlic in a medium-size pan. Toss potatoes in the mixture to coat well. Roast potatoes in preheated 375-degree oven for 35 to 45 minutes until potatoes are tender, turning gently every 10 minutes. Sprinkle with salt and freshly ground pepper to taste before serving. Serves 6-8.

ELEGANT CIRCLE OF CREME

2 cups heavy cream
1 cup sugar
1 envelope unflavored gelatin
2 cups sour cream
1 teaspoon vanilla
1/4 teaspoon almond extract
4 cups fresh raspberries, strawberries,
  blueberries; or a combination of all
OR
1 recipe Berries Romanoff (See index)

Mix cream and sugar in saucepan. Heat gently until sugar dissolves. Add gelatin and stir until gelatin is dissolved. Do not allow to boil. Remove from heat and cool in refrigerator until mixture begins to congeal, stirring occasionally.

Mix extracts with sour cream and fold into cooled mixture, whisk until quite smooth.

Pour into a large (4-cup) or 8 small (1/2 cup) oiled mold(s), cover and chill until set, at least several hours.

To unmold, dip mold in hot water to loosen edges. Invert mold onto platter and surround with berries of choice.

Jo says, "I like to have a bowl of light brown sugar and cinnamon on the table so guests can sprinkle some on top of the berries and creme if they desire."

For The Good Times

Intimate Valentine Dinner

Bellinis
Artichoke Dip
Crackers and Relishes
Carol's Broccoli Salad
Herbed Chicken Piccata
New Potatoes and Cherry Tomatoes
Herbed Dinner Rolls (See index)
Creme Caramel (See index)
Coffee - Courvoisier

Shared moments and a quiet evening for two will make this a very memorable Valentine's Day; an invitation to romance which says "I love you."

This would be the perfect time to serve dinner at your coffee table. Forget chairs and have pillows for seating; or an intimate table for two by the fire is always very cozy.

Your centerpiece can vary from elaborate red and pink sweetheart roses and baby breath to the always tastefully elegant single rose in a vase.

Remember, personal touches make anything more special and say "I love you" without uttering a word. Dim the lights; use lots of candles, the more the better and soft music in the background will enhance the mood of the evening.

The red rose whispers passion...
and the white rose breathes of love.
The red rose is a falcon,
And the white is a dove.

— *J. O. Reilly*

BELLINIS

2 fresh peaches or 1 cup frozen, sliced
1 tablespoon sugar
2 tablespoons brandy
2 teaspoons lemon juice
Champagne, chilled

Peel and quarter peaches. Freshly crushed and pressed peaches make the best juice; but fresh frozen will work well. Combine in blender with sugar, brandy and lemon juice; puree. To serve, 1/4 part peach puree to 3/4 part champagne is the correct ratio. For a proper Bellini, good champagne is the crucial ingredient. If you prefer, just use peaches and champagne, omiting other ingredients. Serves 4.

ARTICHOKE DIP

1 cup mayonnaise
1 cup Parmesan cheese
1 can artichoke hearts, chopped

Mix ingredients together. Bake at 350 degrees for 30-45 minutes until top is lightly browned. This is delicious with chips or relishes. Makes about 2 cups.

For The Good Times

CAROL'S BROCCOLI SALAD

1 large bunch broccoli, broken into flowerets
1 large cauliflower (optional) broken into floweretes
1 bunch scallions, diced
1/3 cup vegetable and olive oil, combined
1/4 cup red wine vinegar
1/3 cup mayonnaise
1 teaspoon salt
1/4 teaspoon pepper
1 teaspoon sugar
Ripe olives, sliced
Feta cheese, diced
Fresh red onion, cut in rings
1 red pepper, diced

Combine vegetable and olive oils, vinegar, mayonnaise and seasonings in blender. Mix well. Pour over broccoli. Top with olives, cheese, onion rings, and diced red pepper. Serves 8.

HERBED CHICKEN PICCATA

6 chicken breasts, skinned and boned
1/3 cup flour
1 1/2 teaspoons poultry seasoning
1/4 cup plus 2 tablespoons butter or margarine
3 tablespoons fresh lemon juice
1 lemon, thinly sliced
1 tablespoon capers

Place chicken breasts between waxed paper and flatten to 1/4-inch. Combine flour and poultry seasoning; dredge chicken in mixture.

Melt 1/4 cup butter in skillet. Add chicken and cook 3 to 4 minutes on each side or until golden. Add additional butter, if needed, a small amount at a time. Remove chicken and drain on paper towels. Place on heated serving platter. Add lemon juice, slices and capers to pan drippings and cook until bubbly. Pour mixture over chicken. Serves 6.

NEW POTATOES AND CHERRY TOMATOES

1 1/2 pounds small new potatoes, peeled
12 small cherry tomatoes
3 tablespoons margarine
2 teaspoons parsley, minced
4 tablespoons Parmesan cheese

Cook potatoes until fork-tender; set aside. In a 12-inch skillet, melt margarine; add potatoes, tomatoes, parsley and stir gently until potatoes and tomatoes are coated. Sprinkle the Parmesan cheese over the mixture until coated. Serve in a warm bowl. Serves 4.

Jan says, "I use new potatoes in many ways and just happened to add the tomatoes one time. Now it is one of our favorites and is an eye-catcher with the colorful veggies."

For The Good Times

Wedding

Of all life's celebrations, the wedding offers the most variations as how the ritual will be performed. It does not matter if your wedding celebration is a large church affair followed by a huge sit-down dinner, or a an intimate gathering of family and friends in your home - your special day follows careful planning.We will not attempt to help you plan your wedding, but offer you our favorite recipes which can be adapted to your own tastes and plans. We suggest you also look in Cheer Delights and The Lady Has Taste for other choices.

CHAMPAGNE COCKTAIL

2 tablespoons cognac
2 tablespoons triple sec
1 sugar cube rubbed with orange
Dash angostura bitters
2 slices orange
8 ounces chilled champagne

Mix together all of the ingredients except the champagne. Divide between 2 oversized wine goblets. Add 1/2 cup champagne to each glass just before serving. Serves 2.

Jo and Jan say, "For those intimate toasts."

BRIDE'S CHAMPAGNE PUNCH

8 1/2 cups orange juice
4 1/2 cups orange liqueur
2 cups superfine sugar
1 1/2 cups fresh lemon juice
1/2 cup fresh lime juice
9 bottles (26-ounce size) champagne, chilled
7 bottles (28-ounce size) club soda, chilled

Combine 4 cups orange juice and 1 bottle of club soda. Fill an 8-cup mold and freeze overnight or until frozen.

Combine remaining orange juice with orange liqueur, sugar, lemon and lime juices. Allow flavors to blend overnight. When ready to serve, add chilled champagne and remaining bottles of club soda, pouring over frozen ice mold. Float berries in the punch, if desired. Serves 50.

BRANDY CHAMPAGNE WEDDING PUNCH

Juice of 6 lemons
4 half pints orange curaco
4 half pints Christian Brothers brandy
6 tablespoons sugar
3 fifths dry champagne, chilled
1 quart ginger ale, chilled

Combine lemon juice, orange liqueur, brandy and sugar. This can be make ahead. Add champagne and ginger ale at the last minute. Serve over ice mold.

SHERRIED MUSHROOMS

1 pound fresh mushrooms
1 tablespoon chopped green onions
1 tablespoon butter
1/2 pint heavy cream
1 tablespoon sherry
1/2 teaspoon salt
1/8 teaspoon pepper
Parmesan cheese, optional

Wash and dry mushrooms. Remove and chop stems finely. Saute stems and chopped green onions in butter. Add remaining ingredients and cook about 10 minutes or until mixture thickens. Fill mushroom caps with cooked mixture, sprinkle with Parmesan cheese and place under broiler until brown and bubbling. Makes about 30.

Jo and Jan say, "We like these because they can be prepared in advance, refrigerated and popped under the broiler just before serving."

CHUTNEY CHEESE SPREAD

1 package (8-ounce) cream cheese, softened
4 ounces sharp cheddar cheese
4 ounces mild cheddar cheese
1/2 teaspoon curry powder
1/4 cup dry sherry
1/2 cup chopped chutney
1/4 cup scallions, chopped

Combine all ingredients and blend well. Chill and serve with crackers. Makes about 2 1/2 cups.

Jo and Jan say, "This is one of our most popular spreads. We have served it at signings and at markets and always get raves on it. Men will fall into the bowl! Try it as a spread on smoked turkey sandwiches sometime for a delicious treat."

CASHEW - CHUTNEY SPREAD

1/2 cup chopped cashews
5 tablespoons chutney, chopped
1 package (8-ounce) cream cheese, softened
1/2 teaspoon lemon juice
1/4 teaspoon curry powder

Combine all ingredients and chill. This is delicious on sliced fresh fruit. Makes about 1 3/4 cups.

TARTARE CANAPES

2 1/2 pounds ground round steak
Juice of 1 lime
4 tablespoons dry red wine
1/2 cup onions, chopped fine
3 cloves garlic, minced
3/4 teaspoon Tabasco sauce
2 teaspoons dry mustard
1 teaspoon salt
2 tablespoons Worcestershire sauce
1 teaspoon hickory smoked salt
1 teaspoon curry powder
1 teaspoon bottled steak sauce
Drained capers (optional)
Fresh parsley (garnish)
Cherry tomatoes (garnish)

Put meat through grinder twice; (Butcher will do this for you). Add other ingredients except capers. Mix all together and make a round mound; refrigerate several hours.

To serve, set bowl of capers beside platter of meat. Arrange parsley and tomatoes around mound and serve with a basket of icebox rye, cut silverdollar thin. Serves 18-20.

Jo and Jan say, "Stuff cherry tomatoes with this delicacy. They make a beautiful presentation."

◆◆

PEPPER JELLY STUFFED SNOW PEAS

1/2 pound fresh snow peas
1 package (8-ounce) cream cheese, softened
1/4 cup green pepper jelly
1 tablespoon green chilies, drained and
  chopped
  OR
1/4 cup chopped nuts

Prepare snow peas as instructed in Pea Pod Boats (See index). Combine cream cheese and rest of ingredients until smooth. Fill pea pods and arrange on plate. Cover and chill for up to 4 hours before serving. Fills 1/2 pound.

STUFFED CHERRY TOMATOES

2 pounds cherry tomatoes
Fresh parsley for garnish

Wash and dry cherry tomatoes. Cut around the stem, remove and hollow out pulp. Turn upside-down on paper towels to drain completely. Stuff tomatoes with filling of choice and tuck a tiny sprig of parsley on top. Makes about 40.

FILLING:
1 package (8-ounce) cream cheese, softened
1/2 cup sour cream
2 tablespoons dry onion soup mix
2 tablespoons milk, or enough to make
  spreadable
1 jar or package chipped beef, chopped fine
1 can deviled ham

Blend ingredients and fill drained cherry tomatoes.

Jo and Jan say, "We really have fun with the stuffed vegetable appetizers! The possibilities are endless. Try some of Tonia's Spinach Dip, Mushroom Appetizer, or the Artichoke-Rice salad mixture (See index). It's impossible to goof with any of these and they are so perfect, being bite-size! Arrange the tomatoes and brussels sprouts on a bed of alfalfa sprouts for a nice presentation.

STUFFED BRUSSELS SPROUTS

Cook brussels sprouts in boiling chicken broth, covered, for about 5 minutes, or until a brilliant green. Rinse under cold water. Cut each sprout about 13 through the center in an X with a small knife. Stuff with Boursin cheese or filling of your choice, if you have another favorite.

Jo and Jan say, "These are pretty and very unusual. Be the first of your crowd to present these."

STUFFED MINIATURE BEETS

1 can (814-ounce) baby beets
Boursin cheese (See index or buy
  commercial brand)
Fresh parsley for garnish

Drain beets well. Scoop out center with melon ball cutter; turn upside-down on paper towels until ready to fill. Do not fill until soon before serving as beets will still "bleed" a bit. Fill with softened Boursin cheese and tuck a sprig of parsley in the top.

CAVIAR CHEESECAKE

CRUST:
1 1/2 cups breadcrumbs
1/2 cup butter or margarine, melted
**3 tablespoons Parmesan cheese, freshly
  grated**

FILLING:
**3 packages (8-ounce size) cream cheese,
  softened**
5 eggs, room temperature
3 tablespoons grated onion
1/2 teaspoon lemon extract
1/4 cup butter, melted
4 cups sour cream, room temperature
7 ounces black caviar, rinsed and drained

Line bottom of 10-inch spring-form pan with waxed paper. Mix crust ingredients and press crumbs firmly against sides and bottom of pan. Refrigerate and prepare filling.

Combine cheese, eggs, onion and lemon extract in blender until smooth. Blend in melted butter and transfer mixture to a bowl. Stir in sour cream and fold in the caviar. Spoon filling into chilled crust and bake in preheated 350-degree oven for 45 minutes. Turn off oven and allow cheesecake to remain in oven 15 to 20 minutes. After this time, the filling will appear to be unset; remove from oven and let cool to room temperature. Cover with plastic and refrigerate at least 12 hours before serving. Serves 20 to 24.

MUSHROOM APPETIZERS

**24 thin bread slices, crusts removed,
  buttered on both sides**
4 tablespoons butter
2 tablespoons grated onion
1 pound fresh mushrooms, finely minced
2 tablespoons flour
1 cup heavy cream
1 tablespoon Dijon mustard
1/2 teaspoon salt
1/2 teaspoon Tabasco sauce
Dash ground nutmeg
**1 tablespoon fresh parsley, chopped or 1
  teaspoon dried**
1 1/2 tablespoons chives, chopped
2 teaspoons lemon juice

Grease 24 small muffin tins; fit one bread slice into each mold. Trim edges as necessary. Bake in preheated 400-degree oven for 10 minutes; remove shells from muffin tins and cool on a rack.

Melt butter in skillet and saute onion. Add mushrooms and cook, stirring often, until all moisture is gone. Stir in flour and blend well; add cream and cook stirring until thickened. Add mustard, salt, Tabasco, nutmeg, parsley, chives and lemon juice; stir to blend. Place cooled shells on cookie sheet; fill with mushroom mixture. Bake in 350-oven for 10 minutes. Cool slightly before serving. Makes 24.

Jo and Jan say, "Use puff pastry instead of bread slices. Cut rounds and bake in tart shells for a dazzling first course, or part of a tea menu. You can also flatten out Crescent roll dough and make the shells from it. The unfilled shells may be frozen. It is not necessary to thaw them before filling and baking. This is truly delicious!"

For the Good Times

ROQUEFORT MOUSSE

3 envelopes unflavored gelatin
1 cup cold water
6 egg yolks
1 cup light cream
2 packages (3 1/4-ounce size) Roquefort cheese
1/4 teaspoon salt
6 egg whites, stiffly beaten
1 cup heavy cream, whipped

Dissolve gelatin in cold water, set aside. Combine egg yolks, light cream, cheese and salt in blender container. Blend until smooth; pour in top of double boiler. Cook over boiling water 10-12 minutes until creamy and slightly thickened, stirring constantly. Add softened gelatin and stir until gelatin is dissolved. Remove from heat and pour into large bowl. Chill until it mounds slightly. Fold in beaten egg whites, then fold in whipped cream.

Spray inside of a 2-quart or 2 smaller molds with cooking spray. Spoon mixture into mold. Chill until firm. Serves 20.

Jo says, "Glass, stainless steel or non-stick molds are recommended so color of the mousse is not affected. This mousse is delicious served with fruits and crackers."

AVOCADO MOLD

1 1/2 envelopes (1 1/2 tablespoons) unflavored gelatin
1/2 cup cold water
3/4 cup boiling water
2 tablespoons lemon juice
1 1/4 teaspoons salt
1 tablespoon grated onion
2 dashes Tabasco sauce
2 1/2 cups well-mashed avocado
1 cup sour cream
1 cup mayonnaise

Soften gelatin in cold water; dissolve in boiling water. Add lemon juice, salt, onion and Tabasco. Cool to room temperature; stir in avocado, sour cream and mayonnaise. Turn in a greased 6-cup mold; chill until firm, (5-6 hours or overnight). Unmold on serving plate. Fill center with curly endive and decorate with pimento or cherry tomatoes. Makes 6 cups.

Jo says, "I have been making this for years. It is so pretty on a Christmas buffet, great with Mexican food, and makes a tremendous luncheon entree filled with a shrimp or chicken salad."

SHRIMP MOLD

2 envelopes unflavored gelatin
1/2 cup cold water
1 package (8-ounce) cream cheese, softened
1 cup celery, finely chopped
1/4 cup grated onion
1 1/2 pounds frozen shrimp, thawed and finely chopped
1 can tomato soup
1 cup mayonnaise

Dissolve gelatin in water; heat over hot water until clear, stirring constantly.

In another pan heat soup but do not boil. Add softened cream cheese, a little at a time until melted, then add gelatin and beat the mixture with a rotary beater or hand mixer. Allow to cool.

Add celery, onion, shrimp and mayonnaise. Pour mixture into a well-greased mold (try greasing with mayonnaise) and refrigerate until firm. We recommend making the mold the day ahead of serving.

Unmold on a bed of parsley or watercress and serve with crackers.

FRUIT AND PASTA PRIMAVERA

1 navel orange, peeled and sliced into thin
   rounds
2 kiwi fruit, peeled and sliced into thin
   rounds
1/2 pint strawberries, hulled
1 carton fresh raspberries, blackberries or
   blueberries
1 cup seedless grapes, can be green and red
1 cup cantaloupe, cut in chunks or balls
1 cup honeydew melon, cut in chunks or
   balls
1/4 cup dark rum
1/4 cup honey
1 pound spaghetti or linguine pasta
2 cups English Pastry Cream (See index)
1/4 cup fresh mint leaves

Toss fruit with rum and honey. Cover and refrigerate for 2 hours, stirring frequently. While fruit is marinating, prepare English Cream. Cook pasta for 10 minutes or until al dente and cool under cold running water, then refrigerate in cold water until ready to be used.

Drain fruit and reserve the marinade. Drain pasta well. Stir fruit marinade into the cooled pastry cream. Toss pasta with half of pastry cream, mound on a chilled serving plate; arrange fruit on the pasta and ladle the remaining sauce over fruit. Sprinkle with mint leaves. Serves 8.

PARTY TORTE

12 crepes, made to fit 8 1/2-inch straight side
   springform pan
3 packages, (8-ounce size) cream cheese,
   softened
3/4 cup mayonnaise
1 tablespoon dill weed, or to taste
1/4 teaspoon Tabasco sauce, or to taste
1 cup green onions, chopped fine
6 ounces Provolone cheese, sliced paper
   thin
6 ounces Mozzarella cheese, sliced paper
   thin
6 ounces salami, sliced paper thin
6 ounces ham, sliced paper thin
6 ounces smoked turkey breast, sliced paper
   thin
1 cup chopped walnuts, for side of torte
1 tomato, cut in narrow wedges, for top of
   torte
3 hard-boiled eggs, minced, for top of torte

Make crepes ahead and refrigerate or freeze. Blend cream cheese, mayonnaise, dill and Tabasco until smooth. This is the spread for crepes.

Spread each crepe with a thin layer of cream cheese mixture, reserving enough to frost the completed torte.

Place the first crepe in the bottom of springform pan (See notes). Top the first crepe with chopped green onion. Place next frosted crepe on top of onions, leaving it with just the cream cheese. Continue to layer cream-spread crepes, alternating with a layer of filling, pressing down as you work, building the edges up more than the center.

The top of the torte will be a crepe; frost top and sides and decorate as suggested in our notes with walnuts, eggs and tomatoes, or garnish your desire. Serves 10-12.

Jo and Jan say, "Expect raves when you present this at your next celebration! It is a meal in itself; toss a light salad, fill a basket with hard rolls and prepare a beautiful tray of fruit. That's it!"

NOTES: Prepare the torte a day ahead because it does take time and needs to be refrigerated to set up. We build it in a greased springform pan; when all the layers are completed and pressed down, release the sides of the pan, frost top and sides with cream cheese mixture, press chopped nuts into the sides, and decorate the top with minced hard-boiled eggs and place tomato wedges around the edges. Refrigerate until serving time. Slice the torte like a pie with a serrated or electric knife. Be innovative, make up your own layers, have fun! Serves 10-12.

For the Good Times

GROOMS CHOCOLATE CAKE

5 cups cake flour, sifted
1 1/2 cups cocoa
2 teaspoons baking powder
1 teaspoon salt
2 cups milk
2 teaspoons vanilla
2 1/2 cups butter, softened
4 cups brown sugar
6 large eggs

Preheat oven to 350 degrees. Grease and flour three 18-inch round cake pans; set aside. Sift flour, cocoa, baking powder and salt.; set aside. Combine milk, vanilla and set aside.

In large bowl beat butter and brown sugar until light and fluffy. Add one egg at a time and beat well after each addition. Alternately add 1/4 flour with 1/3 milk mixture until all flour and milk has been used. Divide evenly among pans. Bake for 25 minutes. Cool cake layers in pans on wire racks.

WHITE CHOCOLATE MOUSSE FILLING:

2/3 cup milk
4 tablespoons creme de cocoa
2 enveloped unflavored gelatin
12 ounces white chocolate, chopped
2 egg whites, large
1/2 cup sugar
2 cups heavy cream

In top of double boiler combine milk, creme de cacao and gelatin. Let stand 1 minute. Place over hot water and stir constantly until gelatin is dissolved. Add white chocolate and stir until melted and mixture is smooth; cool.

In small bowl, beat egg whites until foamy. Gradually beat in sugar until stiff peaks are formed. Stir about 1/2 cup meringue into gelatin mixture, fold in remaining meringue. Whip cream until stiff and fold into meringue mixture. Chill until spreadable. Spread half of Mousse on each of the two cake layers and chill in freezer until firm.

CHOCOLATE-MOUSSE FROSTING:

12 squares semisweet chocolate
20 tablespoons butter
6 large eggs, separated
2/3 cup sugar
1 cup heavy cream

In medium saucepan, over low heat, melt chocolate and butter. Remove from heat and whisk in egg yolks one at a time; cool 10 minutes. In a large bowl beat egg whites until foamy. Gradually beat in sugar until stiff peaks are formed. Blend about 1/2 cup meringue into chocolate mixture and fold in remaining meringue. Whip cream until stiff. Fold into meringue mixture and chill until firm enough to spread. Spread frosting on side and top of cake; refrigerate. Decorate with White Chocolate Leaves, below.

WHITE CHOCOLATE LEAVES

4 ounces white chocolate
Rose leaves or ivy leaves, rinsed and patted dry

Melt chocolate in double boiler over hot water. When melted, take knife and spread chocolate on backs of leaves, making sure the leaves are covered well. Set on baking sheet and chill until firm. Gently pull off leaves. The cake may be decorated with the white chocolate leaves and clusters of frosted grapes.

For the Good Times

✦✦

Ladies Only

We though it would be helpful to bring you some of our ideas and special touches for your entertaining. There is much to take into consideration when you start to plan a party, be it large or small, formal or informal. Menus, table decorations and guests should be carefully thought out; your anticipation, enthusiasm and eagerness will show.

A pretty table for a fancy or casual affair always sets the mood. Don't be afraid to improvise and use your imagination. It is not necessary to have an expensive floral arrangement in the center of the table. Use a few cut flowers for an airy look or use the tiny bud vases or miniature liqueur bottles with a flower tucked into each; setting them at random on the table. Look around your house and you will find a certain vase, bowl, basket or soup tureen that would suffice with one of your potted plants, some fruit or vegetables, depending on the time of the year. Candles, whether tall or votives, are lovely and certainly warm the atmosphere. If you are having a large sit-down luncheon or dinner using separate tables, your plates do not have to match and you may harmonize your tablecloths. Variety is the spice of life and your party should reflect your personality.

If you are having a buffet and room is no problem, set up several tables and keep the guests flowing. Have a table for plates, napkins and silverware; another for food and a separate small table for dessert. We all know how popular white wine is, particularly at a luncheon, while waiting for all guests to arrive. A stemmed water glass is nice for wine if you do not have enough wine glasses. If no man is around, let us tell you how to uncork your wine.

1. Cut the foil below the lip of the bottle with a sharp knife.

2. Wipe off the top of the bottle before pouring.

3. Do not ram in the corkscrew. Take time to center it and turn the screw in slowly. Pull or lever up with steady pressure, holding the bottle with the other hand.

Pour the wine in a decanter. If you do not have one, use other glass containers such as water carafes, flower vases or martini pitchers.

1 wine bottle - 24 ounces
1 wine glass - 4 ounces
1 fifth - 16-1 1/2-ounce jiggers

Ladies, if you are going to entertain other ladies between the hours of two to four o'clock you will need no more than 5 or 6 hors d' oeuvres per guest. Since the party will end at four o'clock you may assume the ladies will not be making the hors d'oeuvres their dinner. Women like the lighter variety of snacks such as pea pods stuffed with cheese, green or red seedless grapes wrapped in a cream cheese and Roquefort mixture and rolled in chopped nuts. We always leave some free of the Roquefort cheese because there are those who do not care for the flavor.

A party for men and women between the hours of five and seven o'clock calls for heartier hors d'oeuvres, perhaps including beef and/or shrimp. Plan on each guest having 8 to 10 pieces. We always like to serve a variety; little sandwiches and dips are enjoyed by all. Have enough for everyone to sample because you want them to go away happy and satisfied; that they were able to taste every one of your tremendous array of hors d'oeuvres.

TIP

• The next time you entertain at a brunch or luncheon dress up your butter. Line a clear glass bowl or juice glass with edible flowers, such as pansies, nasturtiums, roses, violets and fill with softened butter; refrigerate until serving time. So pretty, and a conversation piece!

Squash blossoms, nasturtium blossoms, violets make a pretty statement on a plate. A beautiful presentation will have your grests raving about your ability as a hostess; women love these special touches.

For the Good Times

SOOTHING FINGER TOWELS

4 tablespoons lemon juice
4 cups water
8 washcloths

Combine lemon juice and water. Wet washcloths in mixture; wring out and roll. Tie each cloth with a cloth ribbon and place in a basket. Cover with plastic wrap. When ready to use, place basket of cloths in microwave on High for 2 minutes. Hand out towels to guests and watch them smile.

BATHE A TIRED BODY

Make strong tea from a blend of chamomile, lavender, rosemary and mint; add to bath water. This herbal bath is very relaxing, refreshing and stimulating to a tired body. Just the answer for one of THOSE days!

RITES OF SPRING FRUIT PUNCH

2 cans (12-ounce size) frozen lemonade
2 cans (6-ounce size) frozen limeade
1 can (32-ounce) pineapple juice
1 can (32-ounce) apricot nectar
8 ounces Grenadine syrup
1 bottle ginger ale
Ice mold filled with fruits or flowers
Vodka (optional)
Brandy (optional)

Combine first 5 ingredients using amounts of water suggested on lemonade and limeade cans. Chill; then just before serving, add remaining ingredients. Pour over ice mold and add ginger ale and, if you desire, 1/2 bottle vodka and 1/2 bottle brandy. Serves 50.

Jo says, "If you desire a yellow punch, omit the Grenadine syrup."

MARIE'S PINEAPPLE, ORANGE, BANANA PUNCH

5 bananas, mashed
48 ounces pineapple juice
2 cans (12-ounce size) frozen orange juice, thawed but not diluted
1 can (12-ounce) frozen lemonade, thawed but not diluted
6 cups water
3 cups sugar
3 quarts ginger ale

Heat and boil sugar and water; cool. Add mashed bananas and thawed juices. Freeze four hours, stirring occasionally. Add ginger ale just before serving.

LUNCHEON EGGNOG

2 ounces dark rum
6 ounces milk
1 egg
Sugar
Nutmeg, freshly grated

Shake rum, milk, egg and sugar to taste with ice. Strain into a Tom Collins glass. Sprinkle with nutmeg. Serves 1.

PEACH ROYALE

5 parts dry white wine
1 part peach schnapps
1 slice fresh peach

Serve with ice or thoroughly chill the wine and schnapps. Garnish with the peach slice. Serves 1.

WILMA'S WOMENS' DAIQUIRI

3 packages (10-ounce size) frozen
  strawberries, partially thawed
4 cans (6-ounce size) pineapple-orange,
  thawed
4 cans (6-ounce size) pink lemonade, thawed
4 cans (6-ounce size) water
1 can or bottle (12-ounce) 7-Up
3 cans (6-ounce size) vodka

Blend all ingredients in blender until well-mixed. Pour into a 3 to 4-quart bowl and put into freezer.

Jan says, "You will have to mix several batches in the blender for this recipe is too much for 1 container. This is a great drink for the girls' get-togethers." Makes 1 gallon.

RASPBERRY FIZZ

8 ice cubes
1 package (10-ounce) frozen raspberries in
  syrup, (undrained), pureed and strained
1/2 cup fresh orange juice
1/2 cup heavy cream
1/3 cup gin
1/4 cup fresh lemon juice
1/4 cup raspberry liqueur
2 eggs
4 teaspoons sugar

Combine all ingredients in blender and mix until smooth. Divide among chilled glasses; serve immediately. Serves 4.

FROSTY SOURS

1 can (6-ounces) frozen orange juice
  concentrate
2 juice cans water
1 juice can bourbon
1 can ((5 3/4 ounces) frozen lemon juice
2 egg whites
1/4 cup sugar
Orange slices
Mint sprigs

Combine all ingredients except orange slices and mint sprigs in an electric blender. Blend on low speed until smooth, then on high until flothy. Pour into ice-filled glasses. Garnish with orange slices and mint. Makes 10 4-ounce servings.

WHISKEY SOUR MIX

1/2 cup water
1 cup sugar
1 1/2 cups fresh lemon juice
2 cups bourbon
2 tablespoons bottled marachino cherry juice
Orange slices (garnish)
Marachino cherries (garnish)

Combine water and sugar in saucepan; cook over medium heat until clear and syrupy. Add lemon juice to syrup and cook until it is frothy. Remove from heat; add bourbon and cherry juice. Refrigerate and serve over ice. Garnish with orange slices and cherries. This will keep in refrigerator for months. Serves 8-10.

For the Good Times

BUBBLY BLOODY MARY

3 ounces vodka
2 1/2 ounces fresh lemon juice
6 ounces bloody Mary mix
1/4 teaspoon Tabasco sauce, or to taste
Dash Worcestershire sauce
2 ounces club soda
Fresh lime wheels
Celery stalks

Combine all ingredients and serve over ice. The soda gives you a light drink; lemon juice adds a zing. Garnish with lime wheels and celery. Serves 2.

LADIES' DAY FRUIT SLUSH

1 can (6-ounce) frozen pink lemonade, undiluted
1 can (6-ounce) frozen orange juice, undiluted
1 can (20-ounce) crushed pineapple, undrained
1 package (16-ounce) frozen raspberries or strawberries, thawed (unsweetened if possible)
1/2 to 1 cup sugar (use 1/2 cup if berries are sweetened)
1 jar (6-ounce) marachino cherries, undrained
3 cans (6-ounce size) water
4 to 5 bananas, sliced

Mix all ingredients in a large container and freeze. Remove from freezer about 20 minutes before serving. Makes 20-24 servings.

IRISH CREAM LIQUEUR

1 cup Irish whiskey
1 can (14-ounce) sweetened condensed milk
1 tablespoon chocolate syrup
1 teaspoon vanilla extract
1/4 teaspoon coconut extract
3 eggs
1 1/4 cups heavy cream

Combine ingredients in blender; store in refrigerator. Serves 12.

SALMON PARTY BALL

1 package (8-ounce) cream cheese, softened
1 can (16-ounce) salmon, drained and flaked
1 tablespoon lemon juice
1 tablespoon grated onion
1/4 teaspoon liquid smoke
1/4 teaspoon salt
1/4 cup pecans or walnuts
3 tablespoons chopped parsley

Mix all ingredients except nuts and parsley. Cover and chill at least 8 hours. Shape into ball, roll in mixture of nuts and parsley. Store no longer than 4 days. Makes 3 cups.

❖◆◆◆❖

CHEESE-STUFFED MUSHROOMS

1 pound fresh mushrooms; caps and stems
1/2 cup butter or margarine, softened
3 cloves garlic, minced
1/2 cup fresh parsley, chopped
1/2 cup Parmesan cheese, grated
6 slices Swiss cheese, finely chopped
3 eggs
2 tablespoons capers

Clean mushrooms, remove stems. Chop stems and reserve. Combine softened butter, garlic, parsley, cheeses and chopped mushroom stems. Lightly beat eggs and add to mixture; fold in capers. Mixture will be sticky. Stuff mushroom caps and bake on lightly greased baking sheet in preheated 400-degree oven for 10 minutes or until brown. Serves 8-10.

Jo and Jan say, "For other cocktail puffs and fillings see the index."

VEGGIE HORS D'OEUVRE

1 package (8-ounce) Crescent rolls
1 package (4-ounce) Crescent rolls
1 package (8-ounce) cream cheese
1 cup mayonnaise
1/2 teaspoon onion powder
1/2 teaspoon garlic powder
1 teaspoon lemon pepper
1/2 teaspoon salt
1 teaspoon dill weed
3 raw carrots, grated
1/4 head raw cauliflower
3 spears broccoli
2 stalks celery
1/2 green pepper
6 red radishes
1/2 red sweet pepper
1 jar (4-ounce) pimento

Unroll Crescent rolls and spread flat into ungreased 10 1/2 x 15 1/2-inch jelly roll pan. Bake in preheated 350-degree oven for 5 to 10 minutes or until golden brown. Cool completely; do not remove from pan. Blend cheese, mayonnaise, onion powder, garlic powder, lemon pepper, salt and dill weed. Spread on cooled crust. Vegetable pieces should be no larger than pea size. Scatter over cheese mixture. Cover with plastic wrap and press vegetables gently into cheese. Refrigerate overnight.

When ready to serve, cut into 1 1/2-inch squares. Makes 70 squares.

Jan says, "This tasty hor d'oeuvre may be refrigerated 3 to 4 days."

MILLIE'S CREAM OF ZUCCHINI SOUP

3 pounds zucchini, unpeeled, chopped
2 teaspoons salt
2 teaspoons onion powder
2 teaspoons garlic powder
1/8 teaspoon while pepper
2 cans (14-ounce size) chicken broth
1/2 cup water
1 1/2 cups half and half
Chives, chopped (garnish)

Wash zucchini, chop and put into a saucepan with rest of ingredients except half and half. Simmer until zucchini is tender. Put mixture into blender, in batches, and blend until smooth. Add back to saucepan, add half and half; heat and serve. Garnish with chives. Serves 6-8.

For the Good Times

COLD BLUEBERRY SOUP

6 cups blueberries
5 cups water
1 cup sugar
2 medium lemons, thinly sliced
1 3-inch cinnamon stick
1/2 teaspoon nutmeg, freshly grated if
    possible
1/4 teaspoon allspice
4 1/2 cups sour cream
1 cup dry red wine

Combine blueberries, water, sugar, lemon and spices in large saucepan and bring to a boil over high heat. Reduce heat to medium-low and simmer 15 minutes.

Strain mixture into large bowl, discarding cinnamon stick and lemon peel. Cover and chill thoroughly. Just before serving, whisk in sour cream and wine. Serves 8.

COLD PEACH SOUP

1 1/2 pounds fresh peaches
2 cups sour cream
1 cup fresh orange juice
1 cup pineapple juice
1/2 cup dry sherry
1 tablespoon fresh lemon juice
Sugar

Peel and slice peaches. Puree in blender or food processor until smooth. Add rest of ingredients except sugar and blend well. It will be necessary to do in batches, depending on size of equipment. Strain soup, add sugar to taste and serve chilled.

Serves 6-8

GLAZED LEMON NUT BREAD

1 cup solid shortening
3 cups sugar
6 egg yolks
3 cups flour
1/4 teaspoon salt
1 cup buttermilk
1 ounce lemon extract
1/2 teaspoon grated lemon peel
6 egg whites, stiffly beaten
2 1/2 cups chopped pecans
GLAZE:
Juice of 2 lemons, strained
1 cup confectioners' sugar

Cream shortening, sugar and egg yolks. Sift dry ingredients and add alternately with buttermilk to the creamed mixture. Add lemon extract and peel. Fold in beaten egg whites, then pecans. Pour into 3 greased loaf pans (bread size) and bake in preheated 350-degree oven for 1 1/2 hours or until a pick inserted near center comes out clean.

Cool on wire rack for 15 minutes. Stir lemon juice into confectioners' sugar until mixture is smooth. Remove bread from pan and rest on rack over waxed paper. Spoon glaze over warm bread; cool completely before slicing. Makes 3 loaves.

LEMON - POPPY SEED MUFFINS

1/4 cup poppy seeds
3 cups flour
1/2 teaspoon salt
1 tablespoon baking powder
1/2 teaspoon baking soda
1/2 cup shortening
1 cup sugar
2 eggs, beaten
1/2 cup lemon juice
2 tablespoons grated lemon peel
2 tablespoons water

Mix poppy seeds, flour, salt, baking powder and soda together in mixing bowl. In another bowl, cream together shortening and sugar. Add beaten eggs, water, lemon juice and grated lemon peel; blend. Make a well in the center of dry ingredients and pour in egg mixture. Stir just enough to moisten. Drop into greased miniature muffin cups, filling 3/4 full. Bake in preheated 375-degree oven for 25 minutes. Makes 2 dozen miniature muffins.

❖❖

NORMA'S FROSTED PARTY SANDWICH LOAF

1 can Swanson Premium White Chicken
1 can Underwood Deviled Ham
6 eggs, hard-boiled (discard ends of whites, chop rest)
1 can Chicken of the Sea - Fancy Albacore Tuna
Kraft Miracle Whip 1
 loaf Thin sandwich bread
2 packages (8-ounce size) cream cheese
Pimento-stuffed olives

12 hours before assembling loaf, set out cream cheese so it will be soft for frosting the loaf when it is finished.

Norma says, "The first thing I do is to get 4 rather large soup bowls; one for each of the chicken, ham, eggs and tuna. I mix each one with Miracle Whip, not mayonnaise, and set the bowls aside. Next, I take my electric knife (it is important to use an electric knife) and cut off the crusts from the bread. Now I am ready to put the sandwich loaf together.

Lay 3 slices of bread side by side (with edges touching on a tray or platter. (You will not want to lift the loaf upon completion, so have it on your serving tray). Then spread the tuna salad on top of all 3 slices. Now lay 3 slices of bread side by side on top of tuna salad. Then spread egg salad on top of all 3 slices. Now lay 3 slices of bread side by side on top of the egg salad. Spread ham salad on top of all 3 slices. Now lay 3 slices of bread side by side on top of ham salad. Then spread chicken salad on top of all 3 slices. Now lay 3 slices of bread for your top layer. (15) slices of bread, (3) side by side (5) times, with your salad spreads in-between.

Now you are ready to spread the loaf with the very soft cream cheese, spreading it thin over the two ends first, then the top and then the two long ends.

I cut my olives in half so each side will have some pimiento on it. I always make a design with my olives. Once I put a big TWA made from olives (Jan and I are ex-TWA hostesses and I used it for one of the meetings).

Cover loaf with plastic wrap and refrigerate overnight." Serves 12.

LADIES' DAY SHRIMP SALAD

3 tablespoons olive oil
2 tablespoons white wine vinegar
1 teaspoon Dijon mustard
Freshly ground pepper
1 pound fresh shrimp, cooked, shelled, deveined and cubed
1 cup mayonnaise
2 tablespoons chili sauce
2 garlic cloves, crushed
Dash of Tabasco sauce
Dash of salt
2 large ripe tomatoes, cut into eighths
3 hard boiled eggs, Cut into fourths
1 large ripe avocado
Juice of 1/2 lemon
2 tablespoons fresh dill, finely minced
2 tablespoons fresh chives, finely minced
Dill sprigs, lemon wedges, avocado slices (garnish)

Combine first 4 ingredients and whisk until well blended. Add to shrimp; toss thoroughly, cover and marinate in refrigerator 2 hours.

Whisk mayonnaise, chili sauce, garlic, Tabasco and salt until smooth and refrigerate.

Peel and cut tomatoes and eggs . Cover separately and chill. Peel, seed and cube avocado. Sprinkle with lemon juice and set aside.

Drain shrimp; add avocado, dill and chives and toss lightly. Fold in enough mayonnaise mixture to coat lightly. Taste and adjust seasoning. Cover and chill if not serving right away.

Divide salad among 4 chilled plates, divide eggs and tomatoes and place around the salad. Garnish with dill sprigs, lemon wedges and extra avocado slices. Serve immediately. Serves 4.

❖❖

CHICKEN - ARTICHOKE - RICE SALAD

4 cups chicken, cooked and diced
1 package (6 ounces) chicken-flavored rice
   mix
6 green onions, thinly sliced
1/2 green pepper, chopped
12 pimento stuffed olives, sliced
2 jars (6 ounce size) marinated artichoke
   hearts
1/2 teaspoon curry powder
1/3 cup mayonnaise
Cherry tomatoes (garnish)
Toasted slivered almonds (garnish)

Cook chicken, cool and dice; set aside. Cook rice as directed, omitting butter. Cool in a large bowl. Drain artichoke hearts and reserve juice. Cut hearts in half and combine with mayonnaise and curry powder. Pour reserved artichoke liquid over rice and add onion, green pepper and olives. Toss artichoke hearts and chicken with the rice mixture. Chill until serving time. To serve, mound on a bed of greens, garnish with cherry tomatoes and sprinkle top with toasted almonds. Serves 8 to 10.

"THE GIRLS' " FAVORITE CHICKEN SALAD

2 cups chicken, cooked, skinned and cut
   into bite-size cubes
1/2 cup mayonnaise
1 tablespoon lemon juice
4 teaspoons grated orange rind
2 teaspoons sugar
1 cup celery, chopped
1 cup fresh orange slices
1/2 cup ripe olives, sliced
1/4 cup green onions, including tops, sliced
1 large ripe avocado

Cook chicken as you desire; (broiling is nice, as it gives a nice coating as well as flavor) and chill until ready to toss with rest of ingredients.

Combine mayonnaise, lemon juice, orange rind and sugar. In large bowl, combine chilled chicken with celery, orange slices, olives and onions. Peel and cut avocado into cubes; add to bowl. Add dressing and toss lightly. Serves 4-6.

Jo and Jan say, "This is very nice served in a hollowed pineapple. If you do this, add some fresh pineapple cubes to the salad or slices as garnish. The Epicurean Dressing (See index) is also wonderful as a dressing for this luncheon salad."

ROSY TOMATO ASPIC

2 cups tomato juice
1 tablespoon grated onion
1 tablespoon horseradish
3 tablespoons vinegar
Pinch of salt
1 package (4-ounce) raspberry Jell-O

Combine tomato juice and seasonings. Bring to a boil and pour over gelatin. Stir well and chill.

SNOW WHITE LAYER:
1 package (3-ounce) cream cheese
1/2 cup mayonnaise
1/2 teaspoon salt
1/2 teaspoon grated onion
1/2 envelope unflavored gelatin
2 tablespoons water

Mix softened cheese with mayonnaise, salt and onion. Soften gelatin in water and dissolve in hot water. Add to cheese mixture, mixing well. To mold, pour 1/2 of tomato aspic in loaf pan which has been rinsed in cold water. Chill; when set add cheese mixture and chill. Lastly add remaining aspic and chill again. Serve on greens with a dollop of mayonnaise and garnished with pimento-stuffed olives. Serves 6-8.

APRICOT SOUFFLE RING

1 cup apricot juice (from can of apricots)
1 cup apricot nectar
1 package (6-ounce) lemon Jell-O
2 cups heavy cream, whipped
Fresh mint leaves (garnish)

Bring apricot juice and apricot nectar to a boil. Add Jell-O and stir until dissolved. Chill until mixture is consistency of honey; check after 45 minutes. Fold in to whipped cream and chill in a greased 6-cup ring mold.

To serve, dip ring very quickly into hot water and unmold on round serving plate. Mound salad in center. Serves 8-10.

Jo and Jan say, "This mold is delicious filled with a chicken salad. It is perfect for a luncheon entree; rolls or muffins and a dessert are all you need to add."

SPINACH SOUFFLE RING

3 packages (10-ounce size) frozen chopped
  spinach
1 teaspoon salt
1/2 teaspoon freshly grated black pepper
1/2 teaspoon freshly grated nutmeg
1 small onion, grated
1 cup mayonnaise
1 tablespoon lemon juice
2 tablespoons unflavored gelatin
1/4 cup water
1 cup heavy cream

Generously brush a 6-cup ring mold with oil and turn over on paper towels to drain off excess; set aside. Cook spinach according to package instructions; drain well and squeeze out all moisture. Chop very fine and place in a large bowl. Season with salt, pepper and nutmeg; stir in grated onion, mayonnaise and lemon juice. Sprinkle gelatin in water to soften and dissolve over low heat. Whip cream and fold into gelatin mixture; fold cream into spinach mixture and pour into prepared mold. Chill at least 2 hours before unmolding on serving plate. Serves 6 -8.

Jo and Jan say, "Fill the ring with a seafood or meat salad. This makes a wonderful luncheon entree!"

PRESBYTERIAN LADIES' CHICKEN CASSEROLE

4 cups diced cooked chicken
1 package (8-ounce) noodles, cooked
2 cans cream of mushroom soup
4 tablespoons butter
4 tablespoons onion, grated
4 tablespoons green pepper, chopped
4 tablespoons pimento, chopped
Dry bread crumbs

Melt butter and saute onion, green pepper and pimento. Place a layer of noodles in 9 x 13-inch casserole, spread diced chicken over noodles. Mix sauteed mixture with soup and spread over chicken. Cover with bread crumbs. Bake in a preheated 325-degree oven for 25 minutes. Serves 12.

Jan says, "This has been a favorite for years at our church dinners. It is so easy and delicious I know you will want to try it."

For the Good Times

CAROL'S CHICKEN DIJON

4 chicken breasts, split, skinned and boned
1/4 cup sour cream
1/4 cup Dijon mustard
Salt and pepper
1/8 teaspoon garlic powder
3/4 cup Italian bread crumbs
2 tablespoons butter or margarine

Lightly pound chicken breasts between two pieces of waxed paper. Combine sour cream, mustard, garlic powder, salt and pepper to taste. Spread chicken breasts with this mixture; roll in bread crumbs. Melt butter in a shallow baking dish and arrange chicken so the pieces do not touch. Bake in a preheated 350-degree oven for 30 minutes. Turn and bake 20 to 30 minutes longer. Serves 6-8.

MARGARET'S CHICKEN

2 whole chicken breasts or 4 halves, skins removed and deboned
1 box chopped spinach, well drained, but not cooked
1 tablespoon butter or margarine
1 cup chopped mushrooms
1/3 cup chopped green onions
1 egg, beaten
1/2 cup blue cheese
1 cup herb stuffing
2 1/2 tablespoons butter or margarine

Pound chicken breasts between plastic wrap. Melt butter or margarine in skillet and saute green onions and mushrooms about 10 minutes or until golden. Add well-drained spinach, cool slightly; add egg and blue cheese, mix well.

Divide mixture among the 4 breasts, spread and roll up. Make crumbs with herb stuffing. Melt butter and mix 1 tablespoon with crumbs. Place chicken rolls in baking dish, sprinkle with herb crumbs, pour rest of melted butter over the top and bake in a preheated 350-degree oven for 25 to 35 minutes.

MINCEMEAT - FILLED PEACHES

Peach halves (fresh, canned or fresh-frozen)
Mincemeat - commercial brand or Mock Mincemeat (See Index)

Fill peach halves with a heaping tablespoon of mincemeat. Place under broiler until hot and bubbly.

Jan says, "These are a beautiful accompaniment to your Holiday turkey. They are perfect for rounding out your luncheon plates. Not only pretty, but oh, so good!"

DOROTHY'S GOOSEBERRY CAKES

1/2 cup margarine or butter
3/4 cup sugar
2 eggs
1 1/2 cups flour
2 1/2 teaspoons baking powder
1/2 cup milk or half-and-half
1 can (16 1/2-ounce) gooseberries, drained or 1 cup fresh
1 cup confectioners' sugar
Milk (about 4 teaspoons)

Grease 24 fluted or grease and flour 15 regular muffin pans. In a large mixer bowl beat margarine on medium speed for 30 seconds. Add sugar and beat until fluffy. Add eggs, one at a time, beating well after each addition. Combine flour and baking powder; add alternately with milk to margarine mixture. Beat on low speed until combined. Stir in gooseberries and fill muffin cups 2/3 full. Bake in preheated 375-degree oven about 15 minutes. Let stand for 15 minutes. Combine confectioners' sugar and milk, to make a consistency for drizzling over the cakes. Drizzle over cakes. Makes 24 or 15 muffins. Store in a closed container. They will freeze nicely.

❖❖

BLUEBERRY CHEESECAKE SQUARES

CRUST:
1 cup graham cracker crumbs
1/3 cup butter or margarine, melted
2 tablespoons sugar
1/4 teaspoon cinnamon

FILLING:
2 packages (8-ounce size) cream cheese,
   softened
1/2 cup sugar
2 large eggs
2 tablespoons heavy cream
1 tablespoon freshly squeezed lemon juice
1 teaspoon lemon peel
1 teaspoon vanilla extract
Dash freshly grated nutmeg

TOPPING:
1 cup sour cream
2 tablespoons sugar
1 pint fresh blueberries, washed and drained

In small bowl combine crumbs, butter, sugar and cinnamon. Press mixture onto bottom of a 9-inch-square baking dish. Chill for 30 minutes.

In large bowl of electric mixer beat cream cheese, sugar and eggs until light. Beat in cream, lemon juice, peel, vanilla and nutmeg until smooth. P our into chilled pan and bake in preheated 350-degree oven for 25 minutes or until set. Remove from oven, leaving temperature at 350. Cool on a rack for at least 10 minutes.

In a small bowl combine sour cream and sugar until well blended; spread on cooked cake. Return to oven and bake for 5 minutes. Let cool to room temperature; sprinkle blueberries evenly over top; chill for several hours or overnight. To serve, cut into 2 1/4-inch squares.

HAWAIIAN CHEESECAKE

CRUST:
2 cups graham cracker crumbs
1/2 cup toasted shredded coconut, chopped
   fine
3 tablespoons sugar
1/3 cup butter, melted

FILLING:
1 can (16-ounce) crushed pineapple in heavy
   syrup
5 packages (8-ounce size) cream cheese,
   softened
1 1/2 cups sugar
1/3 cup cornstarch
5 eggs
2 egg yolks
Grated peel of 1 lemon
1/2 cup canned cream of coconut
1/3 cup dark rum

TOPPING:
Reserved drained, crushed pineapple and
   liquid
1 tablespoon cornstarch
1/4 cup sugar
1/4 cup dark rum

Combine cracker crumbs, coconut, sugar and melted butter. Stir to moisten and press crumbs on bottom and half-way up sides of 10-inch springform pan; set aside.

Drain pineapple, reserving juice. Beat cream cheese and sugar in the large bowl of electric mixer until fluffy; slowly add cornstarch. Beat in eggs and yolks, one at a time and beating well after each addition. Blend in lemon peel, cream of coconut and rum. Stir in 1/2 of the drained pineapple and pour filling into prepared crust.

Place pan in a larger pan of hot water and bake in a preheated 350-degree oven for 1 hour 15 minutes. Prepare Topping.

Blend together until smooth the reserved pineapple juice and cornstarch in a medium saucepan. Stir in pineapple, sugar and rum. Heat to a boil, stirring occasionally, until clear and thickened; allow to cool.

Spread cooled topping over cooled cheesecake (room temperature) and chill several hours or preferably overnight. Serves 12.

❖❖❖

KATIE'S COCONUT CRISPIES

2 sticks margarine
1/2 cup sugar
1/2 teaspoon soda
1/2 teaspoon vinegar
1/2 teaspoon vanilla
1 1/2 cups flour
1 package (7-ounce) flaked coconut

Mix margarine, sugar, soda, vinegar and vanilla until blended. Add flour and coconut; mix until flour is mixed well. Drop by teaspoon on cookie sheet, flatten with fork. Bake in preheated 350-degree oven for 15 to 20 minutes, until lightly browned. Makes 3 dozen.

MINT SHERBET RING

3 pints lemon sherbet
1/3 cup creme de menthe
1 quart fresh strawberries, blueberries or
    raspberries, sweetened

Slightly soften sherbet in mixing bowl. Beat quickly with electric mixer; blend in liqueur. Cut 6 strips wax paper I-inch wide by 12 inches long. Lay them in a 5-cup ring mold crosswise with ends hanging over the edge. Pack in sherbet and freeze until firm.

3 hours before serving, dip mold quickly in warm water. Run a knife around edge and turn upside down on a baking sheet or serving plate so ends of wax paper are out from under the mold. Lift off mold and peel off paper. Refreeze until serving time; then fill center of ring with berries. Garnish with waxey leaves or fresh mint. Serves 6-8.

TROPICAL SHERBET

3 mangoes
2 papayas
1 cup fresh orange juice
1 basket (4-5 ounce) fresh raspberries

Blend all ingredients in blender and pour mixture into freezer dish and freeze until crystals begin to form around edges. Remove from freezer and beat until smooth but not liquid. Return to freezer for several hours or until firm. Makes about 1 quart.

TONIA'S PUNCHBOWL FROZEN FRUIT TRIFLE

2 angle food cakes, baked
1 package (3-ounce) strawberry Jell-O
1 package (3-ounce) lime Jell-O
1 package (3-ounce) orange Jell-O
1/2 gallon vanilla ice cream
1 small can mandarin oranges
1 package frozen strawberries
1 package frozen blueberries
Kiwi fruit for top

This makes a very large dessert so use a big bowl! Tear cake into pieces and layer with ice cream, sprinkling Jell-O on the ice cream and dividing the frozen fruit among the layers. Work quickly with the ice cream and frozen fruit. Freeze again until serving time. Arrange kiwi slices on top before serving.

DESSERT EGG NOG

1/2 cup sugar
6 eggs
4 cups milk
1 cup chocolate syrup
1 cup Amaretto
1/3 cup instant coffee granules
2 cups whipped cream
Nutmeg

Beat sugar and eggs until fluffy. Gradually beat in milk; add chocolate syrup. Combine Amaretto and instant coffee and stir until coffee dissolves. Add to egg mixture and stir. Pour into a bowl and chill. Top with whipped cream and sprinkle with nutmeg.

For the Good Times

Brunches

COFFEE NOG

1 pint coffee ice cream
2 cups hot strong coffee
1 cup rum, 80 proof
1/2 cup Kahlua

Pour coffee over ice cream and stir to melt. Add rum, Kahlua and stir until blended. Cover and chill overnight before serving. Pour into small glasses or punch cups to serve. Makes 3 1/2 cups.

Jo and Jan say, "This is wonderful for a brunch!"

KENTUCKY DERBY SLUSH

1 can (12-ounce) frozen orange juice
    concentrate
1 can (12-ounce) frozen lemonade
1 cup sugar, or to taste
9 cups water
3 cups bourbon
1 bottle 7-Up (2-liter) more or less as desired
Fresh mint sprigs

Combine orange juice and lemonade, sugar, water and bourbon in a large plastic container; freeze.

At serving time, place frozen mixture in punch bowl and carefully pour in 7-Up. Float mint sprigs in punch. Makes about 50 4-ounce servings.

MINT JULEP PUNCH

1 fifth bourbon
2 bottles Welch's white grape juice
1 bottle gingerale
Fresh mint

Combine ingredients and serve cold. The sprigs of fresh mint can be imbedded in ice rings, but we also float some on top. We also tuck a small sprig in the punch cups or glasses.

Jo and Jan say, "This is the perfect punch for a Kentucky Derby party."

FROZEN FRUIT COMPOTE

1 can (6-ounce) frozen lemonade, slightly
    thawed
1 can (6-ounce) frozen orange juice, slightly
    thawed
1 cup sugar
1 can (No. 2 size) crushed pineapple
1 bag (16-ounce) frozen blueberries
1 bag (16-ounce) frozen peaches
1 bag (16-ounce) strawberries
2 bottles (16-ounce size) 7-Up
4 large bananas, sliced

Mix sugar with juice. Add 7-Up and fruit; freeze 24 hours. Thaw to slightly slush. Serves 20-25.

Jan says, "A delightful summer compote that may be served as a dessert, salad or at a brunch. Can be served attractively in a crystal bowl or individual sherbet dishes. To prepare for a picnic, spoon into small paper cups and freeze ahead of time. Can prepare it days ahead of time and it is ready to put on ice in the picnic hamper."

For the Good Times

FRESH FRUIT GAZPACHO

1 cup diced cantaloupe
1 cup diced honeydew melon
1 cup whole strawberries, hulled
1 large green apple, pared and diced
2 teaspoons sugar
1 teaspoon grated orange peel
1/4 teaspoon grated lemon peel
1 cup orange juice
1/2 cup fresh blueberries

In processor or blender, combine melons, strawberries, apple, sugar and peels with orange juice; process until smooth. If using blender, do half at a time.

Pour into serving bowl; stir in blueberries. Cover and chill at least 1 hour or up to 6 hours.

Serve in chilled bowls. Garnish with lemon and lime slices and additional blueberries, if desired. Serves 8.

SPINACH BALLS

1/2 cup sesame seeds
2 packages (10-ounce size) frozen chopped
  spinach
2 cups herb or garlic seasoned croutons or
  bread stuffing mix
1 medium onion, finely chopped
1/2 cup water chestnuts, chopped (optional)
6 eggs, lightly beaten
3/4 cup butter, softened
1 cup Parmesan cheese
1/2 teaspoon garlic powder
1/2 teaspoon thyme (omit if using herb
  croutons or stuffing mix)
1/2 teaspoon white pepper
Tabasco to taste (optional)

Toast sesame seeds in a heavy skillet; stirring constantly until golden, about 2 to 3 minutes, and set aside.

Cook spinach following package directions. Drain well and mix with remaining ingredients, thoroughly blending. Shape into small balls, about 1 rounded teaspoon, and dip tops in sesame seeds.

Place balls on greased baking sheet and bake in preheated 350-degree oven for 8 to 10 minutes or until firm but not dry. Watch closely. Makes 60.

Jo and Jan say, "These will be a hit whenever you serve them, be it a brunch or garden party. They freeze beautifully. To freeze before baking, place in a layer on baking sheet until frozen, then transfer to an airtight container. If frozen, bake for 10 to 12 minutes or until done."

CHUTNEY EGGS

12 hard-boiled eggs
6 slices bacon, cooked crisp and crumbled
  fine
1/4 cup chutney, finely chopped
3 tablespoons mayonnaise
1 green onion, chopped fine
Paprika, for garnish

Cut eggs in half lengthwise and remove yolks. Mash yolks; add crumbled bacon, chutney, mayonnaise and onion. Fill whites and sprinkle with paprika. Makes 24 halves.

❖❖

QUICHE TARTLETS

2 1/2 cups sifted flour
1 1/2 teaspoons salt
1 cup shortening
6 to 8 tablespoons ice water
1 egg yolk, beaten with 2 teaspoons water
16 slices bacon or 1 cup sliced stuffed green
   olives or 6 medium onions, sliced
1 1/2 cups (6 ounces) grated Swiss cheese
4 eggs, slightly beaten
2 cups heavy cream
1/4 teaspoon salt
1/4 teaspoon nutmeg
Dash cayenne pepper
Dash black pepper

Sift flour and salt in a bowl. Blend half of shortening into flour mixture, using pastry blender, until mixture looks like coarse corn meal. Cut in remaining shortening until the size of large peas.

Sprinkle ice water, 1 tablespoon at a time, over the flour mixture, quickly stir and mix with a fork after each addition; blend just until mixture holds together. Turn out on waxed paper and press into a ball. Roll out 1/4 dough at a time. Carefully fit pastry into tartlet pans. Combine beaten egg yolk and water. Brush this mixture onto each tartlet shell before filling to prevent soggy crusts.

Fry bacon until crisp and drain on paper towels. Crumble into pastry-lined tartlet pans.

If making olive quiche, put a few olive slices into each pan. If making onion quiche, saute sliced onions in butter or margarine until golden; drain well and put about 1 teaspoon onion in each tartlet pan.

Sprinkle 1 heaping teaspoon grated cheese into each tartlet pan, Combine beaten eggs, cream, salt, nutmeg and pepper. Pour 1 to 1 1/2 tablespoons of this mixture over cheese in tartlets. Bake in preheated 400-degree oven for 8 minutes; reduce heat to 350 and bake 5 to 8 minutes longer, or until filling puffs up and is golden-brown. Serve hot. Makes about 40 tartlets, 2 1/2 to 3 inches wide.

Jo and Jan say, "You can add crab or ham to the filling. Also, these can be baked early in the day, just do not brown completely. When ready to serve, brown in a preheated 400-degree oven for 3 to 5 minutes. This filling recipe will also make one 8-inch quiche. Bake a large one for 15 minutes in a preheated 425-degree oven; reduce heat to 300 degrees and bake 40 minutes or until knife inserted in center comes out clean. Let stand 15 minutes before cutting. You can get 2 large shells out of this pastry recipe."

CAROL'S SPINACH QUICHE

3 3/4 cups sifted flour
1 1/2 teaspoons salt
1 cup solid shortening, chilled
3/4 cup water
1 egg beaten with 1 tablespoon milk

FILLING:
2 cups (8-ounces) Swiss cheese, grated
1 package (10-ounce) frozen chopped
   spinach, thawed and moisture squeezed
   out
1 3/4 cups light cream
4 eggs, beaten
1 tablespoon butter or margarine, melted
1 teaspoon salt
1/8 teaspoon white pepper
1/8 teaspoon grated fresh nutmeg

Combine flour and salt in a large mixing bowl. Cut in shortening until mixture resembles coarse meal. Sprinkle water over top, 1 to 2 tablespoons at a time; mix in lightly with a fork until pastry holds together. Gather into a ball.

Roll pastry out on a lightly floured surface to a 13 x 18-inch rectangle. Fit it into a 10 1/2 x 15 1/2 x 1-inch jelly roll pan; making sure there are no holes in the crust. Prick bottom and sides with a fork; brush with beaten egg and bake in preheated 425-degree oven for 20 minutes or until lightly browned. Cool completely on a wire rack; When cool, sprinkle cheese over bottom of crust.

Combine remaining ingredients ; pour over cheese and bake in 425-degree oven for 15 minutes. Reduce heat to 350 degrees and bake 10 to 15 minutes longer or until golden brown on top and a knife inserted halfway between center and rim comes out clean. Cool on wire rack about 10 minutes; cut into squares or diamonds. Makes 35.

Carol says, "These can be baked, cut, wrapped and frozen. Great for entertaining! To serve, just unwrap and heat at 325 degrees for 25 minutes or until hot."

MOCK BLINIS

2 loaves Pepperidge Farm bread. Cut off crusts and roll each slice flat
2 egg yolks
2 packages (8-ounce size) cream cheese
1/2 cup sugar
Brown sugar and cinnamon mixture - as much as needed
2 sticks butter or margarine
Sour cream, for dipping

Combine egg yolks, cream cheese and sugar; spread on bread slices. Melt 2 sticks butter or margarine. Roll up each slice of bread. Then roll in butter or margarine mixture, then in mixture of brown sugar and cinnamon. Place on cookie sheet. Freeze.

When ready to serve, cut in thirds. Bake at 350 degrees for 20 minutes. To serve, pass on trays or place on buffet table with a bowl of sour cream so guests can dip. Jo says, "Be ready to replenish because they do not last long."

ZUCCHINI PANCAKES

3 cups zucchini, coarsely grated
2 large eggs, beaten until frothy
2 tablespoons milk
2 teaspoons flour
1 tablespoon parsley, chopped
1/2 teaspoon salt
1/4 teaspoon pepper
2 tablespoons salad oil

Drain grated zucchini in colander until most of moisture is out of it. Add remaining ingredients except oil, to beaten eggs and fold into the zucchini.

Heat oil in a large skillet. Spoon 1 tablespoon batter for each pancake, adding more oil if necessary. Cook 1 minute on each side until golden-brown. Keep warm on platter while you finish the batter. Serve with sour cream as a dip. Serves 6.

JEANNE'S BRUNCH EGGS

SAUCE:
1/4 cup soft butter
1 teaspoon salt
4 tablespoons flour
1/4 teaspoon white pepper
1/4 teaspoon dry mustard
2 cups hot milk
4 tablespoons diced Swiss cheese
4 tablespoons Parmesan cheese
EGGS:
8 hard-boiled eggs
1/4 pound fresh mushrooms, sauteed in butter, drained and finely chopped
4 tablespoons soft butter
4 tablespoons Sauce
Grated Parmesan cheese

Place all sauce ingredients into blender, cover and blend at low speed until ingredients are thoroughly mixed. Turn to high speed for 30 seconds. Pour into top of double boiler and cook over simmering water for 15 minutes, stirring occasionally.

Meanwhile, halve eggs lengthwise. Remove yolks and reserve whites. Mix yolks with an equal amount of cooked and chopped mushrooms, butter and sauce. Fill egg whites with mixture, mounding it high.

Spread a layer of sauce in a shallow baking dish, place eggs in sauce and cover with more sauce. Sprinkle with Parmesan cheese and brown under broiler. Can be made a day or two ahead of time, covered and refrigerated.

If refrigerated, set out at least 1 hour before heating. Place in a preheated 325-degree oven for 30 minutes or until sauce is bubbly in center of baking dish. Serves 10 - 12.

EDDIE'S EGGS FLORENTINE

1 package (10-ounce) frozen chopped
   spinach
2 tablespoons butter or margarine
3 tablespoons grated Parmesan cheese
Poached eggs
1 recipe Bechamel Sauce (See Index)
Toasted English Muffins

Thaw spinach, drain well and squeeze dry. Melt butter and saute spinach with Parmesan cheese. Toast muffins, arrange spinach on toast, arrange poached eggs over spinach and cover with Bechamel sauce. Run the dish under the broiler until sauce bubbles and browns slightly.

Eddie says, "This is one of my brunch favorites. I add a few grains of cayenne pepper and a dash of lemon juice to my Bechamel sauce to zip it up just a bit."

GARLIC CHEESE GRITS

1 cup quick-cooking grits
1 roll garlic cheese
1 stick butter
2 well beaten eggs
3/4 cup milk
Paprika

Cook grits according to package directions. Add cheese and butter; cool. Combine eggs and milk, add to grits mixture. Spoon into a buttered 2-quart casserole and bake, uncovered, for 1 hour in a preheated 375-degree oven. Dust top with paprika before serving. Serves 8.

CHILLED ORANGE - GLAZED RICE RING

1 quart milk
2/3 cup converted rice
1/2 teaspoon salt
Juice of 1 large orange, strained
2 envelopes unflavored gelatin
Grated rind of 1 large orange
1/2 cup sugar
3/4 cup heavy cream, whipped
1 jar (12-ounce) apricot jam
6 tablespoons sugar

GARNISH:
5 large oranges, peeled and sectioned
1/3 cup Grand Marnier liqueur

Grease a 4-5 cup ring mold with vegetable oil and turn upside down on paper towels to drain. Bring milk to a boil in heavy saucepan. Add rice and salt; bring to a boil again. Reduce heat to a simmer and cook, stirring occasionally until almost all the milk has boiled away, about 1 1/2 hours.

Sprinkle gelatin over orange juice, then stir into rice with orange rind and sugar. Cook 10 minutes more. Place plastic wrap over surface and refrigerate until cool. Fold in the whipped cream and spoon the mixture into the greased mold. Seal with plastic wrap and refrigerate overnight.

GLAZE: Combine the apricot jam and 6 tablespoons sugar. Stir over low heat until sugar has dissolved. Bring to a boil and cook until mixture reaches 220 on a candy thermometer. While still warm, spoon over rice ring, reserving some to toss with garnish. Refrigerate.

GARNISH: Combine orange sections, not the juice, with the Grand Marnier and remaining glaze. Just before serving, spoon into center of ring. Serves 8-10.

SAUSAGE RING

2 pounds medium-hot sausage
1 1/2 cups cracker crumbs
1 teaspoon sage
2 eggs
1/2 cup milk
1/4 cup onion, minced
1 cup apples, unpeeled and finely chopped

Combine ingredients and press into a greased 6-cup ring mold. Place on baking sheet and bake in preheated 350-degree oven for 1 hour.

Let stand for 10 minutes before unmolding on serving platter. Fill center with watercress or parsley and garnish with a few cherry tomatoes. Serves 8-10.

PARTY PERFECT CHICKEN

1 cup wild rice
1 quart cold water
1 teaspoon salt
1 tablespoon butter
1/2 cup dry sherry
Salt and pepper
4 cups cooked chicken, diced
2 cups mushrooms, sliced
2 tablespoons butter

CREAM SAUCE:
2 tablespoons flour
4 tablespoons butter
2 cups boiling milk
1/2 cup light cream
Salt and pepper

MORNAY SAUCE:
1/4 cup butter, softened
1 teaspoon salt
4 tablespoons flour
1/4 teaspoon white pepper
1/4 teaspoon dry mustard
2 cups hot milk
4 tablespoons diced Swiss cheese
4 tablespoons Parmesan cheese
Parmesan cheese (For topping)

Place rice in cold water; add salt and bring to a boil. Cook, covered for 20 minutes and cool. Melt butter and saute rice. Add sherry, then salt and pepper to taste. Saute for a few minutes and set aside. Set cooked, diced chicken aside also.

Melt 2 tablespoons butter in small skillet; add mushrooms and saute until tender and set aside. Prepare cream sauce.

Melt butter, add flour and stir until smooth. Gradually add boiling milk until creamy. Cook 10 to 15 minutes then add light cream. Salt and pepper to taste. Remove from heat and add diced chicken and sauteed mushrooms. Prepare Mornay Sauce.

Place all sauce ingredients into blender, cover and blend at low speed until thoroughly mixed. Turn to high speed for 30 seconds. Pour into top of double boiler and cook over simmering water for 15 minutes, stirring occasionally.

To serve, form a ring of wild rice mixture, mound chicken mixture in the center, top with Mornay Sauce and sprinkle with Parmesan cheese. Place under broiler until sauce just becomes golden. Serves 4-6.

GEORGIA'S ZESTY SAUSAGE SQUARES

1 cup buttermilk biscuit mix
1/3 cup milk
4 tablespoons mayonnaise
1 pound hot-seasoned pork sausage
1/2 cup onion, chopped
1 egg
2 cups grated cheddar cheese
2 cans (4-ounce size) green chilies, drained and chopped

Mix biscuit mix and milk with 2 tablespoons mayonnaise and spread in a well-greased 9 x 13-inch baking pan; pat down.

Saute sausage and onion; drain and spread on biscuit mixture. Beat eggs and add 2 tablespoons mayonnaise, cheddar cheese and chilies. Spread on top of meat layer. Bake in preheated 375-degree oven for 25 minutes.

Cut into 1-inch squares for appetizers or larger squares for a brunch buffet. Makes 100 small or 12 to 16 large.

JACK'S CRAB SUPREME

1 1/2 pounds crabmeat, cut into bite size
  pieces
1/2 head coarsely shredded iceburg lettuce
1 1/4 cups mayonnaise
3-4 chopped green onions, including tops
1 tablespoon seasoning salt
1 teaspoon white pepper
Juice from 1/2 fresh lemon
12 tomato slices (2 or 3 large tomatoes)
6 English muffins, split and buttered
12 thin slices Swiss cheese

Mix crab, lettuce, mayonnaise, onions, salt, pepper and lemon juice.

Place tomato slice on each muffin half. Divide crab salad equally on top of tomato slices. Top with Swiss cheese slices. Place on baking sheet and bake in preheated 350-degree oven until cheese melts, about 15 minutes. You can use the microwave to prepare this recipe without warming up your oven, but only for a short time, as your muffins will get tough. Serves 6.

Jack says, "This is a recipe we used at The Embers, our restaurant in Wellington, Kansas until 1987, for an entree at those very special occasions like Easter or Mother's Day. It was also a favorite for "brunchy" type occasions like lady golfer gatherings, etc. It's delicious!"

BAKED PINEAPPLE

2 cans (20-ounces each) chunky pineapple,
  drained
6 tablespoons liquid from pineapple,
  reserved
6 tablespoons flour
1 1/2 cups sugar
1 cup shredded Cheddar cheese
2 cups Ritz crackers (crushed)
1 stick margarine (melted)

Combine sugar, flour, juice over low heat until some of the sugar melts. Stir in pineapple chunks and cheese. Pour into 1 1/2 quart casserole. Put crushed crackers on top. Pour melted margarine over crackers. Bake in preheated 350-degree oven for 20 to 25 minutes. Serves 6 to 8.

Jo and Jan say, "This dish is addictive! It is a wonderful accompaniment to brunch or luncheons."

GRAND MARNIER FRENCH TOAST

4 cups half-and half
4 eggs, beaten
2 tablespoons sugar
4 tablespoons Grand Marnier liqueur
2 tablespoons grated orange rind
6 to 8 slices French bread or Texas toast
1/2 cup cooking oil
Confectioners' sugar

Combine first 5 ingredients and pour into a flat pan. Soak bread 1 hour; turn bread over and soak 1 more hour.

Heat oil in large skillet; fry bread on both sides to a golden color or as desired for crispness. Remove bread from skillet and drain on paper towels. Place on baking sheet and allow to bake in preheated 400-degree oven for 3 to 5 minutes or until puffed. Remove from oven, sprinkle with confectioners' sugar and serve with Grand Marnier Butter (See index).

For the Good Times

FRENCH TOAST

12 slices white bread
Butter, to spread
12 tablespoons brown sugar
1 3/4 cups flour
1/2 teaspoon salt
1 1/4 teaspoons baking powder
2 eggs, separated
1 cup milk
3 tablespoons butter, melted
Confectioners' sugar

Butter the 12 slices of bread well. Sprinkle 6 slices with brown sugar allowing 2 tablespoons per slice; turn 6 slices, buttered side down on top of brown sugar slices to make a sandwich and set aside.

Sift flour, salt, baking powder; add egg yolks, milk and butter. Beat with rotary beater until smooth. In a separate bowl beat egg whites until stiff and fold into the yolk mixture. Slice the bread into halves or fourths. Dip sandwich into batter and fry in l-inch of oil. Turn only once to allow pieces to become golden brown. Remove from skillet and sprinkle with confectioners' sugar. Top with warm syrup or preserves. Serves 6.

Jan says, "Forget that diet! What a way to go!"

SUGAR - GLAZED BACON

1 pound high quality sliced bacon
1/2 cup dark brown sugar

Arrange bacon on a jelly roll pan. Bake in preheated 350-degree oven for 10 to 12 minutes or until fat is rendered and bacon is a deep golden brown. Drain and sprinkle with brown sugar. Return to oven and bake until sugar has melted. Serves 4-6.

FRESH FRUIT TART

3/4 package refrigerator sugar cookie dough
1 package (8-ounce) cream cheese, softened
1/3 cup sugar
1 tablespoon milk
2 tablespoons fresh orange rind
Assorted fruits in season - peaches, strawberries, blueberries, kiwi, grapes, pears, etc...

GLAZE:
3/4 cup water
1 cup orange juice
1/4 cup lemon juice
1 teaspoon orange rind
1 teaspoon lemon rind
1 cup sugar
3 tablespoons cornstarch
Salt

Make crust by rolling cookie dough in a thin layer on a pizza pan or 9 x 13-inch baking pan. Prick dough with fork and bake according to package directions. Let cool.

Make cream filling by whipping cheese, sugar, orange rind and milk together. Spread evenly over top of crust. Cover and chill. Decorate with fresh fruit and top with glaze.

Combine sugar, cornstarch and salt. Add liquids and bring to a boil. Cook one minute, then add rinds. Let glaze cool then careful pour it over fruit and toss to coat well. Chill thoroughly.

Jo says, "This is one of my family favorites for brunch. You can use just one fruit or mix. Personally, the fresh peach is my favorite!"

❖❖❖

TIP ON FREEZING CREPES

• Be sure crepes are frozen in air-tight bags and because they are so delicate and easily damageed around the edges, we suggest you store the bags inside two paper plates stapled together or perhaps foil plates taped.

BASIC CREPE BATTER

4 eggs
1/4 teaspoon salt
2 cups flour
2 1/4 cups milk
1/4 cup melted butter

In medium mixing bowl, combine eggs and salt. Gradually add flour alternately with milk, beating with electric mixer or whisk until smooth. Beat in melted butter. Refrigerate at least 1 hour before cooking crepes.

Melt a teaspoon of butter in a 5-inch crepe pan and heat over medium-high heat until butter bubbles. If drops of water "dance" on the surface, you are ready to begin. Pour in about 1/4 cup of batter, lift skillet from burner and tilt quickly in all directions to distribute batter evenly. The amount of batter used should be just enough to coat the bottom of the pan.

Cook the crepe until the edge begins to brown and surface is bubbly, about a minute. As crepe begins to brown around edge, loosen by running spatula around the edge. Turn crepe and cook the second side until golden brown, about 15 seconds. Slide the crepe onto a plate. Stack with waxed paper in between.

Brush pan lightly with oil in between every 1 or 2 crepes. Repeat until all crepes are cooked. Makes 36 crepes.

To freeze, put in freezer bags and seal. To defrost, set at room temperature for a short time, they can be heated in a low oven or microwave. They can be refrozen and thawed again.

Jo and Jan say, "If crepe batter is too thick after the hour of refrigeration, thin it with 1 or 2 tablespoons of milk or water. Too thin? Thicken with a little flour. Mix the batter into the flour first, then add to the batter so you don't have lumps."

BUSY DAY CREPES

1/3 cup plus 2 tablespoons flour (may need more)
1 tablespoon sugar
1 egg
1 egg yolk
3/4 cup milk
1 tablespoon melted butter
Dash of salt

Combine ingredients in mixing bowl. Beat with electric beater until smooth. Lightly grease a 6-inch skillet or crepe pan. Heat until a drop of water beads on surface. Remove skillet from heat and pour about 2 tablespoons of batter onto surface using a measuring cup. Quickly tilt pan until batter evenly covers bottom of skillet. Return to heat and cook until under side is lightly browned. Invert skillet over a paper towel to remove crepe. Repeat process to cook rest of crepes. Store or freeze with paper toweling between crepes to prevent sticking.

If you are going to double or triple this recipe, do it in separate batches; don't try to multiply ingredients. Makes 8 crepes.

For the Good Times

HERB CREPE BATTER

1 1/2 cups sifted flour
1 cup milk
1 cup water
4 eggs
Freshly grated nutmeg
1/4 cup butter, melted
1 tablespoon fresh parsley, finely minced, or
   1 teaspoon dried
1 tablespoon fresh chives, finely minded or
   1 teaspoon dried
Butter

Combine flour, milk, water, eggs and nutmeg in blender or food processor until smooth; scrape sides of bowl to incorporate all of ingredients. Pour mixture into mixing bowl; add melted butter and herbs; whisk until blended. Cover and let stand at room temperature for 2 hours.

Melt 1 teaspoon butter in a 6-inch skillet or crepe pan. Add about 1/4 cup batter, or just enough to coat the bottom of pan. Brown crepe on each side; repeat process with remaining batter, adding more butter as necessary. Makes about 20 crepes.

CREPES A LA REINE

12 Basic Crepes (See Index)
2 tablespoons minced onion
4 tablespoons butter
4 tablespoons flour
1 cup milk
1 cup chicken stock
3 tablespoons white wine
Salt and Pepper
1 egg yolk
2 cups cooked chicken, chopped
1 cup fresh mushrooms, sliced and sauteed
1/2 cup canned pimientos, chopped
Parmesan cheese

Saute onion in butter until golden. Blend in flour; stir in 1/2 cup milk and chicken stock; simmer, stirring until thickened. Add wine, salt and pepper to taste; then beat egg yolk into 1/2 cup of milk and add to mixture. Bring to a simmer and thicken, but do not boil. Set aside 1/2 cup.

To remaining sauce add chicken, mushrooms and pimiento. Spread crepes with chicken filling and roll, tucking in the ends. Place seam-side down in a baking dish. Spread with reserved sauce and sprinkle with Parmesan cheese. Place under broiler to glaze. Serves 6.

Jo and Jan say, "You might like to try topping the crepes with Hollandaise Sauce for a different flavor. (See index)."

LOBSTER CREPES

12 Basic or Herb Crepes (See index)
4 tablespoons butter
4 tablespoons flour
2 cups milk
3 tablespoons white wine
1/4 cup grated Parmesan cheese
1 egg yolk, beaten
4 tablespoons cream
Salt and freshly ground pepper
2 cups cooked lobster, cut into bite-size
   pieces

Melt butter and blend in flour. Add milk and wine; stir, cooking slowly until thickened. Add cheese and stir until melted. Add beaten egg yolk to cream; add some of hot mixture to egg-cream mixture, stir back into hot mixture in pan. Simmer until thickened; salt and pepper to taste. Reserve 2/3 cup of sauce; set aside.

To remaining sauce add lobster. Divide amount on 12 crepes; roll, tuck ends under and place in a shallow, greased baking dish. Spread reserved sauce over crepes and sprinkle with additional Parmesan cheese. Place under the broiler until tops are glazed. Serves 4 to 6.

❖❖

CRAB CREPES

12 Basic or Herb Crepes (See index)
2 tablespoons onion, finely chopped
4 tablespoons butter
4 tablespoons flour
1 1/2 cups milk
3 tablespoons sherry
1/2 cup chicken stock
Salt and freshly ground black pepper
1 egg yolk, beaten
3 tablespoons half-and-half
2 cups crab meat, chopped
1/2 cup mushrooms, chopped and cooked
2 teaspoons chopped chives
2 teaspoons chopped fresh parsley
4 tablespoons heavy cream, whipped
Nutmeg

Saute onion in butter, stir in flour; add milk, sherry and chicken stock. Season to taste with salt and pepper. Cook, stirring, until thickened. Add beaten egg yolk to cream. Stir a small amount of hot mixture to egg-cream mixture, then stir back into the hot mixture. Simmer, but do not boil, until thickened. Reserve 1/2 cup of sauce.

Add crab meat, mushrooms, chives and parsley to remaining sauce; stir until heated. Divide mixture on 12 crepes; fill and roll, tucking ends under. Place in a lightly greased baking dish. Mix whipped cream and a pinch of nutmeg into the reserved sauce; spoon over crepes and place under broiler to glaze. Serves 4 to 6.

SHRIMP CREPES

12 Basic or Herb Crepes (See Index)
2 tablespoons minced onion
4 tablespoons butter, melted
4 tablespoons flour
2 teaspoons curry powder
2 cups milk (we sometimes use less milk, add some white wine)
Salt and Freshly-ground black pepper
2 cups tiny shrimp, cooked and cleaned
1 tablespoons freshly parsley, chopped
Chopped peanuts (optional)

Saute onion in melted butter until golden; blend in flour and curry powder. Stir in milk (and wine) and cook until thickened. Salt and pepper to taste; reserve 1/2 cup of sauce and set aside. Add shrimp and parsley to remaining sauce; stir until heated. Divide mixture among crepes; roll and tuck in ends; Place in a lightly greased baking dish and spoon reserved sauce over crepes. Sprinkle with peanuts if desired. Glaze under the broiler. Serves 4 to 6.

HAM CREPES

12 Basic or Herb Crepes (See index)
4 tablespoons butter, melted
4 tablespoons flour
1 1/2 cups milk
Salt and Freshly ground black pepper
1 egg yolk, beaten
2 cups cooked ham, chopped
3/4 cup chopped, cooked mushrooms
2 tablespoons fresh parsley, chopped
1/3 cup Parmesan cheese, freshly-grated

Blend melted butter and flour over heat; Stir in milk and simmer, stirring until thickened. Season to taste with salt and pepper. Add small amount of hot mixture to beaten egg yolk, then stir it into the hot mixture, stirring constantly. Bring to a simmer until thickened; do not allow to boil.

Add ham, mushrooms and parsley to sauce; spread filling on crepes and roll, tucking in the ends. Place in a lightly-greased, shallow, baking dish; sprinkle with cheese and place dish under broiler to glaze. Serves 6.

For the Good Times

FLORENTINE FILLING FOR CREPES

12 Basic or Herb Crepes (See index)
1/2 pound fresh mushrooms, finely chopped
2 tablespoons butter
1 box (10-ounce) frozen chopped spinach,
    cooked and well drained
1/3 cup dry onion soup mix
2 cup ham, cooked and finely chopped
6 tablespoons flour
6 tablespoons butter
2 cup milk
1 cup Swiss cheese, grated
1/2 teaspoon Worcestershire sauce

Make crepes and set aside. Melt butter and saute mushrooms. Add drained spinach, soup mix and ham to mushrooms and set aside. Melt 6 tablespoons butter and add flour, blending well. Gradually add milk, stirring constantly. Cook until thickened; add cheese and Worcestershire sauce and heat until cheese is melted. Blend 1/2 cup of the sauce into the spinach mixture. Fill crepes with spinach mixture and roll. Place seam-side down in a greased baking dish. Spoon remaining sauce over top of crepes. Cover and heat in preheated 350-degree oven for 15 to 20 minutes. Serves 6.

CREAM CHEESE - MUSHROOM FILLING FOR CREPES

12 Basic or Herb crepes (See index)
2 tablespoons butter, melted
1/2 pound fresh mushrooms, minced
2 tablespoons green onion, finely minced
Salt and freshly ground pepper
1 package (8-ounce) cream cheese, softened
2 cups sour cream
3 tablespoons Parmesan cheese
2 tablespoons fresh dill, minced or 2
    teaspoons dried
6 tablespoons butter, melted

Add mushrooms and green onion to melted butter in a heavy skillet. Cook until liquid has evaporated; season with salt and pepper to taste and set aside.

In a large mixing bowl combine cream cheese and sour cream. Add mushroom mixture, cheese and dill; mix well. Adjust seasonings to taste. Divide mixture among crepes; roll up and place seam side down in a shallow baking dish. Pour butter over top and bake in a preheated 325-degree oven for about 20 minutes. Sprinkle with additional Parmesan cheese and place under broiler until cheese is slightly browned. Serves 4-6.

JACK'S HOLLANDAISE SAUCE

9 egg yolks
1 tablespoon water
3 sticks butter, melted and cooled to room
    temperature
3 tablespoons fresh lemon juice or to taste

Combine yolks and water in small saucepan. Whisk over low heat until mixture begins to thicken. Watch closely so it doesn't curdle. Slowly whisk in cooled butter, mixing constantly until thick. Blend in lemon juice. Cover and let stand at room temperature for up to 2 hours. Makes 2 cups.

Jack says, "If you like, you can add rinsed and drained red caviar; gently fold it into the sauce. It is a nice variation on eggs benedict or asparagus hollandaise."

BLENDER HOLLANDIASE

3 egg yolks
4 teaspoons lemon juice
Dash cayenne pepper
1/2 cup butter or margarine

Place egg yolks, lemon juice and cayenne in blender container. Cover and quickly turn blender on and off. Melt butter or margarine until almost boiling. With blender on high speed slowly pour in hot butter, blending until thick and fluffy; about 30 seconds. Makes 1 cup.

VARIATIONS OF HOLLANDAISE SAUCE

SAUCE CAPRES

Add 3 tablespoons finely minced or smallest whole drained capers to 1 recipe of hollandaise sauce. Serve with fish, poultry or it is delicious on cauliflower.

SAUCE MARSEILLAISE

Add 2 tablespoons tomato puree, salt and pepper to taste to 1 recipe of hollandaise sauce. Sprinkle with chopped parsley, oregano or chives if desired. Serve with fish or meat.

SAUCE MOUTARDE

Add 2 tablespoons prepared mustard to 1 recipe hollandaise sauce. Serve with cold meats or fish.

SAUCE MALTAISE

Add 3 tablespoons strained orange juice and grated rind of 1 orange to 1 recipe of hollandaise sauce. Serve with asparagus, broccoli, artichokes and cauliflower.

SAUCE NOISETTE

Add 1/4 cup grated hazelnuts or filberts to 1 recipe hollandaise sauce and season well. Serve with chicken or asparagus.

ORANGE HOLLANDAISE SAUCE

2/3 cup freshly squeezed orange juice
1 1/2 teaspoons distilled white vinegar
1 teaspoon finely grated lemon rind (blanched)
4 teaspoons finely grated orange rind (blanched)
3 egg yolks
1 tablespoon hot water
3/4 cup butter, melted
Dash of pepper

Boil orange juice, vinegar and blanched rinds in a non-aluminum pan until sauce has reduced to about 3 tablespoons; about 8 minutes. Set aside.

Place egg yolks and hot water in blender and process on low speed. Keeping on low, slowly pour in the hot melted butter, orange mixture and pepper; continuing to blend until the sauce is thick and smooth. Makes 1 cup.

Jo and Jan say, "Do not reheat this over direct heat. Place in a small pan and set it in another pan of hot, not boiling water."

WHIPPED BUTTER

2 sticks butter, room temperature
1/2 cup heavy cream

Beat softened butter with cream with electric mixer on low speed until cream is absorbed and mixture is fluffy. Spoon into a bowl and serve at room temperature. Makes 1 1/2 cups.

For the Good Times

❖❖❖

WHIPPPED HONEY BUTTER

1/4 pound butter
1/4 pound margarine
1/4 cup honey
1/4 cup half-and-half

Bring butter and margarine to room temperature. Mix together with electric mixer until well blended. Add honey, a tablespoon at a time and whip until fluffy. Beat in half-and-half, a tablespoon at a time, until smooth and fluffy. Cover and refrigerate. Bring to room temperature before serving.

For variation, add finely chopped lemon peel or grated orange peel. Makes 1 1/2 cups.

GRAND MARNIER BUTTER

6 ounces butter, softened
Juice of 1 orange
1 tablespoon Grand Marnier liqueur
1/2 cup confectioners' sugar
1 tablespoon grated orange rind

Blend all ingredients and whip until smooth. Chill if not serving right away.

BRANDY BUTTER

6 tablespoons unsalted butter
6 tablespoons lightly packed dark brown sugar
Grated peel of 1/2 lemon
1 tablespoon fresh lemon juice
2 tablespoons brandy or rum, or to taste

Cream butter with electric mixer. Gradually add sugar, lemon peel and juice. When mixture is smooth add brandy to taste. Spoon in small container and chill. Serve with crepes, puddings, pancakes, waffles, French toast.

PEACH BUTTER

1/2 cup peeled, sliced fresh peaches
1 cup unsalted butter
1/2 cup confectioners' sugar

Combine ingredients in blender or food processor until smooth. Chill and spread on toast, muffins, waffles, pancakes or crepes.

STRAWBERRY SPREAD

1 package (10-ounce) frozen strawberries, thawed
1 cup powdered sugar
1 cup soft spread margarine

Combine and beat with electric mixer for 10 minutes. Use as a spread in place of butter.

Jo and Jan say, "Use this spread with Strawberry Bread (See index). It is also delicious on English muffins'!"

❖❖

Bed and Breakfast

IRENE'S FRIENDSHIP CAKE

1 cup Greetings
1 large Handshake
1 teaspoon Sympathy
1/2 cup Smiles
2/3 cup Love
2 cups Hospitality

Cream Greetings and Smiles thoroughly. Add Handshake separately. Slowly stir in Love. Sift Sympathy and Hospitality and fold very carefully. Bake in a Warm Heart. Serve Often.

ORANGE JULIUS

1 can (6-ounce) frozen orange juice,
   undiluted
1 cup milk
1 cup water
1/4 cup sugar
2 teaspoons vanilla
2 cups ice cubes

Combine ingredients in blender, mix well and pour into glasses. Serves 2.

TROPICAL FRUIT DRINK

2 1/2 cups pineapple juice
1 large or 2 small bananas
1 package frozen strawberries, unsweetened
1/2 of can (14-ounce size) coconut syrup
Grenadine syrup, to taste
Rum

Blend pineapple juice, bananas, strawberries, coconut syrup and grenadine syrup. Blend well; pour half of mixture into another container and set aside. To remaining mixture, add desired amount of rum, fill blender with cracked ice. Blend and serve. Repeat with the reserved mixture. This keeps well in the freezer; nice to have on hand for summer "drop-ins." Makes 10 cups.

ICED CINNAMON COFFEE

4 cups strong coffee (use 2 to 4 teaspoons
   instant coffee to 1 cup boiling water)
1 piece (3 inches) stick cinnamon, broken
   into pieces
2/3 cup heavy cream
Coffee Syrup (See Index)
Sweetened whipped cream (optional, as
   garnish)

Pour hot coffee over cinnamon pieces; cover and let stand about 1 hour. Remove cinnamon and stir in the cream. Chill thoroughly.

To serve, pour into ice-filled glasses. Stir in desired amount of Coffee Syrup. If desired, top with sweetened whipped cream and sprinkle with ground cinnamon. Use cinnamon sticks as stirrers. Serves 4.

For the Good Times

FRIED APPLES

6 medium-sized apples
2 tablespoons margarine
1/8 cup brown sugar
1/4 teaspoon cinnamon

Wash and quarter apples. Take out cores and slice apples 1/4-inch thick. Melt margarine in a medium-sized skillet and add apple slices. Cook until apples are shiney and beginning to look limp; sprinkle sugar and cinnamon over them and lightly mix. Serve hot. Serves 4.

Jan says, "This is a wonderful side dish and this recipe would be enough for me with no one's help. Remember that apples shrivel up and it always takes more than the recipe states."

POACHED PEARS

4 firm pears with stems intact
1 quart water
2 cups sugar or use a sugar substitute
4 1-inch strips lemon zest

Peel pears and cut a thin slice from the bottom so pears will stand upright. Dissolve sugar in water in a large saucepan; bring to a boil. Add zest and stand pears in water. Cover, reduce heat and simmer until pears are fork tender. Leave in the cooking liquid and cool to room temperature; then remove and refrigerate until serving time. Serves 4.

Jan and Jo say, "Serve the pears with Raspberry, Black Currant Sauce or do Carol's Variation on Poached Pears (See index)"

KRISTI'S BAKED PEACHES

3/4 cup blanched almonds, finely ground
1/2 to 1 cup sugar
1/8 teaspoon almond extract
3/4 cup white wine
2 fresh peaches, peeled and halved

Combine almonds, half of sugar and almond extract. Add about 1 tablespoon wine and beat mixture until creamy but firm. Divide mixture among peach halves and press firmly into cavities. Place in a shallow baking dish with remaining wine and sugar in bottom of dish. Bake in preheated 350-degree oven for 20 to 25 minutes, or until golden on top, basting twice during baking time. Place peaches in serving dishes, spoon syrup over tops. Serve warm or cold. Serves 4.

Jan and Jo say, "These are very pretty served in a crystal stemmed dish."

◆◆◆

FRESH LIME CREAM FRUIT TART

3/4 package refrigerator sugar cookie dough
2/3 cup sugar
1/4 cup cornstarch
1/4 teaspoon salt
1 1/2 to 1 2/3 cups milk
2 eggs, lightly beaten
1 1/2 teaspoons grated lime rind
1/3 cup freshly squeezed lime juice, (about 3
  limes)
3 nectarines, sliced
2 bananas, sliced
1 cup blueberries
1 cup grapes
1 cup fresh raspberries, blackberries or
  sliced strawberries
2 tablespoons corn syrup (optional)

Make crust by rolling cookie dough in a thin layer on a pizza pan or a 9 x 13-inch baking pan. Prick dough with fork and bake according to package directions. Let cool.

In medium saucepan, combine sugar, cornstarch and salt; mix well. Gradually stir in milk. Cook over medium heat, stirring constantly until mixture boils and thickens. Boil 1 minute. Remove from heat; slowly stir hot mixture into beaten eggs. Return to low heat; cook, stirring constantly, 2 minutes. Remove from heat and stir in lime rind, lime juice and butter. Pour into prepared cookie crust; cool and chill. Before serving, arrange fruits in a decorative pattern on top of pie. If desired, brush with corn syrup to glaze fruits. Serves 8.

A TIP ON FRITTERS

• Fritters may also be frozen. Place in single layer on cookie sheet and quickly "flash-freeze." Remove and wrap in heavy-duty foil. To reheat, unwrap and place unthawed in a preheated 375-degree oven for 15 to 20 minutes.

PRUNE FRITTERS

1 cup flour
1/3 teaspoon salt
2 tablespoons sugar
2 eggs, well-beaten
1/2 cup milk
1 cup prunes, cooked, drained, sweetened
  and pitted
Powdered sugar

Sift flour, measure and sift with sugar and salt. Combine eggs and milk. Add dry ingredients and mix until smooth. Add prunes and mix well.

Drop by spoonfuls into deep fat (365 degrees). Fry until evenly browned and drain on paper towels. Sprinkle with powdered sugar. If desired, serve with Lemon Sauce (See index).

BANANA FRITTERS

3 bananas
1 tablespoon sugar
2 teaspoons lemon juice
1 teaspoon orange juice
2 teaspoons grated orange rind
1 cup flour
1/3 teaspoon salt
2 tablespoons sugar
2 eggs, well-beaten
1/2 cup milk

Peel bananas and quarter. Sprinkle with sugar, lemon and orange juice and rind. Cover and let stand 30 minutes.

Meanwhile, sift flour, measure and sift with sugar and salt. Combine eggs and milk. Add dry ingredients and mix until smooth.

Dip banana pieces in fritter batter. Fry in deep fat (365 degrees) until brown. Drain on paper towels, sprinkle with powdered sugar. Makes 12. If desired, serve with Lemon Sauce (See index).

For the Good Times

KATHY'S FRESH APPLE FRITTERS

1 cup milk
1 egg, beaten
4 tablespoons margarine
1/2 cup sugar
1 teaspoon vanilla
1/2 teaspoon salt
1 orange, grated rind and juice
1 cup apples, chopped fine (peel may be left on)
3 cups flour
2 teaspoons baking powder
Confectioners' sugar

In mixing bowl combine beaten egg, milk, melted margarine. Add orange juice and rind, chopped apples and vanilla. Sift together flour, salt, baking powder and sugar. Stir into egg mixture with spoon until blended. Do not over mix. Preheat oil in skillet or fry kettle to 350 degrees. Drop batter from tablespoon into hot oil and fry to a golden brown. Turn so they brown evenly. Remove from oil, drain on paper towels and allow to cool. Roll in confectioners' sugar. Makes 4 dozen.

DERELYS' LEMON FRENCH TOAST

8 slices extra thin-sliced bread
3 eggs
1/4 cup cream
1/4 cup oil, scant
2 lemons, squeezed
Confectioners' sugar

Beat eggs until frothy and light. Add cream with a couple extra beats. Soak bread, a few pieces at a time, so that they absorb egg-cream mixture thoroughly. In a skillet or griddle, heat oil and fry bread on both sides to a golden color or as desired for crispness.

Remove bread from skillet and drain on paper towels if needed. Pour lemon juice over toast and sprinkle confectioners' sugar very generously over the toast. Serve immediately.

Jan says, "I cannot say how many this will serve. I could and would eat all 8 slices by myself! This delectable morsel was served to us by our dear friend, Derelys, at her home on Laguna Beach with the ocean in the background. But, you know, I don't even miss the ocean when I eat this great lemon French toast."

CINNAMON LOGS

1 loaf (1-pound) firm white bread, crusts trimmed
1 cup milk
1 cup heavy cream
5 eggs, beaten
2 tablespoons sugar
1/2 to 3/4 teaspoon cinnamon
1/4 teaspoon grated nutmeg
1/2 teaspoon vanilla

Cut bread into 4x2x2-inch rectangular logs. Let stand to dry out slightly. Blend milk, cream, eggs, sugar, cinnamon, nutmeg and vanilla in medium bowl. Pour mixture into a shallow pan large enough to hold bread in 1 layer. Arrange bread in milk mixture, turning to coat all sides. Chill until liquid is absorbed, several hours or overnight.

In a skillet heat 1/2 cup cooking oil. Fry logs in batches until golden on all sides, or as desired for crispness. Remove from oil and drain on paper towels. Place on baking sheet and bake in preheated 400-degree oven for 3 to 5 minutes or until puffed. Serve immediately with whipped butter, powdered sugar with cinnamon, warm syrup or preserves. Serves 6.

Jo and Jan say, " Texas toast makes wonderful Cinnamon Logs."

BUTTERMILK PANCAKES

1 egg
1 cup buttermilk
2 tablespoons vegetable oil
1 cup flour
1 teaspoon baking powder
1/2 teaspoon baking soda
1 tablespoon sugar

Beat egg, add buttermilk. Mix flour, baking powder, soda and sugar. Add to buttermilk mixture then add oil. If mixture is too thick, add a little more buttermilk. Cook pancakes on a hot griddle.

Jo says, "Add a crushed banana or blueberries to these pancakes for a special brunch dish."

NANCE'S PANCAKES

1 1/2 cups flour
1/2 cup sugar
3 teaspoons baking powder
Pinch of salt
3 tablespoons oil
1 1/2 cup milk
1 egg, beaten
1 mashed banana (optional)

Combine dry ingredients; add oil, milk and egg. Stir to blend. Add mashed banana if you desire. Pour onto hot griddle, serve with melted butter and hot syrup. Serves 4.

CINNAMON - HONEY - PECAN SAUCE

2 cups maple syrup
1/2 cup honey
3/4 cup pecans, coarsely chopped
3/4 teaspoon cinnamon

Combine ingredients; stir well and store at room temperature in a tightly closed container. Makes 3 cups.

Jo and Jan say, "This is delicious with French toast, pancakes, waffles or desserts."

LEMON MUFFINS

1/2 cup sugar
1 stick margarine
2 egg yolks, beaten
1 tablespoon lemon rind, finely grated
1 cup flour
1/4 teaspoon salt
1 teaspoon baking powder
4 tablespoons fresh lemon juice
2 egg whites

TOPPING:
3 tablespoons sugar
1/8 teaspoon cinnamon
1/4 cup pecans, chopped (optional)

Cream sugar and margarine. Add egg yolks and lemon rind. Sift dry ingredients and add to creamed mixture alternately with lemon juice. Beat egg whites until stiff and fold into batter. Fill greased miniature or medium size muffin tins 2/3 full. Combine topping ingredients and sprinkle a bit on each muffin. Bake in preheated 375-degree oven for 20 minutes or until toothpick inserted in center comes out clean. Makes 12 medium size muffins or 24 miniature.

For the Good Times

APRICOT MUFFINS

2 cups flour
4 teaspoons baking powder
1/3 cup sugar
1/4 teaspoon salt
1 cup milk
1/2 cup dried apricots, chopped
1 egg yolk
2 tablespoons melted shortening
1 egg white, beaten

Combine dry ingredients; add milk, apricots and egg yolk. Beat 2 minutes and fold in rest of ingredients. Half fill greased muffin tins and bake in preheated 350-degree oven for 15 to 20 minutes. Makes 16.

CINNAMON RAISIN BISCUITS

1 cup flour
2 teaspoons baking powder
1/4 teaspoon salt
1 1/2 tablespoons shortening
1/3 cup milk, scant
1 tablespoon melted butter or margarine
1 tablespoon sugar
1/4 teaspoon cinnamon
1/2 cup raisins, chopped

Sift flour, salt and baking powder together; cut in shortening. Add milk to form soft dough. Turn out on lightly floured board; knead lightly. Pat into sheet 1/2-inch thick. Spread 1/2 of dough with melted butter, sugar, cinnamon and raisins. Fold dough 1/2 over and cut with a floured cutter. Place on unoiled baking sheet and bake in a preheated 425-degree oven for 10 minutes.

RUTHIE'S ORANGE COFFEE RING

2 cans prepared biscuits
1/4 cup butter, melted
3/4 cup sugar
1 tablespoon orange juice
1 tablespoon orange rind
1/2 of 3-ounce package cream cheese
/4 cup confectioners' sugar
1 tablespoon orange juice
1/4 teaspoon vanilla

Dip biscuits in butter, then combine sugar, orange juice and rind; dip buttered biscuits in mixture and place in an overlapping circle in a 9-inch round pan. Bake in a preheated 400-degree oven for 15 to 20 minutes. Prepare frosting by combining cream cheese, confectioners' sugar, orange juice and vanilla. Blend well and frost biscuits while warm. Serves 6-8.

GAILE'S COFFEE CAKE

3 cups flour
2 cups sugar
1/2 teaspoon salt
1/2 teaspoon cloves
1/2 teaspoon nutmeg
1/2 teaspoon cinnamon
3/4 cup shortening
3 tablespoons butter or margarine
3 tablespoons brown sugar
2 cups buttermilk
2 teaspoons soda
1/2 cup cut raisins
1/2 cup chopped nuts

Sift together the flour, sugar, salt and spices. Blend in the 3/4 cup shortening. Take out 1/2 of this mixture; add the butter and brown sugar; blend this and set aside for topping.
Add buttermilk, soda, raisins and nuts to the remaining flour mixture. Stir to blend well. Pour batter into greased and floured bundt pan; sprinkle topping on top of batter and bake in preheated 350-degree oven for about 45 minutes.

❖❖❖

CINNAMON SOUR CREAM COFFEE CAKE

1/2 cup butter or margarine, softened
1 cup sugar
2 large eggs
1 cup sour cream
2 cups flour, sifted
1 teaspoon baking powder
1/2 teaspoon baking soda
1 teaspoon almond extract
3/4 cup chopped almonds
2 teaspoons cinnamon
2 tablespoons dark brown sugar

Cream butter and sugar until light and fluffy. Add eggs, one at a time, beating well after each addition. Stir in sour cream. Sift together the flour, baking powder, soda, and add to creamed mixture. Stir in almond extract.

In another bowl combine almonds, cinnamon and brown sugar. Grease and flour a bundt or 8-inch tube pan. Spoon half of batter into pan and sprinkle half of cinnamon mixture on top. Cover with remaining batter and top with cinnamon mixture.

Bake in preheated 350-degree oven for 1 hour or until toothpick inserted in center comes out clean. Serves 12.

BLUEBERRY COFFEE CAKE

1/2 cup shortening
1 cup sugar
2 eggs
1 teaspoon vanilla
2 1/4 cups flour
1 tablespoon baking powder
2/3 cup milk
2 cups blueberries, fresh or frozen
2/3 cup sugar
2/3 cup flour
1/2 cup margarine
1/4 teaspoon almond extract

Beat shortening and sugar until light and fluffy. Add eggs and vanilla; beat well. Stir together 2 1/4 cups flour and baking powder. Add to beaten mixture alternately with milk. Spread in 2 greased 9 x 9-inch baking pans. Top each with 1 cup of blueberries. Combine remaining sugar and flour; cut in margarine and extract until mixture crumbles. Sprinkle over blueberries. Bake in preheated 350-degree oven for 40 minutes. Cool slightly and cut into wedges. Makes 2 coffee cakes.

Jan says, "This is a wonderful coffee cake to serve for a special breakfast or brunch. I have found it takes longer to bake than the 40 minutes, so check it carefully to see that the toothpick comes out clean when you test."

SUGAR TWIST

1/2 cup milk
1/2 cup warm water
2 packages yeast
1/2 cup sugar
1/2 teaspoon salt
2/3 cup oil
3 eggs
5 1/2 cups flour

Scald milk and cool to lukewarm. Dissolve yeast in warm water; add yeast, sugar, salt, oil, and eggs to milk and mix well. Add flour and mix well; knead and let rise, covered for 1 hour. Roll out and cut into ropes about 6 inches long. Brush with oil and roll in cinnamon - sugar mixture. Twist into a loose knot. Place on a greased baking sheet and let rise for 30 to 45 minutes. Bake in a preheated 375-degree oven for 10 to 15 minutes, watching the sugar so it doesn't burn. Remove immediately, turn upside down and cool. Makes 24.

Jo says, "This reminds me of the Bohemian sugar twists which were deep-fried, then rolled in sugar. They are called Ceske. You might like to try them fried instead of baked sometime."

For the Good Times

PECAN ROLLS

3/4 cup brown sugar
1/2 cup margarine, melted
54 pecan halves
2 packages yeast
1/2 cup warm water
1/4 cup granulated sugar
1 1/4 teaspoons salt
3 cups flour, sifted
1 egg
2 tablespoons soft shortening

Measure into the bottom of 18 muffin cups 1 1/2 teaspoons brown sugar, 1/2 teaspoon melted margarine and 3 pecan halves; set aside. Add yeast to 1/2 cup water; stir until dissolved. Add granulated sugar, salt and 11/2 cups of the flour. Mix together and blend until smooth. Add egg, shortening and remaining 11/2 cups of flour all at once. Blend and beat until smooth. Spoon batter into muffin cups to 1/2 full. Let rise in warm place until batter is level with top of muffin cups. Bake in preheated 375-degree oven for 24 to 30 minutes or until golden brown. Let stand 1 minute before turning out of pans. Makes 18.

QUICK DANISH ROLLS

1 package (8-ounce) cream cheese, softened
1/2 cup sugar
1 tablespoon lemon juice
2 cans (8-ounce size) refrigerated Crescent rolls
4 teaspoons preserves
1/2 cup powdered sugar
1 teaspoon vanilla
2 or 3 teaspoons boiling water

In a medium-size bowl cream the cheese, sugar and lemon juice until smooth. Separate dough into 8 rectangles. Spread about 2 tablespoons cream cheese mixture on each rectangle. Starting at the long side, roll up and press edges to seal. Gently stretch each roll to about a 10-inch strip. Coil loosely into spirals and seal the ends good. Make deep indentation with thumb in center of each roll and fill with 1/2 teaspoon preserves. Bake on ungreased cookie sheet in a preheated 350-degree oven for 20 to 25 minutes. Blend the powdered sugar, vanilla and water to make a smooth glaze and drizzle over each roll. Makes 8 rolls.

AL'S GRAVY TRAIN

1 pound medium or hot sausage
2 tablespoons butter
4 tablespoons flour
1/2 teaspoon salt
1/4 teaspoon pepper
2 cups milk
English muffins or toast points

Crumble and fry sausage until done; drain and set aside. Heat butter in a saucepan; blend in flour, salt and pepper. Heat and stir until bubbly. Gradually add the milk, stirring until smooth. Bring to a boil; cook and stir 1 to 2 minutes longer. Add cooked sausage and mix well. Serve over toasted English muffins or toast points and garnish with parsley. Serves 6.

❖❖

OVERNIGHT POTATO BREAKFAST CASSEROLE

1 box (6-ounce) dehydrated hash brown
   potatoes
5 eggs
1/2 cup cottage cheese
1 cup shredded Swiss or Monterrey Jack
   cheese
1 green onion, chopped
4 drops tabasco sauce
6 slices bacon, fried crisp and crumbled
Salt and pepper
Paprika

Soak potatoes according to directions on box; drain. In a small bowl, beat eggs slightly. Stir in potatoes, cheese, green onion and seasonings. Turn into a slightly greased 9 x 13-inch casserole. Sprinkle bacon and paprika on top. Cover tightly with foil and refrigerate overnight.

Place in a cold oven; set temperature to 350 degrees and bake 40 minutes. Serve immediately. Serves 8-10.

JAN'S BREAKFAST PIZZA

1 package Crescent rolls or pizza dough
1 cup Hash Brown O'Brians
1 package brown and serve sausages,
   chopped
1 jar sliced mushrooms (drained)
1 1/2 cups Colby cheese, shredded
1 1/2 cups Mozzarella cheese
4 eggs
1/4 cup milk
Parmesan cheese

Press rolls into bottom of 9x13-inch baking dish. Sprinkle with hash browns, then chopped sausage, mushrooms, and cheeses. Beat eggs with milk and pour over entire mixture. Top with Parmesan cheese. Bake in preheated 350-degree oven for 40 minutes.

OMELETS

Jo and Jan say, "Here are two recipes for omelets for you to try with fillings of your choice. We could give you a complete book of just omelet fillings, but we have found that often times people will add extras, so try everything from artichokes to zucchini, chicken, ham, Mexican omelets, Italian, sweet and sour, and on and on. When Jo's daughter, Tonia, makes a Sunday omelet, half the refrigerator is included. Her omelets rank among the world's best, if we do say so."

THE BASIC OMELET

3 eggs
1 tablespoon water
1/4 teaspoon salt
Dash of pepper
1 tablespoon butter or margarine

In a small bowl beat together the eggs, water, salt and pepper with a fork until the mixture is blended but not frothy. For an herb-flavored omelet, add 1/8 to 1/4 teaspoon of your favorite dried crushed herb.

Heat the butter in an 8-inch skillet with flared sides. When butter sizzles and browns slightly, lift and tilt the pan to coat the sides.

Pour in egg mixture. Continuing to cook over medium heat, use a fork to rapidly stir just through the top of the uncooked eggs in a zigzag pattern. While stirring the cooked portions will come to the center. While stirring, also shake the skillet constantly to keep the the egg mixture moving, shaking carefully so that the depth of the omelet remains even. When the eggs are set on the bottom but still shiny and soft on top, remove the skillet from the heat.

Spoon desired filling across the center. Using a spatula, carefully lift 1/3 of the cooked omelet and fold over filling. Tilt skillet and with spatula, gently fold remaining third of omelet over filling. Invert skillet to roll omelet out onto serving plate. Top with sauce or garnish as desired. Serve immediately. Serves 2.

For the Good Times

❖❖

THE PERFECT FLUFFY OMELET

4 egg whites
2 tablespoons water
1/4 teaspoon salt
4 egg yolks
1 tablespoon butter or margarine

In a large mixer bowl, beat egg whites until frothy; add water and salt. Beat until stiff peaks form, about 1 1/2 minutes.

In a small mixer bowl, beat egg yolks at high speed on electric mixer until thick and lemon-colored, about 5 minutes. With a spatula, gently fold egg yolks into egg whites, turning bowl as you fold.

In a 10-inch skillet with oven-proof handle,
heat butter or margarine. A drop of water should sizzle when temperature is right. Pour in egg mixture; spread evenly, leaving the egg mixture higher at the sides. Cook slowly, uncovered, for 8 to 10 minutes, or until puffed and set. Lift edge of omelet with a metal spatula; the bottom will be golden brown.

Place skillet in preheated 325-degree oven and bake for 10 minutes or until a knife inserted in center comes out clean.

Loosen the sides of omelet with a spatula. Make a shallow cut across the omelet, cutting slightly above and almost parallel to the skillet handle; tilt the pan. Spoon filling of choice onto lower half of omelet. Fold the upper half of omelet over the lower half. Slip omelet onto platter. Serves 2.

For a Mob

ROB'S SHRIMP FOR A MOB

4 pounds rendered chicken fat
4 pounds flour
4 gallons chicken stock
20 egg yolks
1 1/2 pounds butter, softened
4 lemons, juiced
Tabasco sauce
5 pounds mushroom caps
Butter
16 tomatoes, cut into wedges
24 ounces white wine
10 pounds asparagus
16 pounds shrimp
Butter
2 cups breadcrumbs
1/4 cup melted butter
Paprika
Parmesan cheese
Parsley

Heat chicken fat; add flour to make a roux. Add chicken stock and set aside. mix egg yolks by hand and add softened butter; this mixture will be lumpy. Now add the lemon juice and a few drops of hot sauce. Combine with the chicken stock sauce. Strain this mixture and set aside.

Saute mushroom caps in a small amount of melted butter; add tomato wedges and saute until tender. Season to taste; add wine and cook for a minute or so, then remove from heat.

Cut asparagus so tips are about 2 inches long. Save the rest of the spears for another use (maybe asparagus soup). Place tops in hot water and cook until tender.

Saute shrimp in melted butter until they are pink; season to taste. Place shrimp in a large ovenproof casserole. Place mushroom-tomato mixture on top, followed by asparagus. Cover with sauce. Combine bread crumbs with melted butter and sprinkle over top of sauce. Sprinkle with paprika and Parmesan cheese. Place under broiler until brown. Garnish with fresh parsley. Serves 100.

Rob says, "This is truly elegant; perfect for that huge buffet party you are planning. Has been used for wedding celebrations."

JACK'S CHICKEN FOR A MOB

Broiler halves or quarters, nurtured over low coals and basted with a flavorful sauce, are one of my favorites on the charbroiler. But three, maybe four chickens, are all that one can handle properly on the broiler without the situation becoming an endurance contest. Chickens require constant attention, frequent turning and basting, and a long vigil at the grill to turn out a worthy product. To over extend the chef is a sure guarantee that the host will be transformed into a human likeness of a fireplace shovel, complete with red watering eyes, blistered lips, and the disposition of an overheated badger. Great fun for host and guests alike!!

Still, if you are dealing with a large group, chickens are a great favorite, eliminating the predictable and inevitable wail of "too done, too rare, you got mine, etc., etc.," that accompany short-stay-at-the-grill items such as steaks or chops. After years of struggle, I've stumbled onto a technique that satisfies the "fix us your broiled chickens, Uncle Jack," request, and at the same time allows me to participate in the day's events with family and friends. Here's what I call Chicken for a Mob. I hope it works for you, and your mob enjoys it. If it fails I don't care and I don't want to hear from you! After years of acting like a badger, I can react quite violently!

NEEDS AND INGREDIENTS

Broiler chickens
Smoker with at least 2 racks
Charbroiler
10-pound bag of charcoal
Lighter fluid
1 cup red cooking wine
1 cup melted butter
Bottle of vegetable oil
3 cloves fresh garlic
Garlic powder
Cracked black pepper
Worcestershire sauce
Tabasco sauce
Small handful of mesquite chips (soaked)
Juice of 1 lemon

Wash, dry and quarter your broiler chickens, rubbing them lightly with oil, cracked pepper and garlic powder. Use plenty of the latter. Set aside while you prepare your equipment.

I use a stacked smoker manufactured by Smoke-N' Pit. There are other similar smokers on the market. You may, however, need to bend these general guidelines to accommodate the traits of your equipment.

Prepare the water pan by combining 1 cup of red cooking wine, 1 cup of melted butter, 1/2 cup oil, the fresh garlic or 3 tablespoons garlic powder, 2 tablespoons cracked black pepper, 2 tablespoons Worcestershire sauce, 2 teaspoons Tabasco and the lemon juice. Top off the pan with water and stir well; you eventually place it in the smoker.

Use about 3/4 of the bag of charcoal. I light the coals by putting about half a can of lighter fluid in a 3-inch circle in the top center of the charcoal. When the initial flame has burned down (several minutes) add the soaked mesquite chips.

Place the water pan in the smoker and stack the chicken quarters equally on the number of racks your smoker utilizes. Don't worry about the fact that the chickens won't brown where they touch. We'll remedy that situation later on. Place the lid on the smoker and don't dare take a peek! The chickens will be ready to remove in 4 to 5 hours.

While the chickens are smoking you need to set up your regular charbroiler for a low-to-medium-heat fire. You want this fire bed to be ready to receive the chickens as they come out of the smoker.

I position the charbroiler in close proximity to the smoker to facilitate the transfer to the grill. Likewise, I can beat the kids (of all ages) away from the smoker as the natural tendency is to lift the lid and thereby lengthen the smoking time.

Now the chef moves the chicken quarters, in numbers that can be easily handled on the grill, to the charbroiler. Our purpose is to mark and brown the chickens. The normal need to baste the chicken has been eliminated. They will be bursting with locked-in juices that will make the basting task unnecessary. Use tongs that are smooth for minimize puncturing the skin—and watch out for flashing if your grill is too low or the fire is too hot.

When quarters are golden brown and marked, remove them to a holding pan, or serve them directly onto the plates of your guests. As our friend from Louisiana would say, "I gar-on-tee" your mob will enjoy this combination of smoked and charcoaled flavors—and you should be at the fire not much more than 30 minutes. WARNING: even some of the average eaters may hit you for a couple of quarters!

Jo says, "Jack prepared chicken quarters for our 4th of July celebration. There were around 30 of us; all the chicken was on the huge tray at the buffet—at the same time! It was the hit of the day, and disappeared fast. Some of us could have eaten more, but were out-maneuvered! It is delicious!"

SALAD FOR A MOB

DRESSING:
1 cup salad oil
1 tablespoon sugar
1 teaspoon dry mustard
2 teaspoons Dijon mustard
1/2 teaspoon garlic powder
Reserved juice from artichokes (See below)
1/3 cup wine vinegar
1/2 tablespoon salad herbs
Salt and Pepper to taste

SALAD:
2 pounds chicken or turkey breast, cooked and diced
2 pounds ham, cooked and diced
2 pounds cheddar cheese, grated
1 dozen hard boiled eggs, grated
4 ripe avocados, cubed
1 pound fresh mushrooms, thinly sliced
1 can (7 3/4-ounce) pitted ripe olives, thinly sliced
4 ribs celery, thinly sliced
2 bunches radish, thinly sliced
2 bunches green onions, thinly sliced
1 pint cherry tomatoes, halved
3 jars (6 ounce size) marinated artichoke hearts, diced, reserving juice
5-6 heads of mixed greens (spinach, iceberg, romaine, or of choice)
Sunflower seeds or walnuts (optional)

Prepare salad dressing and marinate mushrooms and artichoke hearts in mixture for 4 hours. To serve, mix remaining ingredients and toss with dressing, mushrooms and artichokes. Sprinkle sunflower seeds or chopped walnuts as you desire before tossing. Serves a mob!

DAVID'S MUSTARD DRESSING FOR A MOB

1 quart salad oil
2 cups wine vinegar
1/2 cup cool water
1 to 2 jars Dijon mustard
2 large white onions, pureed
2 3/4 ounces salt
1 ounce white pepper
1/4 ounce tarragon

Combine all ingredients except oil and slowly add the oil. This dressing is delicious on spinach, Boston lettuce and red fringe romaine salads.

David says, "Use real bacon bits on the salads, it's a catalyst on the mustard."

KATHIE'S SHERRIED CHICKEN STRIPS

12 pounds chicken breasts, boned and
  skinned (24 breasts)
3 cups flour
1 tablespoon salt
1 1/2 teaspoons garlic powder
2 teaspoons Hungarian paprika
1/2 teaspoon white pepper
2 cups butter or margarine, melted
2 cups dry sherry
1/3 cup chopped fresh parsley

Cut chicken breasts in half, then into 1-inch strips, crosswise. Combine flour, salt, garlic powder, paprika and pepper in a plastic bag. Add chicken pieces, a few at a time, and shake to coat well.

Saute about a quarter of the strips in 1/2 cup of butter until golden brown. Add 1/2 cup sherry, cover and simmer 5 to 7 minutes or until chicken is tender. Remove chicken from skillet and repeat procedure three more times. Serve strips garnished with fresh parsley.

Jo and Jan say, "This is wonderful party fare because it can be prepared ahead and just reheated. After cooking the chicken pieces, freeze them in layers, separating layers with aluminum foil. To reheat, simply place, covered in a 325-degree oven for 45 minutes." Serves 50.

RUM SAUCE FOR A MOB

15 cups sugar
150 egg yolks
3 pounds butter, melted
1 quart rum
3 quarts heavy cream

Beat sugar and egg yolks together; place over hot water and cook until slightly thickened. Add melted butter to mixture and blend well; slowly add rum. Remove from heat and slowly add heavy cream. Serve over pound cake, Blitz Torte, angel food cake, etc..

Jan says, "This recipe was given to me by Evalina at the Wichita Country Club. She personally took me into the kitchen to show me the ingredients as she was about to make up a 'batch.' It's truly overwhelming to see 150 egg yolks. So here it is, direct from the kitchen. This is wonderful spooned over Blitz Torte."

SUELLEN'S MONSTER COOKIES

4 cups granulated sugar
2 pounds brown sugar
1 pound butter
1 dozen eggs
3 pounds peanut butter
1 tablespoon white Karo syrup
11 teaspoons soda
2 teaspoons vanilla
18 cups oatmeal
12 ounces M & Ms
1 package (12-ounce) chocolate chips
2 cups chopped nuts

Cream together the sugars and butter; add eggs. Add peanut butter, syrup, soda and vanilla. In a separate bowl mix oatmeal, M & Ms, chocolate chips and nuts. Add to creamed mixture and mix with your hands.

Using an ice cream scoop, drop on cookie sheet (1 to a sheet) and bake for 15 minutes in preheated 350-degree oven. Do not overbake. Makes 9 1/2 dozen.

◆◆◆

Boy's Club

When we were writing "A Cooking Affaire" we asked fellows for their favorites. We had talked about writing a cookbook for so long no one took us seriously (sort of like the boy who cried wolf); and alas, we went to press without our mens' section.

When the guys saw the completed book (and loved it!) we began receiving a flood of recipes -- and here is the completed project -- a mini-book, complete from appetizers to desserts. All mens' favorites and many are their own creations.

We ask you to notice our headings for each section and the guys' tips which are found in the Locker Room.

◆◆◆

The 19th Hole

19th HOLE MARGARITAS

1 can (6-ounce) frozen limeade, undiluted
1 limeade can beer
1 limeade can tequila
Juice of 1 lime
Salt
Crushed ice
Fresh limes (garnish)

Pour partially thawed limeade in blender. Fill can with beer; add to blender. Fill can with tequila and add to blender. Process, gradually adding crushed ice, until of desired thickness. Dip rims of glasses in lime juice, then in salt. Pour in blended margarita mixture and garnish with lime slices. Serves 6 - 8.

THE CLASSIC MARGARITA

1 1/2 ounces tequila
1/2 ounce Triple Sec
Juice of 1/2 lime

Prepare a cocktail glass by rubbing the rim with lime peel and dipping it in coarse salt. Combine ingredients and shake thoroughly with cracked ice and strain into glass. Garnish with a slice of lime. Serves 1.

JIM'S MARTINIS

3 parts Smirnoff 80-proof vodka
1 part Martini & Rossi vermouth
1 slice lemon peel
1 small cocktail onion
Dash of onion juice
Chipped ice
2 cocktail onions

Combine vodka, vermouth, lemon peel, cocktail onions, onion juice and ice in a pitcher. Stir to blend. Place a cocktail onion in each of 2 martini glasses and pour blended mixture without the ice into the glasses. Serves 2.

Jim says, "If you want a drier martini, go 4-1 vodka and vermouth."

SNEAKY PETE

3 cans (6-ounce size) frozen orange juice
3 cans (6-ounce size) frozen pink lemonade
2 cans (12-ounce size) frozen cranberry juice
6 cans (12-ounce size) lemon-lime soda
4 cups vodka

Combine all ingredients. Pour into a square or round deep container and freeze until ready to serve. Serves 24.

SPARK PLUG

1 1/2 ounces Cognac
1 1/2 ounces Amaretto
2 glasses of ice
Coke
Fresh lime

Add 3/4 ounce of Cognac and Amaretto to each glass of ice. Fill glass with Coke; stir and garnish with wedges of fresh lime. Serves 2.

CAFE BRULOT

2 cinnamon sticks or 1/2 teaspoon ground
   cinnamon
3 whole allspice berries
5 whole cloves
2 tablespoons finely minced orange zest
2 teaspoons finely minced lemon zest
8 sugar cubes
6 ounces (3/4 cup) brandy
2 ounces (1/4 cup) curacao
4 cups strong black coffee

Combine cinnamon, allspice, cloves, zests and sugar in hot chafing dish; mash together with ladle. Add brandy and liqueur; stir briefly and ignite. Continue mixing until sugar dissolves and gradually stir in coffee. When flames go out, serve immediately in demitasse cups. Serves 8.

IRISH COFFEE

24 ounces hot coffee
4 teaspoons sugar
1 cup heavy cream, whipped
4 jiggers Irish whiskey
2 jiggers Kahlua
Cinnamon

Fill mugs 3/4 full with coffee; add 1 teaspoon sugar to each. Pour 1 jigger whiskey and 1 jigger Kahlua into coffee; top with whipped cream and sprinkle with cinnamon. Serves 4.

DRAMBUIE COFFEE

8 tablespoons Drambuie
1 teaspoon brown sugar
Freshly brewed strong hot coffee
Whipped cream

Place 1 tablespoon Drambuie and 1/8 teaspoon brown sugar in each of 8 serving cups or mugs. Fill with hot coffee and top with whipped cream. Serves 8.

CAPPUCCINO

4 cups half-and-half
2 cups extra strong coffee
1/4 cup honey
1 tablespoon unsweetened cocoa
1 tablespoon vanilla
6 ounces brandy
5 ounces coffee liqueur
4 ounces rum
1 tablespoon Galliano
Whipped cream (garnish)
Shaved chocolate (garnish)

Combine cream, coffee, honey, cocoa and vanilla in saucepan. Place over medium-high heat and stir until hot; do not boil. Remove from heat and stir in next 4 ingredients. Pour into warmed mugs; garnish as desired. Serves 8-10.

UNO CAPPUCCINO

1 packet sweet chocolate mix
1 ounce Cognac
6 ounces strong, hot coffee

Mix chocolate and cognac; add coffee. Stir well and top with whipped cream. Serves 1.

❖❖

ROB ROY

3/4 ounce sweet vermouth
1 1/2 ounces scotch
Dash angostura bitters

Stir well with cracked ice and strain into a cocktail glass. Serves 1.

WHITE ELEPHANT

2 ounces vodka
2 ounces white creme de cacao
2 ounces milk
Ice

Fill 2 glasses with ice; pour 1 ounce of vodka, creme de cacao and milk in each glass and stir. Serves 2.

LIGHTS OUT EGGNOG

1 quart milk
5 egg yolks
1/3 cup sugar
1/4 teaspoon salt
3 egg whites
3 tablespoons sugar
1/2 cup bourbon, brandy or rum
Fresh grated nutmeg

Scald milk but do not boil; remove from heat. Beat egg yolks with sugar until thoroughly blended. Add salt and slowly add hot milk; stir well. Return mixture to medium heat and cook stirring constantly until mixture thickens, do not boil; remove from heat. Beat egg whites until foamy. Add 3 tablespoons sugar gradually beating until stiff peaks form. Fold beaten whites into hot milk mixture. Blend in liquor of choice; sprinkle with fresh nutmeg and serve hot.

KENTUCKY DERBY MINT JULEP

1 fifth bourbon
6-7 sprigs of fresh mint
Simple Syrup (See index)
Rum
Fresh sprigs of mint (garnish)
Orange slices (garnish)

Crush mint leaves and marinate overnight with bourbon. To serve, fill 6-8 ounce glasses with crushed ice; float with 2 ounces of minted bourbon and 1/2 ounce of Simple Syrup. Stir until frosty. After mixture settles a bit, float 1 teaspoon of rum on top of each glass. Garnish with orange slices and fresh sprigs of mint. Makes 12.

GIN PUNCH

1 can (12-ounce) frozen orange juice
   concentrate
1 can (6-ounce) frozen pure lemon or lime
   concentrate
1 fifth 90-proof gin
18 ounces water
1/3 cup grenadine syrup
1 quart ginger ale

Combine all ingredients in punch bowl with ice. Will keep in refrigerator if well sealed. Makes 1 gallon.

SON OF A PEACH

8 ounces peach schnapps
8 ounces pineapple juice
1 ounces sweet and sour mix
Fresh mint

Combine ingredients in blender with crushed ice. Blend well and strain into cocktail glasses. Serves 4.

SNAPPY BOB'S TOMATO COCKTAIL

1/2 bushel tomatoes
4 onions (use 6 to a bushel)
1 celery stalk
6 green peppers
12 whole cloves
2 cups sugar
3 tablespoons salt
Juice of 3 fresh lemons
1 1/2 tablespoons oregano
1 1/2 tablespoons marjoram
1 1/2 tablespoons cumin
1 cup Worcestershire sauce
Tabasco sauce to taste

Wash, core and quarter tomatoes. Clean celery, onions and peppers; chop coarsely. Combine first 5 ingredients and boil over low heat until celery and peppers are soft, about 15 minutes. Strain mixture and add remaining ingredients. Bring to a boil; pour into sterilized jars and seal. Makes about 10 quarts.

Bob says, "This makes great Bloody Marys or use as you would any tomato cocktail juice; soups, stews, goulash, etc."

ARTILLERY PUNCH

6 cups strong black tea
3 cups orange juice
1 1/2 cups lemon juice
3/4 pint cognac
3/4 pint gin
3 ounces Benedictine
1 1/2 pints dark rum
1 1/2 fifths claret
1 1/2 fifths whiskey

Combine all ingredients in a large container; let stand at least 2 hours. To serve, pour over a large block of ice in punch bowl. Serves 20 - 25.

FISH HOUSE PUNCH

36 lemons, halved
4 gallons water
6 cups sugar
1 fifth dark rum
1 fifth bourbon
1 fifth peach brandy

Place halved lemons, water and sugar in a large pan and bring to a boil. Reduce heat and simmer until liquid is diminished by half. Remove lemons and discard. Add rum, bourbon and peach brandy. Garnish with lemon slices and chill for a day. The longer it chills the better it gets. To serve, pour over a large cake of ice and pour over ice into individual glasses.

Jo and Jan say, "This punch was invented by members of the Fish House Club founded in Philadelphia in 1732. There were 30 original members who kept the recipe a secret; and following generations also kept it a guarded secret for almost 200 years."

BOB'S TIA MARIA

6 tablespoons instant coffee granules
4 cups sugar
2 cups boiling water
2 cups blended whiskey
2 vanilla beans

Dissolve coffee, sugar and water; allow to cool and add whiskey. Using 2 quart bottles, cut the vanilla beans in half and put two half beans in each bottle. Divide mixture to each bottle and fill with water. Screw on bottle tops and tape shut.

Place bottles on sides and turn each week for four weeks. Then you can bottle into smaller bottles for gift giving.

Bob says, "These make truly delicious and very neighborly Holiday gifts. But mark on your calendar to start the process early."

VODKA CONVERSATION PIECE

Fifth vodka
Half-gallon milk carton, empty
Mint leaves or other decorative leaves
Napkin

Place vodka bottle in the milk carton; pour water up to the neck of the bottle and insert leaves if desired. Stand in the freezer until water is completely frozen. Run cool water on container to loosen ice block. Set the ice-coated bottle on a tray or plate and wrap a pretty napkin around the neck of the bottle. Pour vodka into small glasses and you have the true authentic Russian way of drinking vodka...straight up and cold!

CHEESE BALL

1 package (8-ounce) cream cheese, softened
1 stick (4-ounces) margarine
1 envelope dried green onion dip mix
Garlic salt
7 green onions, chopped
3/4 cup toasted pecans or walnuts, finely chopped

Combine cream cheese and margarine. Add onion dip mix, a dash of garlic salt and green onions. Form into a ball; roll in toasted nuts and chill. Good with crackers or veggies. Makes about 1 1/2 cups.

BEER-CHEESE APPETIZERS

2 packages (8-ounce size) cream cheese, softened
1/2 cup beer
2 tablespoons parsley, finely chopped
1 teaspoon paprika
3 cups smoked sharp Cheddar cheese, shredded
Almonds, sliced

In large bowl beat cream cheese, beer, parsley, and paprika until well blended. Stir in the cheese. Chill 1 hour, then mold the cheese into a bowl or a pinecone shape, inserting the almonds on the mold to resemble a pinecone. Cover and chill several hours. Place on a large platter and surround with apple and pear slices or assorted crackers. Makes 4 cups.

JOHN'S HOT CHEESE DIP

2 pounds Velvetta cheese
1 tablespoon butter or margarine
2 medium onions, chopped
2 tortilla peppers
1 can (20-ounce) tomatoes, drained
Salt and pepper

Melt cheese in top of double boiler. Melt butter in small pan and saute chopped onions until soft. Add to cheese; squeeze juice from peppers into cheese. Put 1 pepper back in jar, open other pepper, discard seeds and chop pepper. Add to cheese mixture then add tomatoes. Salt and pepper to taste. Makes about 5 cups. Serve hot with dippers.
"You guys will love this! It is great to have ready for those T.V. sports events."

COCKTAIL SAUSAGES

24 cocktail sausages
1 tablespoon oil
3/4 cup thinly sliced onions
1 cup beer
1 bay leaf

Prick the sausages in 1 or 2 places. Heat the oil in skillet, saute onions until browned. Add beer and bay leaf, bring to boil and add sausages. Cover and cook over low heat 15 minutes. Drain and pierce with cocktail picks.

TOM'S SPICY DOGS

5 packages hot dogs
2 cups thick barbecue sauce
1/2 cup honey

Cut dogs into bite size pieces. Place in crock pot or baking dish. Pour honey and sauce over dogs and cook on low all day. Serve hot.

CRAIG'S BARBECUED MEAT BALLS

3 pounds lean ground beef
2 eggs, well beaten
1 tablespoon prepared mustard
2 teaspoons MSG
2 teaspoons salt
2 teaspoons seasoned pepper
2 teaspoons garlic powder
2 cups dry bread crumbs
Commercial brand barbecue sauce

Combine all ingredients except bread crumbs. Add enough bread crumbs to hold mixture together. Shape into balls (1-inch for appetizers or larger for entree size). Bake in preheated 375-degree oven for 20 to 30 minutes, until brown. Remove from oven and drain off any excess grease. Pour your favorite barbecue sauce over the meatballs and return to a 225-degree oven until ready to serve.

Craig says, "These can be made several hours ahead of time and kept in a warm oven. This also allows the barbecue flavor to 'soak in.' "

BARBECUED MINI DRUMSTICKS

50 chicken wings
1 cup brown sugar, packed
3/4 cup sherry
1/2 teaspoon dry mustard
1 cup soy sauce
2 cloves garlic, crushed

Cut chicken wings at drumstick joint. Bag up discarded tips and freeze to use for making chicken broth in the future. Combine brown sugar, sherry, soy sauce, mustard and garlic in sauce pan and bring to a simmer. Place drumettes in a shallow baking dish and pour sauce over, covering well. Bake uncovered in preheated 325-degree oven, turning occasionally, until sauce cooks down and wings are well glazed. Makes 50.

STEAK APPETIZER

1/4 cup olive oil
3 tablespoons wine vinegar
1 tablespoon Dijon mustard
1 teaspoon onion salt
1 teaspoon celery salt
1/4 teaspoon garlic salt
1 teaspoon dried oregano leaves
1/2 teaspoon black pepper
1 bay leaf
1 teaspoon fresh parsley, chopped
1 1/2 pounds boneless sirloin steak, cut into
  1-inch pieces

Combine all ingredients except meat in a 1 1/2-quart casserole. Heat in microwave until boiling. Cool slightly. Add beef and mix to coat. Marinate 6 hours or overnight. Cover with plastic wrap. Microwave on medium-high for 5-7 minutes. Makes 36 pieces.

Jan says, "This is a great appetizer for the working person to prepare. Not only as an appetizer, but with a tossed salad and French bread, it is a terrific quickie dinner for 2. Marinate it one night, enjoy the next."

COCKTAIL GARLIC STEAK

1/4 cup olive oil
2 tablespoons butter
2 garlic cloves, crushed
1 tablespoon dry mustard
1 1/2 teaspoons Worcestershire sauce
1 teaspoon red pepper sauce
1 1/2 pound sirloin steak, cut 3/4-inch thick

Combine olive oil, butter and garlic in small pan, over low heat for 5 minutes. Stir in mustard, Worcestershire sauce and red pepper sauce; cook 1 minute longer. Pour sauce into baking dish; add steak, turn to coat and refrigerate 1 hour. Preheat broiler; place steak on rack in broiling pan and broil 10 minutes for rare, turning once.

Reheat garlic sauce, cut steak into cubes and place on warm platter, pouring sauce over steak. Serve with cocktail picks. Makes 16 cubes.

Jan says, "If you have a chafing dish, it is nice to keep these warm while serving.

DR. LONNIE'S WILD DUCK HORS D'OEUVRES
This is Dr. Lonnie's Rx. as given to us.

Allow 1/2 wild duck breast per person, skinned and deboned. Season meat with salt and pepper to taste. Place in foil-lined pan in a single layer. Put a dot of butter or margarine on each piece. Broil until meat is as done as you like, just pink in the middle is good. Remove pan from oven; pour sherry (Bristol Creme) over meat and let stand 5 minutes. Cut meat into bite-size pieces. Serve with Dijon mustard as a dip for the meat.

Lonnie says, "For a first course, serve pieces on wild rice. Pour the sherry sauce over top."

PHEASANT PATE

2 tablespoons butter
1 small shallot, finely diced
1/4 teaspoon salt
1/4 teaspoon pepper
1/4 teaspoon dry mustard
1/2 cup pheasant livers
2 tablespoons Marsala wine
1 raw egg yolk

Melt butter in skillet; add the shallot, salt, pepper and mustard. Saute until shallot is soft; add livers and wine. Saute until livers are done (about 3 minutes per side), stirring constantly so they do not stick. Place mixture, including pan drippings in blender or food processor; add egg yolk and puree. Spoon mixture into a bowl and chill until serving time. Will keep in refrigerator several days. Makes about 1 cup.

TOM'S HUNTER'S PATE

1 1/4 pounds mixed game livers (goose, duck, pheasant, venison)
4 large mushrooms, chopped
1/2 onion, chopped
2 large shallots, chopped
1 garlic clove, chopped
3 tablespoons butter
1/2 teaspoon sage
1/8 teaspoon dry mustard
Dash nutmeg
Salt and pepper to taste
1/2 cup brandy
4 to 5 tablespoons mayonnaise
1/4 cup heavy cream
Green onions (garnish)

Cut up all meat so it is the same size pieces. Saute livers with mushrooms, onion, shallots and garlic in butter until lightly browned. Sprinkle with seasonings and continue to cook 3 to 5 minutes at medium temperature. Add 1/4 cup brandy; cover and simmer 5 minutes. Add rest of brandy and allow to cook covered over medium heat for 20 minutes.

Spoon mixture into blender or food processor and process until all is evenly chopped. Add mayonnaise and cream and continue processing until well mixed and smooth. Spoon mixture into a well oiled 4-cup mold and refrigerate for several hours before serving.

To serve, carefully turn onto a platter and garnish with chopped green onions. Serves 6-12.

Tom says, "I like to arrange fresh watercress and a generous amount of chopped hard-boiled egg surrounding the pate. Serve with crackers."

❖❖

ESCARGOT BOURGUIGNONNE

12 to 14 clean snail shells (can be purchased in specialty shops)
1 can (4 1/2-ounce) snails, rinsed and drained
1/2 cup butter, melted
1/3 cup green onion, finely chopped
2 tablespoons garlic, crushed
1 tablespoon freshly minced parsley
Salt and pepper
1/2 cup dry red wine

In a 9-inch skillet over medium heat, melt butter and saute onion and garlic. Pour some into each shell. Add parsley, salt, pepper and wine to remaining mixture. Add snails and saute for just a minute or two; stuff snails into shells. Place under preheated broiler for 10 minutes. Serve with remaining sauce. Serves 2.

OYSTER SHOOTERS

1 cup tomato catsup
1/2 cup celery, chopped
1 tablespoon onion, chopped
1/4 cup prepared horseradish
1/2 cup lemon juice
1/4 teaspoon Tabasco sauce
18 freshly shucked oysters
Lemon wedges (Garnish)

Combine first 6 ingredients in blender. Refrigerate until serving time. When ready to serve, place 1 oyster in each shot glass and spoon sauce over or place 3 oysters in each of 6 cocktail glasses, spoon sauce over and garnish with a wedge of lemon. Pass cocktail forks. Serves 6 (3 per serving).

OYSTERS LOUISIANNE

Fresh oysters
Green onions
Cracked pepper
Mornay sauce (see index)
Paprika
Snipped parsley

Shuck desired number of oysters, placing each individually on a rinsed half shell. Sprinkle with thinly sliced green onions and cracked black pepper. Spoon Mornay Sauce over each oyster. Place uncovered, in microwave on High for a minute or two (time depends on equipment and number of oysters) until heated thoroughly. Sprinkle with paprika and snipped parsley. Serve with toast points.

Jack says, "Here's an appetizer conceived at the Slate Creek Depot, our fun-filled restaurant in Wellington, Kansas, that was destroyed by fire in 1982. It's a wonderful alternative to more traditional baked oyster offerings."

HOT CRABMEAT DIP

1 package (8-ounce) cream cheese, softened
1 tablespoon milk
1 can (61/2-ounce) flaked crab meat
1 tablespoon onion, finely chopped
1/4 teaspoon creamy horseradish
1/4 teaspoon salt
Dash pepper

Mix all ingredients. Bake in preheated 375-degree oven for 15 minutes. Serve in chafing dish accompanied with crackers. Makes about 2 cups.

❖❖❖

The Pepper Grinder

DOCTOR SYLER'S FAMOUS DELICIOUS, NUTRITIOUS HAMBURGER SOUP

1 1/2 pounds hamburger
Garlic salt
1 can Italian tomatoes, whole, peeled and
    mashed (undrained)
6 cups water
1 medium onion, chopped
1 green pepper, chopped
6 teaspoon beef bouillon or 6 cubes
1/2 teaspoon thyme
1 teaspoon sweet basil
1 cup celery chunks, heaping
1 cup carrot chunks, heaping
1 cup diced potatoes, heaping
1 can green beans (undrained)
1/2 cup barley
Salt and pepper to taste

Brown hamburger in a skillet; season lightly with garlic salt. Drain off grease. In a separate, large kettle combine tomatoes, water, onion, green pepper, bouillon, thyme and basil. Bring mixture to a boil; add celery and boil gently 1 minute. Add carrots and boil 15 minutes. Add diced potatoes, beans and barley. Pour browned hamburger into pot and boil gently for 15 minutes or until potatoes are about done. Remove kettle from burner to cool. Salt and pepper to taste. Serves 8 - 10.

Doctor Syler says, "This soup will keep for 10 days in the refrigerator. It's a balanced meal in itself."

Jo and Jan say, "Bet it doesn't last for 10 days! It's too good!"

JACK'S BEEF STOCK

1 pound ground beef
1 quart cold water
1 carrot, chopped
1/2 teaspoon salt
1/2 teaspoon pepper
1 large onion, chopped
1 stalk celery, chopped

Combine all ingredients into pan and simmer, partially covered for 1 hour. Skim fat and strain through cheese cloth. Discard all bits and pour into jars. Refrigerate for several days or freeze. Makes 1 quart.

Jack says, "When I have time I like to make my own broth for stock in my soups."

JAY'S CHAMPIONSHIP CHILI

2 1/2 pounds chuck roast
3 pounds lean ground beef
3 large onions
1 can beer
1 can (16-ounce) tomato sauce
1 can (8-ounce) Rotel tomatoes and pepper
1 teaspoon black pepper
1 teaspoon salt
2 tablespoons red chiles, ground
2 tablespoons cumin
1 teaspoon paprika
1 teaspoon garlic powder or 3 garlic cloves,
    chopped fine
1 teaspoon Accent
4 cans red beans
2 packages Williams Chili Seasoning

Bake roast for 2 1/2 hours. Cool; remove fat and dice meat. Combine roast and pan broth in a large kettle. Saute ground beef and onions; drain off all grease, add to kettle with remaining ingredients. Cook for 2 hours. If mixture becomes too dry, add another can of beer. Serves 8-12.

Jay says, "This chile has been entered in cook-offs and has won many prizes."

Jo and Jan say, "Don't let Jay know we told you, but he is a very good cook!"

❖❖

BOB'S CHILI

1 3/4 pounds ground beef
1 medium onion, chopped
1 or 2 packages William's Chili seasoning
3 tablespoons flour
1 can (15-ounce) tomato sauce
1 can (46-ounce) tomato juice
2 cups water
1 teaspoon garlic powder
1/2 teaspoon oregano
1/4 teaspoon cumin
1 teaspoon salt
1/2 teaspoon pepper
1 tablespoon vinegar
1 tablespoon brown sugar
2 cans (15-ounce size) chili beans
4 tablespoons chili powder

In a large kettle, brown meat, onions and chili seasoning until meat is brown. Add rest of ingredients and simmer slowly for several hours. Serves 8-10.

CHEF MICHAEL'S CHILI

6 pounds ground chuck (3 of which are
    coarse ground)
2 tablespoons olive oil
2 onions, chopped
1 teaspoon garlic powder (or to taste)
Salt to taste
Accent to taste
2 cans (14-ounce size) stewed tomatoes,
    chopped
1 can (46-ounce) V-8 Juice
2 tablespoons paprika
1 1/2 tablespoons cayenne powder
3 tablespoons chili powder
3 tablespoons flour, blended into 1 cup
    warm water

Saute beef in olive oil; strain off most of grease. Add onions, garlic powder, salt, Accent to taste to meat mixture. Stir well and simmer for a few minutes. Add V-8 Juice, paprika, cayenne, and chili powder. Simmer for 2 hours. Add flour combined with warm water and continue to simmer for 1 hour, stirring occasionally.

Mike says, "You may wish to add some Pace's Picante Sauce at this time, depending on how hot you like your chili. Eat a big bowl and get prepared to say, "Come on Ice Cream!"

JOHN'S CHILI BRICKS

5 pounds ground beef
4 tablespoons chili powder
4 tablespoons paprika
2 medium onions, chopped
2 cans (8-ounce) tomato sauce
2 cups finely crushed soda crackers
1 can chili beans
1 can tomatoes

Brown beef slowly. Add next 3 ingredients and simmer until onions are tender. Add tomato sauce and cook slowly at least 2 hours. Remove from heat and add cracker crumbs. Pour into 9x13-inch pan. Cool and freeze; cut into 3 bricks and package. Return to freezer. To serve, add 1 can chili beans and 1 can tomatoes, chopped, to each brick. Heat and serve. Serves 6-8.

◆◆◆

BLACK-EYED PEA CHOWDER

1/2 pound bacon
2 cups celery, chopped
2 cups green pepper, chopped
2 cup onion, chopped
1 clove garlic, crushed
1 can beef consomme
2 cans (16-ounce size) tomatoes
2 cans (16-ounce size) black-eyed peas
Tabasco sauce to taste

Dice bacon and saute with celery, green pepper, onion and garlic. Add remaining ingredients; simmer 30 minutes. Serves 6-8.

Jo and Jan say, "This will be terrific for that New Year's Day game-watching! Toss a salad and serve with jalapeno cornbread. You might want to double this recipe though, as one bowl will not be enough for most guys!"

TOM'S WINTER STEW

3 slices bacon, diced
1 pound small white onions
2 pounds beef, cut in 2-inch chunks
1 can (12-ounce) beer
1 teaspoon instant beef bouillon
1 teaspoon dried thyme
1/2 teaspoon dried marjoram
1 teaspoon sugar
1 teaspoon salt
1 1/2 cups water
1 bag (16-ounce) carrots
1 large acorn squash
1/2 pound green beans
3 tablespoons flour
1/4 cup water

Cook bacon and onions in Dutch oven until well browned; set aside. Cook beef, a pound at a time, in drippings until well browned; remove to bowl. Return all beef to kettle; stir in beer, bouillon, thyme, marjoram, sugar, salt and water; bring to a boil over high heat. Reduce heat to low, cover and simmer 30 minutes. Add bacon and onions; cover and simmer 30 minutes more. While meat is cooking, cut carrots into 2-inch pieces and slice squash in half; remove seeds and cut into chunks

After beef has cooked 1 hour add vegetables to cooked mixture and cook about 30 more minutes or until vegetables are tender. Mix flour and water and stir into stew. Cook over medium heat until stew boils and thickens. Serves 8.

Tom says, "This is great for Poker Night. I serve it with cornbread or hard rolls. If fresh vegetables are not available, use bags of frozen. Sometimes I change the vegetables too."

CHEESE - BEER SOUP

2 cans condensed cream soup (celery, mushroom or chicken)
1/4 teaspoon seasoned salt
1/4 teaspoon paprika
1 teaspoon Worcestershire sauce
24 ounces beer
2 cups shredded Cheddar cheese
Croutons (optional, as garnish)
Bacon bits (optional, as garnish)
Minced parsley (optional, as garnish)
Chives (optional, as garnish)

Combine soup and seasonings in saucepan; add beer gradually, stirring constantly. Bring to a simmer over heat. Add cheese and heat slowly while stirring constantly, to melt cheese. To serve, ladle into bowls and garnish, as desired. Makes 7 cups.

AL'S STEAK SOUP

1/2 pound margarine
1 cup flour
1/2 gallon water, or to individual desired thickness
1 package (10-ounce) frozen mixed vegetables
4 tablespoons beef granules
1 large carrot, diced
1 medium onion, diced
1 can stewed tomatoes
Fresh ground pepper
1 pound sirloin, cubed and sauteed
1 pound ground beef, browned and drained

Melt margarine in large kettle. Stir in flour; cook for 2 minutes and gradually add 2 cups water. Stirring constantly, add rest of water to desired thickness. Stir in all other ingredients except meat. Saute meat and add to other ingredients. Simmer at least 1 hour.

Al says, "We like the soup thick, so do not add all the water. This is tremendous for tail-gate picnics and after-the-game get togethers." Serves 6-8.

DADDY'S OYSTER STEW

1 pound canned oysters, drained; reserving liquid
6 medium potatoes, thinly sliced
1 onion, thinly sliced
1 cup water
2 tablespoons butter
1 tablespoon flour
1 teaspoon salt
1/4 teaspoon pepper, or to taste
3 cups milk
2 green onion tops, sliced lengthwise in thin strips (Garnish)

Boil potatoes and onion in reserved liquid with water; cook until tender. In a saucepan, melt butter, blend flour, salt, pepper and add to butter, blend well. Gradually add milk, stirring constantly. Add oysters and cook 2 minutes. Combine with potatoes, onion and the liquid. Garnish with green onion strips. Serves 6.

It takes four men to make a salad:
A spendthrift for the oil
A miser for the vinegar
A philosopher for the seasoning
And a madman for the tossing!
Told to us by Vicki Savage...

FLAVOR YOUR OWN OIL

Garlic, pepper and herb-flavored oils are made from a good quality olive, peanut or safflower oil. Heat the oil until it boils then remove from heat. Add the flavoring, such as garlic, herbs, black or red pepper or lemon pepper. Strain the oil through a cheesecloth and store in the refrigerator.

Oriental chili oil is a peanut or vegetable oil that has chili pods in the oil which have steeped for some time. Put oil and chili pods in a jar and let it sit on the counter overnight. The longer you let it sit the hotter the flavor becomes. Very good in stir-fried dishes, salad dressings, rice and butter sauces.

Mesquite oil is used to marinate or baste food while you are charcoaling. If using the flavored mesquite oil with garlic, pepper or soy oil it gives a smoke flavor to a dish or meat which has not been charcoaled. We would like to suggest you try it on popcorn and vegetables; it gives a wonderful zest.

MICHAEL'S MAYONNAISE

4 egg yolks
2 cups oil
1 1/2 teaspoons lemon juice
Pinch of salt and pepper

Have all ingredients at room temperature. Combine egg yolks, lemon, salt and pepper in a mixing bowl and whisk until well mixed. Slowly add oil while beating briskly. Continue adding oil, slowly at first and then faster until the oil is incorporated.

Mayonnaise can separate if you add the oil too fast or if you don't whip it enough. Should it separate take another egg yolk in a fresh bowl and add the mixture mixing well (hard and fast).

If you are close with the first attempt, a tablespoon of warm water instead of another egg will do well to correct the separation.

And finally, to prevent the finished Mayonnaise from separating in storage, bring 2 tablespoons vinegar to a boil and whip it into the Mayonnaise while the vinegar is still hot.

BEEF SALAD

3 cups cooked beef, cut in strips
3/4 cup salad oil
1/2 cup red wine vinegar
1 garlic clove, crushed
1 1/2 teaspoons salt
1/4 teaspoon ground pepper
1/8 teaspoon Tabasco sauce
1 tablespoon chili powder
Salad greens
Fresh mushrooms, sliced
Avocado slices, brushed with marinade
Onion rings
Green pepper rings
Tomato wedges
Ripe olives

Prepare marinade of salad oil, vinegar, garlic, salt, pepper, Tabasco and chili powder. Place all ingredients in a bottle or jar and shake well. Pour over beef strips, cover and marinate several hours or overnight.

Remove beef from marinade and arrange on crisp green. Garnish with remaining ingredients and serve the marinade as a dressing. Serves 4 - 6.

JOHN'S PERFECTION SALAD

1 envelope unflavored gelatin
1/4 cup sugar
1/2 teaspoon salt
1 1/4 cups water, divided
1/4 cup white vinegar
1 tablespoon lemon juice
1/2 cup finely shredded cabbage
1 cup chopped celery
1 pimento, cut in small pieces, or 2
   tablespoons chopped sweet red or green
   pepper

Mix gelatin, sugar and salt thoroughly in a small saucepan. Add 1/2 cup of the water. Place over low heat stirring constantly until gelatin is dissolved.

Remove from heat and stir in remaining 3/4 cup of water, vinegar and lemon juice. Chill to unbeaten egg white consistency. Fold in shredded cabbage, celery and pimento or pepper.

Turn into individual molds or a 2-cup mold and chill until firm. Unmold on serving plate and garnish with salad greens. Serves 4.

Jo says, "This was one of my Daddy's favorite salads. He loved to make a beautiful tossed garden salad and no-one could do it better, but this was his favorite molded salad."

CRAIG'S FRESH BROCCOLI SALAD

1 pound bacon, fried and crumbled
1 onion, chopped
1 cup shredded cheese
1 bunch broccoli, cut up
1/4 cup sunflower seeds

DRESSING:
1 cup mayonnaise
1/2 cup sugar
4 teaspoons vinegar

Mix all ingredients together and pour dressing over; mix to coat well. Can garnish with cherry tomatoes.

JACK'S SPINACH SALAD

5 packages (10-ounce size) frozen chopped spinach
1 cup onion, finely chopped
1 can water chestnuts, drained and finely chopped
2 cups Monterrey Jack cheese, grated
8 hard-boiled eggs, finely chopped
1 cup mayonnaise
1 1/2 teaspoons white vinegar
Salt and pepper to taste
Grated hard-boiled egg (garnish)
Horseradish
Cherry tomatoes

Cook and drain spinach according to package directions. Remove as much liquid as possible by squeezing, pressing and draining. Add water chestnuts, cheese and eggs to thoroughly drained spinach. Combine mayonnaise, vinegar, salt and pepper; mix well and add to spinach mixture and chill.

To serve, mound on a lettuce leaf, with ice cream scoop portions. Garnish with grated egg, a teaspoon of horseradish on the side and cherry tomatoes. Serves 12.

SPINACH-CUCUMBER SALAD

1 1/2 pounds fresh spinach
3/4 cup celery, chopped
2 medium cucumbers sliced thin
1/2 cup green stuffed olives
1/2 cup black pitted olives
1/2 cup almonds, toasted and sliced

DRESSING:
1/4 cup salad oil
2 tablespoons red wine vinegar
1/2 teaspoon salt
Dash of pepper
1/4 teaspoon oregano

Tear spinach into bite-size pieces and place in large salad bowl. Combine celery, cucumbers, green and black olives and almonds with spinach.

Combine dressing ingredients and pour over salad. Serves 4-6.

LARRY'S TACO SALAD

1 1/2 pounds ground beef
1/2 cup chopped green pepper
1 cup chopped onion
1/3 cup chili powder
1 box (1 pound) Velvetta cheese, diced
1 can Ro-Tel tomatoes and green chili
1 head iceberg lettuce, shredded
2 large tomatoes
1 large bag corn chips

Brown ground beef in a large skillet. Add green pepper, onion and chili powder to the meat and cook thoroughly. Place cheese and tomatoes in the top of a double boiler; heat until smooth and hot. In individual soup-size bowls, place some shredded lettuce first, then some diced tomatoes, then 1 or 2 handfuls of crushed corn chips, then 1 or 2 serving-size spoonfuls of the meat mixture. Top with 2 ladles of the hot cheese mixture. Makes 6 servings.

Larry says, "This is a BIG CLUE AND HINT! This is not a salad, but a main meat dish. Two bowls of this is a complete meal! Also, better double the recipe because people will want seconds, and they'll be eating this all evening."

Jo and Jan say, "Thank you, Larry, for sharing this. Isn't this a great idea for a T.V. sports watching party?"

The Loafer

AL'S BEER BREAD

3 cups self-rising flour
1 can beer, room temperature
5 tablespoons sugar

Mix all ingredients and pour into greased loaf pan. Let set for 15 minutes before baking. Bake loaf in preheated 350-degree oven for 1 hour. Brush top with butter and Krazy Salt.

Jo and Jan say, "You must try this with Beer Bread Spread (see index).

GARLIC-CHEESE BREAD

1 loaf (16-ounce) French bread
2 packages (8-ounce size) mozzarella cheese
1/2 cup margarine
1/2 teaspoon garlic powder
1/4 teaspoon oregano leaves, crushed
1/4 teaspoon basil leaves, crushed
1/4 teaspoon parsley leaves, crushed
1/8 teaspoon ground red pepper

Cut bread crosswise into 18 slices, unless the bread is already cut. Place cut side down on large baking sheet and broil on each side until golden; set aside. In a small saucepan, melt margarine, stirring in garlic powder, oregano, basil, parsley and red pepper. Brush each slice of broiled bread with mixture. Top each slice with mozzarella cheese. Bake in preheated 250-degree oven for 5 to 8 minutes or until cheese melts. Serves 10.

HUSH PUPPIES

1 1/2 cups corn meal
1/2 cup flour
1 chopped onion
1 egg
1/8 teaspoon salt
2 tablespoons baking powder
1/2 teaspoon soda
1 cup buttermilk
4 tablespoons bacon drippings, melted

Mix all ingredients and drop by teaspoon into 1/2 to 3/4 inch of hot oil until golden brown. Drain on paper towels and serve warm with fried fish.

ONE HOUR HAMBURGER BUNS

4 1/2 to 5 cups flour
2 packages dry yeast
1 cup milk
3/4 cup water
1/2 cup oil
1/4 cup sugar
1 tablespoon salt

Stir 2 cups flour and dry yeast together. Heat milk, water, oil, sugar and salt until very warm (120 to 130 degrees). Add liquid all at once to flour-yeast mixture and beat until smooth; about 3 minutes at medium speed on mixer or 300 hand strokes. Add enough flour to make a soft dough and mix well, either by hand or with mixer. Let rest 10 minutes; roll out on well-floured surface to 1/2-inch. Cut with 3-inch round cutter and place on greased baking sheets. Let rise in warm place 30 minutes. Bake in preheated 425-degree oven for 12 to 15 minutes or until lightly browned.

Jo and Jan say, "Want to make an impression at your next barbecue? Hamburgers will taste even better on these homemade buns."

HERB BREAD

2 sticks butter or margarine
2 teaspoons dried parsley
1/2 teaspoon dried thyme
1 teaspoon garlic powder
Salt, as desired
1 loaf Italian or French bread

Soften butter; blend herbs in butter and allow to mellow for several hours. Cut bread on the diagonal, almost through the bottom crust. Spread with seasoned butter. Wrap loaf in aluminum foil and heat in 400-degree oven for 20 minutes. Bread can be frozen and heated without thawing at 400 degrees for 30 minutes.

CORN FRITTERS

2 1/2 cups cooked corn
1 cup flour
3/4 cup milk
2 eggs
1 teaspoon salt
1 teaspoon sugar
3/4 teaspoon baking powder
1/4 teaspoon freshly ground pepper

Heat oil in large skillet. Combine remaining ingredients in medium bowl and mix well. Drop by spoonful into hot oil. Fry until golden brown on each side, turning once. Drain on paper towels and serve immediately. Serves 4-6.

PETE'S QUICKIE BREADSTICKS

12 8-inch breadsticks
6 slices bacon
2 tablespoons grated Parmesan cheese

Cut slices of bacon in two and wrap around breadsticks. Line a 9 x 13-inch baking dish with paper toweling. Place breadsticks in dish and sprinkle Parmesan cheese over each stick. Cover dish with paper towel and place in microwave on high for 6 minutes or until bacon is crisp. If you do not have a turntable, rotate the dish once.

Pete says, "These breadsticks are great with soup, chili or salads. You may substitute 1/4 cup Cheddar cheese for the Parmesan."

BEER BREAD SPREAD

4 slices bacon
1 package (8-ounce) cream cheese, softened
1 cup sour cream
1/4 cup onion, finely minced
1/4 cup celery, finely minced
1/4 cup chopped pecans
1/2 teaspoon salt

Fry bacon until crisp; drain on paper towel and crumble. Combine cream cheese and sour cream; beat until smooth. Stir in onion, celery, pecans, salt and crumbled bacon. Cover and refrigerate. Delicious served with Al's Beer Bread (See index).

JERRY'S "GREAT AMERICAN GRIDDLE CAKES"

1 cup self-rising flour
4 1/2 tablespoons powdered milk
2 1/2 teaspoons baking powder
1/2 teaspoon salt
1 tablespoon sugar
1 egg
1 tablespoon melted butter or margarine
1/2 cup water

Sift together the flour, milk, baking powder and salt; add sugar.

Beat egg lightly, add water and melted butter. Beat liquid into flour mixture until smooth.

Heat frying pan or griddle; grease and pour in 1/4 cup of batter. Cook until bubbly and browned at edges, turn and cook on the flipped side. Serve warm, buttered or with honey or syrup.

HOT ITALIAN LOAF

2 loaves frozen bread dough, thawed
24 slices cold cuts, ham or turkey
24 slices Swiss, Monterey Jack cheese
3 tablespoons Dijon mustard
1 teaspoon dried parsley
1/2 pound fresh mushrooms, steamed and
    sliced
1/2 teaspoon Italian seasoning
1/2 teaspoon garlic powder
1/2 teaspoon onion powder
3 tablespoons sesame seeds

Defrost dough in refrigerator overnight. Lightly grease and flour cookie sheet. On lightly floured surface, roll one loaf of dough into a 15 x 5-inch rectangle. Spread 1 tablespoon of mustard on dough within 1/2 inch of all edges.

Divide meat and cheese slices in half. Alternately layer half of meat and cheese slices over top of dough to within 1/2 inch of all edges. Combine mushrooms, parsley, Italian seasonings, garlic and onion powders. Spoon on top of first half of layered meat and cheese. Top with reserved second half of meat and cheese. Spread remaining mustard on top of second layer of meat and cheese. Brush edges of dough with water and roll second loaf into 15 x 5-inch rectangle. Place over top of meat. Gently stretch down to cover meat; pinch edges of dough together and brush top of loaf with warm water and sprinkle with sesame seeds.

Bake in preheated 375-degree oven for 30 minutes; serve warm.

Jo and Jan say, "This is a great sandwich to have when Super Bowl rolls around or any other time when you are wanting to wow your guests."

SUPER BOWL SANDWICH

1 loaf French bread
1/2 cup sour cream
1/2 cup mayonnaise
2 tablespoons horseradish sauce
1 teaspoon Dijon mustard
1 1/2 teaspoons dry onion soup mix
Leaf lettuce
2 tomatoes, sliced
1/2 red onion, thinly sliced - if small use
  whole onion
Bread and butter pickles
1/2 pound deli ham, thinly sliced
1/2 pound deli roast beef, thinly sliced
1/2 pound deli turkey, cooked and thinly
  sliced
8 slices Cheddar cheese
8 slices Monterey Jack cheese
Cherry tomatoes (garnish)

Slice loaf lengthwise. Combine sour cream, mayonnaise, horseradish sauce, mustard and soup mix; refrigerate for 2 hours.

Spread each bread half with chilled mixture. Layer bottom slice with lettuce, tomatoes, onion, pickles, meats and cheese slices. Cover with top loaf. Secure with wooden picks and top each pick with cherry tomatoes. Serves 6-8.

ROB'S GYRO SANDWICH
(Pronounced "yee-ro")

1 1/4 pounds lean ground beef
1 1/4 pounds lean ground lamb
1/4 cup oregano
1 1/2 tablespoons onion powder
1 tablespoon freshly ground pepper (or to
  taste)
1 teaspoon thyme
3/4 teaspoon salt
1 cup plain yogurt
1/4 cup cucumber, finely chopped
1/4 cup onion, finely chopped
2 teaspoons olive oil
Garlic powder
1/2 teaspoon dill weed
Salt and freshly ground white pepper
8 large pita bread rounds, cut in half
Thinly sliced onion rings

Combine beef, lamb, oregano, onion powder, salt, pepper, and thyme. Mix thoroughly and shape into 16 thin patties.

Combine Yogurt, cucumber, onion and olive oil in small bowl. Add seasonings to taste; set aside.

Preheat broiler or barbecue. Broil patties until done as desired; turning once. Place 1 meat patty in each pita half and top with yogurt sauce; garnish with onion slices. Makes 16 sandwiches.

DELI HAM ROLLS

12 round club rolls
12 slices smoked ham
8 cups deli marinated vegetable salad
12 slices mozzarella cheese

Cut a thin slice off top of rolls, hollow out centers leaving a 1/2-inch shell. Place ham inside roll bottoms; fill with vegetable salad, drained. Top with cheese slices and broil until cheese starts to melt. Recap with roll top and serve. Serves 6.

ANTONE'S ITALIAN BEEF SANDWICHES

1 boneless rump roast, 5 pounds
2 cans (10 1/2-ounce size) beef broth
2 garlic cloves, minced
2 tablespoons Worcestershire sauce
1/2 cup finely chopped green pepper
1 teaspoon oregano
1 teaspoon marjoram
1 teaspoon basil
1/2 teaspoon thyme
Bottled hot sauce to taste

Place meat on rack in a roaster and roast for 2 hours in a preheated 325-degree oven. Cool for 20 minutes; slice as thin as possible and set aside. Pour broth into roaster; set over medium-high heat on top of stove and stir to loosen drippings. Add remaining ingredients and bring to a boil. Reduce heat to a simmer and cook 15 minutes. Add sliced meat to mixture; cover and let marinate in refrigerator at least 4 hours; preferably overnight. Reheat and serve on crisp Italian bread. Makes about 12 hearty sandwiches.

Jo and Jan say, "We use an electric knife to slice the meat. You can really get paper-thin slices."

TONY'S ITALIAN SANDWICH

8 round club rolls
3/4 pound ground beef
1 can (8-ounce) tomato sauce
1/4 cup dry onion soup
1/4 teaspoon dried oregano
1/4 teaspoon dried basil
1 beaten egg
3/4 cup cream-style cottage cheese, drained
1 cup mozzarella cheese, shredded

Cut thin slices off tops of buns and hollow out centers. Leave at least 1/2-inch thick; set aside. In a skillet brown beef; drain off fat and add tomato sauce, soup mix and herbs. Cook slowly over low heat for 10 minutes, stirring frequently. Remove from heat and set aside.

In a small bowl combine egg, cottage cheese and 1/2 cup of mozzarella cheese. Spoon half the meat mixture into rolls; top with cheese mixture then remaining meat mixture. Top with remaining mozzarella cheese. Replace bun tops. Serves 8 (or 4 guys).

HE-MAN STEAK SANDWICHES

1/2 stick margarine
2 medium onions, sliced
1/2 teaspoon sugar
Salt and pepper
1 tablespoon flour
1/2 cup dry red wine
1/4 cup water
1 tablespoon minced parsley
1 pound sirloin steak cut 3/4-inch thick
1/2 teaspoon dried basil
1/2 teaspoon dried parsley
6 slices whole wheat bread

Melt margarine over low heat in 12-inch skillet; add onions, sugar, salt and pepper. Cook until onions are tender, stirring occasionally. Stir in flour and cook 1 minute; add wine and water, stirring until mixture thickens slightly and is smooth. While onions are cooking, preheat broiler. Place steak on rack and broil 5 minutes; turn steak and sprinkle with herbs. Broil 5 minutes longer or until done.

While steak is broiling, toast bread; remove broiled steak to a cutting board and slice thin. Place toast on serving plates, top with steak slices and spoon onion mixture over top. Makes 3 servings.

REUBEN LOAF

1 loaf (16-ounce) rye bread
1 bottle (8-ounce) Russian dressing
3 packages (4-ounce size) sliced corn beef
1 package (8-ounce) Swiss cheese, sliced
1 can or jar (14-ounce) sauerkraut, well
    drained

Slice loaf into 12 slices. Spread 6 slices with Russian dressing. Arrange corned beef and cheese on them and top each with sauerkraut and more dressing. Cover each with a slice of bread; stack sandwiches on top of each other and secure the long loaf with a skewer. Wrap loaf tightly with foil and bake in preheated 350-degree oven for 1 hour or until cheese melts. Take a quick peek half way through so they don't get too done. To serve, place loaf on warm platter; remove skewer and separate into individual sandwiches. Serves 6.

NEW YORK HOT DOGS

1 tablespoon butter or margarine
3/4 cup onions, chopped
1/4 cup green pepper, diced
2 cans (8-ounce size) tomato sauce
1 tablespoon Worcestershire sauce
1 teaspoon chili powder
1/2 teaspoon cinnamon
1/2 teaspoon dry mustard
1/2 teaspoon garlic salt
1/4 teaspoon cayenne
Hot dogs, warmed
Buns, split, buttered and warmed

Melt butter or margarine in a small skillet; add onions and green pepper and saute until soft. Stir in rest of sauce ingredients and simmer for about 5 minutes. Place hot dogs in warm buns and top with sauce. Makes 3 cups.

BENNIE'S BEER BURGERS

1 1/2 pounds ground beef or ground chuck
1 can (12-ounce) beer
Dash of salt
3/4 stick margarine
3 large red onions, sliced
4 hamburger buns
1 tomato, thinly sliced
2 dill pickles, sliced lengthwise

Combine beef, 3/4 cup beer and salt in medium sized bowl; mix well. Shape into 4 patties and set aside. Melt margarine in 12-inch skillet; add onions and cook until tender. Stir in remaining beer; bring to a boil. Cook stirring occasionally until most of liquid is absorbed.

Place patties on rack in broiling pan and broil 5 minutes on each side or until desired doneness. On each of hamburger bun bottoms, place a hamburger patty, some onion mixture, some tomato and pickle slices and top with bun. Serves 4.

LITTLE PIZZAS

1 1/2 cups sharp Cheddar cheese, grated
1 cup ripe olives, sliced
1/2 cup green onions, sliced
1/2 teaspoon chili powder
1/2 cup mayonnaise
Salt to taste
6 English muffins

Combine olives, onions, chili powder, mayonnaise and salt; set aside. Cut muffins in half and butter each half with mixture; sprinkle cheese on top. Place on baking sheet and broil until cheese is melted. Yummy! Makes 12.

❖❖

BOY'S CLUB SCRATCH PIZZA

3/4 cup milk
tablespoons sugar
1/2 teaspoon salt
1 egg, well beaten
1 package yeast, dissolved in
   1/4 cup lukewarm water
1/4 cup oil
3 3/4 cups flour

Add:
1 jar Spaghetti sauce; spread over dough
Any ingredients you desire; build your own
   creation
6 ounces shredded Mozzarella cheese;
   sprinkle over top of pizza

Scald milk; add sugar and salt. Cool to lukewarm; add egg, yeast, oil and half of flour. Beat with rotary beater until smooth. Add remaining flour 1/2 cup at a time. Knead for 10 minutes. Place dough in a well greased bowl, cover and let rise until double. Roll out into 2 big circles.

Bake in preheated 425-degree oven for 20 minutes.

Side Kicks

STUFFING FOR BAKED POTATOES

6 baked potatoes
6 tablespoons butter or margarine, softened
3/4 cup sour cream
6 slices cooked bacon, crumbled
6 shredded Cheddar cheese
2 tablespoons chopped fresh chives or
   green onions
Salt, pepper and paprika to taste

Cut baked potatoes in half lengthwise and scoop out pulp, leaving 1/4-inch thick shell. Place hot pulp in bowl and mash with potato masher or electric mixer. Add butter, cream, bacon, 1 cup cheese and chives to mashed potatoes and mix well. Season with salt and pepper, spoon into shells and sprinkle remaining 1 cup cheese over potatoes and garnish with paprika. Place on baking sheet and place in hot oven until stuffing is heated through, or in microwave oven on 50 percent power for 9 to 12 minutes.

ANDY'S BAKED POTATO CHIPS

3 1/2 pounds red or white potatoes
6 tablespoons olive oil
3 cloves garlic, crushed
2 teaspoons Italian herbs
Salt and freshly ground black pepper
Paprika

   Combine olive oil, garlic and herbs; set aside while you prepare potatoes.
   Clean potatoes and cut crosswise into 1/8-inch slices. Lightly grease 2 baking sheets. Place sliced potatoes in a large bowl; pour olive

oil mixture over and toss potatoes well so all are coated with oil. Arrange potato slices in a single layer on the sheets. Position racks in upper and lower third of oven and preheat to 500 degrees. Place sheets on racks and bake 7 minutes; switch pans and bake until potatoes are crisp and browned around edges, about 8 minutes; watch closely! Remove sheets from oven and transfer potatoes to a heated platter. Sprinkle with salt, pepper and paprika; serve while hot. Serves 6.
   Jo and Jan say, "If you desire to cut the potatoes in French fry slices, time will vary a bit; just keep an eye on the oven."

◇◆◇

CRISP BAKED POTATOES

1 1/2 cups dry bread crumbs
1 tablespoon ground nutmeg
1 teaspoon salt
1/2 teaspoon pepper
8 medium potatoes, pared and cut in 1/4-
 inch slices
1 cup melted butter

Combine bread crumbs, nutmeg, salt and pepper. Dip potatoes in butter; roll in bread crumb mixture. Place on greased baking sheets in single layer. Position racks in upper and lower third of oven and preheat to 400 degrees. Place sheets on racks and bake 10 minutes; switch pans and bake until potatoes are crisp and browned around edges, about 10 to 15 minutes. Watch closely. Remove from oven and transfer to a heated platter. Serves 8.

LEE'S BAKED CORN ON THE COB

Pick the freshest ears of corn you can find. Pull down the husks but do not remove them. Clean all the silk from the ears, brush with butter, pull the husks back up over the ears and wrap in foil. Place in a shallow pan and bake for 45 minutes in a preheated 350-degree oven.

ROASTED CORN ON THE COB

4 or more ears of fresh corn
8 ounces fresh butter
1 teaspoon brown sugar

Corn cooked in its husks on hot coals remains sweet and firm. The fresher the corn, the better it will taste. Peel back the green husks without removing them from the stalk, which should be intact. Remove corn silk and replace green husks back over the corn, smoothing them tightly over the raw kernels. Tie the tops of husks together with string and briefly dampen each ear under cold running water. Place corn directly on the grill over hot coals and cook for 10 to 15 minutes, turning so that all sides get toasted. Melt butter and stir in brown sugar. Serve corn in the husks with the bowl of butter on the side.

Jo says, "A new, small paint brush will make spreading the butter easy."

MIKE'S HERBED GRILLED CORN

1/2 cup butter, softened
2 tablespoons chopped parsley
2 tablespoons chopped chives
1/2 teaspoon salt
Dash of pepper
8 ears of corn, husks and silk removed, ends
 trimmed

Blend butter with other ingredients. Spread 1 heaping tablespoon on each ear; wrap individually in heavy-duty foil. Grill over glowing coals 15-20 minutes, or until tender, turning occasionally. Serves 4-8.

D. DEEMS' WEST TEXAS BEANS

1 pound pinto beans
1 large onion, diced
Smoked ham hocks or pork chops
4 tablespoons brown sugar
4 teaspoons chile powder

Place beans in a kettle; cover with cold water and allow to sit overnight. Pour off water and cover with fresh water. Add onion and ham hocks or pork chops. Cover and simmer until beans are tender.

Drain beans, remove any meat from bones and discard bones. Add brown sugar and chili powder. Mix well and reheat before serving. Serves "1 Texas-Size Appetite!"

WILD RICE CASSEROLE

1 box Long Grain & Wild Rice
1/4 cup margarine
1 small onion, chopped
1/2 cup green pepper, chopped
1 1/2 cups celery, chopped
1 small can mushrooms, undrained
1 can mushroom soup
1 can water chestnuts

Cook rice following instructions on box. Saute onion, green pepper, celery in margarine until golden. Add undrained mushrooms, soup, water chestnuts and rice to onion mixture and mix gently. Pour into greased 2-quart baking dish; bake in preheated 325-degree oven for 45 minutes. Serves 8 - 10.

Jan says, "A wonderful accompaniment to Pot Roast."

PASTABILITY HINTS

• When cooking your favorite pasta, undercook the entire package. Drain in a colander and rinse immediately under cold running water. Drain again and refrigerate up to five days in a large covered container or package and freeze individual portions in re-sealable plastic bags.

• If you want to cook your pasta ahead of time and use it for dinner, do the same as above but set the colander on your counter and use the pasta when your sauce is ready.

• When making the cream sauce for your fettuccini, pour cream in a heavy pan or skillet and bring it to a rolling boil. Boil a few seconds and then reduce heat and add the butter which will calm down the cream. Go from there with your other sauce ingredients.

Jan and Jo say, "Thanks to Chef Michael! These hints are wonderful and really work."

MACARONI AND CHEESE SUPREME

1 package (8-ounce) small elbow macaroni
2 quarts boiling water
1 tablespoon salt
2 tablespoons butter
1/2 pound Velvetta cheese
1 1/2 cups milk
8 slices bacon, fried crisp and crumbled
1/4 cup chopped green pepper
1 jar (2-ounce) sliced pimiento
1 can (4-ounce) mushrooms and liquid
1/4 teaspoon Tabasco sauce
1/4 teaspoon paprika
1/2 teaspoon black pepper
1 package (8-ounce) sharp Cheddar cheese
Paprika (garnish)

Cook macaroni in boiling, salted water according to package directions and drain. Pour into a buttered 9 x 13-inch baking dish. In top of double boiler, combine butter, Velvetta cheese and milk; cook until cheese melts. Add other ingredients except sharp cheese and paprika garnish. The sauce will be thin. Pour over macaroni and stir to mix; top with grated sharp cheese and sprinkle with paprika. Bake in preheated 350-degree oven for 40 minutes. Serves 10 - 12.

CHEF MICHAEL'S BECHAMEL SAUCE

3 ounces butter
2 1/2 ounces flour
1 quart boiled milk
Pinch of nutmeg
Salt and white pepper

Melt butter in saucepan; add flour and cook 2 minutes while stirring with a whisk. Slowly add milk, nutmeg, salt and pepper; whisking constantly until smooth and cook 10 minutes at a gentle boil. Strain through a cheese cloth or fine strainer. Makes 4 cups.

CURTIS' MUSTARD SAUCE

1 cup cider vinegar
4 ounces dry mustard
2 eggs
1 3/4 cups sugar

Mix vinegar and mustard together. Let set overnight at room temperature in a jar. Beat eggs well and add sugar. Add this mixture to the vinegar and mustard; heat to a <u>barely boil</u>, do not burn. Refrigerate overnight.

Curtis says, "This is a very good recipe and many folks ask for it."

TOM'S MUSTARD SAUCE

1/3 cup Grey Poupon mustard
2 eggs, beaten
1 cup cream
1 tablespoon vinegar
1/4 teaspoon tarragon, or dill weed

Heat ingredients in saucepan over low heat. Stir constantly until mixture thickens. Makes 1 1/2 cups.

The Stock Market

CHEF MICHAEL'S SPAGHETTI MEAT SAUCE

4 pounds ground chuck
2 tablespoons olive oil
1 1/2 pounds Italian sausage
1 large yellow onion, chopped
1 large green bell pepper, chopped
1 large red bell pepper, chopped
1 apple, chopped
4 medium carrots, chopped
2 cans mushrooms, drained and chopped
1 quart Ragu spaghetti sauce
2 cans (15-ounce size) stewed tomatoes, chopped
Brown sugar
Spices of preference (I use Italian herbs, garlic powder, MSG, seasoned salt and seasoned pepper).

In a medium skillet, saute sausage until lightly browned. In a larger pot saute ground chuck in olive oil until browned then pour off most of the fat. Add chopped vegetables to ground chuck. Cover and simmer for 20 minutes, stirring frequently. Add sliced sausage to pot. Add all seasonings and Ragu; slowly bring to a boil, stirring often to prevent sticking. Add about 1 1/2 handfuls of brown sugar and stir well. Cover and simmer for as long as you like, stirring occasionally, about 3 to 4 hours. If you prefer fresh garlic, add the finely chopped garlic cloves to the olive oil and brown prior to sauteing the ground chuck.

Mike says, "I like to make up my sauce several days prior to serving in order for the flavors to become 'married'." Serves 18 - 20.

CHRIS' BEEF STROGANOFF

1 1/2 pounds ground beef
1 small onion, chopped
1 small garlic bud, chopped
1 tablespoon Worcestershire sauce
Tabasco, to taste
1 can tomato soup
1 cup sour cream
Salt and pepper to taste

Brown meat until pink; add onion and garlic. Add Worcestershire sauce and 6 drops of Tabasco. Simmer 10 minutes; add tomato soup, sour cream, salt and pepper. Simmer 30 minutes longer and serve over spaghetti or noodles. Serves 4-6.

Chris says, "This has been one of my family favorites over the years."

CABBAGE ROLLS

1 pound ground beef
1 pound ground pork
1 1/2 cups uncooked rice
1 can (8-ounce) tomato sauce
1 1/2 cups onion, chopped
1/3 cup celery, chopped
3 cloves garlic, minced
1/2 cup green pepper, chopped
4 teaspoons salt
1/4 to 1/2 teaspoons cayenne pepper
1/2 teaspoon black pepper
2 large heads cabbage
6 strips bacon
1 46-ounce can V-8 Juice

Mix all ingredients except cabbage, bacon and V-8. Core cabbage and place in boiling water. As leaves wilt, peel off and drain well. Place about 1 large tablespoon of mixture on a leaf at stem end. Fold sides in toward center and roll up. Place open edge down in large oven roaster. Continue with mixture and leaves until mixture is gone. Place bacon strips on rolls; pour juice over top to almost cover rolls. Cover roaster and bake in a preheated 350-degree oven for 1 1/2 to 2 hours.

Jo says, "If cabbage leaves are very large, cut them in half from core end to edge and make two rolls. This makes a very large amount so it is an excellent buffet dish. The recipe can be divided or the entire amount can be made and frozen. For added zip, substitute a Bloody Mary mix for the V-8 Juice. If so, you might want to cut down on the cayenne pepper." Makes 6 - 7 dozen.

TOSTADO PIE

1 9-inch pie shell, baked
1 pound ground beef
1/2 cup onion, chopped
1 tablespoon dry beef bouillon
1 can (16-ounce) refried beans
1 can (4-ounce) green chilies, drained
1/4 cup tomato sauce
Sour cream
Lettuce, shredded
Tomatoes, chopped
Cheddar cheese, grated

Prepare pie shell, bake and set aside. In large skillet brown beef, onion and bouillon until bouillon dissolves. Remove from heat and stir in beans, chilies and tomato sauce. Pour mixture into pie shell and bake in preheated 375-degree oven for 20 to 25 minutes or until edges are bubbly. Remove from oven and let stand 10 minutes. Garnish with the remaining ingredients. Serves 4 - 6.

Jan says, "I fill small bowls with the sour cream, lettuce, tomatoes and cheese. That way, your family or guests may help themselves to them. You might also want to make up some Guacamole."

MEAT LOAF
— Just Like Mom Used To Make —

2 pounds ground beef
1 pound ground pork
2 cups corn flakes
1 egg
1 small can tomatoes (pour off juice and reserve)
Salt and pepper
Dash of Worcestershire sauce
1 small onion, grated

Mix all ingredients; form loaf in baking dish. Pour reserved tomato juice over top and bake in preheated 350-degree oven for 1 hour or until done.

Jo and Jan say, "This makes great sandwiches; serve cold or hot."

❖❖

JIM'S LIVER AND ONIONS

4 slices liver
16 strips bacon (4 per person)
2 large onions, sliced
Flour
Salt and pepper

Tenderize liver well; (Jim uses the back of a kitchen knife; some use the edge of a saucer).

Fry bacon crisp and drain on paper towels. Saute onions until barely limp; remove and set aside.

Dredge tenderized liver in flour seasoned with salt and pepper. Fry in bacon grease until done. Return onions, placing them on top of liver. Add 1/4 cup water to skillet, cover and cook until liver is very tender.

Remove liver to serving plater, top with onion and bacon slices. Serves 4.

Jo says, "Jim is the proclaimed liver and onions expert at our house. When he prepares this dinner it always tastes so much better than mine!"

SMOKED SAUSAGE, BEANS AND POTATOES IN HERB-WINE SAUCE

2 can green beans, drained, reserve liquid
6 medium boiling potatoes
1 pound smoked Polish sausage
1/2 pound smoked knockwurst
1/2 pound smoked bratwurst
1 1/2 cups dry white wine
6 tablespoons olive oil
1 teaspoon dried thyme
1/2 teaspoon dried tarragon
1/2 teaspoon dried marjoram
1 tablespoon minced scallions
1 tablespoon white wine tarragon vinegar
1/4 teaspoon Dijon mustard
1 egg yolk
1 tablespoon snipped fresh parsley
1 tablespoon snipped fresh chives
1/2 teaspoon salt
1/4 teaspoon ground white pepper

Cook potatoes in reserved bean liquid in a Dutch oven just until tender, about 20 minutes. Drain, saving liquid; cool slightly and peel. Cut into 1/4 inch slices. Keep warm.

Pierce sausages with fork. Combine sausages, wine, 1/4 cup of oil, thyme, tarragon and marjoram in large skillet; simmer partially covered, turning sausages frequently for 10 minutes. Reserve sausages and wine mixture separately.

Saute scallions in 1 tablespoon oil in small saucepan until soft, about 2 minutes. Add reserved wine mixture; heat to a boil. Simmer until reduced to 3/4 cup, about 10 minutes. Stir in vinegar and mustard. Remove from heat. Gradually whisk wine mixture into egg yolk in small bowl. Stir in half the parsley, half the chives, the salt and pepper; pour over potatoes; cover.

Cut sausages into 1/2-inch slices. Brown in remaining oil in a large skillet. Heat beans in reserved bean liquid, drain well, then add to potato mixture and arrange with sausages in a serving bowl. Sprinkle with remaining parsley and chives. Serves 6 - 8.

TONY'S MEAT MARINADE

1/2 cup Italian salad dressing
1/4 cup Worcestershire sauce
1 teaspoon Lawry Seasoning Salt
1/4 teaspoon pepper
1/4 teaspoon garlic powder
2 teaspoons honey
1/2 cup Heinz 57 Sauce

Combine all ingredients in a quart jar and shake well. Pour over steaks, ribs or chops, turning every 2 hours until time to cook meat. As you barbecue, brush remaining sauce over the meat. Makes about 1 1/3 cups.

RICK'S MARINADE FOR BEEF OR CHICKEN

1 quart pineapple juice
1 cup sugar
2/3 cup red wine vinegar
1 1/2 teaspoon granulated garlic
2 cups sherry (not cooking sherry)

Combine ingredients and mix well. Immerse meat in mixture and leave covered for 12 - 24 hours; the longer, the better. Charcoal meat to taste, using marinade as basting liquid.

Jo and Jan say, "Rick's recipes were the first we received for our Boy's Club section. We knew we were off to a good start!"

KENT'S TARRAGON MARINADE FOR SIRLOIN STEAKS

3 tablespoons tarragon vinegar
2 large onions, sliced
1 lemon
5 garlic cloves, slivered
1 teaspoon dried tarragon, crumbled
1 bay leaf
1/2 teaspoon dry mustard
1/2 cup dry red wine
1 cup olive oil
1 teaspoon salt
Freshly ground pepper

Line a baking dish with 3/4 of onions. Squeeze lemon juice over onions. Add garlic, herbs, mustard, salt and pepper. Pour in vinegar, wine and oil. Lay steaks in marinade and spread rest of onions on the meat. Marinate for at least 3 hours, basting frequently. Serve the marinated onions raw with the cooked steaks. Marinates 2 pounds of sirloin, 2 inches thick.

JAKE'S SPICY BEEF TENDERLOIN

1 cup port wine
1 cup soy sauce
1/2 cup olive oil
3 tablespoons Meat Seasoning Blend (See index)
5 to 6 pound tenderloin, trimmed
Fresh watercress (garnish)
Cherry tomatoes (garnish)

Combine wine, soy sauce, olive oil and Seasoning Blend; mix well. Place tenderloin in large shallow dish; pour wine mixture over top and cover tightly. Refrigerate for 8 hours, turning frequently.

Remove tenderloin from marinade, reserving marinade. Place meat on rack in roasting pan inserting meat thermometer. Do not let it touch fat. Bake in preheated 425-degree oven for 45 to 60, basting occasionally with marinade, until thermometer registers 140 degrees for rare; 150 for medium-rare and 160 for medium.

Transfer meat to a warm serving platter and garnish with watercress and cherry tomatoes. Serves 10 - 12.

DAVID'S "POOR MAN'S" FILET

6 pounds fresh rump roast
1 large garlic clove
Fresh peppercorns

Sliver garlic and insert in roast, then insert several fresh peppercorns. Roast in a preheated 350-degree oven for 1 1/2 hours, then cool for 5 hours at room temperature.

David says, "This is delicious served with Pasta Primavera (See index)."

Jo and Jan say, "We found this is really delicious made up in Mary's Steak Salad (See index). It makes a wonderful second day dish."

BUTTERFLIED SIRLOIN STEAK

1 sirloin steak (1-pound)
6 tablespoons butter
2 shallots, diced
3 tablespoons onion, chopped
1/2 teaspoon Escoffier Sauce Robert
Black pepper, freshly ground
1 1/2 ounces white wine
Fresh parsley, chopped

Trim steak of all fat and butterfly it by cutting from flat to rounded side; do not cut all the way through. Lay steak on board and pound thin. Melt butter in large skillet on medium-high heat; add shallots and onion and saute until golden. Add Escoffier sauce and mix well. Place steak in butter mixture and saute about 3 minutes on each side or until as you desire. Grind pepper over steak each time you turn it, giving it a good amount of pepper. Remove steak to heated platter; add wine to the butter in skillet and simmer for 3 to 4 minutes. Spoon sauce over steak and sprinkle with chopped parsley. Serves 4.

STEAK AU POIVRE

4 - pound boneless sirloin steak, 1 1/2 inches thick, room temperature
2 tablespoons freshly cracked black pepper
1 teaspoon garlic powder
2 tablespoons butter or margarine
2 tablespoons salad oil
1/2 cup dry red or white wine
2 tablespoons brandy
1 teaspoon salt
2 tablespoons chopped fresh parsley

Your steak should weigh 4 pounds after the butcher has boned it. the reason for boning it is so it will fit into a skillet. Try it for size in the skillet when you take it from the refrigerator to bring it to room temperature. You may have to tie or skewer the meat.

Wipe steak with damp paper towels. If you have a pepper mill that grinds coarsely, use it; otherwise, crack your pepper by hand using a rolling pin or mortar and pestle. Freshly-cracked pepper has more flavor. Rub 1 tablespoon pepper and 1/2 teaspoon garlic powder into each side. Press into meat with the heel of your hand and let stand at room temperature.

Slowly heat the large skillet and add 1 tablespoon butter and the oil, stirring until butter is melted.

Add steak; over high heat, brown steak well about 2 minutes on each side, turning meat with 2 wooden spoons so as not to puncture the meat. Reduce heat to medium and cook 8 to 10 minutes per side for medium rare. Remove steak to a heated platter.

Add remaining butter, wine, brandy, salt and parsley to skillet. Simmer for 3 minutes to de-glaze. Pour mixture over the steak and serve immediately. Serves 6.

CHEF MICHAEL'S SCALOPPINA ZAGARA

6 slices (8-ounce each) veal
Salt and pepper to taste
2 tablespoons butter or margarine
1 teaspoon shallots, finely diced
6 ounces mushrooms, sliced
2 tablespoons Grand Marnier liqueur
1 teaspoon orange peel
Juice of 1 1/2 oranges
2 tablespoons Demi-glaze or Beef Stock (See index)
3/4 cup heavy cream
1 teaspoon butter or margarine

Saute veal in butter until just done. Remove from skillet and place in a covered warm container. Saute shallots and mushrooms in skillet until tender. Add liqueur; (it will flame) then add orange peel and juice. Cook to reduce mixture by 1/2. Add beef stock and cream; cook until thickened. Place veal on serving plate; drop 1 teaspoon butter in sauce, mix in and pour sauce over the veal and serve. Serves 6.

Mike says, "This recipe is delicious with duck breast. Prepare 2 duck breasts in 4 portions. Clean breasts free of bones and trim to neat portions. Lightly pound meat until uniformly shaped; but don't overdo it.

Lightly roll breasts in flour, salt and pepper and saute in butter until almost done, leaving a little pink in center. Remove to a warm, covered dish and proceed as with veal." Serves 4.

CHICKEN-FRIED STEAK WITH WHITE GRAVY

1 1/2 pounds round steak, cut into 4 pieces
Salt and pepper
1 teaspoon baking powder
3/4 cup flour
1/2 cup milk
Vegetable oil
WHITE GRAVY:
1/4 cup flour
1/4 cup oil
1 1/2 cups milk
1/2 teaspoon salt
1/2 teaspoon black pepper, or to taste
1/4 teaspoon nutmeg

Pound steaks until 1/3-inch thick and fork tender. In one bowl combine baking powder and flour; in another bowl combine milk and eggs. In a heavy skillet, pour enough oil to come halfway up the sides of the meat. Heat oil to 375 degrees. Dip steaks in milk mixture, then dredge in flour; repeat process. Fry meat until golden brown on one side, about 7 minutes then turn and fry an additional 3 to 4 minutes. Note: steaks will float on top of oil when they're done. Remove from skillet and drain on paper towels; keep warm in oven while preparing gravy.

Drain oil from skillet, reserving 1/4 cup. Heat oil in same skillet, stirring to loosen any browned bits. Sprinkle flour over oil and cook, stirring constantly over medium-high heat for 1 minute, until flour just begins to color. Slowly stir in milk, keeping gravy smooth; add seasonings and cook until gravy is thick. Serve over steaks. Serves 4.

Jo and Jan say, "Chicken-fried steak should be fork tender, so pound it well; also it should not be greasy and batter should be crisp. Add pepper to the gravy as you like; some guys really like it poured on, Texas-style."

MARINATED LOIN OF PORK

1 boned, rolled loin of pork, about 3 pounds
1/2 cup soy sauce
1/2 cup dry sherry
2 cloves garlic, crushed
1 teaspoon dry mustard
1 teaspoon ground ginger
1 teaspoon dried thyme leaves, crumbled
1 teaspoon paprika

Combine soy sauce, sherry and seasonings in a small bowl and blend well. Place pork loin, fat-side up, in a shallow roasting pan. Using sharp knife, score fat in crisscross fashion; pour marinade over. Let set at room temperature, turning loin occasionally. You can marinate it overnight; but cover and refrigerate. Cover pan tightly with foil and bake in preheated 325-degree oven for 11/2 hours. Remove foil and bake 1 more hour, basting frequently with pan juices. When meat is tender and temperature reaches 170 degrees, transfer to a heated platter. Remove fat from pan juices and use juices for a sauce. Serves 4 - 6.

GLENN'S MANDARIN PORK ROAST

5 to 8 pound pork roast
Garlic salt
Onion salt
2 tablespoons margarine
3/4 cup chopped onion
1 cup red plum preserves
2 cups Dr. Pepper
2 tablespoons prepared mustard
3 drops Tabasco

Sprinkle roast generously with garlic and onion salt. Place fat side up in a roasting pan. Place in a preheated 325-degree oven for 2 hours.

Meanwhile melt margarine in a small saucepan and add onions. Cook until tender; add remaining ingredients and simmer 15 minutes.

Pour fat off partially roasted meat; pour 1/2 of the sauce over meat and continue roasting and basting until done. Serves 8 - 10.

Glenn says, "I serve the other half of the sauce with the sliced roast. Figure roasting time as 35 to 45 minutes per pound."

CHEF MICHAEL'S PORK ROAST

3 - 4 pound pork loin roast with rack
Salt and pepper
2 tablespoons olive oil
1 bay leaf
2 garlic cloves, whole and peeled
1 stalk celery, sliced
1 carrot, peeled and sliced
1 onion, sliced
1/2 teaspoon thyme
1 cup dry white wine
1 1/2 cups beef broth

Measure olive oil in a heavy skillet. Salt and pepper your roast and place fat side down in the hot skillet. Brown on all sides; remove to a separate plate and keep warm.

Place bay leaf, thyme, carrot, onion, celery and garlic in skillet and saute for 3 to 4 minutes. Place roast on top of the vegetables and cook for about 2 more minutes. Add wine and cook an additional 2 minutes.

Place uncovered pan in a preheated 475-degree oven for 10 minutes and then cover for the remainder of the cooking time. Figure your cooking time to be 15 minutes per pound.

Baste roast several times with pan juices. When roast is done, remove from roaster and keep warm.

Strain and press all liquid from vegetables. Place strained liquid in a saucepan and discard vegetables. Reduce liquid over high heat by 1/3.

Slice roast and keep it warm; spoon reduced stock over meat. Serves 6.

Mike says, "I like to slice my roast at tableside and make a production of the presentation. Guests enjoy that."

AL'S PORK CHOPS

4 thick boneless pork chops
Garlic powder
Teriyaki marinade

Sprinkle pork chops with garlic powder and marinate for several hours in teriyaki.

Grill about 20 minutes per side or until done.

Jo and Jan say, "Al prepared these delicious chops for us and what a treat! They are so easy to prepare and we think they are delicious served cold; sliced in slivers they are perfect for picnics!"

COUNTRY GENTLEMAN PORK CHOPS

1 corn bread recipe for 8
8 pork chops cut 1 1/4 inches thick
1 medium-size bottle horseradish
1 pound mild sausage
6 cups dried bread crumbs
2 teaspoons sage
1 teaspoon poultry seasoning
2 teaspoons parsley
1/2 cup onion, chopped
3 chicken bouillon cubes dissolved in 1
    cup hot water
Flour

Prepare corn bread following package directions to serve 8; cool and crumble. Trim excess fat from pork chops and set it aside. Marinate chops in horseradish at least 6 hours. Brown meat in a hot, ungreased skillet for 8 to 10 minutes. Fry sausage until partially cooked; drain on paper towels. Combine in a 9 x 13 x 2-inch baking dish the crumbled corn bread, crumbs, sausage, herbs, onions and dissolved bouillon. Mixture should be light and crumbly. Top with pork chops.

Render out reserved pork fat and combine with enough flour and water to make 4 cups of thin gravy. Pour this over casserole. Bake in preheated 350-degree oven for 1 hour. Serves 8.

❖❖

LEE'S PRIZE WINNING ROAST LEG OF LAMB

5 - 7 pound leg of lamb (boned)
1 cup salad oil
1 cup chablis wine
1/2 cup lemon juice
1/2 cup wine vinegar
2 tablespoons marjoram
1 tablespoon garlic juice
1 garlic clove
2 medium onions
2 teaspoons coarse ground black pepper
1 teaspoon salt

Combine oil and rest of ingredients in blender and mix until properly blended. Place lamb in container and marinate in refrigerator overnight, turning occasionally in marinade. Roast in preheated 325-degree oven for 3 to 3 1/2 hours or until doneness is achieved, basting frequently with marinade.

Lee says, "You can baste with chablis instead of the marinade. A few drops of red food coloring in the marinade improves the color of lamb. I serve the lamb on a bed of buttered popcorn rice."

LEE'S ROAST LEG OF LAMB IN GARLIC SAUCE

1 boned leg of lamb (6 1/2 pounds, weight after trimmed)
Salt and freshly ground pepper
1 teaspoon dried marjoram
1 teaspoon dried thyme
1 teaspoon dried rosemary
1 1/2 teaspoons paprika
1 1/2 teaspoons Dijon mustard
2 large garlic cloves, peeled and crushed
8 anchovy fillets
3 tablespoons butter
1 tablespoon oil
2 cups hot beef bouillon
SAUCE:
16 large garlic cloves, peeled
2 tablespoons butter
1 small onion, finely minced
2 large ripe tomatoes, peeled, seeded and chopped
Salt and freshly ground black pepper
1 teaspoon dried thyme
1 small can tomato paste
GARNISH:
Sprigs of fresh watercress or romaine lettuce

COOKING TIME: 1 hour 30 minutes, Oven 2 hours approx., Charcoal Grill

1. 2 hours before roasting, season the lamb with salt, pepper, marjoram, thyme, and rosemary. Rub the roast with paprika and mustard. Arrange anchovy fillets across top of roast. Set lamb aside at room temperature for 2 hours.

2. Preheat oven to 375 degrees. If using charcoal grill start 10 pounds of charcoal 20 minutes before you are ready to roast.

3. Place roast on an elevated rack in a large flame-proof baking dish and spoon some of the melted butter over it. Place lamb in oven and roast for 1 hour, 20 minutes or 12 minutes per pound, basting it every 10 minutes with a little of the hot beef bouillon.

To Charcoal, same as above except use a metal cake pan instead of baking dish. Since it is difficult to maintain consistent heat in a charcoal grill a meat thermometer is essential. 140 degrees on meat thermometer for rare, 150 degrees for medium rare.

4. While lamb is roasting make the sauce. In a small saucepan bring salted water to a boil; add garlic and cook for 5 minutes or until tender. Drain the cloves and mash them to a paste or puree them in blender. Set garlic paste aside.

5. In a small heavy skillet heat the butter. Add onion and cook for 2 minutes without browning. Add tomatoes, salt, pepper and thyme. Optional: You may wish to use a small amount of tomato paste to increase volume of sauce. Cook the mixture until it is reduced to a thick puree. Add the garlic paste and reserve.

6. When the lamb is done transfer it to a serving platter, cover and keep warm. Taste sauce and correct seasoning. Garnish lamb roast with sprigs of fresh watercress or romaine and serve the garlic sauce on the side.

Lee says, "Poaching the garlic cloves renders them quite harmless and they will add an interesting and somewhat sweet taste to the sauce. I like to serve the lamb on a bed of popcorn rice with corn on the cob, snow peas and cherry tomatoes."

❖❖

TIP

- If smoking a leg of lamb, insert slivers of garlic in the meat. Add 1 bay leaf, 1/2 teaspoon dried rosemary and 1/2 teaspoon dried thyme to the smoking liquid.

Greats for Steaks

BASTING SAUCE

3/4 cup olive oil
3/4 cup dry red wine
1 tablespoon lime juice
1 garlic clove, mashed
1/3 cup onion, finely chopped
1 teaspoon oregano
1/2 teaspoon thyme
1 teaspoon sugar
1 teaspoon salt
Freshly ground pepper

Combine ingredients and beat until well blended. Spread liberally over steak while cooking, both before and after turning.

WESTERN HERB SAUCE

2 tablespoons chopped scallions
1/2 pound mushrooms, sliced
1/4 cup olive oil
1/4 cup butter
2 tablespoons chives, chopped
2 tablespoons tarragon, chopped
3 tablespoons parsley, chopped
3 tablespoons bottled Escoffier Sauce Diable
   or steak sauce
1/2 teaspoon salt
Freshly ground black pepper

Saute scallions and mushrooms in olive oil and butter for 5 minutes. Add rest of ingredients and simmer for 5 more minutes. Makes about 3 cups.

Jo and Jan say, "Serve this hot with broiled steak. It is a thick sauce which you can thin by adding 1/2 cup beef bouillon and simmer an extra 5 minutes."

JACK'S FRENCH SAUCE FOR STEAKS

1 1/2 sticks butter
2 tablespoons Worcestershire sauce
1 tablespoon dry mustard
1 cup finely chopped shallots
Salt to taste
Freshly ground black pepper; I use a lot!
2 teaspoons garlic powder
1/8 cup freshly chopped parsley

Melt butter and add remaining ingredients; parsley goes in right before using. Brush on meat while cooking and across the top before serving. Makes 1 1/2 cups.

Jack says, "Use this sauce on KC strips. An extra-thick KC for two, cut in slices and held to form is wonderful with this sauce."

BERNAISE SAUCE

1 tablespoon tarragon wine vinegar
2 tablespoons dry white wine
2 tablespoons shallots, chopped
Freshly ground pepper
3 egg yolks
Pinch of salt
3/4 cup butter

Combine vinegar, wine, shallots and pepper in small saucepan and cook until most of liquid has evaporated; remove from heat and cool slightly. Place egg yolks, salt and cooked mixture in blender. Melt butter and heat until bubbly but not brown. With blender running, add butter in a slow, steady stream. Makes about 1 cup.

Jan and Jo say, "Serve this over tenderloin or beef fillets. The flavor is exceptional! It can be prepared early in the day, but do not let it boil when reheating. If you desire more tarragon flavor, you can add a pinch of dried tarragon to the cooked mixture; be careful though, the flavor should be subtle."

MOCK BERNAISE SAUCE

1/2 cup dry white wine
1/2 cup parsley sprigs
1/4 cup white vinegar
1 small onion, quartered
2 large cloves garlic
2 1/2 teaspoons dried tarragon leaves, crushed
1/4 teaspoon dried chervil leaves, crushed
1/8 teaspoon pepper
1 cup mayonnaise

Combine first 8 ingredients in blender; cover and blend on high speed until uniform. In small saucepan, stir over medium heat until reduced to 1/3 cup. Strain and return liquid to saucepan. Add mayonnaise and stir over medium heat just until warm. Makes 1 1/4 cups.

JEFF'S BORDELAISE SAUCE

2 tablespoons butter or margarine
1 shallot, finely chopped
1 garlic clove, finely chopped
1 onion slice
2 carrot slices
1 parsley sprig
6 whole black peppercorns
1 whole clove
1 bay leaf
2 tablespoons flour
1 cup canned beef bouillon, undiluted
1/4 teaspoon salt
1/8 teaspoon pepper
1/3 cup Burgundy
1 tablespoon finely chopped parsley

Melt butter in a medium skillet. Add shallot, garlic, onion and carrot slices, parsley sprig, peppercorns, clove and bay leaf. Saute until onion is golden. Remove from heat; add flour, stirring until smooth. Over very low heat, stir and cook until flour is lightly browned, about 5 minutes. Remove from heat.

Gradually stir in bouillon and bring to a boil over medium heat, stirring constantly. Reduce heat; simmer gently 10 minutes, stirring occasionally. Strain and discard vegetables. Add remaining ingredients and reheat slowly. Makes 1 cup.

Jeff says, "This is excellent served with beef."

Jo and Jan say, "To make this a mushroom sauce, saute 1 cup thickly sliced mushrooms in 1 tablespoon butter until tender. Strain from liquid and add to prepared sauce."

ADAM'S RIB ROUND - UP - BARBECUE BASICS

So, you want to become an outdoor chef! Well, you're in good company. Barbecuing has become an important part of the American scene for outdoor fun. Here are some tips to help you get started on your new endeavor.

Outdoor cookery has become so popular that many stores have a complete section devoted to the subject. We suggest you visit one, familiarize yourself with all equipment from smokers and grills to all the "extras," and make up your "wish list." Family and friends will appreciate it at gift-giving times.

If purchasing utensils for barbecuing, choose sturdy ones with extra-long handles. Asbestos mitts are a must and you should have a pair of pot holders, a couple of kitchen towels, and a spray bottle of water to calm things down when dripping fat or sauces flame.

There are two methods used for grilling. The first is the DIRECT METHOD - placing the food over the hottest part of the grill. This method is used for burgers, chops and steaks.

The INDIRECT METHOD is for fish, vegetables, ribs and roasts. To use this method, wrap food in foil, or place your food on a foil-covered grill. Another way of accomplishing INDIRECT heat is simply to arrange the charcoal on one side of the broiler and cook on the other side.

Line the bottom of the grill with a 1-inch layer of pebbles to prolong the life of the grill and also help reflect heat to the food. Basting the grill with olive oil will prevent sticking and food will turn easier.

Arrange charcoal briquettes in a pyramid. Squirt with charcoal lighter and wait 1 minute before lighting. When coals begin to turn grey on the edges, spread them out. Coals should be glowing red to cook. Wait 30 minutes before beginning; grilling over flames will give food a bitter taste.

You can barbecue with wood chips—using the above methods—which will give a smoky, outdoor flavor. Soak chips in water at least 30 minutes before sprinkling them evenly over the hot coals. If using a gas grill, preheat at least 10 minutes on high. If a charcoal-type grill is being used, wait until coals are hot and covered with white ash. Begin cooking food when chips begin to smoke. You can also add aroma to coals by putting lemon or orange peel or dried spices among them.

As you begin, you must maintain coals at just the right temperature for perfectly done grilled food. If coals are not hot enough, gently shake the grill or tap the coals with the tongs to shake off excess ash. If the coals are too hot, cover the grill and reduce airflow to the coals for several minutes. To make sure the coals aren't too hot, hold your palm over them at grill height for about 8 seconds. If you can stand the heat, you're ready to proceed.

Important facts to remember as you begin—don't salt meat of fish before grilling; the food will become soggy as it absorbs moisture. However, you can salt chicken—on the inside. Olive oil is ideal for high temperature cooking; don't use butter because it burns quickly if you are going to be cooking for more than just a few minutes. And lastly, don't ever stick a fork into the food because the juices will run out, causing the coals to flare and burn the food. It also makes the meats dry and takes away the flavor.

RIBS: When buying ribs, figure a pound per person. But we recommend a bit more; better to have some left than to run short. Pork ribs, usually referred to as spareribs, are more tender and flavorful if you choose the smallest and meatiest. Try to get back ribs, from near the loin. Country style spareribs may be used but they have more fat.

Beef ribs, the long bones cut from the standing rib roast, should be chosen for small size and meatiness.

Preliminary parboiling of pork spareribs and lamb, especially when it's done in an herb-flavored liquid, makes for moister, tastier meat than dry heat alone. Parboiling shortens barbecue time by almost half. Cover ribs with boiling water. Simmer, covered, until tender, 45 to 60 minutes for pork sparerib/loin ribs; 50 to 60 minutes for beef chuck ribs. Grill, covered, indirectly over medium-slow heat for 15 minutes or until done.

Without precooking, grill pork sparerib/loin ribs, covered, indirectly over medium heat 10 minutes. Put a foil pan under the grill to catch the drippings and place hot coals around the pan. Place ribs on the grill over the pan and cover it. Then uncover, grill 15 to 30 minutes more or until done.

SEAFOOD: When purchasing seafood, plan on 1 pound of whole headless and dressed fish for 2 servings or 1 pound of fillets or steaks for 3 servings. Plan to cook fish within 1 to 2 days of purchase.

When coals are covered with a grey ash, spread them evenly in an area slightly wider than the food to be cooked on the grill.

BARBECUE BASICS CONT.

Fish should be buttered before being placed on the grill, and should be brushed well with butter or marinade several times during the cooking process. Steaks or fillets without skin will need more basting than whole fish.

Avoid over-handling the fish during cooking and serving. Cooked fish is delicate and will flake apart easily. Turn only once during cooking. Some fish doesn't even need turning; follow your recipe.

Fish and seafood should be moist and tender with a delicate flavor. It is better to have it slightly under-cooked than overcooked. Fish is done when the flesh is translucent and flakes easily when tested with a fork. Great grilling choices are halibut, tuna, monkfish, trout, salmon, shark and swordfish.

SHELLFISH: Grilling shellfish is easy. Wrap them in foil and place over the coals and you will get a steamed product without much of a smoky taste. Or, you can poke a few holes in the foil to allow some of the smoke to permeate the fish. Shellfish can be cooked a little slower by dividing the ashy white charcoal into 2 small banks along 2 sides of the barbecue bottom. Lay the shellfish in center of the grill away from the direct heat of the charcoal. Place a pan in the center of the barbecue bottom to catch drippings. The fish is cooked partly by the heat, partly by hot smoke. The smoky flavor will be intensified it the grill is covered.

KABOBS: Allow 4 servings per pound of meat or fish, 3 servings per pound of shrimp with shell or chicken with bone. Plan 1 cup vegetable or fruit per person.

Place meat in a marinade in a plastic bag. Chill 2 to 4 hours for fish, seafood or chicken; 6 hours or overnight for lamb, beef or pork, turning at least once.

Start the barbecue 40 minutes before you are ready to cook. When cooking kabobs over charcoal, place skewers at an even heat on an uncovered grill. Turn the skewers frequently for even cooking, whether cooking indoors or out.

When brushing with marinade, remove skewers from over coals to prevent marinade from dripping and causing unnecessary flaming. Total cooking time will be from 10 to 15 minutes, varying with the number of kabobs as well as the type of food you grill.

PARBOILED SPARERIBS

1 side of ribs
1 medium onion, quartered
2 cloves
1 bay leaf
1 celery rib with top
1 teaspoon thyme
1/4 teaspoon freshly ground pepper

Place ribs in a large pot and barely cover with cold water. Add remaining ingredients. Bring to a boil, reduce heat and simmer, covered, 40 to 45 minutes. Drain and cool. Marinate and grill.

PREROASTED RIBS

2/3 cup flour
2 garlic cloves, minced
1 tablespoon paprika
1 teaspoon lemon pepper
Salt
2 racks of beef ribs, about 3 pounds each

Combine flour, garlic, paprika, lemon pepper and salt. Rub uncut ribs with seasoned flour. Place on rack in roaster, rounded side up, and bake in preheated 325-degree oven for 1 to 1 1/2 hours. Remove from oven and allow to cool. Marinate and grill.

LEMONED RIBS

10 pounds spareribs
1 can (12-ounce) vegetable juice cocktail
1 cup chili sauce
1 cup catsup
1/2 cup lemon juice
1/4 cup Dijon mustard
Dash Tabasco
1/4 cup vegetable oil
3 tablespoons Worcestershire sauce
3 tablespoons brown sugar
1 tablespoon grated lemon peel
1 teaspoon salt
1/8 teaspoon pepper

Parboil ribs (See index). Combine remaining ingredients in saucepan, bring to a boil and cook, uncovered for 5 minutes. Separate ribs and dip each into sauce and roast or grill 40 to 45 minutes or until tender; basting frequently and turning to evenly brown. Serves 8 - 10.

CHILI RIBS

8 pounds spareribs
3 cans (8-ounce size) tomato sauce
1/2 cup chicken stock
1/2 cup minced onion
3 tablespoons Worcestershire sauce
3 tablespoons brown sugar, packed
2 tablespoons honey
1 tablespoon lemon juice
2 garlic cloves, crushed
2 teaspoons dry mustard
1/2 teaspoon nutmeg
2 to 3 teaspoons chili powder
1 teaspoon salt

Parboil ribs, (See index for directions). Combine remaining ingredients in saucepan. Bring to a boil; reduce heat and simmer, uncovered for 30 minutes. Brush ribs with sauce and grill for 45 minutes or until tender, basting and turning frequently. Cut ribs into serving portions. Serve with remaining sauce. Serves 8.

Jo and Jan say, "This sauce is excellent for chicken and beef ribs also. We have also done the ribs in the oven. Baste and turn ribs frequently in a 425-degree oven for about 1 hour or until tender."

GINGER SAUCE MARINADE

1/2 cup soy sauce
1/2 cup catsup
1/4 cup chicken stock or water
3 tablespoons brown sugar
2 teaspoons dried ginger

Combine ingredients and pour over meat. Cover and refrigerate overnight, turning once or twice. After removing from marinade, reserve for basting while grilling. Will marinate 6 pounds of ribs.

TERIYAKI SAUCE

1 cup chicken stock
1/2 cup soy sauce
1/2 cup honey
1/2 cup white vinegar
2 garlic cloves, minced
1 teaspoon dried ginger

Combine ingredients and spoon over chicken or ribs. Cover and refrigerate 3 hours or overnight, basting occasionally. Grill or bake as desired. Will marinate 4 pounds.

❖❖

CHINESE RED DIPPING SAUCE

1/2 cup catsup
1/2 cup chili sauce
4 tablespoons horseradish (not creamy
  style)
2 teaspoons lemon juice
Dash of hot pepper sauce

Combine all ingredients and mix well. Serve with ribs, chicken, shrimp or kabobs.

CHINESE MUSTARD DIPPING SAUCE

1/2 cup boiling water
1/2 cup dry mustard
4 teaspoons vegetable oil
1/2 teaspoon salt

Add water to mustard and mix to blend well Stir in oil and salt. Serve with barbecued ribs or chicken. Makes 1 cup.

BOB'S BARBECUE SAUCE

1 pound butter
1 bottle Worcestershire sauce
1/2 cup catsup
1 cup water
1 cup vinegar
2 tablespoons sugar
Salt and Pepper to taste
2 cloves garlic (optional)

Combine ingredients in a saucepan as listed. Heat until sugar melts, stirring constantly. Will baste 12 chickens.

Bob says, "This is an old family recipe from Texas. We halve or quarter the chickens; place on the grill over a low fire and baste with the sauce about every 20 minutes. Cook a 2-pound chicken approximately 1 1/2 to 2 hours."

BILL'S BARBECUE SAUCE

4 tablespoons butter or margarine
1 medium onion, chopped
1 bottle (44 to 48-ounce) catsup
1 1/4 cups brown sugar, firmly packed
5 tablespoons vinegar
1/2 to 2/3 teaspoon garlic powder
1 to 1 1/2 tablespoon chili powder
4 tablespoons mustard
1 tablespoon cumin
1/3 cup Worcestershire sauce
2 1/2 ounces liquid smoke

Saute onion in butter; add rest of ingredients and bring to a slow boil for 8 to 10 minutes. Turn heat to low, cover and simmer for 30 to 40 minutes. Can use immediately or store in refrigerator. Makes about 2 quarts.

Fin and Feather

Fish cooks quickly, so start testing with a fork before the cooking time is up, so you can catch it just as it begins to flake, because it will continue to cook briefly after being removed from heat.

TIP FOR FRYING FISH

• Float a kitchen match on your oil. When match ignites, start frying.

BEER BATTER FISH

1 egg
3/4 cup beer, room temperature
1 cup all-purpose flour
1 teaspoon salt
1/4 teaspoon pepper
1 teaspoon baking powder
1 pound fish fillets
1/4 cup additional flour for dredging
Vegetable oil for frying

Beat egg lightly then beat in the beer. Whisk in the flour, salt, pepper and mix until smooth. Cover and let stand 30 minutes. Just before frying, stir in the baking powder. Pour enough oil in a fryer or deep pan to cover the fish, but not more than two-thirds full because batter will bubble. Heat to 375 degrees. Cut fish into serving pieces and pat dry with paper toweling. Dip into flour, then into batter. Place into hot oil and fry about 3 minutes, or until golden brown and puffy. Be careful to not overcrowd your pan. Remove from pan and drain on paper towels. Serves 4.

FISH COATING

1 cup flour
1/2 cup cornstarch
1 1/2 tablespoons baking powder
1/2 tablespoon soda
1/2 tablespoon vinegar
1/2 tablespoon salt
1 cup water

Combine all dry ingredients in a small bowl. Add water slowly, blending well, until of a medium sauce consistency. Stir until smooth. Makes 2 1/2 cups.

MIKE'S PARMESAN FISH COATING

Milk
1/2 cup Parmesan cheese
1/2 cup bread crumbs
Fish fillets
Lemon pepper
Fresh lemon

Wash and pat dry the fish fillets; dip in milk then in mixture of cheese and bread crumbs. Place under oven broiler for 4 minutes to each side or until fish flakes with a fork. Remove from oven and sprinkle with lemon juice.

Michael says, "I like this coating with orange roughy and it is excellent on catfish."

BASTING MARINADE FOR FISH

1 onion, minced
2 teaspoons parsley, chopped
1 garlic clove, minced
1 teaspoon Worcestershire sauce
1/4 teaspoon dill
1/4 cup butter, melted

Combine ingredients to make a sauce. Brush over fish and use as a baste while broiling. Bastes 2 fish.

FRIED CATFISH

6 small catfish, or fillets
1 teaspoon salt
1/4 teaspoon pepper
2 cups self-rising cornmeal
1 quart peanut oil

Lightly salt and pepper catfish and set aside. Measure cornmeal into a brown paper bag and drop fish into it; shaking bag so fish is completely covered.

Pour oil in a large skillet to half-full level and heat to very hot but not smoking. Place each piece of fish in oil separately and cook on high until fish has reached a golden brown and has floated to the top of the oil. Remove from oil; drain well and keep on paper toweling until ready to serve. Serves 6.

❖❖❖

STOCK FOR POACHING FISH

1 cup white wine
1 cup water
1 bay leaf
1/2 teaspoon crushed black pepper
Sprig of thyme
1/4 cup chopped green onion
1/4 cup chopped celery
1/4 cup chopped parsley
1 garlic clove, crushed
1 tablespoon lemon juice

Combine all ingredients in a large pot; bring to a boil and let simmer for 10 minutes, then strain and proceed with poaching of fish. Makes 2 3/4 cups court bouillon.

CHEF MICHAEL'S METHOD FOR FISH MEUNIERE

Clean your fish well. It may be whole (trout, sole, flounder, perch, etc) or fillet (snapper, red fish, bass, etc.).

Use 2 tablespoons of butter and 1 tablespoon olive oil per 10 to 14 ounces of fish. Dry off fish and flour each portion on all sides. Heat butter and oil until it is hot enough to have lost all its water content. Place the floured fish in the oil and cook each side until it is crispy brown, 4 or 5 minutes on a side is usually enough. Please don't over-cook the fish; it should be moist, not dried out.

Place fish on serving plate but leave the butter-oil in the skillet. Place skillet back on heat and add 1 tablespoon butter per portion into skillet. As this is melting, squeeze 1/4 lemon per portion into skillet with 1/2 tablespoon chopped fresh parsley per portion. Let the ingredients blend well together and cook 30 seconds to 1 minute and pour this sauce over the fish.

GRILLED SWORDFISH

2 1-pound swordfish steaks, 1-inch thick
2 fresh limes
1 bottle (12-ounce) teriyaki sauce

Fire up your coals on the grill about 1/2 hour before cooking the fish; you want coals hot but not flaming. Wash steaks and pat dry. Squeeze limes over both sides. Place steaks in one layer in a shallow dish. Add any remaining lime juice to teriyaki sauce and marinate fish in 8 ounces of sauce for 20 minutes, turning once. Grill 5 to 7 minutes per side; if smaller steaks are used, reduce cooking time. Brush with additional teriyaki sauce once on each side while fish is cooking. Cut steaks in half for serving 4.

LEMON - BROILED FISH FILLETS

2 pounds fish fillets
1/2 cup melted butter
1/4 cup lemon juice
2 teaspoons salt
1/2 teaspoon Worcestershire sauce
1/4 teaspoon pepper
Dash of Tabasco sauce

Combine butter, lemon juice, salt, Worcestershire, pepper and Tabasco. Baste fish with mixture and place on grill, four inches from hot coals for 8 minutes. Baste with remaining sauce; turn and cook 7 to 10 minutes longer, until fish flakes easily when tested with a fork. Serves 6.

Jo and Jan say, "When we grill fish fillets, we really prefer using a hinged broiler rack. You don't have to worry about the fish falling apart when you turn it."

BILL'S BAKED HALIBUT STEAKS

2 pounds halibut steaks
3 tablespoons butter or margarine
1 green pepper, cut into thin strips
1 onion, chopped
1 cup celery, sliced thin
1 teaspoon salt
1/8 teaspoon pepper
3 tomatoes, chopped
1/2 teaspoon oregano leaves
2 garlic cloves, crushed
2 teaspoons chili powder
1/4 cup fresh parsley, minced
1/3 cup sliced ripe olives
1 cup dry red wine

Melt butter or margarine in a heavy skillet; add pepper, onion and celery and saute. Add remaining ingredients, except fish and simmer 10 minutes. Pour half the sauce into a lightly oiled baking dish. Place the steaks over sauce in a single layer and pour remaining sauce over the steaks. Bake for 15 minutes in a preheated 350-degree oven. Serves 4-6.

SHRIMP SAUCE FOR FISH FILLETS

1/4 cup butter or margarine
1 tablespoon minced celery
1 tablespoon minced green onion
1 can shrimp, drained or 4 ounces fresh
   cocktail size
1 teaspoon paprika
1/4 cup flour
2 cups half-and-half
2 tablespoons dry sherry
1 teaspoon dill
Salt and pepper to taste

Melt butter in a saucepan and saute celery and onion. Finely mince 1 tablespoon shrimp and add to butter mixture. Saute for 2 minutes; add paprika, stir and remove from heat. Add flour, whisk to blend; return to heat and cook several more minutes. Stir in cream, sherry, dill and seasonings. Reserve a few shrimp for garnish, then chop remaining shrimp and stir into thickened sauce. Spoon over cooked fish fillets. Makes about 2 1/2 cups.

CAMPFIRE TROUT

For cooking over the open fire you can use vegetable oil, butter or bacon grease. You can also render out pork fat.

Clean your fish, wash and pat dry. Roll in seasoned flour; it may be a combination of flour and cornmeal. Just a bit of salt and a touch of dill or marjoram and pepper can be added.

Heat oil in a heavy skillet; add fish and cook over medium coals. You want to cook it slowly and have the outside crispy and golden. Turn the fish often so it does not stick to the pan.

CHRIS' GRILLED TROUT

Trout
Italian or French Salad Dressing

Prepare coals on your broiler. Clean fish, wash and pat dry. Brush fish inside and out with dressing. Place fish in an oiled, hinged, mesh grill. Baste fish frequently with dressing and turn often. Grilling time will be 8 to 12 minutes, depending upon the size of the fish.

ISLAND TROUT

1 pound trout fillets
1/2 cup sesame seeds, toasted to a light
  brown
3 green onions and tops, sliced
2 tablespoons vegetable oil
1/4 cup soy sauce
1 garlic clove, crushed
1 teaspoon fresh ginger root, minced

Combine onions, oil, soy sauce, garlic and ginger in a bowl and let stand at least 15 minutes.

Preheat broiler. Line broiler pan with foil; lightly oil the foil. Place sesame seeds in a flat dish. Dip the fish in the soy mixture then in the seeds; place on foil. Fillets cook very fast; time depends on thickness. If thick, will need to be turned; thin do not. Serves 2.

BROILED SHRIMP

2 pounds jumbo shrimp
1/4 cup flour
1/4 cup olive oil
1/4 cup melted butter
2 tablespoons minced garlic
4 tablespoons minced parsley
1 cup Drawn Butter Sauce

DRAWN BUTTER SAUCE:
4 tablespoons butter
2 tablespoons flour
1 teaspoon lemon juice
Fresh ground black pepper
1 cup hot water

Shell shrimp, leaving tails on. Dry, dust with flour. Stir oil and butter into flat baking dish; place shrimp in dish, broil at medium heat for 8 minutes. Add garlic and parsley to Drawn Butter Sauce. Pour over shrimp; stir until shrimp are coated. Broil for 2 minutes and serve immediately. Serves 6.

Melt 2 tablespoons butter; add flour, lemon juice and pepper. Stir until smooth; add water, bring to a boil, stirring constantly. Reduce heat and cook 5 minutes. Add remaining 2 tablespoons butter and stir until melted.

SEAFOOD KABOBS

1 pound shrimp and/or scallops
1 can (13 1/2-ounce) pineapple chunks,
  drained
1 can (4-ounce) button mushrooms, drained
1 green pepper, cut in 1-inch squares
1/4 cup butter, melted
1/4 cup lemon juice
1/4 cup parsley, chopped
1/4 cup soy sauce
1/2 teaspoon salt
Dash pepper

Combine all ingredients in a large bowl and blend well. Let marinate about 30 minutes, stirring occasionally. Using long skewers, alternate shrimp and/or scallops and pineapple, mushrooms, and green peppers until skewers are filled. Broil 4 inches from hot coals for 5 minutes; baste with sauce, turn and cook 5 to 7 minutes longer. Serves 6.

GRILLED WHOLE SALMON

1 whole salmon, 2 to 4 pounds
1 large onion, cut into rings
Sprigs of fresh parsley
Dill, Fennel (optional)
Melted margarine or cooking oil
Salt and pepper

Thaw fish if frozen. Remove fins and leave tail on. Slash fish on both sides at 3-inch intervals. Insert rings of onion and sprigs of parsley alternately in slashes. Brush with margarine or oil, sprinkle with seasonings and wrap in foil. Broil over moderate heat for 10 to 15 minutes on each side or until fish flakes. Delicious served with Lemon Dill Sauce (See index).

BLACKENED FISH

4 fresh or frozen fillets (pompano, pollock, catfish)
1/2 teaspoon onion powder
1/2 teaspoon garlic salt
1/2 teaspoon lemon pepper
1/2 teaspoon ground red pepper
1/2 teaspoon dried basil, crushed
1/4 teaspoon dried thyme, crushed
1/8 teaspoon ground sage
1/4 cup margarine, melted

Thaw fish if frozen, wash and pat dry. Combine remaining ingredients except margarine in a small bowl. Brush fillets on both sides with seasonings. Place a cast iron skillet directly on hot coals. Heat the skillet for 5 minutes. Add fish; drizzle with margarine. Grill until blackened; turn fish, repeat. Serves 4.

Jan and Jo say, If the fillets are different sizes, you may have to remove the smaller ones and cook the larger ones a bit longer."

HOW TO EAT A WHOLE MAINE LOBSTER
Follow the Numbers

1. Twist off claws at dotted line.

2. Crack open claws with nutcracker and remove meat.

3. Twist off tail at dotted line.

4. Twist off tail flippers and discard.

5. Remove meat from tail by inserting fork or fingers where flippers were broken off and push meat out.

6. Unhinge back shell from theabody. The liver is considered quite a delicacy and is located in the back.

7. Crack the remaining part of the body along the dotted line and remove meat with a small fork.

8. Remove small claws; there is meat inside which you can suck out like if using a straw. Lobster meat is delicious dipped in melted butter, and try it cold in salads.

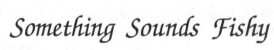

Something Sounds Fishy

SIMPLE BUTTER BASTE

1/4 cup butter or margarine, melted
Lemon juice, white wine, fresh herbs

Add lemon juice, wine, herbs of your choice to melted butter and spread on fish as it is broiling.

BARBECUE MARINADE

1/4 cup salad oil
1/4 cup vinegar
2 tablespoons brown sugar
1 can tomato sauce
1 tablespoon Worcestershire sauce
1/2 teaspoon garlic powder
1/8 teaspoon pepper

Combine ingredients and marinate fish in mixture for 2 hours, turning occasionally. For a milder flavor, just baste on fish as it is cooking.

HERB - WINE MARINADE

1 cup dry white wine
1/4 cup lemon juice
2 tablespoons white wine vinegar
2 garlic cloves, crushed
1 teaspoon salt
1 teaspoon tarragon
2 tablespoons butter, melted (can use salad oil)

Combine all ingredients and bring to a simmer. Remove from heat, cover and let stand for 1 hour. Pour into a dish, place fish in marinade, cover and chill 1 hour, turning once.

HERB - BUTTER SAUCE

1/4 cup soft butter or margarine
3 tablespoons white wine
1/2 teaspoon salt
Dash cayenne pepper
1 tablespoon chopped parsley
2 tablespoons chopped chives
1 teaspoon dill

Beat butter until creamy. Gradually stir in wine then rest of ingredients. Makes 1/2 cup.

Jo and Jan say, "This is a nice sauce for any seafood, whether it is broiled or fried fish or shellfish such as shrimp, scallops, or lobster tails."

LEMON DILL SAUCE

2 egg yolks
2 1/2 tablespoons lemon juice
1/8 teaspoon white pepper
1/4 teaspoon dill weed
1/2 cup butter, melted

Place egg yolks, lemon juice, pepper and dill in a blender and process for 10 seconds. Pour melted butter slowly into blended mixture while processing at high speed. Serve warm over fish. Makes 3/4 cup.

Jo and Jan say, "You might like to substitute chicken broth for the melted butter."

CHUCK'S TUNA CASSEROLE

1 can (6 1/2-ounce) tuna
1 can cream of mushroom or chicken soup
1 soup can milk
1 cup celery, thinly sliced
1/2 cup minced onion
1/4 pound cashew nuts
1 can (5 1/2-ounce) Chow Mein noodles

Combine all ingredients, reserving some of noodles to sprinkle on top. Spoon into casserole dish and top with noodles. Bake in preheated 350-degree oven for 40 minutes. Serves 4 - 6.

GRANDPA'S BREAKFAST CASSEROLE

1 package (8-ounce) Crescent rolls
1 package (10-ounce) Monterey Jack cheese
2 cups ham, chopped, diced or shredded
10 eggs
1 cup half-and-half

Press rolls into bottom of 9 x 13 x 2-inch casserole. Slice the cheese and lay over the rolls. Spread ham over cheese. Beat eggs, add half-and-half. Pour slowly over other ingredients. Place the casserole in a pre-heated 350-degree oven and bake for 45 minutes. Serves 8 - 10.

Glenn says, "This is a full meal; however, I find that a fruit bowl goes very well with this casserole."

JACK'S SMOKED TURKEY

1 turkey (12 pounds)
1 stick butter, melted
1 cup red wine
1 cup cooking oil
2 tablespoons cracked pepper
1 tablespoon garlic salt
2 tablespoons Worcestershire sauce
Juice of 2 or 3 lemons
2 onions, cut into eighths
Water
1 cup chopped celery with leaves
4 cups soaked hickory or mesquite chips
10 pounds charcoal briquettes.

Prepare coals in smoker (See instructions, Summer and Smoker). If using frozen turkey, defrost tightly wrapped in plastic, in refrigerator 24 to 36 hours. Whether using fresh or frozen turkey, remove giblets and reserve for other use. Rinse turkey inside and out under cold water. Pat dry with paper toweling.

Combine melted butter, wine, oil, pepper, garlic powder, Worcestershire sauce and lemon juice. Rub turkey with mixture inside and out; sprinkle cavity with salt and pepper. Fill with onions and celery; truss loosely.

Rub outside of turkey; place on smoker rack. Pour butter, wine mixture in water pan of smoker and add water to fill the pan. You can add more wine if you prefer.

Close smoker and smoke turkey until it is a deep brown and an instant-reading thermometer inserted into the thickest part of the thigh near the bone registers 170 degrees; about 7 or 8 hours. Allow to stand 10 to 20 minutes before carving. Serve warm or cold.

The appearance of smoked turkey is different than oven roasted. The meat closest to the skin and throughout may have a rose color.

This recipe can be used with chickens (See Jack's Chicken For A Mob; index) or Rock Cornish hens. Smoke chicken 4 to 5 hours, hens 2 to 3 hours.

SESAME FRIED CHICKEN

2 chickens (3-pounds each) quartered
4 tablespoons sesame seeds
11/4 cups flour
1 teaspoon poultry seasoning
2/3 cup evaporated milk
1/2 teaspoon paprika
11/2 teaspoons salt
Ground black pepper
1/2 cup butter
1/2 cup oil

Combine sesame seeds, flour, poultry seasoning, paprika, salt and pepper. Dip chicken quarters into milk, then roll them in the sesame seed mixture. Saute chicken in combined butter and oil for 30 minutes or until golden brown and tender, turning frequently. Serves 6 - 8.

JACK'S ELEGANT GLAZED CHICKEN BREASTS

2 chicken breasts, halved, deboned and
    skinned
1/3 cup margarine
1 teaspoon garlic powder
Pepper to taste
1 package chicken gravy mix
1/2 to 1 teaspoon dried tarragon
6 large mushrooms, sliced
1/3 cup white wine

Melt margarine; add garlic powder and stir to mix well. Add chicken breasts and pepper and lightly brown on each side. While chicken is cooking, prepare gravy according to package directions, adding the tarragon.

When chicken is done, remove from skillet, add wine, turn up the heat and stir to de-glaze mixture in skillet. Add chicken gravy and bring to a boil. Add mushrooms and chicken to skillet and spoon sauce over chicken, watching mushrooms so they do not over-cook. To serve, place chicken on plates, top with a glaze of sauce and sliced mushrooms. Serves 4.

The Wild Life

CHRIS' HERB - BAKED PRAIRIE CHICKEN

1 prairie chicken
1/4 cup flour
1/2 teaspoon salt
1/4 teaspoon pepper
1/2 teaspoon savory
1/4 cup milk
Dash of thyme
Dash of basil
1 strip bacon
1 tablespoon butter or margarine

Clean prairie chicken; set aside while combining flour, salt, pepper and savory. Dip bird in milk and dredge in flour mixture. Sprinkle thyme and basil on bacon strip; roll it up and insert in the bird's cavity, close with tooth picks. Melt butter in skillet and brown the bird. Remove and place in baking dish, cover and bake in preheated 325-degree oven for 1 hour or until tender; checking occasionally if skin starts to look dry. If so, baste with some melted butter or margarine. Serves 2 - 4.

CAPON STUFFING

5 packages (10-ounce size) frozen chopped
   spinach
2 packages (8-ounce size) cream cheese,
   softened
1 tablespoon olive oil
3 eggs
1 cup grated Parmesan cheese
3/4 cup fresh bread crumbs
1 medium onion, chopped and sauteed
Salt and Pepper
Nutmeg (optional)

Thaw spinach, drain thoroughly and squeeze dry. Combine with other ingredients in a large bowl and mix well. Stuff capon and roast. If you prefer not to stuff the bird, place stuffing in a greased souffle dish, dot with butter and bake in a preheated 350-degree oven for 30 to 45 minutes. Stuffing will fill a 6 to 8 pound bird. Serves 8 - 10.

ROCK CORNISH HENS

1 cup uncooked wild rice
6 tablespoons butter
1/2 cup chopped onion
1/2 pound fresh mushrooms, sliced
1 1/2 cups cooked ham, chopped
1/2 teaspoon salt
1/2 teaspoon marjoram
1/2 teaspoon thyme
6 Rock Cornish game hens
1 teaspoon salt
6 slices bacon
2 tablespoons butter
SAUCE:
Juice of 4 large oranges
Rind of 1 orange
1 tablespoon cornstarch
2 tablespoons brown sugar
2 tablespoons granulated sugar

Wash and cook rice according to package directions and drain. Melt butter in medium size skillet and saute onion, mushrooms and ham for 5 minutes. Mix with rice; add salt, marjoram and thyme. Sprinkle cavities of hens with salt; stuff with rice mixture and truss. Lay 2 half slices of bacon over each bird and roast uncovered, in a preheated 350-degree oven for 1 to 1 1/2 hours, or until tender. Baste occasionally with pan drippings to which you have added 2 tablespoons butter.

While hens are baking, prepare sauce. Combine ingredients and simmer until clear and thickened, about 10 minutes. Spoon sauce over hens before serving. Serves 6.

❖❖❖

STOVE TOP SQUAB

3 tablespoons butter or margarine
12 to 15 pearl onions
3/4 cup chopped carrots
3/4 cup chopped celery
4 squab
2 tablespoons butter or margarine
4 tablespoons flour
4 tablespoons chopped, fresh parsley
2 tablespoons margarine
2 bay leaves
1 teaspoon thyme
Salt and pepper to taste
2 cups red wine
2 cups chicken stock
Brandy to taste
1/2 pound sauteed mushrooms

Melt butter in small skillet and saute onions, carrots and celery. In a separate skillet melt 2 tablespoons butter and brown birds. Remove squab and add flour, parsley, margarine, bay leaves, thyme, salt and pepper. Mix well; combine mixtures and add 2 cups red wine and chicken stock. Turn into a deep pot; add squab, cook, covered, on top of stove for 1 hour. Thicken sauce with a bit of flour; add brandy to taste and mushrooms. Serves 4 (1 bird per person).

BAKED DOVE

12 doves, cleaned
Salt and pepper
Flour
6 tablespoons butter
1 cup chopped celery
1 cup chopped onion
1/2 teaspoon garlic juice
1 tablespoon Worcestershire sauce
2 cups beef consomme
1/2 cup red wine
8 to 10 fresh mushrooms

Season doves with salt and pepper and dust with flour. Melt butter in a large heavy skillet. Add doves and brown slowly on all sides over medium heat. Transfer to a large Dutch oven or casserole. Add celery, onion, garlic juice, Worcestershire sauce and consomme to the casserole. Cover and bake in a preheated 350-degree oven for 2 hours. During the last 1/2 hour of cooking, add wine and mushrooms. Serves 6 - 8.

PHEASANT WITH WINE SAUCE

1 cup butter
4 garlic cloves, crushed
4 pheasants, cleaned
2 onions, quartered
4 sticks celery
1/4 cup Worcestershire sauce
Pinch of dried whole leaf thyme
2 cans (10-ounce size) cream of mushroom
  soup
1 cup dry Sherry
1/2 cup dry red wine

Melt butter; add garlic and saute. Add pheasant and brown lightly. Stuff pheasant with onion and celery (dividing vegetables among the birds). Place pheasants breast side down in a covered casserole with the pan juices, and bake in a preheated 350-degree oven for 15 minutes. Uncover casserole and sprinkle birds with Worcestershire sauce and thyme. Again cover and bake another 15 minutes. In a mixing bowl, combine the soup, Sherry and wine. Remove birds from oven and baste with the soup mixture; cover and return to oven. Continue to bake the pheasant for about another hour, basting often with the soup mixture and pan juices. Serves 8 - 10.

❖❖❖

KANSAS JAYHAWKERS' QUAIL

8 tablespoons butter
24 quail, cleaned and left whole
1/2 cup bourbon, warmed
1/2 cup sherry
Salt and pepper to taste
1 cup chicken stock
2 cups heavy cream

Melt half the butter in a large skillet over moderately high heat. Place 6 or 7 quail in butter, do not let the touch. Brown on all sides; remove from skillet and repeat with remaining birds, using the same butter. When all have been browned, return all to skillet and pour in warm bourbon and sherry; ignite. When flame burns out, salt and pepper the birds and add chicken stock. Cover and simmer on low for 20 minutes. When birds are tender, add cream; simmer uncovered, for 5 more minutes. Taste and adjust seasonings. Serves 6 - 8.

Jo and Jan say, "This is straight from the Jayhawks' beak; this is a popular fall and winter brunch dish. The guys who love to hunt even like to cook, too."

DADDY'S ROAST QUAIL

8 quail
4 tablespoons butter
Flour
Salt and pepper
2 cans golden mushroom soup
1 can chicken rice soup
1/2 cup sherry
1 bunch green onions, sliced
1 can (4-ounce) mushrooms

Roll quail in seasoned flour. Melt butter in skillet and saute birds until golden brown; remove to a casserole. Add 1 can mushroom soup and chicken rice soup to skillet drippings. Stir in sherry and green onions. Heat and pour over birds. Cover pan and bake 2 to 2 1/2 hours.

Remove quail to platter, add second can of mushroom soup and if necessary, thin with a little more sherry until mixture is the right consistency for gravy. Serve with wild rice and a tossed salad. Serves 4.

BAKED WILD TURKEY

1 wild turkey (12-16 pounds)
Salt and pepper
Garlic salt
Cayenne pepper
2 medium onions, quartered
2 bell peppers, quartered
4 ribs celery
3 garlic cloves, slivered
Margarine, softened

Prepare turkey the day before baking. Wash turkey thoroughly and wipe dry. Season cavity with salt and pepper, garlic salt and cayenne pepper; stuff with onions, bell peppers, celery, and garlic. Season outside of bird with salt, pepper and garlic salt rubbing the skin well.

Cover entire bird with margarine and re-season if necessary. Place bird in a cooking bag and refrigerate until ready to bake.

With turkey in cooking bag, place in a shallow baking pan, breast up in preheated 400-degree oven. Bake for 1 hour. Check to see if bird is browning. If not, continue baking for 1/2 hour more or until bird is brown. Reduce temperature to 300 degrees and continue baking with bag closed for 1 to 2 more hours, depending on size of bird. Test for doneness by checking to see if turkey leg starts to separate from body. At this point turkey is done and should be removed from bag. Reserve gravy; remove turkey to serving platter and cover loosely with foil. Spoon gravy over dressing and carved turkey. Serves 10 - 12.

SAM'S GRILLED WILD DUCK

1 cup soy sauce
1 cup oil
1 garlic clove, crushed
1 1/2 tablespoons Liquid Smoke
Salt and pepper
1/2 teaspoon Worcestershire sauce
1/4 teaspoon dry mustard
Breasts of 8 wild ducks (mallards are best) split, boned and skinned, giving you 16 pieces

Combine all ingredients in a large bowl; add duck breasts, turning to coat completely. Cover and refrigerate overnight if possible, at least 8 hours.

Prepare coals in grill and when they are moderately hot, add breasts to grill. Cook for 3 1/2 to 4 minutes to a side, basting constantly with marinade. Breasts should be pink inside. Serve whole or sliced. Serves 6 - 8.

GAME SEASONING BLEND

1 teaspoon dried marjoram, crumbled
1 teaspoon dried thyme, crumbled
1/2 teaspoon crushed bay leaf
3/4 teaspoon cayenne pepper
1 tablespoon whole white peppercorns
1 1/2 teaspoons dry mustard
1/2 teaspoon ground cloves
1 teaspoon ground ginger
1 teaspoon nutmeg, freshly grated
3/4 teaspoon juniper berries

Crush all ingredients to a powder and store in an airtight container in a cool, dry place. Use 2 teaspoons of seasoning per pound of game. Makes 1/2 cup.

CHEF MIKE'S VENISON ROAST

Marinade for Red Meat (See index Spicy Beef Tenderloin)
2-pound venison roast
3 tablespoons olive oil
Salt and pepper to taste
1 onion, sliced
1 carrot, chopped
1 stalk celery, chopped
1 bay leaf, crumbled
2 cups veal stock (chicken or beef can be used)
1 bottle (8-ounce) chestnuts, drained
1/2 cup heavy cream
3 tablespoons butter

Prepare marinade and marinate roast for 24 hours. Remove meat from marinade; dry completely and save marinade.

Measure olive oil in roasting pan. Place on top of stove, turn on high and when oil is hot, brown roast on all sides. Salt and pepper to taste. Reduce heat and place vegetables and bay leaf in pan to saute until tender. Add 1 1/2 cups stock to pan and stir. Cover and bake in preheated 475-degree oven for 20 minutes per 2 pounds of meat. For best results, use a meat thermometer.

Remove roast to a warm place; strain liquid and discard vegetables. Place 1/2 cup stock to pan, deglace bottom of pan; pour this stock in a saucepan along with strained cooking stock.

Puree drained chestnuts in blender with 1 cup of the strained stock. Bring remaining stock to a boil in saucepan and reduce it a little. Add pureed chestnuts to pan and continue to boil for 1 or 2 minutes. Add heavy cream and return to a slow boil for 4 or 5 more minutes. Slice roast; remove saucepan from heat; stir in butter and 2 tablespoons of reserved marinade; adjust salt and pepper. Mix well and serve over sliced roast. Serves 6 - 8.

JIM'S VENISON JERKY

1 1/2 pounds venison round steak (trimmed
   of all fat)
1 teaspoon seasoned salt
1/2 teaspoon garlic powder
1/2 teaspoon pepper
1 teaspoon onion powder
1/4 cup Worcestershire sauce
1/4 cup soy sauce

Slice meat, along the grain, into 18 1/4-inch strips. If meat is chilled, it is easier to thinly slice. Combine seasonings and sauces and coat the bottom of a Pyrex dish. Place one layer of meat in sauce; brush with more sauce. Cover with more strips of meat and brush on rest of sauce. Marinate meat overnight in the refrigerator.

Place foil on bottom of your oven and preheat oven to 140 degrees. Lay strips of meat in a single layer on oven racks. Dry meat in oven for 6 to 8 hours or until it has reached the desired degree of chewiness. Store in airtight containers. Makes about 1/2 pound.

Jim says, "This same procedure can be done with flank steak to make Beef Jerky."

MARINATED GRILLED VENISON WITH WINE SAUCE

4 pounds venison filet, cut into 1 - 1 1/2-inch
   pieces
1 cup olive oil
1 cup vegetable oil
3 tablespoons soy sauce
3 tablespoons lemon juice
1 tablespoon seasoned salt
1 tablespoon paprika
2 garlic cloves, crushed
2 tablespoons dried tarragon
1 cup white wine
1 stick butter or margarine, melted

Combine oils, soy sauce, lemon juice, salt, paprika, garlic and tarragon. Mix well and pour over meat in a large glass or nonmetallic bowl. Cover and marinate in refrigerator overnight. Remove meat and reserve marinade. Place meat on barbecue grill over low heat. Baste frequently with marinade for approximately 20 minutes. Drippings will smoke and perhaps flame; this is desirable in the flavor. Transfer meat to a large shallow baking dish; add wine and melted butter. Bake in a preheated 250-degree oven for 15 minutes. Serves 6 - 8.

Jan and Jo say, "If you do not use venison filet, you might want to add 1 tablespoon meat tenderizer to the marinade ingredients. This is an excellent dish to accompany with wild rice."

The Closing

ROY'S BREAD PUDDING

1 cup warm water
1 cup Carnation Coffee Mate
3 medium eggs
1/4 cup margarine
1/2 cup sugar
1 teaspoon vanilla
1/4 teaspoon salt
4 slices white bread
1/4 cup raisins
Cinnamon

In small mixing bowl, combine first two ingredients until free of any lumps. Add margarine and beat 30 seconds; add eggs and beat 1 minute. Add sugar, vanilla and salt. In a non-greased casserole place 1 1/2 cups of mixture and sprinkle with raisins; then add bread cut in 1-inch squares. Toss lightly and add remaining mixture, pouring evenly over bread and sprinkle lightly with cinnamon. Bake in preheated 325-degree oven 40 to 45 minutes. Remove and cool slightly; top with warm Nutmeg Sauce (See index). Serves 6.

❖❖

ROY'S NUTMEG SAUCE

1/2 cup sugar
1 tablespoon cornstarch
1/2 teaspoon nutmeg
1 cup milk
1/4 cup margarine
1 teaspoon vanilla

In a small saucepan combine sugar, cornstarch and nutmeg. Stir in milk and margarine; cook over medium heat until mixture starts to thicken slightly. Add vanilla and stir constantly until mixture becomes thick; do not boil. Remove from heat and pour over bread pudding. Makes 1 1/3 cups.

FUZZY NAVEL CAKE

1 package (2-layer size) yellow cake mix
1/2 cup vegetable oil
1 package (5 1/2-ounce) instant vanilla
  pudding mix
4 eggs
3/4 cup peach schnapps
1/2 cup orange juice
1/2 teaspoon orange extract
GLAZE:
4 tablespoons peach schnapps
2 tablespoons orange juice
1 cup confectioners' sugar, sifted

Combine all cake ingredients in large mixing bowl and blend thoroughly with electric mixer. Pour into lightly greased and floured 9 1/2-inch or 10-inch tube pan. Bake in preheated 350-degree oven for 45 to 50 minutes or until cake springs back when lightly touched.

To prepare Glaze, combine schnapps, juice and sugar in a small bowl. When cake is done, but still warm, poke holes in cake with a bamboo skewer or long wooden pick and pour Glaze mixture over. Allow cake to cool in pan at least 2 hours before removing. Serves 12 - 16.

ROY'S OATMEAL COOKIES

1 cup ground raisins
1 cup shortening
1 cup brown sugar, packed
1 cup white sugar
2 eggs
2 teaspoons vanilla
2 cups flour
1 teaspoon salt
2 teaspoons soda
2 cups quick rolled oats

Grind raisins in food grinder or food processor. Combine shortening, brown sugar, white sugar and eggs, blending thoroughly; stir in ground raisins, vanilla, flour, salt, soda and oats. Drop from teaspoon onto greased cookie sheets. Bake in preheated 375-degree oven for 8 to 10 minutes; cool on racks. Makes 4 dozen.

Roy says, "Grinding the raisins is the great secret to these cookies."

CRAIG'S DEATH BY CHOCOLATE

1 family-size box brownie mix
3 packages (3.5-ounce size) Jell-O Chocolate
  Mousse
8 Skor or Heath bars
1 carton (16-ounce) Cool Whip

Make brownies according to directions in a 9 x 13-inch pan. Do not frost. Cool and break into small pieces. Break up candy bars into small pieces. Prepare mousse according to package directions (you do not have to let it sit).

In a large, glass, straight-edged bowl, layer 1/2 brownies, 1/2 chocolate mousse, 1/2 broken candy bars and 1/2 Cool Whip. Repeat layers using other half of all ingredients. Serves 10 - 12.

Craig says, "Before breaking up the brownies, you can pierce them with a fork and pour Kahlua or a mixture of strong coffee (4 tablespoons) and sugar (1 teaspoon) over them."

❖❖

CRAIG'S FRESH STRAWBERRY CREAM CHEESE PIE

1 1/2 pounds fresh strawberries
1 package (8-ounce) cream cheese
1 tablespoon sugar
1 Keebler prepared cookie crust
3 tablespoons cornstarch
1 cup sugar
1 cup boiling water
1/2 of 1 package (3-ounce) strawberry gelatin
Cool Whip (Garnish)

Soften cream cheese and stir in sugar to sweeten. Spread in bottom of cookie crust. Wash, hull and halve strawberries. Place berries in crust, standing upright. (Line outside of shell with the back-sides of the berries). Mix cornstarch and sugar together; add boiling water and cook until mixture is clear and thick, stirring frequently or it will burn. Remove from heat and stir in 1/2 package of gelatin. When mixture cools, pour over strawberries. Garnish with Cool Whip if desired.

GOOEY BUTTER CAKE

1 box yellow cake mix
1 stick butter, melted
2 eggs
TOP LAYER:
2 eggs
1 package (8-ounce) cream cheese, softened
1 box confectioners' sugar

Mix cake mix, melted butter and eggs. Spread batter in a greased 9 x 13-inch baking pan. Spread with Top Layer.

Beat eggs, cream cheese and confectioners' sugar with mixer until smooth. Pour over bottom layer and bake in preheated 350-degree oven for 30 minutes or until top is golden brown.

Jo and Jan say, "Try slicing some fresh fruit; peaches, apples, pears, plums, or berries over the bottom layer before spreading on the top layer. When it bakes, it will be a sweet surprise."

RICK'S PUMPKIN BROWNIES

1 1/4 cups oil
2 cups all-purpose flour
2 cups sugar
1 can (29-ounce) pumpkin
4 eggs
2 teaspoons baking powder
2 teaspoons baking soda
1 teaspoon salt
4 teaspoons cinnamon
ICING
1/2 stick butter
1 package (8-ounce) cream cheese
1 teaspoon vanilla
1 package (16-ounce) confectioners' sugar
1/2 cup chopped nuts

Mix ingredients and pour into 2 (9 x 13-inch) pans. Bake in preheated 350-degree oven for 25 minutes.

Melt butter, add cream cheese and other ingredients. Ice brownies while still hot.

◆◆

MICHAEL'S CRUNCHY CHOCOLATE CHIPPERS

2 sticks plus
2 tablespoons unsalted butter
1 1/2 cups light brown sugar, packed
2 eggs
4 teaspoons vanilla
2 cups flour
1 teaspoon soda
1 teaspoon salt
1/2 teaspoon baking powder
1 1/2 cups granola
2 cups pecans, coarsely chopped
3 cups chocolate chips

In large electric mixer bowl cream butter and sugar until smooth. Add eggs and vanilla; beat on high for 3 minutes. Combine flour, soda, salt and baking powder; mix well and stir in granola, nuts and chocolate chips. Drop batter by tablespoonsful on lightly greased cookie sheet about 2 inches apart. Bake in preheated 350-degree oven for 9 to 10 minutes depending on your oven. Remove and cool on wire rack or newspaper that has been spread on your counter. Eat! Makes 70 - 80 cookies.

Jan says, "Oh, the shades of his mother and his idea of how to cool the cookies!"

GRANDMA BILL'S BROWNIES

1/2 cup shortening (Bill recommends butter flavored Crisco)
1 square (1 ounce) unsweetened baking chocolate
3/4 cup all-purpose flour
1/2 teaspoon (heaping) baking powder
1/2 teaspoon salt
2 large eggs
1 cup sugar
1 teaspoon (overfull) vanilla
1 cup (rounded) nuts

Melt shortening and chocolate together; set aside to cool. Sift flour, baking powder and salt together. Beat eggs until light in color and continue beating as the sugar is added. Beat slowly as the chocolate and shortening mixture is added; continue beating until well blended. Add the flour mixture slowly, beating until well blended; add the vanilla.

Add nuts and pour batter into a buttered 8-inch square pan; spread mixture evenly in pan. Bake in preheated 350-degree oven for 30 to 35 minutes. Cool and frost with chocolate icing (Bill uses Betty Crocker creamy deluxe milk chocolate). Cool and cut into squares. Enjoy!

Jo says, "My friend Rustee tells me that Bill is such a good cook and does all the baking. So when the grandchildren come to visit, guess who is in the kitchen? Grandma Bill!"

RALPH'S MICROWAVE CHOCOLATE PUDDING CAKE

3 cups water
2 tablespoons margarine, melted
1 cup flour
1/2 teaspoon baking soda
1 teaspoon vanilla
1/4 teaspoon salt
1/2 cup buttermilk
1/2 cup chopped pecans
1 1/2 cups sugar, divided
10 tablespoons baking cocoa, divided

Bring water to a boil in saucepan. Meanwhile, combine flour, soda, salt, vanilla and buttermilk. Stir in 3/4 cup sugar and 3 tablespoons cocoa; add nuts and stir. When water boils, stir in remaining 3/4 cup sugar, 7 tablespoons cocoa and bring to a boil again. Pour into a 9 x 13-inch glass baking dish; spoon batter into hot liquid. Microwave on MED (50% power) for 6 minutes. Turn dish; microwave on HIGH for 5 to 7 minutes, until cake is done. Serve warm with sauce spooned over cake.

If you aren't concerned about cholesterol, use butter instead of margarine; it makes a richer sauce. Serves 8 - 10.

❖❖

RICK'S NUT CLUSTER COOKIES

1 cup sugar
1 stick butter
2 eggs
1 teaspoon vanilla
3 squares melted unsweetened chocolate
1 1/2 cups flour
1/2 teaspoon baking powder
1/2 cup pecans
1 teaspoon salt

Cream together butter and sugar. Add eggs and vanilla; beat until fluffy. Stir in chocolate; add flour, baking powder and salt. Mix well, then add nuts. Drop by teaspoonful onto cookie sheet and bake at 350 degrees for 8 to 10 minutes.

LARRY'S CHOCOLATE RUM STRIPPED PIE

1 package (12-ounce) semi-sweet chocolate
    morsels
1 cup milk
1/4 cup sugar
1 envelope unflavored gelatin
1/2 teaspoon salt
2 eggs, separated
1/3 cup rum
1/2 cup sugar
2 cups heavy cream
4 tablespoons confectioners' sugar
2 9-inch pie shells, baked or 2 graham
    crackers shells

Combine in top of double broiler over hot (not boiling) water the chocolate morsels, milk, 1/4 cup sugar, gelatin and salt. Heat until gelatin is dissolved and mixture is smooth. Quickly beat in egg yolks and continue cooking for 2 minutes, stirring constantly. Remove from heat; stir in rum. Chill in refrigerator until completely cooled and slightly thickened (about 1 1/2 to 2 hours).

In a small bowl, beat egg whites until frothy. Gradually beat in 1/2 cup sugar and continue beating until stiff, glossy peaks form. Fold into cooled chocolate mixture; set aside.

In another small bowl, combine heavy cream and confectioners' sugar; beat until stiff peaks form . Pour the chocolate mixture evenly into the 2 pie shells. Divide the whipped cream and spread over the chocolate mixture in each shell. Chill until firm (at least 1 hour). Serves 16.

Larry says; "This makes 2 of the best chocolate pies you will ever eat!"

LARRY'S KENTUCKY COLONEL BOURBON BALLS

1 cup chopped pecans
3 jiggers bourbon
1 box (1 pound) confectioners' sugar
1 stick butter or margarine, softened
1 package (12-ounce) semi-sweet chocolate
    morsels
1/3 block paraffin

Soak chopped nuts in the bourbon overnight in a small bowl. Mix sugar, nuts and butter; form into small balls about 3/4 to 1 inch in diameter and freeze.

Melt chocolate morsels and paraffin in the top of a double boiler. Using a spoon, dip each frozen ball into the chocolate mixture. Line a cookie sheet with wax paper and drop balls on paper. Return to the freezer for about 1 hour. They are now ready for great eating and snacking. Makes 36 to 48.

Larry says, "Be careful not to overheat the chocolate and also leave balls frozen until ready to serve, as they melt at room temperature after a while."

❖❖❖

STEVE'S CHOCOLATE PEANUT BUTTER PIE

1 baked pie shell (8-inch pie)
Peanut butter
1 package (3 1/8-ounce size) chocolate
   pudding and pie filling mix
Whipped cream

Spread peanut butter over baked and cooled pie shell; thickness as you desire. Prepare chocolate pudding according to package directions. Cool and pour over peanut butter layer. Chill until ready to serve. Spread whipped cream over top of pie before serving. Serves 8.

Steve says, "This will remind you of your favorite peanut butter cups."

VIENNESE COFFEE

1 gallon vanilla ice cream
2 cups strong black coffee
2 cups hot milk
Brandy or coffee liqueur to taste

Mound ice cream balls in a large bowl; place in freezer until serving time. Combine coffee and milk; bring bowl of ice cream balls to table and carefully pour coffee mixture over ice cream. Stir gently and when the hot coffee mixture has melted the ice cream, add the brandy or liqueur. Makes 20 cups.

The Locker Room

MAKING THE PERFECT COCKTAIL

If you need to brush up on making that "perfect cocktail" let us give you a few pointers. Use the best liquor you can afford and always measure, don't guess your amounts. Make sure your ice is fresh and clean; we tend to forget that is essential to a good cocktail.

Use only fresh fruit juices as mixers and when using them, pour the liquor in last.

Use superfine sugar, not powdered for sweetening and always use only egg white, never a chemical mix for foaming drinks.

Stirring makes a clear drink and shaking makes one cloudy; so do as your recipe calls for; if it says stir, do just that. and lastly, if possible, chill your cocktail glasses and drink the cocktails as soon as possible; don't let them stand.

STOCKING THE BAR

If your party will go on for 4 hours and you are entertaining around 20 people here are some helpful tips. Figure on 1/2 gallon of vodka, 1 bottle each of gin, bourbon, rum, scotch and dry vermouth. 3 bottles each of tonic water, club soda, and cola, 2 bottles of lemon-line soda; 1 bottle ginger ale and 1 bottle mineral water. Be sure to get a couple of quarts of orange juice, 1 quart each of grapefruit and cranberry juice or the new bottled fruit drink 'coolers.'

White wine is so popular now, it is hard to figure how many might be drinking wine; check with your liquor dealer, he can tell you how your area trends are running. Also, check with him to see if any unopened bottles can be returned for credit.

You can figure approximately 21 drinks can be served from 1 quart of liquor, based on a 1 1/2-ounce shot per drink.

When stocking your bar, don't forget fruit slices, cocktail onions and olives; fresh mint if available and figure on 1 pound of ice per person.

❖❖

HOW TO BUY A FINE OLD WINE

- Stick with wine types that improve with age and purchase only the best vintages.
- Buy from stores that specialize in old wines and have good, cool storage. Ask how the wine is stored and if it has been tasted recently.
- Look the bottle over carefully. Avoid wines with yellowed labels or excessive airspace. When the bottle is upright, the level of the wine should not fall below the bottom of the bottle's neck.
- For serving, stand reds and ports upright for a day or two to settle. Decant just before serving.

WINE FOR GAME DISHES

- Quail and pheasant - Choose a medium-bodied red Pinot Noir
- Duck and Goose - Deep-flavored Merlot
- Venison - California Cabernet Sauvignon or a top Italian red wine.

WINE AND CHEESE PARTNERS

- Strong cheese - Serve with red wine such as Cotes du Rhones or Barberas
- Mild cheese - Serve with a Bordeaux or Burgundy
- Swiss cheese - Serve with whites such as Rieslings or Pinot Gris
- Roquefort - Is very good served with a sweet Sauterne
- Beaujolais is a wine that goes with many different cheeses. The flavor of fine wines is ruined by pungent cheese.

HOT TIPS FROM BUTCH THE BUTCHER

- When carving, remember knives should be made of high-quality steel and be extremely sharp. If you use a dull knife your meat slices will not be thin and even and the meat will shred.
- For smooth even slices, each cut should be direct and sharp with long sweeping strokes.
- Cutting against the grain is the usual rule in carving all meat.
- Use knives of the correct size for your carving. 9-inch blade for roasts, 7-inch blade for steaks.
- When carving, use a proper fork. Insert fork and leave in one position while carving. The fork will keep the meat in place.
- After the first incision has been made, the angle of the knife should never be changed.
- Remember when you are buying meat, prime is best and choice is second. Do not buy any meat below these two grades.
- The best quality of meat has a minimum of outer fat. The fat should be cream-colored and have a slightly reddish coloration. The meat should be firm, finely grained and generally a bright red color.
- The best budget cut of beef for roasting is the first 6 inches cut from chuck. Second is the first six inches of shoulder and then top round.
- When you roast the less tender cuts you would be wise to marinate the meat for 24 hours and cook it at a lower temperature. Another method is to cover the roast with cabbage leaves to provide it with extra moisture.
- The best buys in steaks are the first-cut chuck steak. Then first-cut club steaks, sirloins, first ribs of a rib roast cut into steaks.
- When broiling the less-tender cuts of steak like chuck and top round, the most important thing is to have the meat at room temperature. Leave it out for two to three hours. At room temperature, the meat cooks more quickly with less shrinkage. It is also less tough. Rubbing the meat with a marinade after removing it from the refrigerator will help tenderize it.
- When serving flank steak allow 6 slices, about 3 1/2 to 4 ounces per serving.
- When serving veal scallops allow 3 scallops, 3 1/2 to 4 ounces per serving. Place scallop between waxed paper and pound to an even thickness, about 1/16th-inch.

❖◆

TIPS FROM A WINE STEWARD

- Serve white wines with fish, but a light red such as Pinot Noir is good with salmon or tuna.
- Serve red wine with red meat, but Chardonnays are wonderful with rare baby lamb chops, and dry Rieslings are great with sausages.
- Serve dry wines before sweet.

- Don't serve wine with spicy foods.
- Serve red wine at room temperature.
- Don't serve wine with salad.
- Don't serve wine with chocolate, but a rich ruby port is wonderful with chocolate desserts that aren't too sugary.
- Let red wines breathe.

TIPS ON SAUSAGE

- Dr. Lonnie says "Squeeze fresh lemon juice on cooked sausage patties. It brings out flavor and cuts grease."

Jo and Jan say, "We never serve sausage without the lemon. It's delicious!"

TIPS ON POT ROAST

Always use a heavy gauge utensil such as cast aluminum, cast iron or an enamel-coated cast iron with a tight-fitting lid. Wipe roast with a damp paper towel and roll in flour until evenly coated. It may be seasoned with garlic powder, salt, pepper and paprika. Pour a small amount of cooking oil into the kettle and add floured meat. This method is called braising. It is an effective method of browning meats to keep in the juices and add a deep savory flavor. Brown the meat on all sides.

Add liquid; anything from water to wine, to tomato juice to bouillon. Pot roasting may be done on top of the stove at a very low heat so it

barely bubbles. Also the roast may be put in a 300-degree oven, the length of time varies according to weight of the roast. It should be fork tender. Add the vegetables the last hour of roasting.

Some prefer the juice from the roast without any thickening. However, you may prefer to thicken the gravy. If so, skim off the fat and for each cup of liquid that remains you will need to stir in 1 tablespoon of flour, made into a paste with 2 tablespoons water. Bring mixture to a boil, stirring constantly. If you desire a darker, richer color, add 1 teaspoon of Kitchen Bouquet.

SUMMER AND SMOKERS

Either a water smoker or a covered grill works well for smoking, though a smoker allows for better circulation of heat and steam around the food. The longer smoking time in a water smoker intensifies the smoke flavor.

Soak wood chips in water to cover 30 minutes to an hour. Hickory, apple wood or mesquite give a delicious flavor.

When smoking, consult your recipe to determine amounts of wood chips, charcoal and

liquid to be used. Arrange charcoal in a pyramid shape in fire pan of smoker; light coals, allowing them to burn until a grey ash covers about 30 per cent of the surface.

Drain wood chips thoroughly and sprinkle evenly over coals. Set smoker over coals. Set water pan in place; add water or liquid to water pan; fit rack or racks into place. Arrange food on rack(s) according to recipe. Cooking time will vary according to recipe and food being smoked. You will find recipes in this section of your book. Enjoy the Great Outdoors!

❖❖❖

Girl Talk

This section was so popular in our first book that we decided to include it again. We have had so many people tell us they "took their book to bed or sat it on their coffee table." They enjoyed reading recipes and all we shared in Girl Talk. We hope you will also delighted with this expanded chapter.

❖❖❖

**Breakfast, Lunch, Dinner
Or just a cup of tea,
Served in the kitchen
Seems more friendly—**

- Bouquets of herbs, especially mint, which grow profusely and flower can fill your home with fresh, delicate fragrances.

- Make your own herb-flavored vinegars by soaking such herbs as tarragon, rosemary, bay leaves, or thyme in vinegar for 10 days. Strain through cheesecloth and keep tightly capped.

- Dry herbs with woody stems for winter use. Tie them in loose bunches of about 12 stems and hang in a warm dry place. In sunny weather, they can be hung outdoors in a shady spot, but must be brought in at night.

- Salad herbs can be kept in oil in a glass jar and will stay green for quite a long time. If they do turn dark, strain them and use the flavored oil for salad dressing or cooking.

- Add fresh herbs to your floral bouquet for a unique arrangement. Dill, for example, resembled baby's breath and has a lacy texture.

- Tie together several sprigs of fresh rosemary or thyme and use to baste sauce on roasted or grilled chicken and lamb.

- Chop fresh parsley and put it into a sectioned ice cube tray, fill with water and freeze. You can drop the cubes into stews, sauces, etc.

- Wash and thoroughly dry fresh basil. Remove stems and place leaves on sheets of aluminum foil in 1-cup batches. Wrap tightly and freeze. They will be handy for sauces or dressing.

- If using fresh herbs in place of dried, use three times the amount. Allow food to simmer at least 30 minutes for the full flavor of the herbs to develop.

- Use wooden berry boxes for a container for fresh or dried flowers. If using fresh flowers, place a small bowl of water in the box. We tie a strip of ribbon around the side of the box. It is an attractive, inexpensive table decoration for outside entertaining; great for a picnic.

- When making pomander balls, try using a nut pick to poke the holes for the cloves.

- You can make your own gift boxes for cookies and candy. Save tubular containers of tin or cardboard (some potato chips and snack items are packaged in these) and cover with your favorite paper. Kids love to help on this project; even the baking part.

- Drop a miniature marshmallow into the point of an ice cream cone before adding the scoop of ice cream. This will prevent the dripping problems so many little children encounter with melting ice cream. They also get a pleasant surprise with that last bite.

- Make your own superfine sugar by grinding granulated sugar in a food processor with quick on-off motions for a few seconds. Store in a covered container. This sugar is great to use when making meringues as it will dissolve very quickly in egg whites, eliminating grittiness. It is also nice to use in beverages.

- Speaking of beverages; to 2 cups of fruit juice or lemonade, add 1/2 teaspoon of cinnamon, nutmeg or allspice. Freeze in ice-cube tray; add to drinks for added zest.

- When setting up for your next party, cool beverage cans and bottles in your punch bowl. Fill bowl with ice around beverages. This is much more attractive than an ice chest and it keeps the folks out of the refrigerator.

- Place crystallized honey or jams, uncovered, in the microwave on high power about 1 minute or until sugar melts. Stir and let cool.

- When you measure liquids, pour into a standard glass or clear plastic measuring cup with a spout. Be sure your cup is on a level surface. Add the liquid to the cup until it reaches the amount you desire.

- When measuring dry ingredients use a measuring cup that holds the exact amount you need. Spoon in your dry ingredients and level with a flat bladed metal spatula. It is important to not dip your cup into the dry mixture because you will get more than you need.

- Make extra gravy or cream sauce and pour into ice cube trays. When frozen, remove them from tray and place in clear plastic bags and store them in the freezer. The cubes will last for three to four months.

❖❖

- A simple splatter lid to use when frying or sauteing is a metal colander placed upside down over your skillet.

- When frying food you want to keep crisp, place a rack under the paper towels you drain the food on. The paper towels absorb grease and the rack lets air circulate, keeping the food crisp.

- If you don't have a microwave oven, the next time you fry bacon, prepare an extra amount; draining well on paper toweling. Freeze in a single layer then store in an airtight container. When ready to serve, warm in oven or skillet.

- Protect recipe cards from splatters by inserting card into a 3 x 5-inch Plexiglass picture frame. Recipe is still easy to read but stays clean.

- If you blanch citrus fruits in hot water for 2 to 3 minutes before peeling, they will peel easier with less white membrane clinging to the segments.

- Also dipping citrus fruits in hot water before squeezing will increase the amount of juices you will extract.

- Rolling a lemon on the countertop while pressing hard with the palms of your hand will increase the juice amount you will extract.

- Raisins can be chopped more easily if you freeze them first. Lightly coat blender or food processor container and blades with vegetable oil and chop 1/2 cup of raisins at a time.

- When making your next relish platter, pare baby carrots and with a sharp paring knife, or skewer, cut a hole in the top end of each. Insert a sprig of parsley or a young spinach leaf (carefully washed, please) in the hole for a carrot top.

- To keep asparagus and parsley fresh and crisp, stand it up in a jar with some water; place a plastic bag over the top and refrigerate.

- Drop tablespoons of unused tomato paste on waxed paper and freeze. When frozen, transfer to an airtight container. The premeasured paste is convenient for use in sauces and soups.

- To make a beautiful tomato rose garnish, remove core from a ripe tomato with a small, sharp knife. Begin at core end and cut a continuous 1/2-inch wide strip of peel around the tomato. Place on a flat surface and rewind peel to form a spiral rose.

- For an interesting effect, stand fresh veggies such as asparagus and endive upright in a bowl as if they were flowers.

- We have a thrifty friend who freezes leftovers in a large freezer container. When the container is full, she makes a vegetable soup.

- To remove sand from vegetables, pour some salt in the soaking water; rinse out well.

- Chop up unpeeled zucchini and freeze in 1 or 2-cup portions for use in sauces and bread making.

- After you've picked the first crop of beans from your garden, mow the plants down about 3 inches from the ground with a hand mower. You'll be able to have another crop of beans that season.

- Place carrots, celery sticks, small pieces of cauliflower in the jar of pickle juice when pickles are all gone. Use the marinated veggies for relish trays.

- Save your vegetable peelings such as carrot, potato, onion; freeze and add to liquid when making stock. They add flavor as well as nutritional value.

- Arugula is a tender salad green with a peppery flavor similar to watercress. The leaves are long and narrow and tend to be sandy so rinse them well. It is delicious served alone with an oil and vinegar dressing seasoned with garlic. We also like to add sliced mushrooms and tomato wedges.

- Keep bean sprouts crisp and white by storing them in a bowl of water in the refrigerator.

- Buy extra mushrooms to freeze when the prices are low. Loosely pack sliced, clean, dry mushrooms in plastic bags. Squeeze to remove as much air as possible and seal. When ready to use, mushrooms will easily separate by smaking the bag against the counter so you can use only what you want.

- Chop canned tomatoes before pouring from the can by inserting kitchen shears into the opened can and cutting into the tomatoes. Several snips and you can pour tomatoes directly into your recipe all chopped.

- When washing greens, always lift them out of water, do not drain water off. By lifting, any dirt will fall out with water droplets.

- Crisp freshly washed spinach and lettuce leaves by spreading them on a clean dry towel, roll up and refrigerate.

- If you put an onion in the freezer for 5 minutes before cutting, no tears.

◆◆◆

- Use dampened paper coffee filters instead of cheesecloth to remove fine sediment that remains even after straining from soups or juices. They will be crystal clear.

- Attention bread bakers! Save cooking water from boiled, peeled potatoes; cool and refrigerate to use within 2 days for bread making. Nutrients, as well as flavor is added to the bread.

- If you wrap a paper towel around each potato you are baking in the microwave oven you will eliminate those soggy skins. The paper towel absorbs moisture and the skin will be crisper.

- For smooth as velvet mashed potatoes, whip hot, drained potatoes with plenty of butter on medium speed of electric mixer until very smooth. Gradually add just enough hot milk to make the potatoes smooth. You might add a pinch of baking soda to the warm milk.

- Quick soaked beans! Place washed and picked-over dried beans with twice their volume of water in microwave oven in a microwave-safe dish. Heat on high power for 8 minutes or until boiling. Remove from oven, cover with plastic wrap and let stand 1 hour. Beans will be ready to be cooked according to package directions.

- If in a hurry to cook beans and have not soaked them overnight, try this: pick over and rinse beans; place in a saucepan and completely cover with water. Boil beans 1 minute; reduce heat and simmer for 2 minutes. Cover; let rest 1 hour. Drain and add fresh water; cook as usual.

- To reheat rice you cooked ahead of serving time, place rice in a well-buttered pan; cover with a buttered piece of foil and heat in a preheated 325-degree oven for 25-30 minutes, stirring occasionally. Rice will be as fluffy as just cooked.

- When you make pasta, save any scraps of dough you have left. Cut into shapes and freeze. Use them for a delicious addition to soups or stews.

- Freeze leftover pancakes, waffles and French toast between pieces of waxed paper and store in a plastic bag. Reheat in microwave on high power for 30 seconds or heat on a baking sheet in preheated 350-degree oven for 6 to 7 minutes. They can also be heated in a toaster.

- If you purchase staples in large quantities, such as granulated sugar, dried beans, rice, macaroni; use clean, dry plastic gallon milk jugs with plastic tops. The contents are visible and are easy to pour into a measuring cup.

- To peel garlic easily, place cloves in microwave oven. Set on high power for 5 to 10 seconds.

- You can also easily remove skin from garlic by placing clove on a cutting board and "spanking" it once or twice with the flat side of a chef's knife; skin comes right off.

- Before adding whole cloves of garlic to oil or dressing for flavor; stick a toothpick through each clove. It makes for easy removal.

- Place peeled garlic cloves in a small jar and cover with olive oil and refrigerate. The flavored oil can be used in salads and cloves are ready to use when needed.

- For easy removal of garlic from oil when you are cooking chopped garlic only to flavor the oil - place garlic in a flat-bottomed strainer and set strainer in the oil; cook garlic as directed then just lift out the strainer.

- Remove prepackaged cheese from the wrapper, wipe dry with paper towels; wrap in a dry paper towel and store in a plastic bag. This will prolong the life of the cheese.

- If you just need a small amount of shredded cheese, use your vegetable peeler instead of a grater or shredded.

- Stop! Don't throw away that cheese dried out from storing too long! Grate the cheese and store in an airtight container. Use on broiler hamburgers, fish, steak.

- A low calorie substitute for sour cream: Blend until smooth in a blender or food processor 1 cup cottage cheese, 2 tablespoons milk and 1 tablespoon lemon juice. Try it the next time you are without sour cream.

- If you purchase staples in large quantities, such as granulated sugar, dried beans, rice, macaroni; use clean, dry plastic

- You can tell the difference between a hard-boiled egg and an uncooked one. A hard-boiled egg will spin on the counter; an unboiled egg will not.

Girl Talk

- Leftover egg whites may be frozen. One egg white measures 1 ounce, if you are using standard-size large eggs.

- Separate egg yolks from whites by using your hand as a strainer. Crack egg over a bowl into your hand; separate your fingers slightly to let the white slip into the bowl, leaving only the yolk in your hand. We find this works best with chilled eggs.

- Butter can be creamed faster and egg whites beaten to greater volume if you warm the bowl and beaters by rinsing them in warm water before starting beating. Dry thoroughly!

- A few drops of Oriental sesame oil will restore the creaminess of peanut butter and add to the nutty flavor.

- Keep flour in a shaker to use when recipes call for flouring a pan. It is easy to shake out just enough to cover the pan.

- To prevent your pies from bubbling over onto the oven floor, place an oven rack below the one the pie is on. Turn up 1/2 inch on all edges of a 12-inch square of foil. Place it on bottom rack to catch the drips.

- If pies bubble over while baking, sprinkle salt on the spills. They'll bake to a crisp and can be easily wiped away once the pie is done and the oven is cool.

- Prevent overbrowning on edge of pie crust by cutting the inside from an aluminum foil pie tin. Use the rim to cover the edge of crust while baking.

- To easily grease pans, keep a plastic sandwich bag inside your can of vegetable shortening. Just slip the bag over your hand and you are ready to grease. Return bag to can for the next time.

- If you add a bit too much water to your pie crust, freeze the unbaked crust overnight before baking. It helps it dry out.

- Remember to cut the fat into flour as much as possible; until like small peas.

- If you are using a wooden rolling pin or wooden board when making a butter pastry such as for croissants, place the wooden pieces in the freezer for a few hours. It helps keep the dough cool and prevents sticking.

- Use a muffin tin for an ice-tray. The large cubes are attractive in punch bowls and last longer if used for packing ice chests for picnics.

- Use your ice-cream scoop to fill cup cake tins quickly and evenly.

- Use a small ice-cream scoop to drop batter onto the baking sheet when making drop cookies. It's fast and efficient.

- Before chopping nuts (to be used in baked goods) in a food processor; sprinkle nuts with a small amount of the flour called for in the recipe. Nuts will not stick to the blades. Do the same if ground nuts are to be incorporated in a batter or dough. They will mix more easily and evenly.

- If you shake nuts, raisins or fruits in a paper bag with just enough flour to cover, they will not sink to the bottom of cake or bread batter.

- Brush a beaten egg white on unbaked pie crust before filling to prevent crusts from becoming soggy. This is especially good for custard pies.

- Sieve confectioners' sugar over meringue before baking that next pie, especially if you have a humid day. This helps form a protective crust.

- To split angel food cake, or other delicate cakes into layers, use a silk or nylon thread. Wrap thread around the cake's sides and tie it in a knot. Gently pull thread through the layer. This is also a good way to cut cinnamon rolls before baking.

- Before wrapping a frosted cake, stick a few toothpicks into top and sides to keep wrap from sticking to frosting.

- 2 or 3 toothpicks stuck halfway into layers will keep frosted layers from sliding.

- A pinch of baking powder added to powdered sugar icings will keep them moist and will prevent hardening and cracking.

- To keep a cut cake fresh, place half an apple in the cake box.

◆◆◆

- Freeze rose petals in ice cubes. Fill ice-cube tray halfway and freeze. Place a petal on each cube, anchor with a teaspoon of water and freeze again; fill completely with water and freeze until ready to serve.

- Throw marigold or chrysanthemum petals into a salad for flavor and color. Keep in mind marigolds are pungent and not to everyone's liking-they have a "nose tickling" fragrance.

- Nasturtium seeds can be pickled and used instead of capers.

- Drop a rose petal in a glass of white wine.

- A beautiful ribbon tied around a cake makes a stunning presentation. Try it sometime and tuck a few flowers into the bow. We think it would be lovely for a luncheon or party.

- If serving cheese as an appetizer, allow 3 to 4 ounces per person if it is the only food served. If other foods will be offered, allow 1 to 2 ounces of cheese.

- When planning a cocktail party, allow 10 bites per person. Figure the number each recipe will serve and divide by 10.

- When planning tea sandwiches figure there are 23 1/2-inch slices in a 12 1/2-inch loaf of bread, 32 1/2-inch slices in a 15 1/2-inch loaf. You can cut six 1/2-inch lengthwise slices from an unsliced loaf of bread. Allow 2 tablespoons of filling for each slice of bread.

- If your tablecloth gets spoiled during the dinner, before you remove the cloth from the table, snap a clothes pin or attach a safety pin to the stain area. It will help you find those spots at laundry time.

- Sheryl tells us she gathers hedgeballs and places them on paper in the basement to ward off crickets.

Food Quantities For 25

Salad Dressing	1 quart
Mixed Green Salad	14 heads of Bibb lettuce
	Or
	5 heads Boston Lettuce
	And
	4 Romaine, combined
	3 cucumbers
	2 large red onions
	12 large tomatoes
Soup	1 1/2 gallons
Crackers	1 1/2 pounds
Cheese	3 pounds
Mixed Filling For Sandwiches (meat, eggs, fish, chicken)	2 quarts
Chicken Salad	4 quarts
Rolls	4 dozen
Butter	1/2 pound
Pasta	7 1/2 pounds
Rice	8 cups raw
Turkey or Chicken	14 pounds
Whole fish with bones	30 pounds
Roasted Meat	12-14 pounds
Ground meat	12 pounds
Potato Salad	4 1/2 quarts
Baked Beans	3/4 gallon
Watermelon	37 pounds
Ice Cream	2 gallons
Cake	1 10x12-inch sheet cake
Strawberries	12 pints

- Coffee - 1 pound coffee plus 2 gallons of water makes 40 cups.

- Tea - 1 1/2 quarts of boiling water and 1/4 pound loose tea makes enough concentrate for 45 cups of hot tea or 30 glasses of iced tea.

- Hot chocolate - 4 1/2 quarts of milk and 3 cups chocolate syrup makes 25 cups of hot chocolate.

HUGGING

Hugging is ... good for your health
Hugging is ... practically perfect; no movable parts, no batteries to wear out, no periodic check-ups, low energy consumption, high energy yield, inflation proof, non-fattening, no monthly payments, no insurance requirements, theft proof, non-taxable, non-polluting, and of course, fully returnable.

Hugging is ... natural, organic, naturally sweet, no pesticides, no preservatives, no artificial ingredients, 100 percent wholesome. The best people, places and times to hug: anyone, anywhere, anytime.

— *Borrowed*

◆◆

◆◆◆

❖❖❖

Butcher Block Press

Butcher Block Press, Inc.
P.O. Box 6
Medicine Lodge, Kansas 67104

Rt. 2 Box 123
Halstead, KS 67056

I can hardly wait for "A Cooking Affaire II!" Please send me _____ copies at $24.95 each, plus $3.50 per copy for shipping.**

I have loved "A Cooking Affaire" and would like to order _____ copies at $24.95 each, plus $3.50 for shipping.**

**Kansas residents, please add $1.60 (6.40%) per copy for tax. TOTAL: $30.05.

Enclosed is my check or money order in the amount of $ _____
Make checks payable to Butcher Block Press, Inc. (Sorry, No C.O.D.'s –Allow time for personal checks to clear.)

We honor   MasterCard   VISA

Account No. (all digits) [ ][ ][ ][ ][ ][ ][ ][ ][ ][ ][ ][ ][ ][ ][ ][ ]   Expiration Date: _____

Signature _____
(required if using credit card)

Total amount of credit card order: $

From:
Butcher Block Press, Inc.
P.O. Box 6
Medicine Lodge, Kansas 67104

To:
Name _____
Address: _____
City: _____
State: _____ Zip: _____

Mailing Label, Please Print

Butcher Block Press

Butcher Block Press, Inc.
P.O. Box 6
Medicine Lodge, Kansas 67104

Rt. 2 Box 123
Halstead, KS 67056

I can hardly wait for "A Cooking Affaire II!" Please send me _____ copies at $24.95 each, plus $3.50 per copy for shipping.**

I have loved "A Cooking Affaire" and would like to order _____ copies at $24.95 each, plus $3.50 for shipping.**

**Kansas residents, please add $1.60 (6.40%) per copy for tax. TOTAL: $30.05.

Enclosed is my check or money order in the amount of $ _____
Make checks payable to Butcher Block Press, Inc. (Sorry, No C.O.D.'s –Allow time for personal checks to clear.)

We honor   MasterCard   VISA

Account No. (all digits) [ ][ ][ ][ ][ ][ ][ ][ ][ ][ ][ ][ ][ ][ ][ ][ ]   Expiration Date: _____

Signature _____
(required if using credit card)

Total amount of credit card order: $

From:
Butcher Block Press, Inc.
P.O. Box 6
Medicine Lodge, Kansas 67104

To:
Name _____
Address: _____
City: _____
State: _____ Zip: _____

Mailing Label, Please Print

Butcher Block Press

Butcher Block Press, Inc.
P.O. Box 6
Medicine Lodge, Kansas 67104

Rt. 2 Box 123
Halstead, KS 67056

I can hardly wait for "A Cooking Affaire II!" Please send me _____ copies at $24.95 each, plus $3.50 per copy for shipping.**

I have loved "A Cooking Affaire" and would like to order _____ copies at $24.95 each, plus $3.50 for shipping.**

**Kansas residents, please add $1.60 (6.40%) per copy for tax. TOTAL: $30.05.

Enclosed is my check or money order in the amount of $ _____
Make checks payable to Butcher Block Press, Inc. (Sorry, No C.O.D.'s –Allow time for personal checks to clear.)

We honor   MasterCard   VISA

Account No. (all digits) [ ][ ][ ][ ][ ][ ][ ][ ][ ][ ][ ][ ][ ][ ][ ][ ]   Expiration Date: _____

Signature _____
(required if using credit card)

Total amount of credit card order: $

From:
Butcher Block Press, Inc.
P.O. Box 6
Medicine Lodge, Kansas 67104

To:
Name _____
Address: _____
City: _____
State: _____ Zip: _____

Mailing Label, Please Print

All copies will be sent to same address unless otherwise specified.

If you wish books sent as gifts, furnish a list of names and addresses of recipients. If you wish to enclose your own gift card with each book, please write name of recipient on outside of the envelope, enclose with order, we will include it with your gift.

All copies will be sent to same address unless otherwise specified.

If you wish books sent as gifts, furnish a list of names and addresses of recipients. If you wish to enclose your own gift card with each book, please write name of recipient on outside of the envelope, enclose with order, we will include it with your gift.

All copies will be sent to same address unless otherwise specified.

If you wish books sent as gifts, furnish a list of names and addresses of recipients. If you wish to enclose your own gift card with each book, please write name of recipient on outside of the envelope, enclose with order, we will include it with your gift.